The Responsibility to Protect

THE RESPONSIBILITY TO PROTECT

THE PROMISE OF STOPPING MASS ATROCITIES IN OUR TIME

Jared Genser and Irwin Cotler

OXFORD
UNIVERSITY PRESS

OXFORD
UNIVERSITY PRESS

Oxford University Press, Inc., publishes works that further Oxford University's objective of excellence in research, scholarship, and education.

Oxford New York
Auckland Cape Town Dar es Salaam Hong Kong Karachi Kuala Lumpur Madrid
Melbourne Mexico City Nairobi New Delhi Shanghai Taipei Toronto

With offices in
Argentina Austria Brazil Chile Czech Republic France Greece Guatemala Hungary Italy
Japan Poland Portugal Singapore South Korea Switzerland Thailand Turkey Ukraine
Vietnam

Published by Oxford University Press, Inc.
198 Madison Avenue, New York, New York 10016

Library of Congress Cataloging-in-Publication Data
The responsibility to protect: the promise of stopping mass atrocities in our time /
edited by Jared Genser and Irwin Cotler.
p. cm.
Includes bibliographical references and index.
ISBN 978-0-19-979776-9 ((hardback): alk. paper)
1. Humanitarian intervention. 2. Atrocities—Prevention. 3. Genocide—Prevention. I. Genser, Jared.
II. Cotler, I. (Irwin), 1940-
JZ6369.R485 2011
327.1'17—dc22 2011015273

---

1 2 3 4 5 6 7 8 9

Printed in the United States of America on acid-free paper

Contents

Funders

HUMAN RIGHTS FOUNDATION CENTER FOR LAW AND DEMOCRACY

The Human Rights Foundation Center for Law and Democracy (HRF-CLD) is a program of the Human Rights Foundation (www.theHRF.org) and seeks to promote legal scholarship in the areas of comparative constitutional law and international law. HRF is an international nonpartisan human rights organization, headquartered in New York, whose mission is to protect and promote human rights globally, with an expertise in the Americas.

THE MORIAH FUND

The Moriah Fund (www.moriahfund.org) is a private foundation that seeks to promote human rights and social justice, help disadvantaged people gain self-sufficiency and control over their lives, foster sustainable development, and promote women's rights and reproductive health.

About the Editors

Jared Genser is managing director of Perseus Strategies, LLC, a law firm focusing on international human rights. He is also founder of Freedom Now, an independent non-profit organization that works to free prisoners of conscience worldwide. Previously, Jared was a partner in the government affairs practice of DLA Piper LLP and a management consultant with McKinsey & Company, the global strategy consulting firm. He has taught semester-long seminars about the UN Security Council at the University of Michigan and University of Pennsylvania law schools. Mr. Genser was a 2006–2007 Visiting Fellow with the National Endowment for Democracy. His pro bono clients have included former Czech Republic President Václav Havel and Nobel Peace Prize Laureates Liu Xiaobo, Aung San Suu Kyi, Desmond M. Tutu, and Elie Wiesel. He holds a B.S. from Cornell University, an M.P.P. from the John F. Kennedy School of Government at Harvard University, and a J.D. *cum laude* from the University of Michigan Law School. He is a Young Global Leader of the World Economic Forum and Term Member of the Council on Foreign Relations.

Irwin Cotler, PC, OC, MP has been a Canadian Member of Parliament since 1999 and served as Minister of Justice and Attorney General of Canada from 2003–2006. Mr. Cotler is currently on leave as a Professor of Law at McGill University, where he is Director of its Human Rights Program and Chair of InterAmicus, the McGill-based international human rights advocacy Center. He has been a Visiting Professor at Harvard Law School, a Woodrow Wilson Fellow at Yale Law School, and is the recipient of nine honorary doctorates, including from the Hebrew University of Jerusalem, whose various citations refer to him as "a scholar and advocate of international stature." Mr. Cotler received a B.C.L. from McGill University and an LL.M. from Yale Law School.

Contributors

President Václav Havel is a Czech writer and dramatist. He was the tenth and last president of Czechoslovakia (1989–1992) and first president of the Czech Republic (1992–2003). He has written more than 20 plays and numerous works of non-fiction, many of which have received international acclaim. Beginning in the 1960s, his work turned to focus on the politics of Czechoslovakia. After the Prague Spring, he became increasingly active in Czech politics. In 1977, his involvement with the human rights manifesto Charter 77 brought him international fame as the leader of the opposition in Czechoslovakia. The communist regime sentenced him to four-and-a-half years imprisonment for subversion of the Republic and he served as a prisoner of conscience from 1979–1983. The 1989 "Velvet Revolution" launched Havel into the presidency. In this role, he led Czechoslovakia and later the Czech Republic to capitalism and multi-party democracy.

The Most Reverend Desmond M. Tutu, Archbishop Emeritus of Cape Town, is a South African cleric and activist who rose to worldwide fame during the 1980s as an opponent of apartheid. In 1984, he became the second South African to be awarded the Nobel Peace Prize. In 1986, he was elected and ordained the first black South African Anglican Archbishop of Cape Town, South Africa. Bishop Tutu also chaired South Africa's Truth and Reconciliation Commission and is currently the chairman of The Elders. He is vocal in his defense of human rights and campaigns for the oppressed in such countries as Burma, Sudan, and Zimbabwe. Bishop Tutu is also an advocate for addressing issues of HIV/AIDS, poverty, and racism.

Lloyd Axworthy, President and Vice-Chancellor of The University of Winnipeg, graduated in 1961 with a B.A. from United College (now The University of Winnipeg), and received an M.A. and Ph.D. from Princeton in 1963 and 1972, respectively. Dr. Axworthy's political career spanned 27 years, six of which he served in the Manitoba Legislative Assembly and 21 in the Federal Parliament. He held several Cabinet positions, notably Minister of Employment and Immigration, Minister Responsible for the Status of Women, Minister of Transport, Minister of Human Resources Development, Minister of Western Economic Diversification, and Minister of Foreign Affairs from 1996–2000. In the latter context, he initiated the International Commission on Intervention and State Sovereignty and served as chairman of its advisory board. Issued in December 2001, the Commission's report provided the key context for the development and later adoption of the Responsibility to Protect doctrine. Upon leaving public office, Dr. Axworthy served as Director and CEO of the Liu Institute for Global Issues at the University of British Colombia prior to his appointment at The University of Winnipeg.

William W. Burke-White is Deputy Dean and Professor of Law at the University of Pennsylvania Law School. His scholarship focuses on the intersection of international law and political science, where he addresses issues related to international tribunals, post-conflict justice, the International Criminal Court, linkages between human rights and national security, and international investment arbitration. From June 2009 though June 2011, he served as a member of the Foreign Policy Planning Staff at the U.S. Department of State. His portfolio included international organizations, global governance, and the Russian Federation. In addition, he served as Principal Drafter of the Quadrennial Diplomacy and Development Review. Previously, Professor Burke-White was Humboldt Fellow at the Max Planck Institute in Heidelberg, Germany and Visiting Professor at MGIMO in Moscow, Russia and Mofid University in Iran, and Lecturer at Princeton University. He holds a Ph.D. and M.Phil. in international relations from Cambridge University, where he was a Fulbright Scholar, a J.D., *magna cum laude* from Harvard Law School, and a B.A., *magna cum laude* from Harvard College.

Tarun Chhabra is a J.D. candidate and Paul and Daisy Soros Fellow at Harvard Law School, and a doctoral candidate in international relations at Oxford University. He previously worked on the staff of UN Secretary-General Kofi Annan's *High-Level Panel on Threats, Challenges, and Change*, and in the Executive Office of the Secretary-General. He also served as a consultant-advisor to the Norwegian Foreign Ministry on nuclear non-proliferation and disarmament initiatives. Mr. Chhabra was a Fulbright Scholar in Russia at the Moscow State Institute for International Relations (MGIMO) and received a Marshall Scholarship to study at Merton College, Oxford, where he earned a M.Phil. in international relations. He received a B.A. from Stanford University.

Jeremy B. Zucker is a partner in the International Trade group of Hogan Lovells US LLP and is the chair of Freedom Now, a non-profit organization that works to free prisoners of conscience worldwide. In 2010, he was named by *Law360* as a Top 10 Rising Star Under 40 in international trade. Mr. Zucker's current human rights clients include Dr. Oscar Elias Biscet of Cuba, and Chief Ebrimah Manneh of Gambia. Previously, he served as a law clerk at the International Court of Justice in The Hague, The Netherlands. He holds a B.A. from Yale University, an M.P.P. from the John F. Kennedy School of Government at Harvard University, and a J.D. *magna cum laude* from New York University School of Law, where he was editor-in-chief of the Journal of International Law and Politics and a Fellow of the Center for International Studies. He is a Term Member of the Council on Foreign Relations.

Nicole Deller has been advocating for and monitoring the development of the norm of Responsibility to Protect (RtoP) since 2004. From its founding in 2008 until July 2010, she was Director of Programs for the Global Centre for the Responsibility to Protect, a research and advocacy institute that promotes universal acceptance and effective operational implementation of RtoP. From 2004 to 2007, she was Senior Program Officer at the Institute for Global Policy where she headed the Responsibility to Protect – Engaging Civil Society project. She is co-author of "The Responsibility to Protect During Emerging and Acute Crises: A Civil Society Proposal for the United Nations" in *Responsibility to Protect: The Global Moral Compact for the 21st Century* (Palgrave Macmillan, 2008) and "Preventing Future Genocide: A Responsibility To Protect" (World Order 36, 2006) with William R. Pace. Ms. Deller received her B.A. from Case

Western Reserve University *summa cum laude* and her J.D. from New York University School of Law. She served as chair of the International Security Affairs Committee of the New York City Bar Association (2004–2007).

Edward C. Luck is Special Adviser to the UN Secretary-General, with the rank of Assistant Secretary-General, in which capacity he primarily focuses on the Responsibility to Protect. Until mid-2011, he served as Senior Vice President for Research and Programs at the International Peace Institute. From 2001 to 2010, Dr. Luck was Professor of Practice in International and Public Affairs and Director of the Center on International Organization, both of Columbia University. A past president and CEO of the United Nations Association of the USA, he has served the UN in a variety of capacities, taught at Princeton and Sciences-Po (Paris), and founded a research center co-sponsored by the NYU School of Law and Princeton's Woodrow Wilson School. Among his books are *United Nations Security Council: Practice and Promise* (Routledge, 2006 and 2011), *International Law and Organization: Closing the Compliance Gap*, with Michael Doyle (Rowman & Littlefield, 2004), and *Mixed Messages: American Politics and International Organization, 1919–1999* (Brookings, 1999).

Ademola Abass is Head of Peace and Security and Capacity-Building Programmes at the United Nations University Comparative Regional Integration Studies (UNU-CRIS) and Professor of International Law and Organisation at Brunel University, West London. Previously, Professor Abass taught at the Universities of Reading, Nottingham, and UWE, Bristol. His publications include: *Regional Organisations and the Development of Collective Security: Beyond Chapter VIII of the UN Charter* (Hart Publishing, 2004); *Protecting Human Security in Africa* (Ed., Oxford University Press, 2010); *Complete International Law: Texts, Cases and Materials* (Oxford University Press, 2011). He received his LL.B., LL.M., and Ph.D. degrees from the Universities of Lagos, Cambridge, and Nottingham, respectively. He also received an Advanced Diploma *magna cum laude* from the Institute of International Public Law/International Relations at Aristotle University.

Noel M. Morada is Executive Director of the Asia-Pacific Centre for the Responsibility to Protect. Previously, he was a Professor of Political Science at the University of the Philippines (Diliman) and was a Distinguished Visiting Professor, Southeast Asian Program at the School of Advanced International Studies (SAIS) at Johns Hopkins University. Dr. Morada has published works on RtoP in Southeast Asia, specifically the roadmap to promoting and building a constituency in the region, as well as the challenges in doing so under the existing ASEAN Charter. He is also director of the Philippines program of the Centre. His publications and research interests also include ASEAN regionalism and external relations with major powers, the ASEAN Regional Forum and cooperative security in the Asia Pacific, and human security and human development issues in the region. He received his Ph.D. from Northern Illinois University, M.P.A. from Cornell University, M.A. from the University of the Philippines (Diliman), and his B.A. from the University of the Philippines (Diliman).

Mark V. Vlasic is an adjunct professor of law at Georgetown University Law Center, a senior fellow at Georgetown's Institute for Law, Science & Global Security, and a partner at Ward & Ward PLLC, where he heads the firm's international practice. A former head of operations of the World Bank's StAR Secretariat, a presidential initiative to recover stolen assets from past dictators, Mr. Vlasic served as a White

House Fellow, special assistant to the Secretary of Defense, and advisor to the president's Special Envoy to Sudan, and was awarded the Secretary of Defense Medal for Exceptional Public Service by Secretary Robert Gates. He has provided commentary to CNN, BBC, FOX, CBS, and NPR, practiced law at Gibson, Dunn & Crutcher LLP, helped train the judges that tried Saddam Hussein, and served on the *Slobodan Milosevic* and *Srebrenica* prosecution trial teams at the UN war crimes tribunal. Mr. Vlasic received his B.S. and J.D., *cum laude*, from Georgetown University, his Certificate in International Law from The Hague Academy, and was a NAF-Fulbright Scholar at Universiteit Leiden in the Netherlands.

Gilberto Marcos Antonio Rodrigues was the inaugural holder of the Brazilian Fulbright Scholarship Program on Human Rights for a Visiting Scholar at the Center for Civil and Human Rights at the University of Notre Dame (2010), with a research focused on Latin American Views on RtoP. He is currently a professor at the Catholic University of Santos, São Paulo, and holder of the Sergio Vieira de Mello Chair in conjunction with the Brazilian UNHCR Office. He is a member of the Group of Analysis on Conflict Prevention (GAPCon) at the Candido Mendes University, Rio de Janeiro, and as a Board Member of the Coordinadora Regional de Investigaciones Económicas y Sociales (CRIES) he is part of the International Coalition for the Responsibility to Protect (ICRtoP). He is co-author of "Brazil" in *Diversity and Unity in Federal Countries* (MacGill, 2010). He holds a Ph.D. in Social Sciences, a LL.B. from the Pontifical Catholic University of São Paulo, a M.A. in International Relations from the UPEACE, Costa Rica, and a Diploma in Conflict Resolution from the Uppsala University.

Mohamed S. Helal is a Third Secretary with the Egyptian Foreign Service, and is currently on study leave to pursue an S.J.D. at Harvard Law School. From 2005–2009 he was a political officer in the Cabinet of the Minister of Foreign Affairs of Egypt, where he was responsible for human rights, humanitarian, and multilateral affairs. During this period he also served as the private secretary to the Minister of Foreign Affairs of Egypt. Before joining the Foreign Service he was an International Fellow at the International Human Rights Law Institute at DePaul University College of Law, a Human Rights Law Lecturer at American University in Cairo, and from 2002–2003 he was a legal officer in the Cabinet of the Secretary-General of the League of Arab States. He holds an LL.M. from Harvard Law School, where he was a Fulbright Scholar and the recipient of the David L. Shapiro Award, an LL.B. from Ain Shams University Faculty of Law, a Diploma in International Criminal Law from Istituto Superiore Internazionale Di Scienze Criminali, and an M.A. and B.A. from the American University in Cairo.

Andrew S. Natsios is Distinguished Professor at the Walsh School of Foreign Service at Georgetown University. From 2001–2006, he served as Administrator of the U.S. Agency for International Development (USAID), the lead U.S. government agency doing international economic development and humanitarian assistance. During this period he managed USAID's reconstruction programs in Afghanistan, Iraq, and Sudan, which totaled more than $14 billion over four years. President Bush also appointed him Special Coordinator for International Disaster Assistance and Special Humanitarian Coordinator for the Sudan. Mr. Natsios also served as U.S. Special Envoy to Sudan from October 2006 to December 2007. Previously, he worked for

World Vision U.S. and served in the Massachusetts House of Representatives from 1975 to 1987. He received his B.A. from Georgetown University and his M.P.A. from Harvard University's John F. Kennedy School of Government.

Zachary Scott is a Field Support Coordinator for the Migration and Refugee Services Department at the United States Conference of Catholic Bishops (USCCB), overseeing refugee resettlement in 14 dioceses across the United States. Before working at USCCB, Mr. Scott was a Program Assistant at the Aga Khan Foundation USA from May 2008–November 2009. He received his M.A. from Georgetown's School of Foreign Service in 2008 and B.A. from Indiana University in 2003.

Paulo Sérgio Pinheiro is associate researcher at the Center for the Study of Violence and professor of political science (retired) at the University of São Paulo, Brazil. He is adjunct professor of international relations, Watson Institute for International Studies, Brown University. Mr. Pinheiro held the position of UN Special Rapporteur on Myanmar (Burma) from 2000–2008. He is a commissioner at the Inter-American Commission on Human Rights (IACHR) with the Organization of America States in Washington, D.C. Mr. Pinheiro also served as Brazil's secretary of state for human rights under President Fernando Henrique Cardoso.

Meghan Barron is an associate in the government affairs practice of DLA Piper LLP. She received her J.D. from the University of Texas with honors and a B.A. from Cornell University. She was named as one of Legal Bisnow's 30 Under 30 of exceptional legal talent in the Washington, D.C. area and has done substantial pro bono work in relation to Burma.

Meredith Preston McGhie is the Senior Program Manager (Africa) for the Centre for Humanitarian Dialogue (HD Centre). She has previously acted as an advisor to the Djibouti Peace Process for Somalia in 2009, and in 2008 supported the Kenya National Dialogue and Reconciliation as part of the HD Centre-team seconded to the Kofi Annan-led Panel. She has led projects focusing on elections and mediation, most recently in Somaliland, and presently leads the HD Centre's support to the Popular Consultations as part of the implementation of the Comprehensive Peace Agreement in Sudan. She also leads the HD Centre's gender and peacemaking work, including managing the Women at the Peace Table Africa program. Ms. McGhie has worked in East and the Horn of Africa for more than ten years, with various UN agencies and NGOs on issues of post conflict reconstruction, DDR and small arms control, with a particular emphasis on gender, inclusion of women, and addressing the needs of disabled soldiers.

Serena Sharma is a research associate at the Oxford Institute for Ethics, Law and Armed Conflict and a research fellow of Wolfson College, Oxford. Dr. Sharma was recently appointed as the United Nations Association (UNA-UK) Special Advisor on RtoP. She completed a Ph.D. in International Relations from the London School of Economics and Political Science (LSE), a Masters in Human Rights from the LSE, and a B.A. in International Relations from the University of British Columbia. Her research focuses on the ethics of war, with a particular emphasis on the just war tradition and the Responsibility to Protect. Elements of her research have been published in the *Journal of Military Ethics*, *Global Governance*, *Global Responsibility to Protect*, *UBC Journal of International Affairs*, and others, as well as chapters in edited volumes.

She has served as an editor and associate editor of *Millennium: Journal of International Studies.* Prior to commencing her graduate studies, Dr. Sharma worked with the former Canadian Minister of Foreign Affairs, Lloyd Axworthy, at the Liu Institute for Global Issues.

Damien Kingsbury holds a Personal Chair in the School of International and Political Studies at Deakin University. He teaches Approaches to Political Development and Conflict Resolution and Development. He has written, edited, or co-edited a number of books including *East Timor: The Price of Liberty* (Palgrave 2009), *Political Development* (Routledge, 2007), *Key Issues in Development* (Palgrave, 2004), *Power and Politics in the Indonesian Military* (RoutledgeCurzon, 2003), *The Politics of Indonesia* (Oxford, 3rd Edition, 2005), among others. His book *Sri Lanka and the Responsibility to Protect: Politics, Ethnicity, and Genocide* is due to be published by Routledge in 2011. Dr. Kingsbury received his Ph.D. and M.A. from Monash University and an M.S. from Columbia University.

Delphine Schrank is an adjunct fellow with the East-West Center in Washington and a journalist focused on resource-rich, fragile states. In the fall of 2008, she traveled to the Democratic Republic of Congo as a fellow with the International Reporting Project. Her reporting from Africa, Southeast Asia, and Europe has appeared in *The Washington Post, The Virginia Quarterly Review, The Atlantic Monthly, Mother Jones,* and *TIME Magazine.* She worked as a reporter and editor for *The Washington Post* from 2005–2008, and as an editor and correspondent for *TIME* in Paris and London. Ms. Schrank received her B.A. and M.A. in Modern History from Oxford University and a Master of International Affairs from Columbia University's School of International and Public Affairs.

Kjell Magne Bondevik was Prime Minister of Norway 1997–2000 and 2001–2005. He was also Minister of Foreign Affairs and Minister of Church and Education. He was a member of the Norwegian Parliament 1973–2005. Mr. Bondevik served as the UN Secretary-General's Special Envoy to the Horn of Africa in 2006–2007. He is the founder and president of the Oslo Center for Peace and Human Rights. In 2006, along with former Czech Republic President Václav Havel and Nobel Peace Prize Laureate Elie Wiesel, he commissioned DLA Piper and the Committee for Human Rights in North Korea to produce *Failure to Protect: A Call for the UN Security Council to Act in North Korea.* The report applied RtoP to North Korea and argued that crimes against humanity were taking place in the DPRK and that this merited international intervention. A sequel to the original report was issued in 2008. Mr. Bondevik holds the degree of Cand. Theol. from MF Norwegian School of Theology and was ordained as a priest in the Lutheran Church of Norway in 1979.

Kristen Leanderson Abrams is International Pro Bono Counsel and Program Manager for New Perimeter, a non-profit affiliate of DLA Piper LLP. She received her J.D. from George Washington University Law School with honors and B.A. from Vanderbilt University *magna cum laude.* She was part of the team of lawyers with DLA Piper that co-authored *Failure to Protect* and its sequel.

Gareth Evans, AO, QC, has been Chancellor of the Australian National University since January 2010, a Professorial Fellow at The University of Melbourne since July 2009 and an Honorary Fellow of Magdalen College, Oxford University, since 2004.

He was formerly a long-serving Australian Cabinet Minister, including Foreign Minister (1988–1996), and president of the International Crisis Group (2000–2009). He co-chaired the International Commission on Intervention and State Sovereignty (2000–2001) and the International Commission on Nuclear Non-Proliferation and Disarmament (2008–2010) and has been a member of several other high-level international panels. He has written and/or edited nine books—most recently *The Responsibility to Protect: Ending Mass Atrocity Crimes Once and for All* (Brookings Institution, 2008)—and published over 100 journal articles and chapters on foreign relations, human rights, and legal and constitutional reform. He received the 2010 Roosevelt Institute Award for Freedom from Fear, for his pioneering work on the Responsibility to Protect, and his contributions to conflict prevention and resolution, arms control, and disarmament.

Preface

Jared Genser and Irwin Cotler

UN Secretary-General Kofi Annan challenged Member States in his Millennium Report to answer the question that haunted his tenure at the United Nations: "If humanitarian intervention is indeed an unacceptable assault on sovereignty, how should we respond to a Rwanda, to a Srebrenica—to gross and systematic violations of human rights that offend every precept of our common humanity?"[1] The International Commission on Intervention and State Sovereignty (ICISS) answered the Secretary-General's challenge by introducing the concept of the Responsibility to Protect, building on Francis Deng and his Brookings Institution colleagues' notion of "sovereignty as responsibility."[2] Four years later, over 150 heads of state and government unanimously adopted the Responsibility to Protect (RtoP) at the 2005 World Summit.

They declared that "[e]ach individual State has the responsibility to protect its populations from genocide, war crimes, ethnic cleansing and crimes against humanity. This responsibility entails the prevention of such crimes. . . The international community, through the United Nations, also has the responsibility to use appropriate diplomatic, humanitarian and other peaceful means . . . to help protect populations . . . we are prepared to take collective action, in a timely and decisive manner . . . should peaceful means be inadequate and national authorities manifestly fail [to exercise their responsibilities]. . . ."[3] The Security Council subsequently affirmed the paragraphs of the Outcome Document regarding RtoP.[4]

These are considerable developments for RtoP and relatively rapid ones in the realm of international norms. Yet, some six years since the introduction of an answer to Secretary-General Annan's challenge, RtoP has yet to be fully implemented—but the need to prevent mass atrocities is greater than ever. Over the past decade, the ending, let alone preventing of mass atrocities has been a subordinate priority in the international community as many nations turned their attention to fighting extremism and responding to the global economic crisis.

This book emphasizes the urgent need for the international community to recommit itself to implementing RtoP in a robust and comprehensive manner. After an introduction by former Czech Republic President Václav Havel and Bishop Desmond

[1] Kofi Annan, "*We the Peoples*": *The Role of the United Nations in the 21st Century: Millennium Report of the Secretary General*, A/54/2000, at 48.

[2] Francis M. Deng, et al., Sovereignty as Responsibility: Conflict Management in Africa (Brookings Institution Press, 1996).

[3] *2005 World Summit Outcome*, A/RES/60/1, Sept. 15, 2005, at ¶¶ 138–139.

[4] S.C. Res. 1674, S/RES/1674, Apr. 28, 2006, at ¶ 4.

M. Tutu, Part I provides the historical, theoretical, and legal underpinnings surrounding the development of RtoP. Part II presents important regional perspectives on the development of the doctrine. Part III examines case studies on actual or potential implementation of the doctrine in Darfur (Sudan) Burma (Myanmar), Kenya, Sri Lanka, Democratic Republic of Congo, and North Korea. And then former Australian Foreign Minister and ICISS co-chair Gareth Evans discusses the kinds of steps the international community might take to advance implementation of RtoP in light of the slow progress to date.

It is worth highlighting that as we edited this book, fast-moving events in Libya led to a historic invocation of RtoP by the UN Security Council to prevent Muammar Gaddafi's slaughter of his own people, which many months after the imposition of a NATO no-fly zone led to his ouster from power by forces of the National Transitional Council. While the implications of this intervention for the development of RtoP is still being assessed, Mohamed Helal included an initial analysis in Chapter 10 on Middle East perspectives.

As is the case of any edited volume, the authors of individual chapters sometimes have differing views from each other and differing views from us personally. Nevertheless, we believe the richness of the perspectives presented represents a diversity of opinion that is important in any major global policy debate.

We would like to thank The Human Rights Foundation and The Moriah Fund for their financial support of this important project, which came with their agreement to forgo any editorial input into the book's content; Kevin Pendergast with Oxford University Press, who was a strong editor and advocate for the project; and Beth Schwanke, who spent countless hours providing her invaluable editorial assistance.

For his part, Jared would like to thank his wife Lisa for her love and support, and his parents Lyne and Sander who inspired his commitment to social justice. He would like to dedicate this book to his children Zachary and Alexandra, on whose generation the burden of truly fulfilling the promise of the Responsibility to Protect will fall.

For his part, Irwin would like to dedicate the book to his wife Ariella, his children, and grandchildren.

Jared Genser
Washington, D.C.
Irwin Cotler
Montreal, Canada

Abbreviations

ACSC	ASEAN Civil Society Conference
AEC	ASEAN Economic Community
AHOS	Assembly of Heads of State and Government
AICHR	ASEAN Intergovernmental Commission on Human Rights
ALBA	Bolivarian Alliance of Peoples of America
AMIS	African Union Mission in Sudan
APRM	Africa Peer Review Mechanism
APSC	ASEAN Political Security Community
ARF	ASEAN Regional Forum
ASC	ASEAN Security Community
ASCC	ASEAN Socio-Cultural Community
ASEAN	Association of Southeast Asian Nations
AU	African Union
BATUK	British Army Training Unit Kenya
BPST	British Peace Support Team
CARICOM	Caribbean Community and Common Market
CEDAW	Convention on the Elimination of All Forms of Discrimination Against Women
CFA	Ceasefire Agreement (Sri Lanka)
CIPEV	Report of the Commission of Inquiry on Post-Election Violence (Kenya)
CJTF-HOA	Combined Joint Task Force-Horn of Africa
CNDP	National Congress for the Defense of the People (Democratic Republic of Congo)
CSCAP	Council for Security Cooperation in the Asia Pacific
CoE	Council of Europe
CPA	Comprehensive Peace Agreement (Sudan)
CRC	Convention on the Rights of the Child
DDR	Disarm, Demobilize, and Reintegrate
DFL	Darfur Liberation Front (Sudan)
DPA	UN Department of Political Affairs
DPKO	UN Department of Peacekeeping Operations
DPRK	Democratic People's Republic of Korea (North Korea)
DRC	Democratic Republic of Congo
ECOWAS	Economic Community of West African States
ECPS	Executive Committee on Peace and Security

EISAS	ECPS Information and Strategic Analysis Secretariat
EITI	Extractive Industries Transparency Initiative
EPG	Eminent Persons Group
EU	European Union
FARDC	Armed Forces of the Democratic Republic of Congo
FDLR	Democratic Forces for the Liberation of Rwanda
HDI	Human Development Index
HHI	Harvard Humanitarian Initiative
HLTF	High Level Task Force
HLP	High Level Panel
HRC	UN Human Rights Council
HRW	Human Rights Watch
ICBL	International Campaign to Ban Landmines
ICC	International Criminal Court
ICCPR	International Covenant on Civil and Political Rights
ICISS	International Commission on Intervention and State Sovereignty
ICJ	International Court of Justice
ICRC	International Committee of the Red Cross
ICTR	International Criminal Tribunal for Rwanda
ICTY	International Criminal Tribunal for the Former Yugoslavia
IRC	International Rescue Committee
IDP	Internally Displaced Person
IHL	International Humanitarian Law
IHRL	International Human Rights Law
ILC	International Law Commission
IMF	International Monetary Fund
IPKF	Indian Peacekeeping Force
JEM	Justice and Equality Movement
KNDR	Kenya National Dialogue and Reconciliation
KWP	Korean Workers' Party
LAC	Latin American and the Caribbean
LAS	League of Arab States
LCD	Least-Common Denominator
LRA	Lord's Resistance Army
LTTE	Liberation Tigers of Tamil Eelam
MDG	Millennium Development Goals
MINUSTAH	United Nations Stabilization Mission in Haiti
MONUC	United Nations Organization Mission in the Democratic Republic of Congo
MONUSCO	United Nations Organization Stabilization Mission in the Democratic Republic of Congo
NAM	Non-Aligned Movement
NATO	North Atlantic Treaty Organization
NDF	National Democratic Front (Burma)
NGO	Non-Governmental Organization
NIF	National Islamic Front (Sudan)
NTC	National Transitional Council (Libya)

OAS	Organization of American States
OAU	Organization of African Unity
OCHA	UN Office for the Coordination of Humanitarian Affairs
ODM	Orange Democratic Movement (Kenya)
OHCHR	UN Office of the High Commissioner on Human Rights
OIC	Organization of Islamic Conference
OLA	UN Office of Legal Affairs
OPT	Occupied Palestinian Territories
OSCE	Organization for Security and Cooperation in Europe
PBSO	UN Peacebuilding Support Office
PNU	Party of National Unity (Kenya)
PSC	Protocol Establishing the Peace and Security Council
REC	Regional Economic Community
RIGO	Regional Inter-Governmental Organization
RtoP	Responsibility to Protect
RUF	Revolutionary United Front (Sierra Leone)
SCDL	Special Court for Sierra Leone
SICA	Central American Integration System
SLA	Sri Lanka Army
SLMM	Sri Lankan Monitoring Mission
SLM/SLA	Sudanese Liberation Movement/Sudanese Liberation Army
SSR	Security Sector Reform
TCP	People's Treaty on Trade
UN	United Nations
USAID	US Agency for International Development
UNAMID	AU/UN Hybrid Operation in Darfur
UNASUR	Union of South American Nations
UNDP	United Nations Development Programme
UNGA	United Nations General Assembly
UNSC	United Nations Security Council
UNFPA	United Nations Population Fund
UNICEF	United Nations Children's Fund
UNOSOM	United Nations Operation in Somalia
UNOCI	United Nations Mission in Côte d'Ivoire
WFP	World Food Programme
WSOD	World Summit Outcome Document

Introduction

Václav Havel and Desmond M. Tutu

The Responsibility to Protect (RtoP) is the most significant development in the defense of human rights since the codification of those rights enshrined in the Universal Declaration of Human Rights in the aftermath of World War II and the Holocaust. Yet, six years and millions of preventable deaths after the adoption of RtoP by the 2005 World Summit, its implementation remains far from a reality. Instead, RtoP is a frustratingly elusive promise—the promise of stopping mass atrocities in our time.

This book seeks to advance the discussion and development of the Responsibility to Protect. It is our sincere hope that it will provide a roadmap for closing the gap between the reality and the promise of RtoP.

The development of a global consensus to stop mass atrocity crimes through the adoption of RtoP has been a horrific journey. It is a journey that began in the gas chambers of the Holocaust and moved through the killing fields of Cambodia to the machetes and rapes in Rwanda and into a stadium in Srebrenica. It is a journey that exposes the sad irony that the rallying cry "Never Again!"—first uttered after the full horrors of the Holocaust were exposed—has been ignored for generations. Time and time again, the world has watched and waited as human beings planned and implemented genocides, war crimes, ethnic cleansings, and crimes against humanity, enveloping states and destroying lives. In Rwanda and Bosnia, the world even watched as UN peacekeepers sat impotent, as innocents were slaughtered.

The enormity of the international community's failure to respond to government-sponsored mass murders demanded a rethinking of traditional notions of state sovereignty. For most of the history of nation-states, state sovereignty was absolute and inviolable. One state could not interfere with another's domestic matters. Yet, the mass atrocities of the 20th century and the expansion of international human rights law has pierced the absolute protection provided to sovereign states. While sovereignty remains the fundamental basis for states' coexistence, an understanding of their rights now incorporates clear duties that states owe to their citizens and residents.

After the tragedies in Rwanda and Bosnia, then Secretary-General Kofi Annan challenged UN member states to reconcile their need for the preservation of sovereignty with the need for protection of global human rights. The Secretary-General poignantly asked, "[i]f humanitarian intervention is, indeed, an unacceptable assault on sovereignty, how should we respond . . . to gross and systematic violations of human rights that offend every precept of our common humanity?"

This is the question that the Responsibility to Protect attempts to answer.

At its core, RtoP is the sovereign's responsibility to protect its populations from genocide, war crimes, ethnic cleansing, and crimes against humanity. It is the obligation of the United Nations, up through and including the Security Council, to act where states fail to meet their duties to their own citizens. The weight of RtoP is appropriately on prevention, not on armed interventionist measures. But if the international community decides through the Security Council that mass atrocities are being committed or are looming on the horizon, such intervention may be authorized.

At the 2005 World Summit, the largest gathering of heads of state ever assembled agreed that the Responsibility to Protect rests on three pillars: (1) the responsibility of the state to protect its population from genocide, war crimes, ethnic cleansing, and crimes against humanity, and from their incitement; (2) the commitment of the international community to assist states in meeting these obligations; and (3) the responsibility of the member states to respond in a timely and decisive manner when a state is manifestly failing to provide such protection.

The agreement was, without a doubt, a historic breakthrough. Yet, enormous questions and concerns about RtoP and its scope remain. There are basic classification questions, such as the definition of ethnic cleansing. And there are concerns about misuse, including fears that RtoP will be used by powerful states to justify neo-colonialist incursions into less powerful states.

The most important question, however, is how RtoP will be implemented. Nevertheless, as the case studies in the book highlight, the reality of implementation remains an open-ended question. Although RtoP has been referenced with regards to a number of country situations, it has only been the primary explanation for action in Kenya and Libya. But both those interventions are more likely attributed to a host of political factors than merely to RtoP.

Despite its limited implementation the Responsibility to Protect is far more than an aspirational doctrine. It is a clear and unequivocal public commitment by world leaders that can and will prevent mass atrocities. Although there will surely be stumbles as the doctrine is implemented, the Responsibility to Protect remains the international community's greatest hope for being able to one day truthfully claim, "Never Again!"

President Václav Havel
Former President of the Czech Republic

Bishop Desmond M. Tutu
Archbishop Emeritus of Cape Town

PART I
THE DEVELOPMENT OF THE RESPONSIBILITY TO PROTECT

1 RtoP and the Evolution of State Sovereignty

Lloyd Axworthy

Since the Peace of Westphalia in 1648, non-interference in the international policies of even of the most repressive governments was the golden rule of international diplomacy. The Canadian-sponsored concept of "responsibility to protect" proposed the most significant adjustment to national sovereignty in 360 years.[1]

Since the Peace of Westphalia of 1648 established ground rules for relations between nation-states, security has been predicated narrowly on the fundamental principles of the integrity and inviolability of territorial borders. This makes less sense in light of today's increasingly globalized and borderless world, where threats are, in the words of former UN Secretary-General Kofi Annan, "problems without passports."[2] It is an environment which demands a new paradigm of understanding and response. These changes have influenced a recent shift in focus from national security to human security, creating a need for an expanded definition beyond the traditional understandings of sovereignty.

One of the most important efforts to re-set the meaning of sovereignty took place at the 2005 World Summit in New York, which adopted as part of its reform package the concept of the Responsibility to Protect (RtoP). The concept grew out of the International Commission on Intervention and State Sovereignty (ICISS), which was sponsored by the Canadian government and formed in 2000 to deal with the issue of protecting civilians in situations of risk, a clear expression of the human security ideal. In the post-Cold War world, the idea of human security argued that the greatest threats

[1] Martin Gilbert, *The Terrible 20th Century*, THE GLOBE AND MAIL, Jan. 31, 2007.

[2] Kofi Annan, *Problems Without Passports*, FOREIGN POLICY, Sept. 1, 2002.

to international peace and security were no longer aggressive attacks between states, but destabilizing events such as genocide, civil war, environmental degradation, terrorism, and pandemics. It reflected the concern expressed by Kofi Annan about the increasing transcendence of security threats to individuals across boundaries, and the need for international intervention to protect innocent people even if it meant challenging the sacredness of sovereignty.

The end of the Cold War and the 1990s introduced a unique kind of international security challenge. Where historically wars were fought between armies, and casualties were made up primarily from the ranks for soldiers, the second half of the twentieth century witnessed the post-colonial history of many developing nations degenerating into situations of civil conflict. While the norm among states is to turn a blind eye to another state's internal affairs, it soon became apparent that crises don't always obey territorial boundaries and that internal conflicts had a spillover effect. It was clear the tools we traditionally used to govern ourselves were less relevant to the intermingling of our common fate in today's global conditions. As a result, something new was required in the interest of global peace and security. The realization that something as sacred as the responsibilities of a sovereign state could evolve was linked to the understanding that in today's globalized world no one state can exist in isolation.

From a realist perspective on international relations that focused solely on the state as the referent object and primary provider of security, this would have been considered heresy, if not revolutionary. Since the signing of the Peace of Westphalia treaties in 1648, the practice of sovereignty established the norm of non-interference by external actors regarding the internal affairs of other states. The importance of non-interference should not be understated—under its umbrella, the norm promoted peace and security and interrelationships between states that were stabilized, allowing for the state system we find ourselves in today. But the norm also provides states with what some say is a license to kill, as violent authoritarian leaders are given free reign over the ways and means of governance.[3]

However, since ICISS released its seminal report, it has become the basis for re-examining how the international community must challenge the notion of state sovereignty in order to establish the tools to manage transcendent global problems or egregious internal threats to innocent people. RtoP does not replace the concept of sovereignty but re-sets its application. It maintains that sovereignty is a necessary concept in global governance, but with its benefits come responsibility as well. In the name of protecting civilians, the legitimate ability to govern is linked to security and protection of its people. Should a state fail to do so, it is up to the international community to step in.

This chapter will address the historical evolution of this point from the perspective of a former Canadian Minister of Foreign Affairs who took the initiative in setting up the ICISS. The first part will begin with a brief discussion about the concept of sovereignty. With its roots in the Peace of Westphalia in 1648, sovereignty has never been a rigid concept. It is a foundational concept in international law and denotes the ulti-

[3] Ramesh Thakur & Thomas G. Weiss, *RtoP: From Idea to Norm—and Action?*, 1 Glob. Resp. to Prot. 22–53 (2009).

mate authority over a given territory. *De jure* or *de facto* in nature, it consolidates a set of norms established by other members of the international community. Sovereignty bestows on the state both rights and responsibilities and it will be argued here that these can be re-interpreted with the changing context of international relations. The second section will address in detail the changing international political context of the 1990s and its impact on the expectations of sovereign states and the creation of RtoP. Today, the state remains the principal entity in the process of maintaining peace and security, but what has changed is the role of people in our understanding of security. With greater support for holding state leaders to account for the protection of their citizens, it is important to address next steps, which the chapter will attend to at its end.

I. DEFINING SOVEREIGNTY

As mentioned earlier, discussions around sovereignty generally begin with the signing of the Treaty of Westphalia in 1648 that put an end to the Thirty Years War in Europe. While this is the date given for its genesis, the concept itself and its interpretation have been continuously evolving. Sovereignty is generally considered necessary for the maintenance of peace and security globally, but it can also present an impediment to cooperative global governance. On the one hand, there is the norm of non-intervention into the affairs of other states and on the other, there is a growing framework of international laws, conventions, treaties, and agreements that sets limits on the supreme authority any government has over a given territory. As it is inevitable that states must interact with one another, it benefits them to enter into agreements and establish norms amongst themselves to create the expectation that certain guidelines will be followed. By agreeing to do so, they are voluntarily reducing their claims on the supreme authority within their borders. So the concerns of the sovereign are in a constant state of tension with the demands and requirements made upon it by the international community within which it operates.

Following the end of World War II, the UN was created to avoid the violence and killing that had characterized the early half of the twentieth century. The UN Charter set out its vision for a world based around an agreement that peace and security would be a priority. The intention was to establish a treaty-based scheme in which states would agree to impose limits on their own right to use force in order to benefit from a collective response to any threats or attacks. The UN Charter, which outlines the rights and responsibilities of its members, was worded through the perspective of a rear-view mirror, with the intention of preventing catastrophes of the likes brought about during the two world wars. The hope was that doing so would prohibit the unilateral use of force for any purpose other than self-defense. Prohibition of the use of force is explicitly stated in Article 2(4) of the Charter: "All members shall refrain in their international relations from the threat or use of force against the territorial integrity or political independence of any state, or in any other manner inconsistent with the purposes of the United Nations."[4]

[4] UN, Charter of the United Nations, Oct. 24, 1945, at art. 2(4).

In addition to discouraging state-to-state violence, the Charter also sought to formalize the established international norm of non-intervention that had its roots in the Westphalian system. Article 2(7) of the Charter prohibits intervention into the domestic affairs of other states by offering: "Nothing contained in the present Charter shall authorize the United Nations to intervene in matters which are essentially within the domestic jurisdiction of any state."[5] This article acts as the base for defending sovereignty within the UN system and acts today as the bulwark upon which the inviolability of sovereign states is defended. However, because the UN is in the business of trying to manage issues that cut across borders, it is constantly faced with tensions between the sovereignty clause and the necessity of forging international agreements requiring collective action that challenge the spirit of Article 2(7). The UN Charter was fashioned in response to interstate wars and therefore was silent on the issue of civil conflicts. The outbreak of internal violence against vulnerable people, very often by the governments themselves, increasingly became the main challenge faced by the UN and one that was poorly handled if at all. While UN peacekeepers may have been present, their inability to protect people was severely limited due to the influence of the Charter. One only has to think of the direst situations in the Balkans or in Rwanda.

The first years of the UN represented a defining time in the promotion of a new human rights framework and the responsibility of protecting civilians from the horrors of war and genocide. Over the next decades it would establish a series of treaties and conventions that would serve to create a stigma against aggressive action between states.[6] The first landmark came with the 1948 Universal Declaration of Human Rights and with that, a growing consensus that all people were endowed with the same basic claims to a life with freedom from fear.[7] Since then, it is a document that has captured the hearts and minds of people through its affirmation of the inherent worth and dignity of every person. And its guiding principles have inspired over 80 treaties, giving life to an international architecture of human rights law.

The second landmark was the passage of an international convention making the crime of genocide a matter of universal jurisdiction. The horror of the Holocaust ushered in a new era of human rights law and the slogan "never again." Raphael Lemkin became a one-man moral force in advancing the concept of genocide as an international crime. He embarked on a personal crusade to enlist support for having genocide included at Nuremberg as a crime. His crowning achievement was the passage, at the UN General Assembly in 1948, of the Convention on the Prevention and Punishment of the Crime of Genocide. Today, 137 nations have joined its membership, marking a near-universal acknowledgement that the most egregious of violent acts against any one group of people should be prevented.

In addition to transitioning out of the first half of the twentieth century, characterized by two world wars, and into the UN system, with its focus on peace, security, and human rights, the second half of the century would also bring with it a wave of decolonization. This would introduce a new group of state actors into the

[5] *Id.* at art. 2(7).

[6] *See* Thakur & Weiss, *supra* note 3, at 30.

[7] *See* Robert Belloni, *The Tragedy of Darfur and the Limits of the "Responsibility to Protect,"* 5 Ethnopolitics 327–346 (2006).

international system, creating a new set of challenges for global governance and the maintenance of peace and security. Sovereignty and its companion, non-intervention, had existed for centuries before the end of the Second World War and the establishment of the UN Charter. But the players in that game were few and far between and were dominated by European powers. The process of colonization had drawn a line between those who were sovereign and those who were not. Being recognized as such meant benefiting from the norm of non-intervention and respect for any one state's territorial integrity. Clearly the new colonies would not qualify and, it follows, the business of their subjugation had been considered legitimate, desirable, and appropriate.

While granting these new states *de jure* sovereignty intended to level the playing field, the colonial economies and government structures that were inherited sometimes offered little in terms of the institutions necessary to assert legitimate authority, and the resulting ability to govern over a given territory differed greatly. Despite the outcome, sovereignty offered a means of protecting a newly independent state's affairs from the meddling reach of former colonizers and other powerful interests. For such states, their inherited colonial government structures and economies proved challenging to overcome from a governance standpoint. By the 1980s, many were struggling to maintain the state capacity and legitimacy to rule, resulting in corruption, state-violence, and all-out civil war in a number of cases. While their borders granted them legitimacy from the perspective of other countries, states such as Uganda, Zaire, Guatemala, and Peru were struggling to maintain authority and were not above asserting it through violence.

The intentions of the UN regarding matters of a humanitarian nature were more or less paralyzed during the Cold War at the hands of both superpowers. The tension between both the Soviet Union and the U.S. and the prospect of "mutually assured destruction" held the world's attention. As new states emerged from their colonial histories, the great war of ideologies would extend itself into them. Battle through such proxies as Vietnam, Afghanistan, and Latin American states marked the time, and the Security Council was bound by its members and their veto powers from intervening. Until the Six Day War of 1967, no resolution had mentioned any humanitarian concern since 1945.[8]

The end of the Cold War provided the UN with a renewed opportunity to take the lead on addressing humanitarian crises. Concern was growing over the increasing numbers of civilian casualties being reported in civil wars. Human rights started to make a comeback early on in the decade. With the UN World Conference on Human Rights in Vienna in 1993, the world was able to reaffirm its commitment to upholding basic human rights. From 1990 to 1994, twice as many resolutions were passed than had been previously since the existence of the UN.[9] The UN was now free to act as it had been intentioned and it would be provided with multiple opportunities.

[8] Thomas G. Weiss, *The Sunset of Humanitarian Intervention? The Responsibility to Protect in a Unipolar Era*, 35 Security Dialogue 136 (2004).

[9] *See id.*

II. SOVEREIGNTY AS RESPONSIBILITY

A. Human Security

This new decade would prove to be a turning point as the nature of violent conflict and the impact on large numbers of innocent people would decidedly shift. This takes us to the introduction of the "human security" concept. This was an idea spawned as the Cold War ended and the inadequacies of the nation-state system to meet the demands of globalization were revealing themselves. What had become evident was that new sets of common risks threatened the security of individuals regardless of nationality. The problem that came out of the Cold War was how to define security in an era where civil conflicts were on the rise and had historically evaded international consideration. However, as I have recalled previously, intrastate violence and war have increasingly been recognized for their significant potential for international destabilization that can occur from the spillover effects of conflict.[10] Old notions of national security predicated on the defense of borders made little sense when the threat posed by violence and conflict, international networks of predators and criminals, global pandemics, and massive natural disasters required a new approach to the protection of peoples.

This "human security" agenda became Canada's approach to foreign policy in the mid-90s. In the search for a new, post-Cold War foreign policy paradigm, Canada along with like-minded nations such as Norway recognized that the security of individuals must have commensurate standing as matters of state security. Furthermore, given the nature of threats confronting individuals, it was widely accepted that a broadening of the definition of security was imminent. Human security is much more than the absence of military threat. It includes the guarantee of fundamental human rights. It recognizes the links between economic development, environmental degradation, and population growth. It encompasses into its framework the influence and power of a constellation of international actors who wield influence and power-corporations, civil society, trans-national institutions, networks of groups and individuals—not normally considered in the formulation of international law—but often more of a factor than many nation-states.

In line with these sweeping international changes, Frances Deng can be attributed with introducing the concept of the Responsibility to Protect in the international dialogue. In the early 1990s, as the Representative of the United Nations Secretary-General on Internally Displaced Persons (IDPs), Deng took it as his responsibility to ensure the safety and security of those who had been forced to flee their homes in search of refuge but who had not crossed state borders. He wrote about the Responsibility to Protect with the idea that it was the host government's responsibility to provide for the protection of the IDPs. In the case where a state is unable to do so, it become their responsibility to request international assistance.[11] In fact, the first time I heard the notion of a Responsibility to Protect was when Deng visited me in

[10] Lloyd Axworthy, *Human Security: An Opening for UN Reform*, *in* The United Nations and Global Security (Richard M. Price and Mark W. Zacher eds., 2004), at 249.

[11] Alex J. Bellamy, *The Responsibility to Protect and the Problem of Military Intervention*, 84 International Affairs 619 (2008).

Ottawa and argued for a clear commitment by the international community to deal with the IDP issue.[12]

There was a growing awareness that a crisis within any given state could have regional or international spillover effects and that turning a blind eye could lead to deleterious outcomes. The 1994 genocide in Rwanda is a case in point. The horror of the event was only made more severe by the absolute failure to prevent it from happening. Paul Heinbecker, former Canadian Ambassador to the UN, has referred to it as, "the worst single failure of the UN."[13] Not only was the international community haunted by the images and knowledge of nearly a million men, women, and children dead, but by the realization that early intervention may have successfully avoided the most horrific outcomes of this campaign. In the months and years that followed, the flow of refugees and Rwandan Hutu militia into the neighboring Democratic Republic of the Congo (then known as Zaire) proved to be a destabilizing force throughout the region and led to a horrific war involving multiple African states and many more armed groups and resulted in the deaths of 3.9 million people.[14] This was the evolving reality of conflict.

In response to these events Canada embarked on a number of initiatives that intended to address the neglectful state of human security in states struggling to maintain control over their territories. One of Canada's earliest human security initiatives addressed the global scourge of landmines. It is an interesting case and one very telling of the changing international political climate that included new actors. With the increasing numbers of human rights organizations, and the easy flow of information through the internet, civil society groups were offering new challenges and opportunities in foreign policy. An essential element of this strategy was partnerships. The Ottawa Process, launched in Canada in 1996, began when the International Campaign to Ban Landmines (ICBL), a powerful coalition of humanitarian groups that included several non-governmental organizations (NGOs), International Red Cross, and a number of committed individuals, partnered with Canada and a number of like-minded governments with the aim of achieving a global ban on landmines. The ICBL initiative, and its targeted pressure which focused on the risks of landmines to individuals, moved the discourse out of the realm of diplomatic and military arms control language and shifted attention instead on the devastating impact on innocent civilians. This work would eventually lead to the Ottawa Treaty to ban anti-personnel landmines, a pernicious weapon that would cause harm indiscriminately.

The next vital step in promoting the security of individuals would also strive to hold state leaders accountable when they fail to uphold human rights. This was the creation of the International Criminal Court (ICC) in the late 1990s. The hardscrabble work of international diplomacy is not usually seen as a joyous occupation. But once in a while there is a moment of exuberant glee where the sheer delight at a surprise outcome after months if not years of effort brings joy to the hardened heart. Such a moment occurred with the creation of such a groundbreaking institution in Rome in the summer of 1997.

[12] Lloyd Axworthy, Navigating a New World 414 (2003).

[13] Paul Heinbecker, Getting Back in the Game: A Foreign Policy Playbook for Canada 114 (2010).

[14] International Rescue Committee, *Mortality in the Democratic Republic of the Congo: An Ongoing Crisis* (2007), at ii.

Ultimately, the Rome Statute led to the establishment of the ICC with jurisdiction over genocide, war crimes, and crimes against humanity. Canada helped to ensure that the definition of these crimes was substantially broadened to include the plight of women and children in armed conflict. The ICC was conceived of as an important mechanism for protecting civilians against atrocities. If people responsible for these crimes are actually held to account, others may make different decisions when weighing the costs of their actions.

Events in the Balkans, most specifically in Kosovo in 1999, brought to a head the crucial decision of international humanitarian intervention. It was to be a catalyst in promoting a serious assessment of the meaning of human security. The ultimate test was a willingness to exercise military force to uphold the principles of protection. While there was strong endorsement of the need to intervene to protect people from the widespread abuse, there was equally strong criticism of the way the actions in Kosovo contravened fundamental articles of national sovereignty without explicit UN Security Council authorization. Ultimately, the Charter system had failed to predict both the significant changes that had occurred since is creation; it also proved to be inflexible and incapable of adequately accounting for the security needs of the current historical context. The time had come to face these issues. Death and destruction from internal armed conflicts had become a scourge of the last part of the century and things were looking no better for the new century. At the next G-8 Foreign Ministers meeting in 1999, I made a presentation in which I said:

> Non-interference remains basic to international peace and security, so the intervention in Kosovo must not be held up as a precedent to justify intervention anywhere, any time or for any reason. However, in cases of extreme abuse, the concept of national sovereignty cannot be absolute . . . the UN Security Council cannot stand aside in the face of outrages we have seen in a variety of violent disputes.[15]

It was also in 1999 that Canada won a seat at the Security Council, and we made our objective to push forward human security as a priority for the UN, and to promote broadening its mandate beyond the realm of traditional security concerns. During our presidency at the Council, we held an informal debate on the issue of civilian protection in armed conflict. Given the gravity of the situation and the lack of attention to that point, there was a pressing need to explore the issue further. Keeping this in mind, we called on the Secretary-General to compile a comprehensive report on the protection of civilians in armed conflict, to which he complied.

The Secretary-General released his report on the protection of civilians in armed conflict later that year.[16] It contained a number of recommendations aimed at improving the physical and legal protections in situations of armed conflict. With the leverage this gave us, Canada promoted the adoption of two important resolutions, which drew the attention and focus of the Security Council toward this important matter. The passing of Resolution 1265 (1999) on the Protection of Civilians in Armed Conflict, followed by Resolution 1296 (2000), together offered the most comprehensive measures

[15] Lloyd Axworthy, Navigating in a New World 190 (2004).

[16] Report of the Secretary-General to the Security Council on the Protection of Civilians in Armed Conflict, S/1999/957 (Sept. 8, 1999).

adopted by the Security Council regarding civilian protection. They created an opening for substantive UN reform by accentuating a number of issues that had hitherto been overlooked by the international community, notably, conflict prevention, adequate training for peacekeepers, the impacts of small arms and landmines on civilians, as well as the humanitarian impacts of sanctions on vulnerable populations.

We had a strong ally in Kofi Annan, who is a consummate diplomat well schooled in the "get-along philosophy" of the UN Secretariat, but also a man of conviction and courage who is unafraid to speak out. In his *Millennium Report* to the General Assembly in 2000, he argued, "If humanitarian intervention is indeed an unacceptable assault on sovereignty, how should we respond to a Rwanda, to a Srebrenica, to gross and systematic violations of human rights that offend every precept of our common humanity?"[17] He challenged the UN to reconsider the notion of sovereignty as a means of ending gross violations of human rights and violence against civilian populations. It was in further discussions with the Secretary-General that it was decided that there was a need for a body to examine the question. There were the beginnings of ICISS, initiated by Canada.

B. International Commission on Intervention and State Sovereignty

With the dramatic events of the 1990s drawing to a close, discussions within the UN made clear that an effort must be made to set out a systematic and responsive framework of rules and procedures for the protection of vulnerable people. The horrors that had characterized that decade begged the following question: If this new norm of protection of people was to become a prime responsibility, and, when necessary, trump the long-held principle of national sovereignty, then was international military intervention justified to enforce this standard, and if so, under what conditions?[18] It was this question, along with further discussions with the Secretary-General that gave impetus to a Canadian government initiative to establish ICISS, as a way of formulating a solution to the dilemma of international intervention. At first it was assumed that this should be a UN-sponsored Commission. But after discussions with highly placed officials at the UN, the view changed to establishing an independent commission, thus avoiding the pitfalls of trying to construct a body that would be created by the UN. The ICISS proceeded on the assurances that the report of such a commission would be given serious acceptance at the highest levels of the UN.

ICISS was made up of fifteen able and knowledgeable individuals, chosen specifically to represent varying perspectives on the topic of humanitarian intervention. The commission was sponsored by Canada, granted resources by major U.S. foundations and spent more than a year in worldwide consultations and issued a report called the *Responsibility to Protect* in December 2001. The question the Commission was asked to respond to was the following, "when, if ever, it is appropriate for states to take coercive—and in particular military—action, against another state for the purpose of

[17] UN GAOR, 54th Sess. UN Doc. A/54/2000, Mar. 27, 2000.

[18] *See* Axworthy, *supra* note 15, at 157.

protecting people at risk in that other state."[19] In the end, it answered as follows: sovereignty is based on the ability and willingness of governments to accept the Responsibility to Protect their own citizens. Failing that, the international community has a right to intervene.

In essence, the Commission crafted a definition of sovereignty centered not on the prerogatives of the state but on its primary Responsibility to Protect its citizens. If a state legitimately protects its citizens, then it is in full right of its sovereign power. Such a responsibility implies an evaluation of the sovereignty from the perspective of the victim, not the intervener. If a state cannot provide the protection or is the author of the crime, then it forfeits its sovereign right and the international community steps in, not just to protect, but to prevent and re-build. The RtoP has resonance as future interventions are contemplated. To protect against that abuse of power of intervention used with such callousness by powerful countries against weaker nations for so much of our recent history, the Commission establishes a number of thresholds or tests that must be met. How heinous are the crimes? Have measures been tried to correct the problem, short of force? Does the intervention have the support of a legitimate multi-lateral body and not just the caprice of one set of rulers or one particularly powerful government? Will the force used be appropriate to the problem, especially in terms of the injury and deaths caused by the intervention? If a state fails in its Responsibility to Protect, or is the perpetrator of a massive attack on the rights of its citizens, then the international community must assume the function. The Commission leaders therefore took to a much broader strategy on how to hold states responsible to the protection of the rights of individuals.

The international responsibility comprises three tasks: prevention, reaction, and rebuilding. The Commission stresses that the "prevention option should always be exhausted before intervention is contemplated. The exercise of the responsibility to both prevent and react should always involve less intrusive and coercive measures being considered before more coercive and intrusive ones are applied."[20] A high threshold must be met, such a large-scale loss of lives of ethnic cleansing, before military action is warranted. Military intervention should be seen as a last resort, and the minimum force necessary should be used. The Commission comes down squarely on the need to work through the Security Council, but suggests that the veto should not be used by the P-5 unless their vital interests are at stake. If the Council stalemates, there should be recourse to the General Assembly.

RtoP was conceived as an attempt to reconcile the ambiguity surrounding cases of proposed military intervention as we saw in the case of Kosovo by ICISS establishing thresholds based on traditional "just war" principles. These include last resort, right authority, right intention, responsible prospects and proportional means. As outlined in the report, "Where a population is suffering serious harm, as a result of internal war, insurgency, repression or state failure, and the state in question is unwilling or

[19] International Commission on Intervention and State Sovereignty (ICISS), The Responsibility to Protect: Report of the International Commission on Intervention and State Sovereignty (International Development Research Centre 2001), *available at* http://www.iciss.ca/report-en.asp [hereinafter ICISS Report].

[20] *Id.*, at XI.

unable to halt or avert it, the principle of non-intervention yields to the international responsibility to protect."[21]

The release of the report was unfortunately timed just following the September 11, 2001 attacks on the United States in New York and Washington. The outcome of that attack was a dramatic shift in American foreign policy, with an intensified focus on rooting out sources of terrorism and an aggressive pre-emptive style of interventionism. These events took the focus away from the civil conflicts of the 1990s and, like the flip of a switch, terrorism became the primary focus. With the U.S. intervention in Iraq looming, debates over the legitimacy of the invasion only introduced further questions around the notion of security in the twenty-first century. However, the RtoP concept got back on track in 2003 when Kofi Annan enlisted a group of 16 eminent individuals from various backgrounds to join the Secretary-General's High-Level Panel on Threats, Challenges, and Change. They were enlisted with the task of analyzing "the threats to peace and security our world faces; to evaluate how well our existing policies and institutions are meeting them; and to recommend changes to those policies and institutions, so as to ensure an effective collective response to those threats."[22]

The panel produced their report, *A More Secure World: Our Shared Responsibility*, in 2004, and it was the basis for preparing a UN reform package leading up to the 2005 UN World Summit. The report included a number of references to RtoP and the responsibility of governments to protect their populations. As it states, "There is a growing recognition that the issue is not the 'right to intervene' of any [s]tate, but the 'responsibility to protect' of *every* [s]tate when it comes to people suffering from avoidable catastrophe—mass murder and rape, ethnic cleansing by forcible expulsion and terror, and deliberate starvation and exposure to disease."[23] The report advocates taking prevention seriously, but also suggests five criteria that should be met in order to evaluate the legitimacy of any intervention proposed under the banner of RtoP. The results of the Panel reflected that changing global dynamic of the end of the last century and the recognition that there had to be a framework governing international action to prevent or halt the suffering of civilian populations. What is revolutionary about this is not the status of the state as the primary agent in the affairs of the world, but it is the shift in how sovereignty is defined that marks a change.[24]

At this junction, we had a blueprint that could well provide a framework with which to re-wire the UN system to make it an effective instrument of responding to the contemporary risks of civil conflict and global calamity. The question that is being asked is whether the international community, which is increasingly economically and socially interdependent, is willing to take on political responsibility for those who are being excluded from the protection of universal laws and rights? Indeed, there is a larger reality that can no longer be ignored by those in the more secure, prosperous enclaves of the world. Our own security interests are also at stake, not so much by the old calculations of national interest but as measured by the personal risk to individuals.

[21] *Id.*, at XI

[22] Kofi Annan, *Courage to Fulfill our Responsibilities*, The Economist, Dec. 2, 2004.

[23] Secretary-General's High-Level Panel on Threats, Challenges and Change, *A More Secure World: Our Shared Responsibility*, A/59/565, Dec. 2, 2004, at ¶ 201.

[24] *See* Thakur & Weiss, *supra* note 3, at 28.

The report served to solidify a new interpretation of sovereignty and collective security that is applicable within the UN framework. As Anne-Marie Slaughter has pointed out, the new conception of security "rests on solidarity more than self-defense, and awareness of common threats hence common responsibilities."[25] It essentially creates a bridge between traditional notions of common security, that through solidarity regarding self-defense, establishing a concept of collective security that takes into understanding what should be considered a threat, while respecting the role of the state in maintaining peace internationally.

Participating in this new collective security requires implementing a kind of conditional sovereignty. States must actively accept two new responsibilities, they are that they must act to protect and defend the basic rights and security concerns of their civilian population, and if they fail to do so, their sovereign rights become null. Conversely, if any given state fails to fulfill this basic responsibility, it becomes the responsibility of other states to intervene. The next step was to get members of the UN to agree.

III. ON THE ROAD TO THE 2005 WORLD SUMMIT

On our side, we clearly had the support of the Secretary-General, but like many high-level panels and reports that had preceded it, RtoP was at risk of biding its time as a document on the bookshelves of diplomats and UN staff for all history. RtoP has faced some skepticism. ICISS couldn't have had more unfortunate timing when it released its report a few short months following 9/11. The world's attention shifted away from the humanitarian tragedies of the previous decade to terrorism. Concerns were brought forward, particularly from developing countries that remain wary of the influence and intervention of more powerful states with interests disguised under a humanitarian mask. One such case used as a unilateral intervention with supposed humanitarian intentions was the U.S. invasion of Iraq in 2003. The fallout from these events drew attention away from the human-focused approach of RtoP and suspicions grew regarding its intentions. Particularly damaging was the attempt on the part of the U.S. to inappropriately sell the Iraq invasion on humanitarian grounds.[26]

Ultimately, RtoP had been conceived with military intervention as the least desirable option, to be considered as a last resort in only the most severe of circumstances. What is promoted above all else is prevention, a topic that is too often neglected in the debate. This was, and still is, a contentious issue among states of the Global South, as the history of colonialism remains fresh, and independence remains fiercely guarded. Thomas G. Weiss is correct in pointing out that more debate and attention should be focused on the fact that the majority of intervention has and will take place in the pursuit of non-humanitarian goals. The death tolls of the genocide in Rwanda and the crisis in Zaire are a case in point to the atrocities that have been allowed to pass with little attention from the international community. The problem that RtoP was intended to respond to was not *too much* intervention, but *not enough* when it matters

[25] Anne-Marie Slaughter, *Security, Solidarity, and Sovereignty: The Grand Themes of UN Reform*, 99 Amer. J. Int'l L. 625 (2005).

[26] *See, e.g.*, John McCain, *The Right War for the Right Reasons*, New York Times, Mar. 12, 2003.

most, what Weiss correctly titles, "inhumanitarian non-intervention."[27] But it was this focus on intervention and the possibility of its abuse that presented a challenge to its adoption.

In September 2005, world leaders gathered together at a summit in New York to review progress since the Millennium Declaration, adopted by all UN Member States in 2000. RtoP was brought into the fold for consideration as part of a reform package for the UN. Earlier that year the Secretary-General released a report outlining the issues up for debate at the summit. In it, he argued that a state's primary duty is to protect its citizens and should it fail to do so, it is up to the international community to step in. For this reason, he implored member states to embrace RtoP.[28]

Despite support from senior officials at the UN, the eventual unanimous adoption of resolution 1674 affirming the 2005 World Summit document's commitment to RtoP was preceded by six months of debate in the Security Council.[29] Many recommendations in the original ICISS report fell away as "deal breakers" in the eyes of various interests. For example, restrictions of any kind on the veto in the Security Council were rejected as unacceptable by the permanent members. The range of threats to which RtoP responded was narrowed considerably due to concerns over threshold criteria for intervention. When would it be deemed appropriate to intervene? Authority to decide was vested exclusively in the Security Council. In fact it was much narrowed to only the most egregious of crimes which differed from the vision set out in the ICISS report which also included more broadly, "Situations of state collapse, and the resultant exposure of the population to mass starvation and/or civil war; and overwhelming natural or environmental catastrophes, where the state concerned is either unwilling or unable to cope, or call for assistance, and significant loss of life is occurring or threatened."[30] Ultimately, what was left and what could be agreed upon where genocide, war crimes, ethnic cleansing, and crimes against humanity.

The pace at which this occurred should not be undervalued. In the world of diplomacy and international governance, such a bold and readily accepted change is a rarity. There is no denying that the success of the campaign to bring this forward in the UN came about through the culmination of a series of events following the Cold War that lead to a reworking of how security was and should be understood. It can also be attributed to the thorough work of both the members of ICISS and the High-Level Panel in successfully delineating and outlining the new security context. It made sense from a foreign policy standpoint and reflected the changing reality and challenges the international community faces regarding threats to security. It should also be attributed to the presence of strong leaders committed to the cause.[31] And it was ultimately more sophisticated than anything previously. The Canadian government took on a lead role, with support from high-level officials in the UN and the commitment of Canadian Ambassador Allan Rock leading up to the World Summit, not to mention to full support of first Prime Minister Jean Chrétien and then Paul Martin.

[27] Thomas G. Weiss. *The Sunset of Humanitarian Intervention?*, 35:2 Security Dialogue 135–153.

[28] UN GAOR, 59th Sess., UN Dox. A/59/2005 (Mar. 21, 2005), at ¶135.

[29] Alex J. Bellamy, *The Responsibility to Protect-Five Years On*, 24 Ethics & Int'l Aff. 145 (2010).

[30] *See supra* note 19, at ¶ 4.20.

[31] *See* Heinbecker, *supra* note 13, at 115.

The support of the Secretary-General, in presenting the idea to the UN and in framing the debate broadly enough to allow for all concerns to be heard, was also fundamentally invaluable. As early as 1998, he stated during a speech: "[s]tate frontiers, ladies and gentlemen, should no longer be seen as a watertight protection for war criminals or mass murderers."[32] From then on he reliably understood the shortfalls of the current UN system, and actively promoted its re-evaluation for the benefit of civilians and the protection of human rights.

RtoP is revolutionary because it acknowledges for the first time in a global declaration that there are limits on the UN Charter's prohibition against international involvement in what goes on inside the sovereign state. RtoP does not displace sovereignty as the source of authority in the world order, it serves to reaffirm and re-enforce it. It recognizes, however, that sovereignty gives rise not only to rights and privileges, but also to duties and obligations. Based on the human security framework, it provide the terms through which the members of the UN can fulfill their mandate to promote collective security, in a world of globalized threats.

[32] Kofi Annan, *Reflections on Intervention*, The Thirty-Fifth Annual Ditchley Foundation Lecture, Jun. 26, 1998.

2 Adoption of the Responsibility to Protect

William W. Burke-White*

Understandings of state sovereignty have changed fundamentally, as outlined in the previous chapter, giving rise to and being shaped by the development of the Responsibility to Protect. RtoP is a powerful analytic construct and an emerging norm of international conduct around which actors' expectations and state behavior are beginning to conform. Although the Responsibility to Protect has not yet emerged as binding international law, it is well grounded in existing international law and shaping international discourse on sovereignty, atrocity prevention, and international intervention. This chapter examines the processes of adoption and development of the Responsibility to Protect, arguing that while not yet an independent rule of international law, the RtoP has significant normative power and potential political impact. Yet both the processes of its adoption and the imprecision of its substantive content have limited RtoP's transformation from norm to law.

The process of the adoption of RtoP also suggests that debates about the norm's legal status may be overdrawn. Advocates of RtoP often overstate that status in an effort to advance the sense of legal obligation. In contrast, this chapter suggests that by embracing the normative, rather than legal, status of RtoP to date, the process of legal development will be more effective and ultimately better serve underlying objectives of human security. Moreover, even without legal obligation, RtoP is already having concrete impact; it has shifted understandings of state sovereignty and increased the political and moral costs of inaction in the face of atrocity. Ultimately this chapter is both an exploration of the processes of development of the Responsibility to Protect, and a call for prudence in its legal codification.

This chapter proceeds as follows. First, it examines the initial articulation of the Responsibility to Protect in the 2001 Report of the International Commission on

* The author is grateful to Amara Levy-Moore and Robert Cooper for research assistance.

Intervention and State Sovereignty. Thereafter it considers the adoption of the Responsibility to Protect by the United Nations General Assembly during the 2005 World Summit. Next, it turns to the reaffirmation of RtoP by the Security Council in 2006 and the 2009 General Assembly debates on the topic. The chapter concludes by arguing that the while RtoP remains a non-legally binding norm, human security is best served through gradual development rather than immediate legal codification.

I. THE ORIGINS OF THE RESPONSIBILITY TO PROTECT

The early origins of the Responsibility to Protect can be traced back to the international community's failures to respond to the genocide in Rwanda and, later, to prevent atrocities in Bosnia and Kosovo. As the consequences of those failures became apparent, thinking about the nature of sovereignty and the duties of states began to shift in both academic and policy communities. In a Security Council statement in 1992, then UN Secretary-General Boutros Boutros-Ghali recognized the interdependence of the international system, whereby domestic atrocity anywhere could have systematic impact everywhere:

> Civil wars are no longer civil, and the carnage they inflict will no longer let the world remain indifferent. The narrow nationalism that would oppose or disregard the norms of a stable international order and the micro-nationalism that resists healthy economic or political integration can disrupt a peaceful global existence. Nations are too interdependent and national frontiers are too porous and transnational realities . . . too dangerous to permit egocentric isolationism.[1]

Soon thereafter, Francis Deng built on this interconnectivity, by reframing the concept of sovereignty as responsibility rather than right[2] such that along with the benefits that attach to sovereignty, states should be seen as bearing responsibilities toward their own citizens and the international community. As outlined in the previous chapter, Deng sought to shift understanding of sovereignty from the classic Westphalian model—according to which the sovereign enjoyed exclusive power over his or her territory and had an absolute right to exclude others from entering onto that territory[3]—toward a framing of sovereignty founded on both rights and responsibilities.[4] This shift in analytic framing uprooted a nearly 400-year tradition of sovereignty as exclusive authority and laid the groundwork for the Responsibility to Protect.

Deng's efforts were academic and, while his writings did lead to broader developments in the academic literature, it was not until 2001 that changing notions of sovereignty entered the political space through the report of the International Commission

[1] UN Security Council, *Security Council Summit Statement Concerning the Council's Responsibility in the Maintenance of International Peace and Security*, UN Doc S/23500, Jan. 31, 1992, at 8–10.

[2] Francis M. Deng, et al., Sovereignty as Responsibility: Conflict Management in Africa (Brookings Institution Press 1996).

[3] Schooner Exchange v. McFaddon, 11 US (7 Cranch) 116, 135 (1812).

[4] *See Id. But see* Stephen D. Krasner, Sovereignty: Organized Hypocrisy (Princeton University Press 1999). *See also* Abram Chayes & Antonia Handler Chayes, The New Sovereignty: Compliance with International Regulatory Agreements (Harvard University Press 1998).

on Intervention and State Sovereignty (ICISS). The Commission, convened by Canadian Prime Minister Jean Chrétien at the UN Millennium Assembly in September 2000, sought to build an "international consensus on how to respond in the face of massive violations of human rights and humanitarian law."[5] The Commission's Report, issued in December 2001, reframed the debate surrounding humanitarian intervention by setting forth the concept of the Responsibility to Protect as an alternative to humanitarian intervention discourse.

The report begins with the proposition that "sovereignty implies responsibility, and the primary responsibility for the protection of its people lies with the state itself."[6] This basic proposition is followed by a second—that "[w]here a population is suffering serious harm, as a result of internal war, insurgency, repression, or state failure, and the state in question is unwilling or unable to halt or avert it, the principle of non-intervention yields to the international responsibility to protect."[7]

The first proposition is inherent in the traditional concept of sovereignty, though the Commission frames it in a more forward-leaning way. Stephen Krasner defines domestic sovereignty as "the formal organization of political authority within the state and the ability of public authorities to exercise effective control within the borders of their own polity."[8] The corollary to that effective control of a polity is the primary responsibility of the state for its people. While, of course, traditional sovereignty would not impose the ends to which that responsibility and authority is exercised—allowing, for example, torture as well as protection—the ICISS Report argues that sovereignty must be exercised consistent with fundamental rules of international law prohibiting genocide, war crimes, and crimes against humanity.

The second proposition of the ICISS Report—namely that where a population is suffering and the state that has the primary responsibility to act fails to do so, the obligation to protect the polity passes from the territorial state to the international community—is a radical departure from traditional sovereignty, yet grounded in the transformations outlined in the previous chapter. In short, the Commission asserts that sovereignty is not absolute and can yield to other norms of international conduct. This shift essentially posits that human security can trump sovereign authority, allowing international action where the territorial state's exercise of sovereignty conflicts with its responsibility toward its people.

After laying out these basic principles, the ICISS Report establishes the ends toward which a state's exercise of sovereignty ought to be exercised and the circumstances within which the exclusive sovereignty of the territorial state gives way to the responsibility of the international community. The report also shifts existing debates by moving beyond the criteria for humanitarian intervention—a tired and often thorny debate to which moral or legal answers remain elusive. Instead the report speaks of a "responsibility to prevent" mass atrocities, such as genocide, war crimes, and crimes

[5] International Commission on Intervention and State Sovereignty (ICISS), The Responsibility to Protect: Report of the International Commission on Intervention and State Sovereignty (International Development Research Centre 2001), *available at* http://www.iciss.ca/report-en.asp [hereinafter ICISS Report].

[6] *Id.*, at XI.

[7] *Id.*, at XI.

[8] Krasner, *supra* note 3, at 4.

against humanity, for which the territorial state has the initial duty but the international community also holds a subsidiary responsibility. The report then turns to what it terms a "responsibility to react," namely that "When preventive measures fail to resolve or contain the situation and when a state is unable or unwilling to redress the situation, then interventionary measures by other members of the broader community of states may be required."[9] Such measures may take a variety of forms, up to and including the use of military force. Finally, the report articulates a "responsibility to rebuild."[10] In the wake of international intervention, there should be a genuine commitment to helping to build a durable peace, and promoting good governance and sustainable development.

While the report's overall goal is to establish the duty of the territorial state and the international community to prevent atrocity, it is perhaps most notable for its argument that the international community has a duty to protect where national governments fail to do so. This duty takes a number of forms, including the provision of technical assistance and capacity-building to assist national governments in exercising their primary duty to protect; building the political will and consensus to pressure unwilling national governments to protect their populations; utilizing tools of pressure such as international sanctions to force national governments to act; and, in appropriate circumstances, advocating for forcible international intervention to prevent or halt mass atrocities. The report thereby articulates a deep and escalating set of international obligations to protect, but clearly recognizes that those international obligations are secondary to the territorial state's primary duties.

Perhaps the most controversial element of RtoP as outlined in the report is a discussion of the legal authorities under which collective intervention is justified. The report's discussion of authority for intervention starts from the basic rule of international law that intervention should be authorized by the United Nations Security Council, consistent with Articles 2(4) and 42 of the UN Charter. Yet the report also asserts that the Security Council has a responsibility to act in the face of mass atrocity and must not abdicate that responsibility for political expediency or internal division.[11] More drastically, the report's assessment of the legal authority for intervention suggests that, where the Security Council fails to act, the General Assembly has residual authorities to act under the "Uniting for Peace" process.[12] The report is careful to note that the "General Assembly lacks the power to direct that action be taken, [but that] a decision by the General Assembly in favour of action . . . would provide a high degree of legitimacy for an intervention which subsequently took place, and encourage the Security Council to rethink its position."[13] The report goes on to recognize that regional organizations may also have legal authority for collective intervention. The discussion of legal authority for intervention concludes with an argument that, should the Security Council fail to act in cases of serious atrocity, its own effectiveness and legitimacy could be undermined.[14] Departing from traditional international law, the

[9] ICISS Report, *supra* note 5, at 29.

[10] *Id.*, at 39.

[11] *Id.*, at 50.

[12] *Id.*, at 53.

[13] *Id.*

[14] *Id.*, at 55.

report suggests alternative sources of legal authorization for international intervention beyond Article 42 of the UN Charter.

Ultimately, the ICISS Report is a significant normative statement about both the transformation of sovereignty and the legal obligations of the territorial state and the international community to prevent atrocities. By introducing the concept of the Responsibility to Protect, the report fundamentally shifts existing academic and political debates from a focus on humanitarian intervention to a broader conversation about the responsibility of states to protect their own populations and of the international community to react to violations. The ICISS Report is not, however, a source of international law, nor even a statement of *opinio juris*, that backed by appropriate state practice could give rise to a rule of customary international law.[15] It is, instead, a politically astute and legally aware statement by a highly distinguished group of individuals.[16] It recognizes and embraces existing legal rules, such as the requirements to prevent war crimes, crimes against humanity, and genocide, as well as the rules governing intervention included in the UN Charter.[17] Yet it also questions the adequacy of those rules.

II. THE WORLD SUMMIT OUTCOME DOCUMENT

By shifting the debate from humanitarian intervention to the Responsibility to Protect, the ICISS Report created new political openings to advance the discussion of atrocity prevention and human security. The transition of the debate from the largely academic to the political space occurred remarkably quickly. By 2005, the Responsibility to Protect was on the agenda of the World Summit, one of the largest gatherings of heads of government in history.[18] Over 170 heads of government participated in the

[15] ICJ Statute Art. 38.

[16] ICISS Report, *supra* note 5, at III. The Commission was co-chaired by Gareth Evans and Mohamed Sahnoun, and its members were Gisèle Côté-Harper, Lee Hamilton, Michael Ignatieff, Vladimir Lukin, Klaus Naumann, Cyril Ramaphosa, Fidel Ramos, Cornelio Sommaruga, Eduardo Stein, and Ramesh Thakur.

[17] Convention for the Amelioration of the Condition of the Wounded and Sick in Armed Forces in the Field [hereinafter First Geneva Convention], Aug. 12, 1949, 75 U.N.T.S. 31; Convention for the Amelioration of the Condition of the Wounded, Sick, and Shipwrecked Members of Armed Forces at Sea [hereinafter Second Geneva Convention], Aug. 12, 1949, 75 U.N.T.S. 85; Geneva Convention Relative to the Treatment of Prisoners of War [hereinafter Third Geneva Convention], Aug. 12, 1949, 75 U.N.T.S. 135; Convention Relative to the Protection of Civilian Persons in Time of War [hereinafter Fourth Geneva Convention], Aug. 12, 1949, 75 U.N.T.S. 287; Protocol Additional to the Geneva Conventions of 12 August 1949, and relating to the Protection of Victims of International Armed Conflicts [hereinafter Protocol I], Jun. 8, 1977, 1125 U.N.T.S. 3; Protocol Additional to the Geneva Conventions of Aug. 12, 1949, and relating to the Protection of Victims of Non-International Armed Conflicts [hereinafter Protocol II], Jun. 8, 1977, 1125 U.N.T.S. 609; Protocol additional to the Geneva Conventions of 12 August 1949, and relating to the Adoption of an Additional Distinctive Emblem [hereinafter Protocol III], Dec. 8, 2005 [hereinafter Geneva Conventions]; Convention on the Prevention and Punishment of the Crime of Genocide, Dec. 9, 1948, 78 U.N.T.S. 277 [hereinafter Genocide Convention]; Guénaël Mettraux, *Crimes Against Humanity in the Jurisprudence of the International Criminal Tribunals for the Former Yugoslavia and for Rwanda*, 43 Harv. Int'l L.J. 1, 237 (2002).

[18] United Nations Department of Public Information, UN Summit Takes on Tough Global Issues (2005), *available at* http://www.un.org/summit2005/press_release_global.pdf.

discussions from September 14–16, 2005, leading to the World Summit Outcome Document, which was formally adopted by the General Assembly in Resolution 60/1 (2005).[19]

In paragraphs 138–140 of the World Summit Outcome Document, heads of government and the General Assembly affirm the "responsibility to protect . . . populations from genocide, war crimes, ethnic cleansing and crimes against humanity."[20] The text of those paragraphs provides the operative basis for the Responsibility to Protect:

138. Each individual State has the responsibility to protect its populations from genocide, war crimes, ethnic cleansing, and crimes against humanity. This responsibility entails the prevention of such crimes, including their incitement, through appropriate and necessary means. We accept that responsibility and will act in accordance with it. The international community should, as appropriate, encourage and help States to exercise this responsibility and support the United Nations in establishing an early warning capability.

139. The international community, through the United Nations, also has the responsibility to use appropriate diplomatic, humanitarian and other peaceful means, in accordance with Chapters VI and VIII of the Charter, to help to protect populations from genocide, war crimes, ethnic cleansing, and crimes against humanity. In this context, we are prepared to take collective action, in a timely and decisive manner, through the Security Council, in accordance with the Charter, including Chapter VII, on a case-by-case basis and in cooperation with relevant regional organizations as appropriate, should peaceful means be inadequate and national authorities are manifestly failing to protect their populations from genocide, war crimes, ethnic cleansing, and crimes against humanity. We stress the need for the General Assembly to continue consideration of the responsibility to protect populations from genocide, war crimes, ethnic cleansing, and crimes against humanity and its implications, bearing in mind the principles of the Charter and international law. We also intend to commit ourselves, as necessary and appropriate, to helping States build capacity to protect their populations from genocide, war crimes, ethnic cleansing, and crimes against humanity and to assisting those which are under stress before crises and conflicts break out.

A. The Status of the World Summit Outcome Document

Despite its adoption by heads of government at the 2005 World Summit, the Outcome Document is not an international treaty or other formal legal instrument.[21] International legal rules can only be created through international treaties, customary law consisting of state practice backed by *opinio juris*, or general principles of international law.[22] The authority of the Outcome Document arises from its adoption by the General Assembly in Resolution 60/1. Yet even a resolution of the General Assembly is not a formal source of international law. Articles 10–14 of the United Nations

[19] GA Res. 60/1, UN GAOR, 60th Sess., UN DocA/60/L.1 (Oct. 24, 2005) [hereinafter Resolution 60/1].

[20] *Id.* at ¶¶ 138–40.

[21] *See* ICJ Statute Art. 38(1)(a).

[22] ICJ Statute Art. 38.

Charter lay out the powers of the General Assembly in this regard, which are limited to discussing matters within the scope of the UN Charter and the maintenance of international peace and security, referring matters or making recommendations to the Security Council, or undertaking studies to promote international cooperation.[23] Hence, while the General Assembly's adoption of the World Summit Outcome Document has significance, it does not create legal obligations.

Some legal scholars have asserted that the adoption of the World Summit Outcome Document by the General Assembly ought to classify it as "soft law." For example, Jennifer Welsh and Maria Banda argue that "RtoP is an example of soft law."[24] This approach is both analytically unhelpful and risks prompting a political backlash. So-called soft law is subject to multiple definitions and often-inaccurate usage. The two main streams of legal scholarship define soft law as either imprecise legal obligations[25] or non-legally binding obligations.[26] Classifying the Outcome Document under the first definition inaccurately suggests that it is legally binding, if imprecise. Neither the ICISS Report nor the Outcome Document has the capacity to establish international legal obligations. Under the second definition of soft law, the Responsibility to Protect is an hortatory norm, rather than a legal rule. That definition is accurate, but, even so, the terminology of soft law is both confusing and unhelpful. Terming a non-legally binding norm as "law" creates the misperception of a legally binding rule and may lead states worried about creeping legalization to denounce the norm in an effort to avoid its legal codification.

Rather than speak of "soft law," positive international law makes clear that the Outcome Document and the Responsibility to Protect contained therein are not a new source of international law. In contrast, the relevant provisions of the Outcome Document are political statements by heads of government and the General Assembly reiterating existing international legal rules, potentially laying the groundwork for the establishment of new legal obligations in the future. More specifically, the document reaffirms existing rules of treaty and customary law prohibiting and requiring the prevention of war crimes, crimes against humanity, and genocide. While shifting the focus from the prosecution of such crimes to their prevention, the Outcome Document builds on, rather than creates legal rules.

In terms of the process of law creation, the Outcome Document may serve as an example of *opinio juris* for certain elements of the Responsibility to Protect that go beyond existing rules of law. *Opinio juris* consists of political statements that provide evidence that a state or states believe they are bound by legal obligation. But for such *opinio juris* to give rise to legal obligation, it must be backed by widespread state practice, which does not yet exist with respect to the Responsibility to Protect.[27]

[23] UN Charter Arts. 10–14.

[24] Jennifer M. Welsh & Maria Banda, *International Law and the Responsibility to Protect: Clarifying or Expanding States' Responsibilities?* 2 Global Responsibility to Protect 3, 213 (2010).

[25] Kenneth W. Abbott & Duncan Snidal, *Hard and Soft Law in International Governance*, 54 Int'l Org. 3, 421, 422 (2000).

[26] *See generally*, Kal Raustiala, *Form and Substance in International Agreements*, 99 AJIL 581 (2005).

[27] *See, e.g.*, North Sea Continental Shelf (F.R.G. v. Neth.), 1968 I.C.J.; North Sea Continental Shelf (F.R.G. v. Den.), 1968 I.C.J.; The Paquette Habana, 175 US 677 (1900).

B. The Meaning of the Responsibility to Protect in the World Summit Outcome Document

Notwithstanding that the General Assembly's adoption of the Responsibility to Protect does not in and of itself give rise to a new rule of international law, the World Summit Outcome Document and the General Assembly's adoption thereof has shaped discourse, altered expectations, and impacted state behavior. Given, however, that the World Summit Outcome Document is not an international treaty, but rather a document adopted by the General Assembly, it is not subject to the rules of treaty interpretation contained in the Vienna Convention on the Law of Treaties.[28] The analysis here, therefore, is based on a plain-text interpretation, with reference to background rules of international law.

The section of the World Summit Outcome Document devoted to the Responsibility to Protect begins with an affirmation of existing international legal rules. Specifically, paragraph 138 provides that "Each individual State has the responsibility to protect its populations from genocide, war crimes, ethnic cleansing and crimes against humanity."[29] This statement summarizes legal rules contained in, among other instruments, the Convention on the Prevention and Punishment of the Crime of Genocide,[30] the four Geneva Conventions of 1949,[31] and customary legal rules regarding crimes against humanity as articulated through the jurisprudence of the International Criminal Tribunal for the Former Yugoslavia, for example.[32] Those rules, requiring states to prevent and punish certain international crimes are well established in treaty and custom, and bind on all states. The only significant departure from existing legal norms in this opening line is the inclusion of "ethnic cleansing" in the list of crimes from which states have a Responsibility to Protect their populations. While the specific definitions of the crimes giving rise to a Responsibility to Protect are addressed in detail in a subsequent chapter, it is worth noting here that "ethnic cleansing" likely would also constitute one of the other crimes listed in the sentence—genocide, war crimes, or crimes against humanity—and does not therefore seek to establish new legal obligations.

The second sentence of paragraph 138 again reflects existing international law by affirming that "[t]his responsibility entails the prevention of such crimes, including their incitement, through appropriate and necessary means." The underlying international treaties establishing international criminal responsibility for genocide and war crimes and the customary rules prohibiting crimes against humanity also include an obligation to prevent crimes, including the prevention of incitement. The Genocide Convention, for example, provides that "The Contracting Parties confirm that genocide, whether committed in time of peace or in time of war, is a crime under international law which they undertake to prevent and to punish."[33] Yet the shift in

[28] *See* Vienna Convention on the Law of Treaties, Arts. 31–32, May 23, 1969, 1155 U.N.T.S. 331 [hereinafter Vienna Convention].

[29] Resolution 60/1, *supra* note 18, at ¶ 138.

[30] Genocide Convention, *supra* note 16.

[31] Geneva Conventions, *supra* note 16.

[32] *See generally*, Mettraux, *supra* note 16.

[33] Genocide Convention Art. 1, *supra* note 16.

emphasis in paragraph 138 from punishment to prevention is significant. Treaties focusing on these sets of crimes tend to be backward-looking, providing for the assessment of *individual* criminal responsibility to promote accountability for the commission of international crimes. While there are prevention obligations inherent in the Genocide Convention and Geneva Conventions, RtoP provides for an opportunity for assessment of the actual or *potential* commission of these crimes by *states* as a trigger for preventative action by the international community.

The third sentence of the paragraph merely provides that states "accept that responsibility," something that they of course do automatically with respect to the underlying international legal rules to which they are party under the doctrine of *pacta sunt servanda*.[34]

The fourth sentence of paragraph 138 does, however, mark an important departure from existing international law and an innovation of the Responsibility to Protect. The sentence provides that "[t]he international community should, as appropriate, encourage and help States to exercise this responsibility . . ." This sentence seeks to transform the direct legal obligation of the territorial state to prevent and punish atrocity into an affirmative duty on behalf of all states to assist the territorial state in its efforts. This statement departs from the normal rules governing international treaties, according to which treaties cannot create obligations for third states.[35] The treaties that establish the responsibility of the territorial state to prosecute international crimes cannot give rise to an obligation for international assistance beyond the "extradite or prosecute" requirements contained in, for example, the Geneva Conventions.[36] Where international crimes occur due to the inability or unwillingness of the territorial state to protect its own people, a potential duty of assistance can go far to improve human security.

While the rhetorical shift toward prevention and the focus on international assistance in paragraph 138 are significant, paragraph 139 of the Outcome Document offers key innovations that seek to advance international law. That paragraph begins with the proposition that "[t]he international community, through the United Nations, also has the responsibility to use appropriate diplomatic, humanitarian, and other peaceful means, in accordance with Chapters VI and VIII of the Charter, to help to protect populations from genocide, war crimes, ethnic cleansing and crimes against humanity."[37] While the treaties or customary rules which seek the prevention and punishment of genocide, war crimes, and crimes against humanity focus on the obligations of the territorial or national state, paragraph 138 of the Outcome Document asserts an obligation of the international community to use peaceful means to protect populations. The Outcome Document seeks to establish a secondary layer of prevention, complementary yet subordinate to protection by national authorities. As the complementary jurisdictional regime of the International Criminal Court has shown, the potential for complementary international action can both encourage action by national governments and provide a backstop where national governments are unable

[34] *See* Vienna Convention Art. 31(1), *supra* note 30.

[35] *Id.*, Art. 34.

[36] First Geneva Convention Arts. 49–54, *supra* note 16; Second Geneva Convention, Arts. 50–53, *supra* note 16; Third Geneva Convention, Arts. 82–88, *supra* note 16; Fourth Geneva Convention, Arts. 45, 70, 121, & 131, *supra* note 16.

[37] Resolution 60/1, *supra* note 18, at ¶ 139.

or unwilling to act.[38] While the concept of an international obligation to prevent atrocity is new, the means of collective action in this sentence of the Outcome Document are limited to measures short of the use of force undertaken by the Security Council, consistent with Chapters VI and VIII of the Charter specifically, Articles 32–38 and 52–54.[39]

The second sentence of the paragraph goes on to discuss more active forms of collective action: "[i]n this context, we are prepared to take collective action, in a timely and decisive manner, through the Security Council, in accordance with the Charter, including Chapter VII, on a case-by-case basis and in cooperation with relevant regional organizations as appropriate, should peaceful means be inadequate and national authorities are manifestly failing to protect their populations from genocide, war crimes, ethnic cleansing, and crimes against humanity."[40] This sentence expressly recognizes that atrocities occur not just where states are unable to protect their populations, but also where they are unwilling to do so. Left unstated is the reality that it isn't always about a failure of protection but that states sometimes are actively responsible for the commission of these crimes.

While the sentence has strong rhetorical power, boldly stating that the international community is prepared to act where national authorities fail to do so, its legal significance is limited. Rather than seeking to create an affirmative duty for international intervention, the sentence articulates a political reality—the preparedness to act—that may or may not actually be true in any particular case. Note, for example, the difference in language between the recognition of an affirmative "responsibility to use appropriate diplomatic, humanitarian and other peaceful means" and the statement that states are "prepared to take collective action" under Chapter VII. That preparedness to take action is far short of an obligation to act.

What is perhaps most noteworthy in this second sentence of paragraph 139 is the statement that collective action under Chapter VII should be "timely and decisive." All too often, as illustrated from cases ranging from Rwanda to Bosnia, collective responses are *ad-hoc* or *post-hoc*, undermining their effectiveness at prevention. Too often, the Security Council has stalled until evidence of crimes is so clear that political pressure to act becomes irresistible. And even when it does act, the Security Council's response is rarely decisive, leaving any intervention unauthorized or ill-equipped to meet the challenges on the ground.[41] As a result, prevention far too often fails. The emphasis on "timely and decisive" action by the Security Council is a critical, if rhetorical, step toward effective prevention and impact amelioration. Yet the Outcome Document does not provide a mechanism for turning that political imperative for timely and decisive response into action.

[38] See William W. Burke-White, *Complementarity in Practice: The International Criminal Court as Part of a System of Multi-Level Global Governance in the Democratic Republic of Congo*, 18 Leiden J. Int'l L. 557 (2005); William W. Burke-White, *Proactive Complementarity: The International Criminal Court and National Courts in the Rome System of International Justice*, 49 Harv. Int'l L.J. 53 (2008).

[39] UN Charter, Arts. 32–38 & 52–54.

[40] Resolution 60/1, *supra* note 18, at ¶ 139.

[41] Roméo Dallaire, Shake Hands with the Devil: The Failure of Humanity in Rwanda (Carroll & Graf Publishers 2003); Samantha Power, A Problem from Hell: America in the Age of Genocide (Basic Books 2002).

The next sentence of the paragraph is merely a call for the "General Assembly to continue consideration of the responsibility to protect . . . bearing in mind the principles of the Charter and international law."[42] This ongoing consideration is, in fact, important given the ambiguities and omissions in the Outcome Document itself—discussed in the next section—and the need to increase the precision of RtoP for it to more effectively impact state behavior.

The final sentence of paragraph 139 again turns to international assistance and capacity-building, noting "[w]e also intend to commit ourselves, as necessary and appropriate, to helping States build capacity to protect their populations . . . and to assisting those which are under stress before crises and conflicts break out." While the emphasis on prevention and international assistance is again important, the statement itself remains rhetorical. It merely expresses an intent to commit as necessary and appropriate. Ultimately, such intent must be translated into action to build the prevention and response capacities of territorial states and the international community. Once again, however, the Outcome Document fails to provide a mechanism to translate intent into action.

Despite its limitations, the Outcome Document is a powerful political statement. It reaffirms critical rules of international law. It shifts the focus from response to prevention. It draws attention to the obligations of states to assist one another in preventing international crimes. And it pulls all of these elements together into an overall concept with normative significance. But the Outcome Document is neither novel nor groundbreaking. The obligations referenced in it are grounded in existing rules of international law. The elements of collective response are confined to the existing mechanisms already available under the UN Charter. And the commitments to collective action or international assistance are hortatory rather than obligatory.

In comparison with the ICISS Report, the Outcome Document is conservative. While it embraces the responsibility to prevent atrocities and affirms a need to react, it does not seek to establish an affirmative duty to react, and largely ignores the responsibility to rebuild included in the ICISS Report. It does not propose a set of criteria or circumstances justifying armed and collective intervention, even under existing Security Council authorities. And, unlike the ICISS Report, the Outcome Document does not consider options when the Security Council fails to react to anticipated or ongoing international crimes. While that conservatism might be viewed as a step back, the fact that the Responsibility to Protect was included in the Outcome Document at all and adopted by the General Assembly is a significant step forward.[43] It is a clear recognition of both how far states have come toward recognizing the Responsibility to Protect as a political imperative and a reminder of ongoing skepticism of the bolder version of the Responsibility to Protect in the ICISS Report.[44]

[42] Resolution 60/1, *supra* note 18, at ¶ 139.

[43] *See* Ramesh Thakur & Thomas G. Weiss, *RtoP: From Idea to Norm—and Action?*, 1 Global Responsibility to Protect 1, 22, 39 (2009).

[44] *See, e.g.*, Jutta Brunnée & Stephen J. Toope, *The Responsibility to Protect and the Use of Force: Building Legality?*, 2 Global Responsibility to Protect 3 (2010).

C. The Omissions and Ambiguities of the World Summit Outcome Document

While rightfully seen as an important endorsement of the Responsibility to Protect, the text of the Outcome Document leaves open as many questions as it answers about the scope and nature of RtoP. These key unanswered questions relate to: (1) a tension between a necessary trigger mechanism for the Responsibility to Protect and the ultimate goal of atrocity prevention, (2) appropriate forms of international assistance, and (3) the failure to consider the possibility of Security Council inability or unwillingness to act. Each of these omissions and ambiguities results from political compromises necessary for adoption of the Outcome Document, but have costs that limit the impact of the Responsibility to Protect.

First, as articulated in the ICISS Report and inherent in the first sentence of paragraph 138 of the Outcome Document, the ultimate goal of the Responsibility to Protect is atrocity prevention. To prevent atrocities, domestic or international action must precede crimes. While paragraph 138 makes clear that the territorial state has an affirmative duty to prevent international crimes before they occur, paragraph 139 is far less clear as to when the complementary duty of the international community is triggered. That paragraph begins by affirming a duty on the part of the international community to help protect populations from such crimes through peaceful means under Chapter VI and VIII of the UN Charter, but does not specify whether such crimes must already be underway for the obligation for an international response to attach. This ambiguity unfortunately creates the possibility that significant crimes will occur in advance of any international response—even one limited to actions under Chapter VI or VIII of the UN Charter. And, given the past practice of the Security Council, delayed action is far more likely than anticipatory action.

With respect to the use of forcible measures, the ambiguity of the Outcome Document is even more acute. Paragraph 139 provides that collective action under Chapter VII of the UN Charter should be undertaken in a "timely and decisive manner" where "national authorities are manifestly failing to protect their populations from genocide, war crimes, ethnic cleansing, and crimes against humanity." While a reference in paragraph 138 to "timely and decisive" action and the need to prevent incitement would seem to suggest that the mere potential for atrocity could trigger international action, the requirement of a manifest failure of national authorities to protect could well be interpreted as limiting at least responses under Chapter VII to circumstances in which actual crimes are ongoing and national authorities are evidently failing to prevent them. For the Responsibility to Protect to meaningfully advance human security, this ambiguity must be resolved in favor of allowing—if not requiring—international action, including under Chapter VII, when international crimes are merely imminent.

A second unfortunate ambiguity in the Outcome Document is the lack of clarity as to the allowable and necessary forms of international response. The document is silent on the types of assistance to be provided to national authorities in their own prevention efforts. Without specifics, the document creates only limited political pressure for states to provide assistance. It is, of course, easy for a state to claim that even inadequate assistance has discharged any potential duties to assist when the nature of requisite assistance is undefined.

With respect to potential international responses, the document simply references Chapters VI, VII, and VIII, again without providing specifics. While the reference to all three chapters of the UN Charter opens the door for the full range of coercive enforcement actions available to the Security Council, the lack of specificity fails to establish a commitment to use those powers and again creates the possibility of an under-reaction that is insufficient to prevent potential crimes or stop those underway. Again, for the Responsibility to Protect to have bite, this ambiguity must be resolved in favor of clear articulation of international assistance and response.

A third troubling ambiguity in the Outcome Document and a significant departure from the ICISS Report is the failure to consider circumstances in which the Security Council itself fails to respond. Whereas the ICISS Report seeks to establish an affirmative duty for the Security Council to react to international crimes, offers a stern warning regarding the consequences of Security Council failure to respond, and strongly hints at possible alternatives in the face of Security Council inaction, the Outcome Document merely notes that states are prepared to take action through the Security Council. It does not suggest an affirmative duty of the Security Council to act nor does it address political stalemate. Likewise, it does not consider any residual obligations or authority that might reside with the General Assembly or regional organizations.[45] It is understandable that the General Assembly might seek to refrain from commenting on the powers of the Security Council, but the UN Charter recognizes steps that the General Assembly can take to recommend action to the Security Council that is not discussed in the Outcome Document.[46] This omission creates the strong potential, as illustrated all too clearly by the failure to respond to the genocide in Rwanda, that despite hortatory statements and even international commitment to react, the Responsibility to Protect will not be discharged by the Security Council and international crimes will continue unabated. Again, for the Responsibility to Protect to have impact, mechanisms must be developed to ensure Security Council response or alternative pathways to legitimate collective international response will have to develop.

Each of these ambiguities created by the agreed text of the Outcome Document limit the effectiveness of the Responsibility to Protect as an international norm and hamper its potential transformation into law. As a political matter, the scope of paragraphs 138–40 reflects the scope of agreement among states in 2005 with respect to the Responsibility to Protect, but also highlights their unwillingness to operationalize it beyond the reaffirmation of existing legal rules.

III. SECURITY COUNCIL RESOLUTION 1674

The next important development in the Responsibility to Protect was its inclusion in Security Council Resolution 1674 in April 2006. In operative paragraph 4 of that Resolution, on the protection of civilians in armed conflict, the Security Council "*Reaffirms* the provisions of paragraphs 138 and 139 of the 2005 World Summit Outcome Document regarding the Responsibility to Protect populations from genocide, war crimes, ethnic cleansing, and crimes against humanity."[47] The inclusion is the first explicit endorsement of the Responsibility to Protect by the Security Council. As a political matter, that recognition is significant. Members of the Security Council

45 UN Charter Art. 12; ICISS Report, *supra* note 5, at XII–XIII.

46 UN Charter Arts. 11(2)–(3).

47 S.C. Res. 1674, S/RES/1674, Apr. 28, 2006, at ¶ 4 [hereinafter Resolution 1674].

were willing to join the General Assembly's endorsement and the five permanent members of the Council did not exercise their veto powers to block adoption. Yet, the Security Council's endorsement followed six months of difficult negotiations in which Algeria, Brazil, China, the Philippines, and Russia argued that it was premature for the Security Council to endorse RtoP.[48] Ultimately, the reaffirmation by the Council required a watering down of the language in the resolution to merely "reaffirm" the relevant paragraphs of the Outcome Document and hard-fought political negotiation to secure adoption. Yet, even this more limited result generated political momentum for the development of the Responsibility to Protect.

From a legal perspective, the key significance of the Security Council's reaffirmation of the relevant paragraphs of the World Summit Outcome Document stems from Article 25 of the Charter, according to which, "[t]he Members of the United Nations agree to accept and carry out the decisions of the Security Council in accordance with the present Charter." While the Council's language in Resolution 1674 falls short of a formal decision requiring that member states implement the Responsibility to Protect, it is part of an ongoing process of legalization.[49] At the very least, the Council's reaffirmation of the Responsibility to Protect strengthens the claim that member states have legal duties to advance the political commitment contained in paragraphs 138 and 139 of the Outcome Document.

A number of factors do, however, limit the legal impact of Resolution 1674. First, the Council merely *reaffirms* the relevant paragraphs of the Outcome Document that are themselves either already binding legal obligations or hortatory, rather than norm-creating. As a result, Resolution 1674 should be read largely as yet another political reaffirmation of the Responsibility to Protect, albeit an affirmation by the critical body ultimately responsible for discharging the international response contemplated by the Responsibility to Protect.

A second limitation is the context of the reference in Resolution 1674. While the reference occurs in an operative, rather than preambular paragraph, it is divorced from any particular case of crimes and does not contain a specific demand for action by member states. Without such a particular case or call for action, the Security Council's statements are difficult to translate into precise expectation, obligation, or action.

Third, given that the operative paragraph of the Resolution does not reference Chapter VII and does not find the existence of a threat to international peace and

[48] Alex J. Bellamy, *The Responsibility to Protect—Five Years On*, 24 Ethics in Int'l Aff. 143, 145 (2010); Security Council, Update Report No. 5: Protection of Civilians in Armed Conflict, Jun. 21, 2006, *available at* http://www.securitycouncilreport.org/site/c.glKWLeMTIsG/b.1806823/k.A5D7/Update_Report_No_5BRProtection_of_Civilians_in_Armed_ConflictBR21_June_2006.htm ; Security Council, Update Report No. 1: Protection of Civilians in Armed Conflict, Jun. 18, 2007, *available at* http://www.securitycouncilreport.org/site/c.glKWLeMTIsG/b.2821453/k.AB59/Update_Report_No_1BRProtection_of_Civilians_in_Armed_ConflictBR18_June_2007.htm; Security ouncil, Update Report No. 1: Protection of Civilians in Armed Conflict, Mar. 8, 2006, *available at* http://www.securitycouncilreport.org/site/c.glKWLeMTIsG/b.1466469/k.EF40/Update_Report_no1brProtection_of_Civilians_in_armed_conflictbr8_March_2006.htm.

[49] For a discussion of the circumstances in which decisions of the Security Council are legally binding on member states, see Hans Kelsen, The Law of the United Nations: A Critical Analysis of its Fundamental Problems 95 (E.A. Prager: 1950). Mere recommendations or affirmations of the Council are presumably not intended to create legal obligations for member states. See *Id.*

security, as well as the fact that reference to collective intervention in the underlying World Summit Outcome Document is of a general, non obligatory, and case-by-case nature, the resolution creates no binding legal obligation on member states of the United Nations.

Finally, the Resolution fails to resolve the ambiguities inherent in the text of the Outcome Document noted above. By merely reaffirming that earlier language through reference, the ambiguities are imported into Resolution 1674. The Security Council, like the General Assembly before it, fails to take on the challenging task of resolving those ambiguities in a manner that would both effectively achieve the purposes of the Responsibility to Protect and be acceptable to the Security Council membership.

IV. THE 2009 GENERAL ASSEMBLY DEBATE

In early 2009, the Secretary-General released a report, entitled "Implementing the Responsibility to Protect,"[50] that seeks to "contribute to a continuing dialogue among Member States . . . on the responsibility to protect."[51] The report begins conservatively, providing that the discussion of the Responsibility to Protect in the Outcome Document "does not alter, indeed it reinforces, the legal obligations of Member States to refrain from the use of force except in conformity with the Charter."[52] The report then examines potential means for implementing three pillars of the Responsibility to Protect: "[t]he protection responsibilities of the State,"[53] "[i]nternational assistance and capacity-building,"[54] and "[t]imely and decisive response."[55]

The lengthy discussions of each of these pillars are likewise conservative, suggesting possible means of implementation of RtoP consistent with both existing international law and the agreed text of the Outcome Document. For example, with respect to "[t]he protection responsibilities of the State," the report suggests that states "should become parties to the relevant international instruments on human rights . . . as well as . . . the International Criminal Court"[56] and that they should strengthen individual criminal responsibility.[57] Regarding international assistance and capacity-building, the report highlights the need to make states aware of the costs of the perpetration of international crimes and the need for region-to-region learning processes particularly as related to human security.[58] Perhaps more boldly, regarding state-to-state assistance, the report suggests the need for assistance programs "to build specific capacities within societies that would make them less likely to travel the path to crimes relating to the responsibility to protect."[59]

[50] The Secretary-General, *Report of the Secretary-General on Implementing the Responsibility to Protect*, UN Doc. A/63/677, Jan. 12, 2009.

[51] *Id.*, at 5.

[52] *Id.*

[53] *Id.*, at 8.

[54] *Id.*, at 9.

[55] *Id.*

[56] *Id.*, at 11.

[57] *Id.*, at 12–13.

[58] *Id.*, at 16–17.

[59] *Id.*, at 20.

Finally, the report turns to the implementation of timely and decisive response. While reaffirming the need for states to operate within existing legal authorities, the report also focuses on the ultimate goal of "saving lives through 'timely and decisive' action."[60] The report draws on the Outcome Document's recognition of the need to prevent incitement as a means of promoting a timely response that in fact serves a preventative function. Thereafter, it explores the potential actions that could be taken by the Security Council and member states, including the use of targeted sanctions.[61] Importantly, the report goes beyond the text of the Outcome Document by acknowledging the need for permanent members of the Security Council to refrain from exercising the veto on issues related to the Responsibility to Protect and the role of the General Assembly, under the Uniting for Peace procedure to address issues including the Responsibility to Protect where the Security Council fails to do so.[62] However, even these discussions do not go so far as to suggest that there are alternatives to the UN Security Council for legitimating collective action in response to atrocity. The report does, however, provide the most detailed discussion of the Responsibility to Protect in an official document to date and offers concrete ways to advance and implement the Outcome Document.

The release of the Secretary-General's Report's gave rise to a lengthy debate in the General Assembly about the Responsibility to Protect and whether the report itself should be adopted in some way by the General Assembly. Those debates got off to a rather unfavorable start. The president of the General Assembly, Father Miguel d'Escoto Brockmann of Nicaragua, released a concept note to frame the discussion that was deeply critical of the Responsibility to Protect and sought to reopen a more general discussion as to its validity and appropriateness.[63] Delegates from Cuba, Nicaragua, Sudan, and Venezuela explicitly called for a reopening of general debate. Yet, throughout the course of discussions, 94 speakers, representing more than 180 governments, spoke, with the vast majority supportive of the Responsibility to Protect and at least some of the implementation steps included in the Secretary-General's report.[64] Most speakers recognized a narrow set of responsibilities to which deep obligations of direct prevention and indirect assistance would attach.[65]

After intense discussions, the General Assembly voted to endorse the Secretary-General's report. While a strongly worded endorsement was initially contemplated, resistance from states such as Cuba, Ecuador, Iran, Nicaragua, Sudan, Syria, and Venezuela, led the endorsement to a more toned down statement.[66] Ultimately, General Assembly Resolution 63/308 (2009) "*recall[s]* the 2005 World Summit

[60] *Id.*, at 22.

[61] *Id.*, at 25.

[62] *Id.*, at 27.

[63] Office of the President of the General Assembly, *Concept Note on Responsibility to Protect Populations from Genocide, War Crimes, Ethnic Cleansing and Crimes Against Humanity* (undated), *available at* www.un.org/ga/president/63/interactive/protect/conceptnote.pdf.

[64] Bellamy, *supra* note 50, at 147.

[65] For detailed discussions of the positions of various states, *see* UNITED NATIONS DEPARTMENT OF PUBLIC INFORMATION, MORE THAN 40 DELEGATES EXPRESS STRONG SKEPTICISM, FULL SUPPORT AS GENERAL ASSEMBLY CONTINUES DEBATE ON RESPONSIBILITY TO PROTECT, GA/10849, Jul. 24, 2009, *available at* http://unispal.un.org/UNISPAL.NSF/0/81137EA84576A7C38525760000492F53.

[66] Bellamy, *supra* note 50, at 147.

Outcome," "*takes note* of the report of the Secretary-General and of the timely and productive debate organized by the President of the General Assembly," and "*Decides* to continue [the General Assembly's] consideration of the responsibility to protect."[67] Again, the General Assembly's decision to take note of the report lent additional legitimacy and political support to the report of the Secretary-General, without creating new legal obligations.

The Secretary-General's report and the debates that followed suggest a growing political consensus in support of the Responsibility to Protect. Despite the efforts of a few detractors, states are willing to accept the relatively minimalist construction of the Responsibility to Protect outlined in the World Summit Outcome Document, even when concrete implementation steps are also contemplated. Second, the report begins to address many of the ambiguities and omissions in the Outcome Document, particularly as regards the forms of assistance states may be able to provide, the need to react with sufficient speed to prevent crimes, and the possibility of the Security Council's failure to act. While the report does not fully resolve those ambiguities and omissions, it recognizes the need to consider them and builds the political momentum that may ultimately lead to their resolution.

V. RECENT DEVELOPMENTS

The most recent developments in the Responsibility to Protect were the release on a follow-on report by the Secretary-General in July 2010 and a subsequent General Assembly dialogue. The report, entitled "Early warning, assessment, and the responsibility to protect" further seeks to operationalize RtoP and focuses on the mechanisms available to provide early warning and prevent, rather than merely respond to, atrocity. The report recognizes gaps in the United Nation's early warning capabilities and notes significant improvements in information-sharing over the past decade. It calls upon United Nations entities to improve "the flow of information from the field to headquarters" and analytic assessment tools.[68]

While information flow, assessment, and early warning are essential, operationalization of the Responsibility to Protect is more often a political than informational challenge. Without addressing the problem of political will head-on, the report does seek to foster mechanisms to link early warning to preventive action. It calls upon the Special Advisor to the Secretary-General on the Prevention of Genocide and the Special Advisor on the Responsibility to Protect to "to convene an urgent meeting of key Under-Secretaries-General to identify a range of multilateral policy options, whether by the United Nations or by Chapter VIII regional arrangements, for preventing such mass crimes and for protecting populations."[69] While such a meeting will not necessarily lead to the action that is needed, it is an important step to facilitating connection between early warning and prevention.

One month after the release of the follow-on report, the president of the General Assembly convened an informal, interactive dialogue on early warning and

[67] GA Res. 63/308, UN GAOR, 63d Sess., UN Doc. A/RES/63/308 (Oct. 7, 2009).

[68] The Secretary-General, *Report of the Secretary-General on Early Warning, Assessment, and the Responsibility to Protect*, A/64/864, Jul. 14, 2010, at 4.

[69] *Id.*, at 7.

assessment. Contributions from 42 member states again stressed the importance of prevention and the need for early warming mechanisms within the UN system.[70] While a few states expressed concern about the ongoing development of RtoP, the overall focus of the discussion remained on concrete steps to advance its implementation, including the creation of a joint office for the Secretary-General's Special Advisors on Genocide Prevention and the Responsibility to Protect. Ultimately, the dialogue should be viewed as a further recognition of a deepening consensus on both the need for and substance of the Responsibility to Protect, but a consensus still marked by lingering concerns about the ways in which RtoP may be implemented.

VI. CONCLUSION

The Responsibility to Protect has developed with extraordinary speed. The ICISS Report was released just a decade ago. Since then, the concept has been advanced, framed in terms of concrete implementation steps by the Secretary-General, endorsed twice by the General Assembly, and reaffirmed by the Security Council. In a world of international politics, where change is slow and international legal codification even slower, this rapid trajectory from idea to norm is remarkable. It reflects an expanding view that far more must be done to prevent atrocities and stop international crimes, that historic approaches to sovereignty are outdated, and that both states and the international community have moral and legal obligations to prevent and react when international crimes are imminent or underway.

What the Responsibility to Protect is not, however, is an international legal *rule*. It has not been codified in an international treaty; it lacks the state practice and sufficient *opinio juris* to give rise to customary international law; and it does not qualify as a general principal of law. Instead, the Responsibility to Protect is best understood as a norm of international conduct. As defined by Cass Sunstein, norms are "social attitudes of approval and disapproval, specifying what ought to be done and what ought not to be done."[71] In other words, norms are expectations around which actors' understandings and behavior ought to conform. Over time, such norms may develop into legal obligations, either through codification into international treaties or through the development of customary law. Or they may remain non-legal, but nonetheless influential understandings that structure the expectations and behavior of actors in the international system. The trajectory of the Responsibility to Protect over the past decade is strongly suggestive of its development toward a rule of international law, but further political development and legal process will be required. That process must clarify both how the Responsibility to Protect goes beyond existing rules of law and the precise obligations on all states to prevent and react to international atrocities.

While advocates of the Responsibility to Protect may advocate its early adoption as a legal obligation, its present normative status should be welcomed and its gradual development toward law embraced. First, the underlying prohibitions of international crimes and obligations to prevent them are already codified in long-standing legal

[70] *See generally*, Global Ctr. for the Responsibility to Protect, Early Warning, Assessment, and the Responsibility to Protect: Informal Interactive Dialogue of the General Assembly held on 9 August 2010, Sept. 2010.

[71] Cass R. Sunstein, *Social Norms and Social Roles*, 96 Colum. L. Rev. 4, 903, 914 (1996).

obligations. Reliance on those existing legal obligations will be more effective as a legal matter than basing a claim on a potential new legal rule.

The power of the Responsibility to Protect ultimately lies in its ability to generate political pressure and compliance pull.[72] The key challenge to human security is ensuring that territorial states do in fact prevent crimes and that the international community responds where territorial states do not. As a political statement and reflection of an expanding political consensus, the Responsibility to Protect goes far to induce the preventive and responsive actions that are so urgently needed.

Second, as the debates at the World Summit and, subsequently, in the General Assembly indicate, most states today are willing to recognize the fact that sovereignty carries with it responsibility. Yet, those same states are unwilling to alter the basic legal rules governing when international interventions to prevent or stop atrocity are allowable, remaining firmly rooted in the UN Charter and the necessity of Security Council approval. Hence, were the Responsibility to Protect to be codified as binding law today, it would result in a relatively thin rule that neither addresses nor resolves the challenge of international intervention in the face of Security Council inaction.

Third, despite the efforts of the Secretary-General in his report on the implementation of the Responsibility to Protect to resolve many of the outstanding ambiguities in the World Summit Outcome Document, the 2009 General Assembly debates suggest that there still exists considerable disagreement on specific forms of assistance to be provided by third states and the appropriate scope of international intervention. Early adoption of the Responsibility to Protect as international law would result in either a legal rule of limited precision (and, hence, limited effectiveness) or an international treaty with very few states parties.

Finally, the processes of the past ten years suggest a strong and growing consensus around the Responsibility to Protect. Yet, as is often the case in international law and politics, when states are asked to transform norm to law, political considerations get in the way. Moving too fast risks undermining that consensus as some states step back from forward-leaning rhetorical positions to avoid legal codification.

Ultimately, the power of any norm or rule of international law is its ability to alter the cost-benefit calculations, preference sets, or value choices of actors in the international system. The Responsibility to Protect has already done so and will continue to do so. As the chapters that follow demonstrate, the norm has already shifted academic and political debates; altered conceptions of sovereignty; changed the way states and international actors talk about international crimes and their prevention; and shifted discussions on the appropriateness and duties of intervention. Because of the emergence of the Responsibility to Protect over the past decade, it is today more costly—in terms of political capital, international sanction, and moral identity—for states to perpetrate international atrocities or to allow them to unfold unhindered. And it is more difficult for the international community to stand by—as it did all too often in the past—when atrocity is perpetrated.

The further codification of the Responsibility to Protect as binding international law would, undoubtedly, increase the costs on states that perpetrate international

[72] Thomas M. Franck, The Power of Legitimacy Among Nations (Oxford University Press 1990).

crimes or allow them to occur. Framing the norm as law would facilitate greater condemnations of violations and might give rise to new sanctions for violation. Yet as history all too clearly shows, even international law is not inviolable and the legal codification of the Responsibility to Protect would offer no guarantees of human security.

Ultimately, timing is everything. The desire to legalize the Responsibility to Protect must be balanced against its further substantive development and expanding political consensus of support. For the time being, a course of patient prudence significantly outweighs the marginal increase in effectiveness of formal legalization. And there is reason for optimism that the Responsibility to Protect will develop over time in ways that make it more precise, more expansive, and more effective. While that development unfolds, the norm itself will continue, as it already has, to shape and impact the behavior of states and the cause of human security.

3 Defining the Crimes

Tarun Chhabra and Jeremy B. Zucker*

Since world leaders in 2005 assented to a two-paragraph description of states' individual and collective "Responsibility to Protect" (RtoP), much of the ensuing debate has focused on whether and to what extent that responsibility entails political, moral and/or legal obligations.[1] This chapter addresses two prior questions: what established international crimes does RtoP address, and what is the relevance of legal definitions of these crimes for implementation of RtoP?

The 2005 World Summit Outcome Document (WSOD) declared that individual states have the Responsibility to Protect populations from "genocide, war crimes, ethnic cleansing, and crimes against humanity"; that there is a collective responsibility to "help to protect" populations from those same crimes through "diplomatic, humanitarian, and other peaceful means"; and that states are "prepared" to take collective action up through and including the UN Charter's Chapter VII enforcement methods "should peaceful means be inadequate and national authorities are manifestly failing to protect their populations."[2] But neither the WSOD nor subsequent UN declarations have articulated precisely how the specified four categories of international crimes should be defined for the purposes of implementing RtoP.

Treaties and custom have clarified the elements of genocide, war crimes, and crimes against humanity. In addition, each of these categories of crimes also has been subject to the jurisprudence of international courts and tribunals such as the International Criminal Court (ICC), the International Criminal Tribunal for the former Yugoslavia (ICTY), and the International Criminal Tribunal for Rwanda (ICTR). Ethnic

* The authors thank Yujing Yue for editorial and research assistance, and Maria Banda, David Bowker and Adam Roberts for helpful comments. All errors are our own.

[1] *See, e.g.,* Carsten Stahn, *Responsibility to Protect: Political Rhetoric or Emerging Legal Norm,* 101 Am. J. of Int'l L. 99, 99–120 (2007).

[2] *2005 World Summit Outcome,* A/RES/60/1, Sept. 15, 2005 [hereinafter WSOD].

cleansing does not constitute a nominally distinct legal category; instead, the crimes it is generally understood to encompass fall into the other three categories incorporated into RtoP.

This chapter discusses how the crimes covered by RtoP have been developed through relevant and authoritative legal sources. It also considers three challenges to the underlying premise that the doctrinal warrens of existing legal consensus are or should be integral to implementation of RtoP. These challenges concern: (1) the transferability of legal doctrines drawn from individual criminal responsibility to state responsibility; (2) the multiple and variable responsibilities entailed by RtoP; and (3) the implications for and of pre-existing state responsibilities enshrined in international law. The chapter then considers acts omitted from the scope of RtoP and finally turns to implications for ongoing debates over the legal versus political character of RtoP. We ultimately suggest that a preoccupation with technical legal precipitants for RtoP may undermine rather than consolidate consensus to prevent and halt mass atrocities.

I. THE CONCEPTUAL EVOLUTION OF RTOP

Although the idea of sovereignty as responsibility has a lineage that can be traced to Lockean and Grotian political and legal theory, recent development of the RtoP concept owes a more proximate debt to scholarship authored by Francis Deng in the 1990s.[3] Drawing on Deng's work, the International Commission on Intervention and State Sovereignty (ICISS) issued a report in December 2001 that, while discussing tripartite responsibilities to "prevent," "react," and "rebuild," focused primarily on the problem of humanitarian intervention and sought to shift the terms of the debate from a "right to intervene" to the "Responsibility to Protect."[4] However, the ICISS report does not clearly articulate the threshold events that might trigger a responsibility to take preventive or other action short of armed intervention; instead, it focuses primarily on the threshold for intervention:

> [T]here are exceptional circumstances in which the very interest that all states have in maintaining a stable international order requires them to react when all order within a state has broken down or when civil conflict and repression are so violent that civilians are threatened with massacre, genocide or ethnic cleansing on a large scale. . . . Generally expressed, the view was that these exceptional circumstances must be cases of violence which so genuinely 'shock the conscience of mankind,' or which present such a clear and present danger to international security, that they require coercive military action.[5]

[3] Francis Deng & William Zartman, Sovereignty as Responsibility: Conflict Management in Africa (Brookings 1996).

[4] International Commission on Intervention and State Sovereignty (ICISS), The Responsibility to Protect: Report of the International Commission on Intervention and State Sovereignty (International Development Research Centre 2001), *available at* http://www.iciss.ca/report-en.asp [hereinafter ICISS Report].

[5] *Id.* at ¶ 4.13.

In elaborating a set of criteria for judging the merits of intervention, the ICISS report draws on the tradition of just war theory to find that a "just cause" criterion would be satisfied by two broad categories of events:

> [L]arge scale loss of life, actual or apprehended, with genocidal intent or not, which is the product either of deliberate state action, or state neglect or inability to act, or a failed state situation; or large-scale 'ethnic cleansing,' actual or apprehended, whether carried out by killing, forced expulsion, acts of terror or rape.[6]

The report goes on to identify more specific acts that would fall under these two broad categories, including acts spelled out by the 1948 Genocide Convention; different manifestations of ethnic cleansing; crimes against humanity and war crimes that involve large-scale killing or ethnic cleansing; situations of state collapse resulting in exposure of the population to mass starvation and/or civil war; and overwhelming natural or environmental catastrophes in which a state is unwilling or unable to cope or call for assistance and significant loss of life is occurring or threatened.[7]

Several aspects of these threshold criteria are noteworthy in tracing the evolution of the current RtoP concept. First, the ICISS criteria seem to focus on intervention generally, which could be undertaken with both preventive and reactive purpose; whether the criteria were to apply to preventive and/or reactive intervention, or to preventive or reactive measures other than intervention—or whether the thresholds vary depending on the stage and type of response—is unclear. Second, ICISS focused on "large-scale killing" as a trigger, not requiring a finding of genocide but requiring that only those crimes against humanity and war crimes involving large-scale killing or ethnic cleansing would meet the ICISS threshold. Third, mass starvation, civil war, and natural disasters were included, with only the latter being qualified by an accompanying threatened or manifest "significant loss of life."

The next major stage of development for the RtoP concept came when it was embraced by UN Secretary-General Kofi Annan's *High-Level Panel on Threats, Challenges, and Change*, which was assembled in the aftermath of the 2003 invasion of Iraq in order to inform Annan's 2005 UN reform effort. The High-Level Panel issued its final report in December 2004 and adopted RtoP as a concept applicable across a continuum spanning prevention to intervention in cases of "mass murder and rape, ethnic cleansing by forcible expulsion and terror, and deliberate starvation and exposure to disease."[8] The panel proceeded to apply threshold criteria for RtoP-based intervention:

> We endorse the emerging norm that there is a collective international responsibility to protect, exercisable by the Security Council authorizing military intervention as a last resort, in the event of genocide and other large-scale killing, ethnic cleansing or

[6] *Id.* at ¶ 4.19. The report identifies six criteria in the "just war" tradition: just cause, compelling evidence, right intention, last resort, proportional means and reasonable prospects (*Id.* ¶¶ 4.15–4.43).

[7] *Id.* at ¶ 4.10.

[8] Secretary-General's High-Level Panel on Threats, Challenges and Change, *A More Secure World: Our Shared Responsibility*, A/59/565, Dec. 2, 2004 [hereinafter *A More Secure World*].

serious violations of international humanitarian law which sovereign Governments have proved powerless or unwilling to prevent.[9]

The High-Level Panel parted ways from the ICISS report by shedding from its intervention thresholds mass starvation, civil war and natural disasters. On the other hand, it possibly lowered the barrier to intervention with respect to war crimes and crimes against humanity by stipulating that qualifying violations must be "serious" but not specifying that they must entail large-scale killing or ethnic cleansing.[10] But perhaps the most noteworthy and controversial aspect of the panel's consideration of RtoP was its choice to label the concept an "emerging norm"—language that suggested an effort to chart a path toward recognition as customary international law.[11]

When Annan produced his own report in the run-up to the 2005 World Summit, he cited the panel's reference to RtoP as an "emerging norm" and endorsed the concept as both an individual and collective state responsibility. In the latter framework, he identified a continuum of responsibility encompassing "diplomatic, humanitarian, and other methods."[12] In articulating the scope of collective responsibility short of force, Annan cited a broad imperative to "protect the human rights and well-being of civilian populations."[13] Isolating the question of intervention in a section of the report some distance from RtoP, Annan posed his threshold position rhetorically: "As to genocide, ethnic cleansing, and other such crimes against humanity, are they not also threats to international peace and security, against which humanity should be able to look to the Security Council for protection?"[14]

After extended and contentious negotiations, the WSOD yielded text that described a:

responsibility to protect its populations from genocide, war crimes, ethnic cleansing, and crimes against humanity. . . . entail[ing] the prevention of such crimes, including their incitement, through appropriate and necessary means.[15]

No direct reference to "military intervention" per se survived the negotiations. Instead, paragraph 139 of the WSOD ties RtoP to "genocide, war crimes, ethnic cleansing, and crimes against humanity" (four separate times) in reference to action under Chapters VI and VIII of the UN Charter; capacity-building; enforcement action under

[9] *Id.* at ¶ 203.

[10] *Id.* The panel appears to have understood "humanitarian law" to encompass war crimes and crimes against humanity. There also is reason to believe that its qualification of "serious" war crimes and crimes against humanity was not so deliberate an attempt at differentiation from ICISS as was the exclusion of mass starvation, civil war, and natural disasters. Interview with secretariat staff of the UN Secretary General's High-Level Panel on Threats, Challenges, and Change (Dec. 2010).

[11] *See, e.g.*, objections such as that submitted by the Russian Federation. A/59/PV.87, at 6. ("the establishment of an international norm presupposes that there is wide support within the international community for such a norm. However, that is not the case here.") *See also* Stahn, *supra* note 1.

[12] UN Secretary-General, *In Larger Freedom: Towards Security, Development and Human Rights for All*, A/59/2005, Mar. 21, 2005, at ¶ 135 [hereinafter *In Larger Freedom*].

[13] *Id.*

[14] *Id.* at ¶ 125. The omission of war crimes was apparently not deliberate. Interview with UN Secretariat staff.

[15] WSOD, *supra* note 2, at ¶ 138.

Chapter VII; and further consideration by the General Assembly.[16] The document furnishes only one set of threshold actions for any form of collective action under RtoP, and, unlike the ICISS report, does not qualify crimes against humanity or war crimes as those that threaten or result in large-scale loss of life. But it also diminishes the significance of its stated thresholds by limiting the collective dimension of RtoP to "help[ing]" to protect populations from the four categories of crimes under Chapter VI (peaceful settlement of disputes) and Chapter VIII (cooperation with regional organizations) actions, and agreeing only to be "prepared" to take enforcement actions under Chapter VII on a "case-by-case basis."[17]

Subsequent action at the UN has not altered this consensus. UN Security Council Resolution 1674 merely "reaffirms the provisions of paragraphs 138 and 139 of the WSOD regarding the Responsibility to Protect populations from genocide, war crimes, ethnic cleansing, and crimes against humanity."[18] In a pithy 2009 resolution—the only one referring to RtoP since the 2005 World Summit—the General Assembly "takes note" of Secretary-General Ban Ki-moon's report on implementation of the concept and "decides to continue its consideration" of RtoP.[19]

II. THE CRIMES

From the ICISS report through the WSOD, the core threshold elements for a Responsibility to Protect have been relatively consistent: genocide, war crimes, crimes against humanity, and ethnic cleansing. War crimes and crimes against humanity were spelled out by Article Six of the Nuremberg Charter[20], and UN General Assembly Resolution 95 "affirm[ed] the principles of international law" recognized by the Charter of the Nuremberg Tribunal and its judgments and directed the International Law Commission (ILC)[21] to codify those principles as "offences against the peace and security of mankind, or of an International Criminal Code."[22] The crime of genocide, meanwhile, was defined and prohibited by treaty: the Convention on the Prevention and Punishment of the Crime of Genocide (Genocide Convention), which entered into force in 1948. The ILC integrated the basic elements of all three crimes—genocide, war crimes, and crimes against humanity—into its 1954 Draft Code of Offences against the Peace and Security of Mankind, and, in 1994 and 1996, into its updated Draft Code and into its draft statute for an International Criminal Court.[23]

[16] *Id.* at ¶ 139.

[17] *In Larger Freedom*, *supra* note 12, at ¶ 139.

[18] S.C. Res. 1673, S/RES/1673 (Apr. 27, 2006).

[19] G.A. Res. 63/308, A/RES/63/308 (Oct. 7, 2009).

[20] Agreement for the Prosecution and Punishment of the Major War Criminals of the European Axis, and Charter of the International Military Tribunal, art. 6 (Aug. 8, 1945) [hereinafter Nuremberg Charter].

[21] Then called the Committee on the Codification of International Law, A/RES/1/95, Dec. 11, 1946.

[22] *Id.*

[23] Draft Code of Offences against the Peace and Security of Mankind, [1954] 2 Int'l L. Comm'n 112, A/CN.4/SER.A/1954; Draft Code of Crimes against the Peace and Security of Mankind, [1996] 2 Int'l L. Comm'n 30, A/CN.4/SER.A/1996/Add.1 (Part 2); Draft Statute for an International Criminal Court, [1994] 2 Int'l L. Comm'n 42, A/CN.4/SER.A/1994/Add.1 (Part 2).

The jurisprudence of the ICC and ad hoc international tribunals has further developed the international legal contours of genocide, war crimes, and crimes against humanity. Ethnic cleansing has yet to be explicitly defined by international treaty or custom, but it is widely understood to fall within the scope of the other three categories of crimes: genocide where ethnic cleansing entails an intent to destroy an ethnic group in part or whole; crimes against humanity where there is systematic and widespread persecution based on ethnic identity in connection with any predicate element of crimes against humanity (in a peacetime or wartime context); and war crimes where certain acts—such as forced deportation, sexual violence, and killing civilians—are part of a plan or policy targeting an ethnic group in a wartime context.

We now turn to the most recent developments in the ongoing legal project of progressively defining these four categories of crime. In doing so, we underline the focus of this jurisprudence on individual criminal responsibility, the wide discretion retained by international judicial authorities, and the ambiguities with respect to individual versus collective state responsibility—all of which raise questions about the relevance of recent international legal jurisprudence for the realization of RtoP obligations.

A. Genocide

The Charter of the International Military Tribunal provided for prosecutors at Nuremberg to try and punish persons guilty of crimes against peace (aggression), war crimes, and crimes against humanity.[24] Genocide was not spelled out as a specific crime in the Nuremberg Charter, though the term appeared in indictments and at trial in the context of crimes against humanity. Even so, the tribunal considered genocide only as an accessory to crimes against peace.[25] Today, genocide is an independent crime under international law, and it may be understood as the gravest subset of crimes against humanity and war crimes.

Article Two of the 1948 Convention on the Prevention and Punishment of the Crime of Genocide defines the crime as

> [A]ny of the following acts committed with intent to destroy in whole or in part, a national, ethnical, racial or religious group, as such: (a) killing members of the group; (b) causing serious bodily or mental harm to members of the group; (c) deliberately inflicting on the group conditions of life calculated to bring about its physical destruction in whole or in part; (d) imposing measures intended to prevent births within the group; (e) forcibly transferring children of the group to another group.[26]

[24] Nuremberg Charter, *supra* note 20.

[25] *See, e.g.*, discussion by Robert H. Jackson in Minutes of the International Conference on Military Trials Session of Jul. 23, 1945, *in* Robert H. Jackson, Report of Robert H. Jackson, United States Representative to the International Conference on Military Trials, London, 1945, at 328–31 (Dep't of State Publication 1949) ("The reason that this program of extermination of Jews and destruction of the rights of minorities becomes an international concern is this: it was a part of a plan for making an illegal war. Unless we have a war connection as a basis for reaching them, I would think we have no basis for dealing with atrocities.")

[26] Convention on the Prevention and Punishment of Genocide, art. 2, Dec. 9, 1948, 78 U.N.T.S. 277.

Article Three of the Genocide Convention makes punishable "(a) genocide; (b) conspiracy to commit genocide; (c) direct and public incitement to commit genocide; (d) attempt to commit genocide; (e) complicity in genocide."[27]

Article Four of the ICTY and Article Two of the ICTR both adopt the definition and description of punishable acts found in Articles Two and Three of the Genocide Convention.[28] The Rome Statute transposes Article Two and, in Article 25, also lists all of the elements in Article Three of the Genocide Convention, with the exception of conspiracy.[29]

As early as 1951, the International Court of Justice (ICJ) suggested in an advisory opinion on reservations to the Genocide Convention that all provisions of the agreement expressed pre-existing customary international law and *erga omnes* obligations.[30] In 2007, the ICJ confirmed this view in more explicit terms and in a contentious case—the *Genocide* case (Bosnia v. Serbia[31]), which held that, while the Serbian government was neither directly responsible nor complicit in the 1995 Srebrenica genocide that claimed the lives of more than eight thousand Bosniak men and boys, it nevertheless breached the Genocide Convention by failing to take adequate steps to prevent and punish the massacre.[32] The ICTY, too, has ruled that the provisions of the Genocide Convention constitute not only customary international law but also *jus cogens*.[33] Thus the crime of genocide is applicable in peace or war, and in internationalized or non-internationalized conflicts. But while states are responsible for preventing, repressing, and punishing genocide within their borders, and also for genocidal events proxi-

[27] *Id.* at art. 3.

[28] Statute of the International Tribunal for the Former Yugoslavia, S.C. Res. 827, art. 4, S/RES/827, May 25, 1993 [hereinafter ICTY Statute]; Statute of the International Criminal Tribunal for Rwanda, S.C. Res. 955, art. 2, S/RES/955, Nov. 8, 1994 [hereinafter ICTR Statute].

[29] *But see* Thomas E. Davies, *How the Rome Statute Weakens the International Prohibition on the Incitement of Genocide*, 22 Harv. Hum. Rts. J. 245 (2009) (arguing that the Rome Statute weakens the prohibition on incitement to genocide by classifying incitement as a mode of participation in the underlying crime, rather than a crime in and of itself).

[30] Reservations to Convention on Prevention and Punishment of Crime of Genocide, Advisory Opinion, 1951 I.C.J. 15 (May 28).

[31] Application of the Convention on the Prevention and Punishment of the Crime of Genocide (Bosn. & Herz. v. Serbia & Montenegro), 2007 I.C.J. 91 (Feb. 26) [hereinafter ICJ Bosnia Judgment].

[32] *Id.* at ¶¶ 425–450 ("the obligation in question is one of conduct and not one of result, in the sense that a State cannot be under an obligation to succeed, whatever the circumstances, in preventing the commission of genocide: the obligation of States parties is rather to employ all means reasonably available to them, so as to prevent genocide so far as possible. A State does not incur responsibility simply because the desired result is not achieved; responsibility is however incurred if the State manifestly failed to take all measures to prevent genocide which were within its power, and which might have contributed to preventing the genocide").

[33] Prosecutor v. Popović et al., Case No. IT-05–88-T, Judgment ¶ 807, n.2910 (Int'l Crim. Trib. for the Former Yugoslavia, Jun. 10, 2010, http://www.icty.org/x/cases/Popovic/tjug/en/100610judgement.pdf [hereinafter Popović] ("'the principles underlying the [Genocide] Convention are principles which are recognized by civilized nations as binding on States, even without any conventional obligation' and "that the norm prohibiting genocide was assuredly a peremptory norm of international law (*jus cogens*)'") (internal citations omitted). *See also* Prosecutor v. Krstić, Case No. IT-98–33-T, Judgment ¶ 541 (Int'l Crim. Trib. for the Former Yugoslavia Aug. 2, 2001), http://www.icty.org/x/cases/Krstić/tjug/en/krs-tj010802e.pdf [hereinafter Krstić], on customary law at time of Srebrenica.

mate to their borders where there are strong military or political ties—provided a state is aware or should be aware that genocide could occur—the question of third-party and collective responsibility remains unsettled.[34] Although Article Eight of the Genocide Convention specifies that contracting parties may call upon competent organs of the UN to prevent or repress acts of genocide, no UN body save for the ICJ has invoked the Convention. Although the UN Secretary-General has appointed Special Advisers on the Prevention of Genocide, UN Member States also have declined to create a special treaty body to track implementation of the Convention. Notwithstanding the ICJ's 1951 advisory opinion on reservations to the Genocide Convention and its 2007 *Genocide* case, legal development of the criminal "elements" of genocide has occurred primarily in the context of international criminal prosecution. We therefore turn to the jurisprudence of the ICTY and ICTR in order to highlight—in the context of individual criminal responsibility—the current legal understanding of three key elements of genocide: substantiality, intent (*mens rea*), and the character of the underlying act (*actus reus*).

1. Substantiality of Part of Targeted Group

The question of a substantiality threshold for obligations under the Genocide Convention is nearly as old as the convention itself. The issue was addressed directly by Raphael Lemkin in a 1950 letter to the U.S. Senate Foreign Relations Committee, in which he concluded that any intent to destroy a group in part must be substantial enough "so as to affect the entirety."[35] Recent ICTY judgments are consistent with this standard. Echoing its *Krstić* judgment, the ICTY in *Popović* decided that, where a group is targeted "in part," it must be "significant enough to have an impact on the group as a whole."[36] More explicitly, this entails consideration of (a) "numeric size of the part of the group targeted, evaluated in absolute terms and relative to the overall group size"; (b) prominence of the targeted part, including whether it is emblematic or essential to its survival; and (c) the area of the alleged perpetrators' activity and any limitations on their "reach."[37] The relative weight attributed to each factor turns on a contextual analysis.[38]

[34] *See, e.g.*, ICJ Bosnia Judgment, *supra* note 31, at ¶ 430 ("the capacity to influence effectively the action of persons likely to commit, or already committing, genocide . . . depends, among other things, on the geographical distance of the State concerned from the scene of the events, and on the strength of the political links, as well as links of all other kinds, between the authorities of that State and the main actors in the events . . . [T]he possibility remains that the combined efforts of several States, each complying with its obligation to prevent, might have achieved the result—averting the commission of genocide—which the efforts of only one State were insufficient to produce.") *But see* Int'l L. Comm'n, Draft Articles on Responsibility of States with Commentary, n. 92, 93, A/56/10 (2001), *available at*http://untreaty.un.org/ilc/texts/instruments/english/draft%20articles/9_6_2001.pdf [hereinafter Draft Articles ILC].

[35] Letter from Raphael Lemkin, *in* Executive Session of the Senate Foreign Relations Committee, Historical Series 370 (Government Printing Office 1976).

[36] 36 Popović, *supra* note 33, at ¶ 831 (quoting Prosecutor v. Krstić, Case No. IT-98–33-A, Appeal Judgment ¶ 4 (Int'l Crim. Trib. for the Former Yugoslavia, Apr. 19, 2004), http://www.icty.org/x/cases/Krstić/acjug/en/krs-aj040419e.pdf [hereinafter Krstić Appeal Judgment]).

[37] *Id.* at ¶ 832 (quoting Krstić Appeal Judgment, *supra*, at ¶¶ 12–14).

[38] *Id.* (citing Krstić, *supra* note 33, at ¶ 14). The targeted part need not be civilians; military personnel may qualify where the other requirements are met. Popović, *supra* note 33, at ¶ 833 (citing Krstić Appeal Judgment, *supra* note 36, at ¶ 226)

This analysis, which confers remarkable discretion on the tribunal, again raises questions about the relevance of a doctrinal threshold in international criminal jurisprudence for state responsibility. The ICJ's reliance on the ICTY's substantiality analysis has provided few answers.[39]

2. Genocidal Intent

Like substantiality, the question of genocidal intent has been treated as a multi-factor analysis that confers significant discretion on presiding judicial officers. A showing of three elements of intent is required: (a) intent to *destroy* the targeted group; (b) intent to destroy the group *in whole or in part*; and (c) intent to *commit the underlying act*.[40] The ICTY has drawn several specific conclusions. For instance, the *mens rea* with respect to the underlying act also can serve as evidence for the element of specific intent to destroy.[41] Forcible transfer alone is not sufficient evidence of the requisite intent but may be a relevant consideration.[42] Personal motives do not preclude genocidal intent.[43] And intent to destroy must involve "physical and biological destruction . . . exclud[ing] attempts to annihilate cultural or sociological elements."[44]

The ICC also may impose a higher threshold for intent than the ICTY and ICTR. Although the Rome Statute itself does not contain such language, the ICC Elements of Crimes, an interpretive document, requires that genocide must be committed in the context of a "manifest pattern."[45] Some scholarship supports this view, finding the *travaux preparatoires* of the Genocide Convention to suggest that intent must be

[39] ICJ Bosnia Judgment, *supra* note 31, at ¶ 296.

[40] Popović, *supra* note 33, at ¶ 808 (citing Krstić Appeal Judgment, *supra* note 36, at ¶ 20 and ICJ Bosnia Judgment, *supra* note 31, at ¶ 186.

[41] Popović, *supra* note 33, at ¶ 823 (citing Krstić Appeal Judgment, *supra* note 36, at ¶ 20).

[42] Popović, *supra* note 33, at ¶ 824 (citing Prosecutor v. Blagojević and Jokić, Case No. IT-02–60-A, Appeal Judgment ¶ 123 (Int'l Crim. Trib. for the Former Yugoslavia May 9, 2007), http://www.unhcr.org/refworld/category,LEGAL,ICTY,,,48ac10ac2,0.html [hereinafter Blagojević and Jokić Appeal Judgment]. A similar conclusion was reached by the 2004 Report of the International Commission of Inquiry on Darfur to the United Nations Secretary General, which did not infer genocidal intent from forcible transfers: "forcibly displacing members of some tribes does not evince a specific intent to annihilate, in whole or in part, a group distinguished on racial, ethnic, national or religions grounds", UN Secretary-General, S/2005/60, Jan. 25, 2005.

[43] Popović, *supra* note 33, at ¶ 825 (citing Prosecutor v. Jelisić, Case No. IT-95–10-A, Appeal Judgment, ¶ 49 (Int'l Crim. Trib. for the Former Yugoslavia, Jul. 5, 2001), http://www.unhcr.org/refworld/country,,ICTY,,BIH,45 62d8b62,4147fcad4,0.html [hereinafter Jelisić Appeal Judgment]).

[44] Popović, *supra* note 33, at ¶ 822 (citing, *e.g.*, Prosecutor v. Blagojević and Jokić, Case No. IT-02–60-T, Trial Judgment ¶¶ 656, 665 (Int'l Crim. Trib. for the Former Yugoslavia Jan. 17, 2005) [hereinafter Blagojević and Jokić Trial Judgment]; Prosecutor v. Akayesu, Case No. ICTR-96–4-T, Trial Judgment ¶¶ 485, 521 (Int'l Crim. Trib. for Rwanda Sept. 2, 1998), http://www.unhcr.org/refworld/publisher,ICTR,,,40278fbb4,0.html [hereinafter Akayesu Trial Judgment]). But such acts are often concurrent and "may legitimately be considered as evidence of an intent to physically destroy the group." *Id.* (quoting Krstić, *supra* note 33, at ¶ 25, n. 39).

[45] International Criminal Court, Elements of Crimes, PCNICC/2000/1/Add.2 (2000), at art. 6 [hereafter Elements of Crimes].

attributed to a state policy.[46] The ICTY and ICTR have eschewed this view, insisting that, as a matter of customary and statutory law, neither a plan nor policy is required to find intent to commit genocide.[47] In *Popović* and *Krstić*, the ICTY specifically rejected claims that it was bound by the ICC approach to intent, finding that "reliance on the definition of genocide given in the ICC's Elements of Crimes is inapposite" because the Elements "are not binding rules, but only auxiliary means of interpretation."[48] This jurisprudence has helped to clarify the requisite *mens rea* for individual criminal responsibility for genocide, but like determinations of substantiality, determinations of genocidal intent entail wide judicial discretion. They are based on "all of the evidence, taken together."[49] To wit, the "[intent to destroy] . . . may be inferred from a number of facts and circumstances, such as the general context, the perpetration of other culpable acts systematically directed against the same group, the scale of the atrocities committed, the systematic targeting of victims on account of their membership in a particular group, or the repetition of destructive and discriminatory acts."[50]

3. The Underlying Act

Legal criteria specifying the underlying act, or *actus reus*, of genocide suggest several fault lines that may distinguish determinations appropriate for individual criminal responsibility from those appropriate for state responsibility. Among the underlying acts that qualify a crime as genocide are killing; acts causing serious bodily or mental harm; forcible transfer of children; acts fundamentally altering conditions of life; and measures intended to prevent births. For killing, the requisite elements are equivalent to those of murder.[51] The ICC Elements of Crimes provides that genocide may occur

[46] *See, e.g.*, William Schabas, *State Policy as an Element of International Crimes* 98 J. Crim. L. & Criminology 953, 962–69 (2008) (arguing that the drafting history of the Genocide Convention implicitly assumed State policy as an element of the crime).

[47] *See, e.g.*, Popović, *supra* note 33, at ¶ 828; Krstić Appeal Judgment, *supra* note 36, at ¶ 223; Jelisić Appeal Judgment, *supra* note 43, at ¶ 48; Prosecutor v. Kayishema and Ruzindana, Case No. ICTR-95–1-A, Appeal Judgment ¶ 138 (Int'l Crim. Trib. for Rwanda, Jun. 1, 2001, http://www.unhcr.org/refworld/publisher,ICTR,,,4 8abd5a31a,0.html. But the existence of such a plan or policy, and knowledge of it can be relevant evidence supporting an inference of intent. Popović, *supra* note 33, at ¶ 830.

[48] Popović, *supra* note 33, at ¶ 829 (quoting Krstić Appeal Judgment, *supra* note 36, at ¶ 224).

[49] Popović, *supra* note 33, at ¶ 820 (quoting Krstić Appeal Judgment, *supra* note 36, at ¶ 134).

[50] Popović, *supra* note 33, at ¶ 823 (citing Jelisić Appeal Judgment, *supra* note 43, at ¶ 47; Blagojević and Jokić Appeal Judgment, *supra* note 42, at ¶ 123 and Krstić Appeal Judgment, *supra* note 36, at ¶¶ 33, 35).

[51] *See, e.g.*, Popović, *supra* note 33, at ¶¶ 787–89; n. 2918 (citing Prosecutor v. Krajišnik, Case No. IT-00–39-T, Trial Judgment ¶ 859(i) (Int'l Crim. Trib. for the Former Yugoslavia Sept. 27, 2006), http://www.unhcr.org/cgi-bin/texis/vtx/refworld/rwmain?docid=48ad29642 [hereinafter Krajišnik Trial Judgment]); Blagojević and Jokić Trial Judgment, *supra* note 44, at ¶ 642; Prosecutor v. Jelisić, Case No. IT-95–10-T, Trial Judgment ¶ 63 (Int'l Crim. Trib. for the Former Yugoslavia Dec. 14, 1999), http://www.unhcr.org/refworld/topic,4565c22538,4565c25f449,4 147fe474,0.html [hereinafter Jelisić Trial Judgment]; Prosecutor v. Seromba, Case No. ICTR-2001–66-I, Trial Judgment ¶ 317 (Int'l Crim. Trib. for Rwanda Dec. 13, 2006), http://www.unhcr.org/refworld/topic,463af22 12,469f2d102,48abd58ed,0.html [hereinafter Seromba Trial Judgment]; Prosecutor v. Semanza,

where a perpetrator kills "one or more persons."[52] This threshold of genocide for purposes of individual criminal responsibility may not be transferable to the context of state responsibility, either for reactive or preventive purposes.

A second *actus reus* is the category of acts causing serious bodily or mental harm. Here the ICTY has required "proof of a result."[53] Such result must reach "beyond temporary unhappiness, embarrassment or humiliation" and inflict "grave and long-term disadvantage to a person's ability to lead a normal and constructive life."[54] Qualifying acts include torture, inhumane or degrading treatment, sexual violence including rape, interrogations combined with beatings, and harm that damages health or causes disfigurement or serious injury.[55] Forcible transfer alone does not qualify but can constitute the act that causes the requisite harm, such as if the transfer leads to death.[56] Ultimately, however, the test collapses into whether an act "threaten[s] [a group's] destruction in whole or in part," which, again, yields a highly contextual inquiry.[57]

The "conditions of life" element that can satisfy the *actus reus* requirement involves "methods of destruction that do not immediately kill the members of the group, but, which, ultimately, seek their physical destruction."[58] Examples of conditions found to meet these criteria are denial of medical services and "circumstances that would lead to a slow death," such as lack of proper housing, clothing, and hygiene; the imposition of excessive work or physical exertion; and systematic expulsion from homes.[59]

Case No. ICTR-97–20-T, Trial Judgment ¶ 319 (Int'l Crim. Trib. for Rwanda May 15, 2003), http://www1.umn.edu/humanrts/instree/ICTR/SEMANZA_ICTR-97–20/SEMANZA_ICTR-97–20-T.htm [hereafter Semanza Trial Judgment]; Prosecutor v. Musema, Case No. ICTR-96–13-T, Trial Judgment ¶ 155 (Int'l Crim. Trib. for Rwanda Jan. 27, 2000) [hereinafter Musema Trial Judgment].

52 Elements of Crimes, *supra* note 45, at art. 6(a), Element 1.

53 Popović, *supra* note 33, at ¶ 811.

54 *Id.* (citing Krstić, *supra* note 33, ¶ 513 and Blagojević and Jokić Trial Judgment, *supra* note 44, at ¶ 645).

55 Prosecutor v. Brđjanin, Case No. IT-99–36-T, Trial Judgment ¶ 690 (Int'l Crim. Trib. for the Former Yugoslavia Sept. 1, 2004), http://www.unhcr.org/cgi-bin/texis/vtx/refworld/rwmain?docid=4146fd744 [hereafter Brđjanin Trial Judgment] (cited in Popović, *supra* note 33, at ¶ 812). *See also* ICJ Bosnia Judgment, *supra* note 31, at ¶ 319 (finding systematic "massive mistreatment [including] beatings, rape and torture causing serious bodily and mental harm" qualify for purposes of the Genocide Convention).

56 Popović, *supra* note 33, at ¶ 813; Blagojević and Jokić Trial Judgment, *supra* note 44, at ¶¶ 650, 654.

57 Prosecutor v. Seromba, Case No. ICTR-2001–66-A, Appeal Judgment ¶ 46 (Int'l Crim. Trib. for Rwanda, Mar. 12, 2008), http://69.94.11.53/ENGLISH/cases/Seromba/decisions/080312-Appeals_judg.pdf (cited in Popović, *supra* note 33, at ¶ 810) [hereinafter Seromba Appeal Judgment]; Blagojević and Jokić Trial Judgment, *supra* note 44, at ¶ 646; Krstić, *supra* note 33, ¶ 513.

58 Popović, *supra* note 33, at ¶ 814 (quoting Akayesu Trial Judgment, *supra* note 44, at ¶ 505).

59 *See, e.g.*, Brđjanin Trial Judgment, *supra* note 55, at ¶¶ 691, 906; Prosecutor v. Stakić, Case No. IT-97–24-T, Trial Judgment ¶ 517 (Int'l Crim. Trib. for the Former Yugoslavia, Jul. 31, 2003, http://www.unhcr.org/refworld/category,LEGAL,ICTY,,,41483ab14,0.html [hereinafter Stakić Trial Judgment]; Akayesu Trial Judgment, *supra* note 44, at ¶ 506; Musema Trial Judgment, *supra* note 51, at ¶ 157; Prosecutor v. Kayishema and Ruzindana, Case No. ICTR-95–1-T, Trial Judgment ¶¶ 115–16 (Int'l Crim. Trib. for Rwanda May 21, 1999), http://www.unhcr.org/refworld/publisher,ICTR,,,48abd5760,0.html [hereinafter Kayishema and Ruzindana Trial Judgment].

With respect to measures intended to prevent births, tribunal judgments have held forced separation of males and females to qualify, and so, too, measures that are psychological as well as physical.[60] Unlike the acts of killing or causing serious bodily or mental harm, the acts to impose genocidal conditions of life or to prevent births do not require proof of a result.[61] International tribunals have therefore looked to "the objective probability" of such acts leading to physical destruction, including the length of exposure to imposed conditions and the vulnerability of the targeted group.[62]

Ultimately, individual state responsibility for genocide within that state's borders remains relatively clear. But the scope of extraterritorial, or third-party, individual and collective state responsibility for genocide remains unsettled. In any of these scenarios, however, the transferability of doctrines of individual criminal responsibility from international tribunals—including those tribunals' substantiality tests and use of highly context-sensitive and discretionary legal standards—is questionable. Indeed, the potential for doctrinal divergence between individual criminal versus state responsibility is apparent even in the jurisprudence of international courts; in its 2007 *Genocide* case, the ICJ elected to revert to its *Nicaragua* "effective control" test rather than follow the "overall control" test established by the ICTY in *Tadić*, effectively demanding a higher threshold for state responsibility.[63] To be sure, the concern about discretionary legal standards is not about the inevitable fact of discretion, but rather, about implicit assumptions embedded in such discretion—assumptions tailored to individual criminal responsibility rather than state responsibility.

B. War Crimes

War crimes generally refer to breaches of the four Geneva Conventions and other violations of the customs of war. The Geneva Conventions and customs of war together comprise what is known interchangeably as international humanitarian law, the law of armed conflict, or the laws of war. Acts categorized as war crimes overlap significantly with those classified as crimes against humanity, but whereas the latter may be committed in wartime or peacetime, war crimes are committed by belligerents in the context of armed conflict. Certain war crimes were codified in the 1907 Hague Convention and Geneva Convention of 1929, and these were consolidated under Article Six of the Charter of the International Military Tribunal at Nuremberg, which defined war crimes as

> [V]iolations of the laws or customs of war. Such violations shall include, but not be limited to, murder, ill-treatment or deportation to slave labor or for any other purpose

[60] Popović, *supra* note 33, at ¶ 818 (citing Prosecutor v. Rutaganda, Case No. ICTR-96-3-T, Trial Judgment ¶ 53 (Int'l Crim. Trib. for Rwanda Dec. 6, 1999), http://www1.umn.edu/humanrts/instree/ICTR/RUTAGANDA_ICTR-96–3/RUTAGANDA_ICTR-96–3-T.htm [hereinafter Rutagana Trial Judgment]; Akayesu Trial Judgment, *supra* note 44, at ¶¶ 507–08).

[61] Popović, *supra* note 33, at ¶ 814; Brđjanin Trial Judgment, *supra* note 55, at ¶ 691. Stakić Trial Judgment, *supra* note 59, at ¶ 517.

[62] Popović, *supra* note 33, at ¶ 816 (citing Brđjanin Trial Judgment, *supra* note 55, at ¶ 906; Kayishema and Ruzindana Trial Judgment, *supra* note 59, at ¶¶ 115, 548; Akayesu Trial Judgment, *supra* note 44, at ¶ 505).

[63] For a discussion, *see*, Antonio Cassese, *The Nicaragua and Tadić Tests Revisited in Light of the ICJ Judgment on Genocide in Bosnia*, 18 Eur. J. Int'l L. 649 (2007).

of civilian population of or in occupied territory, murder or ill-treatment of prisoners of war or persons on the seas, killing of hostages, plunder of public or private property, wanton destruction of cities, towns or villages, or devastation not justified by military necessity.[64]

The Geneva Conventions of 1949 subsequently codified and elaborated on the war crimes prosecuted at Nuremberg, and today all states are parties to the four Geneva Conventions. The provisions of these agreements are also considered customary international law.[65] Many of the customary rules applicable to internationalized armed conflict also apply to non-internationalized conflicts, but the extent of the overlap beyond Common Article Three of the Geneva Conventions (which obligates states to treat humanely all persons not taking an active part in hostilities) remains subject to disagreement.[66] It is generally agreed that prohibitions and standards of state responsibility in the context of internationalized conflict remain both more expansive and clear-cut in application than prohibitions in a non-internationalized context. In addition, designated "grave breaches" of the laws of war incur a higher order of state responsibility than other, "serious violations" not least in that such responsibility includes the obligation to punish individual perpetrators.[67]

More recently, Article 8 of the Rome Statute has defined war crimes for the purposes of international criminal prosecution.[68] Although Article 124 of the Rome Statute permits states to opt out of the ICC's war crimes jurisdiction for a period of seven years, no states currently party to the Statute remain outside the war crimes jurisdiction of the Court.[69] Article 8(2)(a) of the Rome Statute defines war crimes as grave breaches of the Geneva Conventions of 1949.[70] Article 8(2)(b) refers to "other serious violations of the laws and customs applicable in international armed conflict."[71]

[64] Nuremberg Charter, *supra* note 20, at art. 6.

[65] *See, e.g.*, Legality of the Threat or Use of Nuclear Weapons, Advisory Opinion, International Court of Justice, ¶¶ 79, 82, 257, 1996 I.C.J. 226, Jul. 8, 1996.

[66] *See, e.g.*, Jean-Marie Henckaerts and Louise Doswald-Beck, Customary International Humanitarian Law (Cambridge University Press 2005).

[67] *See* Beatrice I. Bonafè, The Relationship between State and Individual Responsibility for Individual Crimes (Martinus Nijhoff Publishers 2009), 74, at note 11. This "grave breaches" responsibility to punish individual perpetrators of certain war crimes should not be confused with the transferability of legal doctrines between individual criminal and State responsibility.

[68] Rome Statute of the International Criminal Court, A/CONF.183/9, Jan. 16, 2002, at art. 8(1) [hereinafter Rome Statute].

[69] France and Colombia exercised the right to opt out of the ICC's war crimes jurisdiction, but France withdrew its opt-out declaration, and Colombia's opt-out period has expired.

[70] These include willful killing; torture or inhuman treatment; willfully causing great suffering or serious injury; extensive destruction and appropriation of property; willfully depriving prisoners of war or other protected persons of a fair trial and conscripting prisoners of war or children into military service; unlawful deportation, transfer or confinement; and taking of hostages. Rome Statute, *supra* note 68, at art. 8(2).

[71] These include intentionally directing attacks against civilians, civilian objects or humanitarian and peacekeeping objects; intentionally launching attacks despite knowledge of disproportionate loss of life or injury to civilians, civilian objects or the natural environment; attacking undefended non-military objectives; killing or wounding surrendered combatants; improper use of flags and insignias resulting in death or injury; transfer of a civilian population into or out of occupied

Article 8(2)(c) provides that, in cases of non-international armed conflict, serious violations of Common Article 3 are prohibited.[72] Article 8(2)(e) expands on Common Article 3 prohibitions by prohibiting in non-internationalized conflict "serious violations of the laws and customs applicable in armed conflicts not of an international character, within the framework of international law."[73] Finally, Articles 8(2)(d) and 8(2)(f) provide that the provisions of Article 8 do not apply to "internal disturbances" such as riots.[74]

Common Article 1 of the Geneva Conventions obligates states to "respect" and "ensure respect" for the Conventions "in all circumstances." The ICJ has held that this obligation applies, as a matter of custom, to internationalized and non-internationalized conflicts, and the ICTY has found the provisions of Common Article One to entail an *erga omnes* obligation.[75] The International Committee of the Red Cross assessment of customary international humanitarian law has read ICTY jurisprudence to provide all states with a legal entitlement to demand respect for the prohibition on war crimes.[76] At the same time, there is no basis in the Geneva Conventions or custom for use of this entitlement or obligation as the "sole basis for resort to the use of force," so "[i]t is therefore expected that measures ensuring respect, beyond those decided by the UN Security Council, be peaceful ones."[77]

The International Criminal Court and international criminal tribunals have imposed their own substantiality requirements for war crimes prosecutions. The ICTR and

territories; intentionally directing attacks against objects cultural or historic, and not military, significance; unjustified mutilation or scientific experimentation; declaring that no quarter will be given; unjustified destruction or seizure of enemy property; failure to recognize in a court of law the rights and actions of nationals of a hostile party; compelling nationals to take part in military actions against their own country; pillaging; the use of certain weapons, ammunition and methods of warfare, including the use of poisonous gases; committing outrages upon personal dignity, including humiliating and degrading treatment; committing sexual violence such as rape, sexual slavery, or enforced prostitution, pregnancy or sterilization; using civilian shields; using starvation as a method of warfare. *Id.*

72 These include actions against any person not taking active part in hostilities, including surrendered, sick, wounded or detained prisoners, violence to life and person, in particular murder, mutilation, cruel treatment and torture; outrages upon personal dignity; taking of hostages; and passing and execution of sentences without a judgment of a regularly constituted court with "all juridical guarantees which are generally recognized as indispensable." *Id.*

73 These include many, but not all, of the relevant elements listed in 8(2)(b). Excluded are prohibitions on methods and means of warfare, such as those indicated in Article 8(2)(b)xxvii-xx. *Id.* "Although some delegations sought during the Preparatory Committee sessions and in Rome to stack Article 8(2)(3) with most, if not all, of the crimes applicable to international armed conflict as listed in Article 8(2)(b), most agreed that customary international law has developed to a more limited extent with respect to internal armed conflicts." David Scheffer, *The United States and the International Criminal Court*, 93 Am. J. Int'l L. 12, 16 (1999).

74 Rome Statute, *supra* note 68, at art. 8(2).

75 Military and Paramilitary Activities in and against Nicaragua (Nicar. v. US), 1986 I.C.J. 14, ¶ 220; Prosecutor v. Tadić, Case No. IT-94–1, Decision on the Defence Motion on Jurisdiction ¶ 71 (Int'l Crim. Trib. for the Former Yugoslavia Aug. 10, 1995), http://www.icty.org/x/cases/Tadić/tdec/en/100895.htm.

76 International Committee of the Red Cross, Customary International Humanitarian Law 512 (Jean-Marie Henckaerts & Louise Doswald-Beck eds., Cambridge University Press 2005).

77 *Id.*

ICTY statutes have required that war crimes be of a "serious" nature for individual criminal prosecution to be appropriate, and Article 8 of the Rome Statute, in addition to requiring the same, confers war crimes jurisdiction "in particular when committed as part of a plan or policy or as part of a large-scale commission of such crimes."[78] But if the Rome Statute in this respect raised the bar for international criminal prosecution, along with the jurisprudence of the ICTY, it has augmented the scope of individual criminal responsibility in the context of non-internationalized conflict[79]; in this sense in particular, the laws of war "developed" faster in the first few years of the establishment of the ICTY than in the 45 years after Nuremberg.[80] More recently, the ICC has consolidated this trend, putting forward war crimes counts in four of its country situations—the Democratic Republic of Congo, Sudan, Uganda, and the Central African Republic—each of which involves non-internationalized conflict. The specific crimes enumerated in these cases range from sexual slavery to pillaging to the use of child soldiers.

As with genocide, individual state responsibility—within its territory or within a theater in which it is engaged in warfare—to prevent, prosecute, and punish war crimes is much clearer than states' collective responsibility to do the same. Thus doctrines arising from individual criminal responsibility for war crimes seem least helpful for consideration of collective state responsibility. It is also unclear whether the substantiality threshold for individual state responsibility overlaps fully or only partially with that of individual criminal responsibility. Any overlap is further complicated by variable levels of state responsibility with respect to internationalized versus non-internationalized conflict. And although international tribunals have expanded the reach of war crimes prosecutions into non-internationalized conflicts, their substantiality thresholds have not been uniform. It is unclear which international criminal threshold, if any, should be applicable to attribution of state responsibility.

C. Crimes Against Humanity

Unlike genocide and war crimes, crimes against humanity were not codified after the Nuremberg trials. Nevertheless, crimes against humanity were deemed to be proscribed by custom with *jus cogens* status. Article 6 of the Nuremberg Charter provided that crimes against humanity included

> [M]urder, extermination, enslavement, deportation, and other inhumane acts committed against any civilian population, before or during the war, or persecutions on political,

[78] Rome Statute, *supra* note 68, at art. 8.

[79] *See, e.g.*, Allison Danner, *When Courts Make Law*, 59 VAND. L. REV. 1, 29 (2006).

[80] *See, e.g.*, Theodor Meron, *War Crimes Law Comes of Age*, 92 AM. J. INT'L L. 462 (1998). For objections to the view that the ICTY or ICTR could create new international standards for international humanitarian law, see the Amicus brief filed by the United States in the Tadić case ("[i]n creating the Tribunal, the Council was acting to deal with a specific urgent situation presenting a serious threat to the peace. It was not creating new standards for international humanitarian law") Submission of the Government of the United States of America Concerning Certain Arguments Made by Counsel for the Accused in the Case of The Prosecutor of the Tribunal v. Duško Tadić, at 14, Case No. IT-94-1, Jul. 17, 1995.

racial or religious grounds . . . whether or not in violation of the domestic law of the country where perpetrated.[81]

Crucially, crimes against humanity may be committed within or outside the context of armed conflict.[82] This category of crimes was expanded and incorporated into the founding statutes of the ICTR, ICTY, and Special Court for Sierra Leone (SCSL), and further expanded (to include forced disappearances and apartheid) by Article 7 of the Rome Statute.[83] The Rome Statute, ICTR, and SCSL also provide a substantiality requirement in that they require the specified acts to be committed "as a part of a widespread or systematic attack directed against any civilian population," and the Rome Statute also has an explicit requirement of "knowledge of the attack."[84] The residual "other inhumane acts" clause of crimes against humanity has been interpreted by the SCSL to include offenses such as forced marriage.[85]

ICTY jurisprudence suggests that cross-border obligations arising from crimes against humanity are more limited than those imposed by the prohibition on genocide.[86] But as with other crimes covered by RtoP, the jurisprudence of international tribunals leaves significant discretion to judges in determining whether the key elements of crimes of against humanity have been satisfied. We provide by way of illustration a brief overview of one element in particular: what constitutes a "widespread or systematic" attack.

The ICTY has found that a "widespread" crime may be established by the "cumulative effect of a series of inhumane acts or the singular effect of an inhumane act of extraordinary magnitude."[87] "Systematic," in turn, has been held to require

[81] As in the case of genocide, individual State responsibility to prevent, prosecute, and punish war crimes is much clearer than States' collective responsibility to do so.

[82] The ICTY Statute confers jurisdiction only for crimes against humanity committed in armed conflict, but this reflected an attempt to limit the jurisdiction of the ICTY to the conflict in the former Yugoslavia, and to address crimes that might not qualify as war crimes, but not an effort to narrow the definition of crimes against humanity. "The armed conflict requirement is a jurisdictional element, not a substantive element of the *mens rea* of crimes against humanity." Prosecutor v. Tadić, Case No. IT-94–1-A, Appeal Judgment ¶ 249 (Int'l Crim. Trib. for the Former Yugoslavia, Jul. 15, 1999, http://www.unhcr.org/refworld/country,,ICTY,,BIH,4562d8b62,40277f504,0.html [hereinafter Tadić Appeal Judgment].

[83] The prohibited acts under the Rome Statute are murder; extermination; enslavement; deportation, forcible transfer or enforced disappearance; imprisonment or severe deprivation in violation of international law; torture; sexual crimes including rape, and enforced prostitution, pregnancy or sterilization; persecution where based on certain group identity in connection with any other crime against humanity; and apartheid.

[84] Rome Statute, *supra* note 68, at art. 7; ICTR Statute, *supra* note 28, at art. 3; Statute of the Special Court for Sierra Leone, S.C. Res. 1315, S/RES/1315, Aug. 14, 2000, at art. 2 [hereinafter SCSL Statute].

[85] The SCSL distinguished forced marriage from sexual violence. Prosecutor v. Brima, Kamara & Kanu, Case No. SCSL-2004–16-A, Appeal Judgment (Special Ct. for Sierra Leone Feb. 2, 2008).

[86] Prosecutor v. Furundžija, Case No. IT-95–17-T, Trial Judgment ¶ 142 (Int'l Crim. Trib. for the Former Yugoslavia Dec. 10, 1998), http://www.icty.org/x/cases/furundzija/tjug/en/fur-tj981210e.pdf.

[87] Prosecutor v. Blaškić, Case No. IT-95–14-T, Trial Judgment ¶ 206 (Int'l Crim. Trib. for the Former Yugoslavia, Mar. 3, 2000), http://www.unhcr.org/refworld/topic, 4565c22538, 4565c25f449, 4146f1b2 4,0.html *see also* Akayesu Trial Judgment, *supra* note 44, at ¶ 579, and Draft Articles ILC, *supra* note 34, at 94–95.

consideration of four elements: (a) a political objective or ideology that drive the destruction, persecution or weakening of a community; (b) perpetration of acts on a "very large scale" against a group of civilians, or else, the "repeated and continuous commission of inhumane acts linked to one another"; (c) preparation and use of "significant" public or private resources; and (d) the implication of "high-level political and/or military authorities" in planning.[88]

Article 7(2)(a) of the Rome Statute requires that a qualifying attack be "pursuant to or in furtherance of a State or organizational policy to commit such attack." And a "policy to commit such attack" is understood to mean that the state or organization actively promotes or encourages such an attack against a civilian population.[89]

There may be some divergence between the crimes against humanity jurisprudence of the ad hoc tribunals and that developed by the ICC. Although all of these venues seem to require some degree of high-level state involvement, thresholds of scale and ideology are absent in the Rome Statute. Another open question with respect to crimes against humanity is whether, for purposes of RtoP, there may effectively be two categories of such crimes, distinguished by a perception of seriousness or proximity to genocide: murder, extermination, systematic rape, and deportation or forcible transfer as one set, and apartheid, torture, enslavement, imprisonment, and other forms of sexual violence constituting another.[90] To be sure, however, any of these crimes committed on a certain scale and/or with certain intent may obliterate any such distinction.

The recurrent problem of individual criminal versus state responsibility appears again in defining crimes against humanity for implementation of RtoP. The wide discretion taken in considering substantiality in criminal tribunals raises significant questions about the transferability of jurisprudential developments in these fora to attribution of individual or collective state responsibility for purposes of RtoP.

D. Ethnic Cleansing

Contemporary usage of the term "ethnic cleansing" gained currency in the early 1990s, in response to deportation and forcible transfer of large numbers of civilians in the Balkans. In 1992, an expert group appointed by the UN Security Council defined ethnic cleansing as "rendering an area ethnically homogeneous by using force or intimidation to remove persons of given groups from the area."[91] As Edward C. Luck, the Secretary-General's Special Advisor on the Responsibility to Protect, has argued,

[88] Prosecutor v. Naletilić and Martinović, Case No. IT-98–34-T, Trial Judgment (Int'l Crim. Trib. for the Former Yugoslavia, Mar. 31, 2003); Prosecutor v. Blaškić, Case No. IT-95–14-T, Trial Judgment (Int'l Crim. Trib. for the Former Yugoslavia, Mar. 3, 2000), http://www.unhcr.org/refworld/topic,4565c22538,4565c25f449,4146f1b2 4,0.html.

[89] Elements of Crimes, *supra* note 45, at art. 7, Introduction, ¶ 3.

[90] *See, e.g.*, David Scheffer, *Atrocity Crimes Framing the Responsibility to Protect*, *in* The Responsibility to Protect: The Global Moral Compact for the 21st Century (Richard Cooper & Juliette Voinov Kohler eds., Palgrave Macmillan, 2008), at 86–87.

[91] Interim Report of the Comm'n of Experts Established Pursuant to UN S.C. Res. 780, S/35374 (10993) (1992), at ¶ 55. The report also found that "policy and practices . . . [of] ethnic cleansing . . . constitute crimes against humanity and can be assimilated to specific war crimes. Furthermore, such acts also could fall within the meaning of the Genocide Convention." *Id.* at ¶ 56.

ethnic cleansing is "likely to constitute at least one of [RtoP's] well-established crimes: genocide, war crimes, and crimes against humanity.[92] Although ethnic cleansing that meets the threshold of genocide is likely to be referred to as such, the term remains a popular expression for crimes which are perhaps more likely to fall within the orbit of crimes against humanity or war crimes. For instance, Gareth Evans, co-chair of the ICISS, has written that ethnic cleansing "has no formal legal definition but can be regarded, like genocide, as subsumed within the scope of both war crimes and crimes against humanity."[93] David Scheffer has argued that the overlap is narrower: "as a matter of law, the invocation of ethnic cleansing in the mandates of R[to]P is a non-technical expression for what in fact is a subcategory of the crime against humanity of persecution."[94] Deportation and forcible transfer remain the crimes most closely associated with allegations of ethnic cleansing.

The ICTY has explicitly dismissed the term "ethnic cleansing," deciding that it would "not trea[t] the term as legally significant."[95] Nevertheless, the crime of "persecution" (a crime against humanity) perhaps comes closest to the concept of ethnic cleansing. As defined by Rome Statute's Elements of Crimes, persecution is focused primarily on *mens rea* and therefore must be carried out in connection with another specified crime against humanity.[96] Ethnic cleansing, too, primarily evokes intent and typically refers to acts classified as crimes against humanity or war crimes. The inclusion of ethnic cleansing in the RtoP concept could be criticized, on the one hand, as legally insignificant, if not redundant. From the standpoint of individual criminal responsibility, this critique has purchase. Consider, for instance, reports that Sudanese leaders have sought the advice of counsel on how to engage in ethnic cleansing without displaying the *mens rea* for genocide.[97] On the other hand, to the extent that the strictly legal parameters of the specified crimes may not be as significant for RtoP and the mobilization of collective responsibility, description of atrocities as ethnic cleansing—singling out crimes against humanity or war crimes driven particularly by ethnic animus—may, as an expressive matter, rival genocide in evoking the horrors of dehumanizing atrocity.

III. THREE QUALIFICATIONS

As we have shown, the contemporary legal consensus on so-called "atrocity crimes"[98] has emerged primarily in the context of international criminal adjudication rather

[92] Edward C. Luck, *The United Nations and the Responsibility to Protect*, Stanley Foundation, Aug. 2008, at 4.

[93] Gareth Evans, The Responsibility to Protect: Ending Mass Atrocity Crimes Once and For All (Brookings Inst. Press 2008), 12–13.

[94] Scheffer, *supra* note 90, at 89.

[95] Krajišnik Trial Judgment, *supra* note 51, at ¶ 293.

[96] Elements of Crimes, *supra* note 45, at art. 7.

[97] Mark Osiel, Making Sense of Mass Atrocity (Cambridge University Press 2009), at 137, 242.

[98] The term "atrocity crimes" has been used as an umbrella term to encompass the four categories of crimes included in the RtoP concept in the 2005 World Summit Outcome Document. *See, e.g.*, David Scheffer, *Atrocity Crimes Framing the Responsibility to Protect*, 40 Case W. Res. J. Int'l L. 111, 113 (2008); Evans, *supra* note 93, at 13.

than state responsibility. Even were this not the case, or were it not problematic, the jurisprudence of these crimes confers considerable discretion over key questions of application. This suggests three important qualifications to the use of the existing international legal consensus in efforts to implement RtoP. First, the substantiality requirements for individual criminal responsibility may not be transferable, as a matter of both law and political wisdom, to the realm of RtoP. Second, even if existing legal consensus is apposite, states' individual and collective obligations may be contingent on the specific RtoP commitment in question: namely, preventive versus reactive responsibility, states' individual versus collective responsibility, and responsibility to assist versus responsibility to coerce. Third, given that there are already pre-existing state responsibilities corresponding to all of the crimes incorporated into RtoP, a focus on legal consensus may unnecessarily encumber, if not stunt, implementation of RtoP, which in the foreseeable future is likely to unfold in the context of political rather than legal fora.

A. Substantiality

The first qualification emerging from consideration of crimes incorporated into RtoP relates to substantiality requirements. Each category of crimes contains a substantiality requirement—"systematic," "plan or policy," or "intent to destroy"—and the jurisprudence of international criminal law has elaborated on these requirements in each of the three legally established categories. The first question this raises is whether consensus understandings for the purposes of international criminal prosecution are necessarily appropriate for the purposes of triggering states' individual and collective Responsibility to Protect populations. Although, for instance, genocide has been interpreted by international criminal tribunals to allow prosecution for killing one person, provided such killing was an act "committed with intent to destroy in whole or in part, a national, ethnical, racial or religious group," such an interpretation may not trigger state responsibility and would be even less persuasive as a trigger for RtoP. More broadly, "seriousness" thresholds for individual criminal responsibility versus state responsibility can diverge. Whereas state responsibility typically requires "systematic" and "widespread" human rights violations, individual criminal liability can arise from a single incident.[99]

When the Secretary-General's Legal Counsel claims that, "[t]he responsibility to protect is now slowly beginning to crystallize," and "[i]ts foundations are firmly placed in existing international law—international humanitarian law, human rights law, international criminal law and the UN Charter itself,"[100] it is worth asking whether multiple foundations in so many fields of law may obfuscate more than they clarify threshold substantiality requirements for state responsibility. The U.S., for instance, has objected to the notion that international criminal tribunals are competent to "creat[e] new standards for international humanitarian law."[101] Although there are

[99] *See supra* note 67; and Thomas Franck, *Individual Criminal Liability and Collective Civil Responsibility: Do They Reinforce or Contradict One Another?*, 6 WASH. U. GLOB. STUD. L. REV. 567 (2007).

[100] Patricia O'Brien, UN Under-Secretary-General for Legal Affairs, Statements to 36th Meeting of the Committee of Legal Advisers on Public International Law, Oct. 7, 2008.

[101] Amicus brief filed by the United States in the Tadić case, *supra* note 80.

good reasons to claim, as Secretary-General Ban Ki-moon did in 2009, that "the provisions of paragraphs 138 and 139 of the Summit Outcome are firmly anchored in well-established principles of international law,"[102] the question of which of those principles apply—and how—to RtoP remains open.

B. Variable Responsibilities

A second qualification emerges from the multiple dimensions of RtoP. That is, individual and collective state obligations may vary by the specific RtoP commitment in question. Collective responsibility, for instance, may be incurred more easily for preventive as opposed to reactive action. A state's individual Responsibility to Protect its own population may be triggered sooner than other states' collective Responsibility to Protect a third state's population. And a collective responsibility to participate in capacity-building and other forms of assistance may require a much lower threshold than a collective responsibility to coerce or intervene. These three dimensions—temporality, the nature of the actor, and the character of the act—may be imagined as three-dimensional axes, with co-varying thresholds incurring responsibility. Thus in cases that do not clearly trigger all forms of state responsibility, uncertainty about the thresholds for variable responsibility diminishes the utility of whatever legal consensus may exist in other realms of international law.

C. Pre-Existing Responsibilities

The correspondence of RtoP crimes with pre-existing treaties and custom raises another problematic correspondence: that of responsibilities under RtoP with pre-existing state responsibility. The Secretary-General has sought to assuage any such concerns by insisting that "the [2005 World] Summit's enunciation of the responsibility to protect was not intended to detract in any way from the much broader range of obligations existing under international humanitarian law, international human rights law, refugee law, and international criminal law."[103] This of course does not mean that RtoP will not or cannot detract from existing obligations, but if we presume for a moment that it will not, unresolved is the question of whether RtoP adds any value to pre-existing obligations. To the extent that international crimes have attained the status of *jus cogens*, or of a peremptory norm, there is live debate about whether states are under affirmative obligation to act to halt their commission.[104] In its Bosnia Judgment, the ICJ has interpreted the Genocide Convention to impose an obligation on all states to "employ all means reasonably available to them, so as to prevent genocide so far as possible."[105] Louise Arbour has argued that "because of the power they wield and due to their global reach, the members of the Security Council, particularly

[102] UN Secretary-General, *Implementing the Responsibility to Protect*, A/63/677, Jan. 12, 2009, at ¶ 3 [hereinafter U.N.S.G. Report on Implementation].

[103] *Id.*

[104] The notion of *jus cogens*, or "general international law," was introduced into treaty law through Article 53 of the Vienna Convention of the Law of Treaties, May 23, 1969, 1155 U.N.T.S. 331.

[105] ICJ Bosnia Judgment, *supra* note 31, at ¶ 430. The Court continued, "if the State has available to it means likely to have a deterrent effect on those suspected of preparing genocide, or reasonably

the Permanent Five Members (P5) hold an even heavier responsibility than other states to ensure the protection of civilians everywhere."[106] In addition, the International Law Commission's Article 41(i) of the Draft Articles on the Responsibility of States for Internationally Wrongful Acts (Articles on State Responsibility) provides that "[s]tates shall cooperate to bring to an end through lawful means any serious breach [of a peremptory norm of general international law]."[107] However, in its commentary, the ILC notes that "it may be open to question whether general international law at present prescribes a positive duty of cooperation, and paragraph one in that respect may reflect the progressive development of international law."[108] Article 50(i)(a) of the same draft provides that counter-measures shall not affect "the obligation to refrain from the threat or use of force as embodied in the Charter of the United Nations"—a limitation that seems consistent with the RtoP principle that intervention be accompanied by Chapter VII authorization.[109] Thus there seems to be some ambivalence on the legal status of both collective state responsibility and extra-territorial individual state responsibility for preventing and halting violations of all *jus cogens* crimes.

If either or both such responsibilities are not yet clearly established, whether the Responsibility to Protect could augment pre-existing obligations is an open question. Suggesting an answer in the affirmative, the president of the General Assembly has urged that "it is for member [s]tates to consider if responsibility to protect in its non-coercive dimensions adds anything to the International Law Commission's Articles or to the provisions of international human rights law and international humanitarian law."[110] The UN Under-Secretary-General for Legal Affairs has argued that the Responsibility to Protect is "a new prism through which to view and, crucially, to connect these existing blocks of international law."[111] However, it is unclear what such a "new prism"—itself subject to interpretive debate—adds to the existing landscape of positive international legal obligation.

A more serious concern is that, despite the best intentions, the controversy surrounding RtoP may undermine compliance with pre-existing obligations. The political controversy attending RtoP may provoke some states to resist calls to fulfill obligations they might otherwise be more willing to fulfill. Moreover, a system of dual and shifting obligations creates the potential of deflective evasion. Individual state responsibility may be abrogated through calls for collective responsibility.[112]

suspected of harboring specific intent (*dolus specialis*), it is under a duty to make such use of these means as the circumstances permit" (*Id.* at ¶ 431).

[106] Louise Arbour, *The Responsibility to Protect as a Duty of Care in International Law and Practice*, Remarks at Trinity University (Dublin), Nov. 23, 2007.

[107] Draft Articles ILC, *supra* note 34.

[108] *Id.* at art. 41, ¶ 3.

[109] *Id.*

[110] Office of the President of UNGA, *Concept Note on the Responsibility to Protect Populations from Genocide, War Crimes, Ethnic Cleansing and Crimes against Humanity*, Jul. 17, 2009, *available at* http://www.un.org/ga/president/63/interactive/protect/conceptnote.pdf.

[111] O'Brien statement, *supra* note 100.

[112] This concern extends to shifting responsibility toward the UN. *See, e.g.*, Jennifer Welsh and Maria Banda, *International Law and the Responsibility to Protect: Clarifying or Expanding States' Responsibilities?*, 2 Global Responsibility to Protect 213 (2010), 225 ("[RtoP may] narrow the vehicle for implementing collective responsibility. It is no longer the challenging framework of

And collective responsibility may be stalled by an emphasis on individual responsibility.[113] Security Council debates on Sudan may be a harbinger of the latter scenario; some states have emphasized the primacy of Sudan's individual state responsibility in order to forestall collective sanctions.[114]

IV. OMISSIONS

Like any definition, the World Summit's take on RtoP is as notable for what it omits as what it includes. In his 2009 report to the General Assembly, Secretary-General Ban Ki-moon articulated the virtues of the 2005 definition:

> The responsibility to protect applies, until Member States decide otherwise, only to the four specified crimes and violations: genocide, war crimes, ethnic cleansing, and crimes against humanity. To try to extend it to cover other calamities, such as HIV/AIDS, climate change or the response to natural disasters, would undermine the 2005 consensus and stretch the concept beyond recognition or operational utility.[115]

The "other calamities" noted by the Secretary-General were excluded from RtoP, as were other potential triggers.

A. Aggression

Aggression, or "crimes against peace," as they were called at Nuremberg, was a predicate offense prosecuted at the International Military Tribunal. While aggression is listed among the four crimes within the jurisdiction of the ICC, a definition of aggression was only recently agreed upon in June 2010; it will not go into effect until and unless states party to the Rome Statute vote to formally approve this definition in 2017.[116] There are two primary reasons for this omission. First, the UN Charter already prohibits the threat or use of force under Article 2(4) and other provisions provide positive obligations for states to cooperate with collective action to counter such threat or use of force.[117] Second

common humanity which creates the moral responsibility, but rather the specific political commitment of states to act through the UN to address potential or real atrocities.")

113 *See, e.g.*, Carsten Stahn's discussion of a "complementarity trap." Stahn, *supra* note 1, at 116–17.

114 *See, e.g.*, Alex Bellamy, *Responsibility to Protect or Trojan Horse? The Crisis in Darfur and Humanitarian Intervention after Iraq*, 19 Ethics & Int'l Aff. 31 (2005).

115 UN Secretary-General's Report on Implementation, *supra* note 102.

116 Rome Statute, *supra* note 68, at art. 5(2). In June 2010, in Kampala, Uganda, state parties to the Rome Statute arrived at the following definition of aggression: "the planning, preparation, initiation or execution, by a person in a position effectively to exercise control over or to direct the political or military action of a State, of an act of aggression which, by its character, gravity and scale, constitutes a manifest violation of the Charter of the United Nations." UN News Service, *After Years of Debate, ICC Member States Agree on Definition of Aggression*, UN News Ctr., Jun. 14, 2010. The Kampala agreement also provides that the ICC may not bring aggression charges against a national of a state that is not a member of the ICC without a Security Council resolution under Chapter VII of the UN Charter. *See, e.g.*, Tod Lindberg, *Aggression in the Court: The International Criminal Court's Latest Authority*, Foreign Aff., Aug. 22, 2010.

117 Charter of the United Nations, art. 2(4), Jun. 26, 1945.

and more to the point, RtoP emerged from a political and academic orientation focused primarily on human rights and human security.[118] Threats to human rights and human security in the context of aggression are addressed by RtoP to the extent that they qualify as genocide, war crimes, or crimes against humanity.

B. Terrorism

Terrorism also is not addressed explicitly by RtoP but would be covered to the extent that terrorist acts qualify as crimes against humanity, war crimes, or genocide. In theory, RtoP could be understood to encompass state responsibility to repress transnational terrorism operating from within its territory. Although there is no consensus definition of terrorism in general, various manifestations of terrorism are subject to 13 major international legal agreements.[119] With respect to intrastate terrorism, RtoP could become relevant to the degree that a state is unwilling or unable to address terrorist acts reaching the threshold of crimes against humanity, war crimes or genocide. However, the omission of the term from RtoP is unsurprising in light of the controversy surrounding the doctrine of preventive force, linked to preventing terrorist attacks, articulated by the Bush administration in its 2002 National Security Strategy.[120] In fact, the same UN reform effort that gave rise to the 2005 agreement on RtoP addressed the question of state responsibility for repressing transnational terrorism—particularly so-called catastrophic terrorism involving nuclear or biological weapons—via the question of the preventive use of force.[121]

C. Natural Disasters

The potential applicability of RtoP to natural disasters was contemplated before the RtoP concept was agreed in 2005, and it has arisen in the aftermath of natural disasters that have occurred since then. However, the consensus at the World Summit seems to

[118] *See, e.g.*, S. Neil MacFarlane and Yuen Foong Khong, Human Security and the UN: A Critical History. (Indiana University Press, 2006).

[119] The Convention on Offenses and Certain Other Acts Committed Onboard Aircraft (1963), Convention for the Suppression of Unlawful Seizure of Aircraft (1970), Convention for the Suppression of Unlawful Acts against the Safety of Civil Aviation (1971), Convention on the Prevention and Punishment of Crimes Against Internationally Protected Persons (1973), International Convention against the Taking of Hostages (1979), Convention on the Physical Protection of Nuclear Material (1980), Protocol for the Suppression of Unlawful Acts of Violence at Airports Serving International Civil Aviation, supplementary to the Convention for the Suppression of Unlawful Acts against the Safety of Civil Aviation (1988), Convention for the Suppression of Unlawful Acts against the Safety of Maritime Navigation (1988), Protocol for the Suppression of Unlawful Acts Against the Safety of Fixed Platforms Located on the Continental Shelf (1988), Convention on the Marking of Plastic Explosives for the Purpose of Detection (1991), International Convention for the Suppression of Terrorist Bombings (1997), International Convention for the Suppression of the Financing of Terrorism (1999), International Convention for the Suppression of Acts of Nuclear Terrorism (2005), *available at* UN Action to Counter Terrorism, http://www.un.org/terrorism/instruments.shtml (last accessed Jan. 27, 2011).

[120] US White House, National Security Strategy of the United States, Sept. 2002, *available at* http://georgewbush-whitehouse.archives.gov/nsc/nss/2002/.

[121] See *A More Secure World* and *In Larger Freedom*, *supra* notes 8, 12.

have been that populations at risk have rights—"vertical" and "horizontal"—to be protected only from active human violence and persecution, but not from state neglect or malice—situations in which state authorities may be found to "manifestly fail" to address large-scale death and suffering in consequence of a catastrophic natural disaster. Such a prospect was raised explicitly by the ICISS.[122] It also was debated vociferously in the aftermath of Cyclone Nargis, which struck Burma (Myanmar) in May 2008, particularly in terms of whether gross neglect and active prevention of aid delivery could constitute a crime against humanity and thereby "trigger" RtoP.[123] The debate among advocates of RtoP is driven, on the one hand, by the same humanitarian concerns that arise in the context of human violence, and on the other, by a fear that disingenuous invocation of RtoP under circumstances of a natural disaster will further discredit the concept among skeptics.

D. Political Repression

Finally, RtoP unsurprisingly does not refer to political repression. Much like the omission of terrorism, certain acts symptomatic of political repression may constitute one of the crimes incorporated by RtoP, but, like terrorism, inclusion for expressive purposes would be costly if not fatal. Potential intervention on claims of a collective Responsibility to Protect against political repression has been and remains the primary source of opposition to the concept, especially after the invasion of Iraq.[124] RtoP, from this perspective, could be a shibboleth for at-will regime change.

V. CONCLUSION

To the extent that RtoP entails commitments beyond pre-existing international legal obligations, the definition and implementation of those commitments will be subject to political contestation. At the same time, because the stakes are high, too narrow a focus on the legal content of RtoP crimes may muddle more than it sharpens the debate over application of the concept. A focus on individual criminal responsibility may distract from state responsibility.[125] A preoccupation with technical legal precipitants for intervention to repress mass atrocities may sap consensus to prevent such atrocities. Legalism of this variety also may undermine the credibility of emerging commitments.[126] And it may stymie the emergence of a variegated RtoP consensus that could encompass both consolidated and aspirational commitments.

[122] ICISS, *supra* note 4, at ¶ 4.20.

[123] *See, e.g.*, Gareth Evans, President, International Crisis Group, Presentation on the Responsibility to Protect in Environmental Emergencies to American Society of International Law 103rd Annual Meeting, Mar. 26, 2009; Stuart Ford, *Is the Failure to Respond Appropriately to a Natural Disaster a Crime Against Humanity? The Responsibility to Protect and Individual Criminal Responsibility in the Aftermath of Cyclone Nargis*, 38 Denv. J. Int'l L. & Pol'y 227 (2010);

[124] *See, e.g.*, Mohamed Mohamed Halal's contribution to this edited volume.

[125] *See, e.g.*, Amabelle C. Asuncion, *Pulling the Stops on Genocide: The State or the Individual?* 20 Eur. J. Int'l L. 1195, 1195–1222 (2009).

[126] *See, e.g.*, Scot Straus, *Darfur and the Genocide Debate*, Foreign Aff., Jan.–Feb. 2005, at 127 (assessing the consequences of U.S. Secretary of State Colin Powell's 2004 pronouncement that genocide was occurring in Darfur).

For RtoP advocates, these are not reasons for despair—nor, for detractors, hope. For camps on both sides of the battle line, Myres McDougal's classic characterization of the development of customary law is impartially instructive:

> [A] process of continuous interaction, of continuous demand, and response, in which the decisionmakers of particular nation [S]tates unilaterally put forward claims of the most diverse and conflicting character . . . weigh and apprise these competing claims . . . and ultimately accept or reject them.[127]

It is a mistake to dismiss RtoP as merely "a political catchword rather than a legal norm"[128] precisely because, in the course of this interaction, innovative heuristics can be powerful tools of political mobilization and norm consolidation. Progressive consensus-building on RtoP has advanced its position along a "continuum of nonadjudicative modes of (de)legitimation."[129] The contest over RtoP will not be confined to the arena of legal doctrine. The "age of rights" is as much a political consciousness as a legal order—one deeply rooted in human tragedy and political mobilization struggling to halt and prevent it.

[127] Myres McDougal, *The Hydrogen Bomb Tests and International Law of the Sea*, 49 Am. J. Int'l. L. 356 (1967).

[128] Stahn, *supra* note 1, at 120.

[129] Jose Alvarez, *Judging the Security Council*, 90 Am. J. Int'l L. 1, 12 (1996).

4 Challenges and Controversies

Nicole Deller

The Responsibility to Protect (RtoP) demands that the international community does not stand by in the face of mass atrocities. From its initial conception, through its adoption in the 2005 World Summit Outcome Document (WSOD), to the present, the doctrine has been challenged. Policy makers and scholars alike have questioned its purpose, criticized its ambiguities, and raised concerns about the potential for its misuse. At the same time, however, the credibility of the United Nations (UN) is increasingly seen to depend on its ability to prevent and halt genocide or other acts of mass violence. And, in what has been described as a "revolution in conscience,"[1] many regional bodies, subregional bodies, and national governments are recognizing mass-atrocity prevention as a priority.

The skepticism about and the hopes for RtoP provide the context for this chapter, which identifies the various challenges that confront the new norm. They are presented in two parts: those challenges that relate to the meaning of RtoP, and those about the institutions that are responsible for its implementation.

I. WHAT IS THE RESPONSIBILITY TO PROTECT? CLARIFYING AMBIGUITIES.

A. Responsibility to Protect, not a "Right to Intervene"

The Responsibility to Protect was designed precisely to move beyond the discredited notion of humanitarian intervention in confronting mass atrocities. The WSOD's

[1] Genocide Prevention Task Force, Preventing Genocide: A Blueprint for US Policymakers 99 (2008).

emphasis on prevention and peaceful measures and the implicit rejection of action outside the Security Council were strongly reaffirmed in the 2009 General Assembly debate on RtoP. Nevertheless, one of the most persistent challenges for RtoP has been to deflect criticism that it is merely a reformulation of humanitarian intervention—"two sides of the same coin"[2]—that remains preoccupied with the rights of powerful states to intervene with military force.

1. Background on Humanitarian Intervention

The appeal to humanitarian reasons as a basis for military intervention has a long and uneven history. Although references to humanitarian intervention[3] date back to 1840,[4] the immediate history that led to the development of RtoP was the international community's response—and failure to respond—to humanitarian crises in the 1990s. This history includes two of the most tragic failures of the UN: the massacre of an estimated 8,000 men and boys in a UN safe area in Srebrenica, Bosnia, and the failure of a UN peacekeeping mission in Rwanda to halt the genocide of an estimated 800,000 people. Beyond these two tragedies, this period saw inconsistent responses by the international community to humanitarian crises: some interventions were authorized by the Security Council but unsuccessful (e.g., Somalia); other more successful regional interventions were only implicitly authorized by the Security Council after the fact (e.g., Liberia and Sierra Leone). Most polarizing for the international community was the NATO intervention in Kosovo, conducted without Security Council authorization because of the threatened veto by Russia and China, two of the Council's five veto-holding permanent members.

The failures and controversies in practice led to calls for clearer rules to guide interventions whose aim was the protection of people, not national security.[5] In his 1999 address to the General Assembly, UN Secretary-General Kofi Annan cautioned supporters of humanitarian intervention: "[I]s there not a danger of such interventions undermining the imperfect, yet resilient, security system created after the second world war, and of setting dangerous precedents for future interventions without a clear criterion to decide who might invoke these precedents and in what circumstances?[6]" But there was substantial opposition among governments from the global South to criteria that would legitimize humanitarian intervention. The history

[2] Remarks of the Government of Sudan to the UNGA, UN GAOR, 63rd Sess., 101st plen. mtg., A/63/pv.101, Jul. 28, 2009, at 11.

[3] Humanitarian intervention is defined as "coercive action by one or more states involving the use of armed force in another state without the consent of its authorities" in order to prevent widespread suffering. Thomas G. Weiss, Humanitarian Intervention 5 (2007) (*quoting* Adam Roberts, *The So-Called "Right" of Humanitarian Intervention*, *in* Yearbook of International Humanitarian Law 3, 5 (2000)).

[4] International Commission on Intervention & State Sovereignty, The Responsibility to Protect: Research, Bibliography, Background 16 (2001).

[5] For an example of factors to guide the judgment of when to intervene, *see* Tony Blair, Prime Minister of the UK, Doctrine of the International Community, Speech Delivered to the Economic Club of Chicago (Apr. 24, 1999).

[6] Secretary-General of the United Nations, *Address to UN General Assembly—Presentation of Report of the Secretary-General on the Work of the Organization*, Sept. 20, 1999.

of colonial interventions left them justifiably skeptical about the intentions of Western powers. The Non-Aligned Movement and the Group of 77, two powerful UN voting blocs representing the developing world, repeatedly rejected the right of humanitarian intervention in their collective statements.[7] Algerian President Abdelaziz Bouteflika summarized objections to the concept in his 1999 address to the General Assembly: "sovereignty is our last defense against the rules of an unequal world."[8]

2. Shift Away From Humanitarian Intervention

What remained unanswered in the North-South divide about states' right to intervene was the question of what was to be done when the state is exercising unlawful power against its people. What of the victims? How are their rights to be protected? This was the very dilemma that Kofi Annan posed to the international community in his address to the General Assembly in 2000: "If humanitarian intervention is indeed an unacceptable assault on sovereignty, how should we respond to a Rwanda, to a Srebrenica—to gross and systematic violations of human rights that offend every precept of our common humanity?"[9]

This plea was the catalyst for the creation of the International Commission on Intervention and State Sovereignty (ICISS), the cross-regional panel of eminent persons that conceived of the term "Responsibility to Protect" in the 2001 report of the same name.[10] The ICISS went to great lengths to distinguish RtoP from humanitarian intervention. Rhetorically and substantively, the idea of a Responsibility to Protect took emphasis away from the would-be intervening states and their rights under international law, and focused on populations at risk of large-scale loss of life or ethnic cleansing.

The ICISS placed intervention within a framework of prevention, reaction, and rebuilding. Military intervention was identified as a measure of last resort that must be contemplated, if at all, as part of a far broader spectrum of actions targeted toward the protection of a population at risk.[11] In those situations where force might be appropriate, the ICISS proposed that the determination be guided by precautionary principles: "right authority, just cause, right intention, last resort, proportional means

[7] *See, e.g.*, Group of 77, *Declaration of the South Summit*, Apr. 14–17, 2000, at ¶ 54, *available at* http://www.g77.org/summit/Declaration_G77Summit.htm ("We reject the so-called 'right' of humanitarian intervention, which has no legal basis in the United Nations Charter or in the general principles of international law."); Non-Aligned Movement, *XIV Ministerial Conference of the Non-Aligned Movement, Final Document* ¶ 8 (Aug. 17–19, 2003), *available at* http://www.nam.gov.za/media/040820.pdf (The Non-Aligned Movement "reiterated the rejection . . . of the so-called 'right' of humanitarian intervention.").

[8] *Quoted in* Humanitarian Intervention, *supra* note 3, at 121.

[9] Secretary-General of the United Nations, *Opening Address at the General Debate of the 54th Session of the General Assembly*, Sept. 20, 2000.

[10] International Commission on Intervention and State Sovereignty (ICISS), The Responsibility to Protect: Report of the International Commission on Intervention and State Sovereignty ¶ ¶ 1.6–1.7 (International Development Research Centre 2001), *available at* http://www.iciss.ca/report-en.asp [hereinafter ICISS Report].

[11] *See Id.* at ¶ ¶ 2.28–2.33.

and reasonable prospects."[12] These principles were intended to "strictly limit the use of coercive military force" and "strengthen the order of states by providing for clear guidelines to guide concerted international action. . . ."[13]

3. Proper Authority for Military Action Under RtoP?

Although the *Responsibility to Protect* report de-emphasized the role of the use of force in the protection of populations from mass atrocities, the ICISS could not avoid confronting the question that lingered after the NATO intervention in Kosovo: is there a source of legitimacy for the use of force if the Security Council fails to act? The ICISS proposed two possible alternatives. First is the resort to the General Assembly (UNGA) under the "Uniting for Peace" procedure. In an eponymous 1950 resolution, the UNGA agreed to address situations that threaten international peace and security where the Security Council cannot act due to lack of unanimity of the permanent five members of the Council.[14] Although the General Assembly itself cannot direct military actions to be taken, "if supported by an overwhelming majority of Member States, [it] would provide a high degree of legitimacy for an intervention."[15] The second alternative is a regional or subregional organization acting within its geographical boundaries.[16] Precedent has shown that regional/subregional interventions might be politically acceptable if these bodies were to receive Security Council authorization subsequent to an initial intervention.[17] The purpose for the ICISS, however, was not to find alternatives to the Security Council, "but to make the Security Council work better than it has."[18]

Longstanding opponents of humanitarian intervention were not convinced.[19] Even if cautionary principles were applied, many viewed the report's consideration of use of force outside the Security Council as implying a right to humanitarian intervention. Gareth Evans, co-chair of the ICISS, has strongly disagreed: "In the absence of a credible self-defence argument, the only source of legal authority is the Security Council, without whose support non-consensual military interventions are illegal under international law. Period."[20] Evans draws an analogy to a plea in mitigation in criminal law, which acknowledges the illegality of an act but claims such action took place "in exceptional and defensible circumstances."[21]

[12] *Id.* at ¶ 4.16.

[13] *Id.* at ¶ 4.32.

[14] G.A. Res. 377 (V), A/1775, Nov. 3, 1950.

[15] ICISS Report, *supra* note 10, at ¶ 6.30.

[16] *Id.* at ¶ ¶ 6.31–6.35.

[17] *Id.* at ¶ 6.31.

[18] *Id.* at XII.

[19] *See, e.g., XIV Ministerial Conference of the Non-Aligned Movement, Final Document, supra* note 7, at ¶ 8, in which the Ministers "observed similarities between the new expression 'responsibility to protect' and 'humanitarian intervention.'"

[20] Gareth Evans, The Responsibility to Protect and the Use of Military Force, Presentation to Seminar on the International Use of Force, World Legal Forum (Dec. 11, 2007), *available at* http://www.worldlegalforum.org/Docs/Speech%20Gareth%20Evans.pdf.

[21] *Id.*; *see also* Gareth Evans, The Responsibility to Protect: Ending Mass Atrocity Crimes Once and For All 147 (2008).

4. The World Summit Outcome Document to Present: Continued Rejection of Humanitarian Intervention

The concerns about humanitarian intervention only deepened after the U.S.-led invasion of Iraq. Not only was the intervention unauthorized by the Security Council, but humanitarian concerns were dubiously put forward as a rationale. By 2005, as the UN deliberated over a package of reforms to be agreed upon by heads of state and government at the 2005 World Summit, the North-South divisions were further entrenched. Although the adoption of RtoP was one of the proposed UN reforms, the specter of humanitarian intervention featured prominently.[22] In this climate, a General Assembly agreement discussing alternative means of authorizing force was not possible, and was not included in the WSOD. The proposal for criteria for the use of force was also dropped.[23] The agreement that was ultimately reached includes, among other provisions:

- A reaffirmation that "each individual State has the responsibility to protect its populations from genocide, war crimes, ethnic cleansing and crimes against humanity" which entails the prevention of such crimes, including their incitement;
- "[T]he international community, through the United Nations, also has the responsibility to use appropriate diplomatic, humanitarian and other peaceful means . . . to help protect populations" from the four listed crimes;
- If peaceful means are inadequate and "national authorities manifestly fail to protect their populations," the international community is "prepared to take collective action, in a timely and decisive manner, through the Security Council, in accordance with the Charter, including Chapter VII, on a case-by-case basis and in cooperation with relevant regional organizations as appropriate. . . ."[24]

This formulation departs from humanitarian intervention in several significant ways. The agreement that the international community should "use appropriate diplomatic humanitarian and other peaceful means" dictates that engagement in a potential crisis must begin well before the only option is military force. The 2009 Report of the UN Secretary-General, *Implementing the Responsibility to Protect*[25] elaborates on the WSOD's discussion of peaceful means. Potential measures identified in the report include threats of criminal prosecution,[26] fact-finding missions and investigations,[27] targeted sanctions,[28] and even military-to-military assistance.[29]

[22] *See* Radzi Rahman, Charge D'Affaires of the Permanent Mission of Malaysia to the United Nations, Statement by Chairman of the Coordinating Bureau of the Non-Aligned Movement on behalf of the Non-Aligned Movement, June 21, 2005, at ¶ 4(g), *available at* http://www.un.int/malaysia/NAM/nam210605.html. *See also* Carlo Focarelli, *The Responsibility to Protect Doctrine and Humanitarian Intervention: Too Many Ambiguities for a Working Doctrine*, 13 J. Conflict & Security L. 191, 201–03 (2008).

[23] *See* Alex J. Bellamy, Responsibility to Protect 84–85 (2009).

[24] *2005 World Summit Outcome*, A/RES/60/1, Sept. 15, 2005, at ¶¶ 138–139 [hereinafter WSOD].

[25] *Report of the Secretary-General, Implementing the Responsibility to Protect*, A/63/677, Jan. 12, 2009 [hereinafter *Implementing the Responsibility to Protect*].

[26] *Id.* at ¶ ¶ 53–54.

[27] *Id.* at ¶ 52.

[28] *Id.* at ¶ 56.

[29] *Id.* at ¶ 29.

Secondly, in the WSOD, UN Member States considered that activities to protect populations might be taken in cooperation with the host state. The report of the Secretary-General makes clear that the aim is not to override sovereignty. To the contrary, "[b]y helping States to meet their core protection responsibilities, the responsibility to protect seeks to strengthen sovereignty, not weaken it. It seeks to help States to succeed, not just to react when they fail."[30]

Finally, one of the greatest concerns about humanitarian intervention is that states will reserve for themselves the right to intervene as they see fit. The Responsibility to Protect as agreed in the WSOD is very clear in its confinement of military measures to those authorized by the Security Council. As Ramesh Thakur and Thomas G. Weiss observed:

> RtoP offers developing countries better protection through agreed and negotiated-in-advance rules and roadmaps for when outside intervention is justified and how it may be done under UN authority rather than unilaterally. It will thus lead to the 'Gulliverization' of the use of force by major global and regional powers, tying it with numerous threads of global norms and rules.[31]

Some observers have argued that because the WSOD's provision on the Responsibility to Protect does not expressly reject use of force outside the Security Council, there is a potential opening for states to act outside the Council.[32] This interpretation goes against the consensus that held in 2005. Indeed, some leading diplomats described the World Summit agreement as having "buried" RtoP.[33] "What they meant, it turned out," Edward C. Luck, the UN Secretary-General's Special Adviser with a focus on RtoP, explained, "was that they had once again resisted the adoption of humanitarian intervention as a unilateral, coercive and largely military doctrine."[34] The Secretary-General's 2009 report also rejected the notion that RtoP permitted unilateral action,[35] as did many participants in the 2009 debate of the General Assembly on RtoP.[36]

During the 2009 UNGA debate, which was convened to consider the Secretary-General's 2009 Report on RtoP, a number of governments continued to express their

[30] *Id.* at ¶ 10(a).

[31] Ramesh Thakur & Thomas G. Weiss, *RtoP: From Idea to Norm—and Action?*, 1 GLOBAL RESP. TO PROTECT 22, 47 (2009).

[32] *See, e.g.*, Carsten Stahn, *Responsibility to Protect: Political Rhetoric or Emerging Legal Norm?*, 101 AM. J. INT'L L. 99, 109 (2007); BELLAMY, *supra* note 23, 90–91.

[33] Edward C. Luck, *Building a Norm: The Responsibility to Protect Experience*, MASS ATROCITY CRIMES: PREVENTING FUTURE OUTRAGES 108, 115 (Robert I. Rotberg ed., 2010). Similar assertions were made in discussions of the UN's Fifth Committee during deliberations about the appointment of Edward Luck as Special Advisor on the Responsibly to Protect. EVANS, *supra* note 21, at 52.

[34] Edward C. Luck, *Building a Norm, supra* note 33, at 115.

[35] UN Secretary-General Ban Ki-moon specifies three ways in which use of force could be authorized: by the UN Security Council; by the General Assembly under the "Uniting for Peace" procedure, or by regional or subregional arrangements "with the prior authorization of the Security Council." *Implementing the Responsibility to Protect, supra* note 25, at ¶ 56.

[36] GLOBAL CENTRE FOR THE RESPONSIBILITY TO PROTECT, IMPLEMENTING THE RESPONSIBILITY TO PROTECT: THE 2009 GENERAL ASSEMBLY DEBATE: AN ASSESSMENT 7 (2009) [hereinafter, GLOBAL CENTRE, 2009 GA DEBATE REPORT], *available at* http://globalRtoP.org/media/pdf/GCRtoP_General_Assembly_Debate_Assessment.pdf.

concerns about the relationship between the two concepts.[37] Very few countries, however, argued for the wholesale rejection of the concept. The Global Centre for the Responsibility to Protect counted only four among the 180 represented in the three-day debate.[38] Instead, there were significant numbers of supporters from all regions expressing readiness to move toward implementation of RtoP.[39] This debate gave supporters an opportunity to educate a still unfamiliar majority of Member States about the crucial distinctions between humanitarian intervention and RtoP as it was adopted in the WSOD. The UNGA debate, which resulted in a resolution agreeing to continue consideration of RtoP,[40] demonstrated the importance of dialogue for addressing fears about the hidden agenda of the doctrine.

Despite the clear distinctions between the concepts, efforts to paint the Responsibility to Protect with the brush of humanitarian intervention persist.[41] These arguments appear to be rooted in two different sets of concerns. For some opponents, the continued use of discussions of RtoP to wage battle on humanitarian intervention is part of a broader resistance to any intrusion into their domestic affairs, no matter the circumstances. RtoP is a direct challenge to this viewpoint. For others, these arguments are not so much a criticism of RtoP itself, as a fear that RtoP will be misused to legitimize the unauthorized use of force. For those skeptics concerned with misuse of RtoP, these fears should be put to rest if RtoP is consistently practiced according to the confines of the WSOD.

B. The Responsibility to Protect From What? Clarifying the Scope of RtoP.

1. Limitation of RtoP to the Four Crimes

As agreed at the World Summit, RtoP addresses four categories of crimes: genocide, war crimes, crimes against humanity, and ethnic cleansing.[42] ICISS had contemplated a broader range of conditions that would warrant action under RtoP, including state collapse and "overwhelming natural or environmental catastrophes."[43]

The WSOD's narrower construction has brought comfort to states concerned about the possible overreach of the concept.[44] As the Secretary-General explains, "[t]o try to extend it to cover other calamities, such as HIV/AIDS, climate change or the response to natural disasters, would undermine the 2005 consensus and stretch the

[37] International Coalition for the Responsibility to Protect, Report on the General Assembly Plenary Debate on the Responsibility to Protect 7 (2009), *available at* http://www.responsibilitytoprotect.org/ICRtoP%20Report-General_Assembly_Debate_on_the_Responsibility_to_Protect%20FINAL%209_22_09.pdf.

[38] Global Centre, 2009 GA Debate Report, *supra* note 36, at 1.

[39] *Id.* at 4.

[40] G.A. Res. 63/308, A/RES/63/308, Oct. 7, 2009.

[41] Global Center for the Responsibility to Protect, Early Warning, Assessment, and the Responsibility to Protect: Informal Interactive Dialogue of the General Assembly held on August 9, 2010, at 8 (Sept. 2010).

[42] Although ethnic cleansing is not defined in international criminal law, "crimes" is used in this chapter to generally describe the four categories that the WSOD defines as the scope of RtoP.

[43] ICISS Report, *supra* note 10 at ¶ 4.19.

[44] *See* Global Centre, 2009 GA Debate Report, *supra* note 36, at 6.

concept beyond recognition or operational utility."[45] Based on the author's experience witnessing negotiations of the WSOD, there was support among RtoP proponents for specifying "genocide, war crimes, and crimes against humanity," because this threshold mirrored the International Criminal Court jurisdiction, and therefore suggested a level of seriousness. According to discussions with diplomats at the time of negotiations, the addition of "ethnic cleansing" was made at the suggestion of delegations concerned that some acts of violence, no matter how grave, might fall outside the narrow legal definition of genocide, and so they opted to include the broader term "ethnic cleansing." Given that acts of "ethnic cleansing" would also be covered under the definition of "crimes against humanity,"[46] this addition carries more political than legal significance. As Ekkehard Strauss remarked, "[h]opefully, the identification of ethnic cleansing as a separate case for the application of the responsibility to protect will enable the international community to address some situations based on their factual appearance rather than their legal qualifications."[47]

Chapter 3 contains a detailed analysis of the four crimes.[48] Nevertheless, it is worth noting that a literal interpretation of these four crimes as the scope of RtoP would expand the focus substantially beyond mass violence against populations.[49] This is particularly the case with war crimes, which can refer to individual incidents by individual soldiers.[50] RtoP was not intended to address "relatively minor or isolated threats" of one of the four crimes. Even in the preventive stage, the threat must be of some "meaningful magnitude."[51]

2. Identifying Threshold for Triggering RtoP

It must also be emphasized that RtoP action cannot await a formal determination that a crime has been committed.[52] This may take years as individual suspects are tried or a judgment is rendered by the International Court of Justice.[53] Rather than making formal legal determinations, policy makers must conduct an assessment based on events unfolding on the ground about the potential gravity of a situation. This will require some reasonable basis to believe that crimes are occurring or will occur,[54] and

[45] *Implementing the Responsibility to Protect*, *supra* note 25, at ¶ 10(b).

[46] *See, e.g.*, David Scheffer, *Atrocity Crimes Framing the Responsibility to Protect*, *in* RESPONSIBILITY TO PROTECT, THE GLOBAL MORAL COMPACT FOR THE 21ST CENTURY 77, 89 (Richard H. Cooper & Juliette Voinov Kohler eds., 2009) ("As a matter of law, the invocation of *ethnic cleansing* in the mandates of RtoP is a nontechnical expression for what in fact is a subcategory of the crime against humanity of *persecution*.").

[47] EKKEHARD STRAUSS, THE EMPEROR'S NEW CLOTHES? THE UNITED NATIONS AND THE IMPLEMENTATION OF THE RESPONSIBILITY TO PROTECT 36 (2009).

[48] For a further discussion of the elements of the four crimes, *see id.* at 28–40.

[49] *See* EVANS, *supra* note 21, at 12, Scheffer, *supra* note 46, at 84–88.

[50] Scheffer, *supra* note 46, at 91.

[51] Scheffer, *supra* note 46, at 83–84.

[52] *See* Stuart Ford, *Is the Failure to Respond Appropriately to a Natural Disaster a Crime against Humanity? The Responsibility to Protect and Individual Criminal Responsibility in the Aftermath of Cyclone Nargis*, 38 DENV. J. INT'L L. & POL'Y 227, 237 (2010).

[53] Scheffer, *supra* note 46, at 93.

[54] For a discussion of a possible evidentiary standard for RtoP, *see* Ford, *supra* note 52, at 240.

some assessment that the potential or actual crimes pose a serious enough risk to require a decisive response by the international community. While these situations, if rapidly unfolding, might be clear in their seriousness, other cases may require a more thorough assessment. Borrowing from the factors used by the Prosecutor of the International Criminal Court (ICC) to determine whether a case satisfies the gravity threshold for admissibility to the ICC, considerations that might go into an assessment of a situation could include:

- Scale, which "may be assessed in light of, *inter alia*, the number of direct and indirect victims, the extent of the damage caused by the crimes, in particular the bodily or psychological harm caused to the victims and their families, and their geographical or temporal spread . . .;"
- Nature of the crimes, which refers to "the specific elements of each offence such as killings, rapes and other crimes involving sexual or gender violence, and crimes committed against children, or the imposition of conditions of life on a community calculated to bring about its destruction;"
- The manner of commission of the crimes, which "may be assessed in light of, *inter alia*, the means employed to execute the crime, the degree of participation and intent in its commission, the extent to which the crimes were systematic or result from a plan or organized policy or otherwise resulted from the abuse of power or official capacity, and elements of particular cruelty, including the vulnerability of the victims, any motives involving discrimination, or the use of rape and sexual violence as a means of destroying communities;"
- The impact of crimes, such as "their consequence on the local or international community, including the long term social, economic and environmental damage; crimes committed with the aim or consequence of increasing the vulnerability of civilians; or other acts the primary purpose of which is to spread terror among the civilian population."[55]

This list is illustrative, not exhaustive, of the considerations that will either implicitly or explicitly be made to assess whether a crisis is of the level of seriousness so to require the application of RtoP. In a preventive context, the assessment would consider whether a situation could unfold in a way that crimes of this scale, nature, and impact could be committed.[56] The related question of who would make such an assessment is addressed in Section II.C.

C. Responsibility to Do What? The Ambiguity Over What RtoP Asks of the International Community.

As explained above, one of the primary distinctions between RtoP and humanitarian intervention is RtoP's emphasis on the prevention of—rather than military reaction

[55] International Criminal Court, Draft Policy Paper on Preliminary Examinations, Oct. 2010, *available at* http://www.icc-cpi.int/NR/rdonlyres/E278F5A2-A4F9–43D7–83D2–6A2C9CF5D7D7/282515/OTP_Draftpolicypaperonpreliminaryexaminations04101.pdf.

[56] For a list of considerations to determine whether a situation "where mass atrocities are not obviously occurring right at the time" is one of RtoP concern, *see* Evans, *supra* note 21 at 74–75.

to—mass atrocity crimes. The association of RtoP with a wide range of preventive strategies, however, now poses the opposite challenge of stretching the meaning of RtoP beyond its practical or political utility.

The identification of RtoP with building state capacity for good governance and upholding human rights, as well as tackling root causes of conflicts, has resulted in what has been described as a "dilemma of comprehensiveness."[57] It has created confusion about what is expected of members of the international community in the name of preventing atrocities. This section considers the proposal that RtoP should be narrowly targeted to galvanize action by the international community in situations where atrocities are imminent or unfolding. A review of some of the recent situations where RtoP might be said to apply, however, shows there may be reasons for policy makers to refrain from invoking RtoP even in these narrower circumstances.

1. Preventive Imperative of RtoP

RtoP stands for a moral imperative of non-indifference in the face of atrocities. It would be illogical to propose that the principle only applies once killings have already begun, perversely waiting for a death toll to mount before a situation could be considered a legitimate concern to the international community.[58] From a policy perspective, a doctrine designed only to address ongoing atrocities is also flawed: as the crisis escalates, measures to dissuade perpetrators become increasingly narrow, costly, and difficult to implement.[59] As for its political viability, it is not likely that RtoP would have survived the World Summit negotiation process had it exclusively focused on coercive, reactive measures. For all of these reasons, RtoP rejects the "false choice"[60] between doing nothing and "sending in the marines,"[61] and instead prioritizes prevention.

Yet the language that was agreed to in 2005 does not offer guidance as to how governments are expected to fulfill their preventive responsibilities. In his 2009 report, Secretary-General Ban Ki-moon gave a broad reading to what fulfilling RtoP could mean, with "examples of policies and practices that are contributing, or could contribute to meeting" three pillars of responsibility: "the state's obligation to protect" (Pillar 1); "international assistance and capacity-building" (Pillar 2) and "timely and decisive response" (Pillar 3). The report's focus on consent-based activities and state-building bolstered support among UN Member States and allowed for common ground with the strongest skeptics, evidenced in the 2009 UN General Assembly

[57] Bellamy, *supra* note 23, at 98, *quoting* Edward Luck, *Prevention: Theory and Practice*, *in* From Reaction to Conflict Prevention: Opportunities for the UN System 256 (Fen Osler Hampson & David Malone eds., 2001).

[58] Secretary-General of the United Nations, *Responsible Sovereignty: International Cooperation for a Changed World*, Jul. 15, 2008, *available at* http://www.un.org/News/Press/docs/2008/sgsm11701.doc.htm.

[59] Edward C Luck, *A Response*, 2 Global Resp. to Protect 178, 181 (2010). Genocide Prevention Task Force, *supra* note 1, at 57.

[60] *Implementing the Responsibility to Protect*, *supra* note 25, at ¶ 7.

[61] Gareth Evans, Statement to United Nations General Assembly Informal Interactive Dialogue on the Responsibility to Protect, Jul. 23, 2009, *available at* http://www.un.org/ga/president/63/interactive/protect/evans.pdf.

debate on the subject.[62] This approach, however, led to confusion about the purpose of RtoP: is it intended to be a framework of prevention that re-labels agendas for statebuilding, human rights, and good governance, or should RtoP be used to trigger action when the risk of atrocities is imminent?

2. RtoP as Everything and Nothing

If RtoP is understood as synonymous with capacity-building, respect for human rights, or fostering a culture of prevention, it risks duplicating, with much less precision, agendas that already have their own political support and momentum. RtoP was created to fill an important gap in international affairs: what to do when a state hides behind sovereignty to avoid international scrutiny while perpetrating or allowing mass violence against its population. The innovation of RtoP was the commitment to collective action by the international community in the face of atrocities perpetrated or permitted by the state. The emphasis on capacity building and other upstream measures threatens to distract from this crucial—and still fragile—commitment.[63]

This concern has been voiced by numerous supporters. According to Eli Stamnes, the more comprehensive approach may de-value RtoP's political utility: "The fact that it is supposed to be flagged in connection to the extreme, extraordinary, not-to-be-ignored cases is what gives it added value compared to already existing international legal obligations and instruments."[64] By labeling as RtoP "the whole plethora of activities associated with preventive RtoP action, it could lose its exclusive character."[65] Gareth Evans argues against viewing "every kind of conflict or human rights abuse" as a possible RtoP situation: "if too much is bundled under the RtoP banner, we run the risk of diluting its capacity to mobilize international consensus in the cases where it is really needed."[66] Roberta Cohen warned that RtoP supporters, in their effort to distinguish RtoP from humanitarian intervention "sometimes go to the other extreme and make its application sound almost harmless, which also is misleading."[67] The efforts to "define the concept in a way that promotes robust collective action" while also presenting RtoP "in a non-threatening way" could turn out to be "mission impossible."[68] The author was also involved in civil society efforts to raise these points to RtoP supporters within the UN administration and governments, arguing that the robust view of RtoP that focuses on those situations when a state is actively doing harm against its populations should not be lost in the attempt to gain the support of a wider UN membership.

Moreover, an expansive view of the commitment to RtoP as statebuilding would set up nearly boundless expectations of what is required by the international community

[62] Global Centre, 2009 GA Debate Report, *supra* note 36, at 5–6.

[63] *See* Jennifer M Welsch, *Turning Words into Deeds? The implementation of the "Responsibility to Protect,"* 2 Global Resp. to Protect, 149, 151 (2010). *See also* Bellamy, *supra* note 23, at 99–100.

[64] Eli Stamnes, *"Speaking RtoP" and the Prevention of Mass Atrocities*, Global Resp. to Protect 70, 75 (2009).

[65] *Id.*

[66] Evans, *supra* note 21, at 68–69 (italics in original).

[67] Roberta Cohen, *The Burma Cyclone and the Responsibility to Protect*, 1 Global Resp. to Protect 253, 254 (2009).

[68] *Id.*

in the name of atrocity prevention. While it stands to reason, as the Secretary-General asserts, that "states that handle their internal diversity well, foster respect among disparate groups, and have effective mechanisms for handling domestic disputes and protecting the rights of women, youth and minorities" are unlikely to follow a path toward mass violence,[69] the commitment to RtoP cannot be viewed as a framework to address all of these goals for each and every state. Sarah Sewall considers the potential impact that such an approach would have in light of scarce resources: as there is no consensus on the root causes of mass atrocities, vague prevention strategies focusing on development or conflict resolution may divert resources to places "not at real risk."[70] These measures "cannot serve as a substitute for a more concerted prevention strategy that confronts the complex challenges" posed by mass atrocities."[71]

3. Narrowing the Prevention Agenda

Untangling this dilemma requires a clearer articulation of what the RtoP doctrine expects of the international community. Calling on members of the international community to fulfill the Responsibility to Protect should not be done for ongoing institution- and capacity-building programs, but for specific crises requiring urgent action. RtoP should be invoked—or the doctrine should "apply"—when there is a clear risk of atrocities being committed, with a known set of perpetrators or potential victims. This moves RtoP from focusing on any environments that may be conducive to mass violence, and looks toward those situations where atrocity crimes are a known risk.

Based on his review of the history of RtoP in the UN, "its legal content and the institutional practice of principal organs and other bodies to date," Ekkehard Strauss suggests that RtoP "would apply to situations that are exceptional for grave and serious violations of human rights and humanitarian law and where such violations would be either imminent or already ongoing."[72] Eli Stamnes argues that "the act of speaking RtoP should be limited to situations in which mass atrocity crises are looming," with the view of putting an emerging crisis "above normal decision-making procedures and give it special attention and treatment."[73]

"Invoking" RtoP would mean calling on members of the international community—through the UN, regional or subregional organizations or in other

[69] *Implementing the Responsibility to Protect, supra* note 25, at ¶ 15.

[70] Sarah Sewall, *From Prevention to Response: Using Military Force to Oppose Mass Atrocities, in* Mass Atrocity Crimes, *supra*, note 33, at *159, 163.* Sewall points to the acknowledgement of the Genocide Prevention Task Force that "there is no consensus as to the causes of genocide and mass atrocities, nor is there one commonly agreed-upon theory that sufficiently explains the key catalysts, motivations or mechanisms that lead to them." Genocide Prevention Task Force, *supra* note 1, at xxii.

[71] Sewall, *supra* note 70, at 163–164.

[72] Strauss, *supra* note 47, at 76; *see also* Evans, *supra* note 21, at 72.

[73] Stamnes, *supra* note 64, at 78. Stamnes does not suggest that the principle should be limited, but that some of the work of mass atrocity prevention "must, for political and efficiency reasons, take place without attaching the RtoP label to it." *Id. But see* Alex J. Bellamy, *The Responsibility to Protect—Five Years On,* 24 Ethnics and Int'l Aff., no. 2 (2010), at 143, 160 ("One cannot sustain a commitment to the long-term prevention of genocide and mass atrocities as part of RtoP while also conceptualizing RtoP as primarily a speech act that acts as a catalyst for action.").

appropriate fora—to fulfill their Responsibility to Protect by developing situation-specific strategies to address the potential or actual crisis. This includes consideration of the appropriate mixture of carrots and sticks necessary to dissuade potential perpetrators and developing contingency plans in the event that prevention fails.[74]

Once the international community is mobilized to respond to a crisis, dissuading perpetrators—that is, defusing the crisis—will only be the first step of a comprehensive approach. To Gareth Evans, there are a number of lessons about what engagement in an RtoP situation must mean for the relevant actors in the international community:

> First, sort[ing] out who should do what and when—immediately, over a medium transition period, and in the longer term—and then allocat[ing] the roles and coordinate them effectively, both in relevant capitals and the ground. Second, commit[ting] the necessary resources, and sustain[ing] that commitment for as long as it takes. Third, understanding[ing] local political dynamics and what outsiders can do. Fourth, hav[ing] an exit strategy . . . Fifth . . . prepar[ing] to stay, subject to local consent, as long as it takes.[75]

4. "Mainstreaming" Atrocity Prevention, Not Re-Labeling

The use of RtoP as a tool for mobilizing action can complement other atrocity prevention initiatives. One important initiative is the effort to "mainstream"[76] atrocity prevention considerations into other UN programs and activities, including human rights, humanitarian affairs, peacekeeping, peace-building, political affairs, and development.[77] Mainstreaming cannot substitute for taking measures in the face of imminent atrocities. Nevertheless, if prevention of mass atrocities is expected to be a priority for global institutions and national governments, potential risks of mass atrocities should be factored into other programs dealing with the peace, stability, and development of a society. For the UN Secretary-General, "mainstreaming the goals relating to responsibility to protect" means "forging a common strategy rather than on proposing costly new programmes or radically new approaches."[78] This approach has obvious benefits: ensuring that UN programs do not exacerbate underlying tensions; allowing those with a presence in the field engaged in these programs to signal early warnings by channeling information about risks and potential triggers; and finally, support of such programs by members of the international community may provide some leverage with potential perpetrators if a crisis does escalate. National governments have also been called on to mainstream mass atrocity prevention considerations within their bureaucracies.[79]

[74] Strauss, *supra* note 47, at 130–132.

[75] Evans, *supra* note 21, at 149.

[76] A useful set of criteria to gauge the success of "mainstreaming" within the UN system can be found Special Representative of the Secretary-General for Children and Armed Conflict, *2009 Report of the Special Representative of the Secretary-General for Children and Armed Conflict*, A/64/254, Aug. 6, 2009, at ¶ 30.

[77] *Implementing the Responsibility to Protect*, *supra* note 25 at ¶ 28.

[78] *Id.* at ¶ 68.

[79] Andrew Block and Claire Applegarth, *Acting Against Atrocities: A Strategy for Supporters of RtoP*, *in* Mass Atrocity Crimes: Preventing Future Atrocities, *supra* note 33, at 128, 148–149.

In sum, a possible approach to narrow the application of RtoP is to invoke the doctrine to galvanize political action to looming crises, while also mainstreaming the goals of preventing mass atrocities into upstream preventative work in development, human rights, and conflict prevention. The latter does not require the RtoP label. Through his work on implementing RtoP, the Secretary-General is advancing both initiatives. To address looming crises, he has instituted a process for senior UN officials to consider policy options on an urgent basis in RtoP crisis situations.[80] His plans for the joint office on the Special Advisor for the Prevention of Genocide and the Special Advisor with a focus on RtoP also emphasize the mainstreaming of RtoP perspectives into the UN's work.[81] As for the political reception to this approach, there appears general support for the Secretary-General to develop his institutional mainstreaming.[82] Appeals to the RtoP doctrine to galvanize action, however, are still at very early stages. As discussed in the following section, recent attempts to invoke RtoP reveal some of the political challenges to its application in actual cases.

D. Applying the Label—Consistency or Selectivity?

As discussed above, when RtoP is invoked to address a looming crisis, it can be "an important tool for moral suasion"[83] to galvanize relevant actors to develop a coordinated response. But RtoP is not self-executing: its invocation does not "set in motion automatic action."[84] Instead, it is a framework through which members of the international community can consider appropriate measures. Other frameworks, such as human rights, humanitarian law, or conflict mediation may also be relevant, although RtoP is unique in its focus on the international community's role in protecting from atrocities. Moreover, RtoP is a political—not legal—concept,[85] and its ultimate value will be assessed by its potential to influence policy decisions.

If RtoP is one of many approaches to a crisis, some have asked whether there are times when, even if the circumstances are appropriate, it is best for policy makers not to invoke it. Recent debates about invoking RtoP in specific crisis situations illustrate this point.

1. Impact of the Threat of RtoP's Coercive Measures

While RtoP is not synonymous with military force, force is expressly considered as a policy option of last resort. As long as this continues to be an aspect of the RtoP

[80] UN Secretary-General, *Early Warning, Assessment and the Responsibility to Protect*, A/64/864, Jul. 14, 2010, at ¶ 18.

[81] UN Secretary-General, *Remarks to the General Assembly Informal Interactive Dialogue on Early Warning, Assessment, and the Responsibility to Protect*, Jul. 23, 2010, *available at* http://www.responsibilitytoprotect.org/Secretary%20General%20-Speech%20to%20the%20General%20Assembly,%20dialogue%20on%20early%20warning%20and%20RtoP.pdf

[82] Global Ctr. for the Responsibility To Protect, "Early Warning, Assessment, and the Responsibility to Protect:" Informal Interactive Dialogue of the General Assembly held on 9 August 2010 (Sept. 2010).

[83] Genocide Prevention Task Force, *supra* note 1, at 98.

[84] *Id.* at 98.

[85] Edward C Luck, *A Response*, *supra* note 59, at 183 (2010).

doctrine, some will perceive RtoP as a premise for external forces to intervene to achieve regime change or advance other non-humanitarian agendas. As a result, even in those cases where the use of force is not credibly on the table, invoking the doctrine poses risks of backlash. This point was succinctly made in a 2010 dialogue on RtoP between funders and civil society organizations: "For RtoP proponents, the true objective is to protect civilian populations in ways that are consistent with the RtoP framework. This sometimes requires setting aside the RtoP label in contexts where it raises political resistance and encouraging policy responses consistent with its principles without semantically invoking the norm."[86]

The situation in Burma (Myanmar) after Cyclone Nargis in 2008 was one such example. The junta's failure to respond to the disaster led to the invocation of RtoP, most notably by French Foreign Minister Bernard Kouchner,[87] as a basis to intervene in Burma to deliver aid to the cyclone victims. Assuming that this was a case where mass atrocity crimes were at risk,[88] there were other less controversial ways to seek access to the victims. As Ramesh Thakur, and Thomas G. Weiss explained:

> Invoking the coercive language of RtoP would have riled the generals . . . It would have risked antagonizing the Southeast Asian countries, whose political support was vital . . . It would have risked alienating China, India and Japan . . . whose backing was essential for delivering any meaningful relief in Burma.[89]

Thakur and Weiss did consider, however, that Kouchner's role as "bad cop" may have helped other actors, including ASEAN and the UN, to gain access.[90] This is an important consideration for using the RtoP label in a crisis: the messenger may be as important as the message. Determination of whether to and also who should publicly invoke RtoP might be factored into a coordinated response strategy.

The response to the 2009 crisis in Kenya also reflected concerns about the RtoP label. The African-Union-mandated mediation that brought an end to ethnically targeted violence following the disputed 2008 elections was held up as a successful application of RtoP after the fact.[91] At the time, however, it was not expressly referred to as an RtoP situation. U.S. Ambassador to the UN Susan Rice explained that it was "explicitly not part of the debate" in the Security Council, as "[r]aising the RtoP flag may be morally

[86] Policy Memo, The Stanley Foundation, Funders Dialogue on the Responsibility to Protect, (Sept. 2010) http://www.stanleyfoundation.org/publications/policy_memo/RtoP_FundersDialogue PM909.pdf.

[87] *See* Seth Mydans, *Myanmar Faces Pressure to Allow Major Aid Effort*, New York Times, May 8, 2008

[88] Although RtoP does not extend to natural disasters, the willful neglect of the junta leading to foreseeable deaths of cyclone victims was raised as a potential crime against humanity. *See, e.g.*, Gareth Evans, *Facing up to Our Responsibilities*, The Guardian, May 12, 2008.

[89] Thakur & Weiss, *supra* note 31, at 48–49.

[90] *Id.* at 49.

[91] Roger Cohen, *How Kofi Annan Rescued Kenya*, 55(13) N.Y. Rev. of Books (no. 13) (Aug. 14, 2008).

satisfying, but it can be politically fraught."[92] Nevertheless, the concept was seen as motivating the international community into action.[93]

2. Lack of Impact on Chronic, Pre-Existing Conflicts

In those situations where the international community has long been engaged to address a chronic conflict or human rights situation, there is caution about invoking RtoP even if mass atrocities have occurred in the past and may recur. Two of the most recent and controversial examples include the 2009 Sri Lanka offensive against the Liberation Tigers of Tamil Eelam (LTTE) and the December 2008–January 2009 Israeli invasion in Gaza. In both situations, governments engaged in military operations in response to atrocities committed by non-state actors. In their military reactions, both governments are believed to have committed crimes covered by RtoP.[94] In both cases, RtoP was raised to call attention to the risks to civilians from both state and non-state actors.[95] Although neither case suffered from a lack of attention by the international community about the underlying conflict or the risk to civilians, there were deep divisions about the policy options that the international community should apply. As the crises unfolded, there was little basis to claim that RtoP was successful in increasing protection to at risk populations.[96]

Assessing the lack of impact in such cases, some supporters may avoid use of RtoP in cases where it will be unlikely to succeed in influencing the outcome. In these early stages of the norm, the political will to implement it remains a challenge, particularly in those situations where the international community is already involved, but unsuccessful, in responding to a chronic human rights situation or long-standing conflict. Attaching the label of RtoP to such cases will not act as a silver bullet that brings about policy change just by raising it. A more cautious approach to applying the norm is to reserve it for those cases where there is the greatest opportunity for dissuading or halting perpetrators, and contributing to saving lives. Calls to protect populations would still continue, but without specifically invoking the commitment to RtoP.

It must be recognized, however, that selectivity cannot endure indefinitely. The damage that might be done by the failure of RtoP to make a difference must be weighed against the risks of non-use of the doctrine when it clearly applies. If RtoP supporters stay silent when a clear RtoP situation exists, questions about the utility of the norm will persist. Moreover, selective application such as this will stoke concerns that RtoP

[92] *Quoted in* Thomas G. Weiss, *Halting Atrocities in Kenya*, in Great Decisions 2010 17, 24 (Foreign Pol'y Ass'n, ed., 2010).

[93] *See id.*, *see also*. Desmond Tutu, *Taking the Responsibility to Protect*, New York Times (Nov. 9, 2008).

[94] For an analysis of crimes committed in Gaza, *see Report of the UN Fact Finding Mission on the Gaza Conflict*, A/HRC/12/48, Sept. 12, 2009; for Sri Lanka, *see* International Crisis Group., War Crimes in Sri Lanka, Asia Report No. 191 (2010).

[95] World Council of Churches Executive Committee, Statement on the Gaza War, Feb. 17–20, 2009, *available at* http://www.oikoumene.org/resources/documents/executive-committee/bossey-february-2009/statement-on-the-gaza-war.html.

[96] *See, e.g.*, Matthew Russell Lee, *Sri Lanka's "Bloodbath on the Beach" Made the UN's Ban Ki-mute Moot: Now What?*, SAIS Review of Int'l Aff., Summer–Fall 2009, at 39.

can only be applied to the weak and not the powerful. This is a longstanding challenge to the acceptance of RtoP and is explored in the following section.

II. WHOSE RESPONSIBILITY TO PROTECT? CHALLENGES ARISING FROM THE GLOBAL BALANCE OF POWER.

If it is possible to "define, refine, and confine,"[97] the doctrine of RtoP in the ways described above, this alone is unlikely to satisfy skeptics who believe its legitimacy depends on uniform application across powerful and weak states. For these skeptics, such a norm cannot be accepted until the risk of double standards and selectivity are eliminated. Advocates for RtoP agree with the goal of consistent application, but recognize that to await major global reforms would mean postponing implementation indefinitely, and prefer to make progress where possible. The danger of too few rather than too many interventions[98] gives cause to support the doctrine, notwithstanding the flaws in the current system of global governance.

Many skeptics also insist that reform of the Security Council take place before RtoP can be fully accepted. Although progress cannot await resolution of the seemingly endless negotiations to expand membership of the Council, the existing Council should not be let off of the hook. Much more could be done to improve the way that it responds to the threat of mass atrocities.

A. Selectivity and Double Standards

The Responsibility to Protect from mass atrocities is not exclusively within the domain of the Security Council. Yet the Security Council has a particular role to play at the point when a state has manifestly failed to protect its population, given its primary role within the UN for the maintenance of peace and security. The concern with this division of labor is that the structure of the Council is inherently unequal: only five of the fifteen members of the Council are permanent—others are elected to two-year terms—and only those five permanent members (P-5) hold a right to veto. Although the members of the Council are mandated to carry out their duties on behalf of the entire UN membership,[99] in reality, the veto allows powerful states to protect themselves and their allies from the Council's measures.

The Council's structure thus creates the risk of selective application of RtoP, either to the weak or friendless countries, or those situations where P-5 countries might have a particular interest in intervening. There is also the related risk of double standards: the full range of measures—up to and including the use of force—could be carried out to address atrocities in a weak state, but they will not be applied to the most powerful. As Don Hubert, who led policy development for the Canadian government on RtoP, acknowledges, "the application of these standards will always be inconsistent—it is built into the doctrine. There simply are fewer levers available to dissuade powerful

[97] Remarks of Gareth Evans *in* UN Department of Information, *Press Conference On General Assembly Dialogue on Responsibility to Protect*, Jul. 23, 2009, *available at* http://www.un.org/News/briefings/docs/2009/090723_GA.doc.htm.

[98] Thomas G. Weiss, Humanitarian Intervention 134 (2007).

[99] UN Charter, art. 24 (1).

states from committing crimes against their own populations."[100] Engaging in military force, in particular, would not be a realistic possibility. Mounting a military campaign against a permanent member of the Council or other major power would be unlikely to succeed and could be expected to lead to a larger conflict putting even greater numbers of lives at risk.[101]

Selective implementation and double standards were among the most "commonly expressed concerns" in the 2009 General Assembly debate, with the failure to protect the populations in Gaza from an Israeli intervention as the most frequently cited example.[102] The president of the General Assembly, Miguel d'Escoto Brockmann, the convener of the UNGA debate, was one of the strongest opponents of RtoP, and claimed that skeptics' resistance was "not out of indifference to the plight of many who suffered at the hands of their own Governments," but because "the system of collective security had not yet evolved to the degree that would allow the doctrine to operate in the intended manner."[103]

1. Concerns Cannot Obstruct Progress Where Possible

These concerns must be factored into the way in which RtoP is implemented, but should not be a basis for abandoning the 2005 commitment. It must be recognized that "the international balance of power cannot be changed by RtoP."[104] As Chilean UN Ambassador Heraldo Munoz reasoned, "It would be morally and politically wrong to conclude that because the international community could not act everywhere, it should therefore act nowhere."[105] The New Zealand ambassador also recognized these concerns but argued that "such issues should not be used as diversions or excuses to stop progress."[106]

These challenges are by no means limited to the norm of RtoP; "no principle has withstood the test of application in a perfect or flawless manner."[107] The UN's promotion of human rights has long been plagued with concerns about selectivity and double standards.[108] The UN Special Advisor on Children in Armed Conflict, Radhika Coomaraswamy, makes the analogy to national criminal justice systems:

[100] Don Hubert, *The Responsibility to Protect: Preventing and Halting Crimes against Humanity*, *in* Mass Atrocity Crimes: Preventing Future Outrages, *supra* note 33, at 89, 99.

[101] ICISS Report, *supra* note 10, at ¶ 4.42.

[102] Global Centre, 2009 GA Debate Report, supra note 36, at 3.

[103] UN GAOR, 63rd Sess., 97th plen. mtg., A/63/PV.97, Jul. 23, 2009, at 3.

[104] Susan E. Mayer, *In our Interest: the Responsibility to Protect*, *in* Responsibility to Protect, The Global Moral Compact for the 21st Century 43, 56 (Richard H. Cooper & Juliette Voinov Kohler eds., 2009).

[105] *Quoted in* Global Centre, 2009 GA Debate Report, *supra* note 36, at 6 (2009).

[106] Statement of Jim McLay, New Zealand Ambassador to the United Nations, *in* UN GAOR, 63rd Sess., 97th plen. mtg., A/63/PV. 97, Jul. 23, 2009, at 25.

[107] Statement of Heraldo Munoz, Chilean Ambassador to the United Nations, *in* UN GAOR, 63rd Sess., 98th plen. mtg., A/63/PV. 98, Jul. 24, 2009, at 12.

[108] *See, e.g.*, Human Rights Watch, *Curing the Selectivity Syndrome: the 2011 Review of the Human Rights Council* (2010), *available at* http://www.hrw.org/en/reports/2010/06/24/curing-selectivity-syndrome.

It is well known that poor people are far more likely to be prosecuted, but does that mean we throw out the criminal law? Surely the more enlightened approach is to say yes there are double standards, we will work to make them more equitable but we will continue to protect children where we can. We cannot afford to throw out these doctrines, they save too many lives."[109]

2. Powerful Governments Must be Held to Account with Tools Available

Notwithstanding the current global structure, big powers are not wholly beyond the reach of RtoP. "No major country in the world, however big and powerful, is today wholly immune from peer group pressure," explains Evans. Powerful states have even agreed to military interventions as a result of international pressure. The "coerced consent" of Indonesia to a multinational intervention to protect populations in Timor-Leste from post-referendum violence is often cited as an example.[110]

Voices outside of government, in particular civil society, can play an important role in ensuring against double standards by naming and shaming governments that are shielding allies or are themselves perpetrators of mass atrocity crimes.

3. Enhancing Role of Regional Organizations

Regional and sub-regional organizations may also be critical to delivering effective and credible responses. Because of the impact that such crises can have on the broader region, regional organizations are often considered to have a legitimate interest in being involved and are often viewed as better informed of events on the ground. A state at risk of an atrocity situation may also be more open to regionally led measures.[111] At the UNGA debate on RtoP, UN Member States were outspoken about the potential for regional/sub-regional organizations, particularly those in the global south, to play an enhanced role in fulfilling RtoP.[112] Building their capacity to lead in RtoP crises (within their borders) would ease concerns that powerful governments are reserving for themselves the authority and means to act under RtoP. Yet action within the region is not assured, as the same concerns that create resistance on the global level can play out on the regional level. Initiatives to involve regional organizations must be aimed at increasing the will to confront atrocities as well as capacity.

[109] Radhika Coomaraswamy, *Responsibility to Protect: A Natural Humanitarian Impulse*, The Island, Apr. 26, 1999, *available at* http://www.island.lk/2010/04/26/features3.html.

[110] *See id. See also* Evans, *supra* note 21, at 63; Bellamy, *supra* note 23, at 147–148.

[111] *See* David Carment and Martin Fischer, *RtoP and the Role of Regional Organisations in Ethnic Conflict Management, Prevention and Resolution: The Unfinished Agenda*, 1 Global Responsibility to Protect 261, 268–269 (2009). *See also* International Coalition for the Responsibility to Protect, *supra* note 37, at 10.

[112] *See* International Coalition for the Responsibility to Protect, Report on the General Assembly Plenary Debate on the Responsibility to Protect 10 (Sept. 15, 2009); Global Centre, 2009 GA Debate Report, *supra* note 36, at 9.

B. Confronting Shortcomings of the Security Council

1. Security Council Reform

The concerns about implementing RtoP are most sharply directed at the Security Council. It has failed miserably to prevent past atrocities and is criticized as unrepresentative and outdated. A few UN Member States have suggested that the existing structure has been so utterly delegitimized that they cannot support any initiative that promotes, or even recognizes, the status quo.[113] For these countries, RtoP cannot be implemented until the Council's makeup better reflects the current global powers.[114] A change in the Council's composition, however, requires an amendment to the UN Charter that must be approved by two-thirds of the General Assembly and the five veto-holding members of the Security Council.[115] Despite years of effort, there is little hope for gaining consensus on who would be included in this expanded membership and how. Awaiting Security Council reform would thus result in "unconscionable delays to the UN's efforts" at preventing mass atrocities.[116]

2. Addressing the Veto

Given the dim prospects for reform of the Council's composition or any changes to the UN Charter, RtoP supporters have instead turned to a more modest proposal targeted at the five permanent members of the Council. All too frequently, P-5 members have "made effective collective action virtually impossible by threatening veto, implicitly or explicitly. This has led to either watered-down, ineffectual resolutions, or no resolution at all."[117] For these reasons, the UN Secretary-General[118] and at least 35 governments[119] have echoed the recommendation in the ICISS report that permanent members of the Council agree to refrain from using their veto in situations of actual or impending atrocities.[120] Although an official agreement is not seen as possible at this time, an informal, mutual agreement among the P-5 is believed to be "achievable and would send an important political message."[121]

A public campaign involving supportive governments and civil society would be an important next step to securing this commitment. Diplomatic pressure and media exposure could be effective on a case-by-case basis if any of the P-5 is holding up

[113] *See* International Coalition for the Responsibility to Protect, *supra* note 37, at 7.

[114] For a discussion of Security Council reform proposals, *see* Thomas G. Weiss, *The Illusion of Security Council Reform*, The Washington Quarterly, Autumn 2003, at 147–161; Thomas G. Weiss, What's Wrong with the United Nations and How to Fix It 55–60 (2009).

[115] UN Charter, art. 108.

[116] Global Centre for the Responsibility to Protect, Frequently Made Assertions 3 (2009), *available at* http://globalr2p.org/media/pdf/Frequently_made_assertions_16_June_Final.pdf.

[117] Genocide Prevention Task Force, *supra* note 1, at 106. For a discussion of recent cases that illustrate the ways in which the veto obstructions action in the face of mass atrocities, *see* Citizens for Global Solutions, The Responsibility Not to Veto: A Way Forward 5–6 (2010).

[118] *Implementing the Responsibility to Protect*, *supra* note 25, at ¶ 61.

[119] Global Centre, 2009 GA Debate, *supra* note 36, at 6.

[120] ICISS Report, *supra* note 10, at ¶ 6.20. *See also* Genocide Prevention Task Force, *supra* note 1, at 6.

[121] Citizens for Global Solutions, *supra* note 117, at 8.

action to address a crisis. A more structured civil society campaign could also build pressure from within P-5 states and their allies.[122] The moral case is compelling: these five countries have the ultimate authority over whether atrocities will be met with decisive action or populations will be left to die.[123]

C. Who Determines When RtoP Applies?

The final challenge explored here is the lack of clarity on how the decision to act under RtoP is taken. Currently there is no one institution mandated to make any such determination. Instead, it has been invoked by a range of actors—governments, UN officials, NGOs and the media—to rally the international community to action in the face of mass atrocities. The establishment of formal criteria to be considered by an official body could help to address concerns about inconsistency of application, but would undoubtedly impede the aim of saving lives at risk of atrocities.

1. The Quest for Clarity

The WSOD considers that at a point of "manifest failure," timely and decisive action should be taken to avert or halt atrocities.[124] Having rejected a more specific threshold involving criteria for military force (discussed above), the WSOD leaves the point of thresholds vague. And this has left supporters and opponents alike to ask: how should the international community determine when a situation has reached the level of manifest failure? Who should make this determination? At the 2009 General Assembly debate, calls for clarity came from Cuba,[125] Gambia,[126] Ireland,[127] Malaysia,[128] Switzerland,[129] and Sri Lanka.[130] The Gambia made the specific proposal for a committee to make non-binding recommendations to the General Assembly, Security Council, and regional organizations on RtoP situations and possible measures to address them.[131] The more skeptical speakers expressed a preference for mechanisms that ensured greater oversight of the Security Council, including an enhanced role for the General Assembly.[132]

[122] *Id.* at 8.

[123] Interview with Sapna Chhatpar, Deputy Director, International Coalition for the Responsibility to Protect (Oct. 14, 2010).

[124] WSOD, *supra* note 24 at ¶ 139.

[125] *See* UN GAOR, 63rd Sess., 99th plen. mtg., A/63/pv.99, Jul. 24, 2009, at 22.

[126] *See* UN GAOR, 63rd Sess., 101st plen. mtg., A/63/pv.101, Jul. 28, 2009, at 12.

[127] *See* UN GAOR, 63rd Sess., 99th plen. mtg., A/63/pv.99, Jul. 24, 2009, at 3.

[128] *See* UN GAOR, 63rd Sess., 101st plen. mtg., A/63/pv.101, Jul. 28, 2009, at 4.

[129] *See* UN GAOR, 63rd Sess., 98th plen. mtg., A/63/pv.98, Jul. 24, 2009, at 5.

[130] *See* UN GAOR, 63rd Sess., 100th plen. mtg., A/63/pv.100, Jul. 28, 2009, at 2.

[131] UN GAOR, 63rd Sess., 101st plen. mtg., A/63/pv.101, Jul. 28, 2009, at 12. For a detailed proposal for a Security Council sub-committee on RtoP, *see* Neville F. Dastoor, *The Responsibility to Refine: The Need for a Security Council Committee on the Responsibility to Protect*, 22 Harv. Hum. Rts. J. 25, 49–50 (2009).

[132] *See* International Coalition for the Responsibility to Protect, *supra* note 37, at 7.

2. Rejecting Call for Process over Substance

In Section I.B.2, this chapter identified some of the factors that might be used to make a determination of an RtoP situation. Any attempts to formally establish such criteria and identify who should apply them, however, would be certain to stoke a political battle that would derail progress toward the norm's acceptance. The creation of a subsidiary body for the Security Council would not satisfy detractors, and the Council members would object to any process outside of the Council that would encroach on their mandate. More fundamentally, even if the establishment of an official process of determination might lessen the risk of selectivity,[133] it would do little to advance the aims of saving lives at risk of atrocities. Adding additional layers of deliberation would only distract policy makers and delay responsible action.

The strategy favored by the Secretary-General is to strengthen systems of early warning to increase the flow of information to the many bodies that have a role in taking action.[134] Calling attention to a potential crisis makes it more difficult for those in positions of powers to stand aside. The Secretary-General is emphatic on this point:

> [T]here is no room for a rigidly sequenced strategy or for tightly defined "triggers" for action . . . In a rapidly unfolding emergency situation, the United Nations, regional, subregional and national decision makers must remain focused on saving lives . . . not on following arbitrary, sequential or graduated policy ladders that prize procedure over substance and process over results.[135]

The determination of when to invoke RtoP should be taken by the many members of the international community best placed to address the crises, not through a political negotiation that would result in a lowest common denominator result.

The onus is now on those with information of potential atrocities—within national governments, international organizations and non-governmental organizations—to ensure that policy makers are made aware of those situations at greatest risk and to present recommendations for action. Ideas for strengthening this capacity beyond those proposed by the Secretary-General include the creation of a non-governmental watchlist of the countries at greatest risk,[136] a standing network of national focal points within governments that would coordinate to enhance efforts to anticipate, prevent, and respond better to mass atrocity crimes,[137] and a network of

[133] *See* Dastoor, *supra* note 131, at 53.

[134] *See UN Secretary-General, Early Warning, Assessment and the Responsibility to Protect*, *supra* note 80.

[135] *Implementing the Responsibility to Protect*, *supra* note 25, at ¶ 50.

[136] *See* Gareth Evans, Making the Responsibility to Protect Work, Presentation to ASEAN-ISIS, 24th Asia-Pacific Roundtable, Jun. 8, 2010, *available at* http://www.gevans.org/speeches/speech413.html.

[137] In a September 2010 meeting of ministers, several governments announced the designation of focal points and agreed to a meeting of focal points within a year. *See* Meeting Summary, the Global Centre for the Responsibility to Protect, Fulfilling the responsibility to protect: Strengthening our capacities to prevent and halt mass atrocities (Sept. 24, 2010), *available at* http://globalr2p.org/media/pdf/Ministerial_meeting_2010.pdf.

like-minded governments, international organizations and NGOs that would constitute "an international working group for considering emerging threats."[138] Such initiatives will only have an impact if those with power to act—in particular the Security Council—are receptive to this information and to willing to adopt a comprehensive strategy with a continuum of steps to "deter, inhibit and dissuade perpetrators."[139] But far more than the creation of formalized processes, a consistent and specific flow of information calling attention to lives that are at risk can increase the pressure to act.

III. CONCLUSION

A number of themes emerge from this review of conceptual and political challenges to RtoP:

- While conceptual clarity is important to guide behavior, it is likely to evolve over time through practice, rather than through the creation of any strict definitions negotiated through a multi-lateral process.
- The decision to invoke RtoP is a political one; invoking it will have greatest value in those situations of emerging or actual crises.
- The rhetorical acceptance of the doctrine has not yet been sufficient to result in action in many of the difficult cases. Concerns that it is too controversial or will not be effective have lead many to be cautious about invoking RtoP, even in cases where it would clearly apply.
- Expecting a standard of perfect consistency for any norm is unrealistic. RtoP cannot be expected to change the global balance of power. To await the reform of global institutions before implementing RtoP is to acquiesce to standing by in the face of atrocities, putting at risk the lives of untold numbers of victims.
- Nor can it be expected that perfect consensus will be reached as to whether or how to implement RtoP. It is encouraging, however, to see an increasing number of states from all regions voicing their acceptance of RtoP.

While a few skeptics will remain content rehashing the same debate of 2005 or even 2009, others are considering the institutional changes necessary to make it easier to know the signs, present recommendations, and pressure the relevant actors into responding. It may be too early to gauge success, and the doctrine has not yet shown enough results, but there is no question, looking back to the time when the ICISS report was issued, that this is progress.

[138] Genocide Prevention Task Force, *supra* note 1, at 104.

[139] Strauss, *supra* note 47, at 131. For proposals of how the Council might improve its approach to atrocities prevention, *see* Global Centre for the Responsibility to Protect, Presentation to the UN Security Council Working Group on Conflict Prevention and Resolution in Africa (Dec. 1 2008), *available at* http://globalr2p.org/media/pdf/WkgGrpConflctPrevAfr.pdf.

5 From Promise to Practice: Implementing the Responsibility to Protect

Edward C. Luck

The implementation of the responsibility to protect (RtoP) is a work in progress. That is true in 2011. It is likely to be so in 2021 and 2031 as well. As a policy tool, not just an aspiration or standard, RtoP is in its infancy. In these formative years, choices are being made, both at the United Nations and in national capitals, that could profoundly shape the future development of this promising, perhaps even historic, concept. This chapter looks at the UN side of this development process over three critical years, from early 2008 to early 2011.

There can be no finality when it comes to the implementation of human rights, humanitarian, or human protection standards. There can be no ironclad assurances against slippage or backsliding, no guarantee against recidivism, no presumption that armed groups or new generations of national leaders will observe fully the commitments made by others. Progress toward implementation can, and should, be assessed from time to time, and place to place. But this should be done with the understanding that such judgments, while potentially helpful for gauging whether mid-course corrections are needed, cannot be considered to be conclusive. Progress—or the lack of it—can be fleeting. Results are likely to be uneven, whether they are measured thematically or situationally.

So strategies for implementing the responsibility to protect provisions of the Outcome Document from the 2005 World Summit—paragraphs 138, 139, and 140—have to be both long-term and to some extent self-renewing.[1] Those provisions, it

[1] G.A. Res. 60/1, UN Doc. A/Res/60/1 (Sept. 15, 2005). Many authors understandably only look to paragraphs 138 and 139 for an account of the Summit's provisions on RtoP, as these contain the only explicit references to the concept. However, in this author's view, the inclusion of paragraph 140 on the work of the Secretary-General's Special Adviser on the Prevention of Genocide in the

should be recalled, did not come with detailed instructions or favorite recipes for implementation. Some provisions enjoyed fuller political support than did others. No doubt some of those who accepted these commitments regarded them as hortatory or aspirational, rather than as binding obligations that would be followed by strategies, doctrines, policies, procedures, and capacities for ensuring their fulfillment. Summit outcomes may make important contributions to soft or customary international law, but they are not, in themselves, binding hard law conventions. This caveat could usefully be born in mind when we turn to a consideration of the strategies and tactics that have guided the United Nations' implementation efforts to date. As the official appointed by Secretary-General Ban Ki-moon in February 2008 to spearhead the conceptual, political, and institutional/operational development of the responsibility to protect (RtoP), this author's account that follows may be more than a little subjective at points.[2]

I. ON THE NATURE OF IMPLEMENTATION

For the purposes of this paper, it would be helpful to clarify from the outset what we mean by "implement" and "implementation." The first Webster's definition is helpful in that regard because of its elegant simplicity: implement is "to carry out" or "fulfill;" especially "to give practical effect to and ensure of actual fulfillment by concrete measures."[3] Implementation, then, would be the process or act of fulfillment. Given the uncertainties noted above, the emphasis should be on the process more than on a single, conclusive act of fulfillment. It is a matter of advancement rather than attainment. In fact, in successful cases, there are likely to be multiple acts of fulfillment over time, each step decreasing the likelihood of slippage or the possibility that precipitating events could occur without notice and comment by civil society, government officials, neighboring countries, or international civil servants based in sub-regional, regional, or global institutions.

The Webster definition does not, of course, refer to "process," favoring more action-oriented words and phrases, such as "carry out," "give practical effect to," "ensure," and "concrete measures." So process is not enough. To meet the Webster standard, it should "give practical effect to" the words agreed at the 2005 World Summit. The purpose of the exercise, as the Secretary-General has often underscored, is to turn "words into deeds" and "promise into practice."[4] During his campaign to be appointed Secretary-General, he had stressed this core theme, in the recognition that the United

RtoP section of the Outcome Document should not be overlooked. As discussed below, this decision suggests that the assembled heads of state and government understood the operational value of integrating the world body's work on the two related mandates.

[2] See UN Docs. SG/A/1120 (Feb. 21, 2008), S/2007/722 and S/2007/721 (Dec. 7, 2007).

[3] Webster's SEVENTH New Collegiate Dictionary (G. & C. Merriam Company, 1967), at 419.

[4] Address by UN Secretary-General Ban Ki-moon, "Responsible Sovereignty: International Cooperation for a Changed World," UN Doc. SG/SM/11701 (Jul. 15, 2008), Report of the Secretary-General, Implementing the Responsibility to Protect, UN Doc. A/63/677 (Jan. 12, 2009), at 28, and "Remarks at a Stanley Foundation Conference on 'Implementing the Responsibility to Protect,'" Tarrytown, New York (January 15, 2010), www.stanleyfoundation.org/publications/policy_memo/SGresptoprotect15jan2010.pdf.

Nations regrettably had earned its reputation of being much better at words than deeds—at the normative than the operational—on any number of difficult subjects over the years.[5] Both privately and publicly, Secretary-General Ban has confided that one factor behind his personal commitment to advancing the responsibility to protect has been a desire to deliver on this 2006 campaign pledge. In his February 2011 Cyril Foster Lecture at Oxford, the Secretary-General also pointed to his searing childhood experiences during the Korean War, when his family was forcibly displaced from their home.[6] In that lecture, he also underlined the importance of the individual responsibility to protect, as it is not only up to governments and international organizations to curb such atrocity crimes.

At the same time, bold action is unlikely without parallel movement toward norm creation. And normative innovations at the United Nations do not come about without lots of talk, usually embedded in overlapping tiers of consultations and political processes. Attempts to gain the acceptance of all, or at least the vast majority, of the world body's 193 Member States on new normative standards are bound to be sustained, complex, and multi-dimensional. If it is to succeed, moreover, that process cannot end with the formal adoption of a particular principle. For all of the concerted conceptual and political work that led to the 2005 Summit agreement, that was only the beginning of the implementation process. The skilled and dedicated norm entrepreneurs who spearheaded that effort, particularly former United Nations Secretary-General Kofi Annan and the co-chairs of the International Commission on Intervention and State Sovereignty (ICISS),[7] former Foreign Minister of Australia Gareth Evans and former Foreign Minister of Algeria Mohammed Sahnoun, would be among the first to acknowledge how much work lies ahead.

Normative development is neither a phase of nor a precursor to the implementation process. Normative development should continue throughout the implementation struggle, accompanied by a continuous cycle of interactive feedback to inform and, if necessary, condition the way in which further implementation steps are carried out. Implementation is bound, to some extent, to be a learning-by-doing proposition. As this author has argued elsewhere, even sophisticated models of norm development, such as the classic one posited by Martha Finnemore and Kathryn Sikkink more than a dozen years ago, tend to be insufficiently dynamic and fluid in that regard.[8] Understandably, such models are prone to pay more attention to the visible tip of the iceberg than to what lies beneath the surface. They usually overvalue persuasion and

[5] Transcript, Address by Ban Ki-moon, Minister of Foreign Affairs and Trade, the Republic of Korea, "Restoring the Vitality of the United Nations" (May 31, 2006), http://www.cfr.org/publication/10833/restoring_the_vitality_of_the_united_nations_rush_transcript_federal_news_service_inc.html (accessed Jan. 24, 2011).

[6] UN Doc. SG/SM/13385 (February 2, 2011).

[7] Report of the International Commission on Intervention and State Sovereignty, The Responsibility to Protect (Ottawa: International Development Research Centre, 2001).

[8] For the model, see Martha Finnemore and Kathryn Sikkink, *International Norm Dynamics and Political Change*, International Organization, 52, 4 (Autumn 1998), 887–917. For commentary on how it fits the development of the responsibility to protect, see Edward C. Luck, "Building a Norm: The Responsibility to Protect Experience," Mass Atrocity Crimes: Preventing Future Outrages (Robert I. Rotberg, ed., Brookings Institution Press 2010), 108–127.

undervalue listening.[9] Their assumptions about progress tend to be too linear and too unidirectional, as if these are marketing not political challenges. As discussed below, each forward step at the United Nations toward the implementation of RtoP has been met—predictably—with some form of pushback from those delegations that remain markedly uncomfortable with the concept. The good news, also documented below, is that their numbers remain small while the ranks of the supportive grow with each forward step.

The discussion below of the implementation steps to date addresses some of the primary conceptual, political, and operational challenges faced from early 2008 to early 2011. This tripartite division is more a matter of convenience than logic. Two caveats are in order at the outset. One, this is not a matter of sequencing, as if one could deal with one challenge at a time. In an ideal world, it would be more orderly to complete the conceptual and political work before addressing situation-specific operational matters. Events did not permit this, as the post-election violence in Kenya erupted while the Secretary-General's conceptual framework, as well as his wide-ranging implementation strategy, was still under construction. Likewise, the high interest of Member States and civil society in this work led to early, ongoing, and candid consultations with influential political actors of various stripes. Two, analytically the three challenges often looked like different aspects of the same thought process. For instance, the conceptual development of RtoP had to make sense in political and operational terms. Beautiful theories that had no chance of attracting wide political support or of being sustained through operational application had no place in such a practice-driven exercise. This chapter first addresses the conceptual and political pieces of the puzzle and then turns to the institutional and operational ones.

II. THE CONCEPTUAL AND POLITICAL CHALLENGES

The nexus between the conceptual and the political was all too evident when I started to work with the Secretary-General on moving the responsibility to protect from promise to practice in mid-2007, prior to my formal appointment as Special Adviser. It soon became apparent that not all Member States and not even all of the key players in the Secretariat shared the Secretary-General's enthusiasm for advancing the responsibility to protect. Conceptual confusion was a key explanation for the divergence of views. There was a wide range of perceptions and preferences concerning the scope and content of the concept, both among supporters and among detractors. These differences in understanding, moreover, were about core elements of the principle, not about shadings of interpretation or meaning. Clearly there was going to be little political convergence until something closer to conceptual clarity and coherence was achieved.

The phrase "responsibility to protect"—coined by the ICISS commission in 2001—had substantial appeal, both as a rallying cry and as a powerful reminder of the obligations that come with state sovereignty. But the words meant different things to different people. Whose responsibility was at the core of the concept: that of the state

[9] It is striking, in that regard, how often the most influential figures in debates among the Member States at the UN are not the ones who give the most dynamic and compelling speeches. Sometimes more modest diplomats have a keener "sense of the house" and ultimately prove to be more persuasive, as well as less threatening to their colleagues.

to protect its people or that of the international community to respond effectively when it fails to do so? The 2005 Outcome Document appeared to embrace both perspectives, as any broad-based strategy would be inclined to do. But most supporters seemed to favor one perspective or the other. To some, RtoP was a more sophisticated and nuanced form of humanitarian intervention and hence should be judged by whether it would help to spur vigorous responses, particularly military ones, by the international community to atrocity crimes. To others—including this author—the key 2005 provision was the pledge by the heads of state and government to protect populations by preventing the four crimes—genocide, war crimes, ethnic cleansing, and crimes against humanity—and their incitement. From this perspective, the use of "protect" was a bit of a misnomer, since the Summit leaders stressed prevention as the key to protection. Some might have believed that it would have been more accurate to call the concept "the responsibility to prevent."

These differences in emphasis in some respects echoed the debate spurred by then Secretary-General Kofi Annan in the late 1990s on humanitarian intervention. He posed to the Member States the quandary of having to choose between legality and morality if the Security Council failed to authorize military intervention in extreme cases of violence against populations.[10] A number of Member States, including key developing countries, underscored in the debate following Annan's September 1999 statement to the General Assembly along these lines that they rejected the very premise of his dilemma.[11] To them, it represented little more than a benign facade for old-fashioned imperialist intervention by powerful northern countries in the global south. This premise was as divisive in 2007 as it had been eight years before. The Kofi Annan-inspired and Canadian-sponsored ICISS project had been intended to find a fresh way out of this political and conceptual dilemma. The creative and powerful result was the phrase "the responsibility to protect." Yet the opening sentence of the Commission's report declared that its subject was humanitarian intervention.[12] Much of the report was devoted to just war guidelines for the use of force and the very title of the Commission suggested that it would address the tensions between international intervention and state sovereignty—exactly the core point of contention in the Assembly in 1999. This ambiguity was not lost on skeptics. And it fostered divisions among supporters as well. Was RtoP supposed to be an antidote for humanitarian intervention or its re-emergence in more attractive attire?

Moreover, was the state to be seen primarily as the problem or the solution, the perpetrator or the protector? The 2001 ICISS report appeared to stress the former and the 2005 Summit the latter. In 2005, some ardent proponents of the 2001 version of

[10] For a collection of his speeches on that theme, see THE QUESTION OF INTERVENTION: STATEMENTS BY THE SECRETARY-GENERAL (United Nations, December 1999).

[11] See UN GAOR, 54th Sess., 8th and 9th plen. mtgs., UN Docs. A/54/PV.8 and A/54/PV.9 (Sept, 22, 1999).

[12] The opening sentence of the Foreword reads: "This report is about the so-called 'right of humanitarian intervention': the question of when, if ever, it is appropriate for states to take coercive—and in particular military—actions against another state for the purpose of protecting people at risk in that other state." ICISS REPORT, op. cit., at vii.

RtoP labeled the Summit's repackaging "RtoP lite."[13] Others, including this author, found instead that a careful reading of the Outcome Document suggested that the Member States had actually added distinctions and nuances that would make RtoP a more useful and effective policy tool, as opposed to being relegated to the long list of good ideas that were never implemented. (These amendments to the ICISS approach are discussed in more depth below.) Tactically, if RtoP was all about generating an international response to abuses by the state, how far was its implementation going to proceed in the United Nations, the pre-eminent inter-state body? Had states been the only perpetrators of such crimes? Or had armed groups and terrorists also committed such crimes? Why should they be excused from responsibility and accountability for their actions in such cases?

Success, it is said, has many fathers (and mothers too), while failure is an orphan. So it may be a good sign that RtoP's lineage is so layered and so contested. On the humanitarian intervention side, Bernard Kouchner's pioneering advocacy of the duty (or right) to intervene (or interfere) in the 1980s was a seminal conceptual contribution.[14] Kofi Annan's statements of the late 1990s, noted above, built on this legacy and tested the notion of humanitarian intervention in a political and charter context. The ICISS report then made the critical conceptual advance of looking at the responsibility of the state in question as well as of the international community to respond in cases of state failure to protect. Its findings, in turn, relied heavily on the notion of sovereignty as responsibility, developed by Francis Deng and colleagues at the Brookings Institution when looking at African conflict in the mid-1990s.[15] Unfortunately, while the ICISS report devoted a short section to sovereignty as responsibility, it never cited the sources of the inspiration.[16] The genius of the ICISS report was its valiant effort to weave the two strands of divergent thought—humanitarian intervention and sovereignty as responsibility—into a single conceptual cloth with a catchy name. Though the concept has evolved and deepened since 2001, that remains a singular achievement.

Secretary-General Kofi Annan became a vocal proponent of RtoP, championing it in his report to the 2005 World Summit, just as his High-level Panel on Threats, Challenges and Change had the year before in its report.[17] Nevertheless, key Member States, especially from the Global South, were not convinced, judging from their comments in the Spring of 2005.[18] At that point, necessity became the mother of invention

[13] See, for instance, Thomas G. Weiss, Humanitarian Intervention: Ideas in action (Massachusetts: Polity, 2008), at 117.

[14] Mario Bettati and Bernard Kouchner, Le devoir d'ingérence (Denoel 1987).

[15] Francis M. Deng, Sadikiel Kimaro, Terrence Lyons, Donald Rothschild, and I. William Zartman, Sovereignty as Responsibility: Conflict Management in Africa (The Brookings Institution 1996).

[16] ICISS report, op. cit., at 13.

[17] Report of the Secretary-General, In Larger Freedom: Towards Development, Security and Human Rights for All, UN Doc. A/59/2005 (Mar. 21, 2005), 34–35, ¶132, 135; Report of the Secretary-General's High-Level Panel on Threats, Challenges, and Change, A More Secure World: Our Shared Responsibility, UN Doc. A/59/565 (Dec. 4, 2004), at 65–66, ¶199–203.

[18] See the statement by Ambassador Maged Abdelaziz, UN GAOR, 59th Sess., 86th plen. mtg., UN Doc. A/59/PV.86 (Apr. 6, 2005) at 13 and the statement by the Chairman of the Coordinating Bureau of the Non-Aligned Movement, Ambassador Radzi Rahman, on behalf of the Non-Aligned Movement at the Informal Meeting of the Plenary of the General Assembly Concerning the Draft

or at least of adaptation. During that creative period in the conceptual evolution of RtoP, it became apparent that various actors, each for its own set of reasons, came to play distinct but largely complementary roles in the development of a politically and operationally workable concept. The ICISS process had the comparative advantage of being free from political responsibilities and constraints, though its composition was geographically diverse. So its work was relatively creative. But it also had the weakness of its strength: its ideas did not have to be tested through multilateral political processes. The same could be said of the High-level Panel. The Summit, of course, was quite the opposite: consumed and defined by high-level political horsetrading, it was not known for creativity. At the Summit, the sustained advocacy of Kofi Annan, the co-chairs of the ICISS Commission, and a handful of Member States, including Canada, came face-to-face with the tough questions and concerns being posed by recalcitrant Member States. Even this all-star team of norm entrepreneurs and their Member State partners had to listen to the concerns of the skeptics and modify their vision to accommodate the skeptics to some extent. In this author's view, at least, the product of the subsequent bargaining process was a stronger, not weaker, RtoP.

Perhaps the most important advance was to limit the scope of application of RtoP to a limited and coherent set of crimes. According to Jean Ping, now Chairman of the African Union Commission but President of the General Assembly in the critical months up to September 2005, it was the Permanent Representative of Pakistan, Munir Akram, who had stressed that such a discrete list would have to be agreed if there was to be any chance of bringing key developing countries on board.[19] The ICISS report, quite frankly, could have been more precise on this score. This would have made its recommendations sound less hortatory and more operational. The relative specificity of the Summit's version of RtoP—applying it only to genocide, war crimes, ethnic cleansing, and crimes against humanity—helps to explain why it has been able to assume a more operational and policy character than the more over-arching and generic concept of human security. If RtoP were to apply to the effects of natural disasters, climate change, or chronic under-development, it would be very difficult to carve out operational, bureaucratic, or policy space for it in the UN's crowded agenda. Looking across the expanse of the UN system, which entity or agency/program head could have assumed RtoP leadership if it had such a broad, crosscutting character? The turf problems could well have been endless.

A more expansive definition and scope for RtoP might well have encountered additional political hurdles as well. As Secretary-General Ban put it, "extending the principle to cover other calamities . . . would undermine the 2005 consensus and stretch the concept beyond recognition."[20] The agreed scope of RtoP was tested when Bernard Kouchner, then French Foreign Minister, and others, contended that the government of Myanmar's slow humanitarian response to Cyclone Nargis in

Outcome Document (Jun. 21, 2005), http://www.un.int/Malaysia/NAM/nam210605.html (accessed Jan. 24, 2011).

[19] Report by the International Peace Institute, the Office of the UN Special Adviser on the Prevention of Genocide, and the InterAfrica Group, The Responsibility to Protect (RtoP) and Genocide Prevention in Africa (International Peace Institute, June 2009), Annex II, at 11.

[20] Secretary-General Defends, Clarifies, "Responsibility to Protect" at Berlin Event, op. cit.

May 2008 constituted an RtoP situation (as discussed further below).[21] The negative reactions of many countries, including of those in the region, to assigning an RtoP label to such a situation appeared to confirm the advisability of maintaining the Secretary-General's narrow but deep approach.[22] In terms of early warning, assessment, and messaging, the grouping of these four crimes has worked well operationally, as well as conceptually and politically, because the other three crimes and violations can be precursors to genocide.

The Summit language added the responsibility to prevent the incitement of these crimes and violations, something missing from the ICISS report. This, too, has been very helpful to our efforts to implement RtoP in practice. Incitement is something one can usually see or hear, as mass crimes such as these generally require the mass mobilization of populations against particular minority groups within the society. The latter are both dehumanized and, frequently, accused of unfairly enjoying certain social or economic advantages not available to the majority of the population. Over the years, much of the work of the Secretary-General's Special Adviser on the Prevention of Genocide has revolved around trying to end incitement, as this is seen as one of the surest routes to the prevention of acts of genocide.

In another operationally helpful step, the Summit agreed that the responsibility to protect extends to all populations within the territory of the state. This would logically include refugees, the internally displaced, and immigrants, whether legal or illegal. Since these crimes are often identity-based, a point often made by Francis Deng, the Secretary-General's Special Adviser on the Prevention of Genocide, the more inclusive coverage matters. The ICISS Commission had been a little loose on this point as well, repeatedly referring to the need to protect "citizens" in its report.[23] The Outcome Document also put a bit more emphasis on the role of regional organizations in implementing RtoP than had the Commission. This, too, is a plus in making the concept operational, given the critical role that neighboring countries and transnational civil society groups can play in such situations. In general, the United Nations has become more accustomed and even dependent on working with regional and sub-regional partners on policy implementation on a host of subjects. As the Secretary-General's report for the 2011 informal interactive dialogue in the General Assembly underscores, this would appear to be the wave of the future for RtoP as well.[24]

[21] See, for example, the remarks of Bernard Kouchner, in *Myanmar Faces Pressure to Allow Major Aid Effort*, N.Y. Times, May 8, 2008; Lloyd Axworthy and Allan Rock, *Responsibility to Protect? Yes*, Globe and Mail, May 9, 2008; Ramesh Thakur, Should *The UN Invoke the Responsibility to Protect?*, Globe and Mail, May 8, 2008; Ivo Daalder and Paul Stares, *The UN's Responsibility to Protect*, I.H.T., May 13, 2008. For a balanced assessment, see Asia-Pacific Centre on the Responsibility to Protect, Cyclone Nargis and the Responsibility to Protect, Myanmar/Burma Briefing No. 2 (Brisbane, Australia, 2008).

[22] Secretary-General Defends, Clarifies, "Responsibility to Protect" at Berlin Event, op. cit.

[23] ICISS Report, op. cit., at viii, 13, 15–16, 34, 49, and 75.

[24] Report of the Secretary-General, THE ROLE OF REGIONAL AND SUBREGIONAL ARRANGEMENTS IN IMPLEMENTING THE RESPONSIBILITY TO PROTECT, UN Doc. A/65/877-S/2011/393 (June 28, 2011). To date, there has been relatively little scholarly or journalistic attention focused on what individual states, regional or sub-regional arrangements, or civil society groups are doing to implement the responsibility to protect. Such studies will be needed to

In the Summit Outcome, the heads of state and government also pledged to "support the United Nations in establishing an early warning capability."[25] On the surface, this might appear to be little more than the endorsement of an obviously essential component of effective prevention. However, given the political opposition to such steps in the past, this was a significant step forward. For instance, the 2000 Brahimi report of the Panel on Peace Operations called for the establishment of an ECPS (Executive Committee on Peace and Security) Information and Strategic Analysis Secretariat (EISAS) to "create and maintain integrated databases on peace and security issues, distribute that knowledge efficiently within the United Nations system, generate policy analyses, formulate long-term strategies for ECPS and bring crises to the attention of the ECPS leadership."[26] Though widely seen as a sensible step forward in terms of expanding Secretariat capacity for conflict prevention, this proposal has never been implemented due to political opposition along with some bureaucratic resistance.

The inclusion, in paragraph 140, of an unequivocal statement of support for the mission of the Special Adviser for the Prevention of Genocide had two positive effects in terms of implementing RtoP. Politically, it helped lay the groundwork for generating Member State support for the merger of the work of the two Special Advisers, something that is moving forward smartly, as discussed below. Conceptually, it acknowledged that genocide prevention was an essential part of the RtoP agenda and that looking at all four crimes and violations would be helpful for the world body's ongoing efforts to prevent genocide. It was an early recognition of the symbiotic relationship between these two mandates, something we now see in practice on a regular and consistent basis.[27]

In paragraph 139 of the Outcome Document, "the need for the General Assembly to continue consideration of the responsibility to protect" was asserted. Some Member States that remain unpersuaded about the value of RtoP suggest that this language implies that this is not yet a fully accepted concept and that it requires further conceptual development in the Assembly. Others see this phrase as a bid by the General Assembly to keep a prominent role in the implementation process that some fear will be dominated by the rival Security Council. A number of advocates have fretted that this provision is an invitation for trouble down the road. From the outset, my view has been, rather, that these words offer a prime opportunity to keep the question before the Member States as a whole, to give them a fuller sense of ownership of the concept, to identify and address areas of ambiguity, and to carry out the kind of interactive development of the concept and its implementation posited at the outset of this chapter. It would be a mistake, in this author's view, to allow RtoP to be wholly identified with or captured by either the Assembly or the Council. Each principal organ—including the Secretariat—has its comparative advantage in the division of labor. The Assembly has obvious advantages as a forum of the whole for normative development

supplement and complement the accounts of the struggles to implement RtoP at the United Nations and to give a fuller and truer picture of the process of its normative and operational development.

[25] UN Doc. A/RES/60/1, ¶138.

[26] UN Doc. S/2000/809 (Aug. 21, 2000) at xi, 12–13.

[27] In an August 2007 letter to the President of the Security Council, the Secretary-General noted that his two Special Advisers on these subjects would "share an office and support staff." UN Doc. S/2007/721 (Dec. 7, 2007).

and the building of broad political support, while the Council's discrete size, working methods, and powers make it a much readier operational player in specific crisis situations.

As discussed below, there is reason to believe that the scheduling of annual RtoP debates or dialogues in the General Assembly, each preceded by a report by the Secretary-General, is having just these effects: more understanding, more refinement of the concept, and more political support over time. Personally, it has provided additional chances to hear the views, concerns, and suggestions of the Member States. It has been a process of learning through listening, as well as through doing. Ironically, there is reason to believe that the first of these informal interactive dialogues, in July 2009, was convened by the president of the General Assembly in part to highlight the concerns of RtoP skeptics. However, it may well have served instead to rally supporters of the concept.[28]

Three other conceptual/political points, the first two flagged earlier, deserve further elaboration. The first is the decision to include non-state armed groups in the Secretary-General's approach to RtoP. The second is the scope of the RtoP toolkit and the role coercive military force plays in it. The third is the use of three pillars to define the Secretary-General's strategy and how they differ from the three elements of the ICISS approach.

Neither the ICISS report nor the Summit Outcome Document included non-state actors either as potential perpetrators of such crimes or as having RtoP responsibilities. Early RtoP formulations focused solely on the state. That seemed to me to be a substantial omission, and one out step with the times. The International Criminal Court (ICC) and regional tribunals had sought to hold individual actors—whether or not they were government officials—accountable for their gross violations of human rights and humanitarian standards. Groups such as the Revolutionary United Front (RUF) in Sierra Leone and the Lord's Resistance Army in the Great Lakes region of Africa had committed terrible atrocities. In the former case, international forces had been required to assist the government in resisting the RUF's advances and in returning order to the country. In Secretary-General Ban's words, it was a clear case of the international community acting "to help States succeed, not just to react once they have failed to meet their prevention and protection obligations."[29] It was a case that featured a coercive, Chapter VII, military intervention with the consent of the host government.[30] Such a scenario had not been addressed before either by RtoP supporters or opponents. In addition, a number of terrorist attacks against innocent civilians have caused sufficient loss of life to be considered RtoP cases. True, adopting such a

[28] See the Global Centre on the Responsibility to Protect, Implementing the Responsibility to Protect: The 2009 General Assembly Debate: An Assessment, available at globalr2p.org/media/pdf/GCR2P General Assembly Debate Assessment.pdf and the International Coalition for the Responsibility to Protect (ICRtoP), Report on the General Assembly Plenary Debate on the Responsibility to Protect, available at responsibilitytoprotect.org/ICRtoPGAdebate.pdf. For this author's statement at the outset of that dialogue, see http://www.ipinst.org/images/pdfs/luck_ga_statement23july2009.pdf (accessed Feb. 2011).

[29] Secretary-General Defends, Clarifies, "Responsibility to Protect" at Berlin Event, UN Doc. SG/SM/11701 (Jul. 15, 2008).

[30] Report of the Secretary-General, implementating the responsibility to protect, UN Doc. A/63/677 (Jan. 12, 2009), at 19, ¶42.

stance probably yielded some political benefits, but instead it was the compelling logic of such cases that led us to add this new wrinkle to what had been agreed in 2005. As expected, the Member States have been largely supportive of this amendment to the 2005 agreement.

The most tendentious dimension of RtoP in 2001, 2005, and 2011 remains the potential use of coercive force across borders and without consent in severe RtoP emergencies, as in Libya. The old debates over humanitarian intervention have been finessed and in some ways replaced by a more positive and forward-looking RtoP agenda, but they have not entirely disappeared. Nor should they. Both the 2005 Outcome Document and the subsequent strategy of Secretary-General Ban underscore that the organization of coercive force, if approved by the Security Council, cannot be ruled out. It should be an integral part of any broad-based and effective RtoP strategy at the United Nations. The question of where it fits in the RtoP toolkit, however, has been subject to considerable debate, even among supporters. Part of the conceptual problem, it seemed to me, was an overemphasis on military force as the centerpiece of RtoP. The ICISS report reinforced that message by focusing so much attention on the proposed guidelines for the use of force and on Security Council decision-making.

The problem, in other words, was less with seeing the military option as a piece of the puzzle than with treating it as the puzzle itself. Too little room was left for a serious consideration of the much wider range of policy tools available to the UN, especially under Chapters VI and VIII of the Charter. To me, one of the keys to effective policy-making is to keep as many options open for as long as possible in order to maintain flexibility in the face of changing and unpredictable circumstances. That is very much the course followed by Secretary-General Ban in enunciating his RtoP strategy. It was clear, as well, that historically there have been very few cases of military intervention for humanitarian purposes. Humanitarian intervention has existed far more in theory than in fact. So it would make little sense to base one's approach to implementing the responsibility to protect on the least likely scenario, especially if targeted, broad-based, and vigorous preventive efforts, including naming and shaming, have a chance of avoiding such difficult choices in the first place.

For me, one of the more challenging pieces of the conceptual puzzle was how to package the 2005 Outcome in a more compelling and coherent manner. As a negotiated text, it needed to be deconstructed to get a better sense of how the diverse pieces should relate to each other. The three elements of the ICISS report—the responsibility to prevent, the responsibility to respond, and the responsibility to rebuild—had not been employed by the Summit leaders. The exact reasons are not known, but it would appear that there was some discomfort that such a scenario might be geared to the use of force or sanctions in the response phase. This could be why a rebuilding phase would then be needed. The heads of state and government in 2005 apparently were more concerned with who decides, who has authority, and who has responsibility. Any international action would have to be in full conformity with the Charter, while the ICISS report is somewhat ambivalent about this when a robust response is needed.

In my view, the summit-level pledge at the outset of paragraph 138 of the Outcome Document—to protect by preventing the four crimes and violations and their incitement—should be taken very seriously and every effort should be devoted to reminding leaders of those obligations. Without widespread respect for this core provision, there would be little chance to make the rest of the package work. Moreover, it should be stressed that these are ongoing responsibilities that cannot be sequenced or delegated.[31] This would become Pillar One of the Secretary-General's strategy.

At various points in paragraphs 138 and 139 there are references to assisting or helping states meet their RtoP responsibilities. For the UN system, this was a natural. So the concurrent and ongoing responsibility of the international community to help states protect their populations became Pillar Two. It was recognized this could include military assistance in some cases, though this would probably not be frequent. Two examples of military assistance were noted in the Secretary-General's report. One was the preventive deployment of peacekeepers, as in the Former Yugoslav Republic of Macedonia in the 1990s. A second possibility would be a Chapter VII military response with the consent of a government that is battling for control of its territory with armed groups that are committing one or more of the four atrocity crimes identified in the Outcome Document. The case of Sierra Leone is noted above.

A more common application of the second pillar, however, would undoubtedly take the form of civilian or institutional capacity-building of one sort or another. At the world body, this entails mainstreaming an RtoP perspective in the work of a wide range of UN agencies, programs, funds, and departments, a process that is still in its early stages. But regional bodies, national governments, civil society, and the private sector could also be involved. The final sentence of paragraph 139 is suggestive about the preventive value of such efforts. "We also intend to commit ourselves, as necessary and appropriate, to helping States build capacity to protect their populations from genocide, war crimes, ethnic cleansing and crimes against humanity and to assisting those which are under stress before crises and conflicts break out." This would require either identifying states "under stress" and/or having them come forward to seek such assistance. Several states have already suggested that events in their past and/or their concerns about a repetition in the future would make themselves prime candidates for such capacity building and assistance. As this author has often noted, however, we are still in a learning stage about which kinds of capacity-building would be most helpful under which circumstances. No two situations are identical, so it would be counter-productive to try to devise and impose a rigid, global template that does not take into account the distinct needs, experiences, and characteristics of each society. This is likely to be both a top-down and bottom-up learning process for all concerned. Here, much more case specific research and analysis is needed.

The Third Pillar (response) is equally important. In 2005, the heads of state and government asserted that "we are prepared to take collective action, in a timely and decisive manner, through the Security Council, in accordance with the Charter,

[31] This distinction is not always observed. For example, in the 2010 U.S. National Security Strategy it is stated that in endorsing RtoP the United States has "recognized that the primary responsibility for preventing genocide and mass atrocity rests with sovereign governments, but that their responsibility passes to the broader international community when sovereign governments themselves commit genocide or mass atrocities, or when they prove unable or unwilling to take necessary action to prevent or respond to such crimes inside their borders." (Washington, D.C.: The White House, May 2010), at 48, http://www.whitehouse.gov/sites/default/files/rss_viewer/national_security_strategy.pdf (accessed Feb. 2011). While it is most welcome that the United States would include RtoP in its national security strategy, it seems unhelpful to assume that states can shed their responsibilities by failing to meet them. These responsibilities, according to the Secretary-General's strategy and the pledges made at the 2005 Summit, are enduring ones.

including Chapter VII, on a case-by-case basis and in cooperation with relevant regional organizations as appropriate, should peaceful means be inadequate and national authorities are manifestly failing to protect their populations from genocide, war crimes, ethnic cleansing, and crimes against humanity." In his January 2009 report, the Secretary-General offered a raft of ways that a "timely and decisive" response might be manifested. From the outset, he has called for "an early and flexible response, tailored to the specific needs of each situation."[32] His report is not shy about military options, whose exclusion would severely weaken any RtoP strategy, but they should be considered as part of a much wider set of policy alternatives. This is for pragmatic, as well as political, reasons. Policymakers should be able to call on a wide and agile toolkit, as noted above. They should not be bound by pre-packaged scenarios or sequences for the employment of the various policy instruments available to them under the Charter.

It may be useful for independent experts to weigh and pose various guidelines for Security Council decision-making, as the ICISS report did. This may provide a means for measuring and assessing the Council's performance. However, it should be recognized that the founders of the United Nations felt that the Council should act as a political body, unencumbered by guidelines or checklists beyond the purposes, principles, and provisions of the Charter.[33] They favored adaptability to changing circumstances over detailed rules or standards for the Council's choices. For over 65 years of practice, of course, the members of the Security Council have studiously avoided any such constraints on their collective decision-making process.

From the beginning of my work with the Secretary-General, it has been evident that some RtoP advocates see the first two pillars as central, while others favor the third. To me, each of the three is essential to a balanced and effective strategy. Using an architectural metaphor, if the three supporting pillars are of different lengths, then the whole RtoP edifice would lean one way or another, threatening to fall over. If the three pillars are of different strengths, then the structure could easily implode. Here, once again, the conceptual, political, and operational dimensions of RtoP's development converge.

III. THE INSTITUTIONAL AND OPERATIONAL CHALLENGES

We did not have the luxury of setting institutional and operational questions aside until the conceptual and political ones had been fully answered. Three sets of realities intruded on any illusions of being able to sequence the work. First, as discussed at the outset of the chapter, was the realization of the interdependent and interlocking nature of these various pieces of the puzzle. None could be properly addressed without reference to the others. Second, world events would not permit such an orderly and leisurely work plan. Neither the post-election violence in Kenya nor the claim that the slow response of Myanmar authorities to the ravages of Cyclone

[32] Secretary-General Defends, Clarifies, "Responsibility to Protect" at Berlin Event, op. cit.

[33] Edward C. Luck, "A Council for All Seasons: The Creation of the Security Council and Its Relevance Today," The UN Security Council and War: The Evolution of Thought and Practice Since 1945 (Vaughan Lowe, Adam Roberts, Jennifer Welsh, and Dominik Zaum, eds., Oxford University Press, 2008), 62–85.

Nargis constituted an RtoP situation could be ignored or left to another day. Third, the very act of appointing a Special Adviser on RtoP matters raised a number of acute institutional, as well as political, issues that had to be addressed early on.

In retrospect, the situations in Kenya and Myanmar appear like bookends that helped to shape and define the UN's early operational development of RtoP. There was no doubt that the world body would be heavily engaged in trying to prevent the post-election violence in Kenya in early 2008 from escalating. Among other factors, Nairobi was the UN's fourth capital, after New York, Geneva, and Vienna, and a major hub of international commercial and inter-governmental activity. From an RtoP perspective, both sides following the disputed election appeared to be inciting violence based on tribal identity as well as on political affiliation. It was a toxic combination. The scale and nature of the violence posed a real danger of widespread ethnic cleansing if it was allowed to fester and spread throughout the country.

On the other hand, the active efforts of the African Union, its chief mediator, former UN Secretary-General Kofi Annan, and major external powers, as well as the United Nations, to defuse the violence by forging a political deal offered some grounds for cautious optimism, as long as the violence was not allowed to swell out of control, hardening the political and identity-based battle lines. To me, this appeared to be a classic opportunity to apply RtoP principles in a preventive mode. Following a meeting of his Policy Committee—the closest thing to a UN system-wide cabinet—Secretary-General Ban decided that the world body would address the conflict from an RtoP perspective. Kofi Annan later declared that he also saw his ultimately successful mediation efforts through an RtoP lens.[34] This permitted the United Nations and the African Union, as well as other actors, to deliver directly and personally the same message to the leaders of both sides of the dispute: cease the incitement of atrocity crimes and restrain your supporters from committing such crimes, for impunity is not what it used to be and the international community, as well as your own people, will hold you accountable if further atrocities occur.[35] For whatever combination of reasons, these appeals and warnings among them, the incitement and violence ebbed and an uneasy political arrangement was achieved.

If the Kenyan case was suggestive of RtoP's preventive potential, the situation in Myanmar following Cyclone Nargis in May 2008, just a few months later, offered a note of caution about possible pressures to extend its scope beyond what had been agreed at the 2005 Summit. French Foreign Minister Kouchner urged the international community to treat the regime's refusal to permit most humanitarian groups into the country to assist the victims as an RtoP violation.[36] In doing so, he arguably echoed the spirit of the 2001 ICISS report. Gareth Evans, on the other hand, contended that it was premature to label it an RtoP situation, but that if the refusal to permit substantial assistance to reach those affected by the cycle persisted, then it could constitute a crime against

[34] Roger Cohen, *How Kofi Annan Rescued Kenya*, The New York Review of Books, vol. 55, no. 13 (August 14,2008).

[35] Statement attributable to the Spokesman for the Secretary-General on the Situation in Kenya (Jan. 11, 2008), http://www.un.org/apps/sg/sgstats.asp?nid=2947 (accessed Feb. 2011).

[36] Bernard Kouchner in Seth Mydans, *Myanmar Faces Pressure to Allow Major Aid Effort*, N.Y. Times, May 8, 2008.

humanity.[37] My view, however, was that this case simply fell outside of what the heads of state and government intended when they embraced the responsibility to protect in 2005. Moreover, it seemed to me that well-established human rights norms and widely accepted principles of humanitarian assistance and internal displacement governed in such a situation, with an RtoP banner adding little other than political controversy that could actually distract from a single-minded focus on helping those in need.[38]

As noted earlier, our nascent efforts to build political support for RtoP, especially in the developing world, would have been irreparably undermined if we had violated our "narrow but deep" rule at the first opportunity. This would have been doubly so if it had appeared that we were doing so at the behest of the Foreign Minister of one of the permanent members of the Security Council. A number of developing countries, it should be recalled, were deeply suspicious that RtoP principles would be captured and misused by powerful countries of the North as a device to justify intervention in the Global South. In the end, Foreign Minister Kouchner decided that this was not an RtoP situation after all and Secretary-General Ban Ki-moon was able to persuade the leaders of the Myanmar regime to open the door a crack to permit a somewhat larger influx of international assistance.[39] Some recent studies suggest that the people of Myanmar had developed their own capacities and techniques for self-protection, so that they were not entirely dependent on international assistance to try to hold down the loss of life from Cyclone Nargis.[40]

The spring of 2008 was also marked by an intensive effort to find common ground across the UN system on how to advance the RtoP agenda. If the Secretariat cannot present a united front on such potentially divisive issues, then the chances of gaining broad political support among the 193 Member States declines markedly. Disgruntled entities in the Secretariat are apt to form informal blocking coalitions with skeptical Member States in such cases. From a bureaucratic perspective, big new ideas, such as the responsibility to protect, can be threatening, especially if they come with wide backing from the public, NGOs, and, especially, the Secretary-General. RtoP's crosscutting nature, moreover, meant that its implementation could have programmatic and institutional implications for many aspects of the UN's work, from human rights, humanitarian affairs, political affairs, and legal affairs, to peacekeeping and peacebuilding.

[37] Gareth Evans, *Facing Up to Our Responsibilities*, The Guardian, May 12, 2008.

[38] See Edward C. Luck, testimony, "International Disaster Assistance: Policy Options," Subcommittee on International Development, Foreign Assistance, Economic Affairs and International Environmental Protection, Senate Committee on Foreign Relations (Jun. 17, 2008). See, also, Lloyd Axworthy and Allan Rock, Responsibility to Protect? Yes, Globe and Mail, May 9, 2008); Ramesh Thakur, Should the UN Invoke the Responsibility to Protect?, Globe and Mail, May 8, 2008); Ivo Daalder and Paul Stares, The UN's Responsibility to Protect, I.H.T, May 13, 2008. For a balanced account of the various positions on this crisis, see Asia-Pacific Centre on the Responsibility to Protect, Cyclone Nargis and the Responsibility to Protect, Myanmar/Burma Briefing No. 2 (Brisbane, Australia, 2008).

[39] Bernard Kouchner, Le Monde, May 20, 2008. Briefing to the Security Council on Myanmar (Jul. 13, 2009), http://www.un.org/apps/sg/sgstats.asp?nid=3970 (accessed Feb. 2011)

[40] See, for example, Ashley South with Malin Perhult and Nils Carstensen, conflict and survival: self-protection in south-east burma, Asia Programme Paper ASP PP 2010/04 (London Chatham House, September 2010).

From the earliest discussions in the summer of 2007, it had been evident that the two Special Advisers on Genocide Prevention, Francis Deng, and on the responsibility to protect, this author, would need to work as much as possible as a team, given their overlapping and symbiotic, but distinct, mandates. Their work, in turn, would depend on close substantive and institutional relationships with the Office of the High Commissioner on Human Rights (OHCHR) and the Department of Political Affairs (DPA), as well as with the Office for the Coordination of Humanitarian Affairs (OCHA), the Department of Peacekeeping Operations (DPKO), and the Office of Legal Affairs (OLA). The implementation of the Second Pillar (assistance) would depend on the degree of buy-in of the United Nations Development Programme (UNDP) and other development and peacebuilding actors, including the Peacebuilding Support Office (PBSO), the World Bank, and many others inside and outside of the UN system. Also critical to implementing RtoP would be other entities mandated to address parts of the broader human protection agenda, such as UNICEF (the United Nations Children's Fund), the Special Representative for Children and Armed Conflict, the High Commissioner for Refugees (UNHCR), the Special Representative on Sexual Violence and Conflict, and others in this growing sector.[41]

In addition to scores of bilateral consultations with these entities, in the spring of 2008 I convened a Contact Group to explore the possibility of developing An Agreed Conceptual Framework for the Responsibility to Protect. To no one's surprise, it had become apparent that the UN Secretariat was every bit as susceptible to varying understandings of what RtoP was all about as had been the Member States, NGOs, independent experts, and scholars. Quite rightly, many of these groups felt that their ongoing work was already making significant contributions to protecting populations from the four atrocity crimes. A number of them had extensive presences in the field, along with sensitive relationships with host country governments and vulnerable populations. They needed assurances both that RtoP would bring added value and that voicing RtoP principles would do no harm. The effective operationalization of RtoP, moreover, would depend on early warning and assessment, things that would require access to information and analysis of local situations developed by the multiple UN entities with extensive field operations. The Office of the Special Adviser for the Prevention of Genocide had developed just such arrangements with most of these groups within the UN system, but adding an RtoP dimension would multiply the information and assessment needs of the Office.

Once there was systemwide agreement on a Conceptual Framework, operational arrangements could follow. After many weeks of intensive and instructive roundtable discussions and multiple drafts, agreement on a detailed Conceptual Framework was completed. This, in turn, provided a basis for me to draft the Secretary-General's first major statement on his vision of the responsibility to protect. Delivered in Berlin in mid-July 2008, it was well received by most Member States and NGOs, as well as by the Secretariat.[42] Many who heard or read the statement no doubt felt some sense

[41] UN Doc. SG/SM/13385, op. cit.

[42] Secretary-General Defends, Clarifies, "Responsibility to Protect" at Berlin Event, op. cit. Berlin seemed an apt location for this initial address, as it served to remind people that mass atrocities can occur—and have occurred—in all regions of the world and in countries at different levels of economic and social development.

of ownership, as its key points reflected many months of consultation with all of these stakeholders. More consultations followed over the summer and fall of 2008, as I wove the main elements of the speech and the Agreed Conceptual Framework into the more elaborate form of the Secretary-General's report on *Implementing the Responsibility to Protect*, which was published in January 2009 after several rounds of comments from throughout the Secretariat.[43]

During the critical months before and after the publication of the report, roundtable meetings were convened by the Stanley Foundation, the International Peace Institute, the Global Centre on the Responsibility to Protect and the Mexican Foreign Ministry, the Permanent Missions of Canada and Rwanda to the United Nations, as co-chairs of the RtoP Friends Group, the Permanent Mission of Egypt to the United Nations, the Permanent Mission of Morocco to the United Nations, and the governments of Switzerland, Argentina, and Tanzania, among others.[44] Our goal was to be as open and inclusive in the process of consultations as possible, delivering identical messages to skeptics and advocates alike. We put a premium on consistency, even redundancy, in pursuing a "no surprises" approach to developing the political and operational dimensions of RtoP. It would be difficult to move the responsibility to protect from words to deeds if important stakeholders were still uncertain of the shape and scope of the concept. And we worked hard to refute the claims that RtoP threatened sovereignty or was a northern creation being forced on the Global South. As Secretary-General Ban put it, "the responsibility to protect has emerged from the soil, spirit, experience, and institutions of Africa." His report "seeks to situate the responsibility to protect squarely under the United Nations roof and within our Charter, where it belongs. By developing fully United Nations strategies, standards, and processes for implementing the responsibility to protect, we can discourage States or groups of States from misusing these principles for inappropriate purposes."[45]

The subsequent debate in the General Assembly in late July 2009 on the Secretary-General's report was lively, prolonged, and largely positive. It suggested both that we were on the right track and that a relative handful of Member States retained deep suspicions about the concept. In September the Assembly adopted, by consensus, a thin RtoP resolution that took note of the Secretary-General's report and called on the Assembly to continue its consideration of RtoP, as stipulated in paragraph 139.[46] The signal seemed to be that the operationalization of RtoP could continue, but cautiously and prudently—as it seemed wise to make haste slowly. There had been little criticism of the steps to establish a joint office on the prevention of genocide and the responsibility to protect, though no funding or posts had yet been sought from the General Assembly for that purpose. More discussion was needed within the Secretariat, in any case, on how the joint office would function and fit into existing structures in

[43] Report of the Secretary-General, Implementing the Responsibility to Protect, op. cit.

[44] See, for example, Actualizing the Responsibility to Protect (Muscatine, Iowa: The Stanley Foundation, June 2008), http://www.stanleyfoundation.org/publications/report/UNND808.pdf (accessed Feb. 2011).

[45] Secretary-General, Upcoming Debate on Responsibility to Protect Not About History, But Character of the United Nations, Secretary-General Tells General Assembly, UN Doc. SG/SM/12374 (Jul. 21, 2009).

[46] G.A. Res. 63/308, UN Doc. A/Res/63/308 (Sept. 14, 2009).

emergency situations. If there was to be "timely and decisive" collective action when "national authorities are manifestly failing to protect their populations," as called for in paragraph 139, the early warning and information assessment functions of the joint office would have to be highly developed without confusing the crisis analysis being developed by other parts of the system at the same time. Following more rounds of high-level consultations within the Secretariat in the fall of 2009 and winter of 2010, the Policy Committee met to consider a series of proposals in late March 2010.

These discussions, the largely encouraging reactions to his 2009 report and the support for a UN RtoP early warning capability expressed in paragraph 138 of the 2005 Summit Outcome Document provided a strong basis for some innovative proposals on early warning and assessment by the Secretary-General. These were contained in his subsequent report on those aspects of his RtoP strategy that I drafted in preparation for an August 2010 informal interactive dialogue in the General Assembly.[47] The relatively succinct report laid out the mandate for the joint office and its early warning and assessment function, described some gaps in the world body's existing capacities that the joint office could help to fill, and explained new emergency procedures, as follows:

> When the Special Advisers, based largely on information provided by, and in consultation with, other United Nations entities, conclude that a situation could result in genocide, war crimes, ethnic cleansing or crimes against humanity, they provide early warning to me and, through me, to the Security Council and other relevant intergovernmental organs. If the situation persists, and if national authorities are manifestly failing to protect their populations from these crimes, I will invoke new internal procedures to expedite and regularize the process by which the United Nations considers its response and its recommendations to the appropriate intergovernmental body or bodies. In such cases, I will ask the Special Advisers to convene an urgent meeting of key Under-Secretaries-General to identify a range of multilateral policy options, whether by the United Nations or by Chapter VIII regional arrangements, for preventing such mass crimes and for protecting populations. Such an emergency meeting will be prepared through a working level process convened by the Special Advisers, and the results, including the pros and cons of each option, will be reported promptly to me or, should I choose, to the Policy Committee. This is without prejudice to the role of the relevant United Nations entities, acting within their mandates, to bring any situation to my attention, and through me, to the Security Council and other relevant intergovernmental organs.

Such an emergency convening process, designed to present the Secretary-General with a range of policy options and the pros and cons of each course, is commonplace in national capitals. However, it had not existed previously in the UN system, which typically operates by consensus, setting aside policy differences before presenting group recommendations to the Secretary-General.

The generally upbeat tone of the General Assembly dialogue[48] led to a decision to finally approach the Assembly in the fall of 2010 for three new posts for the joint office

[47] Report of the Secretary-General, Early Warning, Assessment, and the Responsibility to Protect, UN Doc. A/64/864 (Jul. 14, 2010).

[48] For summaries of the August 9, 2010, informal General Assembly interactive dialogue on "Early Warning, Assessment, and the Responsibility to Protect," see the International Coalition for

and its broader RtoP function. The decision, however, was not an easy one given the continuing opposition to RtoP implementation by a determined and vocal minority of Member States, led by Venezuela, Nicaragua, and Cuba. Indeed, the debate, especially in the Assembly's Fifth Committee, proved to be every bit as contentious, layered, and drawn out as anticipated. In the end, however, all three posts were approved and the crucial vote on whether to delete the RtoP language from the Secretary-General's proposal turned out to be one-sided, with a four-to-one margin (68 to 17) favoring its retention.[49] Though the Assembly's approval of the joint office and the new posts was a milestone in the efforts to operationalize RtoP, there is no reason to believe that its adversaries are about to quit the field of battle. Both supporters and skeptics will be watching closely as the office continues to implement its mandate in specific situations. It will have to prove itself through practice.

As of February 2011, the two Special Advisers have taken joint positions on Kenya, the Democratic Republic of the Congo, Kyrgyzstan, Guinea, Côte d'Ivoire, Sudan, and Libya among others. In some cases, they have sought to shape the messages of the Secretary-General and other top UN officials, so that they would include RtoP considerations, such as warnings about incitement, the targeting of minorities, and other provocative actions, as well as reminders about the new age of accountability.[50] We have issued joint statements in several of these cases.[51] The joint office staff has continued to monitor these and a number of other situations of potential concern. As this author told the General Assembly informal interactive dialogue in 2010, "our goal should be early understanding, not just early warning. We need to understand why certain things are happening, not just what is happening." Hence, "we need a moving picture, not a snapshot. . . . Assessment entails understanding the mosaic not the pieces, the pattern not a single act."[52] What is needed, therefore, is early engagement and early understanding, not just early warning.

Seen in this larger context, the work of the joint office is part of a much wider enterprise that encompasses local and transnational civil society, regional and local experts, field-based organizations and groups, regional and sub-regional organizations, governments, and colleagues throughout the UN system. Each partner has a distinct set of insights, experiences, and judgments that can be helpful in trying to

the Responsibility to Protect at www.responsibilitytoprotect.org/Summary%20of%20EW%20dialogue%20on%209%20August%202010(2).pdf and the Global Centre for the Responsibility to Protect, see globalr2p.org/resources/(accessed Feb. 2011).

[49] There were, however, a large number of abstentions or absences, possibly because of the late hour or because many delegations objected to voting on substantive matters in the Fifth Committee, which is to address administrative and budgetary matters. For a useful account of the process, see the report of the Global Centre on the Responsibility to Protect, ACABQ AND FIFTH COMMITTEE NEGOTIATIONS ON THE JOINT OFFICE 2010, http://www.globalr2p.org/advocacy/index.php.

[50] UN Doc. SG/SM/13385, op. cit.

[51] To access the statements of the Special Advisers, see the website of the Office of the Special Adviser for the Prevention of Genocide, http://www.un.org/en/preventgenocide/adviser/statements.shtml (accessed Feb. 2011).

[52] Edward C. Luck, Special Adviser to the United Nations Secretary-General, General Assembly Informal Interactive Dialogue on Early Warning, Assessment, and the Responsibility to Protect (August 9, 2010), http://www.un.org/ga/president/64/thematic/responsibility/Luck.pdf (accessed Feb. 2011).

understand the unique dynamics of each society that may face a risk of atrocity crimes. Clearly, each situation has to be judged on its own merits and seen in the flow of its own history and internal dynamics. Modesty is in order in assuming the likely course of events in such cases. But it should not lead to timidity or undue hesitation on the part of the joint office, given its early warning and assessment responsibilities, as well as its strong preference for preventive action. Waiting can be a form of deciding, limiting options and potentially putting populations at risk.

At this early stage of implementing the responsibility to protect, there have been some encouraging signs, as well as several unanticipated challenges. On the plus side, the practice of RtoP to date in the cases cited above appears to be reinforcing rather than jeopardizing political support for the concept. It is our hope and expectation that the invocation of RtoP principles in appropriate situations will, over time, ease fears of its misuse and raise comfort levels across the board. On the other hand, a misjudgment on our part or evidence that our appeals are being ignored in difficult situations could undermine support for the larger RtoP enterprise. So far, this does not appear to be the case and there is reason to believe that the invocation of RtoP principles has had added value in the cases to date. But the final chapter has not been written in most of these situations and it remains to be seen whether RtoP has made much difference in a couple of the toughest and most stubborn cases, such as Darfur, the DRC, and Somalia. Within UN crisis deliberations, however, RtoP has gained a stronger foothold over the past year, as the need to prevent atrocity crimes and their incitement has become a regular feature of the decision-making process in the higher reaches of the Secretariat.

As expected, the Security Council has been cautious about employing precise RtoP language, usually preferring to use RtoP-like terminology instead. Important exceptions have been Security Council resolutions 1706 (2006) on Darfur and 1970 (2011) and 1973 (2011) on Libya.[53] While there was little opposition in the Council to the references to RtoP in the two resolutions on Libya, its association with the NATO-led use of force may have reinforced the belief of some members that the phrase "responsibility to protect" carries implications for their individual and collective obligation to respond robustly to situations where they would prefer a more cautious response.[54] Building bridges to the Council for a more focused interactive dialogue on the responsibility to protect has proven difficult, despite the encouraging progress along these lines with the General Assembly. In July 2011, the Assembly is expected to have an informal interactive dialogue on the regional and sub-regional dimensions of the Secretary-General's RtoP strategy, to be the subject of his next report. Given the prominent role of the Security Council in Chapter VIII of the Charter on regional arrangements, it would be awkward to limit that discussion to the Assembly alone. Despite the Council's caution toward RtoP, it should be acknowledged that it has

[53] Also, in a thematic resolution on the protection of civilians in armed conflict (UN Doc. S/RES/16April 74, 28, 2006), the Security Council reaffirmed the provisions of paragraphs 138 and 139 of the Outcome Document.

[54] Even in 2005, John Bolton, then U.S. Permanent Representative to the United Nations, expressed such reservations at the World Summit. See Edward C. Luck, Sovereignty, Choice, and the Responsibility to Protect, Global Responsibility to Protect, 1, 1 (2009), 10–21.

made impressive strides over the past decade in championing and operationalizing the wider human protection agenda of which RtoP is a part.

Less expected have been several challenges that have arisen with the more frequent incorporation of RtoP considerations in Secretariat decision-making. One is the need to develop clearer distinctions between conflict prevention and atrocity prevention.[55] Though this is not always the case, atrocities frequently occur in situations of armed conflict. In some situations, as in Rwanda in 1993–1994, concerns over sustaining the conflict resolution process appeared to trump the voices warning of a pending genocide. In several recent cases, such as Kenya, Guinea, South Sudan, Côte d'Ivoire, and Libya, the two agendas appeared to be mutually reinforcing. But a better understanding is needed of how these efforts interact in different kinds of situations. A second, and not unrelated, challenge is messaging: who should say what, and when should they say it? The Secretary-General has a host of Special Representatives, Advisers, and Envoys. Some have situation-specific mandates and others thematic ones, like children and armed conflict, sexual violence and armed conflict, genocide prevention, and RtoP. The coordination and sequencing of messages can be a complicated business in an unfolding crisis.

A third operational challenge has been distinguishing between situations where there are egregious and chronic human rights violations and those where a sudden escalation to atrocity crimes could be imminent. Sometimes the very chronic nature of the violations may make sudden changes in the situation, either of a positive or negative sort, less likely. Such cases may be intolerable from a human rights perspective, yet not ready candidates for attention by the joint office. Finally, it may be easier to predict that atrocities are likely in a particular place than to predict precisely when and how they will occur. In more than one situation over the past year, the trend line was evident enough but it was impossible to know what would spark the violence or how quickly it would escalate. Instigators try not to advertise their plans in advance, of course, though sometimes an intensification of acts of incitement can provide the needed clues.

As noted earlier, efforts to build capacity and to help states succeed are still at an early phase, as is the parallel process of mainstreaming RtoP throughout the UN system. For all the political buy-in for the first two pillars of the Secretary-General's strategy, their actual operationalization will take considerable time. Paradoxically, for all the controversy about the Third Pillar (response), arguably its implementation has actually proceeded more rapidly. Most of the specific cases cited above are ones in which the national authorities either have manifestly failed to protect or appear to be on the brink of failing to do so. These are emergency situations. They might well benefit from assistance and capacity building over time, but the immediate need is to help them avoid an RtoP meltdown. Most of the work of the joint office in those specific cases has involved early warning, assessment, working with partners, messaging, and naming and shaming. This is the stuff of Chapters VI and VIII of the Charter, not Chapter VII. However, in several of these cases, the Security Council, the African Union, or others have imposed political and economic sanctions on one or more

[55] This is raised in Edward C. Luck, The Responsibility to Protect: Growing Pains or Early Promise?, Ethics and International Affairs, 24, 4 (Winter 2010), 349–365.

parties to the conflict. This has not been done only to advance RtoP principles, but atrocity prevention has become part of the rationale for their retention. In Côte d'Ivoire, ECOWAS has threatened to intervene militarily. In several of these situations, the UN has deployed peacekeepers, sometimes with a Chapter VII mandate. These factors, once again, underscore the need to have a fuller understanding of the relationship between conflict prevention and atrocity prevention. In the early thinking about RtoP, the scenarios seemed to assume that atrocity prevention was the only concern and that the UN and regional organizations were not already engaged on the ground in these situations. Instead, we are often finding that RtoP forms another layer of international engagement in already complex situations.

So the learning process regarding RtoP implementation continues. It is not going to be a quick or simple process. We are learning, to some extent, by doing. Hopefully it will not be a course of trial and error, but one in which positive lessons are absorbed about what works when and where. As noted earlier, it is already proving to be both a top-down and bottom-up process, in which the UN is only one of many players and partners. Taken day by day, the results are not likely to appear dramatic or decisive. But seen over time, we may find that RtoP has proven to be a more essential element and a more useful instrument of the world's peace, security, human rights, and humanitarian agendas far sooner than anyone would have had the right to expect, even from the Olympian heights of the 2005 Summit.

PART II
REGIONAL PERSPECTIVES

6 Africa

Ademola Abass*

Africa has been widely credited with playing a pivotal role in the ultimate evolution of the Responsibility to Protect (RtoP) as an international norm.[1] The African Union (AU), in particular, has been eulogized for precociously enshrining certain principles of RtoP in Article 4(h) of its Constitutive Act. Nonetheless, several questions arise as

* Many thanks to my Research Assistants and Interns, Dominique Mystris and Morenike Olatunji, for their excellent work.

[1] For a general discussion on RtoP, *see* Alicia L. Bannon, *The Responsibility to Protect: The U N World Summit and the Question of Unilateralism*, 115 Yale L. J. 1157 (2005–2006); Matthew Kalkman, *Responsibility to Protect: A Bow Without an Arrow* Cambridge Student L. Rev. 75 (2009); Paul D. Williams, *From Non-Intervention to Non-Indifference: The Origins and Development of the African Union's Security Culture*, 106/423, African Affairs 253 (2007); Jeremy Sarkin, *The Role of the United Nations, the African Union and Africa's Sub-Regional Organizations in Dealing with Africa's Human Rights Problems: Connecting Humanitarian Intervention and the Responsibility to Protect* 53(1) Journal of African Law 1 (2009); Christopher C. Joyner, "*The Responsibility to Protect*": *Humanitarian Concern and the Lawfulness of Armed Intervention* 47 Va. J. Int'l L. 693 (2006–2007); Dan Kuwali, *The Conundrum of Conditions for Intervention under article 4(h) of the African Union Act*, 17 African Security Review 90 (2008); Louise Arbour, *The Responsibility to Protect as a Duty of Care in International Law and Practice* 34 Review of Int'l Studies 445 (2008); Teresa Chataway, *Towards Normative Consensus on Responsibility to Protect* 16 Griffith L. Rev. 193 (2007), Alex Bellamy, *The Responsibility to Protect–Five Years On* 24(2) Ethics and Int'l Aff. 143 (2010); Jutta Brunnée & Stephen Toope, *Norms, Institutions and UN Reform: The Responsibility to Protect* 21 Int'l L & Int'l Rel. 121 (2005–6); Damien Helly, *Africa, the EU and RtoP: Towards Pragmatic International Subsidiarity?* Internationale Politik und Gesellschaft, International Pol. & Soc., Friedrich-Ebert-Stiftung (01/2009); Alex Bellamy, *Conflict Prevention and the Responsibility to Protect* 14 Global Governance 135 (2008); Siobhán Wills, *Military Interventions on Behalf of Vulnerable Populations: The Legal Responsibilities of States and International Organizations engaged in Peace Support Operations* 9 J. Conflict & Sec. L. 387 (2004); Juan Garrigues, *The Responsibility to Protect: From an Ethical Principle to an Effective Policy* in La Realidad de la Ayuda (Intermón Oxfam, 2007).

to whether the notion of intervention, embodied by the AU Act, coincides with RtoP. In addition, this chapter considers the implementation of RtoP in Africa, given the preference of the 2005 World Summit for collective action under the UN Security Council. It is argued that while the AU, and, arguably, all regional collective security mechanisms, are empowered to implement RtoP under *certain* circumstances, several legal and policy constraints threaten RtoP in Africa.

In his 2009 *Report on Implementing the Responsibility to Protect* to the UN General Assembly,[2] Secretary-General Ban Ki-moon, observed:

While the Organization of African Unity emphasized non-intervention, its successor, the African Union, has stressed *non-indifference*. In 2000, *five years before* the 2005 World Summit endorsed the responsibility to protect, the Constitutive Act of the African Union provides, in article 4(h), for "the right of the Union to intervene in a Member State pursuant to a decision of the Assembly in respect to grave circumstances, namely: war crimes, genocide, and crimes against humanity . . . It made a clear a distinction between Member States, which were not to interfere "in the internal affairs of another" (article 4(g), and the Union, which could do so in response to the three "grave circumstances.")[3]

In a similar vein, while addressing a Round-Table High-Level Meeting of Experts on "The Responsibility to Protect in Africa"[4] in 2008, the AU Chairperson, Jean Ping, noted

[a]s you are no doubt aware, even *before the adoption* of the Outcome Document on the responsibility to protect, African states had already committed themselves to protect human rights and promote good governance in the continent even at the expense of using force as entrenched in article 4(h) of the Constitutive Act of the African Union.[5]

It is beyond doubt that the Constitutive Act of the African Union encompasses a radical vision of civilian protection in Africa, and that at the inception of the AU, African states embraced a fundamental change to the way their premier organization deals with the scourge of conflicts within the continent. The history of armed conflict in Africa, and the particularly irresponsive nature of the UN's collective security systems to the most brutal of these conflicts (recall the 1994 Rwandan genocide), makes the reorientation of the AU towards intervention in members' conflicts a twenty-first century necessity.

However, contrary to what a cursory read of the AU chairperson's statement quoted above might seemingly imply, African states did not fully embrace the idea of military intervention in their conflicts, either within the context of the negotiation of the AU itself, or during the 2005 World Summit of the UN General Assembly. During the discussion leading to the emergence of the AU, striking a balance between the rather antithetical desires, that the AU should be endowed to intervene in its members'

[2] A/63/677, Jan. 12, 2009.

[3] Emphasis added.

[4] Keynote Address by Jean Ping, Chairperson of the African Union Commission, Roundtable High-Level Meeting of Experts on "The Responsibility to Protect in Africa" Oct. 23, 2008.

[5] Emphasis added.

conflicts on the one hand, and that the Union's activities vis-à-vis its Member States should respect their sovereignty on the other hand, proved to be one of the most divisive issues on the agenda.

Similarly, during the 2005 World Summit of the General Assembly,[6] which led to the adoption of RtoP by the international community, opponents of military intervention, including several African states, introduced two legitimate fears: First, that such interventions could become a façade for meddlesomeness, a concern that was not unwarranted given the situation prevalent in the world around the time the Summit was held, specifically the wars in Iraq and Afghanistan. Secondly, a greater, yet related concern, several opposing states worried about the fate of sovereignty if a State, or group of States, were to be empowered to the point where, once certain thresholds were crossed, prudent action transforms into unfettered license to rain bombs and bullets on the territory of another state, all in the name of protecting humanity.[7] Although RtoP was eventually adopted by the World Summit—the fears of dissenting states having been arguably temporarily assuaged by the doctrinal distancing of RtoP from humanitarian intervention (see below)—considerable doubts linger as to whether there is or will be any real distinction between the two doctrines in practice, or whether, indeed, one is different, and differentiable, from the other.

What *modus operandi* the international community will ultimately favor in implementing RtoP, notwithstanding huge concerns over sovereignty remains, at the moment, largely conjectural; it is plausible, however, to anticipate that several actors will fall back on certain *modu vivendi* in the interim, in the hope that at the end of the day, human security will not be sacrificed due to the conceptual murkiness of RtoP. Whether such temporary measures did or did not play out (or should have played out) in the AU's intervention in Kenya is an interesting question, as indeed is the AU's intervention in the Darfur crisis; it is a query that invariably turns on a realistic interpretation of the principle embodied by the AU Act. But it is equally important to examine the *how*, *when*, and by *what* means the AU will implement RtoP in Africa.

As the organization believed to be the first to enunciate RtoP-like ideals in its constitutive instruments, even without the conceptual clarity and elaborateness of the World Summit Outcome Document, the AU practice, since 2002, offers the best opportunity to attempt to provide answers to the questions raised above. In Kenya and Darfur, the AU had situations which, if they do not qualify as RtoP scenarios, then *de minimis* they fall squarely within the parameters of Article 4(h).

It is important to set out a few caveats at the onset. While the implementation of RtoP is not a question of military intervention only and, in fact, this kind of measure is last resort, this chapter focuses principally on military actions for three main reasons. First, diplomatic measures, which are the preferred method for exacting pressure on States to comply with their international obligations, rarely achieve desired results. Secondly, considering that diplomatic measures do not threaten State sovereignty, they are naturally favored by some States that pursue them often while unleashing mass atrocities on their people simultaneously. Thirdly, since States, whether acting individually or collectively, do not require the authorization of the

6 *2005 World Summit Outcome*, A/RES/60/1, Sept. 15, 2005 [hereinafter WSOD].

7 *See* N. D. White, *The Legality of Bombing in the Name of Humanity* 5(1) J. Conf. Sec. L. 27 (2000).

ultimate guardian of RtoP, the Security Council, to deploy diplomatic measures, recourse to such measures can create tension between the Council and potential residual actors in RtoP implementation, such as regional organizations. As will be seen later, forcible implementation of RtoP by bodies other than the Security Council give rise to serious legal and policy issues.

Concerning the implementation of RtoP by African organizations—which is the focus of this chapter—the most attention is devoted to the African Union for several reasons. As far as the legality of regional implementation of RtoP is concerned, the same international legal rules govern the AU and all other organizations in Africa, as long as they are deemed regional; hence, analysis of international legal rules vis-à-vis the AU apply *mutantis mutandi* to African sub-regional organizations, also known as Regional Economic Communities (RECs). That said, some discussion of certain specific aspects of RECs which may be indispensable will certainly be entertained.

Finally, this chapter is not concerned with the historical evolution of RtoP as a concept, or any elaborate discussion of the concept of sovereignty, both themes having been covered by other chapters in this volume.

The overarching goal of this endeavor is to discuss the role of the AU in implementing RtoP in Africa, especially the relation of Article 4(h) of its Act to the principles of "non indifference" and "non-interference." It considers whether (African) regional organizations have a residual role in implementing RtoP, especially in light of the AU "Ezulwini Consensus" and the 2005 World Summit Outcome Documents. Additionally, the chapter briefly examines the relevance of the African Peace and Security Architecture (APSA), especially concerning the powers of the AU Peace and Security Council (PSC), and the Union's cooperation with RECs. Finally, the chapter examines the legality of regional implementation of RtoP under international law.

I. THE EMERGENCE OF THE AU: CRITICAL HISTORICAL CONTEXTS

It is pointless to rehash here the multitudinous challenges that rendered the OAU virtually irrelevant to the post-Cold War landscape in Africa. Suffice to say that by the turn of the twentieth century, the nasty wars in Liberia and Sierra Leone, to mention but a few, had convinced many African rulers that the OAU would be totally out of sync with the pace of events in Africa in the immediate future. The turning of a blind eye to Idi Amin's murderous regime in Uganda, the ignoring of Jean Bokassa's reign of terror in Central Africa, and the OAU's inglorious silence in the ascent of totalitarianism in many of its Member States had irreparably damaged the organization's meager reputation for seriousness before the multiple devastating civil wars of 1990s in respect of which the OAU was totally ineffective.

The process of revolutionizing conflict resolution in Africa, which was begun with the decisive Fourth Extraordinary Session of the organization's highest decision-making body, the Assembly of Heads of State and Government (AHOS or AU Assembly) in Sirte, Libya, September 8–9, 1999,[8] led to the establishment of the AU.

[8] *See* EAHG/Decl. (IV) Rev. 1, *Fourth Extraordinary Session of the Assembly of heads of State and Government*, Sept. 8–9, 1999, Sirte, Libya (on file with the author).

Although the Draft Constitutive Act of the AU was adopted at the Thirty-Sixth Ordinary Session of the OAU Assembly in Togo on July 11, 2000,[9] and the AHOS declared AU's establishment at its Fifth Extraordinary summit held at Sirte, Libya on March 1–2, 2001, the organization was not formally launched until 2002 in Durban, South Africa, a timeline that often leaves commentators uncertain as to what date to adopt for the existence of the AU. It is perhaps best to state that as an international legal entity, the AU existed from the moment its constitutive instrument entered into force on May 26, 2001, following the deposition of the required instruments of ratification by two-thirds of the AU Member States,[10] while the Union started functioning, properly so called, with its launch in 2002. Hence, the later date is adopted for the present purpose.

Doubtless the Sirte Summit was critical to the evolution of the AU, it is much more significant for envisioning a process that would have more radically transformed how the continental organization would, henceforth, protect human security in Africa, had Libya had its way.

At the 1999 Sirte Summit, Libya presented the Assembly with a Draft Act for the establishment of a United States of Africa.[11] Article 1 of the Act establishes a "United Sovereign independent Nation embracing all African States based on principles of equality."[12] The core principles of this draft act included an "African Nationality" for all Africans,[13] specified official languages,[14] territorial integrity of the entire continent,[15] freedoms of movement, education, religion, right to remain innocent until proved guilty, and so on.[16] Article 8 of the Draft Act deals with consular relations for the whole continent, defense policies, wars and public security, international trade, and currency and economy. While Article 9 deals with matters of judiciary, health, intellectual property, Article 10 recognizes the right of every Member State of the United States of Africa to "preserve within its boundaries their constitutions, full legislative, executive and judicial powers in all matters which do not come within the jurisdiction of the United State of Africa."

In Libyan leader Muammar al-Gaddafi's original agenda, which he fully re-articulated during the 2001 Sirte extraordinary summit of the AU Assembly, he explained:

> [t]he Organization is one thing and the Constitutive Act is another thing. When I personally requested for the Charter to be amended so that we transform the Organization into the African Union, I had to do this by submitting a note to the General Secretariat which had to circulate same to member States and I had to wait for one year in accordance with the Charter. After one year, we met. I expressed my views and we agreed on

[9] AHG/Dec.143 (XXXVI).

[10] Article 28, AU Act.

[11] *Draft of the Establishment of a State of the United States of Africa*, Sirte, Libya, Sept. 9, 1999 (on file with the author).

[12] *Id.* at art. 1.

[13] *Id.* at art. 4.

[14] *Id.* at Art 3.

[15] *Id.* at art. 5.

[16] *Id.* at art. 6.

them. This is because the Organization is made of States, whereas the Union is composed of institutions.[17]

Clearly, Libya wanted a Union with supranational powers and functions, whose institutions would be different from those of its Member States and, arguably would function with total independence. The overall aim of the Libyan proposal—and its main relevance to the issue at hand—becomes all the more clear if we recall that what the Libyan leader spoke about at the 1999 Sirte, and reiterated at the 2001 Sirte, was indeed an articulation of an idea which he had already set before his peers at the Thirty-Fifth Ordinary Session of the OAU Assembly held in Algiers, Algeria, from July 12–14, 1999.[18] Speaking to an agenda item on "Collective Security and Conflicts on the Continent,"[19] Gaddafi had hoped that the proposed extraordinary session in Sirte would discuss

> [W]ays and means of making the OAU effective so as to keep pace with political and economic developments taking place in the world and the preparation required of Africa within the context of globalization so as to preserve its socio-economic and political potentials.[20]

From the records, African leaders were initially disposed to the idea of strengthening the capacity of their organization, especially towards making it more effective and responsive, but many found Gaddafi's ultimate agenda to be too radical and revolutionary which, in plain terms, meant encroaching too far into their sovereignty. A full appreciation of Gaddafi's proposal, and the fears of his peers, will necessitate a detailed consideration of the Draft Act for the United States of Africa, the original proposal from which the AU Act emerged, which is not a goal of this endeavor. Nonetheless, the concerns of Gaddafi's peers prevailed on the day, and citing a rather perfunctory "due to time constraints"[21] reason, they did not discuss his proposal at the Sirte Summit (and later the 2000 Togo summit), which culminated in the adoption of the current AU Act, a more mellow version of the original Act.

What the African leaders said at the 2000 Togo Summit where Gaddafi made a last-ditch effort to generate support for his vision, was

> To establish a Union in conformity with the objectives of the Charter of our Continental organization [which will] accelerate the process of implementing the Treaty Establishing the African Economic Community and, in particular, shorten the implementation periods of Abuja Treaty, ensure the speedy establishment of all institutions provided for in the Abuja Treaty such as the African Central bank, the African Monetary Union, the

[17] *Speech by the Leader of the revolution at the Evening Session of the African Summit* (Closed Session), Jul. 10, 2001, at 6 (on file with the author) (emphasis added).

[18] *See Fourth Extraordinary Summit of the Heads of State and Government*, Sept. 8–9, 1999, Sirte, Libya, (Sirte Declaration).

[19] *See id.*

[20] EAHG/2 (IV), at 1.

[21] *See Report of the Ministerial Conference on the Establishment of the African Union and the Pan-African Parliament* May 31–Jun. 2, 2000, Tripoli, Libya, CM/2162 (LXXII).

African Court of justice and, in Particular, the Pan-African Parliament. The Union will also strengthen and consolidate the "regional Economic Communities as the pillars for achieving the objectives of the AEC and realizing the envisaged Union.[22]

More bluntly, President Abdoulaye Wade of Senegal, in his statement to the session, said that the path towards the African union would need to take into consideration the "definition of a system that *does not affect national sovereignty.*"[23] Consequently, he encouraged the

[c]reation of a Union by an organ or an institutional arrangement other than the OAU, in this case a regrouping of African states that includes Morocco, and finally the vesting of the Union with competencies consistent with the interests of member States.[24]

The point of interest to legal analysis in the narrative of the AU emergence is principally that an understanding of the context and the vision that propelled the original decision to establish the organization, and the compromise reached on the nature of its constitutive instrument, is critical and definitive to interpreting the principles embodied by the AU Act.

Thus, the initial conclusions to be drawn therefore from the above exercise are that (a) the AU was originally conceived to be a supranational organization, endowed with institutions that could function with full powers and authorities separate to those of its component units; (b) that the originally proposed organization would necessarily be able to take actions that would override the sovereignty of its Member States where the predilections of those States and the organization's objectives diverge; and, (c) that the rejection of the Draft Act proposed by Libya implies the rejection of *all* elements of supranationality embodied by that organic document including, in particular, that the proposed organization could possess powers greater than its Member States.

The legal analysis of the AU relations to RtoP would have been a much easier task if the African States, which resolutely rejected all notions of a supranational AU, had then not gone ahead to adopt a constitutive Act which, although remarkably feebler than Gaddafi's Act, contains some of the principles envisioned by the latter. Granted that Article 4(h) imbues the Union with a right to intervene in Member States once certain thresholds are crossed, it does not contain a schema such that aligns the application of this provision with the criteria laid down at the Togo Summit that the Union's activities must be "consistent with the interests of member States" and "not affect the national sovereignty." The prime question therefore is how does the AU intend to assert its right under Article 4(h) despite the insistence of its members on respect for their sovereignty? As a prelude to delving into this inquiry, it is proposed to first examine what Article 4(h) actually entails, especially given the tendency of its purpose to either be misrepresented or misunderstood, or sometimes totally misconceived, in commentaries.

[22] Sirte Declaration, *supra* note 18.

[23] *Id.* (emphasis added).

[24] *Id.*

II. THE AFRICAN UNION AND INTERVENTION: DOES "NON-INDIFFERENCE" MEAN "MILITARY INTERVENTION?"

A. Article 4(h) as a Groundbreaking Provision

Under Article 4(h) of its Constitutive Act, the AU asserts its right "to intervene in a Member State pursuant to a decision of the Assembly in respect of grave circumstances, namely war crimes, genocide and crimes against humanity." This provision, which is commonly regarded as embodying the doctrine of humanitarian intervention, has generated a considerable amount of interest largely due to the fact that it is revolutionary in the annals of regional organizations in particular, and affects the discourse of humanitarian intervention in general.[25]

Up until the AU Act, the controversy about the right or legality of humanitarian intervention had remained largely an academic exercise. Prior to 2000, no single international organization had provided for humanitarian intervention in its treaty. The UN Charter contains no such provision, nor does the Charter establishing the Organization of American States (OAS) in 1948, another major actor in the field of collective security.

Aside from this, the substance of the controversy about the doctrine has, in most cases, arisen by the figment of academic imagination. States, in favor of or against whom the right of humanitarian intervention is frequently canvassed, hardly ever assert such a right in their conducts. Despite the effusive commentary that trailed NATO's aerial bombardment of Serbia and Montenegro during the Kosovo crisis,[26] that organization never formally or collectively claimed that it acted out of humanitarian consideration, although some of its Member States, in particular Belgium, included the claim in its defense in the case brought against ten NATO States by Serbia at the International Court of Justice.[27] Not even in what may be described as probably the best instance of humanitarian intervention yet, that is, Tanzania's forcible expulsion of Idi Amin from Uganda in 1979, did Tanzania claim to have acted out of humanitarian considerations. Rather, President Julius Nyerere said he was responding to a previous attack on his country by Uganda, especially the seizure and annexation of the Kagera Salient, a Tanzanian border area with Uganda.

Indeed, it was not until 1989, when the Economic Community of West Africa States (ECOWAS) intervened in Liberia, apparently "to stop the senseless killings," and the U.S., UK, and France established a safe haven over the 36th parallel in Northern Iraq to shield the revolting Kurdish population from Saddam Hussein's atrocities in 1991,[28] that international organizations and individual states began to formally attribute their

[25] Nsongurua J. Udombana *When Neutrality is a Sin: The Darfur Crisis and the Crisis of Humanitarian Intervention in Sudan* 27(4) Human Rights Quarterly 1149 (2004); *See* Kithure Kindiki, *supra* note 1; Jeremy Sarkin, *supra* note 1.

[26] Antonio Cassesse, *"Ex Iniuria Ius Oritur": Are We Moving Towards International Legitimation of Forcible Humanitarian Countermeasures in the World Community?* 10 EJIL 23 (1999); Bruno Simma, *NATO, The UN and the Use of Force: Legal Aspects,* 10(1) EJIL 1 (1999).

[27] ICJ Reports, Serbia and Montenegro v. Canada (and seven other NATO States), I.C.J., (Dec. 15, 2004).

[28] New York Times, Apr. 11, 1991.

unilateral uses of force to humanitarian intervention.[29] Even then, the fact that the bold and groundbreaking ECOWAS Collective Security Protocol,[30] adopted ten years after its claim to humanitarian intervention in Liberia did not incorporate humanitarian intervention, and the UK lack of reference to that doctrine in its public justification of the NATO action,[31] ten years after protecting Kurds in Northern Iraq allegedly on the same ground, arguably underscores reluctance by States and international organizations alike to constitutionally legislate for, or formally recognize humanitarian intervention in their practice.

The principle embodied by Article 4(h) of the AU Act is widely regarded as humanitarian intervention, insofar as it apparently empowers the organization to intervene with its Member States to halt or prevent violations of human rights that have reached certain predetermined proportions. Accordingly, it has been argued that the Article gives the Union the right to intervene in its members' conflicts *regardless* of such members' preference, and irrespective of the lack of consent to such an intervention by the target State. Certainly, if an action is considered to be a humanitarian intervention, then, regardless of who is undertaking it, it necessarily precludes the consent of the target State. Humanitarian intervention is an *enforcement* action, whether unilateral or authorized by the Security Council, designed to bring the target State to comply with international law in spite of itself. It is anomalous to speak of humanitarian intervention and State consent.

Several commentators have also argued that Article 4(h) provides a legal basis for the AU to use force to protect civilians caught in conflicts. Proponents of this argument resolutely rely on a transparent and literal interpretation of that provision. It is also often argued that the right to protect human lives in times of conflicts accords generally with the paradigmatic shift of the AU from the "non-interference" stance of its predecessor, the OAU, to the widely acclaimed "non-indifference" stance of its own. However, several questions arise against these conclusions, especially the grounding of humanitarian intervention argument on the so-called non-indifference principle.

B. Gross Misconceptions about the Nature and Purpose of Article 4(h)

There is no doubt that Article 4(h) of the AU Act encapsulates the principle that the Union cannot afford to be indifferent in the face of tragedy in its Member States. But what exactly does this principle entail in *reality*, notwithstanding its relative textual clarity, and how may it be reconciled with another major principle of the Act, "non-interference by any Member State in the internal affairs of another" embodied by Article 4(g)? In short, does "non-indifference" mean the same thing as "military intervention," as many commentators tend to argue, or has the purpose of this article

[29] Interestingly, Christine Gray had quite rightly said "there was no well-established doctrine of humanitarian intervention at that time." International Law and the Use of Force, 29 (1st ed. 2000). The UK Government had, nonetheless, asserted that it acted out of humanitarian consideration.

[30] *See* Ademola Abass, *The New Collective Security Mechanism of ECOWAS: Innovations and Problems*, 5(2) Journal of Conf. & Sec. L. 211 (2000).

[31] Instead, Jack Straw, the then Foreign Secretary of the UK, had claimed, *inter alia*, that NATO's action was to support the Security Council resolution against Iraq.

simply been over exaggerated? This query is critical to a consideration of how the AU intends to implement RtoP for the precise reason that such a task implicates interfering in the internal affairs of its member states.

There are two possible ways of interpreting the principle embodied by Article 4(h). First and the more widely subscribed is the straightforward and literal interpretation, which suggests that the principle of "non-indifference" somewhat implies the "use of force." This perspective thrives on the ordinary construction of the provision although, as is well known, there is always a difference between what states say and what they actually do.

It can be argued that the AU did not intend that its "non indifference" principle should be read as the right to take military actions against its Member States. Aside from that there is no reference to "conflicts" in Article 4(h), there are credible grounds to hold that when African leaders agreed on the AU Act, nothing was farther from their minds than the pretext that they thereby agreed that the organization may use force on their territory for whatever reason or purpose without their consent.

During the 1999 Sirte Summit, which considered the texts of the AU Act, the OAU Secretariat identified some benchmarks that should guide the process of the institutional and structural changes and the transformation of the OAU into the African Union. The first relates to the determination, stipulated in preambular paragraph 10 of the Act, "to take all necessary measures to strengthen our common institutions and provide them with the necessary powers and resources to enable them discharge their respective mandates effectively."[32] Secondly is that the objectives and principles of the African Union, enshrined in Articles 3 and 4 of the Constitutive Act, provide an *advanced degree of political cooperation* covering, *inter alia*, the promotion and defense of African common positions on issues of interest to the continent and its peoples.[33]

As a matter of fact, while speaking in regard to the proposed Pan-African Parliament, the then Malian president, Alpha Konare (who would later become the first chairperson of the AU), made it clear that "it was not necessary for such an institution to be a supranational body, but rather a forum that allowed for discussions and exchange of views on the African Union, as well as the participation of the civil society in the project."[34] Konare's view was echoed by virtually all his peers who even extended the proposition to cover all the institutions and organs of the Union, including, of course, the Union itself. Not for once did any of the African leaders present at Sirte refer to Article 4(h) in terms of unconsensual military intervention by AU in its member conflicts. This might explain why the word "conflict" is omitted from the provision of Article 4(h).

Certainly, if the AU intervenes politically in its Member States during a national crisis, it would be seen to have chosen the path of "non-indifference"; but it does not then follow that it *must* intervene militarily in the situation, much less that it has an obligation or duty to undertake humanitarian intervention. To be sure, the AU assumes an obligation under Article 4(h) of its Act, but that obligation is to *intervene in Member States*, not invariably to *use force in its Member States' conflicts*; the two are not the same, and it is highly susceptible to controvertibility to argue that the Union

[32] *See* EAHG/Dec.1 (V), at 4.

[33] *Id.* at 4.

[34] *Id.* at 12.

possesses the *right* of humanitarian intervention under Article 4(h). If it could be said that the AU possesses such powers courtesy of a literal and textual interpretation of that provision, as indeed a simplistic reading of that provision instructs, there are various counterpoints, drawn from the *travaux preparatoire* of the AU Act and several policy instruments, that make such an interpretation at best naïve.

The view that Article 4(h) confers the AU with a right of humanitarian intervention undoubtedly has doctrinal solidity, nonetheless, it underscores an acute lack of awareness of both the history of negotiation of the Union and its practice in the ten years of its existence. It is one thing to say that "non-indifference" principle suggests that the AU will not keep silent in the face of wanton destruction of lives and property in any of its Member States, but it is quite another thing to imply that the Union would always go gun-blazing into any of its Member States to protect human lives on the basis of Article 4(h).

The intervention by the African Union Mission in Sudan (AMIS) shreds any modicum of doubt relating to the conclusion drawn above.[35] AMIS' intervention happened literally in the shadows of the Ezulwini Consensus where the AU empowered itself to intervene in its member states regardless of the Security Council or the General Assembly, and the World Summit that fully endorsed RtoP. Yet, despite that, there was a near universal clamor for the AU to take military action against the *Janjeweed* militia to halt the extermination of the African tribes. The organization had implored the Government of the Sudan (GoS) to allow it deploy a peacekeeping operation. In several of the meetings held at the Union's Headquarters in Addis Ababa related to the mission, not for once did any of the AU States or its officials canvass for humanitarian intervention, or any type of unconsensual action for that matter.

Yet, the AU intervention in Darfur presented the Union with the best opportunity to authorize force to protect human lives which, as seen below, it asserted as its right over Ezulwini without the Security Council's approval. And going by ECOWAS' precedents in Liberia and Sierra Leone,[36] it was highly unlikely that the Security Council would have had issues had the AU so acted, especially given that AMIS deployment coincided with the euphoric adumbration of RtoP at the World Summit that same year.

However, the Kenyan debacle is a different matter. Quite clearly, human lives were lost, and at the critical time in the impasse no one could predict how the situation might turn out. The AU nonetheless deployed a considerable diplomatic effort such that is *sine qua non*, in the schema of the World Summit Outcome Document, to any eventual recourse to military intervention by the international community. Thus, Kenya actually could be read as a perfect example of how RtoP is meant to work. The Government of Kenya, like any of the other States, has the primary Responsibility to Protect its people. But when that government itself became implicated in fraudulent elections, which instigated a massive revolt and subsequent killings, it became obvious that the state was either "unwilling or unable" to protect its people, as required by paragraph 138 of the World Summit Outcome Document.[37] However, such failure

[35] *See* Ademola Abass, *The United Nations, the African Union, and the Darfur Crisis: Of Apology and Utopia*, 54(3) Netherlands Int'l L. Rev. 414 (2007).

[36] *See* Ademola Abass, *The Implementation of Security Council Resolution 1270 in Sierra Leone: New Developments in Regional Intervention* Miami Int'l & Comp. L. Rev. 177 (2001–2002).

[37] *2005 World Summit Outcome*, A/RES/60/1, Sept. 15, 2005.

does not automatically entitle the international community to deploy military force to protect Kenyans. As is clear from paragraph 139 of the Outcome Document, the world must first render assistance towards enabling the State to vindicate its own responsibility under paragraph 138.[38] Only if despite that assistance, the situation persists then the international community's own responsibility can be activated. In Kenya, the fact that the Kofi Annan-led initiative, at the behest of the AU, succeeded, shows that the staggered process for implementing RtoP envisioned by the World Summit Outcomes Documents was indeed effective.[39]

Measured against the two scenarios discussed above, the conclusion seems inevitable that while there may be merit in construing the text of Article 4(h) as conferring a right of humanitarian intervention, state practice and the history of the AU Act reveal that African States intended the article to be no more than an embodiment of a continental policy, agreed by all African States, to empower their Union to intervene *politically* in matters occurring in their territories. If the AU were to ever use force on the territory of its member states, it will be to stop non-state actors or rebel groups, the likes of *Interahamwe* and the *Janjaweed*, which caused havoc in Rwanda and Darfur, respectively. Even then, only insofar as such groups are not acting as mere fronts for their governments as the *Janjaweed* militia is widely believed to be. Whatever may be the case, the AU will still require the consent of the State to come into the country, anyway, before dealing with such groups.[40]

Consequently, the unwritten law of the AU Act is that Article 4(j), entitling the AU Member States to request its intervention (thus, peacekeeping provisions) will remain the basis for any intervention by the Union in the internal affairs of its Member States. As far as conferring a *right* of humanitarian intervention in its Member States' conflicts is concerned the future of Article 4(h) remains, tragically, bleak. It is just as well, therefore, that in their explication of RtoP the authors of the ICISS Report,[41] and the World Summit, deliberated avoided adopting the phrase "humanitarian intervention" given the strong emotional sensitivity it evokes among states in general.

[38] *See id.*

[39] Some believe that the UN was responsible for success of RtoP in Kenya. According to Edward C. Luck: "[T]he only time the UN has actually applied [RtoP], was in the case of Kenya, early in 2008 after the disputed elections. When there's seven or eight hundred people . . . killed, it was not clear there was full-scale ethnic cleansing, but it could well become that or even something greater, and the UN decided to apply RtoP criteria and to really make it the focus of the efforts there. And Kofi Annan, the former . . . Secretary-General who was doing mediation on ground at the time, has said since that RtoP was the lens through which he saw his whole efforts there," *restated in* Mark Schneider, *Implementing the Responsibility to Protect in Kenya and Beyond*, *available at* http://www.crisisgroup.org/en/publication-type/speeches/2010/implementing-the-responsibility-to-protect-in-kenya-and-beyond.aspx.

[40] One of the core requirements of peacekeeping operations is that deployment must be based on consent by the host state. Although the UN Charter contains no rules on peacekeeping, it is generally believed that customary international law underwrites peacekeeping operations.

[41] International Commission on Intervention and State Sovereignty (ICISS), The Responsibility to Protect: Report of the International Commission on Intervention and State Sovereignty (International Development Research Centre 2001), *available at*: http://www.iciss.ca/report-en.asp [hereinafter ICISS Report].

III. THE TENSION BETWEEN THE NON-INTERFERENCE AND INTERVENTION PRINCIPLES IN THE AU ACT

The foregoing analysis begs the question how to interface the antithetical provisions of Article 4(g) with Article 4(h), the former codifying the "non-interference" principle, and the latter endowing the Union with the so-called right of intervention. Even though the possibility of a clash between these two provisions in reality is remote, given that, as said above, the AU may never deploy an unconsensual military action in its Member States, there is a theoretical benefit to be derived from the clarification of the relationship between the two principles.

The solution to the apparent tension between the two provisions lies, it seems, in a purposive interpretation of the article. Article 4(g) forbids AU members states, as opposed to the Union itself, from interfering in matters that occur in other states. In contrast, the right to intervene under Article 4(h) is addressed to the AU, acting as an organization per se. Regardless of whether the AU is or is not a supranational organization, it is well established in international law that an international organization has a separate identity from its members. Thus, whereas an AU Member State may not interfere in another State's affairs, the AU can. By contrast, although Article III(2) of the OAU Charter also forbade its members to interfere in their internal affairs, unlike Article 4(h) of the AU Act, it does not provide the OAU itself with any authority to intervene in its Member States.

The AU Act overtakes the UN Charter, Article 2(7) of which contains a similar injunction to Article 4(g) of the AU Act. However, unlike the AU, it is the UN itself that is forbidden to interfere in matters occurring within its Member States,[42] while individual UN members may not interfere in other States' affairs by virtue of customary international law principle of non-interference. Nonetheless, the distinction between Articles 4(g) AU Act and 2(7) of the UN Charter is of little practical importance. Article 2(7), which prohibits the UN from intervening in Member States' affairs, is reserved against collective security actions authorized by the UN Security Council under Chapter VII of the UN Charter. That said, unless and until that caveat applies, the UN may not interfere in its Member States. The AU, in theory, is under no such restraint as the UN provided, of course, that one of the thresholds enumerated under Article 4(h) has been crossed.

If the argument convinces—that it is unsafe to assume that the AU will ever rely on, or cite Article 4(gh) of its Act as the basis for militarily intervening in its Member States to protect human lives—then it raises the question as to how, then, the organization can discharge its Responsibility to Protect its people in times of conflicts, a responsibility which it has acknowledged and accepted in several fora and by means of various legal and policy instruments? As already argued above, Article 4(h) is more of a policy framework, despite apparently conferring the right to intervene on the AU. In practice, the AU states have neither said that the organization possesses powers to act without their consent, nor have they acted in that manner as seen in the analysis of the

[42] "Nothing contained in the present Charter shall authorize the United Nations to intervene in matters which are essentially within the domestic jurisdiction of any state or shall require the Members to submit such matters to settlement under the present Charter; but this principle shall not prejudice the application of enforcement measures under Chapter VII." UN Charter, art. 2(7).

actions in Kenya and Darfur. On the contrary, the AU itself has on several occasions disavowed the obvious legal import of that provision.

It needs to be stressed, however, that the argument being made here is not that the AU *cannot* or *should* not, as a matter of desirability, take military actions to protect human lives in its member states. Nowhere is there a greater need, and reasons, for regional organizations to possess constitutive authority to take military actions against their member States, regardless of the latter's preferences, than in Africa. The soul of the argument here is that such legal empowerment of the AU should be sought from other sources than through a simplistic and somewhat naïve reading of Article 4(h). The next issue for consideration therefore is: from where does the AU have authority to implement RtoP?

IV. THE AU AND RESIDUAL RESPONSIBILITY TO PROTECT THE "EZULWINI" PRECEDENT

It is beyond controversy that the AU recognizes it bears the Responsibility to Protect its citizens from war crimes, crimes against humanity, and genocide. And if we add the obligations accepted by the AU when it signed up to the World Summit Outcome Document in 2005, then, in addition to these three crimes, it also bears Responsibility to Protect its people from ethnic cleansing, although there is some doubt whether a distinction can be made between this crime and genocide.

In March 2005, the African Union adopted the "Ezulwini Consensus," a common African position in response to the proposed UN reform, contained in the UN Secretary-General's *Report of the High Panel on Threat, Challenges, and Change.*[43] Although the principal objective of the Ezulwini gathering concerned the agitation for two permanent seats for Africa on the UN Security Council, the AU Assembly used the opportunity to roll out its position on many other issues. Regarding RtoP, the Consensus states that

> an authorization for the use of force by the Security Council *should be* in line with the conditions and criteria proposed by the Panel, but this condition *should not undermine* the responsibility of the international community to protect.[44]

This statement is quite telling particularly because, six months before the world would haggle and banter about RtoP, Africa had not only recognized the inevitability of the concept, but was already pondering ways of ensuring that the concept does not become hostage to the Security Council power like many initiatives before it. For in grounding the primacy of the Security Council as the ultimate authority to implement RtoP on the premise that the organ does not behave irresponsibly, the AU broached one of the most sensitive issues that would dominate the World Summit of the General Assembly: the ability of the international community to implement RtoP in lieu of a Security Council action.

[43] Secretary-General's High-Level Panel on Threats, Challenges and Change, *A More Secure World: Our Shared Responsibility*, A/59/565, Dec. 2, 2004 (Hereinafter *A More Secure World*).

[44] Ext/EX.CL/2(VII), at 6, Executive Council 7th Extraordinary Session, Mar. 7–8, 2005, Addis Ababa, Ethiopia (emphasis added).

After States had reached a broad agreement on the content of RtoP at the World Summit, *inter alia*, questions arose as to who should take military action, if a military intervention were to become necessary. This option, of course, becomes available not immediately after a state has manifested its unwillingness or instability to protect its people, but when the international community has equally discharged the obligation.

In 2001, ICISS, the body that first dealt with the concept of RtoP on a major scale and to which, it must be said, the concept owes its popularity, did attempt to provide some answers this question. In its report, ICISS states

> the Commission is in absolutely no doubt that there is *no better or more appropriate* body than the Security Council to deal with military intervention issues for human protection purposes. It is the Security Council which should be making the hard decisions in the hard cases about overriding state sovereignty . . . That was the overwhelming consensus we found in all our consultations around the world. If international consensus is ever to be reached about when, where, how and by whom military intervention should happen, it is very clear that *the central role of the Security Council will have to be at the heart of that consensus*. The task is *not to find alternatives to the Security Council as a source of authority*, but to make the Security Council work much better than it has.[45]

ICISS emphasized that "[w]e have made abundantly clear our view that the Security Council should be the first port of call on any matter relating to military intervention for human protection purposes."[46]

ICISS' insistence on the Security Council taking a lead role in the implementation of RtoP is to be understood against the background of the fear expressed by many states about leaving such an important decision as to use of force within sovereign states to individual states. Also, the body was clearly guided by the collective security structure of the UN Charter as it explicitly referred to Charter VII provisions.[47] Given that the Security Council is already vested with the primary responsibility to maintain international peace and security (Article 24 UN Charter), and is empowered to take enforcement actions against States (Chapter VII), its seems natural that it is the organ favored with the central role for implementing RtoP. Additionally, it is ICISS' strategy of choice to distance RtoP from humanitarian intervention by laying the responsibility for the former squarely and solely on the Security Council, a move that may be counterproductive in the long term but which, in the short term, helped sell RtoP to many States.

It would be recalled that in the 2004 High-Level Panel Report,[48] which reiterated ICISS' advice about making the Council work better,[49] the permanent members of the Security Council were urged "to pledge themselves to refrain from the use of the veto in cases of genocide and large-scale human rights abuses,"[50] a statement which was

[45] ICISS Report, *supra* note at 41, at ¶ 6.14.

[46] *See id.*, at ¶ 6.28.

[47] *See id.*, at ¶ 6.16.

[48] *See A More Secure World*, *supra* note 43.

[49] *See id.*

[50] *See id.*, at ¶ 256.

originally included in the Summit Outcome Document.[51] Obviously, this is a proposal towards concretely achieving ICISS' idealistic suggestion of making "the Security Council work much better." At the World Summit, the United States vehemently rejected this idea, leading to the removal of the proposal for the final document, but opening the door for states insisting on residual actors to implement RtoP.

As seen above, the stance taken by ICISS that only the Security Council may authorize military actions in an RtoP situation, if one becomes inevitable, is not shared across board. In paragraph 139 of the Outcome Document,[52] states pledge their preparedness

> to take collective action, in a timely and decisive manner, through the *Security Council*, in accordance with the Charter, including Chapter VII, on a *case-by-case* basis and in *cooperation* with relevant regional organizations as appropriate, should peaceful means be inadequate and national authorities manifestly fail to protect their populations from genocide, war crimes, ethnic cleansing and crimes against humanity. We stress the need for the *General Assembly* to continue consideration of the responsibility to protect populations from genocide, war crimes, ethnic cleansing and crimes against humanity and its implications, bearing in mind the principles of the Charter and international law. . . .

The exact nature of the obligation States assume under this paragraph is far from clear. It has been suggested that this sentence merely points "toward a voluntary, rather than a mandatory, engagement," and that "states commit themselves to act only on a case-by-case basis through the Council, which again stands in contrast to the assumption of a systematic duty."[53] Whether this is an accurate interpretation of paragraph 139 is debatable, but, to be sure, states rarely assume international obligations under non-binding instruments, such as the World Summit Outcome, on mandatory terms. Yet, adopting flexible or voluntary expressions, as they do in paragraph 139, does not suggest bad faith: on the contrary, it may simply manifest states' desire to leave themselves wriggle room for future negotiation.

What is certain though is that paragraph 139 falls short of unequivocally recognizing residuality regarding the authority to implement RtoP. Nonetheless, the provision contains many deft nuances that could be interpreted as permitting at least regional organizations and the General Assembly to play some role towards implementing RtoP.

Chapter VIII of the UN Charter is the clear undercurrent to the reference made in paragraph 139 to "cooperation with relevant regional organizations," whereas Articles 10–14 of the UN Charter guide the role of the UN General Assembly in international peace and security. While a full analysis of these provisions goes beyond the remit of this endeavor, it is necessary to highlight their importance in the present context.

[51] See revised Draft Outcome Document of the High-Level Plenary Meeting of the General Assembly, Sept. 2005, submitted by the President of the General Assembly, UN Doc A/59/HLPM/CRP.1 Rev.2, Aug. 10, 2005, at ¶ 120.

[52] A/60/L.1, Integrated and coordinated implementation of and follow-up to the outcomes of the major United Nations conferences and summits in the economic, social and related fields.

[53] Carsten Stahn, *Responsibility to Protect: Political Rhetoric or Emerging Legal Norm?* 101 AJIL 99, 108 (2007).

Article 53(1) of the Charter enjoins regional arrangements or agencies not to undertake enforcement actions without the authority of the Security Council. Enforcement action, it is generally agreed, include the use of military force, though whether non-forcible measures such as economic sanctions fall within the term remains controversial. This provision ensures that the use of force by regional organizations does not contravene the general prohibition of force under Article 2(4) of the Charter. Except where States acts in individual or collective self-defense (Article 51), or where they take actions to prevent a renewal of policy of aggression by former enemy states (Article 107),[54] only enforcement actions authorized by the Security Council are legally permissible under the Charter. Though regional organizations act under Chapter VIII when they take regional enforcement action, the authorization derives from the Security Council acting under Chapter VII.

The cooperation envisaged by paragraph 139 of the World Summit Outcome implies a situation where the Security Council delegates its RtoP functions to an "appropriate" regional organization. Obviously an "appropriate" regional organization, for the purpose of RtoP, will invariably be one drawn from within the geographical area of the conflict, nothing in the UN Charter so restricts the Security Council's ability to cast its net wider. As argued elsewhere by this writer, the fact that the Security Council delegated its authority to the European Union during the Operation Artemis in the Democratic Republic of Congo in 2003 justifies this position.[55]

Should regional organizations stringently adhere to paragraph 139 and accept, always, to cooperate with the Security Council, it would mean that only the Security Council may implement RtoP since if a regional organization acts pursuant to a Security Council authorization, it does so as its agent. The question is, what did the states participating at the World Summit actually intend in paragraph 139?

During the Ezulwini retreat, the AU provided its own interpretation of how it envisaged its cooperation with the Security Council in future efforts to protect its people during arm conflicts. In a remarkably bold and blunt passage, the AU states

> Since the General Assembly and the Security Council are often far from the scenes of conflicts and may not be in a position to undertake effectively a proper appreciation of the nature and development of conflict situations, *it is imperative* that Regional Organisations, *in areas of proximity to conflicts, are empowered to take actions* in this regard. The African Union agrees with the Panel that the intervention of Regional Organisations should be with the approval of the Security Council; *although in certain situations*, such approval could be granted "after the fact" in circumstances requiring urgent action. In such cases, the UN should assume responsibility for financing such operations.[56]

From this statement, the AU obviously intends that, like any other regional organization, it should be able to implement RtoP in conflicts occurring in Africa. While the Union does agree that Security Council approval is required for such actions, it reserves for itself the right to act first and then seek a retroactive approval as the situation may

[54] This provision is now considered obsolete given that all states are now UN Member States.

[55] *See* Ademola Abass, *Extraterritorial Collective Security: The European Union and Operation Artemis*, in European Sec. L.134 (Martin Trybus & Nigel White eds., 2007).

[56] Ezulwini Consensus B(i) (Ext/EX.CL/2 (VII)).

dictate. In other words, the AU does not forever bind itself to the structure of Article 53(1) of the UN Charter under which regional organizations have no choice as to *whether* they should seek Security Council authorization for their enforcement actions. For the AU, this disaggregated authorization regime is a sound compromise between those advocating that only the Security Council may implement RtoP (such as the ICISS) and those who believe, as the U.S. argued at the World Summit, that unilateral actions should be permitted under certain circumstances.

It may be argued that because the AU, Ezulwini's position antedated the World Summit, its stance on residuality has been overtaken by the World Summit. This is not the case. On the contrary, since the World Summit several AU members States have reiterated their stance on the role of regional organizations in implementing RtoP. During the Security Council "Open Debate on Maintenance of Peace and Security in Africa," the representative of Benin Republic Jean-Marie Ehouzou, stated

> It is clear that the United Nations system in conducting peacekeeping operations has, until recently, operated with marginal involvement by regional organizations. The time has come to make the necessary changes in order to make it possible for the organizations to fully play their role in the collective security system established by the Charter—both in terms of the doctrine of peace operations and in the allocation of related resources.[57]

Moreover, in 2008 the AU Chairperson said that the Union would no longer sit and do nothing just because the international community (read the Security Council) decides to do nothing. As Ping observes, "the provision of the AU Constitutive Act was informed . . . by the realization that one cannot be indifferent to a fire engulfing a neighbor's house because it could very well end up razing his house as well."[58]

The Ezulwini Consensus also mentions the General Assembly as one of UN organs that are often far from theaters of conflicts. This implies that the AU recognizes the Assembly as a potential actor in implementing RtoP, although the World Summit Outcome does no more than urge the Assembly to continue to consider the Responsibility to Protect people from crimes.

However, while regional interventions in lieu of the Security Council actions may not be objectionable to the Security Council given precedents of ECOWAS in Liberia and Sierra Leone, such actions by the General Assembly should be expected to draw the ire of the organ. In history, whenever the Security Council was immobilized by the veto vote and the General Assembly intervened under the Uniting for Peace Resolution, a huge tension had always arisen between the two, which prompted the Assembly to seek clarification of its role before the ICJ in the *Certain Expenses* case.[59] There is no doubt that the undemocratic nature of the Security Council representation and decision-making process, coupled with the dwindling of states' trust in its ability to behave responsibly and equitably towards all UN member States, contributes to the ever

[57] UN Security Council, Aug. 28, 2007, *available at* http://www.responsibilitytoprotect.org/files/government-excerpts-28-aug-07(2).pdf.

[58] www.africaunion.org/root/au/Conferences/2008/october/bcp/KEYNOTE_ADDRESS_CP_23_october.doc.

[59] I.C.J. Reports 1962, at 151.

increasing clamor for a greater role for the General Assembly in the international peace and security arena. Yet, one seriously questions whether the General Assembly is suited to play the kind of role that is required for implementing RtoP.

It is highly unlikely that the General Assembly will deal with an RtoP situation, which the Security Council is already dealing with. This is due to the stifling provision of Article 12 of the UN Charter, which states that "[w]hile the Security Council is *exercising* in respect of any dispute or situation the functions assigned to it in the present Charter, the General Assembly shall not make any recommendation with regard to that dispute or situation unless the Security Council so requests."[60] There is no last word as to when the Security Council can be said to be "exercising" in respect of a dispute, and random activities, such as merely placing an item on the Council's agenda, is often thought to be within the purview of that phrase.

Undoubtedly, the Assembly may discuss any peace and security issues at its meetings, and may even make general pronouncements on such, it cannot, however, make recommendations to the concerned states or to any other UN members for that matter concerning the situation. To be sure, in situations where the international community needs to protect human lives, more than mere recommendation will be required, so that even if the Assembly is empowered to make recommendations these will be grossly inadequate. A "decision," which, unlike a recommendation, is binding on all UN members by virtue of Article 25 of the Charter, will be absolutely necessary. The General Assembly cannot take a *decision* since Article 39 of the Charter empowers only the Security Council to so act. The World Summit Outcome Document cannot alter the structure of the UN Charter and does not pretend to do so. Little wonder then that the Document does not allocate a residual role for RtoP to the General Assembly.

Even if we overlook the inhibition of Article 12, and assume that the Assembly can, in fact, deal with a matter already being exercised by the Security Council, a major danger still lurks. It must be remembered that even in the past when the General Assembly had supplanted the Security Council, it did not undertake enforcement actions, such that would definitely be needed by the international community to protect human lives under paragraph 139 of the Summit Outcome. In 1956, following an outbreak of military hostilities between Israel and Egypt over the Suez Canal strait, the General Assembly deployed a peacekeeping operation—the United Nations Emergency Force (UNEF)—as a buffer between Israel and Egypt, acting under the "Uniting for Peace Resolution," adopted six years earlier.[61] But when Egypt's President Abdel Nasser requested that the UN withdrew its forces, the organization had no choice but to comply. This mission was a perfect example of the working of classical peacekeeping, but its type would be unsuitable where hundreds or thousands of lives are at stake. The last stop in implementing RtoP is a muscular, multilateral collective military action, not a feeble, consensual, and pacificatory operation.

The ongoing debacle in Côte d'Ivoire shows that, in contrast to the General Assembly, the Security Council possesses, when and if it does decide to act, the mettle, means, and a considerable legal authority, to act decisively *against* any UN member States to protect human lives. Following a general election, the results of which the incumbent

[60] Emphasis added.

[61] G.A. Res. 377 (V). G. A. O. R., 5th Sess. 302nd plen. Mtg, at 341, A/PV. 302 (Nov. 3, 1950).

Laurent Gbagbo was widely believed to have manipulated in his favor, civil unrest broke out among party factions. The Security Council adopted many resolutions including, most importantly, Resolution 1962.[62] Therein, the Council decides to renew the mandate of the United Nations Mission in Côte d'Ivoire (UNOCI) "to use all necessary means to carry out its mandate, within its capabilities and its areas of deployment."[63] This, in practical terms, means that UNOCI can and will use force against the government if needs be. It should be recalled that UNOCI was originally deployed as a peacekeeping operation. In Resolution 1962, the Security Council upgraded the mission's mandate to enable it to meet its obligations, which includes ensuring that the electoral wishes of the Ivories people are respected. Thus, when the incumbent president requested the UN to leave Côte d'Ivoire, as he would have been entitled to had UNOCI remained essentially a peacekeeping mission, the UN made it clear that it "will fulfill its mandate and will continue to monitor and document any human rights violations, incitement to hatred and violence, or attacks on UN peacekeepers,"[64] a stance that would have been legally untenable had UNOCI been a General Assembly deployment.

It is almost certain that, given the manifest reluctance of the Outcome Document, the ICISS and the High-Level Panel Reports, the implementation of RtoP will not suffuse with the General Assembly-led missions or the "coalitions of able and willing" deploying unilaterally (that is without the Security Council authorization). However, different dynamics will surely play out at the regional level where regional organizations are especially active. In Africa, the AU and sub-regional organizations, such as ECOWAS, will most likely assert their right to intervene on the basis of the World Summit Document, which clearly envisages some sort of cooperation between the Security Council and regional organizations, and the Ezulwini Consensus, which fully endorse regional organizations functioning instead of the remotely located Security Council or General Assembly. Of course, whether the organization has the requisite human resources and allied capacities to physically undertake such a task is another issue altogether.

Precedents including ECOWAS' intervention in Liberia and Sierra Leone indicate that such sub-regional organizations, in particular ECOWAS, should be expected to deploy military intervention to their Member States to protect peoples' lives. Fortunately, ECOWAS does not suffer the legal ambiguity of Article 4(h) of the AU Act.[65] In 1999, the organization adopted a very important protocol, which entitled it to take enforcement actions in any of its Member States without their consent.[66] Since 1999, ECOWAS has applied the protocol on several occasions, including to repel Faure Eyadema's unconstitutional ascendancy to the Togolese presidency after the death of his father, and imposed an arms embargo on Guinea and Niger in 2009. Indeed, it is

[62] S/RES/1962 (2010).

[63] *Id.*, at ¶ 14.

[64] Tom Burgis & Harvey Morris, *UN Refuses to Pull Troops from Ivory Coast*, WASHINGTON POST, Dec. 19, 2010.

[65] For analysis and a text of this protocol, *see* Ademola Abass, *supra* note 36.

[66] It is interesting that up-to-date, no ECOWAS State has challenged the legality of ECOWAS' enforcement action on the basis of the protocol, although at least one State decided to withdraw from the organization.

fair to say that when it comes to residual responsibility to implement RtoP forcefully, ECOWAS has shown more courage than any other organization in Africa, including the AU.[67]

The indignation of African States against conferring the Security Council with exclusive Responsibility to Protect peoples derives from a history of costly disappointments and betrayals suffered by Africa from the notoriously selective collective security of the UN. Such great letdowns have occasionally instigated African states to openly defy some decisions of the Security Council. For instance, the OAU Assembly of Heads of State and Government adopted the Ouagadougou decision,[68] which mandated its members to disregard the Security Council sanctions imposed on Libya after the Lockerbie bombing.[69]

However, one must be cautious in interpreting such rare acts of defiance. It is true the deep frustration often felt by many African states sometimes makes full compliance with their international obligations difficult. But to then describe such disregarded Charter rules, (e.g., that the Security Council must authorize regional enforcement actions), as mere "legal niceties" is to totally miss the point.[70] When states ignore Security Council's decisions, including their obligations under the UN Charter, it is usually not because they believe that such decisions and obligations are worthless or because it directly opposes its interests: it is rather sometimes a cold reminder to jolt the Council's conscience to the fact that its irresponsible behavior and discriminatory practices pose a serious threat to its legitimacy, and to how much it could inspire cooperation from States.

The High-Level Panel recognized the inconsistency of the Security Council but advised strengthening the organ from within rather than weakening it:

> One of the reasons why States may want to bypass the Security Council is a lack of confidence in the quality and objectivity of its decision-making. The Council's decisions have often been less than consistent, less than persuasive and less than fully responsive to very real State and human security needs. But the solution is not to reduce the

[67] For a full analysis of this episode, see Ademola Abass, (ed.), Protecting Human Security in Africa (2010).

[68] AHG/OAU/AEC/Dec.1 (II) Jun. 8–10, 1998; Assembly of Heads of State and Government, Thirty-Fourth Ordinary Session/ Second Ordinary Session of the African Economic Community Jun. 8–10, 1998 Ouagadougo, Burkina Faso.

[69] *AHG/Dec.127 (XXXIV)*. In operative paragraph 2, the Assembly "DECIDES not to comply any longer with Security Council Resolutions 748 (1992) and 883 (1993) on sanctions, with effect from September 1998, if the United States of America and the United Kingdom refuse that the two suspects be tried in a third neutral country pursuant to the verdict of the International Court of Justice by July 1998, date on which the sanctions will be due for review, owing to the fact that the said resolutions violate Article 27 paragraph 3, Article 33 and Article 36 paragraph 3 of the United Nations Charter, and the considerable human and economic losses suffered by Libya and a number of other African peoples as a result of the sanctions."

[70] Ben Kioko, *The Right of Intervention under the African Union's Constitutive Act: From Non-Interference to Non-Intervention*, 85 (852) International Rev. of the Red Cross 807 (2003), writing that African leaders "have shown themselves willing to push the frontiers of collective stability and security to the limit without regard for legal niceties such as the authorization of the Security Council," at 821.

Council to impotence and irrelevance: it is to work from within to reform it, including in the ways we propose in the present report.[71]

V. THE PLACE OF APSA IN THE IMPLEMENTATION OF RTOP: THE AU AND RECS

Consistent with Article 5(2) of the AU Act, it adopted the Protocol Establishing the Peace and Security Council (PSC or PSC Protocol) in 2002. The PSC, which is a "a collective security and early-warning arrangement to facilitate timely and efficient response to conflict and crisis situations in Africa"[72] has, as its objectives, promoting "peace, security and stability in Africa, in order to guarantee the protection and preservation of life and property, the well-being of the African people and their environment, as well as the creation of conditions conducive to sustainable development,"[73] among others. Modeled after the Security Council, the PSC comprises ten members elected for a term of two years, and five members elected for a term of three years in order to ensure continuity.[74]

The PSC has enormous powers under Article 7, the high point of which is to "approve the modalities for intervention by the Union in a Member State, following a decision by the Assembly, pursuant to article 4(j) of the Constitutive Act."[75] This provision is enabled by the fact that the PSC operates under the principles contained in Article 4(h) of the AU Act,[76] and as such, is empowered to "recommend to the Assembly, pursuant to Article 4(h) of the Constitutive Act, intervention, on behalf of the Union, in a Member State in respect of grave circumstances, namely war crimes, genocide and crimes against humanity, as defined in relevant international conventions and instruments."[77]

Considering the enormity of its collective security powers, the PSC can be regarded as Africa's equivalence of the UN Security Council, except that it does not have a veto. Nonetheless, the PSC can bind AU member states to its decision by virtue of Article 7(3) of its Protocol,[78] just as the Security Council could do under Article 25 of the UN Charter.

The overall architecture of peace and security in Africa centers on the interactions among the AU, the PSC, and several other elements established for the purpose of maintaining peace in Africa. The relations between the AU Assembly and the PSC are clear: The former is the Union's highest decision-making body and the latter is the organization's collective security powerhouse. That means that the task of implementing RtoP rests squarely on the PSC. It is for the Chairperson of the AU to bring matters, which are considered as likely to threaten peace and security of the continent

[71] High-Level Panel Report, at ¶ 197.

[72] Protocol Establishing the Peace and Security Council, African Union, art. 1 (PSC Protocol).

[73] *Id.* at art. 3(a).

[74] *Id.* at art. 5(1)(a), (b).

[75] *Id.* at art. 7(1)(f).

[76] *Id.* at art. 4.

[77] *Id.* at art. 7(e).

[78] "The Member States agree to accept and implement the decisions of the Peace and Security Council, in accordance with the Constitutive Act."

to the PSC,[79] although the Chairperson's good offices may also be used to resolve disputes.[80]

Both the AU Assembly and the PSC are assisted by the Panel of the Wise, a quaintly named group of five eminent Africans[81] whose responsibility it is to "advise the Peace and Security Council and the Chairperson of the Commission on all issues pertaining to the promotion, and maintenance of peace, security and stability in Africa."[82] There is no provision that entitles the Panel to directly engage with states in attempts to resolve conflicts. Nevertheless, such possibility is recognized by the fact that the Panel is able to, on its own initiative, take measures towards supporting the efforts of the Assembly and the PSC.[83]

Underlining this structure is a continental early-warning system designed to enable the AU to act proactively to address emerging conflicts.[84] However, once violence erupts, diplomatic activities are intensified and expected to be coupled with some forms of military interventions. What type of mission is to be deployed comes down to the decision of the PSC. According to Article 8(13) PSC Protocol,

> Decisions of the Peace and Security Council shall generally be guided by the principle of consensus. In cases where consensus cannot be reached, the Peace and Security Council shall adopt its decisions on procedural matters by a simple majority, while decisions on all other matters shall be made by a two-thirds majority vote of its Members voting.

How the PSC deals with this provision will have a direct impact on its ability to take enforcement actions when African lives are threatened. Clearly, in procedural matters the organ may apply the simple majority rule, while in all other matters, especially those involving peace and security, a two-thirds majority is required.

On the one hand, the absence of the veto vote from the PSC guarantees that no single state can hold the fate of nearly one billion Africans hostage as it is possible with the UN Security Council. On the other hand, the insistence on a two-thirds majority, although desirable for the purpose of achieving broad-based support for an action, will achieve a result that in reality will almost make enforcement actions impossible. Certainly, in an organization where one rich member state has been known to pay the financial dues of several poor members to the Union in order to elicit their support for its position, a requirement of a two-thirds majority for important decisions leaves too much to be desired. It would have been preferable if such decisions as concerning peace and security are subject to the "simple majority" rule with procedural matters left to the two-thirds majority. Had this been the formulae adopted by the Act, it would have been easier to obtain decisions on important issues, such as whether or not to deploy an enforcement action with as many as a majority of one. For instance, in a 54-member AU Assembly, a simple majority will be twenty-eight members as against

[79] *Id.* at art. 10.

[80] *Id.* at art. 10(2)(c).

[81] *Id.* at art. 11(2).

[82] *Id.* at art. 11(3).

[83] *Id.* at art. 11(4).

[84] *Id.* at art. 12.

a two-thirds which is 31 members, although this proposal is, in itself, not watertight, especially since whatever formulae is adopted can always be hijacked by the AU super states such as Algeria, Egypt, Libya, Nigeria, and South Africa.

Arguendo, in order to deploy a military operation, the PSC requires the cooperation of the concerned regional organization, a prospect that has been facilitated by Article 16 of the PSC Protocol which not only makes those organizations part of Africa's peace and security architecture, but also obligates the PSC and the AU Chairperson to coordinate and harmonize their activities with regional mechanisms.

The schema for AU/RECS cooperation is neither detailed in the AU Act nor elaborated in the PSC protocol. Such details are left to the Memorandum of Understanding between the AU and RECs in the field of peace and security, which is not a concern of this chapter. What is important to note, however, is that the bone of contention, in the AU/REC cooperation, is as regards the deployment of the regional elements of the African Stand-by Force, a continental interventionist powerhouse envisaged by Article 13 PSC protocol. Details of who will authorize what are still being worked out both at the AU and at the RECs levels, but it is important that the AU and RECs clearly delineate the areas of responsibility.[85]

Obviously, there exist legal and institutional frameworks such that will enable the AU and RECs to implement all elements of RtoP. However, the mere fact that regional organizations may take enforcement action for the purposes of RtoP does not automatically imply that such actions are invariably legal under international law. It is to a consideration of the legality of regional enforcement action to implement RtoP that the chapter now turns.

VI. IMPLEMENTING RTOP: THE AU AND INTERNATIONAL LAW

Except if the AU is explicitly or implicitly authorized by the Security Council to take enforcement action in a Member State, an enforcement action by the Union, even to protect human lives, risks illegality under the Charter rules.[86] If the AU undertakes an enforcement action, which the Security Council does not authorize prior to the action, or take steps towards retroactively approving, the action is potentially a candidate of illegality. It will be seen to have breached Article 2(4) of the UN Charter.

However, if the AU takes the action pursuant to a request by the concerned Member State, then presumably such is a peacekeeping operation under Article 4(j) of the AU Act which does not require the Security Council authorization. But if the AU later employs military force within that operation against, say a rebel group within that Member State, but not the state itself, this is still an enforcement action, insofar as it is aimed at extracting compliance by the target party with international law. What makes an action *enforcement* is not the party against which it is directed, but the purpose it seeks to achieve.

A regional enforcement action taken for the sole purpose of implementing RtoP may receive accolades from the whole world, but it does not escape the legal

[85] *See* Ademola Abass, (ed.) Protecting Human Security in Africa (2010), at Ch. 11.

[86] UN Charter, art. 53(1).

requirements of the UN Charter. The World Summit Outcome Document, and other allied instruments, may confer some authority on the international community to protect people against the most reprehensible crimes in the world, but these obligations are derived from international instruments *other than* the UN Charter; hence, by virtue of Article 103 of the Charter, such obligations are prevailed over by those of the Charter should there ever be a conflict between the two.

The argument may be made that since Article 103 is addressed to states and not to international organizations, and since the latter are not signatories to the UN Charter, their use of force (unauthorized by the Security Council) to implement RtoP is not in collision with Article 103. Sound as this argument may seem, it is difficult to see how states could escape collectively from obligations that they individually assume under the UN Charter. And it is Member States of the United Nations and AU that contribute troops to regional peacekeeping missions. In any case, the action will still violate Article 53(1) of the Charter.

From a policy standpoint, the risk of AU using force against "the territorial integrity and political independence of its member States" is extremely low given the little probability that the Union will ever deploy military force without the concerned Member State's consent. But what if, against all odds, it does? Then the crux of the matter is whether such a force breaches Article 2(4) of the Charter, even if it clearly breaches Article 53(1) of the Charter, which regulates such uses of force by regional organizations.

The time-honored argument is that any use of force, except for self-defense or [that is] authorized by the Security Council, invariably breaches Article 2(4). Proponents of humanitarian intervention have tried, without much success, to build an exception into customary international law. They argue, *inter alia*, that although the UN Charter does not recognize humanitarian intervention, it seems acceptable to states in their practice. Alternatively they argue that since one of the purposes of the UN is to protect peoples from scourges of war, the use of force to prevent massive human-rights violations or to protect people does not violate Article 2(4). Some even go thus far to argue that since Article 2(4) is only directed against uses of force that violate the "territorial integrity or political independence" of States, the use of force for purposes other than these does not contravene Article 2(4).

This line of argument is prone to many pitfalls. To start with, customary international law is at best inchoate on humanitarian intervention. Furthermore, the Charter, which prescribes protecting people from scourges of war as one of the UN purposes, is the same that specifies the means of achieving that: the Security Council actions or actions authorized by it. Those who argue that "territorial integrity or political independence" is not violated by RtoP obviously discountenance the preference of the target state, in addition to attaching undue importance to the physical structure of a State rather than its political essence. That argument is always thin, and has been since Anthony D'Amato first made it in regard to the U.S. military intervention in Panama in 1984.[87] Certainly, the use of force to protect people will in all aspects violate the territorial integrity and political independence of the concerned state. Thus, the

[87] Anthony D'Amato, *The Invasion of Panama was a Lawful Response to Tyranny* 84 AJIL 516 (1990).

"D'Amatorian" argument is not available for RtoP purposes, that is, if it ever makes any sense at all.

ICISS attempted to escape this kind of debate by deliberately avoiding using the phrase "humanitarian intervention" allegedly because many stakeholders it consulted in the course of its work objected to a militarization of humanitarianism. In the Commission's view, "it is anathema for the humanitarian relief and assistance sector to have this word appropriated to describe any kind of military action."[88] Obviously there is a hint of cynicism about this argument. For some time, the UN has used military force to deliver humanitarian aid, beginning with Somalia in 1994. Does such an action then cease to be "humanitarian" because it is one delivered by military force? It is highly doubtful that humanitarian organizations and workers will object to military protection in war zones for fear of the action being seen as a militarization of humanitarianism.

It is possible that, in future, commentators will seek refuge in the doctrinal exposition of the concept of RtoP by ICISS in order to justify the use of force against a State without its consent. The argument will be that since RtoP is designed to help states to discharge their Responsibility to Protect their people, it is a benevolent act made for altruistic reasons, those reasons which are ensconced in the six conditions prescribed by ICISS to guide RtoP. Thus, the contention will be that the use of force by the international community is resorted to with great pains, and *only* because the State could not protect its own people and could not even take advantage of the assistance rendered it by the international community to achieve that aim. By undertaking RtoP, the international community is actually helping the State to exercise its sovereignty which, in RtoP vocabulary means responsibility towards its people, not control over them. Clearly, the new meaning of sovereignty drawn up by ICISS was skillfully delivered to States through a process that was apparently cajoling, but subliminally akin to a gentle blackmail.

VII. CONCLUSION

The emergence of RtoP as an international norm in 2005, five years after the adoption of the Millennium Development Goals (MDGs), undoubtedly reflects the mood of the international community and its desire to rigorously concern itself with improving the lots of humanity and protecting human lives from wanton destruction both natural and, more importantly, man-made.

To be sure, 2005 was not the first time the world had sworn to "never again" allow the scourges of war, which have blighted humanity several times over. After the Second World War, and again after nearly one million lives were exterminated in Rwanda under the UN peacekeepers' watch are two stark examples. Yet, like a recidivist criminal, the international community will no doubt be a prisoner of its own resolve due to the shenanigans of international politics, likely before the ink dries on the pages where the familiar mantra is once again inscribed.

The Darfur crisis is a somewhat bitter pill in the mouths of a resolute international community. It took nearly five years after the catastrophe began before the world

[88] ICISS Report, *supra* note 41, at ¶ 1.40.

started to seriously engage in the protection of human lives there. It mattered little that the Darfur crisis, which began in 2003, worsened in 2005—the same year the world recommitted itself to protect human security.

There is a great desire to leave the core tasks of protecting human lives to the Security Council. The combined provisions of the UN Charter, the clear preference of States that participated in the 2005 World Summit, the various efforts that antedated and predated that summit, such as the salutary ICISS report reviewed above, all demonstrate that much of the world earnestly desires that the Security Council take full charge.

However, history too tells us that the UN Security Council is often found wanting in the darkest moments of humankind when decisiveness, courage, and forthrightness are the crucial actions needed for a threatening international situation. Many times, Africa has deliberately or inadvertently become a prime example of the Security Council's most profound inaction. Thus, asking Africa to *once again* trust a body that has repeatedly proved to be totally useless when human lives are at stake is like squeezing a stone to yield water. Yet, with no other recourse, Africans have little choice but to trust and hope that the Security Council will employ the sacred Responsibility to Protect with alacrity to ensure their safety and enforce their human rights. In entertaining this request, however, Africans clearly reserve for themselves the right to go it alone, if and whenever they deem fit. This is, to be fair, a small price for the Security Council to pay for squandering its legitimacy.

7 Asia and the Pacific

Noel M. Morada

The Responsibility to Protect (RtoP) is still far from having taken root in China, Southeast Asia, and the larger Asia Pacific region. The novelty of this emerging political norm is appreciated by the informed public, particularly intellectual elites, given its focus on redefining sovereignty as responsibility in protecting peoples against mass atrocities. At the same time, however, there are still serious reservations in this part of the world among governments and non-state actors in embracing the principle in the absence of acceptable universal standards and mechanisms in implementing it, especially if there is manifest failure of states in protecting their people.

This chapter examines the context and dynamics of promoting RtoP in the Asia Pacific, focusing mainly on China and Southeast Asia and the role of the Association of Southeast Asian Nations (ASEAN). A discussion of other Asia Pacific countries' positions on the RtoP debate in the United Nations in July 2009 is also presented to show whether there is an emerging consensus in the region about the principle and its application. The main argument of this chapter is that, notwithstanding a number of challenges and constraints, a stronger commitment in protecting peoples against mass atrocities is possible in the long run. This would depend largely on how RtoP is adapted and operationalized in the context of the principle of non-interference in the internal affairs of states, which is still valued by many states in the region. At the same time, there is a need to promote constituency-building around RtoP at both regional and domestic levels.

What follows is a discussion of China's position on RtoP as well as its views and behavior in dealing with international humanitarian crisis situations and protection of civilians in armed conflicts. Thereafter, the chapter presents a discussion of ASEAN's views and position on RtoP, including Southeast Asia's geopolitical and historical context, which provides an important background to how traditional norms in ASEAN have evolved.

I. CHINA AND THE RESPONSIBILITY TO PROTECT

China has supported the RtoP in the 2005 World Summit and UN Security Council Resolution 1674. It has also affirmed its support for the principle based on subsequent official statements, particularly with regard to enhancing the United Nation's capacity in preventing mass atrocities. Even so, Beijing has been averse to the use of force and sanctions, especially if these are neither based on consensus nor supported by pertinent regional organizations. Its qualified support for the use of force is limited to its application 1) as a last resort to fulfill civilian protection mandate; 2) which must have the consent of the concerned state; and 3) which must be authorized by the UN Security Council. To some extent, China's position on RtoP is anchored mainly on the belief that it is important to build the capacity of states to prevent mass atrocities and that the UN should assist states in this regard, particularly through humanitarian, diplomatic, and other peaceful means.[1]

Just like member states of ASEAN, China adheres to respect for sovereignty and non-interference, which is an important pillar of its foreign policy.[2] Given its problems in Tibet and Xinjiang (East Turkistan), China understandably remains cautious about RtoP given the potential for invoking this principle against the Chinese government. In recent years, China was severely criticized by Western countries in the way that it violently cracked down on protesters in Tibet and Xinjiang province in 2008 and 2009, respectively.[3] While this adherence to policy of absolute non-interference may, on the surface, contradict the core rationale for RtoP, there are nonetheless notable transformations in China's thinking and policies that may contribute significantly to operationalizing the norm.[4] For example, some conservative members of the country's foreign policy elite do not consider committing mass atrocities as part of the state's sovereign prerogative. They also think that the international community can and should respond to extreme humanitarian crises situations through various multilateral means even as the UN is obliged to assist states in putting an end to excessive violence.[5] Specifically, in 2007, Chinese Foreign Minister Yang Jiechi argued during the UN Security Council High-Level Meeting on Africa the necessity of making comprehensive efforts at national, regional, and global levels in promoting peace and noted that the international community "has a moral obligation to help Africa."[6]

[1] Sarah Teitt, *China and the Responsibility to Protect* 2 (Asia-Pacific Centre for the Responsibility to Protect, Dec. 18, 2008), http://www.r2pasiapacific.org/images/stories/food/china_and_r2p.pdf.

[2] This position is based on the Five Principles of Peaceful Coexistence, which include: 1) mutual respect for sovereignty and territorial integrity; 2) mutual non-aggression; 3) non-interference in each other's internal affairs; 4) equality and mutual benefit; and 5) peaceful coexistence.

[3] *See* Edward Wong, *Clashes in China Shed Light On Ethnic Divide*, New York Times, Jul. 7, 2009; Sumini Sengupta & Hari Kumar, *Dalai Lama Won't Stop Tibet Protests*, New York Times, Mar. 16, 2008.

[4] Teitt, *supra* note 1, at 6.

[5] *Id.*

[6] *Id.*

A. RtoP and China's Role in Peacekeeping

China has backed up its rhetoric supporting action on humanitarian crises with continuing involvement in UN peacekeeping operations since the 1990s. It also supported the dispatch of UN peacekeeping missions authorized to use force to protect civilians in intrastate conflicts. Since 2000, China has shown its commitment to international peace by contributing a significant amount of military and civilian police personnel to peacekeeping operations as well as administration and reconstruction efforts in host countries.[7] At the end of 2010, China ranked 13th among the top 20 contributors of uniformed personnel to UN peacekeeping missions and contributed more troops than any other permanent member of the Security Council. It ranked 7th (with 3.94 percent share) among the top 20 contributors to the UN peacekeeping budget after the U.S., Japan, UK, Germany, France, and Italy.[8]

There is no question China has opposed the adoption of a number of UN Security Council resolutions directed at states that sponsor or condone violence against civilian populations. This has effectively limited the practical impact of RtoP, especially when situations merit coercive response from the Security Council. However, China had also resorted to informal or "backdoor" diplomacy to persuade concerned state leaders to practice more restraint and pursued political solutions to emerging crisis situations. More recently, however, a Chinese scholar noted a remarkable change in Chinese diplomacy with regard to the crisis in Sudan. Specifically, Chinese diplomats held press conferences after their visits to Darfur and Khartoum where they described China's efforts to put pressure on the Sudanese government.[9] Another notable change was the meeting between Chinese diplomats and rebel leaders in Darfur in February 2008, which is a departure from the usual adherence to strict interpretation of sovereignty and non-interference to a country's internal affairs. Compared to its stance in the Kosovo crisis, China appears to have adopted a much softer position concerning humanitarian intervention in Darfur.[10] A more flexible Chinese diplomacy was also noted in Burma (Myanmar) in October 2007 when Beijing secured a visa for UN Special Envoy Ibrahim Gambari to enable the latter to meet with top officials in Yangon. This example suggests that Beijing is apparently open to the "conceptual and normative underpinnings" of RtoP and not just "adhering to an unyielding and static concept of sovereignty."[11]

B. RtoP and Protection of Civilians

Notwithstanding some notable changes in China's thinking and diplomatic practice regarding humanitarian crisis situations as enumerated above, China remains wary of the application and interpretation of RtoP in open debates related to protection of

[7] *Id.* at 7.

[8] UN Dep't of Peacekeeping Operations, UN Peacekeeping Background Note, DPI/2429/Rev. 9, Jan. 2011, *available at* http://www.un.org/en/peacekeeping/documents/backgroundnote.pdf.

[9] Wu Chengqiu, *Sovereignty, Human Rights, and Responsibility: Changes in China's Response to International Humanitarian Crises*, 15 J. Chinese Pol. Sci. (2010), at 83.

[10] *Id.*

[11] Teitt, *supra* note 1, at 8.

civilians (POC) in armed conflicts within the Security Council. In June 2006, for example, China pointed out that Resolution 1674 reaffirmed only the World Summit's commitment to RtoP, which applies only to the four crimes (genocide, ethnic cleansing, war crimes, and crimes against humanity) even as its ambassador to the UN argued that "it is not appropriate to expand, willfully to interpret or even abuse this concept."[12] In the 2007 POC debate, the Chinese delegation also argued that the Security Council should avoid invoking the concept given the varied interpretations and understandings of Member States about what RtoP is all about.[13] In 2009, the Chinese delegation in the POC debate underscored the importance of exercising caution in the use of force and avoiding emphasis on military options, even as they also endorsed further discussions on mandating peacekeeping operations to protect civilians.[14] During a meeting in Beijing in November 2009 that looked into the direction of UN peacekeeping, Vice Foreign Minister He Yafei emphasized the need to giving equal importance to traditional approaches to peacekeeping such as conflict prevention, dispute mediation, crisis management, and post-conflict peace-building.[15]

China also opposed the creation of an informal Security Council Expert Group on POC, which was supposed to hold "transparent, systematic and timely consultations on POC concerns, particularly, but not only, in the context of the establishment or renewal of peacekeeping mandates."[16] Specifically, it argued that protection of civilians should be considered on a case-to-case basis as seen in the context of the peace process and political situation for each country.[17] In any case, China's support for the idea that states bear the responsibility to prevent the four crimes is anchored on the belief that conflict prevention and capacity-building are necessary to enhancing protection of civilians.[18] It further contends that the Security Council is not the only one charged to pursue civilian protection in armed conflicts but should also be shared by the General Assembly and other UN agencies, global and regional organizations, as well as non-government organizations. They are seen as playing an important role in enhancing the state's capacity in conflict prevention strategies, including protection of civilians, which are directly linked to operationalization of RtoP.[19]

C. RtoP and China's International Image

Overall, China's cautious support for RtoP does not necessarily mean that it has significantly altered its adherence to the principles of non-interference and protection of state sovereignty. As was noted by one Chinese author, the concept of RtoP has neither received significant attention in the public media nor has it been fully debated

[12] *Id.*

[13] *Id.*

[14] Sarah Teitt, *The Responsibility to Protect and China's Peacekeeping Policy*, J. INT'L PEACEKEEPING (forthcoming 2011) (manuscript at 12) (on file with author).

[15] *Id.*

[16] *Id.* at 13.

[17] *Id.*

[18] Teitt, *supra* note 1, at 9.

[19] *Id.* at 9–10.

among Chinese scholars.[20] If anything, China's "second degree internalization" of this norm is more about its concern for its national and international images. More specifically, if RtoP "represents a new trend in international human rights and humanitarian norms, it has not been fully internalized by China. China has acted generally in accordance to international human rights and humanitarian norms in dealing with some international incidents in this regard, in particular the Darfur crisis, not because China has embraced these norms wholeheartedly, but because these incidents have affected China's interest: they would undermine China's national image had China acted otherwise." [21] As well, its support for RtoP is part of enhancing its international image as a "responsible great power" because, given that Chinese officials seldom mentioned the norm, "China has great incentive to act in accordance with other countries' expectation. It becomes more willing to take responsibility and more sensitive to international human rights and humanitarian norms in its foreign policymaking."[22]

II. RTOP AND ASEAN: GEOPOLITICAL AND HISTORICAL CONTEXTS

Southeast Asia is essentially made up of multi-ethnic societies that are still in the process of nation-state building. Except for Thailand, countries in the region have been administered by post-colonial states whose independence were either granted by Western powers after the Second World War or won through wars of independence up until the mid-1970s. In the aftermath of the Vietnam War in 1975, a prolonged civil war ensued in Cambodia that saw the rise and fall of the notorious Khmer Rouge and the subsequent occupation of that country by Vietnam in 1979 that lasted for a decade. Even today, the legitimacy of the state is continually being challenged internally in some countries through armed rebellion or separatist movements, notably in the island of Mindanao in the Philippines, West Papua (Irian Jaya) in Indonesia, and ethnic-based separatism in Burma. In the case of Thailand, its three southernmost provinces that are predominantly Muslim Malay have been plagued by violence as some extremist groups who refuse the mainstream Buddhist Thai culture continue to attack both civilians and government troops in the area. For other countries, modernization and sustained economic growth for decades have not necessarily mitigated underlying ethnic and religious tensions that surface every now and then, particularly in times of economic downturns or crises.

A. Traditional Norms

It is against this backdrop that many Southeast Asian states continue to value national sovereignty, territorial integrity, and the principle of non-interference. In fact, these traditional norms form the core principles on which the Association of Southeast Asian Nations (ASEAN) was created in 1967 among five original members (Indonesia,

[20] Wu Chengqiu, *Sovereignty, Human Rights, and Responsibility: Changes in China's Response to International Humanitarian Crises*, 15 J. Chinese Pol. Sci. (2010), at 90.

[21] *Id.*

[22] *Id.* at 94.

Malaysia, the Philippines, Singapore, and Thailand) and have been underscored even in the ASEAN Charter that was ratified in 2008 by its ten members.[23]

In the 1980s, the original five members of ASEAN invoked international law and its traditional norms in opposing Vietnam's occupation of Cambodia after ousting the Khmer Rouge in 1979. At the time, ASEAN did not consider the Vietnamese invasion of Cambodia as a form of humanitarian intervention, which was Hanoi's main excuse for ending the mass atrocities committed by Pol Pot. ASEAN's diplomacy in support of the anti-Vietnamese coalition government's taking the Cambodian seat in the United Nations basically reflected the members' adherence to protecting sovereignty and non-interference principle.

Unlike the European Union (EU), which operates under the framework of supranationalism (surrendering part of national sovereignty of members to regional institutions), ASEAN's version of regionalism still values the protection of sovereignty of Member States. Discussion of internal affairs of states remains taboo in ASEAN meetings, even among state or government leaders. In fact, two operative principles in ASEAN decision-making—consensus and "least common denominator" (LCD)—contribute to strengthening sovereignty and non-interference norms in the organization. Consensus decision-making, often referred to as the "ASEAN Way", protects members' national interests as each state could exercise veto on matters that may be perceived as interfering in the state's internal affairs. For example, in 2007, following violent crackdowns against demonstrations in Rangoon, Burma, led by Buddhist monks, the prime minister of Burma during the ASEAN Summit in Singapore objected to the UN Special Envoy giving a briefing to the leaders meeting on the situation in that country.[24] In 2005 former Thai Prime Minister Thaksin Shinawatra, during the ASEAN Summit in Kuala Lumpur, reportedly threatened to walk out of the meeting of leaders if the issue of southern Thailand was raised.[25]

The LCD principle may also be invoked by a Member State if it is unwilling to accept any initiative, project, norm, or principle for immediate adoption by the group if these are perceived as undermining its national interest as well. In some ASEAN documents, the LCD principle is also translated as ASEAN proceeding "at a pace comfortable to all." A good example of Member States invoking this principle was during discussions and negotiations concerning the creation of a regional human rights body in ASEAN. Specifically, in the drafting of the ASEAN Charter in 2006 and 2007, some new members opposed the inclusion of a provision for establishing such a regional body, citing their fears that it could lead to interference in domestic affairs of Member States.

[23] ASEAN was formed as a vehicle to promote regional cooperation among its founding members. Prior to ASEAN's creation, other attempts at regionalism (through the Association of Southeast Asia (ASA) and MAPHILINDO (Malaysia, Philippines, Indonesia)) were made but faltered due to territorial conflicts among its members. Indonesia served as the main stabilizer in the region and a natural leader in ASEAN as it promoted the idea of regional resilience through peace and cooperation among its members, which allowed countries in the region to focus on their national development.

[24] *See* Wan Hamidi Hamin, *Gambari Will Not Brief Leaders On Myanmar*, The New Straits Times, Nov. 20, 2007, http://findarticles.com/p/news-articles/new-straits-times/mi_8016/is_20071120/gambari-leaders-myanmar/ai_n44378795/.

[25] *See* Ukhrist Pathmanand, *Thaksin's Achilles Heel: The Failure of Hawkish Approaches in the Thai South*, 38 Critical Asian Stud. 73, 84 (2006); *ASEAN-China Free Trade Proposed*, Manila Bull., Nov. 27, 2004, http://www.mb.com.ph/node/188073.

To break the deadlock over the issue, a second paragraph was added in the draft Charter that left the design of the terms of reference of the regional human rights body to a separate ad hoc panel that was created later on. Eventually, the terms of reference of the ASEAN Intergovernmental Commission on Human Rights (AICHR) that was created in 2009 did not give the regional body monitoring and sanctioning powers over member states on the protection of human rights.

B. Variations in Political Systems and Cultures

At a deeper level, the difficulties faced by ASEAN in generating consensus on a number of issues in the region—and especially on sensitive political matters—stem largely from the diversity of political systems and cultures, as well as gaps in economic development among its members. For example, some members adhere to one-party rule or single-party dominance, others have multi-party systems, while some have transitioned from authoritarian to democratic orders, and the rest still remain under absolute monarchy or military-dominated rule. More often, the less democratic states in ASEAN have been slow in embracing liberal principles or norms that they perceive to be potentially undermining the authority or legitimacy of the state. In fact, in the late 1980s following the "people power revolution" in the Philippines in 1986, some ASEAN Member States (notably Singapore and Malaysia) at the time even invoked the Asian values argument to parry the wave of "Western liberal values" sweeping the region. For them, the latter's emphasis on individual freedom is not compatible with those of Asian societies that value more filial piety and social harmony. They even argued that instead of giving priority to political rights, they prefer to give more attention to economic and social rights as part of their economic development goals. New members that were admitted after 1995 even invoked the same arguments in resisting calls by civil society groups in the region for the creation of a regional human rights mechanism in the late 1990s. In 2003, when Indonesia was chair of ASEAN and proposed the idea of an ASEAN Security Community that promotes democracy as one of the core values in the organization, a number of members—particularly the newer ones—opposed the idea. Despite this, however, Indonesia remained steadfast in promoting the idea of an ASEAN Community whose members adhere to the principles of democracy, good governance, and justice, which was later embodied in the ASEAN Political Security Community blueprint adopted by the group in 2009.

C. State- Versus People-Centered Regionalism

ASEAN members also remain divided on the idea of allowing greater participatory regionalism. In 2005, calls for transforming ASEAN into a more "people-centered" organization during the 11th Summit of ASEAN leaders apparently created expectations among civil society groups in the region that the ten-member bloc is ready to engage non-state actors in policy formulation.[26] The first ASEAN Civil Society

[26] *See* Noel M. Morada, *ASEAN at 40: Prospects for Community Building in Southeast Asia*, 15 Asia-Pacific Rev. 36 (May 2008).

Conference (ACSC) was held in Kuala Lumpur, which saw for the first time an "interface" meeting with ASEAN leaders during the Summit. The meeting lasted only for about ten minutes where a civil society representative presented the ACSC report to the leaders, which was later appended in the ASEAN Chair's statement.[27] Many civil society groups expected the meeting with ASEAN leaders will become a regular feature of future Summits, but in 2009 the meeting was called off because leaders from Cambodia and Burma did not agree to the process of selecting civil society representatives to the meeting. This clearly indicates that some Member States in ASEAN are still not comfortable with the idea of giving more opportunities for non-state actors to participate in regional policy process.[28]

The discomfort of some ASEAN members towards greater participatory regionalism is also reflected in drafting the ASEAN Charter. In the 2005 Summit, the Eminent Persons Group (EPG) on the ASEAN Charter was created to draw a blueprint of the charter and make recommendations. It was mandated to "think out of the box" and propose bold and innovative ideas on what the ASEAN Charter should look like.[29] The EPG conducted consultation meetings with various sectors, including think tanks and civil society groups in the region to generate ideas for its proposals. In its Report submitted to the ASEAN leaders, the EPG's recommendations, among others, included alternative non-consensus decision-making, provisions for sanctions (including expulsion) of erring members, and creation of a consultative body composed of representatives from civil society groups, academia, business, and industry. On ASEAN principles, the EPG Report also included people-centered recommendations that upheld the protection of human rights, international humanitarian law, prevention of genocide and mass atrocities covered by Responsibility to Protect (RtoP) principle, rule of law, as well as promotion of good governance, among others.[30]

However, the High Level Task Force (HLTF) that later drafted the ASEAN Charter did not adopt the bold recommendations of the EPG that were unacceptable to some member states. The final version of the Charter that was ratified in 2008 upheld consensus decision-making, did not contain provisions for sanctions against erring members, and gave priority to traditional norms protecting sovereignty, territorial integrity, and non-interference even though human-rights protection, good governance, rule of law, and international humanitarian law were also incorporated in its principles.[31] Essentially, the ASEAN Charter was a watered down version that simply formalized the state-centered traditional norms and principles of ASEAN. Amendments to the Charter may be introduced five years after ratification and only based on consensus among members. For many civil society groups that participated in the consultation meetings held by both the EPG and HLTF, the final version of the ASEAN

[27] Chairman's Statement on the 11th ASEAN Summit "One Vision, One Identity, One Community" (Dec. 15, 2005), http://www.aseansec.org/18039.htm.

[28] Kavi Chongkittavorn, *Split between ASEAN Leaders and Civil Society Groups Widens*, The Nation (Oct. 12, 2009), http://www.nationmultimedia.com/2009/10/12/opinion/opinion_30114237.php.

[29] *See* ASEAN, *Declaration on the Establishment of the ASEAN Charter* (Dec. 15, 2005), http://www.aseansec.org/18030.htm.

[30] *See* ASEAN, *Report of the Eminent Persons Group on the ASEAN Charter* (Dec. 2006), http://www.aseansec.org/19247.pdf.

[31] *See* ASEAN, *Charter* (Jan. 2008), http://www.aseansec.org/publications/ASEAN-Charter.pdf.

Charter was a major disappointment, as it did not contain many of their ideas on participatory regionalism, particularly in making Member States more transparent and accountable.

One may be tempted to conclude that ASEAN is less than prepared to embrace emerging political norms like RtoP simply by looking at the ASEAN Charter's pertinent provisions and articles.[32] Specifically, its state-centered norms and principles, coupled with the absence of sanctions against erring members, do not encourage greater transparency and accountability of Member States. Even though a regional human rights body is already in place as provided for in the Charter, its current terms of reference do not allow it to either monitor or even entertain complaints about human rights violations in the region. Apart from this, only four out of ten members have national commission on human rights—Indonesia, Malaysia, the Philippines, and Thailand—even though this does not necessarily imply that these national bodies are effective in promoting the protection of human rights within their respective borders.

The ASEAN Charter and the AICHR, however, are not the sum total of ASEAN. It is also important to look at ASEAN's community-building project as providing more opportunities for advancing RtoP in the region. Specifically, the first pillar of the ASEAN Community idea, which is the ASEAN Political Security Community (APSC), includes political development, norm building, as well as conflict prevention, resolution, and post-conflict peace-building as important dimensions of this project. The next section of this chapter discusses in more detail the pertinent elements of the APSC and how it provides opportunities for RtoP norm internalization in ASEAN.

III. ASEAN COMMUNITY BUILDING: OPPORTUNITIES FOR RTOP NORM INTERNALIZATION

Since 2003, community-building has been the main preoccupation of ASEAN following the Bali Concord II agreement. Specifically, the ASEAN Community idea is composed of three pillars, namely, the ASEAN Security Community (ASC, later changed to ASEAN Political Security Community or APSC), the ASEAN Economic Community (AEC), and the ASEAN Socio-Cultural Community (ASCC).[33]

Of particular significance to promoting RtoP in the region is the first pillar, which is Indonesia's initiative in transforming the regional bloc into a security community, which is envisaged "to bring ASEAN's political and security cooperation to a higher plane to ensure that countries in the region live at peace with one another and with the world in a *just*, *democratic*, and harmonious environment."[34] In a subsequent ASC

[32] For an elaborate discussion of RtoP and the ASEAN Charter, see Noel M. Morada, *The ASEAN Charter and the Promotion of RtoP in Southeast Asia: Challenges and Constraints*, 1 Global Responsibility to Protect 185 (Mar. 2009).

[33] *See* ASEAN, *Concord II (Bali Concord II)* (Oct. 7, 2003), http://www.aseansec.org/15159.htm; ASEAN Secretariat, *Political Security Community Blueprint*, Jun. 2009, *available at* http://www.aseansec.org/5187–18.pdf; ASEAN Secretariat, *Economic Community Blueprint*, Jun. 2009, *available at* http://www.aseansec.org/5187–10.pdf; ASEAN Secretariat, *Socio-Cultural Community Blueprint*, Jun. 2009, *available at* http://www.aseansec.org/5187–19.pdf.

[34] ASEAN, *Declaration of ASEAN Concord (Bali Concord II)*, ASEAN Knowledge Kit 7–8 (Nov. 2006), *available at* http://www.aseansec.org/publ-bali-concord.pdf.

Plan of Action adopted in 2004, the major areas for security community-building were identified as political development, shaping and sharing of norms, conflict prevention, conflict resolution, and post-conflict peace-building. Among the specific activities under political development are: 1) strengthening democratic institutions and popular participation; 2) promoting understanding and appreciation of political system, culture, and history of ASEAN member countries; 3) strengthening the rule of law and judiciary systems, legal infrastructure, and capacity-building; 4) promoting free flow of information among and within ASEAN member countries; 5) enhancing good governance in public and private sectors; 6) establishing a network among existing human rights mechanisms; 7) protecting vulnerable groups including women, children, people with disabilities, and migrant workers; and 8) promoting education and public awareness on human rights.[35]

In the area of conflict prevention, the Plan of Action identified specific activities that include: 1) strengthening confidence-building measures (e.g., utilizing civilian and military personnel in disaster relief operations); 2) strengthening preventive measures (e.g., developing an ASEAN early warning system based on existing mechanisms to prevent occurrence and escalation of conflict); and 3) strengthening ASEAN Regional Forum (ARF) process in support of the ASC (e.g., moving the ARF to the preventive diplomacy stage and beyond). It also identified activities under conflict resolution, such as: 1) developing regional cooperation for maintenance of peace and stability (e.g., promoting technical cooperation with the UN and relevant regional organizations; establishing/assigning national focal points for regional cooperation for maintenance of peace and stability; and utilization of national peacekeeping centers to establish regional arrangement for maintenance of peace and stability); and 2) developing or supporting initiatives (e.g., promoting exchange and cooperation among ASEAN centers of excellence on peace, and conflict management and resolution studies; and considering the establishment of an ASEAN Institute for Peace and Reconciliation).[36]

Finally, in the area of post-conflict peace-building, some of the activities identified in the Plan of Action include: 1) strengthening ASEAN humanitarian assistance (e.g., providing safe havens in conflict areas; ensuring delivery of basic services or assistance to victims of conflict; orderly repatriation of refugees/displaced persons and resettlement of internally displaced persons; ensuring safety of humanitarian assistance workers; promoting humanitarian relief assistance organizations; considering the establishment of an ASEAN Humanitarian Assistance Centre; and intensifying cooperation with the UN and other regional organizations/donor countries); 2) developing cooperation in post-conflict reconstruction and rehabilitation in affected areas (e.g., undertaking human resources development and capacity-building; assisting in institutional building and promoting popular participation; reducing inter-communal tensions through education exchanges and curriculum reform; and increasing cooperation in reconciliation and promotion of a culture of peace); and 3) establishing a mechanism to mobilize necessary resources to facilitate post-conflict peace-building (e.g., a Stability Fund), including through cooperation with donor countries and international institutions.[37]

[35] *Id.* at 41–42.

[36] *Id.* at 44–48.

[37] *Id.* at 49–50.

In 2009, the ASEAN Political Security Community (APSC) Blueprint was adopted by member states, which built on the previous ASC Plan of Action. Specifically, the Blueprint stated that the principal characteristics and elements of the APSC include: 1) promotion of political development "in adherence to the principles of democracy, rule of law and good governance, *respect for and promotion and protection of human rights and fundamental freedoms*"; 2) promotion of "*a people-oriented ASEAN* in which all sectors of society, regardless of gender, race, religion, language, or social and cultural background, are encouraged to participate in, and benefit from, the process of ASEAN integration and community-building"; 3) that in the implementation of the Blueprint, ASEAN should "strive towards promoting and supporting gender-mainstreaming, *tolerance, respect for diversity*, equality and mutual understanding;" and 4) that the APSC "subscribes to a *comprehensive approach to security*, which acknowledges the interwoven relationships of political, economic, social-cultural and environmental dimensions of development."[38]

Based on the above, the APSC Blueprint could serve as the main framework in promoting RtoP norm internalization in the region. Although the above ASEAN documents do not use the language of RtoP, the essential elements of APSC are related to the norm of Responsibility to Protect, particularly in regard to human rights protection, conflict prevention and resolution, and post-conflict peace-building. To some extent, RtoP could even enhance the APSC Blueprint if this norm could be incorporated in the framework, especially in developing the capacity of ASEAN states to prevent genocide and mass atrocities. In a region that is made up of multi-ethnic societies and governed by states with a variety of political systems and culture, the language used in the APSC documents that are undoubtedly linked to RtoP include "people-oriented ASEAN", "promoting tolerance, respect for diversity, and equality", and "comprehensive security." Given that ASEAN members have adopted the APSC Blueprint, it could then serve as a useful benchmark for measuring progress in the areas of political development, norm building, and conflict prevention. Non-state actors and civil society groups that advocate human rights protection, RtoP, and participatory regionalism could also exert pressure on governments to implement the APSC Blueprint and make substantial progress in realizing the goals of this particular pillar of the ASEAN Community.

But what are the prospects for advancing RtoP in the context of ASEAN's community-building efforts? What is the current thinking, views, and perspectives of governments and non-state actors in the region about RtoP? To what extent have member states of ASEAN embraced this emerging political norm since the 2005 UN World Summit? The next section presents a discussion of these issues.

IV. DEBATING RTOP IN SOUTHEAST ASIA: IS IT ABOUT INTERVENTION OR PREVENTION?

In early 2005, this author conducted an initial survey of attitudes and perspectives on RtoP among representatives from academia, civil society, government, and think tanks in the region who were based in major capitals of seven out of 10 countries in ASEAN.

[38] *ASEAN Political Security Community Blueprint*, *supra* note 33, at 1–2.

Most participants in the various workshops and interviews had not heard of RtoP at the time but were generally more positive towards the idea as it attempts to redefine the concept of state sovereignty as including the Responsibility to Protect its people. However, quite a number of them expressed concerns about RtoP being about humanitarian (military) intervention based on the report of the International Commission on Intervention and State Sovereignty (ICISS).[39] Interestingly, most participants expressed interest in developing the preventive aspect of RtoP, which was not fully developed at the time the ICISS Report came out. Some of them even thought of developing a set of regional norms and principles parallel to RtoP that are anchored on existing practices and experiences of countries in dealing with various intra- and inter-state conflicts. Even so, there were real concerns in the region about the prospects of advancing RtoP on a global scale without corresponding reforms in the structure and powers of the United Nations, particularly because of the unilateralist and hyper-power tendencies of the United States under President George W. Bush.[40] The belated adoption of humanitarian intervention by the U.S. as a pretext for invading Iraq in 2003 certainly did not sit well with many countries in the region and did not help in advancing RtoP in this part of the world.

Among other concerns raised with regard to RtoP were: 1) whether it is essentially a Western concept or norm; 2) the difficulties in defining what a humanitarian crisis situation is that merits invoking RtoP; 3) the standards and mechanisms to be used in humanitarian intervention and the role of the UN and regional organizations; and 4) whether the potential targets of humanitarian intervention are most likely the developing countries even as the UN remains a weak institution.[41] Despite these concerns, however, there is agreement among participants that RtoP, as a concept and principle, should be examined further in the context of conflict prevention in Southeast Asia. Specifically, they recognize that many civil society groups in the region have made important contributions to peace-building and post-conflict reconstruction.[42] In fact, there were more ideas and proposals about conflict prevention that were generated in connection with RtoP that seem to parallel those that were identified in the ASC Plan of Action in 2004, as enumerated in the previous section. This indicates that even among intellectual elites and the informed public in the region, RtoP as a concept or norm that advocates prevention—more than military intervention—resonates better in Southeast Asia. To some extent, ASEAN leaders also reflected these views in the UN World Summit in September 2005, as discussed in the next section below.

A. Beyond the 2005 UN World Summit Consensus on RtoP

The unanimous support of UN member states to paragraphs 138–140 on RtoP in the 2005 World Summit Outcome Document apparently indicates that a preliminary international consensus has been reached around the principle that the primary responsibility in protecting people against genocide and mass atrocities rests on states.

[39] *See* Noel M. Morada, *RtoP Roadmap in Southeast Asia* (UNISCI Discussion Papers, No. 11, May 2006), *available at* http://revistas.ucm.es/cps/16962206/articulos/UNIS0606230059A.pdf.

[40] *Id.* at 1–2.

[41] *Id.* at 4–6.

[42] *Id.* at 7.

In Southeast Asia, the support for RtoP by ASEAN Member States should be seen from a more nuanced perspective. Despite endorsing RtoP, Indonesian and Malaysian leaders in their speech at the UNGA in 2005 expressed concerns about the lack of clarity as to when the principle should apply and its potential to sanction the use of force.[43] Although Cambodia and Laos welcomed the UN Secretary-General's *In Larger Freedom* and the 2005 World Summit Outcome Document, they have not overtly endorsed RtoP. Brunei, the Philippines, and Singapore categorically endorsed RtoP in the 2005 World Summit even as Singapore joined the informal "Friends of RtoP."[44] Thailand used to be a vocal advocate of RtoP in 2005 but has since remained quiet, although its former foreign minister and now ASEAN Secretary-General, Dr. Surin Pitsuwan, is a known advocate of the principle.[45] For its part, Vietnam remains a cautious supporter of RtoP and is concerned about the implications of the principle to the norm of non-interference in ASEAN. Burma is the only ASEAN member who expressed concern over the inclusion of RtoP in the World Summit Outcome Document (along with North Korea) even as it also stressed that reforms in the UN should respect the principle of non-interference and equality of states.[46]

Notwithstanding the reservations of most ASEAN members about RtoP, one could identify some common positions based on their policy pronouncements that are linked to implementing the principle. This include support for: strengthening humanitarian response and assistance; enhancing the capability of the UN in deploying peacekeeping troops; adhering to international human rights conventions, rule of law, and good governance; and containing illegal trade in small arms and light weapons. ASEAN members also give importance to the role of regional organizations in assisting the UN in peacekeeping operations. Overall, support for RtoP in the region will be determined by reaching a consensus on: 1) limiting the applicability of the principle to the four crimes (i.e., genocide, ethnic cleansing, war crimes, and crimes against humanity); 2) applying coercive intervention within the framework of the UN Charter; 3) securing the cooperation and consent of states in international engagements in operationalizing the principle, preferably through relevant regional and sub-regional organizations; and 4) implementing RtoP consistent with the principle of non-interference.[47] Limiting the principle to the four crimes would mean that strict standards based on relevant international treaties and conventions would be used to validate claims or allegations about state-sponsored mass atrocities.[48] At the same

[43] *See* Asia-Pacific Centre for the Responsibility to Protect, *The Responsibility to Protect in Southeast Asia* 19, 33 (Jan. 30, 2009) [hereinafter *Southeast Asia*], http://www.r2pasiapacific.org/images/stories/food/r2p%20in%20southeast%20-asia.pdf

[44] According to the former executive director of the Global Center for the Responsibility to Protect, the initial strong interest of the Philippines to join the "Friends of RtoP" in 2009 following the UN GA interactive dialogue appeared to have waned following a change of ambassadors in the Philippine Mission to the UN in New York in 2010.

[45] *Id.* at 53.

[46] Alex Bellamy & Sara E. Davies, *The Responsibility to Protect in the Asia Pacific*, 40 Security Dialogue 566 (Dec. 2009).

[47] *Southeast Asia*, *supra* note 43, 66–67.

[48] For an elaborate discussion of the definition of the four crimes and the criteria used to identify acts that constitute these crimes, *see* Rome Statute of the International Criminal Court, A/CONF.183/9, Jan. 16, 2002.

time, however, it is important to underscore the fact that among member states of ASEAN, only Cambodia has so far ratified the Rome Statute that created the International Criminal Court (ICC), which has jurisdiction over the four crimes. A consensus on the narrow scope of RtoP however does not necessarily imply that states in the region would be ready to submit themselves to the jurisdiction of the ICC. As well, the use of coercive intervention may be easier to accept if it was based on a clear set of criteria (e.g., as a last resort and when all other peaceful means have failed) even as it also has to adhere to the UN Charter. Nonetheless, states in the region are likely to prefer more traditional approaches to managing crisis situations such as mediation, peace talks, backdoor diplomacy, and other political means over the use of military intervention. The consent and cooperation of states is also an important element in securing the legitimacy of any intervention—military or otherwise—given the aversion of many states in this part of the world to external interference. At the same time, however, there are ASEAN members that have advocated the idea of "positive interference" or "constructive engagement" especially in the context of crisis situations that directly or indirectly have an impact on the security and stability of other member states. Thus, for RtoP to be consistent with non-interference principle, consent of states is the key to its implementation.

In July 2009, six members of ASEAN—Indonesia, Malaysia, Burma, the Philippines, Singapore, and Vietnam—participated in the Informal Interactive Dialogue on RtoP in the UN General Assembly, where they reaffirmed their support for the principle based the 2005 agreement. Burma's more positive attitude towards RtoP was a surprise to many, even as it underscored that the consensus in 2005 was a collective obligation and not a unilateral right to act. It also argued that the scope of RtoP should be limited to the four crimes and expressed support for the Secretary-General's appeal in moving the debate on RtoP towards implementing the 2005 agreement.[49] For its part, Indonesia demonstrated its commitment to implementing RtoP and indicated strong interest in expanding measures related to prevention, which it considered to be the key in implementing the 2005 agreement and the Secretary-General's three-pillar approach.[50] Although Malaysia reiterated its commitment to the RtoP, it raised some concerns regarding its implementation. It even argued that a consensus has yet to be reached on the parameters of the principle.[51]

The Philippines also expressed its support to the three-pillar approach in implementing RtoP and argued that the principle clearly applies only to the four crimes. It also stressed that the UNGA debate should work towards a "fair, reasonable, responsible, responsive, effective, and expeditious operationalization of RtoP."[52] Singapore reiterated its commitment to RtoP although it also raised some issues about its operationalization. It argued that the 2005 agreement, specifically paragraphs 138 and 139, provided a clear mandate and that the debate must therefore move forward. It also strongly supported the idea that RtoP is an "ally" and not an "adversary" of

[49] Asia-Pacific Centre for the Responsibility to Protect, *Implementing the Responsibility to Protect: Asia-Pacific in the 2009 General Assembly Dialogue* 22 (Oct. 2009), http://www.r2pasiapacific.org/documents/final_un_ga_debate_july_2009.pdf.

[50] *Id.* at 19.

[51] *Id.* at 21.

[52] *Id.* at 23.

sovereignty.[53] While affirming the 2005 agreement on RtoP and arguing that the international community should no longer debate about the necessity and scope of the principle, Vietnam expressed concern about paragraph 139 of the World Summit Outcome Document. It opted for a holistic interpretation of the paragraph by giving equal emphasis to five "qualifiers", namely: 1) voluntary engagement of states; 2) timely and decisive collective action; 3) "case by case basis"; 4) conformity with the UN Charter; and 5) appropriateness of cooperating with regional organizations. Just like Indonesia, Vietnam also emphasized that prevention is the best approach to protecting people and that the structural causes of conflicts must also be addressed. [54]

Apart from the six ASEAN members, nine other Asia Pacific countries participated in the July 2009 dialogue on RtoP in the UNGA—Australia, China, East Timor, Japan, North Korea, Papua New Guinea, New Zealand, Solomon Islands, and South Korea. Altogether, their statements reflect some points of consensus about RtoP in the Asia Pacific region, which may be summarized thus: 1) the primary Responsibility to Protect people first and foremost rest with the state; 2) the scope of the principle is limited only to the four crimes—genocide, ethnic cleansing, war crimes, and crimes against humanity; 3) the implementation of the principle must be in accordance with international law and the UN Charter; 4) as a universal principle, its application must be done fairly, equally, and non-selectively; and 5) measures related to pillar three of the principle must not be limited to coercion or use of force.[55]

In addition, India expressed its support for RtoP during the 2009 dialogue in the UNGA. However, it highlighted the importance of adhering to the UN Charter in implementing the norm and underscored the need to coordinate with regional organizations if Chapter VII measures are to be used, and only if peaceful means have been inadequate and there is manifest failure on the part of national authorities in discharging their duties.[56] For its part, Pakistan reiterated its support for RtoP but underscored the importance of a comprehensive approach and utilization of UN mechanisms in preventing genocide and other mass atrocities. It also highlighted the need for further dialogue about RtoP in order to clarify the parameters for its implementation in order to avoid the misuse or abuse of the concept.[57] Meanwhile, Sri Lanka pointed out that it recognizes the state as the cornerstone of RtoP and that it is only if it manifestly fails in carrying out its obligations under international law that the international community must assist, with the consent of a democratically elected government, and play a complementary role. Accordingly, a key to operationalizing RtoP is to devise an acceptable approach to defining the triggers and parameters of its application. It also argued that expanding the scope of RtoP beyond the four crimes would not be helpful

[53] *Id.* at 24.

[54] *Id.* at 27–28.

[55] *Id.* at 11.

[56] Amb. Hardeep Singh Puri, Permanent Rep. of India to the UN, Statement to the General Assembly Plenary Meeting on Implementing Responsibility to Protect, Jul. 24, 2009, *available at* http://www.responsibilitytoprotect.org/India_ENG.pdf.

[57] Abdullah Hussain Haroon, Permanent Rep. of Pakistan to the UN, Statement at the Thematic Debate on Responsibility to Protect Populations from Genocide, War Crimes, Ethnic Cleansing, and Crimes Against Humanity, Jul. 23, 2009, *available at* http://www.responsibilitytoprotect.org/Pakistan_ENG.pdf.

in increasing support for the norm even as it also emphasized that its application should be predicated on region-specific context and situations.[58] From Central Asia, Kazakhstan reiterated its support to the 2005 World Summit Outcome Document on RtoP and expressed its full agreement with the UN Secretary General's report and recommendations on implementing the norm. It highlighted its belief that the protection of civilians against the four crimes is a moral imperative and its adherence to the principle of "non-indifference", and called on members of the UN to collaborate in introducing RtoP elements into the UN principles.[59]

B. Between RtoP 1.0 and 2.0

Overall, the debate on RtoP in Southeast Asia as well as in the broader Asian region has been mainly about the tension between understanding the concept or principle as either mainly about military intervention (version 1.0), which was highlighted in the 2001 ICISS Report, or about prevention (version 2.0) based on the 2005 consensus on paragraphs 138–140 of the UN World Summit Outcome Document (WSOD).[60]

To some extent, RtoP 1.0 still overshadows RtoP 2.0 if one considers the issues and concerns raised by states and non-state actors in the region, as discussed in the previous sections of this chapter. Much of this could be attributed to the fact that there is still a very low level of awareness and understanding of how the RtoP has evolved since the concept was introduced in 2001 and the complex issues involved in implementing the 2005 agreement. There is also an apparent lack of familiarity with paragraphs 138, 139, and 140 of the 2005 WSOD, which compose the three equally important and non-sequential pillars of RtoP. There is also a misconception that the principle is primarily a Western idea given the emphasis on military intervention, especially in RtoP 1.0, even though the intervention principles set out in the ICISS report focused on the UN Charter and were not formally adopted in the WSOD. Not many people in the region are aware of the African origins of "sovereign responsibility" in the 1990s from which the RtoP as a concept evolved. Together with the colonial experience of most countries in the region and the strong adherence of states to respecting territorial integrity and non-interference principle, promoting and deepening the appreciation especially for RtoP 2.0 in this part of the world indeed remain a formidable task.

With its focus on prevention and developing the capacity of states to prevent genocide and mass atrocities, one would think that RtoP 2.0 should be easier to promote in the region. However, there are still lingering fears that the principle is open to abuse and misuse in the absence of agreed-upon standards and mechanisms for its implementation. That some permanent members of the UN Security Council have wrongly invoked the principle—e.g., the United States invasion of Iraq in 2003 on a

[58] Palitha T.B. Kohona, Permanent Rep. of Sri Lanka to the UN, Statement at the July 2009 General Assembly Debate on the Responsibility to Protect, Jul. 21, 2009, *available at* http://responsibilitytoprotect.org/Sri%20Lanka.doc.

[59] Byrgamyn Aitimova, Permanent Rep. of Kazakhstan to the UN, Statement at the General Assembly Plenary Session on the Responsibility to Protect under Agenda items 44 and 107, Jul. 24, 2009, *available at* http://www.responsibilitytoprotect.org/kazakshtan_ENG.pdf.

[60] *2005 World Summit Outcome,* A/RES/60/1, Sept. 15, 2005 [hereinafter WSOD].

belated but weak pretext of humanitarian intervention against the tyrannical rule of Saddam Hussein; Russia in its conflict with Georgia over Ossetia in early 2008;[61] and France in the case of Burma in the aftermath of Cyclone Nargis also in 2008[62]—only serve to deepen fears and suspicions of many developing countries in this part of the world about RtoP.

Meanwhile, ASEAN's experience in dealing with Burma after Cyclone Nargis may prove to be instructive as far as managing humanitarian crisis situations in the region are concerned. Clearly, neither the outrage of the international community nor the condemnation of RtoP interventionists convinced the military junta in Burma to open its doors to international humanitarian assistance. Instead, it was ASEAN's quiet backdoor diplomacy that ultimately proved to be more effective. Much of this could be attributed to the fact that no member of ASEAN overtly condemned the military junta for not responding to humanitarian assistance being offered by Western countries led by the U.S. and France. Instead, there was only sympathy and understanding for the constraints faced by the government in Burma. That ASEAN had to secure the consent and cooperation of the military junta to allow international humanitarian assistance to come in is another important lesson as it demonstrates the importance of respecting sovereignty and territorial integrity of a Member State even in a crisis situation. More importantly, the role of ASEAN as the main vehicle for coordinating international humanitarian assistance cannot be overemphasized. Apparently, the military junta in Burma trusted ASEAN given its adherence to traditional norms more than Western countries that were viewed with much suspicion if not absolute paranoia.

Of course, some civil society groups in the region expressed extreme disappointment with ASEAN's soft approach towards the Burma military junta during the Cyclone Nargis crisis. Some strong RtoP interventionist advocates sought to invoke the principle based on contrived legal arguments, alleging for example that the ruling junta was guilty of committing a "sin of omission" when it initially refused to accept international humanitarian assistance.[63] However, they fail to acknowledge that first, the humanitarian crisis situation was mitigated when the military junta eventually

[61] *See* Gareth Evans, *Russia and the 'Responsibility to Protect'*, L.A. Times, Aug. 31, 2008, http://www.latimes.com/news/opinion/commentary/la-oe-evans31–2008aug31,0,3632207.story; *Application of RtoP to the Georgia/Russia Conflict/August 2008*, International Crisis Group (2010), http://www.crisisgroup.org/en/key-issues/responsibility-to-protect.aspx#situations.

[62] *See* Asia Pacific Centre for the Responsibility to Protect, *Cyclone Nargis and the Responsibility to Protect, Myanmar/Burma Briefing No. 2* (May 16, 2008), www.r2pasiapacific.org/documents/Burma_Brief2.pdf.

[63] Some international law experts used this argument during an international conference on RtoP organized by the Amsterdam Centre for International Law, University of Linkoping, and the Global Center for Responsibility to Protect in Linkoping, Sweden in June 2010. The problem with arguing that the military junta was guilty of a so-called "sin of omission" is that it presupposes that the government knew immediately the extent of damage after Cyclone Nargis and that it had the wherewithal to respond to a crisis situation. It also fails to take into account the domestic political context of the country where, in November 2007, demonstrations led by Buddhist monks against the military regime—along with calls for regime change primarily by Western countries—have contributed to the persistent paranoia of the military junta that partly explain its refusal to accept humanitarian aid from the West. For an examination of the various arguments invoking RtoP in the aftermath of Cyclone Nargis. *See id.*

backtracked from its initial intransigent position after ASEAN mediation;[64] and, second, RtoP cannot be invoked under the circumstances given its limited scope even as it would also be quite difficult to prove that the Burmese junta committed any of the four RtoP crimes when it initially declined to accept international humanitarian assistance.

Overall, debating RtoP and attempting to reach a consensus in the region would seem meaningless if the principle does not cascade at the domestic level where constituency-building plays an important role. The next section discusses the importance of a bottom-up approach in promoting RtoP in Southeast Asia and the larger Asia Pacific region.

V. TOWARDS A BOTTOM-UP STRATEGY IN PROMOTING RTOP

A. Constituency-Building

The internalization of RtoP in Southeast Asia must be anchored on constituency-building, particularly at the domestic level. Without strong advocates or "champions" of RtoP from within, states may just be content with having signed international documents or agreements committing themselves to the norm. Indeed, many states have signed international conventions and treaties (e.g., human rights protection, against genocide, and the Rome Treaty that created the International Criminal Court (ICC)), but quite a number of them have not ratified these agreements. Among ASEAN members, only Cambodia has ratified the Rome Statute although other members of the group have signed it.[65] Most ASEAN members are also parties to the Convention on the Elimination of Discrimination Against Women (CEDAW) and Convention on the Rights of the Child (CRC), but many have not ratified these treaties due to certain constraints of domestic law, or passed appropriate domestic laws in support of these agreements.[66] Together with China, only seven members of ASEAN are parties to the 1948 Convention on the Prevention and Punishment of the Crime of Genocide.[67]

Building awareness about the importance of preventing genocide and mass atrocities is one key objective of domestic constituency-building. Currently, there is a very low level of public awareness about RtoP in all countries of Southeast Asia. For those who have heard of the principle, they have some misconceptions about its scope and

[64] This is not to say, however, that the situation improved remarkably after the Burmese junta accommodated ASEAN's intercession. Indeed, ASEAN has acknowledged more than a year after Cyclone Nargis that there is much work to be done to alleviate the suffering of the people in Burma.

[65] As of October 12, 2010, 115 states have become parties to the Rome Treaty, of which 15 are from Asia. In Southeast Asia, only Cambodia and Timor-Leste have ratified the treaty. See *The States Parties to the Rome Statute*, International Criminal Court (updated Oct. 12, 2010), http://www.icc-cpi.int/Menus/ASP/states+parties/.

[66] *See* UN Treaty Collection, *Status of Convention on the Elimination of All Forms of Discrimination Against Women* (updated Feb. 4, 2011), http://treaties.un.org/Pages/ViewDetails.aspx?src=TREATY&mtdsg_no=IV-8&chapter=4&lang=en#EndDec.

[67] *See* UN Treaty Collection, *Status of Convention on the Prevention and Punishment of the Crime of Genocide* (updated Feb. 4, 2011), http://treaties.un.org/Pages/ViewDetails.aspx?src=UNTSONLINE&tabid=2&mtdsg_no=IV-1&chapter=4&lang=en#Participants.

perceive it to be mainly about military intervention. Many have not followed the evolution of the concept since 2001 and are not familiar with progress since the 2005 consensus on RtoP based on the WSOD.

Engaging critical sectors—government, academia, civil society, think tanks, media, and local government—form part of building awareness and constituency on RtoP. In the government sector, for example, prevention of genocide and mass atrocities should form part of a people-centered national security framework that should guide policies and operations of the state. This becomes even more important in countries that have experienced mass atrocities in the past (such as Cambodia) or those with past or ongoing internal armed conflicts (such as Indonesia, the Philippines, and Thailand). Adopting RtoP as part of the national security framework will also contribute to building awareness about human rights protection among soldiers and law enforcers who are also in the frontline in conflict areas. Academia should also play a critical role in building awareness about prevention of genocide and mass atrocities. Specifically, scholars and educators could respectively pursue research and develop course curriculum and instructional materials on crimes covered by RtoP, conflict prevention, and peace-building. They could also conduct seminars, workshops, and training for government and other sectors on these issues. Universities and academic institutions could also encourage students to play an active role in promoting awareness about RtoP through activities such as debates and conferences, setting up student organizations, and networking with other students in universities across the region.[68]

Civil society groups, particularly those involved in human rights protection, conflict prevention, and peace-building advocacy, are also potential RtoP champions in the domestic sphere. Specifically, they could incorporate RtoP in their advocacy framework that could enable them to actively engage the state or government in enhancing the rule of law, promote protection of civilians in conflict areas, prevent or contain extrajudicial killings, and pursue inter-faith or inter-civilization dialogue, among others. Non-government organizations (NGOs) that also campaign for ratification of international treaties such as the Rome Statute could engage national legislators for ratification these conventions and lobby for passage of domestic laws that enhance the protection of human rights and punishment of crimes covered by RtoP. At the community level, NGOs involved in conflict prevention and peace-building could also play a critical role in developing early warning and response systems, in partnership with local government and law enforcement agencies, that can contribute to building state capacity in preventing genocide and mass atrocities. At the regional level, civil society groups could use their extensive networks across Southeast Asia and the Asia Pacific to engage ASEAN, ARF, and AICHR in implementing agreements and action plans (e.g., APSC Blueprint) signed by Member States, which could certainly contribute to the protection of human rights, enhancing good governance, access to justice, and rule of law.

The media is another critical player in promoting awareness about RtoP although many journalists are unfamiliar with this principle. The media has a direct role in increasing public awareness about human rights violations and crimes against humanity through its reporting or coverage of these issues on the ground. For example, the

[68] The University of Queensland St. Lucia, for example, already has a RtoP Student Coalition that was set up in 2009 and has started to network with students from top universities in the Philippines.

Maguindanao massacre of November 2009—where some 58 people including 30 journalists were killed by members of a political clan, the Ampatuans, who is a close political ally former President Gloria Macapagal Arroyo[69]—was relentlessly covered by television networks and newspapers in the Philippines.[70] Given the strong public outrage, President Arroyo was forced to declare a state of emergency in Maguindanao and later put the province under martial law to prevent further escalation of violence in the area.[71] Three weeks after the incident, President Arroyo signed the first domestic law, Republic Act 9851, against genocide and crimes against humanity, which ironically was already passed into law in July 2009, or four months before the massacre.[72] To date, the media in the Philippines continues to cover the trial of the Ampatuan clan. To some extent, the media could potentially contribute to developing an early warning and response system as journalists can alert law enforcement, local or national government agencies, and civil society groups in conflict areas about violence taking place that could escalate into a crisis situation.

B. The Role of the Asia Pacific Centre for the Responsibility to Protect

Constituency-building on RtoP is an important strategy of the Asia Pacific Centre for the Responsibility to Protect to complement regional efforts in promoting the principle in the region. The Centre has four country programs (Cambodia, Indonesia, the Philippines, and Thailand) that focus on building awareness about RtoP through a series of seminars and workshops involving representatives from various sectors. The first constituency-building workshop was held in Manila, the Philippines on June 25–26, 2009, where some 50 participants from government, academe, and civil society groups discussed the relevance of RtoP in the Philippines and generated some initial ideas on how to promote the norm in the country.[73] This workshop played a critical role in providing inputs to the Department of Foreign Affairs that helped shaped a more positive position of the Philippines in the subsequent UN General Assembly's informal interactive dialogue on RtoP in July 2009.

Another important result of the Philippine workshop is the commitment of the Foreign Service Institute (FSI), which is the research and training arm of the Department of Foreign Affairs, to have a program on RtoP geared towards conducting research and training for government staff on the relevance of the norm not just in the

[69] Manny Piñol, *Ampatuan Patriarch Gave GMA Big Win that Fueled His Rise to Power*, PHIL. DAILY INQUIRER, Dec. 29, 2009, http://newsinfo.inquirer.net/inquirerheadlines/nation/view/20091229-244432/AMPATUAN-Patriarch-gave-GMA-big-win-that-fueled-his-rise-to-power.

[70] *Asia Pacific Journalists Prod GMA On Massacre*, PHIL. STAR, Mar. 17, 2010, http://www.philstar.com/Article.aspx?articleId=558739&publicationSubCategoryId=63.

[71] *Arroyo Orders Martial Law In Maguindanao*, ABS-CBNNEWS.COM, Dec. 4, 2009, http://abs-cbnnews.com/nation/12/04/09/arroyo-orders-martial-law-maguindanao.

[72] Marvin Sy, *New Law Addresses War Crimes, Genocide*, PHIL. STAR, Dec. 12, 2009, http://www.philstar.com/ArticlePrinterFriendly.aspx?articleId=531746.

[73] *See* Asia-Pacific Centre for the Responsibility to Protect, *RtoP Constituency Building in the Philippines Workshop Report* (Sept. 2009), http://www.r2pasiapacific.org/documents/manila_workshop_report_2009.pdf.

Philippines but also in ASEAN and the Asia Pacific region. Specifically, RtoP has been included in the cadetship training of new foreign service officers as part of their seminar on international relations. As a followup to the Philippine workshop in 2009, a series of seminars on RtoP were conducted in Manila in November 2010 with academia, civil society, students, and government that focused on these sectors' respective RtoP action plans in the next two to three years. Overall, there was strong interest and commitment on the part of many participants from these sectors to include RtoP in their current programs and projects, with a number of them expressing interest in further training on RtoP and prevention of genocide and mass atrocities.

In June 2010, the first constituency-building workshop was held in Phnom Penh, Cambodia with some 50 participants from government, civil society, and academe.[74] There is no question that RtoP resonates very strongly among Cambodian participants during the workshop given the country's history under the Khmer Rouge. Many of them were quite interested in knowing more about the principle and one of the important recommendations that emerged from the meeting was the need to translate pertinent reports and documents on RtoP into the Khmer language. There was also strong interest among Cambodians to develop instructional materials for schools and universities on RtoP, conflict prevention, and peace-building. In the government sector as among civil society groups, there were suggestions for training and seminars on RtoP as part of building awareness about the principle in Cambodia. Some participants have also expressed interest in conducting research on RtoP and how this may be linked to human security, good governance, and rule of law. Others have expressed interest in drawing lessons from the experience of the Extraordinary Chambers in the Courts of Cambodia (ECCC) in the ongoing trial of former Khmer Rouge leaders charged with crimes against humanity. Indeed, more than any member of ASEAN, Cambodia should have a keen interest in promoting RtoP and could even play a leading role in pushing for a regional convention in preventing genocide and mass atrocities.

In Indonesia, a project on mainstreaming Responsibility to Protect in the country is ongoing. Following the conduct of interviews with key sectors, a national workshop on RtoP will also be conducted in 2011 that aims to promote the principle and build awareness about it. Meanwhile, in Thailand, a national workshop on RtoP constituency-building is planned in the near future. The 2001 ICISS Report has been translated into Thai and it would be interesting to know whether this effort has contributed to building awareness about RtoP at least among the informed public in Thai society. To some extent, the political crisis in Thailand has also had an impact on the Centre's program in that country.

C. CSCAP Study Group on RtoP

One of the projects administered by the Centre is the Council for Security Cooperation in the Asia Pacific (CSCAP) Study Group on RtoP. Its main goal is to contribute in forging regional consensus on the principle among participating states in the ARF and identify specific areas where cooperation may be pursued. A series of meetings have

[74] *See* Asia-Pacific Centre for the Responsibility to Protect, *Responsibility to Protect Constituency Building in Cambodia Workshop Report* (Aug. 17, 2010), http://www.r2pasiapacific.org/documents/Cambodia%20Workshop%20Report%20Aug%202010.pdf.

been conducted amongst CSCAP think tank institutions in the Asia Pacific that will result in a report that will be eventually submitted to the ARF for consideration. The study group had focused mainly on regional arrangements that may contribute to promoting RtoP in the region, which include developing early warning system, strengthening ties with the UN, preventive diplomacy, supporting capacity-building, and strengthening peacekeeping and humanitarian response capabilities. As part of the Track II process, the recommendations of the CSCAP study group could hopefully be adopted in the Track I process through the ARF's inter-sessional and eminent expert group's meetings.[75] Many of these recommendations may contribute to the enhanced role of regional arrangements that the UN could take advantage of in the long run, particularly in managing conflicts and potential humanitarian crisis situations this part of the world. Through the ASEAN and ARF, the Secretary-General of the UN could utilize the role of the ASEAN Chair and the ASEAN Secretary-General in promoting preventive diplomacy and mediation in intra-state conflicts in the region. With regard to building capacities of states to prevent mass atrocities, the UN could also engage ASEAN and the three Northeast Asian states—China, Japan, and South Korea through the mechanism of ASEAN Plus Three—to encourage the passage of domestic laws and regional conventions against genocide and other crimes covered by RtoP. The AICHR may eventually be a useful vehicle to encourage other member states of ASEAN to create their own national human rights commission and contribute—with the help of the UN—to education about international humanitarian law, human rights, peacekeeping and peace-building, as well as protection of civilians. Apart from the UN, Western-developed countries like Australia, Canada, the U.S., as well as members of the EU could also contribute to RtoP operationalization in the region through assistance in security sector reform, development of early warning systems for protection of civilians in conflict areas, and post-conflict reconstruction and rebuilding.

VI. CONCLUSION

This chapter analyzed the challenges in promoting and building regional consensus around RtoP. Specifically, it examined the views and positions of China and the member states of ASEAN on RtoP. It also explored the geopolitical and historical contexts of countries in Southeast Asia and how the traditional norm of non-interference and protection of territorial integrity have shaped the debate on RtoP in this part of the world. And it reflected on the perspectives of the informed public and policy positions of respective governments on the principle, highlighting the tensions and discomfort in embracing this emerging political norm. Despite some constraints, there are opportunities for RtoP to be internalized in the region, particularly in the context of promoting the idea of an ASEAN Political Security Community. Constituency-building plays a significant role in increasing public awareness about RtoP and there are critical sectors that need to be the focus of this effort.

[75] E-mail from Professor Alex J. Bellamy, former Executive Director of the Asia-Pacific Centre for the Responsibility to Protect (Oct. 8, 2010) (on file with author).

Overall, promoting RtoP in Asia needs the concerted efforts of various sectors both at the domestic and regional levels. The interest and commitment of stakeholders in promoting and internalizing the norm must also be sustained as constituency and capacity-building efforts take time to grow and take root. Ultimately, the support of the international community—particularly donor countries—will determine to a large extent the success of norm internalization in this part of the world.

8 Europe and North America

Mark V. Vlasic

Occupying four of the five permanent seats on the United Nations Security Council (UNSC), European and North American states—working together via the United Nations (UN) or North Atlantic Treaty Organization (NATO) or working in their own capacity—may have done more than any other block of countries to aid the victims of humanitarian crises. For these countries, the ideals and principles that compose RtoP are central to their national identities. And although they may find it difficult to move a RtoP intervention forward unilaterally, these countries certainly have the power to stop one in its tracks. They are also the states most financially and militarily capable of shouldering the burden of RtoP interventions, and their efforts over the past two decades have shaped and legitimized the policy both in theory and in fact.

Through their interventions and support in intergovernmental organizations, Europe and North America have worked to develop RtoP over the past two decades, but for all of their support, colonial history and selective application of the concept may have hurt the doctrine's legitimacy. Part I of this chapter discusses the role of Europe and North America in developing RtoP. Part II is a case study considering Russia's invocation of RtoP during its assault in Georgia in 2008. Part III discusses criticisms of RtoP. And Part IV discusses the potential role of four regional organizations in the future of RtoP.

I. EUROPEAN AND NORTH AMERICAN DEVELOPMENT OF RTOP

In the two decades following the end of the Cold War, Europe and North America actively contributed, conceptually and practically, to the development of the RtoP. In the first decade following the Cold War, European and American actions increased international acceptance of humanitarian interventions and increased attention to the atrocities around the world, so that in the second decade, members of the international community were prepared to accept the theoretical underpinnings of RtoP and the notion of sovereignty as the responsibility of sovereigns to protect their own citizens.

The end of the Cold War and a revised balance of power between European and North American states brought both positive and negative consequences for international humanitarian law. As argued by many foreign policy scholars, in concept, the break up of the Soviet Union and the transition to a somewhat unipolar world meant that the UNSC, formerly manacled by the inevitable veto of either the United States or the Soviet Union, would finally have the opportunity to cooperate and pass constructive resolutions. In many ways, the pundits have been right; the UNSC passed twice as many resolutions between 1990 and 1994 as between 1945 and 1990.[1] But the fragmentation of the Soviet Union also produced a group of new states, free from Soviet imperialism[2] and skeptical of external intervention in their domestic affairs. In addition, with communism no longer playing the foil to capitalism, world power foreign aid programs benefiting former client-states became increasingly motivated by morality and humanitarian interests.

A. Practical Contributions in the Early 1990s: Iraq, the Former Yugoslavia, and Somalia

Throughout the 1990s, the West intervened—diplomatically, economically, and when necessary militarily—in sovereign states whose sovereigns had dramatically failed in their duty to protect citizens from genocide, crimes against humanity, ethnic cleansing, and war crimes. Interestingly, over the last decade or so, the UNSC has actively approved the use of force under Chapter VII of the UN Charter for humanitarian reasons, likely because its members have come to understand that internal conflicts constitute a threat, not just states internally, but also to international peace and security. These interventions were often controversial and, at times, placed a strain on political will in Europe and North America, but without a decade of consistent intervention, RtoP might have taken significantly longer to become an emerging norm or to garner its current level of international acceptance.[3]

1. Iraq

The swift expulsion of Iraqi forces from Kuwait in March 1991 inspired many Kurds in Northern Iraq to seek independence from what they perceived to be a weakened leader.

[1] Thomas G. Weiss, *The Sunset of Humanitarian Intervention? The Responsibility to Protect in a Unipolar Era*, 2 SECURITY DIALOGUE 135, 136 (2004). The author wishes to acknowledge and thank Peter Atlee, his research assistant, for his outstanding contributions to this work.

[2] The end of the Cold War produced skepticism not only in the former Soviet republics, but also in existing States, whose domestic affairs had been subject to manipulation by both East and West as part of the client-state system.

[3] *See, e.g.*, UN GAOR, 63d sess., 105th plen. mtg., A/63/PV. 105, Sept. 14, 2009 (debate of the UN General Assembly, adopting and expressing overwhelming support for a resolution to move forward with RtoP); UN GAOR 63d sess., 105th plen. mtg., A/RES/63/308, Sept. 14, 2009 (unanimous resolution to move forward with RtoP).

Whereas Iraqi President Saddam Hussein had previously suppressed Kurdish independence movements with chemical weapons,[4] this time he sent troops to attack Kurdish villages. By April 5, 1991, a total of two million civilians had been displaced, with approximately half fleeing to Turkey.[5] Reports estimated that another 10,000 to 30,000 died from exposure and malnutrition in squalid refugee camps.[6] The UNSC passed several resolutions condemning Hussein's violence and demanding that it end.

In an effort to deliver aid to affected areas of Iraq, the United States, United Kingdom, and France began conducting aid drops in northern Iraq, and the United States committed troops to build encampments in northern Iraq.[7] Neighboring Turkey, likely troubled by the influx of displaced persons, was the first state to propose the creation of "safe havens," an idea that France and Britain would expand into the "no-fly zone." On April 10, 1991, the United States demanded that Iraq cease all military activity north of the 36th parallel (and ultimately added a second safe zone south of the 32nd parallel); at the height of the allied operation, 20,000 soldiers from 13 countries[8] patrolled the "no fly" zones.[9]

2. Former Yugoslavia

Less than a year after the Iraqi intervention, European and American forces were forced to intervene again when ethnic conflict, driven largely by political leaders—in particular Slobodan Milošević—seeking nationalistic-inspired power, led to the "Death of Yugoslavia." Starting on June 25, 1991 and continuing until the end of the year, individual republics of the Socialist Federal Republic of Yugoslavia[10] slowly began to claim independence. These new states had violent births, and by the end of 1992, ethnic violence had killed 6,000 to 10,000 civilians, wounded 10,000, and displaced 100,000.[11] As fighting spread, the numbers reached to 250,000 displaced Serbs and 100,000 displaced Croats.[12] The violence that engulfed the Balkans brought forth a new household word—"ethnic cleansing"—as various ethnic groups used murder, rape, torture, detention camps, forcible transfers, and deportation to reshape the ethnic makeup of various parts of the former Yugoslavia. While crimes were committed on all sides, Muslims in Bosnia bore the brunt of these atrocities at the hands of Serbian forces.

On May 30, 1992, the UNSC passed a resolution imposing broad sanctions on Serbia and Montenegro, and in 1993, the Council passed further resolutions establishing safe

[4] International Commission on Intervention and State Sovereignty (ICISS), The Responsibility to Protect: Report of the International Commission on Intervention and State Sovereignty 96 (International Development Research Centre 2001), *available at* http://www.iciss.ca/report-en.asp [hereinafter ICISS Report].

[5] S/PV. 2982 (1991), at 6.

[6] *See* ICISS Report, *supra* note 4.

[7] *Id.* at 97.

[8] ICISS Report, *supra* note 4, at 97.

[9] Including Slovenia, Croatia, and Bosnia and Herzegovina.

[10] ICISS Report, *supra* note 4, at 98–99.

[11] *See id.* at 100.

[12] The use of so-called "safe areas" was not fully successful. Indeed, the single largest massacre of the war, the slaughter approximately 8,000 Bosnian Muslim men and boys by Bosnian Serb forces after the fall of Srebrenica on July 11, 1995, proved to be the first "genocide" in Europe since World War II.

areas in Bosnia. Troubled by the return to Europe of concentration camps and ethnic cleansing less than a half-century after the Holocaust, the UNSC authorized the use of air power and ground forces in and around designated "safe areas."[13] NATO and Croatian offensive coerced the warring factions into negotiations, and the conflict quickly ended with the Dayton Peace Accords.

3. Somalia

Unfortunately, while North American and European powers worked to bring peace and stability to the Balkans, they were less successful in Somalia, where warring factions have ruled since 1991. Fighting between these factions created a refugee crisis in Somalia that displaced thousands of individuals both externally and internally[14]—of Somalia's 6 million people: 4.5 million were affected by malnutrition, 1.5 million were at immediate mortal risk, and 300,000 had died in 11 months.[15]

In an effort to defuse the humanitarian crisis, the United States agreed to provide 20,000 troops to help UNISOM, the UN's mission in Somalia, to deliver aid to affected individuals, and the UNSC passed a resolution citing humanitarian interests and approving the use of "all necessary means."[16]

The humanitarian aid mission was arguably successful as it provided aid to nearly five million individuals, but the UN's more ambitious plan to depose Somali warlords proved to be a failure. The expanded mission led to serious confrontations with Somali militias, including the infamous episode involving downed American Black Hawk helicopters.[17] Somalia quickly came to represent the potential risks and horrors of humanitarian intervention—and gave many foreign policy professionals and politicians pause as they weighed the value of humanitarian intervention.[18]

B. Practical Contributions in the Mid- to Late-1990s: Rwanda, Haiti, and Kosovo

1. Rwanda

Rwanda's minority Tutsis and majority Hutus had clashed multiple times since independence in 1962, but none of those clashes compared to the genocide that occurred in 1994. Short on political will following the debacle in Somalia, European and North American powers were wary of humanitarian interventions. So, when 10 Belgian troops were killed and mutilated in April 1994, UN officials decided to begin

[13] ICISS Report, *supra* note 4, at 103.

[14] A/47/553, Oct. 22, 1992.

[15] *See* S.C. Res. 794, S/RES/508 (Dec. 3, 1992); Walter Goodman, *Somalia: How Much Did TV Shape Policy?*, New York Times, Dec. 8, 1992.

[16] *See generally* Mark Bowden, Black Hawk Down: A Story of Modern War (1999) (recounting the infamous 1993 firefight in Mogadishu, Somalia that resulted in the deaths of 18 Americans soldiers).

[17] This so-called "Somalia syndrome" is perhaps one of the reasons the West stood by as 800,000 Tutsis were slaughtered by Hutus in Rwanda in 1994.

[18] *See generally* Roméo Dallaire, Lt. Gen. (ret.), Shake Hands With The Devil: The Failure of Humanity in Rwanda (2003).

withdrawing their forces, and Under-Secretary-General of Peacekeeping Operations, Kofi Annan, opted not to provide General Romeo Dallaire with additional troops to help prevent what the General saw as a possible bloodbath.[19] Unfortunately, with an insufficient peacekeeping presence, little stood in the way of the genocidal Hutu forces, who killed approximately 800,000 Tutsis, and displaced 5 million[20]—all in about 100 days.

Despite several UNSC resolutions condemning the atrocities, the UN was unable to mount any sort of military involvement for months. Finally, on June 20, 1994, France stepped forward and announced that it would lead a European-African intervention in Rwanda and put an end to the massacres. Despite widespread suspicion owing to France's colonial ties to the murderous Hutus, the UNSC approved its use of force, and the Hutu militias quickly declared a cease-fire.[21]

While it is notable that France summoned the political will to intervene, Rwanda is important not for European and North American action, but for their inaction. The sheer immensity of the Rwandan genocide served notice to the world that ignoring atrocities would not make them disappear. If not for the gravity of the crisis in Rwanda, European and North American states might not have recognized the importance of humanitarian intervention—and, alternatively, the consequences of nonintervention. Indeed, as discussed more fully in CHAPTER 6, it was the memory of inaction in Rwanda and Srebrenica that motivated many political leaders to back RtoP-related action in Libya.

2. Haiti

In Haiti, in 1994, the United States intervened to reinstall democracy and forestall a growing refugee crisis. On September 30, 1991, the democratically elected government of Jean-Bertrand Aristide was replaced by a *coup d'etat.* The Organization of American States (OAS) condemned the action and called for both diplomatic and economic sanctions,[22] a move that was blocked by China and the non-Aligned Movement (NAM).[23] The UNSC eventually approved economic sanctions in the summer of 1993, but the military dictators refused to reinstate Aristide's government. Although very little actual fighting occurred, an estimated 60,000 to 100,000 Haitians fled poverty and human rights abuses to seek shelter in the Dominican Republic and Florida.[24]

The United States, still cautious of potentially explosive situations after Somalia, waded into the conflict slowly, only realizing the necessity of regional action in the spring of 1994, when several formerly high-ranking American officials traveled to Haiti and secured an agreement with the parties. A few weeks later, 21,000 American

[19] ICISS REPORT, *supra* note 4, at 107; *see also* 2 INT'L PEACEKEEPING NEWS 7, 7 (Mar.–Apr. 1996).

[20] Canada also made a contribution to RtoP, sending troops to eastern Zaire to stabilize a situation that had deteriorated due to the influx of hundred of thousands of Rwandan refugees. *See* S/1996/941, Nov. 14, 1996; S.C. Res. 1080, S/RES/1080, Nov. 15, 1996.

[21] *See* OAS MRE/RES 1/91 (1991); OAS MRE/RES 2/91 (1991); OAS MRE/RES 3/91 (1991).

[22] DAVID MALONE, DECISION-MAKING IN THE UN SECURITY COUNCIL: THE CASE OF HAITI, 1990–1997 63–64 (1998).

[23] ICISS REPORT, *supra* note 4, at 111.

[24] *Id.* at 113.

and over 1,000 international soldiers peacefully deployed to Haiti.[25] The multinational force soon handed power over to a long-term UN mission. The United States action in Haiti in 1994, motivated by prodemocratic interests and a growing refugee crisis, foreshadowed RtoP interventions' use of military force to quell human rights atrocities and then begin rebuilding.

3. Kosovo

The last major undertaking of the twentieth century, the NATO intervention in Kosovo, was perhaps the most influential on the formation of RtoP. Long-standing ethnic and political tensions between the Albanians (in Kosovo/Serbia) and Serbs (in Serbia proper) were inflamed in 1998 when Serbian police killed dozens of Albanian separatists. The UNSC condemned both the excessive force of the Serbians and the terrorist activities of the Albanians, but as the massacres continued, the UNSC could only threaten further resolutions with no military teeth.[26]

In a move that a future commission found to be "legitimate but not legal,"[27] NATO began conducting a phased air campaign, noting that Security Council Resolution 1199 (1998) had tacitly authorized the use of force—Russia and China disagreed. As ethnic cleansing escalated and NATO bombings commenced, the situation grew temporarily worse with 750,000 refugees displaced to Albania and Macedonia, and another 250,000 individuals displaced within Serbia.

The NATO campaign was ultimately successful in suppressing the violence in Kosovo, and its intervention—and a lack of prosecution by the International Criminal Tribunal for the former Yugoslavia[28]—laid the groundwork for future RtoP interventions. The leaders of both the United States and the United Kingdom stressed their exhaustion of diplomatic options leading up to military intervention, a factor missing from other humanitarian interventions. North American and European states (minus Russia and Belarus) defended the action both to the UNSC, which voted 12 to 3 not to end the airstrikes, and to the International Court of Justice.[29] Finally, the EU and OSCE pursued a lengthy rehabilitation and rebuilding process in Kosovo.

[25] Russia had pledged to veto any authorization of military force. *See* Youssef M. Ibrahim, *UN Measure Skirts Outright Threat of Force Against Milosevic*, New York Times, Oct. 25, 1998; S/PV. 3937, Oct. 24, 1998.

[26] Indep. Int'l Comm'n on Kosovo, The Kosovo Report: Conflict, International Response, Lessons Learned 289 (2000) [hereinafter, The Kosovo Report].

[27] *See* Andreas Laursen, *NATO, The War Over Kosovo, and the ICTY Investigation*, 17 Am. U. Int'l L. Rev. 765, 770–71 (2002).

[28] The United States, Canada and France all claimed that the UNSC resolution authorized their use of force in the face of Serbia's continued defiance: Germany, Spain, the Netherlands, and Britain, on the other hand, argued that their actions were legal and necessary as a response to a "humanitarian catastrophe." S/PV/. 3988, Mar. 24, 1999, at 4–6, 8–9, 12, 17. At the ICJ, Belgium further laid out an elaborate justification based on previous UNSC resolutions, the doctrine of humanitarian intervention, and humanitarian necessity. Legality of Use of Force (Provisional Measures), 1999 I.C.J., pleadings of Belgium (May 10).

[29] European and North American powers continue to appeal to humanitarian interests when it suits their national interests. *See* Part III, *infra* (discussing the use of RtoP as a justification for regime change in Iraq).

C. Practical Contributions in the 2000s: Burma, Kenya, and Libya

After September 11, 2001, European and North American attentions shifted to fighting and preventing international terrorism, and, whether for lack of interest or simple lack of capacity, until NATO-led action in Libya in 2011, it appeared that the regional powers became less interested in humanitarian intervention.[30] Still, in the days of 24-hour news cycles and rapid information sharing, it is challenging for democratic administrations to eschew human suffering, even thousands of miles away, and as a result, while military action might have been difficult, European and North American states did take diplomatic and economic action to quell atrocities in the new century.

1. Burma

In early May 2008, Cyclone Nargis struck Burma, assaulting the nation's already-poor citizens and devastating the Irrawaddy Delta. The storm killed (or disappeared) approximately 130,000 people and affected about 2.4 million more.[31] Lacking any sort of meaningful infrastructure for delivery of aid, disease and hunger quickly enveloped Burma, and the ruling junta, likely in an effort to appear in control, imposed severe restrictions on aid workers, including restricting their access to certain affected regions. Three weeks after the disaster, aid was reaching only 25 percent of those in need,[32] leading British and American officials to criticize the junta as inhuman.[33]

Frustrated by the dizzyingly slow distribution of aid, French Foreign Minister Bernard Kouchner remarked, "We are seeing at the United Nations if we can't implement the Responsibility to Protect, given that food, boats, and relief teams are there, and obtain a United Nations resolution which authorizes the delivery and imposes this on the Burmese government."[34] Kouchner further suggested that the junta's reaction to the crisis might constitute crimes against humanity, and several other European governments made similar statements.[35]

[30] Rebecca Barber, *The Responsibility to Protect the Survivors of Natural Disaster: Cyclone Nargis, A Case Study*, 14 J. Conflict & Security L. 3, 3–4 (2009).

[31] Stuart Ford, *Is the Failure to Respond Appropriately to a Natural Disaster a Crime Against Humanity? The Responsibility to Protect and Individual Criminal Responsibility in the Aftermath of Cyclone Nargis*, 38 Denv. J. Int'l L. & Pol'y 227, 232 (2010).

[32] *Id.* at 233. The junta was already at odds with both the United States and United Kingdom governments for attacking ethnic minorities and for the widespread use of sexual violence by the military. *Id.* In January 2007, the UNSC narrowly defeated a resolution calling on the junta to stop these atrocities due to vetoes from China and Russia. *Id.*

[33] *Id.*

[34] *Id.*

[35] *See* Press Release, Bernard Kouchner, Violence in Kenya: Statement Made by French Foreign and European Affairs Minister Bernard Kouchner (Jan. 31, 2008) *available at* http://www.diplomatie.gouv.fr/en/country-files_156/kenya_209/situation-in-kenya-2008_6019/situation-in-kenya-statement-by-bernard-kouchner-january-31–2008_10767. html ("In the name of the responsibility to protect, it is urgent to help the people of Kenya. The United Nations Security Council must take up this question and act.").

2. Kenya

In January 2008, when ethnic cleansing and deadly violence gripped Kenya after its election, France again invoked RtoP and called on the UNSC to support the African Union in addressing the Kenyan atrocities.[36] France's response to Cyclone Nargis and the Kenyan crisis is indicative of its recent efforts to expand the scope of RtoP and the definition of crimes against humanity.[37]

3. Libya

In March 2011, faced with what many believed was to be an imminent slaughter of civilians in Benghazi, Libya, by Col. Muammar el-Qaddafi's government forces, European and North American countries, relying on RtoP rational and a UN mandate, took the lead in conducting military action against Libyan government forces and command structures.[38] With the memory of the Srebrenica and Rwanda genocides still lingering in many minds, France and the United Kingdom took leadership roles in mobilizing UN and NATO support for the military intervention, while the United States provided the majority of the military force to enable the NATO-led coalition intervention.[39]

D. Theoretical Contributions

The struggle between sovereignty and intervention has been highlighted in the new century, especially given U.S. military action following September 11, 2001. Still, the contest has played out mostly in theory, while atrocities continue to haunt the world in practice, as is evident from the crisis-in-slow-motion in Darfur. With the exception of Libya, European and North American states have largely transitioned away from military humanitarian intervention, but are still active in developing the doctrine in theory. Aside from Russia, which is a fierce proponent of sovereignty and the view that states are masters of their own internal affairs,[40] most of Europe and North America generally support RtoP.

Appalled by the genocide in Rwanda, UN Secretary-General Kofi Annan (who, ironically, served as Under-Secretary-General for Peacekeeping Operations at the time of the Rwandan genocide) famously asked, "If humanitarian intervention is, indeed,

[36] INT'L COALITION FOR THE RTOP, JULY 2009 UN GENERAL ASSEMBLY DEBATE ON THE RTOP: WHAT DID MEMBER STATES FROM EUROPE SAY?, *available at* http://www.responsibilitytoprotect.org/GA%20Debate%20MS%20Positions—Europe%20region.pdf. In fact, during the General Assembly debate on RtoP in August 2009, France expressed its view that inadequate responses to natural disasters should be subject RtoP interventions. *See* Jean-Pierre LaCroix, Chargé d'Affaire, Permanent Mission of France to the United Nations, Speech to UN GAOR, 63d Sess., Jul. 23, 2009, at 5–6.

[37] See, for example, Russia's threat to veto any resolution specifically authorizing the use of force during NATO's intervention in Kosovo. *See* Youssef M. Ibrahim, *UN Measure Skirts Outright Threat of Force against Milosevic*, NEW YORK TIMES, Oct. 25, 1998; S/PV. 3937, Oct. 24, 1998, at 12.

[38] *See* Jeremy Bowen, *Libya crisis: The story so far*, BBC NEWS, Jun. 22, 2011 *available at* http://www.bbc.co.uk/news/world-africa-13860458.

[39] *Id.*

[40] Kofi Annan, "*We the Peoples*": *The Role of the United Nations in the 21st Century: Millennium Report of the Secretary General*, A/54/2000, Mar. 27, 2000, at 48.

an acceptable assault on sovereignty, how should we respond to a Rwanda, to a Srebrenica—to gross and systematic violations of human rights that offend every precept of our common humanity?"[41] Prior to Annan's challenge, several governments—the Danish government, the Dutch government, the Swedish government, and the United States government—had written policy initiatives to consider the same question.[42] But Canada met Annan's challenge and, in September 2000, formed the International Commission on Intervention and State Sovereignty (ICISS). The Canadian Prime Minister said that the Commission would "endeavor to build a new international consensus on how to respond in the face of massive violations of human rights and humanitarian law."[43] The panel included members from Canada, the United States, Russia, Germany, and Switzerland, and issued a report outlining an entirely new concept of sovereignty and principles guiding the use of force for humanitarian intervention. Importantly, the report also suggested other avenues of authorization for the use of force should the UNSC refuse to take action to quell atrocities. France, Norway, the United Kingdom, Russia, and the United States also helped to write the High-Level Panel Report. However, unlike the ICISS report, the High-Level Panel limited use of force authorization to the UNSC.

Still, during the creation of the 2005 World Summit Outcome Document, Europe and North American governments were somewhat less helpful. While Canada worked to secure adoption of the document, the Non-Aligned Movement expressed concern about potential abuse of RtoP, especially after the United States' invocation of the doctrine to justify its invasion of Iraq.[44] Given its colonial history, much of Europe was unhelpful in allaying these concerns.[45] The 2005 Outcome Document again made no recognition of non-UNSC authorized action and did not adopt precautionary principles to guide the use of force.

Finally, on September 14, 2009, the UN General Assembly passed a resolution in support of RtoP. During the debate, the United States and Canada both expressed support for the Secretary-General's three-pillar approach to RtoP and for the need for early warning mechanisms and rapid reaction forces. The United States also expressed support for expanding the capacity of regional organizations to take on peace-building operations.[46]

[41] Ved P. Nanda, *The Global Challenge of Protecting Human Rights: Promising New Developments*, 34 DENV. J. INT'L L. & POL'Y 1, 3 n. 11, 12, 13 (2006).

[42] INTERNATIONAL COMMISSION ON INTERVENTION AND STATE SOVEREIGNTY, THE RESPONSIBILITY TO PROTECT: REPORT OF THE INTERNATIONAL COMMISSION ON INTERVENTION AND STATE SOVEREIGNTY (2001) [hereinafter, ICISS Report].

[43] *See* Gareth Evans, *From Human Intervention to the Responsibility to Protect*, 14 WIS. INT'L. L.J. 703, 714–15 (2006).

[44] *Id.* at 715.

[45] *See* UN GAOR, 63d sess., 105th plen. mtg., A/63/PV. 105, Sept. 14, 2009 (debate of the UN General Assembly, adopting and expressing overwhelming support for a resolution to move forward with RtoP).

[46] The EU representative stated, "The EU welcomes and supports the steps to implement the responsibility to protect set out in the report, and particularly the Secretary-General's emphasis on the responsibility of State themselves, the importance of early prevention; and helping States build their capacity to shoulder their own responsibilities." *See* Anders Liden, Ambassador and Permanent Representative of Sweden to the United Nations, General Assembly Debate on the Responsibility to

Similarly, Europe expressed overwhelming support for the norm, with 31 states and the EU speaking in support of it.[47] Even Russia supported the resolution, claiming that responsibility should be placed initially on national governments with timely reaction coming from the UN. The European states expressed general support for prevention as critical to RtoP and for the new interpretation of sovereignty as responsibility. They also expressed some concerns. Serbia and Switzerland were bothered by the lack of criteria guiding the use of force, and some of the small states called on the permanent members of the UNSC (P5) to abstain from vetoing resolutions to stop mass atrocities. Overall, Europe expressed overwhelming support and provided almost half of the unanimous resolution's 67 cosponsors.[48]

Thus, one might argue that humanitarian interventions in the 1990s began to develop the ideas that sovereigns have certain responsibilities to their citizens, that coercive force should be used only as a last resort, and that the international community should attempt to rebuild war-torn nations after humanitarian interventions. Since the turn of the century, these ideas have been recorded in and validated by various internationally recognized documents. Thus, both the practical and theoretical development of RtoP would be lacking without the support of Europe and North America.

II. CASE STUDY: THE SOUTH OSSETIA WAR OF 2008

A. The War

In the summer of 2008, Russia invaded neighbouring Georgia to (as they claimed) defend the citizens of South Ossetia—a breakaway enclave in northern Georgia. The war lasted just over one week, but it escalated quickly as Russia invaded both Abkhazia—another breakaway enclave—and Georgia proper. Both sides claimed that the other had violated international law, and Russia attempted to justify its actions using RtoP,[49] though much of the international community was reluctant to accept that explanation.

For centuries, the Georgians and the Abkhaz have shared the eastern piece of the Black Sea coast, an important region for the flow of oil from the Caspian Sea. The Bolsheviks declared Abkhazia a Soviet republic in 1921, but when Joseph Stalin (a Georgian) took power in the Soviet Union, he made the region an autonomous piece of Georgia.[50] Stalin's secret-police chief then attempted to shift the ethnic balance by relocating thousands of Georgians to the region and closing Abkhaz

Protect, 63d Sess., 97th plen. mtg., Statement on Behalf of the European Union, Jul. 23, 2009, *available at* http://www.responsibilitytoprotect.org/EU_ Sweden_ENG. pdf.

[47] *See* UN GAOR 63d sess., 105th plen. mtg., A/RES/63/308, Sept. 14, 2009 (unanimous resolution to move forward with RtoP); Int'l Coalition for the RtoP, July 2009 UN General Assembly Debate on the RtoP: What did Member States from Europe say?, *available at* http://www.responsibilitytoprotect.org/GA%20Debate%20MS%20Positions—Europe%20region.pdf.

[48] *See* Interview with Sergey Lavrov, Minister of Foreign Affaires, Russian Federation to BBC, in Moscow, Russ. (Aug. 9, 2008), *available at* http://www.un.int/russia/new/MainRoot/docs/warfare/statement090808en.htm.

[49] *Georgia, Abkhazia and Russia: Tales from the Black Sea*, The Economist, Jul. 3, 2008, at 64.

[50] *Id.*

schools.[51] When the Soviet Union collapsed, the ethnic tensions between the two groups boiled over. In August 1992, Georgia started a conflict with Abkhazia, and troops reportedly pillaged the autonomous region.[52] The war continued for two years with the Abkhaz ultimately repelling the Georgians, thanks to Russian and Chechen support; both sides allegedly committed atrocities, and 250,000 individuals were forced out of the country by ethnic cleansing.[53]

Since the 1994 ceasefire, Russia has acted as a self-proclaimed peacekeeper, though not an impartial one. In 2002, Russia changed its citizenship laws to allow for mass distribution of passports to South Ossetians and Abkhazs,[54] enlisting about 90 percent of the Abkhaz population as Russian citizens.[55] But according to reports, Russia was not the only antagonist in this story. In 2004, Georgian President Mikheil Saakashvili chose to abandon negotiations with both Abkhazia and Russia[56] to campaign on national unification,[57] and in 2006, he sent Georgian forces that entered and took control of the Kodori gorge, inside Abkhazia.[58]

Relations between Georgia and Russia further deteriorated in early 2008, when, perhaps emboldened by international recognition of Kosovo's independence,[59] Russia announced its support for the separatist movements in South Ossetia and Abkhazia.[60] After a string of random bombings in July 2008, the situation finally came to a head, though not in Abkhazia.

Intermittently throughout the night of August 7, 2008, Georgian forces shelled Ossetian villages—including Tskhinvali, where a week earlier a roadside bomb had killed six police officers[61]—claiming that Georgian villages were under fire and that the government had to take action to "restore constitutional order."[62] Georgia also claimed that Russia troops had entered its territory through the Roki tunnel early that day.[63] The fighting continued through the next week with Russia sending tanks, artillery, and ground assault aircraft August 9.[64] Russian bombers and war planes attacked troops and civilians in Tskhinvali and airports in four other cities; Russia also assaulted Georgia proper, bombing Sevaki, Zugdidi, Gori, and Poti, a commercial seaport and export point for oil from the Caspian Sea.[65]

[51] *Id.*

[52] *Id.*

[53] *The Russia-Georgia War: The Blame Game*, THE ECONOMIST, Oct. 1, 2009, at 65–66.

[54] *Tales from the Black Sea*, *supra* note 48, at 64.

[55] *Id.*

[56] Michael Schwirtz, Anne Barnard, & C.J. Chivers, *Russia and Georgia Clash Over Breakaway Region*, NEW YORK TIMES, Aug. 9, 2008, at A9.

[57] *Tales from the Black Sea*, *supra* note 48, at 64.

[58] *The Blame Game*, *supra* note 52, at 65–66.

[59] Schwirtz, *supra* note 55, at A9.

[60] Schwirtz, *supra* note 55, at A9; C.J. Chivers & Ellen Barry, *Accounts Undercut Claims by Georgia on Russia War*, NEW YORK TIMES, Nov. 7, 2008, at A16.

[61] Chivers, *supra* note 59, at A16.

[62] *Georgia and Russia: Tense Times*, THE ECONOMIST, Sept. 25, 2008, at 67; Chivers, *supra* note 59, at A16. News outlets were able to confirm neither the shelling of Georgian villages nor the presence of Russian troops on August 7. Chivers, *supra* note 59, at A16.

[63] Schwirtz, *supra* note 55, at A1.

[64] *Id.*; *The Caucasus: After the War*, THE ECONOMIST, Oct. 16, 2008, at 35–38.

[65] *After the War*, *supra* note 63, at 35–38; Chivers, *supra* note 59, at A16.

When Russia entered the war, it claimed that Georgia had committed genocide and killed two thousand civilians in Tskhinvali.[66] According to post-war reports, however, both sides were allegedly responsible for massive destruction, looting, and ethnic cleansing both in and around South Ossetia;[67] thousands of refugees fled the fighting.[68]

On August 7, Russia asked the UNSC to condemn the Georgians use of force and take action to quell the conflict,[69] but the United States, France, and Britain objected to language in Russia's initial draft resolution, which they feared would prevent Georgia from defending itself.[70] Belgium, which held the rotating UNSC presidency at that time, circulated a revised draft resolution that addressed these concerns,[71] but the UNSC never passed the resolution because French President Nicholas Sarkozy brokered a peace agreement early the next week.[72]

The peace agreement recognized Georgia's sovereignty but not its integrity and was based on six points: (1) no recourse to the use of force; (2) cessation of hostilities; (3) access to humanitarian aid for all; (4) Georgia agrees to withdraw its troops to their permanent positions; (5) Russia agrees to withdraw its troops to their August 7 positions; and (6) the international community would discuss the status of South Ossetia and Abkhazia.[73] The agreement also stipulated that the European Union (EU) would send three hundred monitors to the breakaway regions.

Unfortunately, the peace agreement was not able to undo what the conflict had wrought, and implementation proved difficult as looting, killing, and raping continued in both Georgia proper and South Ossetia.[74] Russia, moreover, refused to allow the EU monitors into the separatist enclaves[75] and, in contravention to the treaty, kept troops in Georgia well into 2009.[76]

[66] *After the War, supra* note 63, at 35–38; *Tense Times, supra* note 61, at 67.

[67] Sources estimate that between 35,000 and 60,000 civilians were displaced during the conflict. *See, e.g., Tense Times supra* note 61, at 67 (30,000 refugees from enclaves, 30,000 from buffer zone); *The Blame Game, supra* note 52, at 65–66 (850 dead; 35,000 civilians displaced).

[68] Schwirtz, *supra* note 55, at A9.

[69] *Id.*

[70] *Id.*

[71] The peace agreement that was signed by Georgia on August 15 and Russia on August 16; leaders of the separatist enclaves would later sign the agreement as well. RFE/RL, *Russian President Orders Halt to Military Operations in Georgia*, GlobalSecurity. org, Aug. 12, 2008, http://www.globalsecurity.org/military/library/news/2008/08/mil-080812-rferl01.htm.

[72] Russian Aggression of Georgia: Six Point Peace Plan, Russ. -Geor., Aug. 12, 2008, *available at* http://smr.gov.ge/uploads/file/Six_Point_Peace_Plan.pdf.

[73] *Russia and Georgia: A Scripted War*, The Economist, Aug. 14, 2008, at 24–26.

[74] *See Tense Times, supra* note 61, at 67. Russia did still allow the 28 OSCE monitors, who had been present since 1994, to enter the regions. *Id.*

[75] *The Blame Game, supra* note 52; *After the War, supra* note 63.

[76] Schwirtz, *supra* note 55, at A9.

B. Russian Invocation of RtoP

Richard Holbrooke, then American Special Representative for Afghanistan and Pakistan and former ambassador to the United Nations, attributed Russia's actions to two goals: annexation of the separatist enclaves and regime change.[77]

However, high-ranking Russian officials, including President Dmitry Medvedev and Prime Minister Vladimir Putin, claimed that their forces entered Georgia for humanitarian reasons. They claimed that the perpetration or imminent threat of atrocities, including genocide,[78] in South Ossetia compelled their military intervention. Russian Minister of Foreign Affairs Sergey Lavrov told BBC, Moscow:

> [U]nder the Constitution [the President] is obliged to protect the life and dignity of Russian citizens, especially when they find themselves in the armed conflict. And today he reiterated that the peace enforcement operation enforcing peace on one of the parties which violated its own obligations would continue until we achieve the results. According to our Constitution there is also responsibility to protect—the term which is very widely used in the UN when people see some trouble in Africa or in any remote part of other regions. But this is not Africa to us, this is next door. This is the area, where Russian citizens live. So the Constitution of the Russian Federation, the laws of the Russian Federation make it absolutely unavoidable to us to exercise responsibility to protect.[79]

One might argue that the invocation of RtoP by high-level government officials from one of the P5 demonstrates the concept's growing importance, but Minister Lavrov's statement betrays a misunderstanding of RtoP, and Russia's alleged RtoP justification is considered by many[80] to be a misapplication of the norm for three reasons.

First, according to his critics, Lavrov confused the distinction between self-defense[80] and RtoP. Whereas self-defense permits a state to protect its nationals in countries under certain circumstances, RtoP requires a state to protect individuals within its own borders and permits other states to intervene if it fails in that responsibility. Russia claimed to have invaded Georgia to protect its own citizens, not those of Georgia. In addition, skeptics question Russia's mass grant of citizenship to South Ossetians and Abkhazs only to claim the need to protect them. Russia's statement, at best, was an attempt to justify its actions on the basis of self-defense and should be judged accordingly.

Second, critics note that there was no legal authority for unilateral RtoP intervention in Georgia; that is, Russia lacked UNSC approval. Russia requested an emergency

[77] Gareth Evans, *Russia, Georgia, and the Responsibility to Protect*, 1 Amsterdam Law Forum 25, 25 (2009). Post-war reports found that Georgia had not committed and was not committing genocide. *See The Blame Game*, *supra* note 52, at 65–66.

[78] Interview with Sergey Lavrov, Minister of Foreign Affaires, Russian Federation to BBC, in Moscow, Russ. (Aug. 9, 2008), *available at* http://www.un.int/russia/new/MainRoot/docs/warfare/statement090808en.htm.

[79] *See, e.g.*, Evans, *supra* note 76, *passim*.

[80] For a description of self-defense norms, see Barry E. Carter, Phillip R. Trimble, & Allen S. Weiner, International Law 990–97 (2007).

session of the UNSC, but only after it had seemingly already decided to engage Georgia and, although the Council did not approve Russia's draft resolution, it would likely have taken some action given some brief pause from Russia. RtoP proponents admit that there will be tough questions where unilateral action may be justified should the UNSC fail to act, but Russia made no effort to gain authorization in the instant case, so it cannot, therefore, be considered a tough question.

Third, critics note that the scale of the supposed threat posed by Georgia to its citizens did not meet the threshold for military intervention, and Russia's intervention was not proportional or narrowly tailored.[81] To accept Russia's RtoP justification would set a dangerous precedent for the application (or misapplication) of RtoP to situations unrelated to mass atrocities or where military intervention is not necessary.

Taking into account the objections by various critics around the world, it is challenging to accept Russia's RtoP invocation. According to independent scholars and news reports, none of the four atrocities—genocide, war crimes, crimes against humanity, and ethnic cleansing—listed as RtoP triggers were occurring in South Ossetia.[82] Georgia's assault on Tskhinvali may have been an overreaction, but it arguably did not justify military action by an outside state.[83] There was little evidence of the atrocities claimed by Russia and, while there was not time for a full investigation prior to the war, one would expect that the international community requires substantiation of Russia's bald assertions. Otherwise, Georgia's reaction likely did not amount to "failing to prevent" any atrocities.

It is important to note, as well, that Russia did not take military action as a last resort. It is quite possible that the UNSC could have quickly pressured Georgia to cease military action and would have likely passed a resolution to that effect given a short amount of time. Despite the presence of peacekeepers and monitors in South Ossetia, Russia made no serious efforts to address the situation by non-military means. Also, Russia's introduction of 200,000 troops and 200 tanks[84] into a situation that had otherwise consisted of sporadic artillery shelling of villages was far from proportional. Russia likely exceeded any potential RtoP justification for protecting the citizens of South Ossetia by entering Abkhazia, establishing a naval blockade, and assaulting Gori, Poti, Zugdidi, and a Tblisi aviation plant (all in Georgia proper).[85]

Finally, according to her critics, the balance of consequences did not justify Russia's military action, which led to the outflow of thousands of refugees, especially into Russia and neighboring states. The intervention also encouraged reprisal acts by angry separatists against Georgians, and it threatened stability in the Caucasus and the surrounding region. Moreover, Russia's unauthorized intervention likely injured the

[81] The five factors used to determine when military intervention is warranted are: (1) seriousness of the threat, (2) primary purpose, (3) last resort, (4) proportionality, and (5) balance of consequences. *See* ICISS Report, *supra* note 41, at xxii, 36–37; High-Level Panel on Threats, Challenges and Change, A More Secure World 66–67, 106–07 (2004); Secretary-General Kofi Annan, In Larger Freedom 43, 83 (2005).

[82] *See The Blame Game*, *supra* note 52, at 65–66.

[83] *See, e.g.*, Evan, *supra* note 76, at 26.

[84] *Id.*

[85] *Id.*

credibility of the UNSC as a check on the ambitions of powerful nations looking to abuse humanitarian norms.

Given the above factors, scholars have concluded that Russia's invocation of RtoP was an improper application of the doctrine.[86] Russia's use of RtoP, arguably to justify its pursuit of national interests, is one example of an RtoP application that may lead developing states to criticize the doctrine for creating double standards and fostering selectivity.

III. SELECTIVITY AND DOUBLE STANDARDS

Russia's questionable invocation of RtoP during its assault on Georgia highlights some of the problems with the doctrine. Defending traditional notions of sovereignty, several developing countries claim that the norm is open to misuse and is susceptible to double standards and selective application.[87]

These criticisms are sometimes dismissed as remnants of European colonial rule and United States imperialism during the nineteenth century. Many countries in the so-called Global South[88] view RtoP as yet another rationalization for unwanted, unwarranted interference by developing nations, and the United States' invasion of Iraq and Russia's invasion of Georgia, both of which cited RtoP as justifications, may have confirmed their fears of such interference. However, due to the challenges of the global environment, it is unlikely that the RtoP doctrine will actually lead to any additional, unwarranted interventions,[89] and, despite its fears, the South may stand to gain the most from the doctrine's success.

A. Double Standards

The ICISS report and the subsequent pronouncements of RtoP have almost universally announced that the balance of consequences should limit the use of force. In theory, this means that an RtoP intervention cannot trigger a larger conflagration or put the international community in a worse position. In practice, however, it means

[86] *See, e.g.*, Evans, *supra* note 76, *passim*; GLOBAL CENTRE FOR THE RESPONSIBILITY TO PROTECT, THE GEORGIA-RUSSIA CRISIS AND THE RESPONSIBILITY TO PROTECT: BACKGROUND NOTE (2008), *available at* http://www.globalRtoP.org/pdf/related/GeorgiaRussia.pdf.

[87] States expressing concerns about RtoP include India, Pakistan, Cuba, Sudan, Venezuela, Egypt, and Nicaragua; some scholars believe these countries might be more supportive of a diluted version of the doctrine or one with more specific restrictions on the use of force. *See Responsibility to Protect: An idea whose time has come—and gone?*, THE ECONOMIST, Jul. 23, 2009, at 58–59.

[88] The global North-South divide is a socioeconomic and political division between developed countries (the North) and less developed or developing countries (the South). This article will use the terms North and South in this context, but note that these terms do not accurately describe the position of countries geographically, as some countries in the North are in the southern hemisphere and some countries in the South are in the northern hemisphere.

[89] The United States and Russia would likely have invaded Iraq and Georgia, respectively, regardless of whether they could invoke RtoP as a justification. Moreover, leaders in powerful states were using humanitarian causes to justify their military actions for decades before RtoP was ever a global norm. In 1938, Adolf Hitler invaded Czechoslovakia, on his way to conquering much of Europe, mainly under the guise of rescuing German nationals who were suffering in the State.

that developing states are subject to a different standard than developed states because any RtoP action against a major power would likely cause more harm than good and have limited prospects for success. This creates a structural double standard that would have likely prevented the UN from intervening in East Timor without the consent of Indonesia, but would possibly permit intervention in Darfur without Sudanese consent. Moreover, if eight of the ten most populous states are considered "major powers," then the principle effectively excludes more than half of the world's population from RtoP protection.

This structural double standard gives the possible impression that "some are more worth protecting than others."[90] But proponents argue that a double standard is better than the Cold War's single standard "to do nothing everywhere."[91] Although RtoP may not be perfect, policymakers should question whether focusing on its faults will simply let the perfect be the enemy of the good. As Secretary-General Kofi Annan wrote, "The fact that we cannot protect people everywhere is no reason for doing nothing when we can."[92]

B. Selective Application

The second major criticism of RtoP is that, even when the balance of consequences is satisfied, the norm is not applied consistently across situations. Selective application is almost inevitable given the UNSC's ad hoc approvals and the lack of clearly defined criteria for the use of military force.[93]

Selective application is driven, largely, by two main forces: (1) limitations on resources/capacity, and (2) political will. A small number of states have the resources necessary for RtoP interventions, and it would be unreasonable to many to expect that they maintain the capacity to intervene in every humanitarian crisis. Only a small percentage of European troops are operationally deployable at any given time,[94] and, in recent years, the United States military has come under even greater strain as a result of its operations in Afghanistan and Iraq. RtoP interventions are accordingly limited and must balance the scale of evil against the scale of capabilities (including what a national government may see as its own limitations).

In addition to objective limitations on numbers of deployable troops, intervening states also face logistical obstacles. Troops cannot always be deployed quickly to every

[90] Christine M. Chinkin, *Kosovo: A "Good" or "Bad" War?*, 93 Am. J. Int'l L. 846 (1999).

[91] International Commission on Intervention and State Sovereignty, The Responsibility to Protect: Research, Bibliography, Background 158 (2001).

[92] *See* Annan, *supra* note 39, at 48.

[93] One author explains that the lack of clearly defined terms leads to a "complementarity trap." The term "manifestly fails" provides cover for States that do not wish to intervene in a situation: while some States argue that intervention is warranted, others will argue intervention is premature because the offenses are not yet "manifest." This argument has been used successfully to block intervention in Sudan where opponents feel the Sudanese sovereign has not manifestly perpetrated or failed to prevent atrocities. In other words, complementarity is a double-edged sword. Carsten Stahn, *Responsibility to Protect: Political Rhetoric or Emerging Legal Norm?*, 101 Am. J. Int'l L. 99, 116–17 (2007).

[94] Gareth Evans, President, Int'l Crisis Group, Keynote Address to London School of Economics, Conference on Ethical Dimensions of European Foreign Policy, Jul. 1, 2005.

conflict. The modern military depends on heavy equipment and long supply chains—all of which take time to transport. These logistical obstacles slow deployment, making intervention particularly ineffective where perpetrators act more quickly than rescuers. For example, even if the UNSC had immediately approved the use of force in Rwanda, it may have taken the United States upto six weeks to deploy 15,000 troops to the country, by which time the vast majority of Tutsis would have already been dead.[95]

Apart from their limited capacity, intervening states also face the daunting task of building the political will necessary to send troops to often-distant places—something that is usually challenging in Europe and North America. States often choose to enter conflicts based on national interests (whether political, strategic, or economic), which leads to inconsistent application and picking friends and enemies. Although this may appear to be self-serving and to corrode the norm, political will and national interests provide states with staying power (particularly in countries in Europe and North American where national legislatures have a strong hand in military spending) and may be a necessary, if insufficient, condition for success.

However, political will also creates a serious prevention gap and often leads to the loss of lives. The will to conduct interventions halfway around the world is often lacking until the media starts to cover mass atrocities, and even then it quickly disintegrates with casualties. It took the UN and United States years to deploy a significant humanitarian force to Somalia, where tens of thousands of civilians had died, and the forces were quickly withdrawn after 18 soldiers died.[96] In Rwanda, the UN had troops on the ground in 1994 but quickly withdrew them after ten were killed on the first day of fighting; the international community took years to reintervene.[97] The need for political support in democratic societies forces most European and North American states to intervene only in situations that implicate their national interests and have a reasonable chance of quick and easy success.

The capability gap and the political will gap arguably lead to selective application and illegitimacy of the doctrine. Nevertheless, egregious suffering requires some response, and the international community should focus on the most heinous crimes in the hopes of eradicating at least those atrocities.

The more disquieting part of selectivity is not that states will only intervene where their national interests are at risk, but that states will intervene where their national interests are at risk even if unwarranted. This is, again, evidenced by the Russian invasion of Georgia, where Russia valued its national interests highly enough to ignore the lack of any atrocities in South Ossetia. Impartiality in decision-making is necessary to protect RtoP from misuse, including as a pretext for political and strategic interests. Reliance on UNSC authorization was meant to achieve some measure of impartiality and legitimacy in RtoP decision-making, but the UNSC is an extremely political body, and there is no guarantee that it will act impartially either to quell or compel interventions.

[95] Alan J. Kuperman, *Rethinking the Responsibility to Protect*, WHITEHEAD J. OF DIPLOMACY & INT'L REL. 19, 22 (2009). In Rwanda, over half of the Tutsi victims were killed within the first three weeks of genocide. In the Former Yugoslavia in 1995, Croatia's army ethnically cleansed nearly all of the 100,000 Serbs in Krajina in less than a week. *Id.* at 21.

[96] *Id.* at 20.

[97] *Id.*

Thus, related to selective application is the question of how the international community should react when, for lack of political will or capacity, the UNSC fails to intervene to stop mass atrocities, as occurred in Rwanda. None of the theoretical manifestations of RtoP have comprehensively addressed this question, and there are no clear ramifications for circumventing the UNSC other than political protest. The best answer seems to lie with the balance of consequences: state actors looking to intervene in a situation must weight the damage to UN credibility against the damage to human life. The UN must, further, be aware of the damage to its own credibility and should be careful not to "drop the ball" in such situations.

C. Moral Hazard

Another concern raised regarding the RtoP doctrine is its potential to create moral hazards. According to some critics, RtoP lowers the expected costs of rebellion and raises the likelihood of success, thereby potentially encouraging rebel groups to provoke sovereigns. Secessionists and rebels can expect that, by provoking an overreaction from the sovereign, they will get international attention and support for their cause, but RtoP, nevertheless, still acts as an "imperfect insurance policy"[98] because international forces are likely to arrive only after violent retaliation against civilians.[99]

D. Addressing the Concerns

RtoP proponents can likely address some of these concerns as the doctrine develops. Proponents should stress that RtoP is not a Western or Northern concept. The first two Secretary-Generals to support RtoP were Boutros-Boutros Ghali and Kofi Annan, both of whom are from Africa.[100] Moreover, the African Union declared its right to intervene in countries for humanitarian purposes in 2000, five years before the World Summit would make the same declaration.[101]

The international community should also consider working to create an RtoP infrastructure that will ensure adequate capacity to address manifest atrocities. If the doctrine is not expanded or abused, if states adhere to right authorization, and if the UN has the capacity to address atrocities as they arise, then concerns over selectivity and double standards will largely fade away.

Third, efforts to clarify the doctrine may pay dividends across the world; the international community, and especially the UNSC, should consider accepting precautionary

[98] Kuperman, *supra* note 95, at 22.

[99] In Kosovo, for example, the local Albanian majority sought independence from an unwilling Serbian sovereign. After nearly a decade of unsuccessful, peaceful resistance, the rebels allegedly attempted to provoke the Serbs into retaliating against Albanian civilians to gain military support from the international community. NATO intervened in 1999, but only after thousands had been killed and displaced. *Id.*

[100] Ban Ki-moon, *Secretary-General Defends, Clarifies "Responsibility to Protect" at Berlin Event*, SG/SM/11701, Jul. 15, 2008, at 2–3.

[101] *Id.* at 3.

criteria to guide the use of force in RtoP situations. Detailed criteria may primarily, provide states in the South with some measure of predictability by preventing abusive interventions and will foster political will in intervening states by specifying when interventions are necessary and reducing mission sprawl. A set of comprehensive criteria for the use of force would put pressure on abusive regimes while also decreasing political abuse from great powers.[102]

Finally, UNSC reforms could alleviate some of the selectivity bias, but a restriction on the use of vetoes in RtoP situations is not likely to meet with success. The current proposal, which would require the P5 to refrain from using their veto power unless a resolution affects their "vital national interests,"[103] contains several challenges. First, "vital national interests" is far from a definitive notion. Second, one might assume that the P5 already reserve their vetoes for situations concerning vital national interests. And third, it is unlikely that the United States—much less China, Russia, or any of the P5—would agree to such a restriction on its foreign policy.

Recognition of non-UNSC approval of use of force may also bolster the RtoP concept, allowing intervention in cases where the UNSC refuses to act. Should the UNSC refuse to approve the use of force, the General Assembly might authorize it under its Resolution 377 "Uniting for Peace" power.[104] States might also seek authorization from regional bodies, as what happened with NATO in Kosovo. Finally, while a bit unconventional (and wrought with potential challenges), states seeking authorization for an RtoP intervention might possibly try to request approval from the International Court of Justice.

IV. ENGAGING EUROPEAN AND NORTH AMERICAN ALLIANCES AND ORGANIZATIONS IN RTOP

As discussed in Part III, one of the major questions surrounding the future of RtoP is how states should respond to humanitarian atrocities when the UNSC refuses to take action or takes action too slowly. Some scholars have suggested that regional organizations might take the place of UNSC in approving RtoP interventions; NATO's "illegal but legitimate" action in Kosovo illustrates how regional approval might legitimate an otherwise unauthorized intervention. European and North American organizations can also make substantial contributions to RtoP policy and practice outside of non-UNSC military interventions. Their resources, long history, and powerful members position these organizations (NATO, Organization for Security and Cooperation in Europe, European Union, and Council of Europe) as major players in the future of RtoP.

[102] The counterargument to this is, of course, that a set of explicit criteria may lead to more close calls, longer decision times at the UNSC, and more suffering where regimes are careful not to cross the line.

[103] ICISS Report, *supra* note 41, at 51; *see also* Neville F. Dastoor, *The Responsibility to Refine: The Need for a Security Council Committee on the Responsibility to Protect*, 22 Harv. Hum. Rts. J. 25, 45 (2009).

[104] *See* A/RES/377(v), Nov. 3, 1950.

A. North Atlantic Treaty Organization (NATO)

Formed at the end of World War II to help protect its members from the threats of the Soviet Union and the Cold War, NATO (or "the Alliance") remains today, in many ways, the world's premiere military and national security alliance. Over the years since the end of the Cold War, however, the Alliance has evolved from one focused on mutual protection against the Soviet Union to an alliance focused on broader national security threats. This broader focus led NATO to act as a quasi-humanitarian intervention alliance—taking military action in the former Yugoslavia, including in Bosnia and Kosovo. In the aftermath of the September 11, 2001 attacks, the Alliance broadened its focus, and it is now increasingly concentrated on international terrorism. Still, NATO members remain concerned about, and often invoke, humanitarian causes to justify their military actions.[105]

As a cornerstone of the transatlantic relationship between Europe and North America, NATO is uniquely situated to engage in RtoP interventions, should it choose to do so. First, NATO can take seemingly "legitimate" action even without the approval of UNSC, as it did with its 1999 bombings of Belgrade and Kosovo.[106]

Second, in practical terms—ever important when it comes to humanitarian intervention—NATO has the capability of "earmarking" troops for international peace operations and then transporting them into harm's way (using either member-state resources or NATO's own C-17 transport planes).

RtoP proponents often face the daunting prospect of identifying and securing military capacity for humanitarian engagements, whether voluntary, peacekeeping missions and coercive, peace-enforcement missions. These challenges are combined with the additional burden of securing the global logistical capabilities and strategic airlift needed to transport any such military capacity—and its required supply chain—to the related "hot spot" in time to help prevent the human crisis that RtoP proponents would be seeking to avert.

Thus, in an increasingly complex world requiring both diplomatic consensus and hard military assets, NATO would likely assume a leading military role in future RtoP interventions (as it has in Libya), rather than engaging in the myriad diplomatic efforts that precede them. The president of the International Crisis Group has even said that the NATO Response Force may be "exactly the kind of 'highly mobile, self-sustaining rapid reaction force . . . uniquely prepared to respond to a fast moving genocide, such as occurred in Rwanda in 1994.'"[107]

[105] For example, the United States often cited atrocities committed by Saddam Hussein in the 1990s as it sought approval for Operation Iraqi Freedom. *See, e.g.*, Samantha Power, *Foreword, in* Responsibility To Protect: The Global Moral Compact for the 21st Century (eds., Richard H. Cooper & Juliette Voïnov Kohler, 2009) xii.

[106] NATO's bombing campaigns in Belgrade and Kosovo were unsanctioned by the UNSC, but they were conducted with little international outcry by many states that promote the RtoP doctrine today. As cited in The Kosovo Report *supra* note 27, at 289, NATO's action was found by a post-war investigation to be legitimate, though illegal.

[107] Gareth Evans, President, Int'l Crisis Group, NATO and the Responsibility to Protect, Presentation at Shadow NATO Summit: Options for NATO: Pressing the Re-Set Button on Strategic Concept (Mar. 31, 2009) (quoting Victoria K. Holt & Tobias C. Berkman, The Impossible Mandate: Military Preparedness, the Responsibility to Protect and Modern Peace Operations 65 (2006)), *available at* http://www.gevans.org/speeches/speech313.html.

As one would expect, NATO members are likely wary of serving as the world's *gens d'armes*, so any decision to adopt a global role, protecting non-members from global atrocities, may be narrowly tailored and met with specific criteria outlining the circumstances of intervention. Moreover, even adopting such a role, NATO's first and foremost concern will likely remain the defense of its Member States. NATO may further rely on UNSC guidance and approval to limit its humanitarian entanglements, but it is unlikely that NATO would agree not to act unilaterally.[108]

Finally, should NATO opt to embrace the RtoP intervention capability challenge and earmark troops for RtoP interventions, it will need to adapt itself to the changing realities of modern warfare and address some of the serious demands on its troops, resources,[109] and political will.[110] NATO may also need to adapt itself to the changing international power structure by engaging with Russia, China, and the European Union to establish a mutual understanding of the "rules of the road" for future RtoP interventions.[111] Protracted operations in Afghanistan have already stretched the Alliance and its resources, both financially and politically. When combined with austerity measures on both sides of the Atlantic, it is easy to imagine a situation where national politics and shrinking defense budgets prohibit consensus and limit NATO's ability to take part in RtoP engagements.

B. Organization for Security and Cooperation in Europe (OSCE)

The OSCE is the world's largest regional organization[112] and plays an important role in non-military security policy. As such, its means are political and diplomatic rather than military, and the OSCE is best employed in the prevention, conflict management, and reconstruction phases of RtoP actions. The OSCE hosts the Conflict Prevention Center and the Office of Democratic Institutions and Human Rights, both of which could play critical roles in developing prevention mechanisms and helping to rebuild war-torn societies. At a recent meeting, OSCE members also expressed a desire to

[108] Indeed, it seems there has been little fallout from NATO's action against Serbia in 1999—an action that included both American and European assets—and where barely a decade later, Serbia is relying on massive international assistance, provided by U.S. and EU-backed aid organizations, to further its effort to become a member of the EU.

[109] Currently only 3–4% of NATO troops are deployable for peace operations at any given time. Evans, *supra* note 107.

[110] NATO expansion, especially into Eastern Europe, may help to mitigate these concerns, but NATO must be careful not to expand too far. Politics play an intrusive role in RtoP decision-making, and NATO expansion may lead to lowest common denominator positions that keep the Alliance from taking action in important conflicts.

[111] NATO leaders have apparently conceived of NATO 3.0 (version 1.0: after World War II; version 2.0: the end of the Cold War until today), which will attempt not only focus on new security threats, such as cybersecurity and missile defense, but also to reassess NATO's relationship with rising world powers. Josh Rogin, *Get Ready for NATO 3.0*, FP.com (Oct. 29, 2010), *available at* http://thecable.foreignpolicy.com/posts/2010/10/29/get_ready_for_nato_30. The US ambassador to the Alliance has stated that NATO will operate globally in the future and will look to work with new States like India, China, and Brazil. *Id.*

[112] Kristin M. Haugevik, *Regionalizing the Responsibility to Protect: Possibilities, Capabilities, and Actualities*, NUPIReport Responsibility to Protect 16–17 (2008).

create mechanisms to protect human rights defenders, who have recently experienced increased danger in the region.[113]

Despite its positioning in conflict-prone regions and its dedication to human rights and democratization, the OSCE faces two significant challenges to its effectiveness with RtoP. First, it should address inefficiencies in its decision-making procedures. With 56 members, varied national interests often block effective decisions, which are made by consensus. Second, in an effort to reach consensus, OSCE mission statements are often broad and vague, which causes mission sprawl and the ineffective use of force. The OSCE should attempt to curtail these problems as it works to develop RtoP policy and practice.

C. European Union (EU)

The EU is one of the largest trading blocks in the world and the organization structured to take a leading role in future European affairs. In addition, the EU has a toolbox of resources, beyond state-based military resources, to expand the acceptance and use of RtoP.

On December 11, 2008, the EU revised its European Security Strategy to include a strong reference to RtoP and the responsibilities of Member States, and the European Parliament has also passed several resolutions condemning the situation in Darfur and invoking RtoP. The EU should consider continuing to pursue RtoP-inspired resolutions at the UNSC, even if they are vetoed, as their discussion will be important to the development of RtoP.[114]

Aside from its political support of RtoP, the EU exercises significant soft power across the globe through its development aid, diplomacy, and conflict mediation. That power provides the EU with a unique opportunity to persuade other states to support RtoP. The EU is also the world's largest economy, giving significant influence to any RtoP policies it wishes to advance; in fact, the EU recently asserted that members of the UNSC willing to undercut RtoP, will also be cut off from Europe.[115] Finally, the EU has recently expanded its influence in Africa by forming a strategic partnership with the African Union to cooperate on human rights and capacity-building.

For all of its soft power, the EU can also contribute to RtoP interventions militarily. Since the turn of the century, the EU has intervened in Macedonia (2003), Bosnia (2004), Eastern Congo (2003, 2006), Chad (2008), and the Central African Republic (2008); and in 2002, the EU was given access to NATO's military resources for situations where NATO as a whole chooses not to act.[116] Still, the EU's greatest military contribution may have developed from its 2004 intervention in the Democratic

[113] Press Release, Organization for Security and Cooperation in Europe, OSCE Meeting in Vienna Calls on States to Increase Support for Human Rights Defenders (Mar. 31, 2006), *available at* http://www.osce.org/item/18580.html.

[114] *See* Richard Gowan & Franziska Brantner, *A Global Force for Human Rights? An Audit of European Power at the UN*, European Council on Foreign Relations 67 (2008). Still, some individuals criticize the EU for not doing more to invoke RtoP during recent crises in Burma and Zimbabwe. *See, e.g., id.* at 6.

[115] *See id.* at 68.

[116] NATO, *Berlin Plus Agreement*, 2002.

Republic of the Congo. That successful action led the EU to form "Rapid Reaction Battlegroups"—small units of 1500 troops, deployable within 10 days, for periods of 120 days. These units are meant for use in connection with the European Security and Defense Policy and are not equipped to handle large-scale or long-term interventions. Nevertheless, for small-scale, rapid deployment actions and for demonstrating a quick "show of force," the EU is arguably better equipped than the UN.[117]

D. Council of Europe (CoE)

Founded in 1949, the Council of Europe is the oldest organization working towards European unity, and its broad membership and cooperation with non-members is a source of strength. The CoE is open to all European states, and permits non-member, non-European states to sign onto its conventions and agreements. In many ways its role in the development of RtoP will follow that of the EU as both groups work closely together and have similar power structures.

Dedicated to development and the rule of law, the CoE could make a singular contribution in Europe through the European Convention on Human Rights (Convention) and the associated European Court of Human Rights (ECHR). The Convention is fairly comprehensive, but could be amended to stress the importance of RtoP to CoE members. In addition, the ECHR is arguably one of the most powerful bodies in Europe and one of the most influential human rights courts in the world. The status of RtoP as customary international law or as a concrete legal obligation is still questionable, but the ECHR may someday find itself in a position to hear cases interpreting the Convention and applying RtoP. In the meantime, the Court may serve as an example to other human rights courts as they confront the crimes that underlie and provoke RtoP interventions.

V. CONCLUSION

Europe and North America have played a major role in the development of RtoP since the end of the Cold War, whether by intervening in Kosovo where a sovereign was failing to protect its citizens from ethnic cleansing, pursuing economic and diplomatic sanctions at the UNSC for the same reasons, intervening in Libya, or supporting the doctrine at the UN General Assembly. Developing states might criticize these actions as demonstrating the selective application of RtoP according to world powers' national interests; still, national interests are likely critical to the success of humanitarian interventions. In the future, should RtoP interventions expand, regional organizations may become increasingly important and will likely provide developing states an opportunity to guide those interventions. RtoP is far from perfect in either theory or application, but the citizens of developing states are nonetheless in a better position today thanks to European and North American efforts to develop the doctrine.

[117] *See* Haugevik, *supra* note 112, at 16; Kofi Annan, Secretary-General, United Nations, Address to the National Forum on Europe (Oct. 14, 2004), *available at* http://www.forumoneurope.ie/index.asp?locID=366&docID=566.

9 Latin America and the Caribbean

Gilberto Marcos Antonio Rodrigues*

Latin America and the Caribbean (LAC) is a region featuring its specific historical, political, economic, and cultural characteristics. Consisting especially of Iberian-tradition countries, which have been colonized by Spain and Portugal, the region also includes the former colonies of France, United Kingdom, and the Netherlands comprising the Francophone, Anglophone, and Dutch Caribbean.[1]

Historically, after the U.S. and Canada, LAC was the first non-European region to gain independence from its colonizers and, strongly inspired and influenced by the American (constitutionalism) and French Napoleonic (highly-centralized Republic) models, it began its state-building process, by creating Republican political regimes (the exception was Brazil which has adopted the Constitutional Monarchy from 1822 to 1889) with a strong concentration of central power during the first half of the nineteenth century. All Latin American countries became independent approximately two hundred years ago,[2] which generally implies detachment from the nationalist politics inherent to the immediate post-independence process. These countries also have a higher level of autonomy, political maturity, stronger institutions when

* This chapter was inspired by dialogues with colleagues and students and based on my research during my period as a Fulbright Visiting Scholar at the Center for Civil and Human Rights (CCHR), University of Notre Dame (2010), and I thank Doug Cassel, Sean O'Brien, Jody Klontz (CCHR) and Allert Brown-Gort (Institute for Latino Studies) for their support. I also thank Andres Serbin (CRIES), Sapna Chhatpar (WFM/ICRtoP), Clovis Brigagão (GAPCon/EPAZ), Claudio José dos Santos (UNISANTOS), Paulo Resende (PUC-SP) and Thiago Rodrigues (UFF) for the great stimulation I've received from them during my research on RtoP in Latin America and the Caribbean.

[1] Gilberto M. A. Rodrigues, *Latin America, A Certain "West"?*, *in* JANUS FOREIGN RELATIONS YEARBOOK 12, 52–55 (2009).

[2] *See generally* THE CAMBRIDGE HISTORY OF LATIN AMERICA 3 (Leslie Bethel ed., 1985).

compared to the countries from other continents, such as Africa and Asia, whose independence processes were only initiated after the Second World War.

Nevertheless, LAC faces severe governance and governability problems, which result from archaic, authoritarian, and corrupt practices of its governments, from old and new forms of populism, and challenges inflicted by the transnational organized crime. Collectively, these problems pose a serious threat to democracy and the rule of law in the region. In addition, the U.S. exercised its hegemony directly over the region throughout the twentieth century in unilateral interventions, ranging from the economic to political-military spheres.

From the cultural and anthropological perspective, it would be more appropriate to refer to the LAC region as Afro-Latin-Amerindian, considering its ethnic and linguistic characteristics shared by autochthonous populations (particularly in the Andean subregion and in Central America), the African population brought as slaves from Africa (especially to Brazil, Venezuela, Colombia, the Caribbean, and Central America), and the colonizers. This differentiated ethnic mix is the focus of huge inequalities and human rights violations in the broad spectrum of civil, political, economic, social, and cultural rights and presents the challenge of the harmonious and egalitarian thriving of diversity within the unity.[3]

As to the economy, LAC is a region comprised mostly of developing countries. Taking the Human Development Index (HDI) as a criterion, the region encompasses from high-development countries (such as Chile, Uruguay, Costa Rica, and Barbados) to low-development countries (such as Haiti and Bolivia).[4] Additionally, there is an issue of social-economic inequality that affects and challenges the management of public policies of the states in the region.[5]

It is in such a peculiar scenario that the Responsibility to Protect (RtoP) is inserted and must be understood within the extent of LAC. An analysis of LAC views of RtoP should take into account both the memories of past foreign interventions during the nineteenth and twentieth centuries and the memories of atrocity crimes under military dictatorships during the Cold War.

I. UNDERSTANDING LATIN AMERICAN AND CARIBBEAN VIEWS

A. The Memories of Past Foreign Interventions

In 1823, U.S. President James Monroe launched the Monroe Doctrine, summarized as "America for the Americans."[6] Amidst the process of independence, the European

[3] Gilberto M. A. Rodrigues & Marcus Faro de Castro, *Brazil*, *in* Diversity and Unity in Federal Countries 75–108 (Louis Moreno & César Colino eds., 2010).

[4] United Nations Development Programme, Human Development Report 2010: The Real Wealth of Nations, http://hdr.undp.org/en/reports/global/hdr2010/(report commissioned by the United Nations Development Programme).

[5] *See generally* An Unequal Democracy? Seeing Latin America Through European Eyes (C. Binetti & F. Carrillo-Florez eds., 2005).

[6] *Primary Documents in America History: Monroe Doctrine*, Library of Congress, http://www.loc.gov/rr/program/bib/ourdocs/Monroe.html.

colonizers did not give up their colonies and continued intervening in the region to preserve or regain their territories. The U.S., on the other hand, launched a hemispherical politics with a view to guaranteeing and consolidating the independence processes of LAC—and ensuring their reserved space of regional hegemony.

Throughout the nineteenth century, the LAC region has experienced different forms of intervention motivated by territorial and economic disputes and interests. For example, Mexico has lost approximately half of its territory to the U.S., while Central America and the Caribbean have been systematically invaded by mercenaries. In South America, the British Empire safeguarded its economic interests in the emerging capitalist economy, either by seeking to collect the foreign debts inherited or acquired by the independent nations or by guaranteeing—with the threat of force if required—the investments made in huge works of rail and infrastructure, with a view to ensuring not only the income from capitals, but also the free trade and export of agricultural and mineral commodities.

The end of the nineteenth century coincided with two important movements for the region: within the regional extent, the First International American Conference (1889), which paved the way for the Pan-Americanism; and in the international sphere, the First Hague Conference (1899), which started the discussion on the legal limits for using armed force (*jus ad bellum*).

Back at that time, there were no mechanisms to protect states from a unilateral armed intervention. While international law theoretically supported state sovereignty, it was not guaranteed in practice and the region had to respond vigorously to threats by European countries. The principle of non-intervention with the internal affairs of sovereign states received strong regional support in two episodes. In 1902, the German, Italian, and British governments threatened the use of force to collect its external debt due by Venezuela through a potential blockade of the ports of La Guaira and Maracaibo. This effort generated an indignant diplomatic note from the Argentinean Chancellor Luis María Drago, whose text laid the basis of Drago Doctrine—the policy that no foreign power could use force against an American country to collect debt.[7] In 1907, during the negotiations of the Second Hague Peace Conference, the Brazilian delegate, Ruy Barbosa, vehemently defended the principle of legal equality of sovereign nations, which for the first time was given recognition under international law.[8]

In the first half of the twentieth century to the end of the Second World War, LAC has witnessed the ascendance of the U.S. and the increasing American interventionism in the region, especially in Central America and the Caribbean. Here, American economic interests have expanded with greater strength and U.S. foreign policy undertook the "big stick" policy under President Theodore Roosevelt.[9]

The political power of multinational companies, such as United Fruit Company, over the Central American and the Caribbean governments, and the strategic American interests related to control over land and maritime routes for trade and between the

[7] Luis María Drago, *The Drago Doctrine*, *in* Grandes discursos de la historia Argentina 128–33 (L. de Privittellio & Louis Alberto Romero eds., 2000).

[8] Ruy Barbosa, *Discursos de Rui Barbosa em Haia*, *in* Obras completas de Ruy Barbosa 175–186 (2007).

[9] *Big Stick Policy*, Encyclopedia-Britannica Online Encyclopedia, http://www.britannica.com/EBchecked/topic/65006/Big-Stick-Policy.

Atlantic and the Pacific, such as the construction and control of the Panama Canal, increased American power in the region. Nevertheless, such an interventionist policy was scaled back voluntarily through the "good neighbor policy" adopted by President Franklin D. Roosevelt in 1933, which aimed at fighting the attraction exercised by the European fascist governments in the region.[10]

With the end of the Second World War, Latin American countries played an important role in the negotiation and approval of the Charter of San Francisco (1945) and the Universal Declaration of Human Rights (1948), which inaugurated a new international order where the use of force as a way to settle conflicts has been expressly forbidden and the human rights gained an increasingly important role.[11]

However, during the Cold War (1947–1989), the LAC region once again suffered from American interventions. The stated U.S. goal was to prevent the communism from expanding in the region especially after the victory of Fidel Castro's regime in Cuba (1959) and, thus, one by one, democratically elected governments featuring any leftist trend were deposed with American interference: Guatemala (1954), Brazil (1964), Dominican Republic (1968), Chile (1973), and Argentina (1976). Legitimate civil governments were replaced by military juntas whose iron grip on the levers of the state indelibly marked the history and the recent life of LAC countries.

During President Ronald Reagan's terms in office, LAC witnessed U.S. support for the United Kingdom against Argentina in the Malvinas/Falkland War, an attempt to overthrow the Sandinista government in Nicaragua, as well as invasions of Grenada and Panama. These actions reinforced the negative perception of the idea of intervention, which was viewed by LAC as a selective instrument wielded by the U.S., based on its own definition of national security.

As part of the memories of foreign intervention of non-military character, it is also worth mentioning the operation of international economic organizations, such as the International Monetary Fund (IMF) and the World Bank. In their processes of re-democratization, LAC countries have endured severe problems of external indebtedness caused by the oil crisis and authoritarian economic management. As a result of these trends in the 1980s, several countries decreed a moratorium on payment of the foreign debts, with declarations invoking the principle of non-intervention in their internal affairs to respond to demands by the IMF and international banks.[12]

The need to recover the investment and development capacity of such countries triggered the Washington Consensus (1990), where the IMF and the World Bank, supported by the U.S. and other partners, imposed a series of economic recovery measures that would have a deep impact on the internal life of LAC countries, such as fiscal policy discipline, redirection of spending from subsidies to investments, tax reform, and trade liberalization.

The memories of foreign political intervention, of either a military or economic character, have nurtured a political and legal culture of resistance and defense in the

[10] *See* Andrew Crawley, Somoza and Roosevelt: Good Neighbor Diplomacy in Nicaragua, 1933–1945 (2007).

[11] Almost half (20) of the United Nations original members (51) were from Latin America and the Caribbean. *United Nations Member States*, United Nations, http://www.un.org/en/members/index.shtml (last visited Feb. 5, 2011).

[12] *See* Alan Garcia, El desarme financiero: pueblo y deuda en America Latina (1989).

region throughout two centuries of independence. International law and the principle of non-intervention in sovereign states comprise the main safeguards for many countries that had limited capability to prevent the threats of intervention. Recent history explains these fears. On account of this history, there is a general uneasiness in the LAC region about any kind of interference or intervention.[13]

B. The Memories of Atrocity Crimes Under Military Dictatorships

With the ascension of the military dictatorships in the LAC region, political sovereignty became a key negotiating point for the U.S., as the leader of the Western capitalist block, and the civil and military elites of the countries undergoing a permanent state of exception. In Central America, particularly in Guatemala, El Salvador, and Honduras; and in South America, in Argentina, Bolivia, Brazil, Chile, Paraguay, and Uruguay, brutal authoritarian regimes were established.

Under the argument of fighting communism and grounded in their respective national security doctrines,[14] state security apparatuses in many of the aforementioned countries perpetrated numerous mass atrocities including enforced disappearances and extrajudicial killings.[15] They responded to criticisms of these human rights abuses by forcibly arguing they had absolute authority as sovereigns to act within their own territory.

Supported by the U.S., "Operation Condor," coordinated by the Chilean government of Augusto Pinochet established an international cooperation between dictatorships for capture, exchange and murder of individuals deemed subversive and communist, projecting its operations beyond its sovereign territory. Most striking was the attack killing former Chilean Minister of Foreign Affairs Orlando Letelier in a car bomb attack in Washington.[16] After President Jimmy Carter took office in 1976, the U.S. began to change its posture by supporting individuals, groups, and parties aligned against authoritarian regimes.[17] With President Ronald Reagan (1980–1988), however, the U.S. returned to supporting some authoritarian right-wing governments and worked to undermine left-wing governments whose policies were viewed as detrimental to U.S. foreign policy interests.[18]

[13] *See* Ricardo Arredondo, *La responsabilidad de proteger en America Latina: su aplicabilidad y desafíos*, Documentos CRIES 16, 7–22 (2011).

[14] The U. S. National Security Council was created in 1947 and became the landmark for the American Foreign Policy against Communism in Latin America and abroad and, based on their guidelines during the Cold War, many LAC countries, like Brazil and Chile, developed their own National Security Doctrines.

[15] The United Nations Human Rights Commission established a Working Group on Enforced and Involuntary Disappearances in 1980, the first international initiative to investigate that new form of mass atrocities. The Rome Statute establishing the International Criminal Court has defined forced disappearances as one of its crimes against humanity.

[16] *See* John Dinges, The Condor Years: How Pinochet and His Allies Brought Terrorism to Three Continents (2005).

[17] Jimmy Carter, *Foreign Policy and Human Rights*, *in* Go Forth and Do Good: Memorable Notre Dame Commencement Addresses 196–203 (Wilson D. Miscamble ed., 2003).

[18] *See, e.g.*, President Ronald Reagan, Remarks on Central America and El Salvador at the Annual Meeting of the National Association of Manufacturers (March 10, 1983), *available at* http://www.reagan.utexas.edu/archives/speeches/1983/31083a.htm.

As LAC countries in the 1980s restored democracy and initiated processes of transitional justice including truth commissions and criminal prosecutions, a true understanding of life under these dictatorships has come to light.[19] This movement has also received important support from the Inter-American Human Rights system, which acknowledged the invalidity of amnesty laws in crimes against humanity.[20]

The memories of atrocities of more than two decades of military dictatorships are still alive today because many still await a full explanation of the extent of the violations and information about what happened to the disappeared. As a result, both civil society and the political class of the LAC region have concluded sovereignty cannot and should not be invoked as a principle of control over territory with a view to justifying or covering up massive violations of human rights.

Amidst the two memories—fear of foreign interventions and fear of atrocities—the LAC region has developed its view on RtoP and builds its peculiar engagement around the new concept.

II. LAC COUNTRIES AND RTOP: PERCEPTIONS, POSITIONS, AND INTERESTS

There is diversity among the perceptions, positions, and interests of the LAC countries in relation to RtoP, which can be casuistically explained and includes a range of positions classifiable into two broad categories—the supporters and the critics.[21] Considering the period comprised between the creation of the International Commission on Intervention and State Sovereignty (ICISS),[22] in 2000, and the presentation in 2009 of the Secretary-General's report *Implementing the Responsibility to Protect*[23] and the subsequent special meeting of the special UN General Assembly that same year, each one of such groups will be analyzed next.

A. Supporters of RtoP

At first, it is worth pointing out the participation of three Latin Americans in two important commissions that resulted in founding documents of RtoP. In the formation of the ICISS, the only Latin American member was the former Guatemalan Foreign Minister Eduardo Stein. Although the ICISS was created by the Canadian government, and members were invited in a personal level, Guatemala is emblematic to RtoP in Latin America: the very first country to overthrow its democratically elected president because of his alleged communist ties (1954) and where, ever since, some of

[19] *See* Henry Steiner & Philip Alston, International Human Rights in Context 1131–1247 (2000).

[20] *See* Gomes-Lund et al. (Guerrilha do Araguaia) v. Brazil, Inter-Am. Ct. H.R. (ser. C) No. 219 (Nov. 24, 2010) (most recent decision), *available at* http://www.corteidh.or.cr/casos.cfm?idCaso=348.

[21] Ricardo Arredondo, an Argentinian jurist and diplomat, proposes a different method for categorizing LAC countries' positions referred to RtoP: *Bolivarians* (Bolivia, Cuba, Ecuador, Nicaragua and Venezuela), which are critics; *Inter-americanists* (Chile, Colombia, El Salvador, Mexico, Peru, Uruguay), which are supporters; and a third group, the *Ecletics* (Argentina and Brazil), which are in favour, with reservations. See Arredondo, *supra* note 13.

[22] *See* Int'l Comm'n on Intervention & State Sovereignty, The Responsibility to Protect (2001), http://www.iciss.ca/menu-en.asp.

[23] UN Secretary-General, *Implementing the Responsibility to Protect*, A/63/677, Jan. 12, 2009.

the most widespread atrocities have been committed by dictatorial governments which held the power until the early 1990s.

The country has been one of the supporters of RtoP in the UN system by taking symbolic diplomatic initiatives—such as pressing for the adoption of the first UN General Assembly resolution on RtoP.[24] However, the fragile institutional situation of the country and the persistence of violations of human rights—fruit of the heritage from the authoritarian period not yet overcome—does not make of Guatemala a leader of RtoP in the region, but rather a possible case for application of the principle. At the same time, the fact that Santiago has been the only Latin American capital in which the ICISS promoted regional inquiries indicated Chile's interest in the theme and anticipated its subsequent outstanding position in favor of RtoP.

The High Level Panel on Threats, Challenges and Change, established by the UN Secretary-General in 2004, produced the organization's first official document to make reference to RtoP.[25] On this panel, two members of LAC participated, also on a personal level: former Brazilian Secretary-General of the Organization of American States João Clemente Baena Soares; and the then Uruguayan President of the Inter-American Development Bank Enrique Iglesias. RtoP was one of the subjects addressed in the panel and Baena Soares and Iglesias were certainly not their highest enthusiasts,[26] nor were their respective countries—Brazil and Uruguay—although they support the concept with reservations.

With distinct histories, but sharing common priority about human rights in their external policies by their governments in that period, Chile and Mexico have become the main promoters of RtoP in the LAC region, being among the most outstanding states to defend the acknowledgment of such a new principle globally.[27] Both countries, in partnership with Japan, presented a paper to the General Assembly to enhance the debate about RtoP at the 2005 World Summit.[28]

Certainly, the most important time to learn the individual positions of Latin American and Caribbean countries on RtoP occurred during the special session of the UN General Assembly on the theme held from July 21, 2009, to July 28, 2009. Out of the 94 countries that positioned themselves, 32 Latin American countries participated, 17 individually and 15 represented by Jamaica speaking on behalf of the Caribbean Community and Common Market (CARICOM).[29]

[24] *See* G.A. Res. 63/308, A/RES/63/308, Sept. 14, 2009, *available at* http://www.responsibilitytoprotect.org/index.php/component/content/article/35-r2pcs-topics/2550-adoption-of-first-un-resolution-on-rtop.

[25] Secretary-General's High-Level Panel on Threats, Challenges and Change, *A More Secure World: Our Shared Responsibility*, A/59/565, Dec. 2, 2004, *available at* http://www.un.org/secureworld/.

[26] *See* J.C. Baena Soares, Sem medo da diplomacia (2006).

[27] Argentina was also a strong RtoP promoter in the early stage, during President Fernando De la Rúa's Administration (1999-2001). Even though his successors have paid less attention to the principle, RtoP has been in the agenda of the Argentinian Council for International Relations (CARI), *see* http://www.cari.org.ar/recursos/cronicas/proteger15-03-11.html.

[28] *See* Heraldo Muñoz, *La Responsabilidad de Proteger: tres pilares y cuatro crímines*, 10 Foreign Aff. Latinoámerica 101 (2010).

[29] *See* the GCR2P report, http://globalr2p.org/media/pdf/GCR2P_General_Assembly_Debate_Assessment.pdf

In general terms, some states from the region have stood out as being among the strongest supporters of RtoP (Argentina, Chile, Costa Rica, Guatemala, Mexico, and Panama).

Others supported the idea with reservations. One example of such a country is Brazil, which sees RtoP as a political but not a legal commitment and advocates for a more active role of the General Assembly in the implementation of RtoP. This position coincides with the Brazilian government's strong advocacy for a reformation of the Security Council, as a condition for an international order with new legitimacy in view of new challenges.[30] A similar understanding was shared by CARICOM group, whose position was even more restrictive.

A commonly shared aspect among the strongest supporters of RtoP in the LAC region is its external policy in line with or close to the U.S. positions. A notable exception is Colombia, whose close relations with the U.S. has not resulted in its full support for RtoP, perhaps because it is viewed as a possible case for application of the principle, as it will be seen hereinafter.

There is a collective view in the LAC that prevention should be the main focus of application of RtoP, under pillars one and two of the UN Strategy.[31] This approach puts the region squarely in support of the Secretary-General's initiative to strengthen early-warning mechanisms as a key strategy for implementing the principle.[32]

From the perspective of regional politics, the fact that Argentina, Brazil, Chile, and Mexico—which are the countries of strongest relative political weight in the region—support RtoP, is a guarantee that it may be regionally implemented.[33]

B. Critics of RtoP

Three LAC countries stand out for their strong opposition to RtoP: Cuba, Nicaragua, and Venezuela. United in their ideology, but also grounded on the history of threats and concrete unilateral interventions by the U.S., they consider RtoP as a euphemism for the previously discredited principle of humanitarian intervention, which they view as a disguised form of interference by superpowers, especially the U.S.

It is possible to understand why these three countries are so viscerally against RtoP. Cuba is the only country that maintains a continuous and uninterrupted position in relation to its resistance to any form of intervention—which can be explained by its perception of permanent threat of invasion by the U.S., whose economic embargo has been upheld since 1959.

[30] *See generally* Alexandre Guido Lopes Parola, A ordem injusta (2007).

[31] According to the UN Secretary-General's report *Implementing the Responsibility to Protect*, a three-pillar strategy was outlined for advancing the RtoP agenda: Pillar One—The protection responsibilities of the State; Pillar Two—International assistance and capacity building; Pillar Three—Timely and decisive response. *See supra* note 23.

[32] Secretary-General, *Early Warning, Assessment and the Responsibility to Protect*, A/64/864 Jul. 14, 2010.

[33] The Libya's case has demanded a more clear Brazilian position: the country was one of the five Security Council members that absteined in the Resolution 1973 (2011) approval on a "No fly zone over Lybia", *See* http://www.un.org/News/Press/docs/2011/sc10200.doc.htm; but it answered positively to a UN consultation to receive refugees from Libya, *see* http://www.estadao.com.br/estadaodehoje/20110702/not_imp739762,0.php.

Throughout the second half of the twentieth century Venezuela was a U.S. ally, but with President Hugo Chávez's ascension to the government, its policy has radically changed.[34] The prompt recognition given by the government of George W. Bush to the leaders of the frustrated attempt of *coup d'etat* against Chávez, back in 2002, aggravated even further the Venezuelan opposition to Washington. Benefited and strengthened by the rising of oil barrel prices in the 2000s and by the approval of reforms enabling it to retain power, Hugo Chávez led the creation of a new group of LAC countries around the Bolivarian Alliance of Peoples of America (ALBA),[35] which currently includes Antigua and Barbuda, Bolivia, Cuba, Dominica, Ecuador, Nicaragua, Saint Vincent and the Grenadines, and Venezuela itself. Initially organized as a counterbalance to the Free Trade Area of the Americas,[36] its legal basis is a People's Treaty on Trade (TCP) entered into between Cuba and Venezuela (2004), which expresses ideologically anti-imperialist positions.[37]

Nicaragua, with the Sandinista government, is not only ideologically aligned with Cuba and Venezuela, but also maintains its opposition to interventionist policies of the U.S. of the 1980s. In this period, President Reagan, supported the Contras, to overthrow the Nicaraguan government. The Sandinistas filed a lawsuit in the International Court of Justice. The Nicaraguan government prevailed against the United States, *in absentia*, setting a historical precedent against the unilateral military intervention as a means of political action.[38]

The analysis of perceptions, positions, and interests of supporters and critics of RtoP must be made based both on ideological and pragmatic elements. For the champions of RtoP, there is a strong relation between the external policy of affirmation of human rights and the internal policies of such countries, either because they have emerged from bloody dictatorships (Chile) or by virtue of a radical change to the governing profile (Mexico).[39] The strongest critics of RtoP (Cuba, Nicaragua, and Venezuela) have an ideological position anchored to the old North-South conflict grounded on the memory of interventions experienced by their countries throughout the twentieth century.

There is also a need to contextualize the positions and interests of the LAC countries in relation to RtoP in the regional political arena, where Brazil and Venezuela, in spite

[34] *See generally* ANDRES SERBIN, CHÁVEZ, VENEZUELA Y LA RECONFIGURACIÓN POLÍTICA DE AMÉRICA LATINA Y EL CARIBE (2011).

[35] ALBA is the Spanish acronym of *Alianza Bolivariana de los Pueblos de las Américas*. ALBA-TCP, http://www.alba-tcp.org/.

[36] OFFICIAL WEBSITE OF THE FREE TRADE AREA OF THE AMERICAS PROCESS (FTAA), http://www.ftaa-alca.org/alca_e.asp (last visited Feb. 5, 2011).

[37] TCP is the Spanish acronym of *Tratado de Comércio de los Pueblos*. ALBA-TCP, http://www.alba-tcp.org/(last visited Feb. 5, 2011).

[38] Military and Paramilitary Activities in and Against Nicaragua (Nicar. v. US), 1986 I.C.J. (Jun. 27), *available at* http://www.icj-cij.org/docket/index.php?p1=3&p2=3&code=nus&case=70&k=66.

[39] In Mexico's case, after the reign of the Institutional Revolutionary Party (PRI) during 70 years, President Vicente Fox's Administration (2000–2006) changed the Mexican foreign policy towards a more aggressive human rights approach in LAC and abroad. An important sign of the Mexican full engagement towards RtoP implementation was the Regional Forum chaired by the Mexican Secretary of Foreign Relations, in collaboration with the GCRtoP, in Feb.2009, that brought together LAC ambassadors, UN officials and Civil Society, *see* http://globalr2p.org/events/index.php.

of being political and economic partners, lead two distinct visions of democracy, human rights, and development.[40]

Taking into account the supporters and critics of RtoP, the LAC region appears willing to support its implementation within clear guidelines, leaving no margins for interpretation by the Security Council, and featuring a multilateral institutionality with no exceptions, nor selectivity.

III. INTERGOVERNMENTAL ORGANIZATIONS: LIMITS AND POTENTIAL ENGAGEMENT

The LAC region has accumulated some of the most permanent and complex institutions of regional multilateralism. Much beyond their specificities and mandates, the LAC Regional Inter-Governmental Organizations (RIGOs) have been important venues for dialogue and formation of consensus on themes of security, peace, democracy, and human rights. The organization of widest coverage, with hemispheric mandate, is the Organization of American States (OAS). It exercises directly the regional subsidiary mandate provided for in Article 52 of the UN Charter. For the theme of RtoP, two subregional organizations should be examined as well: the Union of South American Nations (UNASUR) and the Central American Integration System (SICA).

Different than the African experience, in which the theme of prevention and repression to mass atrocities is part of the very statute of the African Union (AU) and its regional debate about human rights, at the LAC RIGOs there are no institutional intervention mechanisms to address the commission of mass atrocities. Neither issue has been expressly included in the agendas of such organizations; however, in line with the UN Secretary-General's *Report on Implementing the Responsibility to Protect*, relevant roles in which the RIGOs from the LAC region operate can be identified, especially in the field of prevention of conflicts, peace-building, protection, and promotion of human rights and democracy.

The regional LAC experience has shown that in extreme cases, such as those of RtoP, there is a clear preference by the countries to accepting the good offices or mediation by the OAS, or by subregional RIGOs, in addition to groups of friends, with aims at preventing or pacifically settling a conflict. In the Latin American experience, action by the UN has been the last resort in limited situations.[41]

A. Organization of American States (OAS)[42]

With a significant accumulated experience with dialogue, prevention, and conflict resolution, the OAS has politically contributed to safeguarding and restoring peace in conflicts that could have resulted in atrocities implicated by RtoP.

[40] *See generally* Michael Reid, Forgotten Continent: The Battle for Latin America's Soul (2009).

[41] Andrés Serbin & Gilberto M.A. Rodrigues, *The Relevance of the Responsibility to Protect for Latin America and the Caribbean Region: Prevention and the Role of Civil Society*, 3 Global Responsibility to Protect (forthcoming 2011).

[42] OAS-Organization of American States, http://www.oas.org/en/default.asp (last visited Feb. 5, 2011).

The OAS has been the main venue of political dialogue in the hemisphere, combining 35 member countries.[43] Under the umbrella of the OAS, important initiatives have had place at times of strong regional tension, such as that of Contadora Group, which had a critical role in the Central American crisis of the 1980s,[44] and in the "group of friends" in the case of the border dispute between Ecuador and Peru in 1995.[45] Similarly, the OAS helped prevent an armed conflict between Colombia and Ecuador in 2008 after Colombian attacks against FARC in the Ecuadorian territory.[46]

As one of the pioneering RIGOs to include the promotion and defense of democracy as part of its mandate, the OAS has also accrued a notable experience in electoral assistance and observation of elections, *in situ*. This practice by the OAS has contributed to the reliability of electoral results in the LAC region, preventing the outburst of mass atrocities post-elections as has been observed in Kenya in 2007–2008. The theme of democracy has progressed considerably in the organization, following the traumatic experience of Peru, during the government of Alberto Fujimori in the 1990s.[47] As a result of the intense debate that was established at the OAS about the Peruvian case, an Inter-American Democratic Charter was approved in 2001. Recently the Charter was applied against Honduras in the *coup d'etat* which overthrew President Manuel Zelaya in 2009. The case mobilized the OAS to such an extreme degree so as to suspend the country from the organization, which contributed to a relatively peaceful transition to President Porfírio Lobo Sosa.[48]

Situations such as that of the crisis between Colombia and Ecuador (2008) and the *coup d'etat* in Honduras (2009) show the role of the political bodies of the Charter of the OAS in heading off potential conflicts that could result in RtoP-implicated crimes.

In the field of human rights, the OAS has overseen the development of the highly sophisticated Inter-American Human Rights System.[49] This system comprises three bodies, including the Inter-American Commission on Human Rights, the Inter-American Court on Human Rights, and the Inter-American Institute on Human Rights. These human-rights bodies, whose recommendations, decisions, and staff

[43] Today there are 34 active members – Cuba did not recover its membership status (although its exclusion approved in 1962 was cancelled in 2009).

[44] The governments of Colombia, Mexico, Panama and Venezuela first met at the Contadora Island, in Panama, in 1983, and since that became the Contadora Group.

[45] The group of friends comprised by Argentina, Brazil, Chile. and the U.S. played an important role as mediator between Equador and Peru, which peace process lead to the Brasilia Peace Agreement of 1998. *See Peace Agreements: Ecuador-Peru*, United States Institute of Peace, http://www.usip.org/publications/peace-agreements-ecuador-peru.

[46] *See* comments on the OAS Resolution related to the Colombia and Ecuador crises, http://www.oas.org/en/media_center/press_release.asp?sCodigo=E-067/08. *See* A América Latina e os Conflitos Fronteiriços (Clovis Brigagão, ed., 2010).

[47] *Fujimorization* was a neologism created to define the so-called "self coup d'Etat" in which President Alberto Fujimori closed the Congress and transformed Peru in a new kind of autocratic regime, in 1992.

[48] *See* Org. of Am. States, *Resolution on the Suspension of the Right of Honduras to Participate in the OAS*, AG/RES. 2 (XXXVII-E/09), Jul. 19, 2009. Honduras recovered its OAS member's status in June'2011. *See* http://www.oas.org/consejo/GENERAL%20ASSEMBLY/41SGA.asp

[49] *See generally* Hector Faundez Ladesma, El Sistema Interamericano de Protección de los Derechos Humanos (2004).

contribute towards promoting and protecting human rights in member countries are key mechanisms for prevention of RtoP situations in the LAC region.[50]

Furthermore, the Inter-American Commission on Human Rights allows direct access for both individuals and civil society organizations.[51] Undoubtedly one may state that the Inter-American System on Human Rights is the main mechanism for prevention and international assistance within the extent of RtoP in the LAC region.

In spite of these strengths, the OAS suffers from severe political and budgetary challenges. Important countries in the system, such as Brazil and Venezuela—for different reasons—have deviated their regional priorities towards the UNASUR, a new subregional organization in South America. The U.S., the main creditor of the OAS as the bulwark of democracy and human rights in the region, wavers and acts ambiguously in relation to the support the organization. As a result of such problems—in addition to past episodes that have generated discredit in the organization[52]—there is a growing skepticism in the OAS by the LAC region in favor of subregional organizations. On the other hand, the OAS's difficulty to open up to civil society for the themes of security and peace renders difficult its opening to a new agenda that includes fundamental actors in the theme of prevention of conflicts and peace-building. But it is exactly with the civil society organizations that the OAS may establish partnerships for a fruitful dialogue, especially on the theme of early warning, with a view to generating conditions for more proactive and less reactive action on the themes of peace and security in relation to RtoP.

B. Union of South American Nations (UNASUR)[53]

UNASUR was organized through treaty in 2008 to promote political cooperation between all countries of South America. It is a new RIGO vested with high power of influence on hemispherical matters. As the result of the leadership of Argentina, Brazil, and Venezuela, UNASUR intends to bring together the experiences of Mercosur,[54] the Andean Pact, and the countries from the Guyana Plateau.

Quite different from other subregional RIGOs, which are focused on economic and commercial integration processes, UNASUR was born also for the purpose of operating in the fields of security, peace, prevention of conflicts, and peacebuilding.[55] Nevertheless, RtoP is not part of UNASUR's agenda or discussions. Under the terms of its organizational treaty, its priority themes regard the threats of terrorism,

[50] *See generally* Paolo Carozza, *From Conquest to Constitutions: Retrieving a Latin American Tradition of the Idea of Human Rights*, 25 Human Rights Quarterly 281–313 (2003).

[51] *See* A.A. Cançado Trindade, *La persona humana como sujeto de derecho internacional*, Revista IIDH 273–329.

[52] Such as the U.S. support to the U.K against Argentina in the Malvinas/Falkland War (1982).

[53] UNASUR is the Spanish acronym of *Unión de las Naciones Suramericanas*.

[54] The South-Common Market, known by its Spanish acronym *Mercosur*, was created in 1991 between Argentina, Brazil, Paraguay, and Uruguay. Venezuela applied to full accession to the block but the Paraguayan Congress did not approve until July 2011.

[55] *See* Andres Serbin, Coordinadora Regional de Investigaciones Económicas y Sociales, OEA y UNASUR: Seguridad regional y sociedad civil en America Latina, (2010).

corruption, the worldwide problem of illegal drugs, human trafficking, small arms and light weapons trafficking, transnational organized crime, and other threats.[56]

The first big political test of the UNASUR as a RIGO capable of preventing conflicts was the crisis in Pando, Bolivia. The intensification of opposition between the Bolivian government of Evo Morales and regional governments governed by the opposition, such as Santa Cruz de La Sierra and Pando, has given rise to a series of political killings in Pando. After a quick intervention by the *pro tempore* presidency of UNASUR, dialogue was established with the Bolivian government and a "Truth Commission" was organized to ascertain the facts. In addition to this political intervention, this Commission, chaired by the Argentinean human rights expert Rodolfo Matarrollo, was able to effectively operate at the site of facts, contributing to the reduction of tensions and dispelling the risk of escalating conflict.[57]

While it is still taking its first steps, UNASUR has strong political support by South American governments. One of the issues raised by the action of UNASUR is to what extent it competes with the OAS or supplements it in themes that were once restricted to the OAS, such as security, peace, and prevention of conflicts. It may be observed that through the UNASUR, the debates about security and peace have a new niche of subregional articulation which once may prescind from the OAS, other times may operate as a supplement to discussions in the OAS.[58]

C. Central American Integration System (SICA)[59]

Central America is a LAC subregion where violations of human rights and the fragility of the rule of law are realities directly related to heritages from authoritarian regimes and civil wars that have devastated societies for many years. With neither sufficient resources or time to be restructured as democratic states, Central American countries are currently forced to face insecurity caused by a series of threats: narcotraffic, human trafficking, robbery and theft of vehicles, money laundering, criminal gangs, terrorism, and illegal firearms trafficking.[60]

After the Framework Treaty on Democratic Security (1995), a subregional approach was created to address the themes of peace and security, prevention of conflicts, and peace-building. The SICA, as the main subregional organization, has had its mandate expanded to encompass the theme of security and peace, taking on the role of coordination of the goals of this new subregional legal regime.[61] According to analysts, this process of coordination performed by the SICA has afforded important spaces for dialogue on public policies for facing these new threats to human security.[62]

[56] This list is according to the UNASUR Treaty.

[57] *See* Informe de Unasur sobre crisis in Bolivia asegura que en Pando ocurrió una matanza, Emol.com (Nov. 21, 2008), http://www.emol.com/noticias/internacional/detalle/detallenoticias.asp?idnoticia=331862.

[58] Serbin, *supra* note 55.

[59] SICA is the Spanish acronym of *Sistema de Integración Centro Americano*, http://www.sica.int/

[60] Daniel Matul & Luis Diego Segura, Coordinadora Regional de Investigaciones Económicas y Sociales, Evolución institucional de la seguridad en el marco del sistema de la integración centroamericana: 1995–2009, at 12 (2010).

[61] *Id.*

[62] *Id.*

Unlike UNASUR, which is supported by resources from its own members, SICA depends to a great extent on international aid to put into practice its policies and projects, which is a particular challenge especially after the recent economic crisis, which has reduced foreign aid coming from Northern countries.

As is the case with all RIGOs, RtoP is not expressly contained in the agenda of the SICA, but the themes addressed are important to expand potential RtoP response in the region.

IV. LAC CIVIL SOCIETY: AN IMPORTANT ACTOR

Among specialists, academics, and practitioners of international relations, it is widely appreciated that civil society is a fundamental contemporary actor in the prevention of conflicts and peace-building.[63] Nevertheless, many governments from the LAC region are suspicious of both non-governmental organizations (NGOs) and their networks of operation. This makes it more difficult for NGOs to access information and meetings, let alone engage in discussions with governments and RIGOs, even when such access is legally required. Nevertheless, these difficulties have not prevented NGOs from organizing to support implementation of RtoP and formulating their own international and regional agenda regarding related themes.[64]

For example, the Regional Coordination for Social and Economic Research (*Coordinadora Regional de Investigaciones Económicas y Sociales-CRIES),*[65] a network of NGOs from the LAC region, became a co-founder and member of the *International Coalition for the Responsibility to Protect (RtoP)*[66] and included RtoP in its permanent work agenda.[67]

From the experience and perspective of civil society, several factors have obstructed the promotion of peace-building and RtoP in the LAC region including: an increasing focus on state control with the aim of preserving national interests; the increased democratic deficit in the new RIGOs and regional agreements (UNASUR, ALBA); and a significant demobilization of civil society from themes of human rights to the detriment of concerns about urban violence, crime, and insecurity.[68] There is also a growing disappointment among NGOs with international organizations and the decreased emphasis on their perspective post-9/11.[69]

[63] *See* Gabriel Aguilera Peralta, *Violencia y y sociedade civil en America Latina y el Caribe. Logros y desafios*, Pensamiento Propio, Jul.–Dec. 2007, at 9–21.

[64] *See generally* De la ONU al ALBA: Prevención de conflictos y espacios de participación ciudadana (Andres Serbin, ed., 2011).

[65] Coordinadora Regional de Investigaciones Económicas y Sociales (CRIES), http://www.cries.org (last visited Feb. 6, 2011).

[66] International Coalition for the Responsibility to Protect (ICRtoP), http://www.responsibilitytoprotect.org/(last visited Feb. 5, 2011).

[67] *Responsabilidad de Proteger*, Coordinadora Regional de Investigaciones Económicas y Sociales (CRIES), http://www.cries.org/?page_id=60 (last visited Feb. 5, 2011).

[68] Serbin & Rodrigues, *supra* note 41.

[69] *Id.* Despite that, some positive steps in the relationship between NGOs and ROGs have taken place, such as the Seminar on Peace, Development and Regional Security: the role of regional organizations and civil society, jointly organized by the OAS and CRIES, in November 2009. *See* Press Release, Org. of Am. States, At OAS, Multilateral Organizations, Governments and Civil Society

In addition to the operation of the networks, there are Latin American NGOs that work individually in several areas related to the scope of RtoP, such as Viva Rio, headquartered in Rio de Janeiro, which has been deeply engaged in rebuilding Haiti.[70]

V. POTENTIAL CASES IN THE REGION[71]

The memories of the massive human rights abuses in the LAC region remain alive to this day. In many cases, practices of torture and other crimes against humanity still haunt societies of the LAC and are potential threats to cause the outbreak of mass atrocities targeted by RtoP.[72] Nevertheless, quite differently from some other regions, such as Africa and Asia, where concrete cases have been identified for potential application of RtoP, the LAC region has not had a situation in the past 15 years in which the application of RtoP has been clearly seen or has been invoked by governments or civil society. On the one hand, this indicates that the LAC region currently experiences a stage of relative peace, if compared to other regions in the world, which does not mean that there are no conflicts that can be considered as situations of RtoP or that there are no potential cases to be faced in the future, such as those analyzed hereinafter.

A. Haiti

The case of Haiti, which since 2004 has been under the mandate of the United Nations Stabilization Mission in Haiti (MINUSTAH), points to a possible case of RtoP. Is the mission playing the role of preventing atrocities between rival groups inside the country, particularly in the wake of Haiti's disputed elections? There is a potential environment for the outbreak of violence in the country in good part due to the lack of police and legal institutions capable of guaranteeing order and security.[73] The lack of minimal state protections and the structural violence that has historically struck Haiti causes one to believe that MINUSTAH would be, even if not explicitly, exercising the role of addressing human security concerns under the terms of RtoP.

B. Colombia

The armed conflict in Colombia is another instance in which there is speculation about the possible application of RtoP. On the one side there are confrontations between

Debate About Peace, Development and Security in the Americas (Nov. 23, 2009), http://www.oas.org/es/centro_noticias/comunicado_prensa.asp?sCodigo=E-392/09.

[70] Viva Rio, http://www.vivario.org.br/publique/cgi/cgilua.exe/sys/start.htm?tpl=home (last visited Feb. 6, 2011).

[71] It is important to clarify that those potential cases are not listed in two of the main organizations and coalitions devoted to RtoP: the Global Centre for the Responsibility to Protect (GCR2P) and the International Coalition for the Responsibility to Protect (ICRtoP). The author's opinion is based on his own research and analysis; moreover, all those cases have been under the International Crisis Group attention, *see* http://www.crisisgroup.org/en/regions/latin-america-caribbean.aspx.

[72] Many cases under the Inter-American Commission on Human Rights and Inter-American Court of Human Rights are related to the practice of torture.

[73] Int'l Comm'n on Intervention & State Sovereignty, *supra* note 22, at 65.

government forces and guerrillas, and on the other side, there is the action of the latter and paramilitary groups against the population inside the country; in both cases there are denunciations of massive violation of human rights and impunity against the state authorities. By virtue of that, the prosecutor of the International Criminal Court has been examining the situation of Colombia, which could generate a case in Court.[74] However, in addition to being a party to the Rome Statute, Colombia has been constructively cooperating with the ICC's work, reducing the international pressure for application of RtoP in relation to the country. Another consequence of the Colombian conflict is the massive internal displacement of people and the forced migration of Colombians, which has continuously generated thousands of refugees in the region. Such facts could also bring about the application of RtoP in Colombia.[75] As to the refugees, Ecuador, Panama, and Venezuela, in cooperation with UNHCR, have played a fundamental role in prevention and international assistance as host countries.[76]

C. Indigenous Peoples

More broadly, the situation of vulnerability of indigenous peoples, particularly in the Andean region and in Guatemala, may generate situations of RtoP, as massive violations of human rights of such populations have intensified, in the dispute for both land and natural resources.

In countries such as Guatemala, Bolivia, Peru, and Ecuador, the indigenous population accounts for more than a half of the country's population. Nevertheless, these populations are vulnerable minorities that have no access to power and essential public assets. Except for Bolivia,[77] indigenous populations still suffer from the stigma of marginality and are preferred victims of all sorts of exploitation. But there has not been strong pressure from the international community to invoke RtoP in relation to the treatment of these peoples, which would need to be grounded in an assessment that what is happening to them constitutes mass atrocities as defined by the principle.[78]

[74] *See* Kirsten Begg, *ICC Warns Colombia Illegal Armed Groups and State It Will Prosecute*, Colombia Reports (Oct. 30, 2009, 5:06 PM), http://colombiareports.com/colombia-news/news/6664-icc-warns-colombian-illegal-armed-groups-and-state-it-will-prosecute.html.

[75] Colombia is by far the most troublesome situation related to forced migration in the Americas: 454,088 refugees have fled the country and there were 3,304,000 to 4,916,000 internally displaced persons within the country in 2009. *Refugees and Internally Displaced Persons Worldwide*, 1 Perspective—A Hum. & For. Aff. Mag. (2010) (citing December 2009 statistics).

[76] "[T]he work of the Office of the United Nations High Commissioner for Refugees in obtaining grants of asylum and protecting refugees has served numerous potential victims of crimes and violations relating to the responsibility to protect." *Implementing the Responsibility to Protect*, *supra* note 23, at 17.

[77] It should be stressed that in Evo Morales's government there has been a radical change towards indigenous people policies in that country.

[78] *See* Report of United Nations High Commissioner for Human Rights Special Rapporteur on the Situation of Human Rights and Fundamental Freedoms of Indigenous People, A/HRC/15/37 (2010).

D. Pando, Bolivia

The case of Pando, Bolivia, as mentioned above, is a worrisome example of how political polarization in Bolivia—and in other countries as well, such as Venezuela—may generate the outbreak of violence and lead into situations where RtoP could be invoked. Although it has not yet been declared by UNASUR or its member governments, from the perspective of civil society, the case of Pando has been characterized as a meeting the threshold for triggering RtoP, given the conflictive and explosive potentiality existing in that region of Bolivia, with potential to contaminate other regions with massive and uncontrolled violence.[79]

E. Other Potential Cases

It is worth considering that there are other situations of severe violence in the LAC region that are unlikely to be classified as RtoP situations. The violence generated by the fight against transnational organized crime, and particularly against narcotrafficking on the northern frontier of Mexico and in the slums of Rio de Janeiro has generated an impressive quantity of deaths and violations of human rights. The use of armed forces in both such situations lend a character of "urban war" to these conflicts.[80]

In Central America, urban violence, especially that practiced by gangs known as *maras*, is a severe problem of security and protection of human rights in the urban sphere. At the same time, the conflicts over the possession and ownership of land and non-renewable natural resources generate situations of severe threat against peasants and indigenous peoples.

RIGOs have tried to update their mandates and agendas to face these new threats; however, there is neither a consensus on how to classify these new conflicts, nor is there speculation that they are situations justifying invocation of RtoP. But this is a discussion that might be raised, mobilizing governments, RIGOs, and civil society in the LAC region in the future.[81]

VI. LAC CONTRIBUTION TO IMPLEMENT RTOP WORLDWIDE

The fact that the LAC region neither presents any emblematic cases of RtoP nor has any interstate and internal armed conflicts, except for Colombia, is a positive indicator that the region benefits from a relatively peaceful environment, especially if compared

[79] Serbin & Rodrigues, *supra* note 41. As an evidence of that, the Brazilian Council for Refugees (CONARE), in an unanimous decision of June'2009, granted refugee status for 118 Bolivians from Pando, who alleged to be threatened by Evo Morales' supporters. *See* http://g1.globo.com/Noticias/Mundo/0,,MUL1186027-5602,00.html.

[80] The Latin American School of Social Sciences (FLACSO) has been conducting research on organized crime and violence related to new threats to democracy and human rights in LAC region. *See* http://www.flacso.org (last visited Feb. 6, 2011); *See also* Thiago Rodrigues, Guerra e Política Nas Relações Internacionais (2010).

[81] An interesting approach to identify the new threats to peace and security is the peace and conflict instability ledger, which tries to rank states on future risks. *See Peace and Conflict 2010*, Center for International Development and Conflict Management, http://www.cidcm.umd.edu/projects/project.asp?id=32 (last visited Feb. 5, 2011).

to Africa and Asia. This peace dividend, combined with regional resistance to interventions of any kind as a way to prevent or solve conflicts, is not translated into lack of interest by the region in the application of RtoP in other regions. On the contrary, LAC has demonstrated great interest and contributed considerably to prevention, international assistance, and capacity building.

Four relevant areas may be highlighted for RtoP, which have been raised in the context of the *Implementing the Responsibility to Protect*—participation in the Peacebuilding Commission; participation in UN peacekeeping missions; broad participation by LAC countries to the Rome Statute of the ICC; and a strong regional policy for refugees.

LAC countries had an outstanding role in the creation of the Peacebuilding Commission and Brazil took over the Presidency of the Specific Configuration of Guinea-Bissau.[82] In the UN peacekeeping missions, several countries from the LAC region have operated intensely in Africa, in the former Yugoslavia, and in Lebanon. The number of LAC countries signing the Rome Statute is a strong indicator of the regional commitment to fight crimes under the umbrella of RtoP. Up through early 2011, out of 33 LAC countries, 25 have signed the Rome Statute.[83] Additionally, the Argentinian Luis Moreno Ocampo, the district attorney who operated in lawsuits for crimes against humanity committed by Argentinian authorities during dictatorship, became the first prosecutor of the ICC.

Finally, with the Mexico Declaration and Plan of Action (2004), regional refugee policy includes new innovative instruments have opened up the possibility for receiving refugees from other continents.[84]

In these four dimensions, the LAC region has decisively contributed to the success of means, mechanisms, and instruments that guarantee the effective application of RtoP in the extra-regional sphere.

VII. CONCLUSION

The LAC region currently experiences a situation of relative peace if compared to other continents, as it does not present any manifest cases of RtoP. Its urgency to discuss and promote the theme is strongly related to the memory of atrocities committed in the period of military dictatorships (1960–1990s), whose sequels are still felt and still affect the safeguard of human rights. In parallel, opposers to RtoP coherently invoke, even if distortedly, the history of political, military, and economic

[82] Among 31 Peacebuilding Commission members, 5 are from LAC region: Brazil, Colombia, Guatemala, Peru, and Uruguay. See http://www.unhcr.org/pages/4a02da6e6.html (last visited Feb. 6, 2011).

[83] LAC signatories to the Rome Statute as of January 2011: Antigua and Barbuda, Argentina, Barbados, Belize, Bolívia, Brazil, Chile, Colombia, Costa Rica, Dominica, Dominican Republic, Ecuador, Guyana, Honduras, México, Panamá, Paraguay, Peru, Saint Kitts and Nevis, Saint Lucia, Saint Vincent and the Grenadines, Suriname, Trinidad and Tobago, Uruguay, and Venezuela.

[84] The Mexico Plan comprises three main pillars that address urban displacement, protection in the sensitive border areas, and resettlement. *See* UNHCR-Americas, http://www.unhcr.org/pages/4a02da6e6.html (last visited Feb. 6, 2011).

interventions made by the U.S. for the sake of democracy. In that regard, the post-9/11 period is viewed as a real threat to future actions in the region.

The LAC RIGOs accrue significant experience and institutionality in the field of prevention of conflicts and peace-building. The option and preference for RIGOs to act in extreme cases has been a regional trait, which dispels interventions from the UN benchmark. The same RIGOs are provided with frameworks and notable experience in handling with the theme of democracy and human rights—whose resolution of many cases has certainly prevented RtoP situations from emerging.

Civil society and the NGO networks play a critical role for the LAC region, but their potential for accomplishment is restricted by the resistance from the states and the RIGOs to open up more intensely and regularly to discussion and joint action.

A crucial issue in the analysis of the LAC region in relation to RtoP is: as there are no concrete cases in the region, why should it be concerned about the theme? Such a question may be answered in two distinct ways: It should be concerned about the theme as there are potential situations of RtoP in the region which require both preventive policies and actions; and, at last, the LAC region sympathetically demonstrates its concern about RtoP as it honors fundamental axes of RtoP, such as PBC, the ICC, and the regional refugee policy, aiding the promotion of such a principle globally.

10 Middle East

Mohamed S. Helal*

In recent diplomatic history, few issues have aroused as much interest and debate as the rise of the Responsibility to Protect (RtoP). Governments, academics, and civil society from around the world have reacted to the emergence of RtoP and debated its effects on international law and world affairs. In this chapter, a Middle Eastern perspective regarding the rise of RtoP, its scope, content, and contours will be presented.

This chapter will survey the spectrum of positions adopted by Middle Eastern countries toward RtoP and will offer an explanation for why these policies were espoused and how they developed as RtoP advanced to the forefront of the international diplomatic agenda. Therefore, this chapter is divided into three parts. Part I defines the Middle East and the territories that will be considered within the region. This part also highlights the salient historic, geographic, and political features of the region that influenced policies regarding RtoP. Part II surveys the positions of Middle Eastern countries as the international community debated the notion of intervention to prevent or halt gross violations of human rights. This part will also chart the development of Middle Eastern positions as the global debate on RtoP progressed and identify the main factors that influenced the policies of regional players. Part III examines the applicability of RtoP to the Occupied Palestinian Territories, which is among the leading issues currently affecting regional attitudes towards RtoP. And Part IV briefly analyzes the international response to the popular revolt against Libyan leader Colonel Muammar Gaddafi, and the question of the applicability of RtoP to the Libyan case.

* The author dedicates this chapter to Professor M. Cherif Bassiouni, a father, a mentor, an inspiration and an indefatigable warrior for peace and justice. The views expressed in this chapter are solely those of the author, and should not be read or construed as representing the views of any governmental institutions with which he is/was affiliated.

I. SETTING THE STAGE: THE COMPLEXITIES OF THE MIDDLE EAST

A. Defining the "The Middle East"

The Middle East is a land of many controversies, one of which relates to defining the region. Governments and scholars have offered numerous definitions of the Middle East and have coined various terms to refer to that part of the world.[1] For some, the region has been associated with the rise of Islam, which meant extending its bounds to include present-day Afghanistan and Pakistan.[2] Meanwhile, others identify the region as the territories formerly under Ottoman control, thus including Turkey and excluding Iran and all territories to its east.[3]

Given the lack of a unanimously accepted definition of the Middle East in both the political and academic worlds, for the purposes of this chapter the region will be considered to include: North African Arab states (Algeria, Egypt, Libya, Mauritania, Morocco, and Tunisia), states and territories of the Levant (Israel, Jordan, Lebanon, Syria, and the Occupied Palestinian Territories), and states of the Arabian Gulf (Bahrain, Iran, Iraq, Kuwait, Oman, Qatar, Saudi Arabia, and the United Arab Emirates), and Yemen. This chapter will also include Turkey within the rubric of the Middle East due to Ankara's greater engagement in recent years in the politics of the region,[4] which has undoubtedly affected and shaped Turkish policy regarding RtoP.

B. The Multiple Identities of the Middle East

The Middle East is a region of multiple, and at times competing, identities and allegiances, all of which have an immense impact on foreign policy, including on attitudes regarding RtoP. Egypt is a prime example of these multiple identities. This is reflected in the foundational theory of modern Egyptian diplomacy,[5] which identifies three spheres of activity—in order of priority—for the country's foreign policy: the

[1] One genealogy of the term the "Middle East" credits the 19th century American strategist Alfred Thayer Mahan for coining it to denote the region between Europe and the Far East, which includes China and Japan. *See* Michael G. Kort, The Handbook of the Middle East 5 (2002). One of the labels frequently used in the United States to refer to the region is the "Near East." This term is used by the US State Department, which includes Algeria, Bahrain, Egypt, Iran, Iraq, Israel, Jordan, Libya, Morocco, Oman, Palestine, Qatar, Saudi Arabia, Syria, Tunisia, United Arab Emirates, and Yemen. *See*: http://www.state.gov/p/nea/index.htm.

[2] Arthur Goldschmidt Jr. and Lawrence Davidson, A Concise History of the Middle East, 1 (8th ed. 2006).

[3] L. Carl Brown, International Politics and the Middle East 7 (1984). *See also* Bernard Lewis, A Middle East Mosaic xi (2001).

[4] Saban Kardas, *Turkey: Redrawing the Middle East Map or Building Sandcastles?*, Middle East Policy Vol. XVII, No. 1, Spring 2010, at 115. *See also* F. Stephen Larrabee, *Turkey Rediscovers the Middle East*, Foreign Affairs, Vol. 86, No. 4, Jul./Aug. 2007, at 103; Ian O. Lesser, *Turkey in a Changing Security Environment*, J. Int'l Aff., Vol. 54, No. 1, Fall 2000, at 184.

[5] This theory was formulated by President Gamal Abdel Nasser in a short book that he authored following the 1952 revolution. *See* Gamal Abdel Nasser, Egypt's Liberation: The Philosophy of the Revolution (1955).

Arab world, Africa, and the Islamic world.[6] This phenomenon is not, however, uniquely Egyptian; indeed, the foreign relations of all the North African Arab states bear features of this diplomatic trinity.[7] Turkey presents an equally complex picture due to the conflicting realities of being an important NATO member and an aspiring member of the European Union, while being an influential Muslim nation with growing interest in Middle Eastern politics.[8] Meanwhile, the foreign policy of the Gulf Arab states is guided by the twin considerations of being both Arab and Islamic nations, which are relatively compatible.[9] Finally, Israel's Jewish character and Iran's Islamic orientation mean that the question of identity poses few challenges for the formulation of foreign policy in those two nations.

Foreign policy in the Middle East is also influenced by the membership of its countries in various regional organizations. Specifically, with the exception of Israel, all the region's countries are members of the Organization of the Islamic Conference (OIC). Concurrently, all the Arab states congregate under the umbrella of the League of Arab States (LAS), while the North African Arab states, with the exception of Morocco, are also active members of the African Union. In addition, all the Middle East's nations, except Israel and Turkey, are members of the Non-Aligned Movement (NAM), which has been the central forum for elaborating the position of the developing world towards RtoP.[10]

Membership in these constituencies, which overlap in many respects but that diverge on some issues, imposed on Middle Eastern states the duty to tread a nuanced line that balances the positions of these various caucus groups. As demonstrated below, the pressures and responsibilities of simultaneously being a Non-Aligned, developing, Arab, African, and Muslim-majority country coalesced to shape regional attitudes regarding RtoP.

C. The Protracted Conflicts of the Middle East

Another aspect of Middle Eastern politics that affects regional perspectives towards RtoP is the existence of numerous protracted conflicts.[11] In many cases, these conflicts

[6] For a detailed expose of how these various sphere's of interact and how they affect the decision making process of Egyptian diplomacy, *see* Boutros Boutros-Ghali, *Egyptian Foreign Policy After Sadat*, FOREIGN AFF., Vol. 60, No. 4, Spring 1982. For an exploration of how the various "identities" of Egypt have affected its foreign policy during the 20th century *see* JOSEPH LORENZ, EGYPT AND THE ARABS: FOREIGN POLICY AND THE SEARCH FOR NATIONAL IDENTITY (1990).

[7] *See generally* BAHGAT KORANY & ALI E. HILLAL DESSOUKI EDS., THE FOREIGN POLICIES OF ARAB STATES (2008).

[8] Ali Karaosmanoglu, *The Evolution of the National Security Culture and the Military in Turkey*, J. OF INT'L AFFAIRS, Vol. 54, No. 1, Fall 2000, at 199–216. *See also* Omer Taspinar, *Turkey's Middle East Policies: Between Neo-Ottomanism and Kemalism*, CARNEGIE PAPERS, No. 10, Sept. 2008.

[9] *See generally*: RAYMOND A. HINNEBUSCH AND ANOUSHIRAVAN EHTESHAMI ED., THE FOREIGN POLICIES OF MIDDLE EAST STATES (2002).

[10] It is also noteworthy that, for the purposes of RtoP, membership in organizations has not always led to unqualified support of the bloc's position, neither has it meant that all states have been vocal in espousing the group policy regarding RtoP, which is partially a function of the varying degree of importance attached to these organizations by the various countries in the region.

[11] There is a wealth of international relations and security studies literature on the phenomenon of protracted conflicts and "enduring rivalries." For example *see* Gary Goertz & Paul F. Diehl, *Enduring*

form the axis around which the foreign policies of regional powers revolve and the lens through which every development in international relations is analyzed. Therefore, an emerging norm that, like RtoP, justifies foreign intervention in conflict situations will, regardless of its humanitarian nature, be evaluated according to its impact on the protracted conflict that is of primary interest to a regional player.

The Arab-Israeli conflict is the most prominent political question for most Middle Eastern governments and their peoples. Indeed, for Israel and some Arab states the entire business of foreign relations gravitates around this conflict.[12] For other countries, particularly the Arab states of the Arabian Gulf, the primary foreign policy priorities pertain to maintaining peace and stability in that sub-region and countering the burgeoning Iranian influence.[13] In addition, the continuous confrontation with Iraq that extended from its 1990 invasion of Kuwait to the 2003 U.S.-led invasion also shaped regional attitudes towards RtoP and the possibilities of its use and misuse.

Finally, the unabated conflict in Sudan, whether between North and South Sudan or in Darfur, and the prospects of foreign intervention in that country, undoubtedly affected the positions of Middle Eastern countries with strategic interests in Sudan, most notably Egypt.[14]

II. SURVEYING MIDDLE EASTERN PERSPECTIVES

Having laid out the background regional setting and political realities that affect Middle Eastern positions towards RtoP, this chapter now proceeds to charting the evolution of these positions.

Rivalries: Theoretical Constructs and Empirical Patterns, INT'L STUD. QRTLY, Vol. 37, No. 2 (Jun. 1993), at 147; GARY GOERTZ & PAUL F. DIEHL, WAR AND PEACE IN INTERNATIONAL RIVALRY (2000).

[12] While the Arab-Israeli conflict is certainly high on the agenda of all Arab states, some governments ascribe greater importance to it than others. Specifically, it is arguable that for Syria the Palestinian question and the confrontation with Israel are the sole and unchallenged concern of Syrian foreign policy. *See* ALASDAIR DRYSDALE AND RAYMOND A. HINNEBUSCH, SYRIA AND THE MIDDLE EAST PEACE PROCESS (1991). For a more recent evaluation of Syrian foreign policy and strategy *see* International Crisis Group, *Reshuffling the Cards (I) and (II): Syria's Evolving Strategy*, MIDDLE EAST REPORTS NO. 92 AND 93, (2009), *available online* http://www.crisisgroup.org. Other countries, like Egypt, pursue a more diversified foreign policy, where the ending of the Israeli occupation of the Palestinian territories constitutes a primary objective, but it is not the unchallenged or singularly most important question.

[13] For example, Anthony Cordesman opined in 2003 that the primary threats to Saudi Arabian security were the developments in Iran and the situation in Iraq. ANTHONY CORDESMAN, SAUDI ARABIA ENTERS THE 21ST CENTURY: THE POLITICAL, FOREIGN POLICY, ECONOMIC AND ENERGY DIMENSIONS (2003). On the foreign policy of the United Arab Emirates, which also exhibits extreme sensitivity to Iranian influence and policies in the region, *see* Peter Hellyer, *The Evolution of UAE Foreign Policy*, *in* UNITED ARAB EMIRATES: A NEW PERSPECTIVE 161 (Ibrahim Al Abed & Peter Hellyer eds., 2001).

[14] For a survey of modern Egyptian-Sudanese relations *see* Yehudit Ronen, *Sudan and Egypt: The Swing of the Pendulum (1989–2003)*, MIDDLE EASTERN STUDIES, Vol. 39, No. 3, Jul. 2003. For an example of the importance that Egypt attaches to Sudan as a crucial ally in ongoing negotiations pertaining to the regulation of the Nile river waters, *see The Battle of the Nile*, AFRICA CONFIDENTIAL, Vol. 51, No. 17, Aug. 2010; *see also* Dan Murphy, *Why Egypt Won't Press Sudan: The Nile*, CHRISTIAN SCIENCE MONITOR, Vol. 98, No. 218, Mar. 2006.

A. Kosovo: The Dilemma of Humanitarian Intervention

Any choice of a starting date for the examination of Middle Eastern positions regarding RtoP will entail a degree of arbitrariness.[15] However, the decision to commence this survey with the 1999 Kosovo War is predicated on the NATO campaign and that its ramifications provided the immediate setting and impetus for developing RtoP as a policy framework for responding to mass violations of international humanitarian law (IHL) and international human rights law (IHRL).[16]

The American-led NATO intervention in Kosovo polarized the international community and sparked heated debates about the concept of humanitarian intervention, its legality, and legitimacy. Indeed, it was the leading topic during the High-Level Plenary debate of the 54th Session of the UN General Assembly (UNGA).[17] Secretary General Kofi Annan kick-started that debate by challenging world leaders to formulate a mechanism to protect civilians from mass atrocities without demolishing the post-World War II collective security system.[18] The first Middle Eastern response to the Secretary General's challenge came only two speakers later when Algerian President Abdelaziz Bouteflika, speaking on behalf of Africa, stated that: "[w]e remain extremely sensitive to any undermining of our sovereignty, not only because sovereignty is our final defense against the rules of an unjust world, but because we have no active part in the decision-making process in the Security Council nor in monitoring implementation of decisions."[19]

Almost every Middle Eastern nation that spoke after Algeria commented on this matter. What emerged was a wide spectrum of Middle Eastern positions. On one side of this spectrum, Algeria was joined by other countries that unequivocally opposed NATO's actions and unwaveringly upheld sovereignty as a sacrosanct principle of both international law and international relations. These states included Iraq, which described humanitarian intervention as a "modern form of neo-colonialism,"[20] Libya that warned that humanitarian intervention "will help erode the little that remains of

[15] One could start a survey of Middle Eastern perspectives of intervention on humanitarian grounds from a number of historical events. Indeed, some scholars have charted a genealogy of the norm requiring international intervention to protect civilians from mass violations of human rights that starts with pre-20th Century situations, such as the Western intervention in Lebanon in 1860, *see* Ian Brownlie, *Humanitarian Intervention, in* Law and Civil war in the Modern World (John Norton Moore ed. 1974). Other academics focused on situations that occurred in the post-World War II, such as: India's intervention in East Pakistan (1971); Syria's intervention in Lebanon (1976); Vietnam's intervention in Cambodia (1978); Tanzania's intervention in Uganda (1979); France's intervention in the Central African Republic (1979); and finally, India's intervention in Sri Lanka (1987). *See* Susan Breau, Humanitarian Intervention: The United Nations and Collective Responsibility 33–69 (2005). For similar analysis of pre-1990 cases of humanitarian intervention *see* Sean Murphy, Humanitarian Intervention: The United Nations in an Evolving World Order (1996); Fernando Teson, Humanitarian Intervention: An Inquiry into Law and Morality (1988).

[16] Alex Bellamy, Responsibility to Protect 33–34 (2009).

[17] The records and statements of the plenary meetings are *available at* http://www.un.org/ga/54/pv54e.htm.

[18] UN GAOR, 54th Sess., 4th plen. mtg., A/54/PV.4, Sept. 20, 1999, at 2.

[19] *Id.* at 14.

[20] UN GAOR, 54th Sess., 12th plen. mtg., A/54/PV.12, Sept. 24, 1999, at 28.

State sovereignty,"[21] and Sudan, which portended that NATO's intervention would "only lead to chaos and the hegemony of the powerful over the weak."[22]

As we move along the spectrum, the positions of Middle Eastern governments gradually become more nuanced. Egypt and Tunisia delivered statements that proposed solutions to address the challenge presented by the Secretary-General. Specifically, Tunisia insisted that deliberations on the appropriate policies to protect populations from grave violations of human rights should not be confined to the Security Council, but ought to extend to the General Assembly.[23] Meanwhile, Egypt described the plight of the Kosovars as a human tragedy, welcomed the adoption of Security Council resolution 1244, and observed that while consensus existed on the need to intervene, there was no agreement on *who* had the right to act. Egypt then opined that:

> Any international action must stem from the Security Council as the competent organ with primary responsibility for the maintenance of international peace and security. If the Council were unable to do so, the General Assembly would be the organ that must deal with any threats to international peace and security, as it represents the common interest of all its members.[24]

Another group of Middle Eastern nations that spoke on the matter avoided taking a clear stand on the central question of how the international community should react in cases similar to the Kosovo crisis, and instead focused on expressing indignation at the suffering of the Kosovars. For example, the United Arab Emirates[25] and Morocco[26] highlighted their participation in relief efforts in Kosovo and called for greater international cooperation to avoid such humanitarian disasters.[27] Bahrain's statement also condemned the inhumane treatment of Kosovo's population and called on the international community to "unfailingly guard against and address the causes of the phenomenon of racism and all its manifestations."[28] Similarly, Iran noted that most countries agreed on the importance of maintaining the integrity of the UN Charter system, and called for an international debate on the matter to be held in the UNGA.[29] Meanwhile, in its statement Lebanon surveyed the divergent views of the international community on the matter and then drew the important parallel between Kosovo and the Palestinian question by calling for "a just and equitable settlement that addresses the issue of the final status of the Palestinian refugees, in accordance

[21] UN GAOR, 54th Sess., 16th plen. mtg., A/54/PV.16, Sept. 29, 1999, at 16.

[22] UN GAOR, 54th Sess., 19th plen. mtg., A/54/PV.19, Sept. 30, 1999, at 29.

[23] UN GAOR, 54th Sess., 17th plen. mtg., A/54/PV.17, Sept. 29, 1999, at 16.

[24] UN GAOR, 54th Sess., 10th plen. mtg., A/54/PV.10, Sept. 23, 1999, at 22.

[25] UN GAOR, 54th Sess., 7th plen. mtg., A/54/PV.7, Sept. 21, 1999, at 37.

[26] *Id.* at 27.

[27] Interestingly, despite being a NATO member, Turkey did not comment on the principle of humanitarian intervention. Instead, it reiterated its commitment to the security and stability of the Balkans and highlighted the need for the long-term reconstruction and stabilization of Kosovo. For the statement of Turkey, *see*: UN GAOR, 54th Sess., 11th plen. mtg., A/54/PV.11, Sept. 23, 1999, at 38.

[28] UN GAOR, 54th Sess., 16th plen. mtg., A/54/PV.19, Sept. 29, 1999, at 20.

[29] UN GAOR, 54th Sess., 12th plen. mtg., A/54/PV.12, Sept. 24, 1999, at 13.

with internationally agreed principles that govern similar situations. Those principles, it should be recalled, were recently applied in Kosovo."[30]

Further along the spectrum of Middle Eastern positions are countries that extended qualified support to NATO's intervention. These governments noted that the Kosovo war represented a serious challenge to the post-World War II legal order, but they favored such intervention if undertaken to save civilians from massive violations of human rights. Syria's statement is emblematic of this approach:

> Marginalizing the role of the UN, using it only on selected occasions and as a cover for initiatives and decisions adopted outside the Security Council will serve the interests of no one . . . But here it must be said that illegitimate intervention outside the framework of the UN Security Council is not as bad as completely ignoring dangerous and bloody crises.[31]

Similarly, Saudi Arabia considered intervention without UN authorization "not to be the ideal way to settle international crises. But it becomes an unavoidable necessity whenever the Security Council, due to disunity and disagreements between its Permanent Members, fails in its role in maintaining international peace and security."[32]

Last on the spectrum are those countries that applauded NATO and voiced unqualified support for its intervention in Kosovo. Oman and Qatar fall in this category, with the latter "expressing satisfaction"[33] at the results of the operation and the former voicing "thankfulness for the timely intervention by NATO."[34] Finally, one country that referred neither to the Kosovo crisis nor to the question of humanitarian intervention was Israel. The statement of Israel focused almost exclusively on the prospects of peace in the Middle East and on combating terrorism.[35]

Accounting for this plurality of Middle Eastern positions requires recalling the complex political landscape of the region discussed earlier. Countries like Iraq, Libya, and Sudan, which expressed extreme opposition to NATO's intervention, were pitted during the late-1990s in an intense confrontation against the Western world generally, and the United States especially.[36] This dictated the rejection of any concept,

[30] UN GAOR, 54th Sess., 11th plen. mtg., A/54/PV.11, Sept. 23, 1999, at 11.

[31] UN GAOR, 54th Sess., 18th plen. mtg., A/54/PV.18, Sept. 30, 1999, at 17.

[32] UN GAOR, 54th Sess., 19th plen. mtg., A/54/PV.19, Sept. 30, 1999, at 35.

Another country that can be included in this group is Jordan, which expressed the view that "upholding the principles of sovereignty should not overturn the obligations to observe human rights and international humanitarian law." UN GAOR, 54th Sess., 4th plen. mtg., A/54/PV.4, Sept. 20, 1999, at. 33.

[33] UN GAOR, 54th Sess., 18th plen. mtg., A/54/PV.18, Sept. 30, 1999, at 6.

[34] UN GAOR, 54th Sess., 13th plen. mtg., A/54/PV.13, Sept. 24, 1999, at 26.

[35] UN GAOR, 54th Sess., 16th plen. mtg., A/54/PV.16, Sept. 29, 1999, at 12.

[36] In the case of Sudan, the United States bombed sites in Khartoum on August 20, 1998, in retaliation for alleged Sudanese complicity in the dual bombings against U.S. Embassies in Kenya and Tanzania. As to Libya, this was before Tripoli reached understandings with Western powers for the dismantling its weapons of mass destruction programs. Finally, Iraq was still under UN sanctions and the U.S. and UK still maintained no-fly zones over the north and south of the country, which were partially justified on the humanitarian grounds of protecting the Kurdish and Shiite communities of Iraq.

regardless of its humanitarian purposes, that justified the unilateral resort to force and that could be employed to legitimize foreign intervention. Indeed, those countries adhered to a narrow interpretation of articles 2(4) and 2(7) of the UN Charter that prohibit both the use of force in international relations and the interference in the domestic affairs of states, which they felt provided them an extra measure of protection.[37]

In addition to fears harbored by those countries from Western armed intervention, Algeria's statement reflected two concerns neither of which is uniquely Middle Eastern. The first is a fear perceived by most developing countries that given the global inequalities of power and wealth, a right of unilateral humanitarian intervention would essentially become the prerogative of powerful countries, which entails a serious diminution of their hard-won independence and sovereignty. This was best reflected in the Final Communiqué of the NAM Ministerial Meeting held alongside the UNGA debate, which "reject[ed] the so-called 'right of humanitarian intervention' which has no legal basis in the UN Charter or in the general principles of international law."[38]

The second concern relates to a general sentiment among developing countries that they are marginalized in the UN decision-making processes. This outlook is most pronounced regarding the Security Council, which is denounced as an undemocratic and unrepresentative institution that lacks transparency and is controlled by its five Permanent Members to the detriment of the other members of the organization.[39] This explains the ambivalence expressed by some Middle Eastern countries towards both humanitarian intervention and RtoP, which were viewed as principles that further expand the powers and prerogatives of the Security Council within the UN system.

As we move along the spectrum of Middle Eastern positions, we discover how the different interests and strategic outlooks of the various countries influenced their

[37] For scholarly positions reflecting this "narrow" interpretation of the UN Charter provisions of relevance to the question of the resort to force, *see* Bruno Simma, *NATO, the UN and the Use of Force: Legal Aspects*, 10 Eur. J. Int'l L. (1999); R. Hofmann, *International Law and the Use of Military Force Against Iraq*, 45 German Y.B.Int'l L. (2002); M. Bothe, *Terrorism and the Legality of Preemptive Force*, 14 Eur. J. Int'l L. (2003); Albrecht Randelzhofer, *Article 51*, *in* The Charter of the United Nations: A Commentary (Bruno Simma et. al. eds., 1994); Christine Gray, International Law and the Use of Force (2004).

[38] Final Communiqué of the Meeting of Ministers for Foreign Affairs and Heads of Delegation of the Non-Aligned Movement, Sept. 23, 1999, at 171, *available at* http://www.nam.gov.za/minmeet/newyorkcom.htm#top.

[39] The question of Security Council expansion and the reform of its working methods has been on the UN agenda for at least 15 years, and the developing world has consistently voiced numerous grievances in this regard. The sentiment among the developing countries is well reflected in a statement delivered by the African Group, which called for making "the Security Council inclusive, representative, democratic and responsive to the current geo-political realities. The status quo is no option and is unacceptable, indeed, we cannot continue like this unless something has to be done sooner rather than later to redress this worrying situation." *See Statement of the Permanent Representative of Sierra Leone on Behalf of the African Group*, Mar. 4, 2009, *available at*: http://globalpolicy.org/images/pdfs/AfricanGroup_StatementOnSCReform_4Mar092.pdf

For an overview of debates on Security Council reform and the views of the various regional groups *see* Dimitris Bourantonis, The History and Politics of UN Security Council Reform (2005).

policies. In this regard, Egypt's and Tunisia's more balanced reactions to NATO's operation are imputable to multiple factors. Both countries endorsed a right of international intervention to protect civilians from mass atrocities. They did, however, place qualifications on this right, the first of which is the requirement that intervention be limited to situations that threaten international peace and security. This is significant because, primarily, it ensures that humanitarian intervention will never be applicable to countries that, like Egypt and Tunisia, frequently face allegations of human rights violations, but that never constitute a threat to international peace and security.[40] Second, it constructs an implicit analogy between Kosovo and the Israeli occupation of the Palestinian territories, which is understandable in light of the priority given to the Palestinian question in the foreign policies of both countries. A second proposal advanced by Egypt was that the UNGA should be authorized, pursuant to the United for Peace formula,[41] to intervene in humanitarian crises should the Security Council fail to execute its mandate. This echoes the desire of the developing world to encourage the UNGA, where developing countries enjoy greater influence, to perform a greater role in international affairs.

A third element of Egypt's position was the requirement that decisions to intervene be taken *multilaterally*. This reflects a deep-seated apprehension from the destabilizing effects that a right to the unilateral resort to force—regardless of its pretext—would have on the Middle East. For countries like Egypt and Tunisia the UN provides a forum that ensures that the resort to force would result from a process of multilateral deliberation that reflected world opinion as opposed to the narrower interests of any particular power.[42] This is particularly true in the case of Egypt, which was especially concerned in the late-1990s about the possibilities of armed intervention against its southern or western neighbors, Sudan and Libya.[43]

Further along the spectrum are those countries that did not adopt a specific position on the question of humanitarian intervention, and that limited their comments to expressing sympathy for the suffering of the Kosovars. Among those countries, Lebanon explicitly called for according the Palestinians the same treatment that was extended to the Kosovars, which reflects the centrality of the Palestinian question to the foreign policy of Beirut. Otherwise, a variety of motives could have led countries in this category, like Morocco and UAE, to adopt this posture. One explanation is that none of these countries feared that humanitarian intervention could be employed against them or in areas where their vital interests would be affected. Furthermore, none of these countries traditionally vie for the political leadership of the Middle East, Africa or the developing world, which meant they could leave other delegations to bear the burden of advancing the NAM agenda. Moreover, the fact that these nations have Muslim majority populations meant that expressing indignation at the

[40] While the human rights record of both countries leaves much to be desired, it is doubtful that the governments of these two countries anticipated that they would ever witness the kinds of violations that could be described as threatening international peace and security.

[41] G.A. Res. 377 (v), UN GAOR, 5th Sess., Nov. 3, 1950.

[42] A prime example of this is the 1991 Gulf War, when Egypt opposed Iraq's invasion of Kuwait and joined the U.S.-led international coalition to end the Iraqi occupation, which was sanctioned and authorized by the UN Security Council.

[43] *See* Ibrahim Nafie, *An Egyptian Agenda*, AL-AHRAM, Sept. 7, 2000, at 5.

plight of the Kosovars would partially placate public opinion. These considerations undoubtedly coalesced to influence Bahrain's decision to vote against the Russian draft resolution presented to the Security Council to demand a halt to NATO's intervention.[44]

The next group of countries includes those which, despite voicing concern over the potentially destabilizing effects of NATO's action, supported intervention to protect civilians if the UN fails to do so. The motivations for those countries are varied. Syria, for example, was probably driven by a desire to utilize the concept of humanitarian intervention to apply greater pressure on Israel to end practices that Damascus considers amounting to RtoP crimes. While Saudi Arabia's traditional role as a leader of the Muslim world necessitated its acquiescence to an intervention that saved tens of thousands of Muslims in Kosovo. However, the status of both these countries as important members of NAM probably persuaded them not to sway too far from the group positions by fully endorsing NATO's intervention. Furthermore, their cautioning about the deleterious effects of undermining the UN collective security system stems from their pivotal role in Middle East politics and their recognition of the dangerous ramifications that further foreign armed intervention would have on the region.

The last group on the spectrum of Middle Eastern positions includes those states that fully supported NATO. This is imputable to the relatively low cost that countries like Qatar and Oman would incur by adopting such a position. Neither of these countries performs a leading role in the developing world blocs at the UN, nor is their security threatened by possible interventions on humanitarian grounds. Furthermore, supporting the U.S.-led intervention was probably well received in Washington, which guarantees the security of these Arabian Gulf nations.[45] Moreover, applauding NATO was in consonance with public opinion in those countries that undoubtedly sympathized with their fellow Muslims in Kosovo.

This survey of Middle Eastern positions regarding the Kosovo War leads to a number of observations. First, the vast majority of Middle Eastern countries endorsed the idea that when faced with mass atrocities the international community is duty-bound to intervene to protect civilians. Second, the ambivalence exhibited by some countries emanated from fears of the possible misuse of humanitarian intervention in areas that affected their national security or strategic interests. Therefore, those countries proposed procedural guarantees, such as multilateral authorization for intervention, to guard against the misapplication of humanitarian intervention. Third, other concerns expressed were not uniquely Middle Eastern, but echoed apprehensions shared by the broader developing world. These ranged from fears of marginalization within the UN system to concerns about a growing unilateralist streak in Western

[44] Susan Breau, Humanitarian Intervention: The United Nations and Collective Responsibility 142 (2005). It is also noteworthy that the Permanent Representative of Iran to the UN communicated the joint position of the OIC in a letter to the President of the Security Council in which the NATO intervention was *not* condemned. Instead, the letter expressed regret that the Security Council could not discharge its responsibilities. *See id.*, at 143.

[45] *See* F. Gregory Gause III, *The Approaching Turning Point: The Future of US Relations with the Gulf States*, Brookings Project on US Policy Towards the Islamic World, May 2003.

foreign policy that threatened to undermine the global multilateral structure that is indispensable to developing countries.

These underlying considerations continued to shape Middle Eastern positions towards RtoP as it emerged as a substitute to the more controversial concept of humanitarian intervention. The direction Middle Eastern policies towards RtoP took, however, was dictated primarily by developments within the region.

B. The Invasion of Iraq

The one event that had the greatest impact on regional positions towards RtoP was the 2003 U.S.-led invasion of Iraq. Scholars and commentators have testified to the harm that this war wrought onto international efforts to advance RtoP. Gareth Evans, a leading advocate of RtoP, even lamented that proffering humanitarian grounds for the invasion almost led the norm to be "choked at birth."[46] This was because it had confirmed "long-standing suspicions on the part of many southern states that a doctrine of humanitarian intervention would be a weapon used by the strong against the weak."[47]

It would be an oversimplification, however, to assume that it was the justification of the invasion of Iraq, *inter alia*, on humanitarian grounds that alone shaped regional attitudes towards RtoP. Rather, it was the objectives and instruments of foreign policy adopted by the administration of U.S. President George W. Bush that had the most significant impact on policies towards RtoP.

In the post-September 11th world, the "democratization" of the Middle East became a top U.S. foreign policy objective.[48] This was predicated on a belief that Islamist terrorism was fueled by the "absence of democracy in the Middle East [which] threatened not only the citizens of Arab countries but U.S. security as well."[49] Therefore, the war on Iraq was touted as being part of an overall strategy of domino-democratization where the fall of Saddam Hussein would, in the words of then-National Security Advisor Condoleezza Rice, spark "the march of freedom in the Muslim world."[50] Beyond Iraq, the prime targets of the drive to liberalize the Middle East were two of Washington's closest allies, Egypt and Saudi Arabia. "Almost overnight, the two countries became U.S. enemies, accused of fostering terrorism by denying their citizens democracy and wealth-generating free market policies."[51] While few in Cairo or Riyadh expected the U.S. to launch an invasion against either country, both nations, especially Egypt, were exposed to immense American pressure to urgently undertake political reforms.[52]

[46] Gareth Evans, *When is it Right to Fight*, 43 Survival 63 (2004).

[47] Nicholas Wheeler, *A Victory for Common Humanity? The Responsibility to Protect after the 2005 World Summit*, 2 Int'l J. of Int'l Rel. 95 (2005–2006).

[48] Jeremy Sharp, *U.S. Democracy Promotion Policy in the Middle East: The Islamist Dilemma*, *in* CRS Report for Congress, Jun. 2006, at 1.

[49] Marina Ottoway, *Promoting Democracy in the Middle East: The Problem of US Credibility*, Carnegie Endowment Working Papers, Mar. 2003, at 7.

[50] James Harding and Richard Wolffe, *Interview with Condoleezza Rice*, Financial Times, 23 Sept. 2002.

[51] Marina Ottoway, *Arab Dictators*, Foreign Policy, Mar./Apr. 2007, at 46.

[52] *Id.*

Of course, U.S. interest in the state of human rights in the Middle East was not novel. What changed was the intensity of U.S. pressure and the adoption of unilateralism, preemptive war and regime change as instruments of U.S. foreign policy in a highly unstable region.[53] It was this environment that most affected regional policies regarding RtoP. The Middle East was now faced with the world's sole superpower implementing a "policy of *force first*, where ad hoc 'coalitions of the willing' preserve homeland security through discretionary war-making [emphasis in original]."[54] This was also an America that was disavowing the post-World War II multilateral structure that is indispensable to the foreign policy of many countries from the developing world.[55] This led these countries to adopt a more belligerent attitude towards RtoP during the negotiations on the 2005 World Summit Outcome Document (WSOD).

C. The 2005 World Summit

The inclusion of the celebrated paragraphs 138–140 in the WSOD in which over 150 Heads of State and Government unanimously endorsed RtoP is considered by many to be the landmark achievement of the 2005 World Summit.[56] These paragraphs and the language in which they were drafted were the result of months of arduous negotiations. Unlike the Kosovo debates, however, most Middle Eastern countries were less vocal during the discussions on RtoP. Meanwhile, the few states that were engaged in the debate, such as Egypt, Syria, Iran, and Algeria, adopted a unfavorable attitude towards RtoP.

Two themes dominated Middle Eastern positions during discussions on RtoP. First was the acknowledgment of the need to protect civilians from mass atrocities committed during armed conflicts. Iran, for example, declared:

> Undoubtedly, the international community cannot and should not sit idly and neglect its high responsibility when faced with heinous crimes of genocide, war crimes, and crimes against humanity. Indeed, it cannot be right for the UN to stand by, when the international community is faced with these crimes, and let them unfold to the end, with disastrous consequences for many thousands of people.[57]

Similarly, Egypt announced that it was "committed to the fundamental orientation to promote the rule of law as a basic foundation for safeguarding international security and human rights."[58]

[53] Moisés Naím, *Casualties of War*, Foreign Policy, Sep./Oct. 2004, at 96.

[54] Harold Hongju Koh, *Setting the World Right*, 2353, 115 Yale L. J. 2350 (2006).

[55] John Ikenberry, *Is American Multilateralism in Decline?*, 1 Perspectives on Politics (2003).

[56] *2005 World Summit Outcome*, A/RES/60/1, Sept. 15, 2005 [hereinafter WSOD]. For a commentary on the results of the World Summit, especially as regards RtoP, *see*: Kofi Annan, *A Glass At Least Half-Full*, Wall Street Journal, Sept. 19, 2005; *see also* Serena Sharma, *Toward a Global Responsibility to Protect: Setbacks on the Path of Implementation*, 16 Global Governance 121 (2010).

[57] Ambassador Mehdi Danesh-Yazdi, Deputy Permanent Representative of the Islamic Republic of Iran to the United Nations, *Statement at the Informal Thematic Consultation of the UN General Assembly on the Report of the Secretary General, In Larger Freedom: Towards Development, Security and Human Rights for All*, Apr. 20, 2005, *available at* http://globalr2p.org/resources/country.php?country=56.

[58] Ambassador Maged Abdelaziz, Permanent Representative of the Arab Republic of Egypt to the United Nations, *Statement at the Informal Thematic Consultation of the UN General Assembly on the*

The second prevailing theme among Middle Eastern delegations was that RtoP should be excluded from the WSOD, a contention that was predicated on two grounds. The first of these was that RtoP is superfluous because it was already established that states are obligated to protect their own populations from grave human rights violations, and that if a situation threatened international peace and security, then the Security Council was already mandated to address such cases. This argument was advanced by Egypt: "[T]here is no shared responsibility outside the responsibility of the state to protect its own citizens and the responsibility of the Security Council to address matters of international peace and security."[59] Meanwhile, Algeria espoused the second ground for sidelining RtoP; namely that the concept required further elucidation and that it did not command consensus.[60] Syria also agreed with this position and called for the exclusion of RtoP because it was not grounded in international law and was in conflict with the principles of the UN Charter.[61]

One common account of these positions considers them "unsurprising when viewed in the larger context of . . . historical attitudes towards humanitarian and human rights causes."[62] It is contended here, however, that this view is both uncorroborated by the evidence and ignores many factors that were fundamental to shaping the policies of Middle Eastern countries.

It should be recalled that during the debates on the Kosovo war, which occurred only six years before the negotiations on RtoP, none of the Middle Eastern countries, with the exception of Iraq, Sudan, and Libya, rejected the notion of humanitarian intervention. Indeed, some Middle Eastern countries, like Syria, supported the NATO operation, and expressed the view that intervention without UN authorization should be allowed if the Security Council failed to execute its mandate. What, therefore, caused many of these countries to make a *volte-face* and express discomfort with RtoP, despite being much less controversial than humanitarian intervention?

The salient reason was the Iraq war and the fundamental changes in U.S. foreign policy in the post-9/11 period. The humanitarian justification for the invasion of Iraq essentially confirmed the worst fears of many Middle Eastern nations about the misuse of humanitarian grounds to legitimize unilateral armed intervention in regional disputes. "The Bush doctrine of preemptive or even preventive self-defense [was] regarded by many States as a general threat that requires a renewed commitment to the non-intervention rule. Thus there [was] more pressure to return to classical Westphalian notions of sovereignty."[63] This accounts, for example, for Egypt's declaration that RtoP "conflicts directly with such well-established principles enshrined in the Charter,

Report of the Secretary General, In Larger Freedom: Towards Development, Security and Human Rights for All. Id.

[59] *Id.*

[60] *Statement of Algeria at the Informal Thematic Consultation of the UN General Assembly on the Report of the Secretary General, In Larger Freedom: Towards Development, Security and Human Rights for All. Id.*

[61] *See State-by-State Positions on the Responsibility to Protect, A Compilation of Government Positions on RtoP*, International Coalition for the Responsibility to Protect, *available at* http://www.responsibilitytoprotect.org/index.php?option=com_content&view=article&id=294.

[62] Claire Applegarth and Andrew Block, *Acting Against Atrocities: A Strategy for Supporters of the Responsibility to Protect*, Discussion Paper #09–03, Belfer Center for Science and International Affairs, Harvard University John F. Kennedy School of Government, Mar. 2009, at 28.

[63] S. Neil MacFarlane, Caroline J. Thielking, & Thomas G. Weiss, *The Responsibility to Protect: Is Anyone Interested in Humanitarian Intervention?* Third World Quarterly, Vol. 25, No. 5, 2004, at 984.

particularly those related to the use of force, sovereignty, territorial integrity and non-interference in the internal affairs of States."[64]

In addition, Middle Eastern unease with RtoP emanated from the lack of conceptual clarity and the ambiguities concerning its application. Specifically, there were, and still are, calls by scholarly and governmental figures to expand the scope of RtoP to other situations. For example, France has repeatedly called for the extension of RtoP to humanitarian crises caused by natural disasters.[65] Meanwhile, two influential American scholars, one of whom previously headed the Policy Planning Staff at the U.S. State Department, advocated a corollary of RtoP in the field of global security in the form of a "collective 'duty to prevent' nations run by rulers without internal checks on their power from acquiring or using WMDs."[66] This caused many Middle Eastern governments to fear that RtoP could be extended beyond cases of genocide, war crimes, crimes against humanity, and ethnic cleansing to include other forms of human rights violations or other international disputes. In the eyes of countries like Egypt, Syria, Algeria, and other Middle Eastern nations, this would turn RtoP into an ever-expanding license for "the strong to judge the weak."[67]

Another cause for concern was the decision not to include any criteria for determining the legitimacy of intervention. Originally, the 16-member High-Level Panel (HLP) established by Secretary-General Kofi Annan to present recommendations on confronting the challenges facing the UN in the twenty-first century, including responding to gross violations of human rights, had proposed criteria to govern the resort to force by the UN.[68] These criteria were then endorsed by the Secretary General and presented to the General Assembly in his report titled *In Larger Freedom: Towards Development, Security and Human Rights for All.*[69]

This proposal was met with considerable opposition, especially by some of the Permanent Members of the Security Council, albeit for starkly different reasons. On the one hand, the U.S. rejected the inclusion of any criteria that might either limit its freedom of action or that might pressure it into acquiescing to or participating in interventions that it opposed. On the other hand, the Russian Federation and China opposed the enumeration of any criteria out of the fear that these might be abused and employed to legitimize unilateral intervention in the internal affairs of states.[70] This came as a disappointment to some Middle Eastern countries which, like many developing nations, sought to curtail the powers of the Security Council and instill

[64] Statement of Egypt, *supra* note 58, at 2.

[65] Jean-Pierre Lacroix, Deputy Permanent Representative of France to the United Nations, *Statement Delivered Before the UN General Assembly on the Responsibility to Protect*, Jul. 23, 2009, *available at* http://www.franceonu.org/spip.php?article4072.

[66] Lee Feinstein and Anne-Marie Slaughter, *A Duty to Prevent*, Foreign Affairs, Jan./Feb. 2004, at 137.

[67] Statement of Egypt, *supra* note 58, at 2.

[68] *Secretary-General's High-Level Panel on Threats, Challenges and Change, A More Secure World: Our Shared Responsibility*, A/59/565, Dec. 2, 2004, *available at* http://www.un.org/secureworld/. The criteria adopted by the HLP included: (1) seriousness of threat, (2) proper purpose, (3) last resort, (4) proportional means, and (5) balance of consequences.

[69] The Secretary General, *Report of the Secretary General: In Larger Freedom: Towards Development, Security and Human Rights for All*, A/59/2005, Mar. 21, 2005, at 132.

[70] Bellamy, *supra* note 16, at 84.

greater transparency in its work.[71] Therefore, Egypt warned against the adoption of norms for international intervention "without clear parameters that would protect the interests of all States."[72] It is also likely that Cairo calculated that there was a high probability that situations would arise in the Occupied Palestinian Territories that satisfy the criteria that were designed to identify cases that necessitated Security Council intervention. This, it was hoped, would have pressured the Council into performing a more proactive and depoliticized role in the Middle East Peace Process and in protecting Palestinian civilians in times of crises.

Despite these reservations and apprehensions, however, none of the Middle Eastern countries adopted an uncompromising attitude towards RtoP. Rather, they all joined the consensus, endorsed RtoP, and were actively engaged in future debates about the concept both in the Security Council and the UNGA. A number of factors account for this relative flexibility of Middle Eastern countries.

The first factor is geographic. Many Middle Eastern countries are also African nations and were part of the emerging African consensus on the importance of timely intervention to prevent mass violations of human rights. This African position was reflected in two documents, the first of which was the Constitutive Act of the African Union (AU) that allowed for intervention to prevent genocide, crimes against humanity and war crimes.[73] The second document was *Ezulwini Consensus* which reflected the common African position on the entire UN reform agenda as outlined in both the HLP report and Kofi Annan's *In Larger Freedom* report. In this latter document, Africa endorsed RtoP, but demanded specific criteria to govern its application, and reaffirmed its view that the AU should be empowered to intervene in African conflicts, even if Security Council authorization was only acquired ex post facto.[74] Therefore, despite the apprehensions harbored by some Middle Eastern governments towards RtoP, it would have been imprudent for North African delegations to adopt policies that collided with the common African position, to which they were deeply committed.[75]

A second factor was linguistic. Paragraphs 138, 139, and 140 were certainly not optimal in the eyes of many Middle Eastern nations, but they did include some essen-

[71] This position was not shared by all developing nations. Some developing countries, most notably India, also opposed the inclusion of criteria to govern the use of force by the Security Council. On the other hand, most African nations were in favor of the enumeration of standards that directed the work of the Council when it considered intervention in humanitarian crises. *See id.*

[72] Statement of Egypt, *supra* note 58, at 2. This position was also the unified position of Africa, which was adopted during Extraordinary Session of the African Union Executive Council, which affirmed that: "Authorization for the use of force by the Security Council should be in line with the conditions and criteria proposed by the Panel." *See*: African Union Executive Council, *The Common African Position on the Proposed Reform of the United Nations, Ezulwini Consensus,* Ext/EX.CL/2 (VII), Mar. 8, 2005.

[73] Constitutive Act of the African Union, art. 4(h).

[74] *Ezulwini Consensus, supra* note 72, at 6.

[75] This is especially true given the reality that there were other aspects of the Ezulwini Consensus that were of much greater interest to North African states. Specifically, the paragraphs outlining the common African position on Security Council reform and expansion were of immense importance to countries such as Egypt and Libya, which harbor ambitions to represent Africa as permanent members in an expanded Council. This meant that adherence to the text and spirit of the Ezulwini Consensus was of considerable importance for these countries, even if it meant living with concepts, like RtoP, that they were not completely comfortable with.

tial elements. First, they required Security Council authorization for the resort to armed intervention, and implied that such intervention would be undertaken only after the exhaustion of other peaceful means. This allayed the central concern that endorsing RtoP in the WSOD would grant a global stamp of approval for a policy of unilateralism guised as humanitarianism. Second, the WSOD limited the application of RtoP to four specific situations, which assuaged fears that it would either extend to less egregious forms of human rights violations or to political disputes. Finally, by requiring the UNGA to further consider the matter, paragraph 139 indicated that RtoP was not yet ripe for implementation. Indeed, the "decisions and proposals laid out in the Outcome Document were not self-authorizing or self-executing but required further decisions by the General Assembly or other relevant Councils."[76] This convinced Middle Eastern countries that they would be given more time and opportunities to participate in the elucidation of the scope and content of RtoP, and to set the safeguards that would protect them against its misuse.

The third factor was developmental. Middle Eastern countries are developing nations, and many of them perform leading roles in the forums in which developing countries coordinate their policies at the UN, especially NAM and the G-77. As Alex Bellamy recounts, during the negotiations on the WSOD various tradeoffs were concluded between Western and developing states. These included reaffirming the former's commitment to the Millennium Development Goals (MDGs) in return for the latter's acceptance of Western proposals on issues including UN Secretariat and management reform, the Human Rights Council, and counter-terrorism efforts.[77] Once Western concessions had been secured on the developmental priorities of NAM and the G-77, despite attempts by U.S. Permanent Representative John Bolton to remove all references to the MDGs, it was difficult for leading countries in these blocs to oppose the WSOD package over RtoP.

These factors coalesced to ensure that the none of the Middle Eastern countries attempted to block the global consensus on RtoP, and encouraged them to engage in future discussion about the concept at the UN.

D. The General Assembly Debate on Implementing RtoP and the Security Council Debates on the Protection of Civilians in Armed Conflict

RtoP remained high on the agenda of the UN since the adoption of the WSOD. On July 23, 2009, the UNGA held a plenary debate on implementing RtoP.[78] The debate focused on a report submitted by Secretary General Ban Ki-moon to the Assembly

[76] Bellamy, *supra* note 16, at 5.

[77] *Id.* at 84–87. *See also* Alex Bellamy, *Wither the Responsibility to Protect? Humanitarian Intervention and the 2005 World Summit*, 20.2 Ethics and Int'l Affairs 143 (2006).

[78] For a synopsis of the debate and the positions adopted by the participating countries, *see Implementing the Responsibility to Protect The 2009 General Assembly Debate: An Assessment*, Global Center for the Responsibility to Protect, *available at* http://globalr2p.org/media/pdf/GCRtoP_General_Assembly_Debate_Assessment.pdf.

titled *Implementing the Responsibility to Protect*,[79] which was prepared pursuant to the mandate issued by the 2005 World Summit to the UNGA to continue to consider RtoP. In addition, the Security Council held periodic debates about the protection of civilians in armed conflict during which the UN Member States exchanged views on RtoP. These two forums provide insights into how Middle Eastern attitudes towards RtoP evolved since the 2005 World Summit.

Surveying Middle Eastern positions in the years since the 2005 World Summit reveals elements of continuity and signs of change. Primarily, none of the Middle Eastern countries disavowed RtoP or called for rolling back the WSOD consensus. Second, almost all delegations welcomed the Secretary General's report and called for further deliberations on operationalizing RtoP. Concurrently, however, the July 2009 UNGA debate revealed that certain concerns continued to persist regarding RtoP.

First, Middle Eastern delegations continued to express uneasiness about the possible exploitation of RtoP as a guise for politically motivated intervention. Egypt's statement in the UNGA debate, delivered on behalf of NAM and endorsed by all other NAM speakers from the region,[80] echoed this fear: "there are concerns about the possible abuse of RtoP . . . to legitimize unilateral coercive measures or intervention in the internal affairs of States."[81]

A second issue highlighted by Middle Eastern delegations was the apprehension that new situations might be added to the four cases that the WSOD identified as triggering RtoP. For example, Jordan emphasized that attempts to expand the scope of RtoP would undermine the entire concept and cast a shadow of doubt over its viability.[82] Similarly, Iran "stressed that the notion of RtoP must be limited to the four grave crimes identified in paragraphs 138 and 139 of the 2005 Summit Outcome Document . . . Any attempt to apply this notion to other situations would only render it more complicated and blurred."[83]

Another matter that aroused concern among Middle Eastern countries was the question of the UN body responsible for elucidating RtoP and developing mechanisms for its implementation. Specifically, many countries insisted that it was the UNGA and not the Security Council that was charged with deliberating on RtoP. Addressing the Security Council during the Debate on the Protection of Civilians in

[79] UN Secretary General, *Implementing the Responsibility to Protect, Delivered to the General Assembly*, A/63/677, Jan. 12, 2009.

[80] The significance of this endorsement lies in the fact that some members of NAM have diverted from the unified position of the bloc regarding RtoP. Specifically, Chile has been vocal in stressing that the NAM position on RtoP, as enunciated in the Final Document of the XV NAM Summit, was not unanimously adopted. It is, therefore, significant that every Middle Eastern member of NAM that spoke during the 2009 UNGA debate chose to explicitly announce its alignment to and endorsement of Egypt's statement.

[81] Ambassador Maged Abdelaziz, Permanent Representative of the Arab Republic of Egypt to the United Nations, *Statement on Behalf of the Non-Aligned Movement on Agenda Item 44 and 107*, General Assembly, Jul. 23, 2009. [Hereinafter: NAM Statement]

[82] Ambassador Mohamed Al-Alaf, Permanent Representative of the Hashemite Kingdom of Jordan to the United Nations, *Statement on the Implementation of the Responsibility to Protect*, General Assembly, Jul. 24, 2009 [Original in Arabic, translation by the author].

[83] Ambassador Eshagh Al-Habib, Deputy Permanent Representative of the Islamic Republic of Iran to the United Nations, *Statement on Agenda Item 44 and 107, General Assembly*, Jul. 28, 2009.

Armed Conflict, Egypt's Permanent Representative insisted that the Council should only discuss the "protection of civilians in armed conflict as defined by the items on its agenda. The Council should not expand its authority by establishing general policies for dealing with humanitarian issues and human rights. The elaboration of such policies falls within the mandates of the General Assembly."[84] Similarly, during the UNGA debate on RtoP, NAM emphasized that should the Security Council fail to discharge its duties pursuant to RtoP, then the General Assembly should be empowered to exercise its responsibility to maintain international peace and security.[85] These positions echo the traditional policy of developing nations of endeavoring to restrict the powers of the Security Council in favor of the General Assembly where they enjoy relatively greater influence.

A fourth element of Middle Eastern attitudes towards RtoP is the emphasis on capacity-building and development assistance as central to the implementation of RtoP and the prevention of gross violations of human rights. During the 2009 UNGA debate, Algeria adopted this approach and highlighted that the crimes covered by RtoP "generally take place in a context marked by extreme poverty, which is the breeding ground par excellence of fanaticism and violence."[86] Similarly, for Iran implementing RtoP first required addressing the political and socio-economic causes of conflict, including "aggression and foreign occupation, foreign interferences and meddlings, poverty and underdevelopment, and exclusion are among the main such causes, to name a few."[87] This reflects the general practice of developing countries to promote the development agenda at the UN. It is also likely that Middle Eastern countries that are the most apprehensive of the coercive aspects of RtoP sought to marginalize those elements by emphasizing its capacity-building side.

Turkey and Israel also highlighted the importance of prevention. Unlike other Middle Eastern delegations, however, they did not focus on development assistance as the primary tool for preventing the four RtoP crimes. Rather, Turkey identified the promotion of the rule of law and the proper administration of justice as "the key deterrent for potential perpetrators of these crimes."[88] Meanwhile, Israel drew attention to the dangers of racism and the incitement to the commission of grave human rights violations. Israel implored the international community to recall that crimes "all begin in the minds of men—they all begin by inciting blind hatred against a group, a tribe, a race, a religion or a nation. Teaching peace and tolerance and eliminating incitement to hatred remain critical elements to overcome these evils."[89] This Israeli

[84] Ambassador Maged Abdelaziz, Permanent Representative of the Arab Republic of Egypt to the United Nations, *Statement on the Protection of Civilians in Armed Conflict, The Security Council,* Dec. 9, 2005.

[85] NAM Statement, *supra* note 81.

[86] Ambassador Mourad Benmehidi, Permanent Representative of Algeria to the United Nations, *Statement on Implementing the Responsibility to Protect,* General Assembly, Jul. 24, 2009.

[87] Statement of Iran, *supra* note 83.

[88] Fazli Corman, Charge' d'Affaires of the Republic of Turkey to the United Nations, *Statement on the Responsibility to Protect,* General Assembly, Jul. 24, 2009.

[89] Ambassador Gabriela Shalev, Permanent Representative of the State of Israel to the United Nations, *Statement on the Integrated and Coordinated Implementation of and Followup to the Outcomes of the Major United Nations Conference and Summits in the Economic, Social and Related Fields,* General Assembly, Jul. 24, 2009.

position is understandable given the tragic history of the Jewish people. It is also probable that Israel's representative was utilizing the UNGA debate to implicitly call for confronting certain forces in the Middle East—such as Iran, Hezbollah, and Hamas—that threaten Israel and that have adopted a deeply hostile vernacular towards it.[90]

Examining the Security Council debates on the Protection of Civilians in Armed Conflicts reveals how another aspect of Middle East politics shaped regional perspectives regarding RtoP. Both Turkey and Israel seemed to invoke their governments' Responsibility to Protect their citizens as grounds for their counter-terrorism efforts. Specifically, Turkey, which is engaged in a protracted confrontation with the Kurdistan Workers Party,[91] deplored the fact that "members of the international community still fail to implement their commitments in the face of terrorist threats and acts. Therefore, we must look into ways and means to further improve and coordinate our joint fights against this scourge, which is an integral part of our responsibility to protect."[92] Similarly, Israel, for whom terrorism is a central security concern, condemned the targeting of civilians by terrorist organizations and, in what seems to echo the foundational principle underlying RtoP, stressed that "it is the obligation of all nations, first and foremost, to protect their people from harm."[93]

Finally, despite the many unbridgeable chasms that separate Middle Eastern countries, one concern regarding RtoP seems to have crossed the many fault lines that divide the region. Almost every delegation warned against double standards and selectivity in the implementation of RtoP. From Iran to Israel to Qatar, Middle Eastern countries cautioned against the discriminatory application of RtoP and the danger of allowing it to be held hostage by political interests. For these countries, the full acceptance of RtoP continues to hinge on whether they can become confident that it will be implemented fairly and universally. Jordan, which is considered an ally of RtoP, declared that its credibility and its implementation remain dependant upon avoiding selectivity of application.[94] Similarly, Iran affirmed that "a key to preventing and suppressing such grave crimes in the future would be to faithfully implement the United Nations Charter and avoid selectivity and double-standards."[95]

For Iran, Turkey, and the Arab world, the depoliticized and universal application of RtoP means ensuring that the Palestinian people enjoy the promise of protection guaranteed by RtoP. This is reflected in Qatar's statement during the 2009 UNGA debate, which pointed to how "recent events in Gaza and, before that, in Somalia, Iraq, and Afghanistan highlighted the international community's reluctance to implement the responsibility to protect principle fairly, justly and without politicization."[96]

[90] For a short account of Israel's threat perceptions, *see* Michael Oren, *Seven Existential Threats*, 127(5) COMMENTARY 15–20 (May 2005).

[91] *See* ALI KEMAL ÖZCAN, TURKEY'S KURDS: A THEORETICAL ANALYSIS OF THE PKK AND ABDULLAH ÖCALAN (Routledge Advances in Middle Eastern & Islamic Studies 2006).

[92] Ambassador Baki Ilkin, Permanent Representative of the Republic of Turkey to the United Nations, *Statement on the Protection of Civilians in Armed Conflict*, Security Council, Jan. 14, 2009.

[93] UN SCOR, 61st Sess., 5577th mtg., S/PV.5577 (Resumption 1), Dec. 4, 2006, at 10.

[94] Statement of Jordan, *supra* note 82.

[95] Statement of Iran, *supra* note 84.

[96] Salem Al-Shafi, Representative of the State of Qatar, *Statement on the Responsibility to Protect*, General Assembly, Jul. 24, 2009.

On the other hand, while not explicitly denying the applicability of RtoP to the Occupied Palestinian Territories, Israel counseled that for the "Responsibility to Protect to develop into an effective means offering true protection from the most serious of crimes, we must also ensure that it does not become a political tool for exploitation and abuse."[97] Meanwhile, Palestine considered that the humanitarian situation in the Occupied Territories represents "a moral and legal failure of those whose duty it is to prevent such disasters,"[98] and proclaimed that

> If we are to apply the RtoP doctrine effectively, we must ensure that the Security Council acts in good faith, without selectivity and with strict adherence to the Charter and international law, for the promotion of international peace and security rather than the narrow interests of those who have inhibited the Council from fulfilling this most crucial responsibility.[99]

This is RtoP's greatest challenge in the Middle East today. It is highly unlikely that the peoples and governments of the region—with the notable exception of Israel—will fully support RtoP if they continue to feel that the international community treats the Palestinian people as an underprivileged class. In a region where recent political experience engenders skepticism towards intervention on humanitarian grounds, the only hope for fostering full Middle Eastern endorsement of RtoP resides in extending its promise of protection to the Palestinians. The arguments surrounding whether RtoP in applicable to the Occupied Palestinian Territories (OPT) are discussed in the next section.

III. THE PROMISE OF PROTECTION: RTOP IN PALESTINE

The question of the applicability of RtoP to the OPT rose to prominence during and following Israel's military operations in Gaza known as Operation Cast Lead, which lasted from December 27, 2008, to January 18, 2009. As outlined above, many Middle Eastern countries opined that Palestinian civilians ought to have benefited from the promise of protection afforded by RtoP. Scholars also voiced the view that RtoP was applicable to the OPT during Israel's military operations in Gaza. For example, Richard Falk, the UN Special Rapporteur on the Situation of Human Rights in the Palestinian Territories Occupied since 1967,[100] argued that the Palestinian people had been left unprotected in situations that, especially in the Gaza Strip, necessitated international intervention according to RtoP.[101]

[97] Statement of Israel, *supra* note 89.

[98] Feda Nasser, Charge' d'Affaires Permanent Observer Mission of Palestine to the United Nations, *General Assembly Debate on The Responsibility to Protect*, General Assembly, Jul. 24, 2009.

[99] *Id.*

[100] The post of a Special Rapporteur on the Situation of Human Rights in the Palestinian Territories Occupied since 1967 was originally established in 1993 pursuant to the resolution of the Commission on Human Rights 1993/2 (E/CN/CHR 1993/3). Richard Falk was appointed to his position since May 1, 2008. *See generally* http://www2.ohchr.org/english/countries/ps/mandate/index.htm.

[101] Richard Falk, *Report of the Special Rapporteur on the Situation of Human Rights in the Palestinian Territories Occupied Since 1967*, Human Rights Council, A/65/331, Aug. 10, 2010, at ¶ 6; *see also* Richard Falk, *Report of the Special Rapporteur on the Situation of Human Rights in the Palestinian*

Gareth Evans, on the other hand, espoused an alternative position. Writing during Israel's military operation in Gaza, Evans argued that RtoP was not the appropriate framework for addressing the crisis, and that a more "relevant and helpful" characterization of the crisis was to consider it a "conflict involving major breaches of international humanitarian law which must be stopped, than as an 'internal' situation in which a sovereign state is either committing, or allowing to be committed, mass atrocity crimes against its own people."[102] Evans predicated his view on the understanding that RtoP was formulated

> Essentially to galvanize international action in situations where the international community had previously resisted involvement based on the notions of sovereignty and non-interference in other countries' internal affairs. Whatever else has inhibited effective international action in relation to the Israel-Palestinian conflict, it has not been unwillingness to interfere in 'Israel's internal affairs'.[103]

Evans seems to be making two claims: first, that RtoP was designed to address mass atrocities perpetrated in "internal situations," and, second, that IHL is more relevant to the OPT than RtoP. Regarding the first claim, it is contended that restricting RtoP to internal conflicts is an overly narrow interpretation that excludes numerous conflict situations and denies countless civilians the promise of protection. For this author, a broader and more appropriate interpretation should not be predicated on the *nature of a conflict* but ought to reflect the underlying *purpose of RtoP*; namely the protection of civilians. Accordingly, RtoP should be understood as reaffirming the responsibility of states to protect all civilians under its jurisdiction from the four crimes prescribed in the WSOD, regardless of whether the conflict situation is internal or external.[104]

This interpretation of the scope of RtoP is in consonance with its legal underpinnings. According to the International Commission on State Sovereignty and Intervention, which authored the groundbreaking report *The Responsibility to Protect*, RtoP is based on "a miscellany of legal foundations (human rights treaty provisions, the Genocide Convention, Geneva Conventions, International Criminal Court statute

Territories Occupied Since 1967, Human Rights Council, A/HRC/13/53/Rev.1, Jun. 7, 2010, at ¶ 33; Richard Falk, *Entry Denied, Detention and Expulsion*, TRANSNATIONAL INSTITUTE, *available online*: http://www.tni.org/article/entry-denied-detention-and-expulsion.

[102] Gareth Evans, *Should RtoP be Invoked in the Context of the Conflict in Gaza?*, International Crisis Group, Jan. 16, 2009, *available at* http://www.crisisgroup.org/en/key-issues/responsibility-to-protect.aspx.

[103] *Id.*

[104] Former UN Under-Secretary General John Holmes espoused this approach of extending the reach of RtoP to all civilians within the jurisdiction of a state, regardless of the nature of the conflict or the context in which crimes are perpetrated. Holmes adopted this understanding of RtoP while addressing the Security Council: RtoP entails the "the primary responsibility of each State to protect its citizens *and those within its jurisdiction* from genocide, war crimes, ethnic cleansing and crimes against humanity [emphasis added]." *See* John Holmes, UN Under Secretary General for Humanitarian Assistance and Emergency Relief, *Statement before the Security Council on the Protection of Civilians in Armed Conflicts*, Jun. 22, 2007, a*vailable at* http://globalr2p.org/resources/document.php?document=87.

and the like), growing state practice—and the Security Council's own practice."[105] A brief survey of these sources, which form the intellectual foundations of RtoP, confirms that the prohibitions on genocide, crimes against humanity, war crimes, and ethnic cleansing are not limited to internal conflicts. The International Court of Justice (ICJ) confirmed this in relation to the prohibition on genocide, which is considered a *jus cogens* norm,[106] by adjudging that it was intended "by the General Assembly and by the contracting parties [of the Genocide Convention] to be definitely universal in scope."[107]

Unlike genocide, the prohibition on crimes against humanity, which is also a *jus cogens* norm,[108] is not enshrined in a specialized convention, but appears in a variety of legal instruments ranging from the 1907 Hague Convention[109] to the Rome Statute of the ICC.[110] In none of these incarnations of the prohibition on crimes against humanity is the protection of civilian populations dependant on the nature or context of a conflict.[111] This is confirmed by Article 7 of the ICC Statute, which defines crimes against humanity as "directed against *any* civilian population [emphasis added]."[112] Similarly, the prohibition on war crimes, many aspects of which have attained the status of *jus cogens* norms,[113] is enshrined in numerous instruments, most prominent of which are the 1949 Geneva Conventions and their two Additional Protocols. A fundamental distinction that underpins the Geneva Conventions is between international and non-international armed conflicts.[114] In the former category, certain violations committed against protected persons are considered to be a special category

[105] International Commission on Intervention and State Sovereignty, The Responsibility to Protect 50 (2001). This position was also adopted by many UN delegations during the 2009 UNGA debate on RtoP. *See Implementing the Responsibility to Protect The 2009 General Assembly Debate: An Assessment, supra* note 105.

[106] M. Cherif Bassiouni, Introduction to International Criminal Law, 139 (2003).

[107] *Reservations to the Convention on Prevention and Punishment of the Crime of Genocide*, Advisory Opinion, 1951 I.C.J. (May 28). It should be noted that the protected "groups" identified within the convention do not discriminate on the basis of citizenship. Even the category of "national" groups, which is identified as one of the beneficiaries of the prohibition on genocide, is not understood as meaning communities distinguishable on the basis of *nationality* or *citizenship.* Rather, the term "national" group for the purposes of the Genocide Convention denotes communities within a broader society that share a distinct historical, linguistic or cultural background. *See* Convention on the Prevention and Punishment of the Crime of Genocide, 78 UNTS 277 (Dec. 9 1948). For commentary and analysis of the convention, *see* William Schabas, Genocide in International Law 134–139 (Cambridge University Press, 2d edition, 2009).

[108] Bassiouni, *supra* note 106, at 141.

[109] Convention Respecting the Laws and Customs of War on Land, 1 Bevans 631 (Oct. 18, 1907).

[110] Rome Statute of the International Criminal Court, A/CONF.183/9, Jan. 16, 2002.

[111] *See generally* M. Cherif Bassiouni, Crimes Against Humanity in International Criminal Law (Springer, 2nd ed., 1999); M. Cherif Bassiouni, *Crimes Against Humanity: The Need for a Specialized Convention*, 31 Col. J. Trans'l L. 457 (1994).

[112] Rome Statute, *supra* note 110, art. 7.

[113] Bassiouni, *supra* note 106, at 141–143.

[114] *See* Commentary on the IV Geneva Convention Relative to the Protection of Civilian Persons in the Time of War (Jean S. Pictet et. al., eds., 1958). M. Cherif Bassiouni, *The Normative Framework of International Humanitarian Law: Overlaps, Gaps and Ambiguities* 8 Trans'l L. Contemp. Prob. 199 (1998).

of war crimes labeled "grave breaches,"[115] while in the latter category, violations are considered war crimes but not "grave breaches" of the conventions.[116] It is highly unlikely that the framers of RtoP intended it to apply solely to internal conflicts, which effectively excludes the entire category of grave breaches from the ambit of RtoP.

The second ground advanced by Gareth Evans for the inappropriateness of applying RtoP to the OPT was that IHL is a better framework for addressing the situation than RtoP. It is contended, however, that the relationship between IHL and RtoP is not a choice among alternatives. Rather, it is a relation of complementarity. Fundamentally, RtoP is a policy mechanism that provides a blueprint for the protection of civilians from crimes that are prohibited by IHL. Specifically, IHL prohibits genocide, crimes against humanity, war crimes, and ethnic cleansing, while RtoP reaffirms the responsibility of states to protect populations from these crimes and then empowers the international community to intervene to protect civilians when states fail to do so. In other words, IHL is a major component of the underlying legal and normative basis of RtoP.[117] While RtoP was designed as a policy tool to address "a fundamental problem in modern international law: the lack of existing mechanisms through which individuals are able to hold States accountable for human rights violations."[118]

The claim here is not, however, that RtoP should be invoked haphazardly or applied indiscriminately in the context of the Palestinian question or the broader Arab-Israeli conflict. Such an approach would be of limited efficacy to the cause of protecting civilians and might undermine the existing areas of agreement on the scope and content of RtoP. Rather, a principal contribution of RtoP could be in the area of prevention. The utility and value of conflict prevention for the protection of civilians

[115] *See* Articles 50 and 51 of the First and Second Geneva Conventions and articles 130 and 147 of the Third and Fourth Geneva Conventions. *See also* William Schabas, An Introduction to the International Criminal Court (2001); William Schabas, The International Criminal Court: A Commentary on the Rome Statute, Part 2, (2010); Otto Triffterer ed., Commentary on the Rome Statute of the International Criminal Court (1999).

[116] *See* Common Article 3 to the Four Geneva Conventions. Lindsay Moir, *Non-International Armed Conflicts*, *in* International Criminal Law (M. Cherif Bassiouni, ed., 2008); Lindsay Moir, the Law of Internal Armed Conflicts (2002); Christopher Greenwood, *International Humanitarian Law and the Tadic Case*, 7 Euro. J. Int'l L. 265 (1996).

[117] In his report to the General Assembly on RtoP, the Secretary-General adopts this understanding of the relationship between IHL and RtoP, which deserves to be quoted at length:

> It should be underscored that the provisions of paragraphs 138 and 139 of the Summit Outcome are firmly anchored in well-established principles of international law. Under conventional and customary international law, States have obligations to prevent and punish genocide, war crimes, and crimes against humanity. Ethnic cleansing is not a crime in its own right under international law, but acts of ethnic cleansing may constitute one of the other three crimes. The Summit's enunciation of the responsibility to protect was not intended to detract in any way from the much broader range of obligations existing under international humanitarian law, international human rights law, refugee law and international criminal law. It should also be emphasized that actions under paragraphs 138 and 139 of the Summit Outcome are to be undertaken only in conformity with the provisions, purposes and principles of the Charter of the United Nations. In that regard, the responsibility to protect does not alter, indeed it reinforces, the legal obligations of Member States to refrain from the use of force except in conformity with the Charter. *See Implementing the Responsibility to Protect, supra* note 79, at ¶ 3.

[118] Margo Kaplan, *Using Collective Interests to Ensure Human Rights: An Analysis of the Articles on State Responsibility*, 79 N.Y.U. L. Rev. 1903 (2004).

has been recognized and reaffirmed innumerable times throughout the twentieth century.[119] It is also undeniable that prevention is one of the cornerstones of RtoP and represents one of the major policy tools available for its effective implementation.[120]

As relates to the OPT, the contribution of RtoP to conflict prevention is best demonstrable through a practical example. In late June 2008, Egypt brokered a six-month ceasefire between Israel and Hamas,[121] which effectively controls the Gaza Strip.[122] As the ceasefire neared is terminus, Cairo single-handedly held talks with Israel and Hamas to renew the ceasefire, but to no avail.[123] Unfortunately, as the International Crisis Group noted, "without bilateral engagement, effective third party mediation or mutual trust, it inexorably came to this: a brutal military operation in which both [Israel and Hamas] feel they have something to gain."[124] The devastating impact of the hostilities on civilians was documented by a UN Fact-Finding Mission on the Gaza Conflict,[125] which found that Israel perpetrated serious violations of IHL, including grave breaches of the Geneva Conventions, war crimes and crimes against

[119] *See generally* Fen Hampson & David Malone Eds., From Reaction to Conflict Prevention: Opportunities for the UN System (2002); Hitoshi Nasu, *Operationalizing the "Responsibility to Protect" and Conflict Prevention: Dilemmas of Civilian Protection in Armed Conflict*, 14 J. Conf. & Sec. L. (2009); UN Secretary-General, *Report of the Secretary General: An Agenda for Peace*, A/47/277, Jun. 17, 1992, at ¶ 23–32.

[120] Gareth Evans, The Responsibility to Protect: Ending Mass Atrocity Crimes Once and For All (2008). *See also Implementing the Responsibility to Protect*, *supra* note 79; *In Larger Freedom*, *supra* note 69.

[121] Isabel Kershner, *Israel Agrees to Truce with Hamas on Gaza*, New York Times, Jun. 18, 2008.

[122] International Crisis Group, *After Gaza*, Middle East Report No. 68, Aug. 2007. In the months between the overtaking by Hamas of the Gaza Strip in June 2007 and the outbreak of Israel's Operation Cast Lead in December 2008, Israel launched a number of military operations, incursions and strikes against the Gaza Strip. The report of the Fact-Finding Mission established by the UN Human Rights Council to investigate violation of IHL and IHRL during Operation Cast Lead (Goldstone Report) provides a chronology of the various Israeli military operations in Gaza and the firing of missiles by Islamist groups against Israel from 2005 till December 2008. *See* Human Rights Council, *Report of the United Nations Fact Finding Mission on the Gaza Conflict*, A/HRC/12/48, Sept. 15, 2009.

[123] *Israel Warns Hamas Over Rockets*, B.B.C. News, *Available online*: http://news.bbc.co.uk/2/hi/7799593.stm.

[124] International Crisis Group, *Ending the War in Gaza*, Middle East Briefing No. 25, Jan. 2009.

[125] Goldstone Report, *supra* note 122. The Fact-Finding Mission was established by the Human Rights Council. *See* A/HRC/S-9/L.1, Jan. 12, 2009. Many Israeli, Palestinian and international non-governmental organizations also contributed to the documentation of the humanitarian impact of Operation Cast Lead. In this regard, *see* B'Tselem, *Guidelines for Israel's Investigation into Operation Cast Lead* (Feb. 2009); Al-Haq, *Field Report on Violations of International Humanitarian Law* (Jan.–Mar. 2009); Human Rights Watch, *Rain of Fire: Israel's Unlawful Use of White Phosphorus in Gaza* (Mar. 25, 2009); Palestinian Center for Human Rights, *War Crimes Against Children: Palestinian Children Killed by Israeli Forces in the Gaza Strip December 27, 2008 to January 18, 2009* (May 11, 2009); Human Rights Watch, *Precisely Wrong: Gaza Civilians Killed by Israeli Drone-Launched Missiles*, Jun. 30, 2009; Al Mezan Center for Human Rights, *Cast Lead Offensive in Numbers: Statistical Report on Persons Killed and Property Damaged in the Gaza Strip by the Israeli Occupation Forces 27 December 2008 to 18 January 2009*, Aug. 2, 2009; Human Rights Watch, *White Flag Deaths: Killings of Palestinian Civilians During Operation Cast Lead*, Aug. 13, 2009; B'Tselem, *Military's Investigations into Operation Cast Lead Focus on Individual Soldiers, Not Unlawful Policies* (Nov. 11, 2009); Amnesty International Annual Report, *Israel and the Occupied Palestinian Territories* (2010), at 182–84.

humanity.[126] The Fact-Finding Mission also found that Hamas and other Palestinian armed groups in Gaza committed war crimes and other actions that may amount to crimes against humanity.[127]

During the conflict, many Middle Eastern countries called for international intervention to protect civilians from grave violations of IHL and IHRL.[128] It is highly unlikely, however, given the political realities of the Middle East and the interests of global powers, particularly the U.S., that the Security Council would have invoked RtoP to intervene during the military operations.[129] A more effective approach would have been for the international community to intervene politically and diplomatically prior to the outbreak of hostilities when the unmistakable signs of impending conflict were abundant. The tools for such preventive intervention are well known and have been exercised by the international community in various settings.[130] The UN, regional, and international players should have assisted Egypt in its efforts to avert the conflict and should have pressured Israel and Hamas into renewing the ceasefire.

IV. RTOP IN ACTION: LIBYA

As this volume was being written, a revolutionary wave swept the Arab World. Starting with Tunisia on December 17, 2010, and then moving to Egypt on January 25, 2011, it reached Libya on February 16, 2011. In both Tunisia and Egypt the armed forces did not forcibly confront demonstrators calling for the toppling of autocratic regimes that had been, respectively, in power for 23 and 30 years.

In Libya, however, events took a different path. While a complete and impartial account of the events that transpired in Libya since the outbreak of demonstrations against Colonel Muammar Gaddafi was not available as of this writing, the Libyan leadership was clearly not willing to peacefully relinquish power. Colonel Gaddafi ordered elements of Libya's military and security forces loyal to him to violently quell demonstrators.[131] Eyewitness and media reports also claimed that thousands of

[126] Goldstone Report, *supra* note 122, at ¶¶ 1716–1733.

[127] *Id.* at ¶ 1747.

[128] *See, e.g.*, Ambassador Baki Ilkin, Permanent Representative of the Republic of Turkey to the United Nations, *Statement on the Protection of Civilians in Armed Conflict, The Security Council*, Jan. 14, 2009; NAM Statement, *supra* note 58.

[129] Indeed, the Security Council adopted resolution 1860 on the crisis and called for an immediate ceasefire and for an Israeli withdrawal from Gaza. This resolution did not, however, allude to RtoP.

[130] The Secretary-General's report on implementing RtoP canvasses the various tools available for the international community to intervene preventively before the outbreak of deadly conflicts. *See Implementing the Responsibility to Protect*, *supra* note 79.

[131] A wide array of military services and security agencies have been identified in Libya. These include: (1) The Libyan Armed Forces (composed of the Army, Navy, Air Force, and Revolutionary Guard Brigades), (2) The "*Kata'eb*" or Brigades, many of which are headed by Colonel Gaddafi's sons, and are employed by the regime to maintain internal security, (3) The Revolutionary Committees, which are mostly composed of plain clothed personnel utilized to quell anti-regime movements, (4) The Internal and External Security Organizations, which correspond to what would be the internal and external intelligence agencies in other countries, but which also have been engaged in confronting anti-Gaddafi forces, and, finally, (5) The Interior Ministry Forces, which include riot police brigades and other undercover police services. This categorization should not

mercenaries flown into Libya from Sub-Saharan African countries were engaged in efforts to pacify demonstrators. Reports indicated that the regime deployed heavy armor, artillery, and even the air force in confrontations with anti-Gaddafi demonstrators. Horrified at the prospect of using their weapons against their compatriots, many members of the Libyan armed forces, including air force pilots, defected from the ranks of their services. In addition, senior Libyan officials, including Cabinet Ministers, and diplomatic officers resigned from their posts to protest the brutality of the Libyan leadership.

As the confrontations with demonstrators intensified, reports appeared, despite the almost complete media blackout imposed by Gaddafi, claiming that thousands of casualties had fallen in clashes between anti-Gaddafi demonstrators and forces loyal to the Libyan regime. This compelled regional and international actors to issue scathing condemnations of Gaddafi's behavior.[132] On February 26, the Security Council unanimously adopted resolution 1970, which reminded Libya of its "responsibility to protect it population," imposed sanctions on the Libyan leadership, including travel bans and an assets freeze, referred the situation to the International Criminal Court, and banned the sale of arms to Libya.[133] Concurrently, the Human Rights Council held its 15th Special Session, which resulted in the issuing of resolution S-15/1 that called upon the Libyan government to meet its "responsibility to protect" its population, recommended the suspension of Libya's membership in the Council, and appointed an independent international commission of inquiry to establish the facts pertaining to the conflict and to determine the responsibility of the various actors.[134]

Meanwhile, in an unprecedented move, the League of Arab States suspended Libyan participation in the organizations' organs and demanded the cessation of violence against demonstrators. On 12 March, the League also called for the imposition of a no-fly zone to shield civilians and rebels from attacks by pro-Gaddafi forces, a decision that was taken days after the Gulf Cooperation Council, which includes the six oil rich

lead the reader to the illusion that there exists in Libya clear lines of command and control of the various military and security services of the Libyan State. Quite to the contrary, it is hard to determine the exact composition and structure of the Libyan armed forces and security agencies. This is due to a number of factors, primary among which is a deliberate policy adopted by Colonel Gaddafi to divide the command and control of the main branches of Libya's armed forces among his sons, family members, tribesmen, and loyalists. According to this policy, a system of checks and balances was instituted, which ensured that none of the various Libyan armed services or security agencies was powerful enough to threaten the rule of Colonel Gaddafi. The result, of course, was that, unlike Egypt and Tunisia, where the armed forces acted professionally and refused to attack the civilian population, command and control of Libya's armed forces disintegrated, and the various units acted on the basis of where their loyalties laid, and were guided, primarily by whether they owed allegiance to Gaddafi. On this matter, *see*: Hanspeter Mattes, *Challenges to Security Sector Governance in the Middle East: The Libyan Case*, Paper presented at the Workshop on "Challenges of Security Sector Governance in the Middle East," held in Geneva 12-13 July 2004. *Available online at*: http://www.dcaf.ch/dcaf/Projects/Details?lng=en&size711=10&id=15793

[132] Condemnations were voiced by the leaders of numerous countries from around the world, and by the League of Arab States, the African Union, and the Organization of the Islamic Conference, and the European Union Foreign Affairs Council.

[133] UN Security Council Resolution 1970, S/Res/1970 (2011), 26 February 2011.

[134] UN Human Rights Council Resolution S-15/1, A/HRC/RES/S-15/1, 3 March 2011.

Arabian Gulf States, urged the League and the international community to deny Gaddafi the vital advantage of air-superiority.[135]

Meanwhile, the international community was initially ambivalent and divided about enforcing a no-fly zone. European powers, especially France and Britain, supported this measure, and announced that they were consulting other countries on adopting a new Security Council resolution to authorize this action. These suggestions received a lukewarm response from Moscow and Beijing, both of whom emphasized the importance of avoiding foreign military intervention against Libya. Washington, on the other hand, remained cautious, with the White House treading a fine line by emphasizing that, while all options were on the table, further discussion was required to assess which course of action was the most suitable.[136]

Despite these differences, and after laborious negotiations, the Security Council adopted resolution 1973 on March 17, 2011, which authorized the use of 'all necessary measures'[137] "to protect civilians and civilian populated areas under threat of attack in the Libyan Arab Jamahiriya, including Benghazi, while excluding a foreign occupation force of any form on any part of Libyan territory [...]."[138] The resolution also imposed a no-fly zone over Libya to "help protect civilians,"[139] and further elaborated the measures required to effectuate the arms embargo placed on Libya pursuant to resolution 1970.[140]

Numerous factors contributed to achieving consensus among the Security Council members on the question of intervention in the Libyan situation. Primarily, reports emerging from Libya, many of which were circulated using Internet based social media platforms, about the brutality of troops and paramilitary formations loyal to Colonel Gaddafi led to global popular indignation and prompted calls for international intervention to protect Libyan civilians against Gaddafi's wrath. This was most palpable in neighboring Arab countries, like Egypt and Tunisia, where the people had just succeeded in ousting their autocratic leaders, and sympathized with Libyans in their quest to overthrow Colonel Gaddafi who had reigned over their country since 1969.[141] Second, the decision of the League of Arab States to call for the establishment of a no-fly zone over Libya effectively eliminated reservations that some Security Council members, especially Russia and China, had harbored regarding the prospect of foreign intervention in the Libya. Third, the Arab World's consent to intervention in Libya placated fears in some Western capitals that the operation might be equated in some quarters of Arab public opinion to the US-led invasion of Iraq, which, as discussed

[135] Aljazeera English, Arab states seek Libya no-fly zone, 12 March 2011. *Accessed online*: http://english.aljazeera.net/news/africa/2011/03/201131218852687848.html

[136] Susan Cornwell and Caren Bohan, *Top U.S. Officials Cautious on Libya No-Fly Zone*, REUTERS, 2 March 2011; David Sanger and Thom Shanker, *Gates Warns of Risks of a No-Fly Zone*, N.Y. TIMES, 2 March 2011; Paul Richter and Peter Nicholas, *Obama administration Taking Cautious Approach on Libya*, L.A. TIMES, 9 March 2011.

[137] As is well known, the phrase "all necessary measures" has become the code-word for the authorization of the use of force by the UN Security Council. *See generally*: THOMAS FRANCK, THE RECOURSE TO FORCE (2002).

[138] UN Security Council Resolution 1973, S/Res/1973 (2011), 17 March 2011.

[139] *Id.*, Para. 6.

[140] *Id.*, Para. 13.

[141] *See generally*: DIRK VANDEWALLE, A HISTORY OF MODERN LIBYA (2006).

above, was partially legitimated on humanitarian grounds. Fourth, the embarrassment that some European capitals, especially Paris, experienced due to their initial hesitation in supporting the Arab popular uprisings of 2011, compelled those countries to adopt an uncompromising attitude toward Gaddafi, who had unleashed the full might of his security apparatus against the civilian population. Fifth, the successes that pro-Gaddafi forces achieved in the early weeks of March, and their threatening of the rebel stronghold of Benghazi convinced the international community that armed intervention had become unavoidable if the rebel forces and civilians were to be saved. Sixth, and finally, fears for the civilian population of Benghazi and other rebel cities were confirmed by the venomous speeches given by Gaddafi and his son Saif-Alislam, both of whom promised to quash the opposition once their forces conquered cities under rebel control.

Air strikes against Gaddafi's forces commenced, pursuant to Security Council resolution 1973, on March 19, 2011 under American, British, and French leadership, and with the participation of token forces from other countries, including the Arab states of Qatar and the United Arab Emirates. On March 31, command of the operation was transferred to NATO. Meanwhile, a Libyan National Transitional Council (NTC), headed by the Gaddafi's former Minister of Justice who defected in the early days of the revolt, was established in Benghazi to provide leadership and direction for the anti-Gaddafi forces. Unfortunately, however, the struggle to dethrone Colonel Gaddafi proved difficult. While Libya's air force was quickly neutralized, the rebel forces on the ground were untrained, under-equipped, and disorganized. NATO-led aircraft provided air cover and support to these rebel forces as they slowly pushed Gaddafi's troops westwards along the costal plain towards Tripoli in a campaign that, as of this writing, extended to almost four months and claimed the lives of thousands of civilians and combatants in each of the cities that the rebels wrested from Gaddafi's control.

On August 24, 2011, Colonel Gaddafi's reign came to an end and ushered in a new political reality in Libya. This is a country that has been ruled for over 40 years by a blend of Gaddafi's idiosyncratic policies and his brutal iron first, and has almost no culture of political participation or democratic governance. This reality presents the Libyan people with formidable challenges as they strive to rebuild their country. Moreover, it is not unlikely that the tensions running along geographical, tribal, and familial lines in Libyan society, which have been violently suppressed by Gaddafi, will reemerge and further complicate post-conflict reconstruction efforts. In addition, the abundance of weapons and the readily available oil wealth might fuel confrontations between these various factions that will probably surface in the post-Gaddafi era.[142]

For RtoP, Security Council resolution 1973 and the intervention in Libya are, undoubtedly, milestones of considerable significance. For the first time, the UN Security Council relied on RtoP to authorize armed intervention to protect a civilian population from the wrath of a tyrannical regime, and allowed the international community to undertake an air campaign to support the dislodging of an autocratic leader. While it is certainly premature to definitively judge this first instance of applying RtoP,

[142] *See*: Dirk Vandewalle, *How Not To Intervene in Libya*, Foreign Policy, 10 March 2011. *Available online:* http://www.foreignpolicy.com/articles/2011/03/10/how_not_to_intervene_in_libya?page=0,1

some preliminary observations can be noted in this regard. Primarily, an important lesson that emerged from the Libya experience was the vital role played by the pertinent regional organizations. The decision of the League of Arab States to call for imposing a no-fly zone over Libya provided indispensible political support for international actors that favored armed intervention to protect civilians. Similarly, the condemnation of Gaddafi's actions by both the African Union and the Organization of the Islamic Conference contributed to creating a global consensus on the need to intervene to halt the serious violations of human rights being perpetrated in Libya. This demonstrates that it is vital to extend discussions on the application of RtoP beyond the chambers of the Security Council, and to involve influential regional players and the relevant regional organizations in deliberations on invoking RtoP in any particular setting.

Second, despite the close cooperation between the UN, other international organizations, and regional partners prior to the commencement of military operations, the Libyan experience revealed the necessity of maintaining constant coordination throughout the conflict, especially on matters relating to the political settlement of the crisis. This was demonstrated, for example, by the divergence of views between the African Union and other international actors on the referral of the Libyan situation to the ICC. On July 2, 2011 the African Union called on its member states to disregard an ICC arrest warrant issued against Colonel Gaddafi and members of his regime because this measure was deemed to "seriously complicate" efforts to reach an agreement on ending the conflict in Libya.[143] Similarly, the Secretary-General of the League of Arab States expressed concerns about the civilian casualties caused by the NATO-led bombing of Libya, and criticized the breadth and scope of military operations for exceeding the original request by the League to impose a no-fly zone over Libyan skies.[144]

Third, the rapidity with which Libya descended into violence, and the brutalities that the Gaddafi regime was willing to perpetrate to crush the rebellion confirmed the soundness of the position adopted by the UN Secretary General in his 2009 report on implementing RtoP regarding the relationship between the three pillars of RtoP. As discussed above, some UN delegations espoused the view that intervention by the international community should be dependent on the exhaustion of all other remedies, and that armed force, as envisioned by Pillar Three, can only be applied after policies included under Pillars One and Two prove ineffectual. The Libyan crisis and the urgency with which it was necessary to intervene militarily to protect civilians from Colonel Gaddafi's advancing troops confirms the Secretary General's recommendation that when applying RtoP the international community should "remain focused on saving lives through 'timely and decisive' action, not on following arbitrary, sequential or graduated policy ladders that prize procedure over substance and process over results."[145]

A fourth, and final, observation relates to the policy objectives of the international intervention in Libya. In the days preceding the launch of air strikes against Colonel Gaddafi's forces there appeared to be two views on the overall objectives of

[143] *African Union Opposed Warrant for Qaddafi*, N.Y. Times, July 2, 2011.

[144] Maria Golovnina and Michael Georgy, *Western Powers Strike Libya; Arab League has Doubts*, Reuters, March 20, 2011.

[145] *Implementing the Responsibility to Protect*, *supra* note 79, at ¶ 50.

the operation. One approach favored the "selective containment" of Gaddafi's troops, which entailed halting their westward advance toward Benghazi and protecting the civilian population against further attacks. The second, and broader, approach recognized that the Libyan crisis had turned into a zero-sum game. Protecting civilians, especially in the eastern Libya, was unsustainable unless Colonel Gaddafi was removed from power. Otherwise, the international community would have been compelled to condone and support a stalemate that effectively meant the partition of Libya, with Tripolitania in the west under Gaddafi's control and Cyrenaica in the east under rebel control.[146] Ultimately, the nations participating in the operation opted for the second approach, and adopted a policy of actively assisting the rebel forces in their quest to depose the Gaddafi regime.[147]

This choice will undoubtedly have implications for RtoP. In essence, the military operations undertaken by the international community in Libya exceeded the protection of civilians and expanded to include the overthrow of a ruler and his regime. While this was probably unavoidable in the Libyan context, it potentially collapses the distinction between RtoP and other concepts that have been employed to legitimize the use of force in international relations, such as pro-democratic intervention.[148] RtoP, strictly and narrowly construed, is limited to protecting civilians from the four crimes listed in the 2005 WSOD, while pro-democratic intervention entails actively working to dislodge an autocratic regime and enabling the establishment of a democratic polity. What the Libyan experience has shown is that circumstances may arise when these two concepts become inseparable, and where pro-democratic intervention becomes necessary to protect civilians from mass crimes. This confirms the need to further elucidate and elaborate the scope and content of RtoP, and determine the policies and procedures that best serve the underlying purpose of RtoP, namely the protection of civilians from egregious violations of their fundamental rights.

V. CONCLUSION

Morally and ethically, RtoP presents a compelling argument. Complacency is simply intolerable when faced with the killing fields of Rwanda or Srebrenica. This is RtoP's greatest potential; to provide impetus for intervention to uphold the basic principles of human dignity. As the evolution of Middle Eastern positions towards RtoP proves,

[146] Dirk Vandewalle, *To the Shores of Tripoli: Why Operation Odyssey Dawn Should Not Stop At Benghazi*, Foreign Affairs, March, 21, 2011. *Accessed online*:http://www.foreignaffairs.com/articles/67669/dirk-vandewalle/to-the-shores-of-tripoli

[147] This policy was not without its detractors, including among the Permanent Members of the UN Security Council. For example, when France starting supplying the rebels fighting Colonel Gaddafi's forces with armaments, both the Russian Federation and the Peoples Republic of China expressed reservations to these measures, and considered them to overstep the limits of the Security Council resolution 1973. *See*: *Russia criticizes France over arming Libyan rebels*, Russia Today, June 30, 2011. *Accessed online*: http://rt.com/news/france-supplying-rebels-country/

[148] On pro-democratic intervention *see*: W. Michael Reisman, *Coercion and Self-Determination: Construing Charter Article 2(4)*, 78 Am. J. Int'l L. (1984); Oscar Schachter, *The Legality of Pro-Democratic Invasion*, 78 Am. J. Int'l L. (1984); Anthony D' Amato, *The Invasion of Panama Was a Lawful Response to Tyranny*, 84 Am. J. Int'l L. (1990); Thomas Franck, *The Emerging Right of Democratic Governance*, 86 Am. J. Int'l L. (1992).

however, its greatest challenge resides in the perils of politics. This is especially true in a region where history breeds cynicism.

In 1999, the vast majority of Middle Eastern countries endorsed the right of the international community to forcefully intervene to protect civilians from mass atrocities. Six years later, however, Middle Eastern nations exhibited considerable apprehension towards RtoP despite being less controversial than its intellectual predecessor, humanitarian intervention. The salient factor in shaping the policies and positions of the Middle East's countries was the strategic and political climate both regionally and globally. The fear of the distortion and misuse of RtoP in an exceptionally volatile region compelled governments to approach this emerging norm with ambivalence.

Nonetheless, the Middle East has not rejected RtoP. As demonstrated above, the region actively engaged in UN debates about the concept and contributed to elucidating its scope, content, and means of implementation. While it is unlikely that Middle Eastern concerns regarding RtoP will be entirely allayed, an essential step in that direction is achieving a *global* consensus on the conceptual and operational contours of this norm. The key to the full endorsement of RtoP by the overwhelming majority of Middle Easterners, however, remains whether it can contribute to ameliorating the plight of the Palestinian people. Indeed, the road to dissipating Middle Eastern skepticism towards RtoP should begin with advocates of this concept showing commitment to the universal application of its promise of protection.

PART III
CASE STUDIES

11 Darfur, Sudan

Andrew S. Natsios and Zachary Scott

This chapter provides a historical overview of Darfur, and discusses the origins of the conflicts that gripped the region from the 1980s to the present day. Particular attention is paid to the role that Libyan and Sudanese political leaders have played in fomenting ethnic tension in Darfur, leading to the outbreak of three civil wars. After describing how and why crimes against humanity were committed in Darfur, the chapter analyzes the exact time frame when RtoP could have been implemented to curb the violence. The chapter proceeds to illustrate the disconnect that existed among advocacy groups' calls for interventionist policies and the reality of killings on the ground. The chapter continues by analyzing what effect, if any, RtoP could have had on Darfur in light of previously ineffectual—and perhaps counterproductive—UN resolutions to stop violence, and then analyzes the causes of excess mortality that took place in Darfur from September 2003 to December 2008. The chapter concludes with three dilemmas confronting the implementation of RtoP in Darfur and holds out little hope that RtoP can affect the Sudanese regime's behavior in Darfur in the near future or be an effective instrument of change without a very different approach to international crisis interventions than the current model.

I. HISTORICAL BACKGROUND ON CONFLICTS IN DARFUR

Peace—not conflict—has been an aberration in Darfur's history through much of the nineteenth century and in particular over the last 25 years. The independent Darfur Sultanate, which had governed the region for three centuries, collapsed in 1916 and was followed by a period of British-Egyptian colonial rule during which little effort was made to develop the region. The British pursued a policy of non-interference and governed through the tribal nobility and existing power structures so long as they accepted colonial authority.[1] The underdevelopment of the region was exacerbated during the latter half of the twentieth century after independence, as recurring droughts in the 1970s intensified and desertification of once verdant pastures of the Sahel increased markedly. The changing climate forced nomadic herders further south in search of pasture and water sources to feed and maintain their livestock, which caused conflicts with farmers in the region. Although the movement of nomads into farmland was by no means a new phenomenon, and had been the cause of past conflict for centuries among the two groups, these previous tensions had been managed by local leaders skilled in negotiating informal arrangements to keep the peace between herders and farmers. These leaders were replaced by local sheikhs and chiefs favored by the British, who lacked the skills and authority to manage the conflicting claims of farmers and nomads.

The movement of tribes in the Sahel reflected a pattern of migration that was occurring across Darfur during the 1980s. Between 1950 and 2000, the population of Darfur increased from one million to six and a half million, increasing the stress on already fragile and arid land. The increase in population also meant a corresponding increase in the number of livestock, which put limited pastureland under additional pressure. Clashes soon ensued between the established farming tribes—particularly the Fur—who made up perhaps a third of the population of the province, and the nomadic, camel-herding Arab newcomers from Chad and northern Darfur. As tensions rose, the winds from the Sahara swallowed up larger tracts of pastureland and drought spread across Darfur in the mid-1980s. In 1984 a famine developed, killing an estimated 95,000 people.[2]

II. EVOLUTION OF DARFUR'S HUMANITARIAN DISASTER 1986–2004

The failure of Sudan's central government to respond to the famine of 1984–1985 led, among other crises, to the overthrow of Jaafar al-Numayri's regime and the emergence of a transitional government before elections were held in April 1986 that brought Sadiq al-Mahdi to power as prime minister of Sudan.[3] Under the new government, a rapprochement between the Sudanese government and the Libyan government of Muammar Qaddafi took place, which had been at virtual war with the Numayri government.[4] The trans-Saharan road from Sudan to the Libyan oasis of Kurfa was opened, allowing victims of the famine to go to Libya for work and send much needed

[1] By 1935, Darfur had only four government primary schools with a total budget for education of only £1,200 a year for a school age population of 300,000. Gérard Prunier, Darfur: The Ambiguous Genocide 30 (2005) [hereinafter The Ambiguous Genocide].

[2] The Ambiguous Genocide, *supra* note 1, at 56.

[3] Sadiq al-Mahdi was the great grandson of the most famous leader in modern Sudanese history; the Mahdi who was a Islamic mystic who expelled the British and Turco-Egyptian colonizers from Sudan in 1885 and established his own government.

[4] Qaddafi had assumed power in 1969, establishing Libya as an Arab socialist republic resembling that of Abdel Nasser's Arab nationalist movement in Egypt. During his more than 40 years in power, Qaddafi has sought to expand Arab influence and his own narrow version of Islam, exerting a greater amount of influence over the course of events in Darfur than successive government in Khartoum.

remittances home to their families. The opening also brought Arab exiles to Darfur who had trained in Qaddafi's military camps as part of the *Tajamu al Arabi*, or Arab Gathering, which was a loose confederation of Arab supremacists who opposed the rule of black Africans and espoused an ideology of Arab superiority which reflected a deep-seated hatred for *zurga* (African blacks) who they viewed as not true Muslims, and thus not entitled to rule Muslim lands.[5] This was a quarrel among Muslims, there being no Christians and few adherents to traditional religions in Darfur.

Although the Arab Gathering never possessed a military forces of its own and was more of a conglomeration of like-minded groups than a formalized union, it did claim the loyalty of Arab militia leaders and brought into Darfur high-powered artillery and automatic weapons that had never before been used in the region. The militarization of Darfur was facilitated even further by Qaddafi's establishment in 1972 of the *Failaka al-Islamiya* (Islamic Legion) and *Munazamat Da'awa al Islamiya* (Organization of the Islamic Call), which recruited Arab Bedouins across North Africa from Mauritania to Sudan and fostered Islamic philanthropy and evangelization in an effort to create an ideology of Arab supremacy in Darfur that was previously unknown. (Many of these Arab Bedouins from across North Africa fought to keep Qaddafi in power during the Libyan civil war that began in early 2011, which may explain why the war dragged on far longer than western diplomats had expected.) Under the Fur Sultanate both Arabic and Fur were spoken in the royal court and in the marketplace interchangeably, and a symbiotic relationship between the cultures and tribes—African and Arab—wove their communities together. It was only later that the Islamic Legion drove them apart and served as the front line of Qaddafi's military incursions into Chad and Sudan to execute his vision of an Arab state that spanned the Sahara and extended into central Africa. He also supplied Sadiq al-Mahdi with weapons and oil for Khartoum's war in the south in exchange for permission to set up rear bases for Libya's war with Chad. Combined, these actions stoked supremacist ambitions among the Bedouins and provided the weaponry—and ideology—for the civil conflicts of Darfur between 1986 and 2004.

III. THE THREE CIVIL WARS OF DARFUR

Subsequent convoys through the trans-Saharan road arrived in West Sudan throughout 1986 with provisions to feed and arm Arab tribes which Qaddafi viewed as local allies. One of the tribes Qaddafi decided to arm was the Um Jalal clan of the Abbala (camel herding) Rizaiqat, then led by Sheikh Musa Hilal. In 1987, Sheikh Musa Hilal's Um Jalal militia, alongside the Islamic Legion and local Arab allies, undertook the first violent displacement of Fur villagers in Jebel Marra, the ancestral home of the Fur. These attacks culminated in an Arab-Fur War in 1987–1989, the first of the three tribal wars that tore Darfur apart between 1987 and 2010. During this war, the Fur received weapons from the Chadian government (which was at war with the Libyans who were

[5] In 1998, a detailed directive entitled Qoreish 1 laid out the Arab Gathering's strategy to ensure Arab supremacy, stating that "volunteers" should be placed in *zurga* areas, "to stop production in these areas, to eliminate their leaders" and to create conflicts among *zurga* tribes "to ensure their disunity." Julie Flint & Alex de Waal, Darfur: A New History of Long War 51 (2008) [Hereinafter Long War].

supporting the Arabs) to attack Arab livestock, while burning pastureland and constructing fences to keep Arab herders away. The Fur and Masalit African tribes began to establish their own militias (*milishiyyat*) to defend their land, while the Arabs organized themselves into units of the *Janjawiid*, which were then referred to for the first time as ethnic militias. The confrontations between the two sides escalated, drawing Darfur in Chad's interethnic conflict which spread across the region killing thousands.[6] The violent, cross-border raids that emerged from these newly established alliances served to worsen the region's ethno-political landscape, creating sharp distinctions between "Arab" and "African" that were reinforced by the Islamic Legion's racist ideology. The compartmentalized view of "Arab" versus "African" gained credibility during this time in a region scarred by famine and in need of scapegoats. While the Fur-Arab War ended just after the Bashir government took power in 1989, the issues that caused it remained unresolved, and the heavy bias of the central government in favor of the Darfuri Arab tribes continued.

Attempts to broker a cessation of hostilities, including returning to the state of affairs before the war concerning land, deportation of illegal aliens, and enforcement of existing laws between Fur and Arabs, made real progress, but Sudanese officials were more preoccupied with their military defeats in southern Sudan than the conflict in Darfur. Sadiq al-Mahdi, under heavy domestic pressure to negotiate a peace agreement on the north-south conflict, was to meet John Garang, leader of the Southern rebellion, in Addis Ababa in July 1989. A week before he was to leave for the peace conference, a group of officers led by Brigadier General Omar Hassan Ahmad al-Bashir staged a successful coup masterminded by the Islamist leader Hassan al-Turabi, overthrowing the government on June 30, 1989, and derailing the peace process.

Hassan al-Turabi, leader of the National Islamic Front (NIF), and the leading Islamist theologian in Sudan was the ideological grand strategist for the new government and was determined to impose an Islamist agenda on all Sudanese, regardless of the fact that only 45 percent of the population of Sudan claims Arab origins and one-third were non-Muslims.[7] The NIF espoused an Islamist ideology which called for the universal application of *Shari'a* law to Muslims and non-Muslims alike, a strict adherence to Islam as interpreted by the first three generations of Islamic scholarship and teaching after the Prophet and excluding all subsequent interpretation, the use of that teaching to govern society, and the violent overthrow of more secular or modernist Arab governments.

From Sudanese independence in 1956 until the present, three Arab tribes—Ja'aliyyin, Shaiqiyya, and Danagla—from the Nile River valley north of Khartoum, which constituted less than 6 percent of Sudan's population, have dominated virtually every aspect of the national life of the country: the police, military, judiciary, business, and economy. The NIF continued this historic domination of state-run institutions by these three powerful but small tribes.

[6] M.W. Daly, Darfur's Sorrow: A History of Destruction and Genocide 244 (2007) [Hereinafter Destruction and Genocide].

[7] That al-Turabi was the undisputed leader of the NIF is illustrated upon his release from Kober prison in September 1989 when Bashir and other high-ranking officials pledged their allegiance through the bay'a, the Islamic oath of allegiance, recognizing him as the leader. Molly Miller, *The Fate of Darfur: Race, Ideology, and Conquest*, Johns Hopkins University Paper, at 14 (2007).

Omar al-Bashir immediately set out in 1990 to recentralize the government, shifting power to Khartoum by giving it control of the judiciary, government treasury, and the right to appoint governors and officials. In 1994, the Bashir government divided Darfur into three separate provinces—North, West, and South—whose senior leadership was appointed by the central government; Darfur's borders were gerrymandered to reduce Fur political power. Administrative positions were given to NIF cronies and, most notably, land registration laws enacted under Numayri were reinstated to dismiss hereditary, but unregistered, rights to land.[8] The effect of this last measure was particularly crippling to tribes in Darfur which had no other way to substantiate their claim to land, even though they had lived on it for centuries.

Administrative reform soon gave way to political exclusion. In 1995, the NIF-appointed governor of West Darfur, where the Masalit tribe was dominant, divided the province into eight new administrative chieftaincies, giving all but one to Arabs, where the Masalit had been dominant before.[9] The new chiefs were given the title *amir* (prince), connoting equality with the Masalit *sultan*—the traditional leader of the Masalit. As such, many Arabs came to believe that they were now entitled to a *dar* (homeland) or *hakura* (land grant) of their own within West Darfur. Since governmental arrangements called for the amirs to elect the sultan, it became clear to the Masalit that their *dar* was no longer viable. This political supremacy strengthened the hand of Arab chauvinists and led to attacks on Masalit villages, leading to local wars that the government did nothing to stop. Arab raids undertaken by *Janjawiid* units continued and by the end of 1996 the entire province was caught up in fighting. This led to the Masalit-Arab War of 1996–1999 which raged in West Darfur—the second of the three civil conflicts in the Darfur over the past 25 years. By 1999, tens of thousands of Masalit had fled to Chad or been killed.[10]

As unrest increased during the fighting of 1996–99, the government began arming Arabs. It was at this time that Sheikh Musa Hilal resurfaced and began to demonstrate the leadership and fighting tactics he had perfected in his attacks around Jebel Marra against the Fur in the late 1980s in the Fur-Arab War. Heavily armed and espousing the racist ideology of the Arab Gathering, Hilal returned to Darfur, launching indiscriminant attacks against the Masalit and other tribes, serving as "spearhead of ethnic cleansing that would spread throughout Darfur" in a few years.[11] Musa Hilal would eventually serve as the de facto captain of all *Janjawiid* forces, operating out of his headquarters at Misteriha in northern Darfur to train militia recruits from Chad and other West African countries to undertake attacks on civilians in their own towns and villages.[12]

[8] Destruction and Genocide, *supra* note 6, at 262.

[9] Long War, *supra* note 5, at 59.

[10] Destruction and Genocide, *supra* note 6, at 263.

[11] *Id.* at 266.

[12] Misteriha was one of many military camps located across Darfur that were used by the government to train and equip militia volunteers. Misteriha contained heavy weaponry, vehicles, a helicopter landing pad and officers' quarters. Other camps contained similar features and were used as paramilitary bases where government forces could work closely with militias to coordinate their joint attacks on rebels and civilians. Long War, *supra* note 5, at 39.

These first two wars—the Arab-Fur and Arab-Masalit—took place in Darfur in a context of severe underdevelopment, the Sahara desert moving south consuming nomadic grazing lands, an influx of automatic weaponry into the hands of Arab militias, population growth, and increasing ethnic polarization. These same trends resulted in the third civil war in Darfur since 1986, which had its formal beginning on July 21, 2001, when Fur and Zaghawa leaders signed a pledge on the Qur'an to organize armed resistance against the Arab supremacist movement that had manifested itself in the Arab Gathering and Islamic Legion and that was now spreading across Darfur under the leadership of Hilal.[13] Masalit activists joined the Fur-Zaghawa movement in November 2001.

To escape government attacks, small groups of Zaghawa began to train the Fur around Jebel Marra—the mountains in central Darfur which were the historic center of Fur power—in July and August of 2001. Although the rebels did not announce themselves publicly until February 2003, their attacks in February 2002 against a southern garrison and a police station in Golo, the district headquarters of Jebel Marra, in June 2002 had made their existence known to the government long before word of their movement reached the outside world.[14] On February 26, 2003 the rebels, first working under the title of the Darfur Liberation Front (DFL) and later renamed as the Sudanese Liberation Movement/Sudanese Liberation Army (SLM/SLA), again attacked Golo. In response to this and other rebel attacks, the government mobilized and trained *Janjawiid* units recruited from the Arab Gathering and Islamic Legion to attack Fur and Masalit villages during the last four months of 2003.[15] In October 2003, with Sudanese military support, the *Janjawiid* from paramilitary camps in South Darfur began the largest offensive on Jebel Marra since the Arab-Fur war of 1987–1989.

The announcement of the formation of SLM/SLA was soon followed by early rebel successes on the battlefield that eclipsed those which had ever been achieved in the twenty-year civil war in southern Sudan. The rebels' victories were, however, a double-edged sword; while serving to bolster the rebel forces with new recruits these victories also frightened Khartoum, heightening its sense of vulnerability and transforming the perception of violence in Darfur from that of a provincial conflict into a direct military threat against the regime.[16] As rebel militias scored successive military victories against the central government, Khartoum panicked, believing it was losing control of Darfur, which could have encouraged revolts in other regions of the country. Khartoum then organized recruitment drives among Arab tribes to expand the Janjiwiid militias which the government now armed, fed, and paid.[17] Not all Arab tribes contributed troops to the *Janjawiid* militia, however. In particular, Ibrahim

[13] Andrew S. Natsios, Sudan, South Sudan, and Darfur: What Everyone Needs to Know, Oxford University Press (Forthcoming 2011).

[14] Long War, *supra* note 5, at 39.

[15] Natsios, *supra* note 13.

[16] The government's weak presence outside of northern Sudan may have caused it to overreact to violence in Darfur and rely even more on peripheral groups such as the Janjawid as supplementary units to the national army. The strategy of supplying money and weaponry to one tribe over another, and encouraging the formation of militias to cause population displacement and undermine Darfur's way of life to put down the rebellion, was first outlined in a paper written by Al-Sadiq al-Mahdi before becoming Prime Minister in 1986 on how to win the war in the South.

[17] Destruction and Genocide, *supra* note 6, at 282.

Musa Madibu—*nazir* of the Baqqara (cattle herding) Rizaiqat of South Darfur and the most influential southern Arab leader—refused to contribute men to the *Janjawiid*, even going so far as to order people under his authority to protect the animals of the Masalit and Fur farmers and herders.[18] The leadership of men such as Nazir Madibu against the central government's strategy underscored a complicated reality in which not all Arabs were perpetrators of ethnic violence in Darfur; some even protected the victims from Khartoum and the *Janjawiid*.

As the government's combat position deteriorated, military leaders changed their tactics, deciding to retaliate not only against the rebels who had defeated them, but against their defenseless tribal villages that were their base of operations. Beginning in late 2003, the target of the government's and *Janjawiid's* focus shifted from rebel militias to their families in their home villages; Darfur became a killing field. The army began its campaign of terror against unarmed civilians using helicopter gunships or jet fighter planes to destroy villages and homes. The *Janjawiid* would then follow, surrounding what remained of the settlements and killing the young men who might join the insurgency. The attacks during this time were far more systematic than attacks up to that point, including the looting of animal herds, burning of fields, mass rape of woman, abduction of children, and demolition of infrastructure. Government-backed Arab militias acted with impunity, while the government turned a blind eye to the violence they had themselves orchestrated. This pattern repeated itself for the next year with the highest frequency of attacks occurring between September 2003 and April 2004.

It is important to note that some rebels' forces committed atrocities against Arabs during 2002–2003, which fed into the cycle of violence and reprisal killings that eventually overtook Darfur in 2003–2004, though these rebel atrocities never reached the scale or fury of the *Janjawiid* and Sudanese government attacks. There is no moral equivalency between the systematic and widespread atrocities of the Sudanese government and its allies and the very real incidents of atrocities by some of the rebel leaders, but which were episodic and not systematic.

From August–September 2003, government and *Janjawiid* forces collaborated to clear a section on the Wadi Saleh between Jebel Marra and the Chadian border in North Darfur, burning villages and adding more internally displaced persons (IDPs) to the already tens of thousands of displaced Fur and Masalit in the area.[19] Mass displacement of villagers continued during clearing of Wadi Saleh, with documented reports of mass executions taking place during this period of time.[20] Rebel forces contributed as well to the spike in killings that took place in the early months of 2004, as they began to steal from Arabs to feed and arm their growing forces and committed killings similar to those inflicted on Fur and Masalit villagers by the *Janjawiid* and government security forces. In particular, the violence inflicted by forces loyal to Minni Minnawi, leader of the Zaghawa insurrection, on the Zadiadiya Arabs is noted for its extreme brutality and contributed to the tribalization of the conflict.[21] Minnawi's actions outside Melli, capital of Dar Berti in West Darfur, played a role in the spike in violence from January–March 2004. A third, smaller peak in violence took place

[18] Natsios, *supra* note 13.

[19] Long War, *supra* note 5, at 131.

[20] *Id.* at 130.

[21] *Id.* at 137.

mostly in South Darfur later in 2004, as the rebels' attacks targeted government positions and civilians and incited the Arab Habbaniya tribe, which had previously been critical of the government, into accepting offers of weapons for self-defense.[22] The pattern of offensives and counter-offensives that moved to the South and East from northern and western Darfur resulted in mass destruction that left hundreds of villages totally or partially destroyed during 2003–2004.[23]

The atrocities committed by both parties to the conflict—rebels and *Janjawiid*/government forces—created a humanitarian catastrophe that included the creation of internally displaced persons with 1.8 million people forced into camps and towns in Darfur and an additional 200,000 who sought refuge in Chad.[24] *Janjawiid* forces positioned themselves outside of the towns and camps, preventing IDPs from gathering firewood or collecting foods that they could use for subsistence.

IV. INTERNATIONAL RESPONSE TO THE THIRD DARFUR WAR

What was the reaction of the international community to the third Darfur War? The United Nations, African Union, and donor governments acted to implement the spirit of the RtoP doctrine even before its passage by the Security Council in September 2005. In fact, since the 1992 Somalia intervention, the international community—principally through the United Nations—has repeatedly intervened in humanitarian crisis to prevent atrocities, save lives, and facilitate peace processes under the existing provisions of the UN Charter without the RtoP doctrine. These interventions have had mixed results: the success or failure of individual interventions is more often determined by the peculiar individual circumstances of each crisis than anything else. International humanitarian law, of which RtoP is the latest addition, can only be implemented through institutions, and the strengths and weaknesses of those institutions and the alignment of political support for robust intervention on the UN Security Council will determine whether the doctrine actually results in the protection of internally displaced people in humanitarian crises, not the language of the doctrine itself. The rule of law is only as good as the institutions used to implement it. The institutionalized system for intervention in humanitarian crisis is rooted in the existing organizational structure of the United Nations and of the Great Powers bilaterally and takes three tracks: *humanitarian* (through the UN Office of the Coordinator of Humanitarian Assistance or UNOCHA and specialized agencies such as UNICEF and the World Food Program or WFP), *diplomatic* (Department of Political Affairs), and *peacekeeping operations* (Department of Peacekeeping Operations or UNPKO). All of these UN Secretariat offices were formed long before the General Assembly approved the RtoP doctrine, and so we know a great deal about their weaknesses and strengths as they have been studied, analysed, and reported on extensively. Let us now look at how these three tracks—humanitarian, diplomatic, and peacekeeping—performed in

[22] *Id.* at 143–144.

[23] *Id.* at 145.

[24] The widely used UN/WFP figure of 2.7 million internally displaced people in Darfur has been proven through a census of the displaced camps to be inaccurate. As of 2010 the UN/WFP has now revised the number more accurately to 1.8 million people.

the Darfur crisis specifically, what problems arose in these efforts, and whether any of these weaknesses can be remedied or whether they are inherent in the power structure of the international system.

To determine the effectiveness of the international system in implementing the RtoP doctrine in Darfur we must employ some rough system of measurement. The best available proxy to demonstrate effectiveness are Darfur mortality rates during the conflict, given that the purpose of the RtoP doctrine is to prevent the death and abuse of civilians during internal conflicts where one side or the other is targeting non-combatants. Public health scientists have studied Darfur mortality rates during the period of the conflict and reached some useful conclusions for our analysis.

V. DEATH RATES IN DARFUR

The January 2010 issue of *The Lancet*, the preeminent British journal of public health, published the most comprehensive and analytically sound study of Darfur mortality rates done by public health scientists based on extensive data collected from the period September 2003 until December 2008. The study reports that there were significant reductions in mortality rates from mid-2004 to the end of 2008. The article argues that "although violence was the main cause of death during 2004, diseases have been the cause of most deaths since 2005, with displaced populations being the most susceptible."[25] Of the 298,000 people who died in Darfur from 2003–2008, 80 percent of excess deaths were not a result of violence, but rather disease which spread as a result of massive internal population displacement. This displacement was driven by *Janjawiid* and Sudanese government attacks.[26] As such, only 20 percent of the excess deaths that took place in Darfur from September 2003 to December 2008 can be attributed directly to violence.[27]

The biggest killers in Darfur from 2005 to the present were diarrheal disease and malaria, dehydration, and malnutrition caused by the mass population displacement, not directly by violent attacks on civilians by the army and *Janjawiid*, as was the case in 2003–2004 (some certainly took place, but were not the cause of most deaths). Three independent sources I spoke to while I served as US Envoy to Sudan in late 2006 reported the Janjawiid units would loot and burn villages, but would tell villagers they were no longer allowed to kill them, which suggests a deliberate change of policy by the Sudanese government. By 2007, civilian deaths caused by violence were usually the result of competition for pastureland among Arab militias and rebels groups or victims of banditry. United Nations officials were by 2008 reporting that the situation

[25] Oliver Degomme & Debarti Guha-Sapir, *Patterns of Mortality Rates in Darfur Conflict*, The Lancet 294 (2010), http://www.thelancet.com/journals/lancet/article/PIIS0140-6736%2809%2961967-X/fulltext#article_upsell [*Hereinafter Patterns of Mortality*].

[26] Patterns of mortality, *supra* note 25, at 297.

[27] While a number of attempts to estimate excess mortality during the third Darfur conflict, the most rigorous, analytically sound, and in depth study to date is the Degomme and Guha-Sapir paper published in Lancet. Eric Reeves, Professor of English Language and Literature at Smith College, has published an extraordinarily high figure of 540,000 excess deaths in Darfur based on methodologies few public health professionals would accept as consistent with accepted scientific and demographic analytical models.

had descended into anarchy. "Darfur today is a conflict of all against all," Rodolphe Adada, the joint African Union-United Nations special representative, told the UN Security Council in April. Between January 1, 2008, and March 31, 2009, he found some 2,000 fatalities from violence, one third of them civilian. The death of some 700 innocent civilians over a 15-month period, out of a total of 60,000 who died violent deaths over the entire course of the conflict indicates a profound shift in the causes of mortality away from killings.[28]

VI. THE INTERNATIONAL HUMANITARIAN RESPONSE

In late 2003 and early 2004, with people's coping mechanisms blocked and the government stonewalling relief operations, IDP death rates soared.[29] Death rates began to subside in early 2005 because of the success of the international humanitarian mission in Darfur, which had managed to provide food assistance to 940,000 people in Darfur and 200,000 refugees in Chad by October 2004.[30] Evidence shows that mortality rates decreased in mid-to late 2004 and early 2005 to levels comparable to those before the war.[31] United Nations agencies such as the World Health Organization, UNICEF, International Red Cross, non-governmental organizations, and donor aid agencies have developed a widely accepted international humanitarian mortality standard used in emergency response: if more than one person dies each day per 10,000 people, an emergency crisis situation exists which requires aid agency interventions.

The reduced mortality rates in early 2005, as compared to late 2003 through early 2004, attest to the international humanitarian response's success in reducing deaths once the aid infrastructure was put in place in 2004.[32] Mortality rates remained below the emergency level from early 2005 until the present (2011). The one major exception to this trend took place between July 2006 and September 2007; a period characterized by a rise in insecurity, which in turn led to an 18 percent reduction in the number of humanitarian staff at exactly the point in time when the number of affected people increased. The result was that the ratio of affected individuals to humanitarian aid workers increased by almost 50 percent per staff member.[33]

[28] Head of Joint African Union-United Nations Operation—Rodolphe Adada, *Briefing by Head of Joint African Union-United Nations Operation*, Security Council, SC/944, Apr. 27, 2009, at ¶ 4.

[29] The rural inhabitants of Darfur, if allowed to roam freely, can find enough food to eat to avoid starvation for months at a time.

[30] Long War, *supra* note 5, at 170.

[31] Debarti Guha-Sapir, Olivier Degomme & Mark Phelan, *Darfur: Counting the Deaths*, Centre for Research on the Epidemiology of Disasters, at 35 (2005), *available at* http://www.cred.be/sites/default/files/DarfurCountingtheDeaths.pdf.

[32] Advocacy groups had claimed that 560,000 people had been killed during the third civil war, but were hard pressed to provide evidence of this level of killings. In a debate in 2008 with Columbia University Professor Mahmoud Mandani, John Prendergast one of the leaders of these advocacy groups and co-founder of the Enough Campaign to end crimes against humanity, said "Most of these figures are wild estimates. They are simply crazily wild estimates." Andrew S. Natsios, Obama, adrift on Sudan, The Nation. 1, ¶ 3 (2009), http://thenationonlineng.net/web2/articles/7907/1/Obama-adrift-on-Sudan/Page1.html.

[33] *Patterns of Mortality*, *supra* note 25, at 298.

The increased level of insecurity during part of this period is more complicated than the earlier period. Between September and December 2006, the Sudanese military began an offensive in which they attempted to defeat Fur militias in the Jebel Marra and occupy the territory. The offensive was a disaster for the government: the Sudanese military suffered heavy losses including high rates of troop desertion and made little headway in taking Jebel Marra against the Fur fighters. From February 2007 until August 2007—probably in preparation for the Darfur peace conference held in Sirte, Libya in October 2007—the Sudanese military did not initiate any major combat operations against the rebels, but the rebels used the time to attack government forces. Thus, the major source of instability during this period stemmed from rebel, not government, attacks.

As such, the international response system, driven by the aid community with strong donor government support and funding, did protect the people of Darfur from further deaths caused by disease and starvation—but through an aid effort, not military intervention. Indeed, it was the reduction in the international humanitarian budget allocated to Darfur—which in turn led to a reduction in the number of humanitarian workers—that resulted in an increased number of disease-related deaths between July 2006 and September 2007.[34] Why did it take six months for the international humanitarian system to begin operations and an entire year for it to become fully operational? Certainly part of the delay was the deliberate obstructionism of the Sudanese government which tried and failed to prevent the aid effort from supporting those people displaced by their attacks. But this was not the only reason, as the timing problems in the humanitarian response to the Haitian earthquake in February of 2010 can attest. No civil war was going on in Haiti at the time and aid agencies (many of which had been in Haiti for decades) were welcome by the people and the government, but they were unable to cope with the magnitude of the earthquake even with significant U.S. military support. Large scale humanitarian aid programs in a crisis take time to set up, even when they are welcome. Approximately 1,000 expatriate aid workers were deployed to Darfur by aid agencies beginning in early 2004 through the end of the year, who themselves had to be fed, housed, supported, protected, offices set up, and provided with vehicles and equipment, before they could help the local population. They in turn had to hire approximately 13,000 Sudanese workers to implement the program. Local staff is essential in humanitarian relief operations because they speak the local languages, know the road system and geography of the country, and understand the complex ethnic and tribal structures and leadership hierarchies, local politics, and culture. Hiring this many local staff cannot be done in a matter of weeks; it takes months. Once the agencies were in place, they had to import hundreds of thousands of tons of food aid, medical supplies, shelter materials, and water purification systems, mostly from donor governments.

The United Nations did not act alone to initiate emergency humanitarian assistance. Early U.S., Canadian, and European Union humanitarian funding resulted in a rapid response on a scale that far exceeded most other previous humanitarian emergencies according to Alex de Waal and Julie Flint in their history of the Darfur conflict. In fiscal year 2003–2004, the U.S. government contributed over three quarters of a

[34] *Id.* at 298–299.

billion dollars in humanitarian assistance for the emergency, which was followed by an additional half a billion dollars during FY2004–2005; this was 60% of total donor funding for the aid effort. Months of planning by the U.S. government in collaboration with other donor governments, the UN, ICRC, and NGOs to channel the increased aid effectively during these early months went largely unnoticed by the press, but were responsible for saving hundreds of thousands of lives.

What compelled the humanitarian response? In March 2004, senior USAID officials took the decision to have the career technical staff from the Office of Foreign Disaster Assistance within the Agency prepare an estimate of *potential future* deaths in Darfur from starvation and disease. This estimate of mortality (see Graph 1) calculated that as many as 300,000 people would die by early 2005 if the UN, NGOs, and donor governments did not organize a massive humanitarian relief effort in Darfur.[35] The mortality chart was an important component of congressional testimony given by Roger Winter, then USAID Assistant Administrator for the Democracy, Conflict and Humanitarian Assistance to spur public debate on Darfur and speed up live-saving relief reaching victims of violence.[36]

We also decided at the same meeting for USAID offices to obtain satellite photographs of the devastation of the Sudanese government's and its allies, the *Janjawiid*, to build the case for a robust humanitarian intervention in Darfur. These photographs, which the Bush White House ordered the US government aerial surveillance system to declassify, provided conclusive evidence that at least 377 villages had been destroyed in Darfur by June 2004. The U.S. delegation made these photographs public during a consultation and pledging conference on Darfur called by the United Nations in Geneva, Switzerland in the summer of 2004 attended by 30 governments and many United Nations humanitarian agencies. These efforts led to a formal statement condemning "grave violations of human rights and international law" in Darfur and played a large role in securing an additional U.S. pledge of $188 million in humanitarian assistance with other countries increasing their financial contributions as well.

In early July 2004, U.S. Secretary of State Colin Powell and the Bush White House instructed me to show the satellite imagery to UN Secretary-General Kofi Annan and his staff, and later to the permanent members of the UN Security Council to prove that the violence in Darfur was not an American invention (some senior staff in the UN Department of Political Affairs privately accused the U.S. government of exaggerating the Darfur atrocities). These U.S. government actions played a significant role in garnering increased media attention on what was happening in Darfur and gaining traction among members of the Security Council for the passage of Resolution 1556 in July 2004.

[35] The study was innovative in that no analytical effort had ever before been done using agricultural, public health, and mortality data to predict potential deaths in a refugee/IDP crisis.

[36] The General Accounting Office, an arm of the U.S. Congress, criticized the USAID study I ordered, arguing some sort of mathematical modeling should have been used. Instead of mathematical modeling, which would have taken a year to develop, the OFDA staff developed some surveys based on retrospective evidence of previous crisis in Darfur, and gave an expert estimate based on health, agricultural, and nutrition status trends, under the premise that the Government of Sudan would continue to lay siege to villages and would not allow humanitarian access.

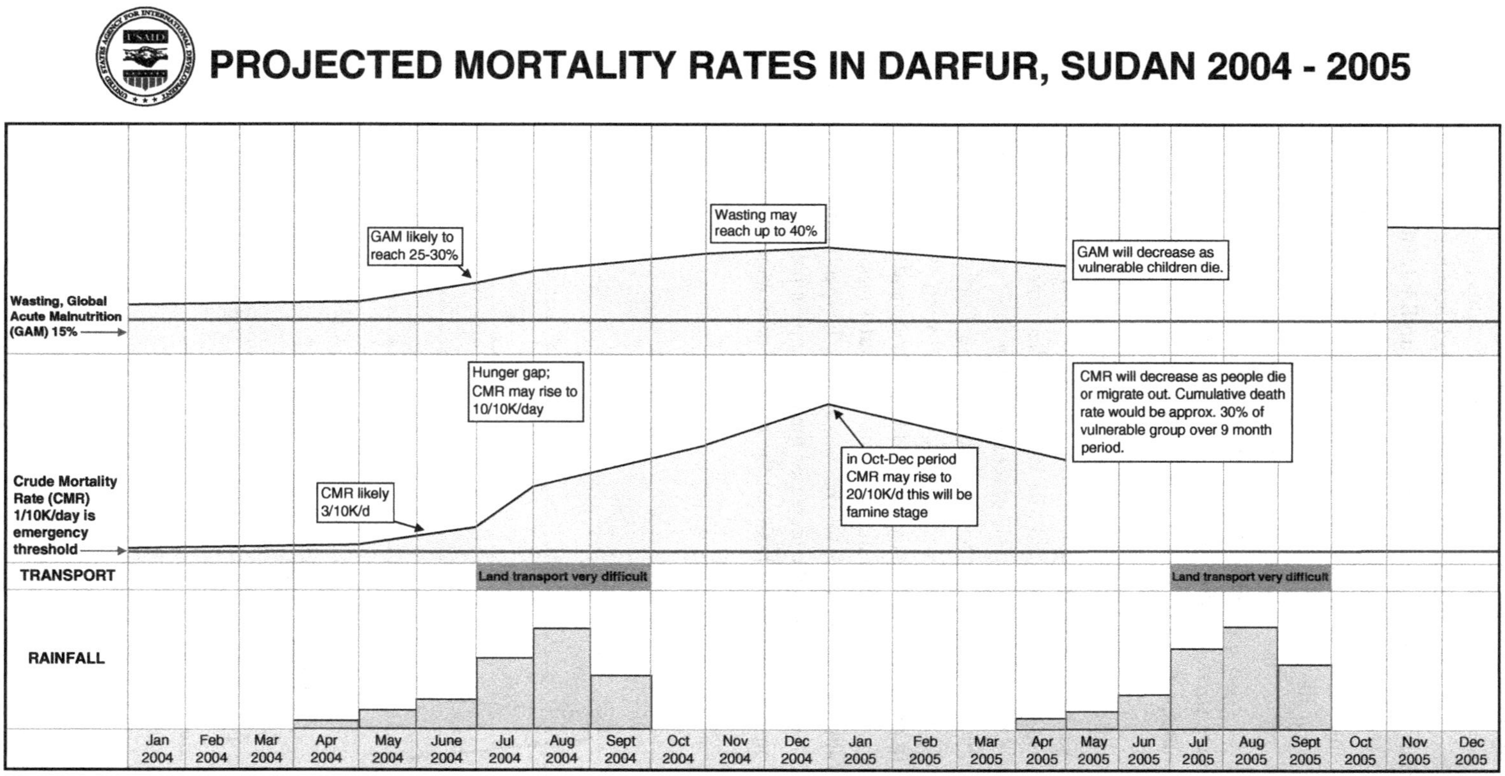

1. *"CMR and Wasting projections from personal communication from field based epidemiology studies in Bahr-I-Ghazal, Sudan 1998 and Ethiopia 2000*
2. *Background on Food Security in Darfur. Collins, Steve, MD "How bad does it have to get? The Nutritional Status in N Darfur, Sudan in Spring 2001" Save the Children (UK).*
3. *Wasting rates, Office of UN Resident and Humanitarian Coordinator for the Sudan, 10 January 2004; FAO Special Report Sudan February 2004.*

Note: Extensive analysis on mortality rates in Darfur was conducted by Peter Morris during his tenure at the Office of Foreign Disaster Assistance (OFDA). His work contributed greatly to the development of the mortality graph.

GRAPH 1 Mortality Rates in Darfur

These U.S. efforts predated the rise in media coverage on the Darfur crisis and the creation of the international advocacy campaign. In fact, the Save Darfur Coalition, created by networks of religious institutions, human rights groups, and civil society organizations, and comprising more than a hundred member groups in the U.S. seeking action on Darfur, was not formally created until July of 2004, months after the U.S. government and the UN agencies had taken action to provide relief and raise the profile of Darfur in the international system. The timeline of these events suggest that outside actors or media coverage did not drive U.S. government in Darfur, but, rather, the inverse: the advocacy campaign was an outgrowth of the visibility of the crisis created by U.S. government actions. These actions were also taken before the passage of the RtoP doctrine at the UN World Summit in September 2005, and subsequent affirmation of the doctrine in April 2006 by the UN Security Council.

While the situation on the ground in Darfur evolved after the end of 2004, advocacy groups and western media outlets reporting on the conflict did not. Engagement of actors such as George Clooney and Mia Farrow did keep media attention on Darfur, ensuring that the amount of press coverage on the topic remained at high levels throughout 2005. But this increased media coverage on Darfur added to the mischaracterization of the conflict and contributed to the growing narrative of a worsening humanitarian disaster alongside accusations of genocide and calls for UN-led intervention when, in fact, judged by declining mortality rates reported in *The Lancet*, this was not the appropriate response to what was actually happening on the ground.

The graph below illustrates the increased media attention paid to Darfur, highlighting the disconnect that existed between the number of newspaper articles published

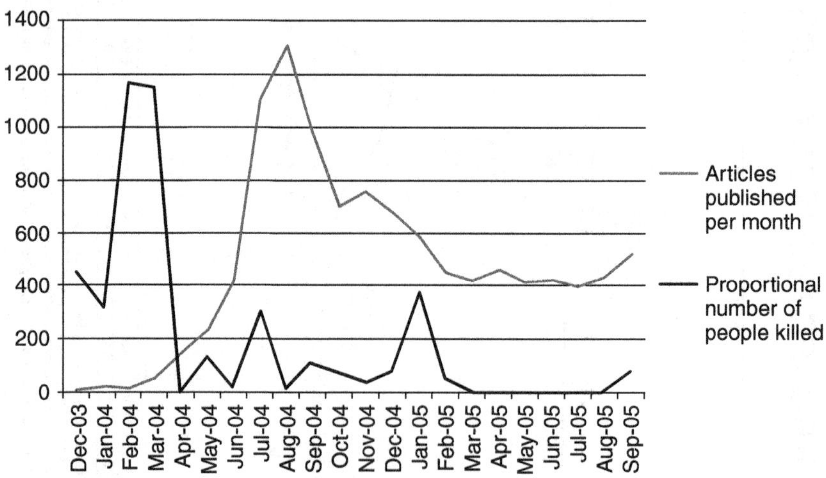

GRAPH 2 Media Attention as Compared to People Killed[37]

[37] Andreas Höfer Petersen & Lise-Lotte Tullin, *The Scorched Earth of Darfur Patterns in Death and Destruction Reported by the People of Darfur*, BLOODHOUND, at 17 (Jan. 2001—Sept. 2005), *available at* http://www.bloodhound.se/06_04_26_DARFUR_report.pdf.

on Darfur as compared to the number of people killed from December 2003–September 2005. As the graph shows, the increase in media attention on Darfur did not correspond to the actual number of killings that were taking place. Indeed, the media began covering the crisis after the killings had climaxed between 2003 and early 2004.

In spite of this disconnect, the media's story of genocide in Darfur prevailed and the region became the focus of international attention and sustained political activism in the United States, making it an issue in U.S. domestic politics and forcing policymakers through explanations of the conflict that oversimplified the reality on the ground. This in turn led to advocacy groups calling for military intervention in Darfur to stop "the ongoing genocide" even before the RtoP doctrine had been approved. Even Nicholas Kristof of the *New York Times*, the most aggressive and persistent columnist covering the crisis, did not write his first article until March 2004, after the killings had peaked and were in decline according to the Lancet study.

But the media's delay in covering Darfur had other implications as well: the absence of coverage made getting international consensus for military intervention much more difficult since what was happening in Darfur was not widely understood. Since Darfur did not have a large pre-existing aid agency or UN infrastructure presence before the conflict and was difficult for reporters to get to (which the Sudanese government stonewalled in any case), information on what was actually happening was very limited until well into 2004. It was between September 2003 and April 2004 that the at-risk population of Darfur most needed protection by an outside peacekeeping force, but it was not until early 2004 that it became clear that widespread atrocities were underway. I traveled to Darfur in November 2003 to see some drought relief programs, and met with the governor of North Darfur who held a dinner for me in El Fasher. He told me, using very carefully worded, deliberately vague language, that horsemen were attacking villages and causing trouble. My delegation and I listened intently to what he was describing, but did not understand how severe the crisis was until early 2004, half way through the peak of the killing. I did say at a press conference in Nairobi after leaving Darfur in December 2003 that a new conflict seemed to be starting in the region, but we certainly did not understand the magnitude of what was happening.

VII. INTERNATIONAL PEACEKEEPING OPERATIONS IN DARFUR

As previously mentioned, *The Lancet* mortality study reported most deaths in Darfur from violence took place before mid-2004. During that period, the Sudanese government with its allies, the *Janjawiid* militias, conducted a massive ethnic cleaning campaign—the looting and burning of villages, executions of local sheikhs and young men, and the mass rape of women—directed among others against Fur, Masalit, and Zaghawa villages to destroy the base of operations of the rebel militias.

Two international efforts to send peacekeeping troops to Darfur were made: one through the African Union and a second by a joint force (the first joint force by the AU and UN in history) of the African Union and United Nations. The African Union force was approved by the Sudanese government and rebel movements at meetings held in N'Djamena, Chad, which began in March 2004 and concluded in April 2004. The African Union insisted that since this was an African problem, they would lead the peacekeeping operation rather than the UN—perhaps the most fateful decision of the military response to the Darfur conflict because the African Union was institutionally wholly unprepared for managing the effort. The Western powers and the UN leadership were unwilling to override African leaders' insistence that this be an AU led effort. The period the peace-keeping troops were most needed—from September 2003 to April 2004—they were not present in any form because no agreement had been reached among the AU and the contestants to allow them to deploy to Darfur. It took a full year—from April 2004 through April 2005—for the full contingent of African Union troops to arrive in Darfur, and once they did arrive, they were unwilling or unable to stop the violence which was subsiding in any case. The African Union did not have the military planning capacity, the weapons systems, the training, or the experience in combat operations to manage an operation of this complexity and magnitude, and so it became clear by late 2006 that a United Nations peacekeeping effort was needed. On July 31, 2007, the Security Council approved a joint AU/UN peacekeeping effort, but a large part of the 26,000 troops and police did not arrive until late 2008.

However, prior to the adoption of RtoP, the developing world had taken positions that could be interpreted as supporting a rejection of the UN's Responsibility to Protect human rights, despite early African Union endorsement for the RtoP doctrine even before the UN World Summit where it was approved.[38] For example, the UN General Assembly's Third Committee, the entity responsible for human rights, adjourned in 2004 without condemning the action of Sudan. The South African delegate of the Committee accused the West of "double standards" for criticism and stated that "the African Group regrets the abuses of a multinational organization like the United Nations to settle disputes on human rights."[39] Khartoum had also met a major requirement of the West before the adoption of RtoP by signing the Comprehensive Peace Agreement (CPA) on the North-South conflict in January of 2005; an agreement that did not include Darfur and had taken years of protracted negotiations to reach.

The opposition of developing countries to military intervention in Darfur was not a historical anomaly, but a chronic reluctance over two decades: they saw humanitarian intervention as a form of western neo-colonialism. During the debate on Resolution 46/182 in the Security Council in 1991, which led to the creation of UNOCHA and its legal mandates, developing countries watered down the interventionist language of the resolution for the same reason—they wanted to constrain, not encourage, the humanitarian enterprise.

Although Darfur was on the UN Security Council's agenda by 2004 when the U.S. government provided the satellite imagery documenting the destruction of villages, there was little appetite among the Security Council members to take measures that western governments and advocates would soon demand. Security Council actions prior to the adoption of RtoP demonstrated that it was not prepared to send peacekeeping troops into Darfur with a robust mandate that included disarming parties to the conflict in order to protect civilian populations. With heavy commitments in the wars in Iraq and Afghanistan, the U.S. government was not about to send troops to yet another Muslim country, particularly where the precise military mission was unclear. These circumstances, however, did not preclude the U.S., alongside Britain and France,

[38] James Traub, *Unwlling and Unable: The Failed Response to the Atrocities in Darfur*, Global Centre for the Responsibility to Protect, at 13 (2010) [Hereinafter *Unwilling and Unable*].

[39] *Id.* at 17.

from taking the most aggressive and interventionist diplomatic positions on Darfur among members of the Security Council by calling for sanctions on the Sudanese government in mid-July 2004 and a no-fly zone. In early September 2004, the U.S. again introduced a resolution calling for sanctions against Sudan. In both instances, the resolutions that the U.S. put forth were watered down by other members of the Security Council and the sanctions were removed.

While it is true that two other permanent members of the Security Council—China and the Russian Federation—both major arms suppliers of Khartoum and in the case of China, owner of a 40 percent stake in Sudan's chief oil consortium, respectively—played a large role in removing sanctions from the resolutions through their veto-wielding power, other non-permanent members of the Security Council also blocked any meaningful resolutions from being passed.[40] Since 2004, two Arab states who served as non-permanent members of the UN Security Council—Algeria and Qatar—either weakened resolutions that included sanctions on the Sudanese government or abstained from voting in a clear message of non-support for military intervention and sanctions.[41] Brazil, Angola, and the Philippines also objected to the threat of sanctions. As such, the Security Council was reduced to considering measures under Article 41, which authorizes coercive but non-military actions.[42]

The result of this dynamic among the members of the Security Council was Resolution 1556. Passed in July 2004, the resolution called on Khartoum to cease all military activities, disarm the *Janjawiid*, and arrest its leaders within a time period of 30 days. The resolution, while calling for the ban on the sale of weapons to "all non-governmental entities and individuals in Darfur" (this was interpreted by Western powers as directed against the *Janjawiid*, while Khartoum's allies interpreted it as limiting weapons distributions to the Darfur rebels) did not preclude future weapon sales to the government in Khartoum. Resolution 1556 proved largely ineffective because it could not be simultaneously supported by military force. Secretary-General Kofi Annan, upon submitting his report required by the resolution, concluded that the Sudanese government had "not met its obligation" to stop "attacks against civilians and ensuring their protection."[43] Ineffective in its first attempt to broker peace in Darfur, the Security Council met again to craft and pass Resolution 1564 in September 2004. Noting with "grave concern" Khartoum's inability to meet its obligations noted in Resolution 1556, the newly passed resolution sought to enhance the capabilities of the African Union Mission to Sudan (AMIS) and establish a commission of inquiry into whether or not the Sudanese government had committed genocide in Darfur.[44]

[40] In 2004, Sudan accounted for 10 percent of China's imported oil. China had helped Sudan construct a pipeline to the Red Sea. Peter S. Goodman, *China Invests Heavily in Sudan's Oil Industry*, WASHINGTON POST, Dec. 23, 2004.

[41] Nadim Hasbani, *About the Arab Stance Vis-á-Vis Darfur*, International Crisis Group, at 1 (2007), *available at* http://www.crisisgroup.org/en/regions/africa/horn-of-africa/sudan/nadim-hasbani-in-al-hayat.aspx.

[42] *Unwilling and Unable*, *supra* note 38, at 10.

[43] UN Secretary-General, *Report of the Secretary-General Pursuant to Paragraphs 6 and 13 to 16 of Security Council Resolution 1556*, Aug. 30, 2004.

[44] Prior to the adoption of Resolution 1564, AMIS consisted of 125 monitors and 305 troops from Rwanda and Nigeria whose orders were to protect UN monitors and provide security for IDPs seeking humanitarian assistance. The troops were not mandated to protect civilians and did not

Resolution 1564, combined with resolution 1556, did little more than limit the UN's involvement in stopping the atrocities in Darfur and support AMIS and further investigations.

The resolutions affected the conflict in other ways, many of which complicated the reality on the ground even further. For one, it could be argued that these resolutions steeled the Sudanese government's will to continue its atrocities, noting that the members of the Security Council were too divided on what to do to pose a credible threat toward its forces wreaking havoc in Darfur. Moreover, through its foot-dragging on the resolutions, Khartoum became more adept at manipulating public opinion in Arab countries, finding other ways to deflect criticism. The regime understood that a relaxation of its bureaucratic restrictions on aid organizations undertaking humanitarian assistance in Darfur would correlate to an easing of pressure from outside groups.[45] In addition, upon closer scrutiny of the amount of killings that took place, a disturbing trend emerged around the time of the adoption of both resolutions. As Graph 3 illustrates, the number of killings that took place at adoption for both resolutions increased, particular in July 2004, to what would be the highest levels until January 2005. This could be interpreted to mean that weak resolutions by the UN, far from doing modest good, may have, at least in the case of Darfur, emboldened perpetrators to increase violence.

Although Chinese and Russian commercial interests probably played a role in their decision not to allow a stronger resolution to pass, their opposition was not solely based on economic grounds, as both countries adhere to a traditional view of state sovereignty. Both countries had ongoing, internal ethnically-based civil unrest themselves—the Tibetans and Uyghurs in China and Chechnians in the Russian Federation—and were very sensitive to outside meddling in their internal

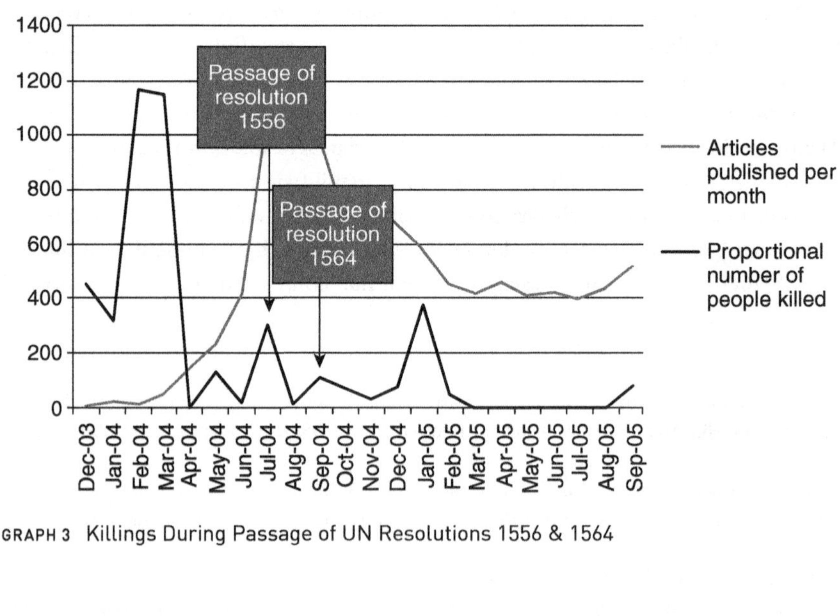

GRAPH 3 Killings During Passage of UN Resolutions 1556 & 1564

constitute a peacekeeping force. In October of 2004, the mandate of AMIS was expanded to a force of 3,320 soldiers, observers, and civilian police.

[45] *Unwilling and Unable, supra* note 38, at 10.

affairs. The language of RtoP is in direct conflict with their long-held views on state sovereignty as a sacrosanct principle of Chinese and Russian statecraft. Wang Guangya, China's then Ambassador to the UN, expressed the Chinese view in a 2007 interview when he stated "[t]o respect sovereignty is the basic norm of international law. In some countries there is a problem, where the protection of their own people is neglected. The UN can come in a quiet way, providing help, providing advice. But the role to play is not to impose it when the government is functioning."[46] This argument of course contradicts the fundamental purpose of RtoP, which clearly states the UN has a Responsibility to Protect citizens whether or not they live in a failed or functioning state, if they are being targeted and their own government for whatever reason refuses to intervene to protect them.

Calls for military action also ignored the historically weak peacekeeping role of the UN in civilian protection. Thus, advocacy groups in particular had inflated expectations about what the organization was capable of achieving under the circumstances. The mandate to use force under Chapter VII of the UN Charter does not provide any clear guidance for how that force was going to be used, let alone which nation would take the lead in commanding the multinational force. Furthermore, it was unclear what peace the purported peacekeepers were going to enforce, since no political agreement had been reached as to the cessation of hostilities among all parties.

The idea that an UN-led force could rapidly deploy and then position their forces across a region as large and remote as Darfur, which had very limited to no infrastructure, ignored reality. A large contingent of troops and civilians under the AU/UN Hybrid Operation in Darfur (UNAMID) with a mandated force of nearly 26,000 personnel was not deployed until late 2008, which was nearly three-and-a-half years after resolution 1556 was approved at the Security Council, three years after the RtoP doctrine was approved by the UN World Summit in 2005, and two years after the Joint AU/UN force was approved at a Darfur strategy conference held in Ethiopia in November 2006 led by Kofi Annan, Salim Ahmed Salim of the AU, and attended by thirty concerned governments.

A considerable amount of time and effort is needed to garner the required political and military support for UN peacekeeping operations to receive approval, funding, and the necessary mandate before they can be deployed. Even if a robust resolution had been approved by the AU and later by the UN, much more rapidly with no opposition, the amount of time required to recruit the troops needed, equip them, construct military bases in Darfur for them to live and support their operations, move the vehicles needed to support the effort, and then transport the troops themselves to Darfur could not possibly be done in a few months. While many proposals have been made for a reform of the current system of UN peacekeeping operations to include a rapid response force, few of these proposals have had much support.

Had any Western power with a military capable of changing the course of the conflict on the ground without the approval or support of the Security Council, the African Union or the Sudanese government sent a large force to Darfur, it would have created a diplomatic firestorm. Such an invasion force would have endangered the humanitarian relief operation, which is always vulnerable to attack and obstructionism by

[46] Unwlling and Unable, *supra* note 38, at 11.

contestants to the conflict. After President Bashir was indicted by the International Criminal Court for crimes against humanity, thirteen international non-governmental organizations were immediately expelled from Darfur by the Khartoum government.

From the vantage point of the Sudanese leadership, the media and activists' calls for intervention and their accusations of genocide from 2005 onward did not provide any incentive for them to stop killing civilians and may have caused the regime to dig its heels in even further against any compromise on the diplomatic front. The Sudanese government used the threat of military intervention to its advantage in the creation of internal propaganda and paranoia that the West wanted to take Sudan's oil, steal Muslim territory, and impose democracy at gunpoint. Most disturbing, however, is that calls for military action against the government jeopardized the lives that advocacy groups sought to save. Khartoum had used food as a weapon in 2003–2004 when it implemented complicated registration requirements for health workers, held up vehicles in Port Sudan and initiated a variety of other bureaucratic entanglements in an effort to block relief operations from taking place. The past behavior of the Bashir government suggested that it would employ similar methods once again to control the distribution of aid to civilians located in camps, just as western governments, the international advocacy campaign and media coverage were increasing the visibility of the crisis. The bellicose Western rhetoric, far from convincing Khartoum to accept an international force to intervene in the conflict, caused the NCP to close ranks and slow down the aid effort.

In the end, the largest peacekeeping force in UN history was deployed to Darfur, but it was much too late to enforce RtoP when it was most needed. And even had the same force been deployed in September 2003, when it was most needed and with clear authority from the Security Council to intervene to protect civilians, it did not have the military fire power or training to stop the Sudanese government and the *Janjawiid* from carrying out their attacks. The Sudanese government insisted that the peacekeeping troops for Darfur come from Africa where it had more diplomatic influence. And when it came time for countries to volunteer their soldiers for the peacekeeping force, the Sudanese government actively recruited them from countries that either had weak militaries or were allies. When the Rwandan government—which had its own experience with mass atrocities in the genocide of 1994 and were committed to trying to stop them in Darfur—offered troops, Sudan initially refused to accept them (a position Khartoum was forced to reverse later under heavy diplomatic pressure).

VIII. DIPLOMATIC EFFORTS TO END VIOLENCE IN DARFUR

Ultimately only a negotiated end to the civil conflict would have permanently protected the people of Darfur and that would have required a political settlement that was enforceable. Of the three tracks—humanitarian, military, and diplomatic—it was diplomacy that offered the only permanent solution to the crisis, and yet it has been on this track that the international system has had the least impact. Why was the diplomacy of the conflict so problematic? What efforts were made by the UN, AU, and concerned governments between 2003 and the end of 2010 to reach a political settlement between the contestants and why did they fail? Why does no permanent Darfur settlement appear to be on the horizon at this writing?

Three prolonged diplomatic efforts were made over the eight-year conflict: one at peace talks held in Abuja, Nigeria in early 2006, the second at Sirte, Libya in late 2007, and the third at a series of talks held in Qatar between 2009 through the present. The first set of talks were organized by the African Union, but were dominated by President Obsanjo of Nigeria for the African Union and Robert Zoellick, then the U.S. Deputy Secretary of State. The Abuja conference came the closest to success in finding an enduring political settlement. In May 2006, the Darfur Peace Agreement was announced, but was only signed by Minni Minawi, at the time the most powerful rebel leader militarily. The other two rebel leaders at the time Abdul Wahid Nur and Khalil Ibrahim refused.

Both Nur and Ibrahim engaged in a public bidding contest with each other as to who could demand of the Sudanese government the most favorable terms and largest financial settlement for the victims. Nur guaranteed his followers would receive $10,000 each, while Ibrahim doubled that and insisted on €15,000 per person (which was more than $20,000 at the time). Khalil also promised his followers an additional twenty billion Euros in reconstruction money from Khartoum before he would be party to the agreement. Wahid had promised Zoellick and Obsanjo he would sign the agreement despite the fact that it had very limited funding, but reversed himself a day later and opposed it. He then organized demonstrations against the agreement in the displaced camps to ensure Minni Minawi, his former deputy who had broken with him, would not get credit for signing it. The Sudanese government did not implement most of the agreement—a common negotiating practice of the Bashir government—probably because two major rebel leaders refused to sign the agreement which was why the rebels were so suspicious of the negotiations to begin with. But that agreement would at least have allowed people to return to their homes and farms.

The second effort was led by Jan Eliasson, former Foreign Minister of Sweden and president of the UN General Assembly, representing the United Nations and Salim Ahmed Salim, former Secretary-General of the OAU and former Foreign Minister of Tanzania, representing the African Union. Because the Libyan government had taken a great interest in Darfur, Libya was chosen as the venue for the talks. The talks failed when the seven major rebel leaders refused to even attend the meeting because they did not trust the Libyan government and wished to hold the negotiations at a more neutral location. The second effort produced no agreement.

The third effort was held in Qatar and chaired by the Qatari foreign minister, Sheikh Hamad bin Jassim Al Thani, with strong UN and AU roles. Their strategy changed at the third round of negotiations and the Sudanese government decided to sign separate agreements with different rebel groups. On February 24, 2010, the Sudanese government signed an individual peace agreement with JEM, after which both parties to the agreement promptly violated its provisions. In June 2010, Minni Minnawi, who had signed the DPA in May 2006 and was rewarded with a senior position in the Sudanese government (in which he had no power but was paid a salary with some of the senior rebel leaders under his command), broke with Khartoum and sought sanctuary in Juba, South Sudan, under the protection of the Southern Sudan government. On December 10, 2010, the Sudanese government suspended its participation in the negotiations. Later in 2010 and early 2011, Minnawi's troops joined Khalil Ibrahim's forces and launched attacks against the Sudanese military.

Why did none of these negotiations yield any lasting results? After the failure of the first round of negotiations, the rebel movements began to fracture into smaller and smaller groups—many of them tribally based—fighting Khartoum and at times each other. This fracturing is a tendency in civil wars where there isn't a single external patron supporting the rebellion to keep them united: rebel movements without this patron will often break into smaller and smaller units over time. This was certainly the case in Darfur where there were multiple external patrons (e.g., neighboring countries such as Chad, Eritrea, and Libya) with conflicting political agendas arming various rebel groups in Sudan. These patrons often abandoned one rebel group to support another, confusing the already chaotic political situation.

But it was also the case that this fracturing was a deliberate policy of the Sudanese government: it used jobs, weapons, and money to divide and conquer the rebels by luring commanders away from the main movement; a practice they aggressively pursued following the failure of the 2006 Abuja talks to produce a universally accepted agreement. By the second round of talks at Sirte, there were at least 27 independent rebel groups—though only 7 of them had a political agenda and any sustainability—and some of these other smaller rebel groups had simply mutated in organized criminal gangs, raiding relief convoys and government offices to support themselves. Successive Sudanese governments used this divide-and-rule tactic in the Southern civil war, and so they had considerable experience before they tried it in Darfur. Despite UN, AU, European, and American efforts to unite the rebels behind one negotiating position with one leader to deal with Khartoum, the rebels remained divided. No Darfuri John Garang (who led the Southern rebellion and negotiated the peace agreement signed in January 2005, which ended the North-South war) existed to unite the movements. With the rebels divided, the tendency was for their leaders to try to outbid each other—as Abdul Wahid Nur and Khalil Ibrahim had done—demanding a higher and higher price for peace, which only made the negotiations more and more dysfunctional and peace all the more unlikely.

More important perhaps than any other factor in negotiating a peace agreement in Darfur is the complexity of the problem. Putting Darfur back together again may have been too difficult a task given the three civil conflicts since the mid-1980s, the polarization of the tribes, the broken economy, the damage to the agricultural system, the memory of atrocities and the demand for retribution, the destruction of the tribal hierarchies needed to implement any peace agreement, and lack of a just system of law and order. It is unlikely an outside diplomatic effort by the UN, AU, neighboring states, or Great Powers can easily remedy the current situation without political will on the part of the contestants in Sudan.

The failure of these interventions suggests that of the three tracks, the diplomatic one is the most important, and yet also the most problematic. International diplomats and the Great Powers can cajole, can offer incentives, and even threaten parties to the conflict, but they cannot easily force the contestants to agree to a lasting settlement and then implement it if the contestants resist it, and yet that is ultimately the most important international tool for ending a conflict and protecting those at risk.

IX. DILEMMAS CONFRONTING RTOP IN DARFUR

Finally, we cannot complete this analysis without observing several dilemmas suggested by this history of outside intervention which complicated the implementation of the RtoP doctrine in the case of Darfur.

- *Sequencing*—To have been effective in reducing violent deaths, RtoP would have had to be implemented at the end of 2003 and early 2004, when violence was the main cause of death. The U.S. government did not commission research on the atrocities until March 2004—and it was the U.S. which had been at the forefront of pressing for action—and the photographs of the burned-out villages were not ready for publication until July 2004. Secretary of State Colin Powell did not declare genocide in Darfur until September 2004, four months after the peak of the violent deaths. In addition, any deployment of a robust peacekeeping force over the objections of the Sudanese government during the period of the greatest violence would most likely have disrupted the speed of the aid operation, leading to much higher mortality rates among the victims whose deaths were caused by malnutrition and disease. Our experience in other crises is that when combatants cannot attack the military force trying to restore order, they will target humanitarian agencies which they see as fronts for Western governments. Advocates of RtoP never confronted the fundamental contradictions in the sequencing of their advocacy, which itself did not begin until after the climax of most of the violence. Put simply, if RtoP had been implemented using robust military force to protect civilians from violence, it would have had the unintended consequence of disrupting the effectiveness of the aid operation, thereby indirectly killing the very people it had a mandate to protect.

- *Military Intervention as Magic Bullet*—The arrival of peacekeeping troops, even if they had had a robust enough mandate to intervene to stop the perpetrators of mass atrocities, took place after violent deaths had declined. The notion that peacekeeping forces could be marshaled, funded, equipped, and deployed to a region as remote and inhospitable as Darfur within a matter of weeks of the beginning of the attacks on civilian targets is a wildly unrealistic expectation when one looks at how UN peacekeeping operations are organized.
- *Ground Reality Versus Outside Perception*—A substantial gap existed between what was actually taking place on the ground in Darfur and what advocacy groups, the media, and western parliamentarians and legislators understood to be happening. They pressed policymakers to take the wrong action at the wrong times. Thus, calls among advocacy groups for military intervention in Darfur reached a crescendo when violent deaths were no longer the main cause of mortality.

Combined, these three dilemmas suggest enforcing RtoP is far more complicated than its authors may have understood when they drafted it. Ultimately the specific local circumstances will determine whether a UN intervention in all of its manifestations—diplomatic, humanitarian, and peacekeeping—will succeed. Darfur is not a good test of the general viability of the RtoP doctrine as a constraint on a government's attacks on its own population nor is it useful as a case study on whether the doctrine will encourage more aggressive Security Council action against these governments. We should not use the failure of RtoP in Darfur to conclude that it will never work anywhere. It depends on the circumstances. Indeed, in conflicts where crimes against humanity are largely spontaneous, the doctrine might prove useful in curbing violence in the future. But the evidence is not particularly encouraging because we know that outside of a few Western democracies for which the protection of human rights is a central foreign policy principle, many countries—China and Russia included—do not share the same worldview and in fact are hostile to the doctrine of humanitarian intervention, particularly when it is imposed against the wishes of a sovereign government. Both nations have veto power over any Security Council resolutions as two of the Permanent Five.

X. THE CONSEQUENCES OF THE RTOP FOR PROTECTION OF AT-RISK POPULATIONS IN SUDAN

The RtoP doctrine, however, may have begun to have an impact on the Sudanese government's actions given events in late 2010—but not in Darfur. The most at-risk population in Sudan in 2010 and 2011 was not in Darfur, but in greater Khartoum where a million southern internally displaced people (IDPs) lived (between the signing of the CPA in January 2005 and 2010, approximately one and a half million IDP's returned to the South, with a million remaining in Khartoum as of this writing). The Sudanese government has long feared the southern IDPs as they see them as the enemy at their gates.

When John Garang, the leader of the Southern rebellion, died in a helicopter crash in July 2005, southern IDPs rioted and burned the city for days as they believed he had been assassinated by Sudanese government's internal security apparatus (though at this writing there is no evidence of this). It was not until Rebecca Garang, his widow, went on national radio and announced that her husband's death had been an accident, that the violence stopped. The Khartoum police lost control of the city and as a result the Northern government continues to fear the IDP population, though as of this writing there has been an organized effort to bring as many of the remaining IDPs back to the South as wish to go voluntarily.

In early October 2010, with the approaching vote in Southern Sudan on whether to secede and form a new independent country (required under the North-South Peace Agreement of 2005), the position of the IDPs around Khartoum grew more untenable and insecure. Sudanese Foreign Minister Ali Kharti, and Information Minister Kamal Obeid, used incendiary language against the Southern displaced, and the latter announced that should the South vote to secede, they would not enjoy citizen rights, jobs, nor would they be treated in hospitals.[47]

Several days later, on October 3, 2010, President Bashir directly contradicted these statements by his own government's ministers, in an uncharacteristic public display of disagreement within the ruling party. In the same speech, Bashir reiterated his responsibility to the protect Southerners in the North, stressing that citizens from Southern Sudan will not have their right to food, jobs, and medical care compromised no matter what the outcome of the January 2011 referendum might be.[48] Bashir's explicit promise to protect Southern IDPs living in the North suggests he was conversant with the language of RtoP and aware of the norm's requirements. The vote did take place on time and with no attempts to manipulate the results; more than 98 percent of the voters supported independence. As we write this chapter, there is no evidence of any retaliatory actions being taken against IDPs around Khartoum or elsewhere in the North. However, on May 25, 2011 Bashir reversed his position on the legal status of

[47] *Sudanese President Pledges to Protect Southerners Living in the North*, Sudan Tribune, Oct. 4, 2010.

[48] *Id.*

the southern IDP's in a belligerent speech in which he said they would be asked to leave the north immediately following independence.

It is premature at this writing to know what the Sudanese government will actually do in practice (there is a large gap historically between their rhetoric and their actions) to protect (or not) the Southern displaced around Khartoum. But President Bashir's earlier public statements do give limited hope that the RtoP doctrine may actually be having some effect on the conversation and public statements of Northern Sudanese politicians, which would be a welcome development indeed, particularly if it is matched with actions.

His comments, however, may be more a tacit acknowledgement of the increasingly precarious position of his own government than an endorsement of the newest principle of international humanitarian law. As we write, a Northern Sudanese coalition may be forming to force true democratic reforms on the Bashir government and in the absence of this, to attempt to overthrow the government. The traditional political parties in Khartoum appear to be forming a coalition with the Darfur rebels, militias of the Nuba mountains, Abyei, Blue Nile Province, and the Beja tribe all of whom had been allies of the South. President Bashir's endorsement of RtoP may be more related to this internal pressure than any fear of international censure or intervention. Or perhaps he and his party apparatus may need the protection of RtoP themselves if they are deposed from power and their enemies take over. Only time will tell.

12 Burma (Myanmar)

Paulo Sérgio Pinheiro and
Meghan Barron

Since the adoption of the RtoP doctrine at the UN World Summit in 2005, there has been much debate regarding its potential application to the human-rights situation in Burma.[1] This chapter examines the first serious attempted application of RtoP to Burma in response to the Burmese military regime's refusal to accept international assistance in the wake of the country's worst natural disaster on record, and explores the reasons for the effort's ultimate failure in the UN Security Council. It then analyzes the doctrine's potential application to Burma more broadly in light of the pattern of ongoing systematic human-rights abuse perpetrated by the military regime. Finally, the chapter considers whether future attempts to apply RtoP to the situation in Burma may serve a useful purpose given that Burma is already on the UN Security Council's permanent agenda.

I. A BRIEF HISTORY OF BURMA

Colonized by the British in the late nineteenth century, Burma was originally a collection of territories ruled by different ethnic groups—including the Arakanese, Burman, Chin, Kachin, Karen, Karenni, Mon, Rohinga, Shan, and Wa peoples, among

[1] In this report, the country examined is referred to as Burma rather than Myanmar. This is the form preferred by the leaders of Burma's democracy movement, the legitimate winners of the 1990 elections. They do not accept that the unelected military regime has the right to change the official name of the country to suit its own ends. Burma (Myanmar) is also the form used by Oxford University Press, which follows the British government's appellation for the country.

others—distinctions which continue to have importance today.[2] Although Japan took control of the country during World War II, in 1945 independence leader General Aung San and the Anti-Fascist People's Freedom League combined with the British to successfully liberate the country. With an eye toward independence and eventually with British consent, the general convinced many of Burma's various ethnic groups to collaborate in outlining a "principle of equality" between the majority Burman people and the other nationalities and create a framework for a federal union that would include political autonomy for ethnic nationality areas.[3]

When General Aung San and other leaders of the Burmese independence movement were assassinated months later, Burma continued along a rocky path toward independence, eventually establishing a fragile parliamentary democracy in 1948.[4] However, tensions quickly emerged throughout the government and within the country as a whole, especially among the various ethnic nationalities. Some military leaders began to question the new democratic system and the restrictions placed on its authority.[5] In 1962, the military, led by General Ne Win, staged a coup that not only overthrew the fragile democratic government but also marked the beginning of Burma's current era of political repression and widespread and systematic human-rights abuses.[6]

Ruling as a dictator until 1988, General Ne Win created a single party system and acted to violently suppress the opposition to his rule posed by armed ethnic nationality groups. These groups had initially emerged in response to concerns regarding the loss of their autonomy under the previous democratic government and some had formed armies designed to combat the Burmese military. Following the 1962 coup, many of these armed ethnic minority groups turned their focus toward combating the tyranny of the new military regime and nine combined to form the National Democratic Front (NDF) coalition, including the Karen National Union, the Kachin Independence Organization, and the New Mon State Party to address issues related to territory, federalism, and the right of secession.[7]

In response to the opposition presented by the armed resistance groups, General Ne Win implemented the devastating "Four Cuts" policy designed to isolate these groups from critical resources, including money, food, information, and reinforcements. This policy resulted in the deaths of thousands of civilians and the widespread destruction of villages and crops.[8] Urban areas were not spared from repression either: the military regime repeatedly cracked down on student-led revolts, most notably in August 1988, when the army attacked hundreds of thousands of students gathered in a peaceful

[2] *See* International Human Rights Clinic at Harvard Law School, Crimes in Burma 7–8 (2009), *available at* http://www.law.harvard.edu/programs/hrp/documents/Crimes-in-Burma.pdf [hereinafter Crimes in Burma].

[3] *Id.* at 8–9.

[4] DLA Piper Rudnick Gray Cary, Threat to the Peace: A Call for the UN Security Council to Act in Burma 8 (2005) [hereinafter Threat to the Peace].

[5] *See* Crimes in Burma, *supra* note 2, at 9–10.

[6] *See* Threat to the Peace, *supra* note 4, at 8–9. These abuses have been primarily directed toward ethnic minorities associated with armed resistance in rural areas and political opposition groups, often students, concentrated in urban areas.

[7] Crimes in Burma, *supra* note 2, at 8–11.

[8] *Id.* at 10.

demonstration in support of democracy, killing thousands, including women and children.[9]

In the face of the military regime's policy of harsh political repression, democratic opposition to the military's rule continued to grow and, when the regime held multi-party elections in 1990, the National League for Democracy, led by General Aung San's daughter, Daw Aung San Suu Kyi, won over 80 percent of the parliamentary seats.[10] However, the military refused to permit the transfer of power and instead focused its efforts on increasing the suppression of pro-democracy advocates, including Daw Aung San Suu Kyi. In 1992, Burma's current ruler, General Than Shwe, assumed power and continued the military's policy of repression and abuse.[11] Since this time, the regime has entered into ceasefire agreements with some of the approximately 20 armed ethnic opposition groups, although in many cases, the ceasefires have either subsequently broken down or have led to the creation of additional armed resistance groups. In other cases, the military has simply ignored the ceasefires in its quest to stamp out opposition through any means possible.

In 2003, in what was likely an attempt to relieve building international pressure, the military regime announced a "roadmap to democracy" consisting of seven steps, including reconvening the national convention to draft a new constitution, holding a national referendum to approve the new constitution, holding parliamentary elections, and forming a new government.[12] The military regime then developed a constitution—without consultation with civil society or any groups outside the military elite—which, among other things, provides for the structural entrenchment of the military, separates the military from civilian justice, and provides immunity for human-rights violations committed by the military.[13] A national referendum on the constitution was announced for May 10, 2008, with national elections scheduled for 2010.

A week prior to the 2008 referendum, a large swath of the country was hit by Cyclone Nargis, Burma's worst natural disaster on record. Despite the devastation caused by the storm—more than 130,000 people killed or missing and millions homeless—and international calls for the government to focus on disaster relief rather than political concerns, the military regime forged ahead with the referendum vote.[14] With much of the population still reeling from the effects of the cyclone, the military regime nevertheless claimed that 26 out of 27 million eligible voters cast ballots, with 92.4 percent of them voting in favor of the new constitution.[15]

On November 7, 2010, the military regime held national elections, later claiming a sweeping victory of over 76 percent.[16] However, most of the main opposition parties

[9] Threat to the Peace, *supra* note 4, at 9.

[10] *Id.* at 10.

[11] *Id.* at 12.

[12] Threat to the Peace, *supra* note 4, at 15.

[13] International Center for Transitional Justice, Impunity Prolonged: Burma and its 2008 Constitution, 31 (Sept. 2009) [hereinafter Impunity Prolonged].

[14] *Id.* at 8.

[15] *Id.* at 9.

[16] Thar Gyi, *USDP Wins 76.5 Percent of Vote*, The Irrawaddy, Nov. 18, 2010, *available at* http://www.irrawaddy.org/election/news/612-usdp-wins-765-percent-of-vote.html.

had opted not to participate given the election's certain fraudulent outcome and many in the international community immediately condemned the vote.[17]

II. AN OVERVIEW OF BURMA'S HUMAN RIGHTS ABUSES

Despite extreme difficulties related to documentation, it is widely acknowledged by the international community that the Burmese military regime has a long history of perpetrating, and continues to perpetrate, severe, widespread, and systematic human-rights abuses against its people. These atrocities, which in some cases rise to the level of both crimes against humanity and war crimes under the Rome Statute,[18] are the manifestation of a state policy designed to suppress opposition forces and are typically committed with complete impunity.

A. Destruction of Ethnic-Minority Villages and Forcible Transfer of Populations

It has been reported that, between 1996 and 2007, the military destroyed or forcibly displaced as many as 3,600 villages in predominantly ethnic minority areas, often through burning or landmines. Nearly half a million people are believed to have been internally displaced by the regime's continuing campaign to suppress and eliminate support for armed resistance in ethnic minority areas. This systematic campaign of destruction has led to mass refugee flows across the border, with an estimated total of three million people forced to migrate both within and outside of Burma.[19] In addition to the military's destruction of villages as a tool to combat support for resistance forces and to control ethnic minority populations, forced displacement has also been caused by the imposition of forced labor, land confiscation, agricultural production quotas, and restrictions on access to fields and markets by the regime.[20] In chronicling the details surrounding the destruction of numerous villages and the forced displacement of hundreds of thousands of individuals in ethnic minority areas, UN Special Rapporteur on the situation of human rights in Myanmar ("Special Rapporteur on Myanmar") Paulo Sérgio Pinheiro noted in 2006 that "the current government strategy of targeting civilians in the course of its military operations represents a willful abrogation of its responsibility under international humanitarian law."[21]

[17] *Western States Dismiss Burma's Election,* THE BBC, Nov. 8, 2010, *at* http://www.bbc.co.uk/news/world-asia-pacific-11707294.

[18] Although Burma has never ratified the Rome Statute, it serves as a useful representation of widely accepted principles of international criminal law and as an important basis for the commonly understood definitions and elements of the international crimes addressed in this chapter.

[19] International Federation for Human Rights, INTERNATIONAL CRIMES COMMITTED IN BURMA: THE URGENT NEED FOR A COMMISSION OF INQUIRY, 15 (2009) [hereinafter FIDH].

[20] *Id.* at 16.

[21] The Special Rapporteur on the situation of human rights in Myanmar, *Question of the Violation of Human Rights and Fundamental Freedoms in Any Part of the World: Situation of Human Rights in Myanmar, Report of the Special Rapporteur, Paulo Sérgio Pinheiro,* E/CN.4/2006/34, Feb. 7, 2006, at ¶ 106 [Hereinafter Myanmar Special Rapporteur February 2006].

B. Murder and Torture

Both as part of, and aside from, the destruction of villages in ethnic minority areas, UN and other human-rights bodies have documented the continued use of extrajudicial killings as a means to instill fear within the civilian population.[22] As one example, a 2008 report by Amnesty International chronicles the killing of detainees, the implementation of a "shoot on sight" policy whereby civilians found outside a village during certain times were immediately shot without question, and killings as collective punishment within the Karen State.[23] The military has also perpetrated murder to repress political demonstrations, such as during the Depayin Massacre in 2003 when thousands of military-backed thugs attacked Daw Aung San Suu Kyi and her supporters at a rally, reportedly killing 10 and causing the disappearance of 108 people,[24] as well as during the more recent crackdown surrounding the September 2007 Saffron Revolution, which caused the death of at least 31 people.[25] In the aftermath of the Saffron Revolution, Special Rapporteur on Myanmar Pinheiro chronicled the use of live ammunition, rubber bullets, tear gas and smoke grenades, bamboo and wooden sticks, rubber batons and catapults, resulting in both the killing and severe injury of monks and men, women, and children. In doing so, he found that the decision by government security forces to shoot to kill and to severely beat protestors to death "constitutes an arbitrary detention of life and violates the right to life, as the lethal force used was unnecessary and disproportionate."[26]

In addition to outright murder, the military systematically utilizes torture as a means to both discourage civilian support for, and as retaliation for sympathizing with, resistance groups, as well as to gain information about their activities. Torture, both physical and psychological, is also routinely used in the interrogation of political prisoners.[27] In 2007, the Special Rapporteur on Myanmar found that political activists and human rights defenders have been "particularly targeted during their arrest, interrogation and detention" while reports have confirmed "appalling detention conditions which fail to meet international standards of the treatment of prisoners and in fact constitute cruel, inhuman and degrading treatment prohibited under international law."[28]

C. Detention of Political Prisoners

The UN estimates that as many as 2,100 political prisoners of conscience are currently being detained in Burma, including monks, students, teachers, lawyers, journalists,

[22] FIDH, *supra* note 19, at 10.

[23] *Id.*

[24] *Id.* at 11.

[25] *Id.* at 13.

[26] The Special Rapporteur on the situation of human rights in Myanmar, *Human Rights Situations that Require the Council's Attention, Report of the Special Rapporteur on the situation of human rights in Myanmar, Paulo Sérgio Pinheiro, mandated by resolution S-5/1 adopted by the Human Rights Council at its fifth Special Session*, A/HRC/6/14, Dec. 7, 2007, at ¶ 30 [hereinafter Myanmar Special Rapporteur December 2007].

[27] FIDH, *supra* note 19, at 18–19.

[28] Myanmar Special Rapporteur December 2007, *supra* note 26, at ¶ 57.

and political activists.[29] These prisoners have often been subject to arbitrary arrest and are without the protection of an independent judiciary or principled rule of law. For example, in the aftermath of the 2007 Saffron Revolution, the Special Rapporteur on Myanmar chronicled the cases of numerous individuals arrested without warrant and detained in unknown locations. Furthermore, many detainees were never brought before the courts or were denied legal representation.[30] A 2009 report from the Special Rapporteur on Myanmar further stated that "from September to December 2008, some 300 prisoners of conscience were given harsh sentences, including a dozen detainees who were given 65-year prison sentences."[31] In addition to the magnitude of the sentences for political opposition, the regime imposes inhumane conditions within the prison system, often transferring prisoners to facilities far from their families and systematically denying prisoners access to adequate medical care.[32]

D. Sexual Violence

The military regularly employs rape and other forms of sexual violence as a tool of repression in ethnic minority areas. In his 2006 annual report, the Special Rapporteur on Torture described this rape as "widespread and systematic violence against women and girls . . . as punishment for allegedly supporting ethnic armed groups. The authorities sanction violence against women and girls committed by military officers, including torture, *inter alia*, as a means of terrorizing and subjugating the population . . . "[33] In fact, rape often occurs in conjunction with other human-rights abuses, such as torture, executions and forced relocation.

Although notoriously difficult to document given underreporting tendencies, a 2002 report documented 43 cases of rape among Karen, Karenni, Mon, Tavoyan, and Shan women and girls, and concluded that the more soldiers were in an area, the

[29] The Special Rapporteur on the situation of human rights in Myanmar, *Human Rights Situations that Require the Council's Attention, Progress report of the Special Rapporteur on the situation of human rights in Myanmar, Tomás Ojea Quintana*, A/HRC/13/48, Mar. 10, 2010, at ¶ 15 [hereinafter Myanmar Special Rapporteur March 2010].

[30] The Special Rapporteur on the situation of human rights in Myanmar, *Human Rights Situations that Require the Council's Attention, Report of the Special Rapporteur on the situation of human rights in Myanmar, Paulo Sérgio Pinheiro, mandated by resolution 6/33 of the Human Rights Council*, A/HRC/7/24, Mar. 7, 2008, at ¶¶ 26–28 [hereinafter Myanmar Special Rapporteur March 2008].

[31] The Special Rapporteur on the situation of human rights in Myanmar, *Human Rights Situations that Require the Council's Attention, Report of the Special Rapporteur on the situation of human rights in Myanmar, Tomás Ojea Quintana*, A/HRC/10/19, Mar. 11, 2009, at ¶ 3 [hereinafter Myanmar Special Rapporteur March 2009].

[32] *See* The Special Rapporteur on the situation of human rights in Myanmar, *Report of the Special Rapporteur on the situation of human rights in Myanmar, Tomás Ojea Quintana, delivered to the General Assembly*, A/63/341, Sept. 5, 2008, at ¶ 42 [hereinafter Myanmar Special Rapporteur September 2008].

[33] The Special Rapporteur on torture and other cruel, inhuman or degrading treatment or punishment, *Civil and Political Rights, Including the Questions of Torture and Detention, Torture and Other Cruel, Inhuman or Degrading Treatment or Punishment, Report of the Special Rapporteur, Manfred Nowak, Addendum, Summary of information, including individual cases, transmitted to Governments and replies received*, E/CN.4/2006/6/Add.1, Mar. 21, 2006, at ¶ 166 [hereinafter Torture Rapporteur 2006].

more rape occurred, perpetrated with impunity by both officers and lower-ranking soldiers.[34] In addition, from 2002 to 2007, women's organizations from Burma documented nearly 400 incidents of rape and other forms of sexual violence committed by the military between 1998 and 2006, affecting nearly 900 victims, almost 130 of whom were younger than 18.[35] In addition, a 2006 report by the Special Rapporteur on Myanmar detailed hundreds of reports of sexual violence between 1996 and 2006, stating that the "failure to investigate, prosecute and punish those responsible for rape and sexual violence has contributed to an environment conducive to the perpetuation of violence against women and girls in Myanmar."[36] A 2008 report further documented sexual abuse against children, including boys.[37]

III. CYCLONE NARGIS AND FRANCE'S FAILED ATTEMPT TO INVOKE RTOP

On May 2, 2008, a Category 4 storm on the Saffir-Simpson Hurricane Scale named Cyclone Nargis made landfall in Burma's Irrawaddy Delta causing massive destruction and widespread devastation. Entire villages were destroyed by both wind and flooding, leaving people without food, potable water, shelter, and basic medical supplies.[38] The international community reacted immediately, offering both supplies and skilled relief workers. Yet, despite the fact that it was doing little itself to aid its suffering people, the Burmese military regime was slow to accept outside assistance and, when it finally did, moved to actively thwart efforts to reach the most vulnerable. As a result of the storm and the military regime's response, it is believed that over 140,000 people lost their lives and at least 3.4 million people were directly affected.[39]

A. Military Regime's Reaction to the Cyclone and Ensuing Disaster

As the cyclone approached, the military regime failed to provide its people with any form of advanced warning, despite the fact it had been warned about the storm by international meteorologists. In the immediate aftermath of the storm, the regime provided little if any assistance with respect to food, clean water and shelter, instead leaving relief efforts to the survivors themselves and local Burmese groups that sprang up in the wake of the cyclone. International supplies, medical personnel, and disaster assessment teams from the region idled for days, waiting for the military regime to

[34] FIDH, *supra* note 19, at 20.

[35] Impunity Prolonged, *supra* note 13, at 15.

[36] The Special Rapporteur on the situation of human rights in Myanmar, *Report of the Special Rapporteur on the situation of human rights in Myanmar, Paulo Sérgio Pinheiro*, A/61/369, Sept. 21, 2006, at ¶ 30 [hereinafter Myanmar Special Rapporteur September 2006].

[37] FIDH, *supra* note 19, at 20.

[38] Emergency Assistance Team (Burma) and Johns Hopkins Bloomberg School of Public Health Center for Public Health and Human Rights, After the Storm: Voices from the Delta, 24–26 (2d ed. 2009) [hereinafter After the Storm].

[39] *Id.* at 13.

grant them entry visas (which, even when ultimately issued, did not allow for access to the most hard-hit regions), while French, British, and American navy vessels laden with thousands of tons of supplies, medics, and relief workers sat for weeks waiting for permission, which never came, to enter the country.[40]

To make matters worse, as aid did begin to mobilize, the military regime actively interfered with its delivery by imposing travel restrictions, checkpoints, and entry fees to limit access to the hardest-hit Delta region.[41] Relief supplies, including those from the international community, were routinely confiscated and never distributed to survivors, and the military further obstructed the flow of aid by intimidating and even arresting relief workers.[42] In addition, the military regime made accurate needs assessment nearly impossible by restricting the flow of information from the Delta and actively downplaying both the extent of the destruction and the needs of those affected.[43] The military regime also forbid the independent collection of data, complicating coordination between relief groups, and restricted the use of communications equipment.

In addition, the military discriminated in the distribution of those resources it did allow to circulate, blocking aid to areas with significant ethnic and religious minority populations, namely the Karen, while ensuring that assistance flowed instead to those with political or personal connections to the military.[44] It also interfered with the establishment of temporary relief centers operated by private groups by forcibly transferring victims from the private centers to military regime-designated relief shelters, then forcing them to return to their destroyed villages without any of the basic necessities for survival and rebuilding.[45] In some cases, the military confiscated land and villages either to rebuild military facilities or for personal gain and further conscripted survivors, including children, as free labor for the reconstruction phase.[46] When the military did provide actual aid-cultivating equipment that was often dysfunctional, poor-quality seeds, and very little fertilizer, it did so as interest-bearing debt payable after the first harvest.[47]

B. The International Community's Response to the Military Regime's Inaction and the Failed RtoP Invocation

In the days and weeks after Cyclone Nargis made landfall, the international community pleaded with Burma's military regime to allow it to help the country's suffering people. After trying to reach General Than Shwe by phone for 11 days, UN Secretary-General Ban Ki-moon finally had to travel to Burma to meet personally with the military regime's leader and exact a guarantee three weeks after the

[40] *Id.* at 52–53.
[41] *Id.* at 7, 29.
[42] *Id.* at 8, 32–33.
[43] *Id.* at 34.
[44] *Id.* at 40.
[45] *Id.* at 41–42.
[46] *Id.* at 41–47.
[47] Asia Society, Current Realities and Future Possibilities in Burma/Myanmar: Options for U.S. Policy, 42 (2010) [hereinafter Asia Society Task Force Report].

cyclone that aid-workers of all nationalities would be given permission to enter the country.[48]

As it became increasingly clear in the early days that the military intended to leave its people to fend for themselves at best, and to actively seek to enhance their suffering at worst, the French Foreign Minister, Bernard Kouchner, threatened to invoke the RtoP doctrine to ensure the delivery of aid from a French naval ship off the Burmese coast, with or without the military regime's consent. However, his remarks, and his apparent conflation of RtoP with the doctrine of humanitarian intervention, touched off a firestorm of controversy that ultimately doomed any potential successful application of the doctrine.

On May 7, Foreign Minister Kouchner first broached the issue publicly by telling reporters at a press conference that he was attempting to invoke RtoP at the UN in order to obtain a resolution imposing the delivery of aid on the military regime.[49] The next day, he issued a sweeping communiqué calling on the military regime to allow the international community access to deliver aid and stating that RtoP is designed to "address human suffering, wherever it may be. . . ."[50] Then, on May 13, Kouchner discussed the potential for an airdrop of supplies and broadly likened RtoP to the "right to intervene."[51]

In each of these three statements, the Foreign Minister went beyond the accepted scope of the RtoP doctrine as outlined in the 2005 World Summit Outcome Document, namely, that "each individual State has the responsibility to protect its populations from genocide, war crimes, ethnic cleansing and crimes against humanity" and similarly, "the international community, through the United Nations, also has the responsibility to use appropriate diplomatic, humanitarian and other peaceful means . . . to help protect populations from genocide, war crimes, ethnic cleansing and crimes against humanity." Instead of cogently linking the Burmese military regime's refusal

[48] After the Storm, *supra* note 38, at 53.

[49] Seth Mydans, *Myanmar Faces Pressure to Allow Major Aid Effort*, New York Times, May 8, 2008 ("We are seeing at the United Nations if we can't implement the 'responsibility to protect' given that food, boats and relief teams are there, and obtain a UN resolution which authorizes the delivery (of aid) and imposes this on the Burmese government.")

[50] Embassy of France in the United Kingdom, *Burma–Communiqué issued by M. Bernard Kouchner, Minister of Foreign and European Affairs (excerpts)*, May 8, 2008, *available at* http://www.ambafrance-uk.org/Bernard-Kouchner-on-Burma-disaster.html ("I again solemnly appeal to the Burmese authorities to lift all restrictions on the distribution of the aid by the most efficient channels. The specialized United Nations agencies and NGOs must immediately be able to have access to the victims. To address human suffering, wherever it may be, is precisely what is meant by the 'responsibility to protect' accepted by the international community and initiated by France. This is what we wanted to remind the United Nations Security Council.")

[51] Embassy of France in the United Kingdom, *Burma–Joint press briefing given by M. Bernard Kouchner, Minister of Foreign and European Affairs, and M. Jean-Pierre Jouyet, Minister of State responsible for European Affairs (excerpts)* (May 13, 2008), *at* http://www.ambafrance-uk.org/Bernard-Kouchner-on-Burma-disaster.html ("the Americans talked about an airdrop if the Burmese authorities delayed opening up the country, if we couldn't get access to the victims. It's a concern which is not just legitimate but has taken international law a step further and which, after being called the duty to intervene, then the right to intervene, is known as the 'responsibility to protect' and was formulated and accepted, virtually unanimously by the United Nations General Assembly. . .")

to accept aid to one of the enumerated crimes that triggers the application of RtoP, Kouchner instead equated RtoP to the right to intervene to provide humanitarian assistance—a related, but separate and even more controversial doctrine—and further appeared to advocate for the doctrine's application in any situation in which human suffering might be present.

In our opinion, Foreign Minister Kouchner did not strengthen his case for the application of RtoP when, in an article published in *Le Monde* on May 20, he distinguished the doctrine from the "principle of freedom of access to the victims of 'natural disasters and other similar emergency situations' to help relief organizations (Resolution 42–131 of December 8, 1988)." After quoting from the 2005 World Summit Outcome Document outlining RtoP, Kouchner then wrote "the legal principle was given a new designation: 'the responsibility to protect.' But it was envisaged only for armed conflicts. And the Burmese situation isn't one. So it is not covered by this text. Consequently, the obligations incumbent on the [m]ilitary regime leaders are based only on the requirement to respect human rights and Resolution 42–131."[52] Having seemingly dismissed the appropriateness of applying RtoP to the ongoing crisis, Kouchner went on to assert that the "[t]he Security Council can decide to intervene to force the passage of the humanitarian assistance, as it has done in the recent past."

Whether due to his approach in raising the doctrine, or because of the doctrine's controversial nature, the fact remains that the Foreign Minister's attempt to invoke RtoP was ultimately unsuccessful. Edward C. Luck, the Secretary General's Special Advisor to RtoP responded that "it would be a misapplication of Responsibility to Protect principles to apply them at this point to the unfolding tragedy in Myanmar." China, Vietnam, South Africa, and the Russian Federation dismissed the invocation outright, while the UN permanent representatives from both China and Indonesia warned against politicizing the issue of aid, with the Indonesian Ambassador saying, "the last thing we would want is to give a political spin to the technical realities and the situation on the ground."[53] British permanent representative John Sawers responded that RtoP "relates to acts of genocide, war crimes, crimes against humanity and so forth, rather than responses to natural disasters . . . I think what's most important is to keep the focus on the needs of the ... upwards of millions of people affected by this appalling disaster."[54] And UN Under-Secretary-General for Humanitarian Affairs and Emergency Relief Coordinator John Holmes declared that Kouchner's approach was "unhelpful" and could be seen as "confrontational."[55]

However, although promptly dismissed by key UN actors as an inappropriate case for the invocation of RtoP, it is not immediately evident that the situation in Burma in the months following Cyclone Nargis did not properly qualify for the application of the doctrine given the Burmese military regime's actions in response to the devastation.

[52] Embassy of France in the United Kingdom, *Burma–Article by M. Bernard Kouchner, Minister of Foreign and European Affairs*, Le Monde, May 20, 2008 *available at* http://www.ambafrance-uk.org/Bernard-Kouchner-on-Burma-disaster.html.

[53] Louis Charbonneau, *China, Indonesia Reject France's Myanmar Push*, Reuters, May 8, 2008.

[54] *Id.*

[55] *Id.*

The most common argument against Foreign Minister Kouchner's suggested invocation of the RtoP doctrine was that the doctrine was not intended to justify intervention in the aftermath of a natural disaster.[56] While even Kouchner appeared to concede that point,[57] the construction of the doctrine does not, on its face, preclude such an application should a government's actions following a natural disaster rise to level of genocide, war crimes, ethnic cleansing, or crimes against humanity. Instead, the doctrine is most likely silent on the issue because there has never been an instance where a country has not only refused foreign assistance, but has actively sought to deny its people relief in the same manner as the Burmese military regime did in 2008.

Indeed, in the two months following the storm, there might have been an appropriate opportunity to invoke the doctrine. As defined in the Rome Statute, one of the enumerated crimes against humanity and customary international law is "other inhumane acts of a similar character intentionally causing great suffering, or serious injury to body or to mental or physical health."[58] As increasing evidence emerged in the weeks following Cyclone Nargis of the Burmese military regime's widespread and systematic efforts not only to discourage, but to actively thwart the effective provision of fundamental and lifesaving supplies, medical care, and assistance to specific segments of its population, some advocated for the invocation of the doctrine based on the grounds that the military regime's actions rose to the level of "other inhumane acts."[59] However, the manner in which France and the Foreign Minister had already unsuccessfully raised the issue made a successful international invocation of the doctrine untenable at this point. Then, as time went on and the Burmese military regime gradually began to lift some restrictions on aid entering the country, public perception of the immediacy of the moment decreased and the window of opportunity for trying to apply RtoP closed.

Furthermore, even in situations that do fall within the generally understood meaning of the doctrine, RtoP has only served as the primary justification for intervention in two cases—Kenya and Libya—and neither had occurred prior to the crisis surrounding Cyclone Nargis.[60] Consequently, the international community's reluctance to invoke the untested and controversial doctrine in imperfect circumstances was unsurprising. Thus, the inherent challenges of applying RtoP generally, when combined with the imprecise manner in which the issue was raised within the UN, ensured Kouchner's failure. Unfortunately, the Foreign Minister's attempt to force the issue within the Security Council effectively poisoned the atmosphere for any real international intervention in Burma following the disaster—and consequently, none occurred. Furthermore, Kouchner's actions created the perception that the RtoP doctrine had been raised, and ultimately failed, with respect to Burma. Unfortunately, this may serve to complicate any future attempts to apply the doctrine to the country—

[56] Asia-Pacific Centre for the Responsibility to Protect, Cyclone Nargis and the Responsibility to Protect, 2–3 (May 16, 2008).

[57] *Article by M. Bernard Kouchner, supra* note 52.

[58] Rome Statute of the International Criminal Court, A/CONF.183/9, Jan. 16, 2002, at art. 7 §1(k) [hereinafter Rome Statute].

[59] Gareth Evans, *Facing Up to Our Responsibilities*, The Guardian, May 12, 2008; Chris Beyrer & Jared Genser, *Burma's Next Wave of Dying*, Boston Globe, May 21, 2008.

[60] Desmond Tutu, *Taking the Responsibility to Protect*, New York Times, Nov. 9, 2008.

either in a similar situation to Cyclone Nargis, or more broadly as a response to the Burmese military regime's perpetration of ongoing crimes against humanity and war crimes against its people.

IV. BURMA'S CRIMES AGAINST HUMANITY AND WAR CRIMES

As described in Section II, the Burmese military regime has undertaken a campaign of horrific abuse against its people for over half a century. Given this history, and aside from the experience at the UN in the aftermath of Cyclone Nargis, there has been much debate over the viability of applying RtoP to the general situation in Burma since the doctrine's adoption. While the likelihood of the international community intervening in Burma on the basis of the doctrine is uncertain—perhaps even more so now following Nargis—it is nevertheless instructive to examine not only the appropriateness of a potential application of RtoP to Burma, but also whether a future attempt to invoke the doctrine on behalf of the Burmese people would be useful from a practical perspective.

A. Overview of Crimes against Humanity and War Crimes

Article 7 § 1 of the Rome Statute defines a "crime against humanity" with respect to the following acts: "murder; extermination; enslavement; deportation or forcible transfer of population; imprisonment or other severe deprivation of physical liberty in violation of fundamental rules of international law; torture; rape, sexual slavery, enforced prostitution, forced pregnancy, enforced sterilization, or any other form of sexual violence of comparable gravity; persecution against any identifiable group or collectivity on political, racial, national, ethnic, cultural, religious, gender . . . or other grounds that are universally recognized as impermissible under international law . . .; enforced disappearance of persons; the crime of apartheid; and other inhumane acts of a similar character intentionally causing great suffering, or serious injury to body or to mental or physical health."[61]

For one of the crimes listed under Article 7 to rise to the level of a crime against humanity, the action must have been undertaken as part of a "widespread or systematic attack directed against the civilian population with knowledge of the attack."[62] "Widespread" generally indicates a large-scale attack with numerous victims, while a "systematic" attack is highly organized, often as part of a pattern or methodical plan.[63] The Rome Statute defines an "attack" as a course of conduct involving multiple commissions of prohibited acts[64] and a "civilian population" is any relatively large body of victims, thus excluding isolated crimes against individuals.[65]

Article 8 § 2 of the Rome Statute addresses war crimes committed within the context of an internal conflict such as in Burma, defining them as any of a number of acts "committed against persons taking no active part in the hostilities" including violence

[61] Rome Statute, *supra* note 58, at art. 7 § 1.

[62] *Id.*

[63] *See* Crimes in Burma, *supra* note 2, at 26.

[64] Rome Statute, *supra* note 58, at art. 7(2)(a).

[65] *See* Crimes in Burma, *supra* note 2, at 26.

to life and persons, in particular murder of all kinds, mutilation, cruel treatment and torture; committing outrages against personal dignity, in particular humiliating and degrading treatment; taking hostages; and the passing of sentences and the carrying out of executions without previous judgment pronounced by a regularly constituted court. In addition, the definition of war crimes also includes, among other crimes, intentionally directing attacks against the civilian population as such or against individuals not taking direct part in hostilities; pillaging a town or place, even when taken by assault; committing rape or other sexual crimes as described in Article 7; conscripting or enlisting children under the age of fifteen years into armed forces or groups or using them to participate actively in hostilities; ordering the displacement of the civilian population for reasons related to the conflict; and destroying or seizing the property of an adversary unless such destruction or seizure is demanded by the necessities of the conflict.[66]

Unlike crimes against humanity, war crimes do not need to fit within a larger pattern of attack and therefore can be individual, or isolated, incidents. However, also unlike crimes against humanity, war crimes must be committed within the context of an armed conflict, either international or, as in the case of Burma, internal.[67]

Although both crimes against humanity and war crimes have distinct elements, it is possible for a crime to fall within both categories. Such is the case with many of the atrocities committed in Burma—while some abuses constitute either crimes against humanity or war crimes, too many qualify as both.

B. Forcible Transfer of Population

As defined by Article 7 of the Rome Statute, the deportation or forcible transfer of population means the forced displacement of persons by expulsion or other coercive acts from the area in which they are lawfully present, without grounds permitted under international law.[68] Similarly, the list of war crimes under Article 8 includes ordering the displacement of a civilian population when the order is not justified by the security of the civilians or military necessity.[69]

As described previously, between 1996 and 2007, as many as 3,600 villages were destroyed or forcibly displaced by the military's forces, often through burning or landmines. Nearly half a million people, particularly in ethnic minority areas, are believed to have been internally displaced as a result of deliberate military actions against civilians to discourage support for resistance groups and to consolidate control over ethnic land and resources. A 2006 report by one co-author, then Special Rapporteur on Human Rights in Myanmar, cited the destruction of villages as "the direct result of systematic human-rights abuse and the conflict between the military authorities and non-State armed groups."[70] That same year, six UN rapporteurs and experts highlighted the targeting of civilians by the military and stated that the operations

[66] Rome Statute, *supra* note 58, at art. 8(2).

[67] *See* CRIMES IN BURMA, *supra* note 2, at 27.

[68] Rome Statute, *supra* note 58, at art. 7 § 2(d).

[69] *Id.* at art. 8 § 2(e)(viii).

[70] Myanmar Special Rapporteur February 2006, *supra* note 21, at ¶ 99.

had resulted in the forcible displacement of thousands of ethnic nationality villagers.[71]

Given these circumstances, the military regime's actions likely rise to the level of both crimes against humanity and war crimes. With respect to crimes against humanity, UN officials have repeatedly identified ethnic minority civilians in Burma as the victims of forced displacement due to the military regime's policy of destroying villages, as well as the military's practice of actively forcing people from their homes. Furthermore, the Special Rapporteur on Myanmar has described this displacement as widespread and part of a deliberate strategy[72] by the military designed to combat armed resistance forces. Regarding war crimes, reports agree that there is a situation of armed conflict in eastern Burma and that the crimes perpetrated in those areas are both related to this conflict and directed by the military against civilians.[73]

C. Murder and Torture

Both UN and other human-rights bodies have repeatedly documented the continued use of murder by the military regime as a means to instill fear in the civilian population, with reports outlining the killing of civilian detainees, the prosecution of the military's shoot on sight policy against civilians in certain areas, and the murder of civilians as an instrument of collective punishment for the actions of armed resistance forces.[74] The military has also repeatedly killed civilians as a means to repress political activity and peaceful demonstrations, as evidenced by the brutal attack on Daw Aung San Suu Kyi and her followers in Depayin and the attacks during the Saffron Revolution.[75]

Like forced displacement, the military regime's perpetration of murder constitutes both crimes against humanity and war crimes. With respect to crimes against humanity, UN reports have described the military's policy of killing civilians as both widespread and systematic,[76] placing particular emphasis on the deliberate shoot on sight policy as executed in the ethnic minority areas of eastern Burma.[77] Because these widespread and systematic attacks are specifically directed toward civilians and are committed in the context of an internal conflict, they also fulfill the requirements necessary to constitute war crimes.

The military also routinely utilizes torture—defined in the Rome Statute as the intentional infliction of severe pain or suffering, whether physical or mental, upon a

[71] Crimes in Burma, *supra* note 2, at 43.

[72] Myanmar Special Rapporteur September 2006, *supra* note 36, at ¶ 47.

[73] *See* Crimes in Burma, *supra* note 2, at 49.

[74] FIDH, *supra* note 19, at 10.

[75] *Id.*

[76] The Special Rapporteur on the situation of human rights in Myanmar, *Human Rights Situations that Require the Council's Attention, Report of the Special Rapporteur on the situation of human rights in Myanmar, Paulo Sérgio Pinheiro*,A/HRC/7/18, Mar. 7, 2008, at ¶ 58–59.

[77] *See* The Special Rapporteur on extrajudicial, summary or arbitrary executions, *Implementation of General Assembly Resolution 60/251 of March 15, 2006 Entitled "Human Rights Council," Report of the Special Rapporteur on extrajudicial, summary or arbitrary executions, Addendum, Summary of cases transmitted to Government and replies received*, A/HRC/4/20/Add.1, Mar. 12, 2007, at 223.

person in the custody or under the control of the accused[78]—as a means to both discourage civilian support for, and as retaliation for sympathizing with, resistance groups, as well as to gain information about their activities.[79] In addition, torture, both physical and psychological is routinely used in the interrogation of political prisoners. In 2010, the Special Rapporteur on Myanmar referenced reports of prisoners of conscience being subject to torture as part of the interrogation process and later while in detention. Citing testimonies from prisoners of conscience who were released, the Special Rapporteur states that "there are systematic patterns of abuse and torture of detainees. Various forms of physical, psychological and sexual abuse by officials have been detailed in reports. Deliberately poor prison conditions combined with purposeful medical negligence cause extreme suffering of prisoners."[80]

With repeated references to the torture of civilians, including prisoners of conscience, as a widespread and/or systematic tool deliberately employed to quash and punish political opposition, UN documentation supports the conclusion that the military's use of torture rises to the level of crimes against humanity. And, as with both forced displacement and murder, the context of internal conflict in which these crimes are committed leads to the conclusion that the military's use of torture further constitutes war crimes.

D. Rape and Sexual Violence

In 2006, the Special Rapporteur on Torture and Other Cruel, Inhuman or Degrading Treatment or Punishment reported that "women and girls are subjected to violence by soldiers, especially sexual violence, as 'punishment' for allegedly supporting ethnic armed groups. The authorities sanction violence against women and girls committed by military officers, *inter alia*, as a means of terrorizing and subjugating the population, particularly those in the Shan state."[81] Despite the chronic underreporting of these crimes, UN actors have described the use of sexual violence against civilian women and girls in Burma, particularly those in ethnic minority areas, as widespread and systematic[82] and human-rights groups have documented hundreds of incidents of rape and other forms of sexual violence committed with impunity by the military.[83]

In describing the repeated attacks against women and girls as widespread, systematic, and part of a deliberate strategy encouraged by military leaders as punishment of civilians connected to the military's fight against domestic resistance groups, UN actors have indicated that these acts rise to the level of both crimes against humanity and war crimes.

[78] Rome Statute, *supra* note 58, at art. 7 § 2(e).

[79] *See* Amnesty International, *Crimes Against Humanity in Eastern Myanmar*, Jun. 2008, at 13.

[80] Myanmar Special Rapporteur March 2010, *supra* note 29, at ¶ 33.

[81] Torture Rapporteur 2006, *supra* note 33, at ¶ 166.

[82] The Special Rapporteur on the situation of human rights in Myanmar, *Human Rights Situations that Require the Council's Attention, Report of the Special Rapporteur on the situation of human rights in Myanmar, Paulo Sérgio Pinheiro*, A/HRC/7/18, Mar. 7, 2008, at ¶¶ 58–59.

[83] Impunity Prolonged, *supra* note 13, at 15.

E. Detention of Political Prisoners

Article 7 of the Rome Statute includes the crime against humanity of "imprisonment or other severe deprivation of physical liberty in violation of fundamental rules of international law."[84] As noted previously, the UN estimates that more than 2,100 political prisoners are being held in Burma and the Special Rapporteur on Myanmar has called for the release of all prisoners of conscience without delay and without conditions.[85]

The military regime regularly pursues a deliberate policy of subjecting civilian political dissenters to arbitrary arrest and no independent judiciary exists to guarantee their right to a fair trial, virtually ensuring the imposition of unduly long prison sentences. As the Special Rapporteur on Myanmar recently noted, "in reality, many trials are conducted behind closed doors within prison compounds, without legal representation, without the presence or knowledge of their family members, without proof of evidence or with defective evidence, and pursuant to arbitrary decisions of the judges."[86] Furthermore, the sentences for prisoners of conscience handed down by the military regime are often overwhelmingly harsh: as cited by the Special Rapporteur, "from September to December 2008, some 300 prisoners of conscience were given harsh sentences, including a dozen detainees who were given 65-year prison sentences."[87] The March 2010 Asia Society Task Force Report further cites sentences exceeding 100 years based on charges under "archaic provisions in the Penal Code criminalizing free expression, peaceful demonstrations, and the formation of organizations not sanctioned by the government."[88] In addition to the magnitude of the sentences for political opposition, the regime imposes inhumane conditions within the prison system, often deliberately transferring prisoners to facilities far from their families and systematically denying prisoners access to adequate medical care.[89] In light of these factors, particularly the widespread practice of arbitrary arrest and lack of due process at the hands of an independent judiciary, international human-rights groups have argued that the prisoners of conscience being held in Burma are victims of crimes against humanity.[90]

V. APPLYING RTOP TO BURMA: A WORTHWHILE PURSUIT?

Given that both UN actors and international human-rights groups have repeatedly acknowledged that the severe human-rights violations perpetrated by the Burmese military regime against its people constitute mass atrocities under international law, it is unsurprising that some have argued for RtoP's application to the situation in Burma in an attempt to alleviate the suffering of the Burmese people. In fact, the Special Rapporteur on Myanmar alluded to the application of the doctrine in his September

[84] Rome Statute, *supra* note 58, at art. 7 § 1(e).
[85] Myanmar Special Rapporteur March 2010, *supra* note 29, at ¶ 15.
[86] *Id.* at ¶ 36.
[87] Myanmar Special Rapporteur March 2009, *supra* note 31, at ¶ 3.
[88] Asia Society Task Force Report, *supra* note 47, at 20.
[89] Myanmar Special Rapporteur September 2008, *supra* note 32, at ¶ 41–42.
[90] *See* FIDH, *supra* note 19, at 17–18.

2010 report, stating, "[i]t is foremost the responsibility of the Government of Myanmar to address the problem of gross and systematic human-rights violations by all parties, and to end impunity . . . If the Government fails to assume this responsibility, then the responsibility falls to the international community."[91] However, while such an application might be technically appropriate, it is unlikely that an invocation of the doctrine at this point would ultimately benefit the Burmese people in a meaningful way.

First, the internal conditions in Burma are such that any international intervention under the banner of RtoP is unlikely to provide lasting security or protection for the civilian population. It is true that the purpose of an RtoP intervention is preventative and, as such, is designed to stop ongoing abuse and alleviate civilian suffering. However, as long as the existing political stalemate between the military regime and opposition forces in Burma continues, the root cause of the military regime's actions will remain unaddressed and any attempt by a divided international community to intervene on behalf of the Burmese people, particularly those in the ethnic minority areas where much of the abuse is concentrated, will be without lasting effect. In other words, while it is important to protect the civilian population, there cannot be a true resolution while the current political standoff endures. Consequently, an international response that seeks to break the existing stalemate is more likely to have the long-term and lasting effects needed most by the Burmese people.

Second, in 2006, the UN Security Council moved to address the human-rights situation in Burma by placing it on its permanent agenda.[92] In the years that have followed, the Security Council has continued to monitor developments in Burma, noting on a number of occasions that it remains "seized of the matter."[93] That said, continued opposition by China and the Russian Federation to meaningful action on Burma human-rights issues has led to a stalemate within the Council that has stymied attempts by other Council members to actively address the continuing atrocities. In 2007, China and the Russian Federation vetoed a Security Council resolution condemning the Burmese military regime and, in the midst of the military's crackdown on peaceful protestors during the Saffron Revolution, China again blocked Security Council action, describing the violence as an "internal situation" and stating that "sanctions are not helpful."[94] Given the stance of both China and the Russian Federation on the issue of human rights in Burma and the fact that any meaningful RtoP action on Burma would likely need to emanate from the Security Council, it is improbable that invoking the doctrine would prompt any additional action on the issue from the Council. Worse, invocation of the doctrine could exacerbate the

[91] The Special Rapporteur on the situation of human rights in Myanmar, *Report of the Special Rapporteur on the situation of human rights in Myanmar, Tomás Ojea Quintana, delivered to the General Assembly*, A/65/368, Sept. 15, 2010, at ¶¶ 67–68.

[92] Press Release, United Nations Security Council, *Security Council, In Procedural Action, Votes to Include Human Rights Situation in Myanmar on Its Agenda*, SC/8832, Sept. 15, 2006.

[93] *See* Press Release, United Nations Security Council, *Security Council Notes Myanmar's Announcement on May Referendum Elections in 2010; Underlines Need for Inclusive Process, Participation of all Actors*, SC/9320, May 2, 2008.

[94] Julian Borger, Ian MacKinnon, Ian Black, *As Burmese Troops Open Fire at Monks, China and Russia Block Global Sanctions*, The Guardian, Sept. 27, 2007.

existing political divisions among the members of the Security Council, thus dampening still further its collective appetite to address the Burma case.

Finally, in addition to the political obstacles—both internally within Burma and externally within the Security Council—the RtoP doctrine itself remains largely untested. It has only served as the primary justification for intervention twice and a lack of clarity continues to exist around when, and in what circumstances, its application is appropriate. Furthermore, the failed invocation of the doctrine in the aftermath of Cyclone Nargis may have poisoned the water when it comes to the international community's willingness to consider the doctrine's application to Burma in particular.

Consequently, while many have asserted that the international community could appropriately apply the RtoP doctrine to the situation in Burma, it is considerably less clear that the doctrine should be invoked. Assuming circumstances remain unchanged both inside Burma and in the international community, an invocation of RtoP appears politically doomed unless there is a high-profile outbreak of mass atrocities which provides the opportunity to give the situation a fresh look. An unsuccessful attempt to apply RtoP to such a complex and controversial case as Burma could impact the international community's willingness to embrace the doctrine more broadly, thus hindering its application in a future situation where an effective and successful outcome might otherwise be more likely.

VI. CONCLUSION

The conclusion that the best course of action for the time being may to be to refrain from advocating the application of the RtoP doctrine to Burma despite its technical applicability does not lessen the severity of the atrocities being perpetrated against the Burmese people, nor does it undermine the need for the international community to engage more actively on the human-rights situation in the country. Instead, it only indicates the importance of the international community coalescing around an alternative course of action.

Multiple Special Rapporteurs on the situation of human rights in Myanmar have repeatedly documented the military's many abuses in reports to the UN General Assembly, the prior UN Commission on Human Rights, and the present UN Human Rights Council. The work of the Special Rapporteurs is just one of the UN's efforts in Burma—since 1990, UN representatives have visited the country more than 40 times in an attempt to facilitate dialogue and promote human rights. They have exhausted all domestic and diplomatic remedies without achieving human-rights protection and national reconciliation. And, while the UN General Assembly and the UN Human Rights Council have passed over 35 resolutions regarding Myanmar, the UN Security Council has yet to pass a single one.[95]

It is clear that the attacks in Burma will continue, just as it is equally evident that the country's domestic legal system will not punish those perpetrating crimes against ethnic minorities. While we do not believe that invoking RtoP at this point is the most effective manner of addressing the issues at hand, we are convinced that it is time for the United Nations to take a more logical next step consistent with the

[95] Paulo Sérgio Pinheiro, *End Burma's System of Impunity*, New York Times, May 28, 2009.

recommendation of the current Special Rapporteur on Human Rights in Myanmar—establishing a Commission of Inquiry into crimes against humanity and impunity in Burma.[96] The Security Council, for instance, has taken similar steps with regard to Rwanda, Bosnia, and Darfur and the situation in Burma is equally as critical. Consequently, the international community must send a strong message to the military regime that it will not tolerate its violation of international humanitarian law and that impunity must end.[97]

The creation of a Commission of Inquiry would accomplish three important goals. First, it could make the military regime accountable for its crimes with the prospect down the road of a Security Council referral to the International Criminal Court—a task that would not be possible under the preventative RtoP doctrine. Second, it would address the widespread culture of impunity in Burma. Third, it has the potential to deter future crimes against humanity in the country.

For two decades, ethnic minorities in Burma have suffered while diplomatic efforts have failed to bear fruit. The time has come for the UN to act more decisively.[98] Similarly, the international community should continue to urge the military regime to address the issue of the atrocities as part of a UN-facilitated dialogue on national reconciliation designed to bring the hostilities between the regime, National League for Democracy, and ethnic groups to a close and restore peace and stability for the Burmese people. This must include releasing the more than 2,100 political prisoners currently being held by the regime and instituting a halt to the military's practice of brutalizing civilians with impunity in areas populated by ethnic opposition forces. Although the regime took an important first step in releasing Daw Aung San Suu Kyi from house arrest in November 2010, this action should not be interpreted as signaling a change in the regime's policies, particularly in light of the fact that her release came mere days after the regime consolidated its political control through fraudulent national elections widely condemned by the international community.

Given the alternatives available, a decision not to invoke RtoP to address the human-rights situation in Burma should not impede the ability of the international community to act now to prevent future atrocities and move toward addressing past crimes and abuses against the Burmese people. Instead, such a decision takes into account the current political realities both on the ground in Burma and within the Security Council and acknowledges the uncertainty that remains within the international community regarding the doctrine itself. In addition, a decision not to invoke the doctrine at this point does not preclude its use in a future crisis or if any of the aforementioned barriers to its practical application should change.

[96] *See, e.g.*, *Quintana Recommends UN War Crimes Commission on Burma*, The Irrawaddy, Mar. 11, 2010.

[97] Thirteen states have already announced their support for this approach, including Australia, Canada, Czech Republic, Estonia, France, Hungary, Ireland, Lithuania, Netherlands, New Zealand, Slovakia, the United Kingdom, and the United States. Burma Campaign UK, Burma Briefing No. 7: Support for a UN Commission of Inquiry, (Jan. 2011).

[98] Pinheiro, *supra* note 95.

13 Kenya

Meredith Preston-McGhie and
Serena Sharma

In late December 2007 and the early days of January 2008, eruptions of violence around Kenya brought the world's attention firmly on the disputed presidential election, held on December 27, 2007. Within days, the country was paralyzed. Transport links had been cut, trade stopped, violence intensified, and the government was unable to function. Equally rapidly, leaders from the continent and abroad flew in to press for a resolution to the crisis and an end to the violence. Ultimately these efforts coalesced around the African Union (AU)-mandated Panel of Eminent African Personalities, under the chairmanship of Kofi Annan, former Secretary-General of the United Nations. After a month and a half of intense mediation, a unity government was established and agreement was reached on a range of governance reforms, aimed at addressing the underlying causes of the post-election violence.

The crisis in Kenya has been highlighted as a unique case of political action and a successful example of mediation as a crisis prevention response. It is regarded as an illustration of African leadership in concert with strong international backing, and a model of rapid and decisive action to forestall an escalation of violence and political upheaval in the country. Most importantly, the situation in Kenya has been hailed as the first example of international intervention under the banner of the Responsibility to Protect—a great success story in the challenging path of the movement for this issue internationally. As Gareth Evans, among others, has argued: "Kenya in early 2008 is probably the best example we have so far of the responsibility to protect appearing to play an important energising role in stimulating an effective response . . . ."[1] As plans advance to translate the rhetorical commitment of RtoP into a global reality, the

[1] Gareth Evans, *Response to Reviews*, 2.3 Global Responsibility to Protect 326 (2010).

identification of an RtoP success story has lent weight to its implementation within the UN system and beyond.

In terms of whether Kenya met the threshold for RtoP, this is a simpler case than many others. As has been confirmed by the International Criminal Court (ICC), the nature and magnitude of violence in the aftermath of the elections, coupled with the prospect of escalation, amounted to crimes against humanity, as laid out in the RtoP-related provisions of the 2005 World Summit Outcome Document.[2] Notwithstanding the seeming clarity around whether this case meets the conceptual provisions of RtoP, the idealization of the political intervention in Kenya's post-election crisis as a simple case of RtoP does not offer an adequately critical or nuanced view of either the international community's response to the Kenya crisis, or the role of RtoP in such circumstances. When considering the broader context in which the Kenya crisis emerged, we argue that many other positive factors converged to push for intervention in the Kenya case.

Contrary to other cases that have exhibited an equal, if not greater magnitude of violence, the prospect of Kenya collapsing was not something international or regional actors were prepared to countenance. Underlying the concern for Kenyan citizens were a set of material considerations brought on by the importance of Kenya in the region, not to mention its stabilizing role on the continent. To the extent that these broader interests sparked the unprecedented global and regional response to the crisis, external actors involved in forestalling the violence were never forced to confront what has been—and continues to be—the fundamental challenge for advancing RtoP: how to galvanize international action in cases of little strategic importance, or where intervention would otherwise be opposed. Owing to the fortuitous convergence between humanitarian concerns and strategic interests, the resolution of the Kenya crisis is not so much a test case for RtoP, but an "ideal case" that has been, and will continue to be, exceptionally difficult to replicate in future cases.

The primary question this case raises is whether or not the atrocities and the state's failure to prevent them and protect their citizens was the overriding motive for the attention and action of the international community. This analysis endeavors to provide a more critical view of the added-value of RtoP in the Kenya case, and of the case of Kenya for RtoP more generally. Has the international response to this crisis improved the capacity of Kenya to prevent such atrocities in the future, and do the lessons from Kenya offer us insights into making RtoP more generally effective in supporting the prevention of such atrocities in the future?

This chapter will proceed in four sections. The first section will establish the background context of the crisis through a consideration of Kenya's strategic role. This will be followed by an overview of the 2007 elections and their aftermath. The third section will analyze regional and global responses to the crisis. The fourth and final section will assess the influence of the Kenya crisis on the broader development of RtoP.

[2] According to paragraph 138 of the 2005 World Summit Outcome Document: "Each individual State has the responsibility to protect its populations from genocide, war crimes, ethnic cleansing, and crimes against humanity. This responsibility entails the prevention of such crimes, including their incitement, through appropriate and necessary means."

I. THE CONTEXT OF THE CRISIS: KENYA'S STRATEGIC ROLE

Kenya has long been viewed as an important stabilizing influence in the East Africa and the Horn of Africa. Kenya hosts one of three United Nations (UN) headquarters as well as large diplomatic missions, and is a hub for humanitarian activities for the Horn as well as Central Africa. The country also hosts a number of regional hubs for international media agencies.[3]

From a security standpoint, Kenya is an important partner on counter terrorism in the region.[4] This has included large-scale partnerships between the United States and Kenya with training and equipping of Kenyan police under programs such as the Anti-Terrorism Assistance, which helped to establish a Kenyan Anti-Terrorism Police Unit between 2003 and 2005. Kenya is a key regional player in the Combined Joint Task Force-Horn of Africa (CJTF-HOA), including acting as a base for military operations in Somalia.[5] Strategic security partnerships are not limited to the U.S.-Kenya relationship. Kenya hosts two of the three main United Kingdom deployments on the African continent, with the British Peace Support Team (BPST) and the British Army Training Unit Kenya (BATUK).[6] The UK Ministry of Defense spends an average of $6.3 million on training of Kenyan security services.[7]

Economically, Kenya is a strategic gateway to Central Africa, with 80 percent of Uganda's and almost all of Rwanda's imported goods passing through Kenya.[8] Kenya has large-scale economic ties globally, as a major exporter of commodities such as tea and cut flowers. Globally, its tourism industry has contributed to a reputation for quintessential "African" safari experiences, and is Kenya's largest source of foreign capital.

By the beginning of January, rapid escalation of violence had shut down large parts of the Kenyan economy, the government was deadlocked with the opposition refusing to recognize President Mwai Kibaki, and the tensions were continuing to rise. Given the strategic importance of Kenya in Africa, it is unsurprising that the region and the world took notice when the country appeared to be, as Prime Minister Raila Odinga has since commented, "dithering on the brink of total collapse"[9] in late 2007 and early 2008. There is consensus around Kenya's significance in the region, as well as globally, by the external players who sought to address the crisis. This sets Kenya apart from other such conflicts, and offers an additional point of convergence for the international community—not a grouping prone to cohesion—to coalesce as quickly as they

[3] Interview with Amb. Adam Wood, Nov. 5, 2010.

[4] Daniel Volman, *US Military Activities in Kenya*, African Security Research Project, Jan. 2008, *available at* http://concernedafricascholars.org/african-security-research-project/?p=3.

[5] *Id.*

[6] UK Ministry of Defence Official Public Information, *available at* http://www.army.mod.uk/operations-deployments/overseas-deployments/932.aspx.

[7] Xan Rice, *MoD Threatens to Halt Training of Kenyan Military Over Claims of Rights Abuses*, The Guardian, Jul. 29, 2008, *available at* http://www.guardian.co.uk/world/2008/jul/29/kenya.military.

[8] Mary Kimani, *East Africa Feels Blows of Kenyan Crisis*, 22 Africa Renewal 3 (2008), *available at* http://www.un.org/ecosocdev/geninfo/afrec/vol22no1/221-kenyan-crisis.html.

[9] Prime Minister Raila Odinga, *Kenya Two Years On*, Hosted by the African Union and Kofi Annan Foundation, Nairobi, Dec. 2, 2010.

did to respond to the instability. As noted by the Regional Parliamentarians from the Great Lakes in their Fact-Finding Report in January 2008:

An unstable Kenya has far reaching impacts on the region. . . . Any animated conflicts would spiral in the region. So far, we have experienced the disruption of transport valves and humanitarian activities geared for Southern Sudan, Somalia and the Great Lakes region. Given the instability in Somalia, the ongoing US-led operations against Al Qaeda and the influx of small arms both in the region, state collapse in Kenya is likely to affect not only Kenya, but the entire African continent . . . Economic resistance, especially the blocking of roads, burning of transport instruments and actions directed at the Rail artery is increasingly asphyxiating not only the state but the region also.[10]

Advocacy around the Kenyan crisis, even by those promoting consideration of the Kenya intervention through the lens of the RtoP, cite the importance of the regional impacts of the crisis.[11]

Compounding the strategic importance of Kenya in the region is the popular perception of the country as "the most stable and economically developed nation in volatile East Africa."[12] One could argue that this perception contributed to a certain amount of complacency prior to the 2007 polls despite clear warning signs. Much of this complacency was nurtured by the view of Kenya as a success story. The economic growth and opening of space under President Kibaki's administration from 2002 cemented the view that Kenya was, despite continually low rankings on corruption indices, on the right track.[13] Many in the international community had watched with trepidation during both the 2002 elections and the 2005 constitutional referendum, and felt that key democratic milestones had been overcome. However, important signals and warnings were present, including increases in hate speech in the months leading up to the elections. The Africa Peer Review Mechanism (APRM) for Kenya's 2006 Report (and the fact that the findings were broadly ignored)[14] offers important insight into Kenya prior to the 2007 elections:

In spite of Kenya's many strengths that have succeeded in containing outbreaks of mass violence, the country still exhibits many of the factors that have been markers of civil strife elsewhere, such as strong ethnic divisions, polarized political issues, political manipulation, rampant violence, socio-economic disparities, deepening levels of poverty and endemic corruption.[15]

[10] *Regional Parliamentarians Fact Finding Mission to Kenya on the Post Election Violence, 13–January 21, 2008,* The Amani Forum–Great Lakes Parliamentary Forum on Peace, Jan. 2008, at 22.

[11] Mary Kimani, *East Africa Feels Blows of Kenyan Crisis,* 22 Africa Renewal 3, *available at* http://www.un.org/ecosocdev/geninfo/afrec/vol22no1/221-kenyan-crisis.html (2008), referencing Don Steinberg and John Holmes.

[12] *How They Stopped the Killing,* Stanley Foundation, Jun. 2009, *available at* http://www.stanleyfoundation.org/resources.cfm?id=596&article=1.

[13] *Messing with Success,* Newsweek, Dec. 22, 2007, *available at* http://www.newsweek.com/2007/12/22/messing-with-success.html.

[14] Bronwen Manby, *Was the APRM process in Kenya a Waste of Time? Lessons that Should be Learned for the Future,* Open Society Institute, African Governance Monitoring and Advocacy Project (Apr. 2008), at 1–4.

[15] *Africa Peer Review Mechanism Country Report for Kenya* (2006), at 14.

Reluctance to act earlier, even in response to some of the more obviously problematic developments prior to the elections—for instance, President Mwai Kibaki's controversial re-engineering of the Election Commission of Kenya-was influenced by Kenya's strategic importance. There was an instinct, prior to the onset of the violence, to support the status quo.

II. THE 2007 GENERAL ELECTIONS: HOW THE CRISIS UNFOLDED

The 2007 elections in Kenya marked an important milestone in its history. Perhaps the most competitive elections that had ever been held, in many ways this offered a greater test to Kenya's cohesion and democracy than the 2002 elections, which were so closely watched internationally. In the lead up to the elections, polling had the incumbent and Party of National Unity (PNU) candidate, President Mwai Kibaki and his main opposition candidate of the Orange Democratic Movement (ODM), Raila Odinga within 1 percent of one another. Both the local polling, Steadman Group, and Gallup polls in November 2007 put the two candidates at 44 percent for Raila Odinga to 43 percent for President Kibaki, and 45 percent for Raila Odinga to 42 percent for President Kibaki, respectively.[16] Importantly, these polls also highlighted the ethnic bases of support for both candidates.[17] While messages in the campaign period had signaled the potential for violence, the diplomatic community in Nairobi, in the region and abroad, did not anticipate the level of violence that erupted in the post-election period.

Polling took place peacefully the December 27, 2007. As the results began to come in the next day, Raila Odinga's lead against President Kibaki grew. In the late afternoon, this margin began to narrow, and continued to narrow. President Kibaki pulled ahead, and after some confusion and controversy at the headquarters of the National Elections Commission, Kibaki was quickly declared the winner and was sworn in approximately 45 minutes later. At this point, the ODM, was already crying foul, and the first pockets of unrest erupted.[18]

Over the course of two months, an estimated 1,300 Kenyans lost their lives as violence swept across the country. The bloodshed that ensued was by no means homogeneous, but varied from region to region throughout the eight-week period. While some of the violence emerged spontaneously in response to the fraudulent elections, there were also signs of organized violence against PNU supporters, and evidence of incitement, particularly in the Rift Valley. Kenya's vernacular FM stations

[16] *Raila Drops in New Ratings*, DAILY NATION, Nov. 9, 2007 (citing Steadman Group polling); *New Poll Predicts Close Race*, DAILY NATION (citing Gallup polling data), Nov, 21, 2007.

[17] Joel Barkan, *Too Close to Call: Why Kibaki Might Lose the 2007 Kenyan Election*, Center for Strategic and International Studies, Nov. 2010, *available at* http://csis.org/blog/too-close-call-why-kibaki-might-lose-2007-kenyan-election.

[18] *See, e.g., Kibaki Declared Winner, Sworn in*, THE STANDARD, Dec. 30, 2007, *available at* http://allafrica.com/stories/200712300027.html; *Kenya Election Update: Violence Erupts After Kibaki Declared Winner; Odinga Makes Counter-claim of Victory*, PANAFRICAN NEWS WIRE, Dec. 31, 2007, *available at* http://panafricannews.blogspot.com/2007/12/kenya-election-update-violence-erupts.html.

played a key role in inciting ethnic hatred both during the electoral campaign, and in its aftermath. The government's banning of public demonstrations also contributed to the escalation of tensions, as it removed a legitimate outlet for citizens to voice their frustrations, and led to excessive use of force by police.[19] Nairobi's Uhuru Park became contested territory, as security services enforced deadly shoot-to-kill policies. Instances of police brutality were, however, most severe within the slum areas in and around the capital. As the violence continued unabated, individuals engaged in reprisal killings in certain parts of the country, namely Naivasha and Nakuru. Prominent local militia, including the notorious Mungiki sect, operated in full force during this time; while ordinary civilians used the absence of law and order to riot, loot, and rape.[20]

Among the associated consequences of violence were widespread levels of internal displacement. Estimates suggest up to 500,000 people were forced to flee from their homes, in a country already suffering from massive displacement. Initial figures indicate that the first wave of displacements were largely among Kikuyus in the North Rift, Western and Nyanza provinces, followed by a second wave of displacements associated with the opposition.[21] As the country continued to spiral downward, the prospect of civil war appeared imminent. As George Wachira ironically observed: "A country with a record for brokering peace in the region was now headed for total collapse."[22] Raila Odinga refused to accept the results of the elections, while President Kibaki claimed victory. With the violence escalating, trade links were being severed. The road from the coastal port of Mombasa to Nairobi and into the interior of Kenya and on to central Africa (Uganda, Rwanda, north to Southern Sudan) was impassable. Humanitarian operations in southern Sudan had to curb activities.[23] Train services were also cut. Looting and destruction of property was widespread.

A Kenya Private Sector Alliance estimate in mid-January warned of 400,000 lost jobs by mid-2008 if the violence was not curbed. It estimated business losses as high as $3.4 billion for this same period. Fears over the economic losses were so great that the private sector became one of the most prominent voices calling for calm and a resolution to the conflict.[24]

Overall, the paralysis and chaos in Kenya in early January 2008 resulted in fuel shortages in Kigali, Juba, and Kampala, and shortages and increase in prices of goods throughout the region.[25] On January 1, reports of a doubling of fuel prices in Kampala

[19] *See, e.g.*, Human Rights Watch, *Ballots to Bullets: Organized Political Violence and Kenya's Crisis of Governance*, Mar. 16, 2008.

[20] Kenya National Human Rights Commission, On the Brink of the Precipice: A Human Rights Account of the 2007 Post Election Crisis (Aug. 15, 2008).

[21] *Kenya in Crisis*, International Crisis Group, Africa Report # 137, Feb. 21, 2008.

[22] George Wachira, *Citizens in Action: Making Peace in the Post-Election Crisis in Kenya–2008*, Nairobi Peace Initiative–Africa, Jan. 2010, at 4.

[23] AMREF UK, *Post election Violence Leads to Humanitarian Emergency in Kenya*, Jan. 7, 2008, *available at* http://uk.amref.org/news/postelection-violence-leads-to-humanitarian-emergency-in-kenya/.

[24] Tom Maliti, *Kenya: The Long Dark Night for Business*, Africa Report, Nov. 21, 2008, *available at* http//www.theafricareport.com/archives2/business/3278865-kenya-the-long-dark-night-for-business.html. *See also*, *Post-election violence causes regional fallout: post-election violence in Kenya has already left its mark on East African business*, Africa Rev. of Bus. & Tech., Apr. 2008, *available at* http://www.entrepreneur.com/tradejournals/article/179048794.html.

[25] *Violence Threatens Kenya's Economy*, BBC News, Jan. 2, 2008.

as a result of the violence.[26] By January 4, fuel rationing was in effect in Kigali and maize prices had risen by 30 percent in Kampala.[27] As the violence continued, fears throughout the region grew that the situation would become even more grave, if the violence in Kenya was not addressed. The media reported 300 deaths on January 4 and 100,000 displaced.[28] By January 8, casualty and displacement estimates were rising, with assessments of 500–1,000 deaths, and 250,000 displaced.[29]

Leaders reacted swiftly. Within a week, Bishop Desmond Tutu, former Presidents Joachim Chissano of Mozambique, Quett Masire of Botswana, and Kenneth Kaunda of Zambia traveled to Kenya to implore the leaders to end the stalemate. International efforts were also being made—both through telephone calls and pressure, as well as visits from leaders such as the U.S. Assistant Secretary of State for African Affairs, Jendayi Frazer. While these visits did not result in an immediate success of either halting the violence or bringing the parties to the table for dialogue, they laid the foundation for the visit of the African Union Chairman, Ghanaian President John Kufour, who visited on January 8, 2008.[30] Though President Kufour's visit did not outwardly yield any agreement, in private, he secured agreement from both President Kibaki and Raila Odinga to mediation by a panel under the leadership of Kofi Annan.[31]

Kofi Annan arrived in Kenya as the Chairman of the AU Panel of Eminent African Personalities (AU Panel) on January 22, accompanied by former Mozambican politician Graça Machel and former Tanzanian President Benjamin Mkapa. The Kenya National Dialogue and Reconciliation (KNDR) process was officially launched on January 24. With the violence continuing, the mediation team was able to work quickly to agree on an agenda. The AU Panel, under Kofi Annan's leadership, took a proactive role in demonstrating rapid progress between the two sides, including a public handshake between President Kibaki and Raila Odinga on January 24, and then the signing of the first two agreements on the February 1 and 4, respectively. Kofi Annan and other members of the AU Panel held regular press conferences and met with a range of civil society and other interest groups, again with a view of restoring public confidence in a negotiated solution, and hence to stem the violence.

[26] *Fuel Shortage Worsens Countrywide*, New Vision, Uganda, Jan. 1, 2008, *available at* http://allafrica.com/stories/200801020053.html.

[27] *Kenyan Violence Hits Fuel Supply*, BBC News, at http://news.bbc.co.uk/2/hi/7171439.stm.

[28] Steve Bloomfield, *Kenya rivals edge their way towards talks after poll violence*, The Independent, Jan. 4, 2007, at http://www.independent.co.uk/news/world/africa/kenya-rivals-edge-their-way-towards-talks-after-poll-violence-768085.html.

[29] *See* Joel Barkan, *Breaking the Stalemate in Kenya*, Center for International and Strategic Studies, Jan. 8, 2008; *Violence, Political Unrest Continues in Kenya*, National Public Radio, Jan. 8, 2008, *available at* http://www.npr.org/templates/story/story.php?storyId=17932927.

[30] For an overview from the African Union, *see Information Note on the Situation in Kenya and the Evolution of the Mediation Efforts*, African Union Peace and Security Council, 115th Meeting, Mar. 14, 2008.

[31] The exact structure and terms of reference of the Panel of Eminent African Personalities were not agreed during President Kufuor's visit. These were developed and agreed in early discussions between the Panel and the parties upon the Panel's arrival in Kenya.

Resolving the political crisis took a considerable amount of time and was the most pressing issue with respect to stemming the violence. The parties reviewed the elections themselves, and considered the various possible mechanisms to address the impasse. Through these deliberations, it became clear that the only workable solution was a political compromise—the "truth" of the elections was beyond reach. However, the nature of a transitional political arrangement, and the type of power sharing this would entail, was highly contested between the two parties. Two weeks of the talks focused on getting the parties to the place where it was agreed that a compromise arrangement was needed—and therefore the details of such an arrangement could be discussed. These details proved even more challenging. Ultimately, when the negotiating teams failed to come to a sustainable agreement on a coalition government, Kofi Annan adjourned the talks and reverted directly to the principals—President Mwai Kibaki and Raila Odinga.[32] This resulted in the power-sharing agreement signed on February 28, at which time the mediation moved on to the last element—discussing long-term reform issues. This is considered in more detail in the following section.

The scale of the violence and the rapidity with which it escalated played an important role in galvanizing regional and international actors to press for the establishment of a mediation process. There was a tangible feeling that Kenya was sliding towards a situation from which it would not be able to quickly emerge. The fact that Kenya could not be allowed to fail given its importance in the region compounded this urgency.

A final aspect, which is important to consider when reviewing the previous history of election violence in Kenya (and the lack of international reaction in the past)[33] is the fact that political forces in the country were deadlocked. The PNU-controlled government of President Mwai Kibaki would continue to be deadlocked against an ODM controlled Parliament, led by Raila Odinga. Governing in this situation was not possible. Further, it became clear that the government was not capable of quelling the violence as it continued to spread.

With respect to the scale of the governance crisis in which Kenya found itself and the broad regional repercussions as outlined above, it is instructive to review some of the other instances of political violence in Kenya's past. In 1984, during what has become commonly known as the Wagalla massacre—over 1,000 people were killed by government security forces in the Wajir District in northeast Kenya—one of the most concentrated and painful in Kenya's history.[34] Similarly, the number of deaths and displacements around both the 1992 and 1997 elections eerily mirror the 2008 statistics. However, despite these severely violent episodes in Kenya's past, none of

[32] For more detail on the trajectory of the talks, *see* Elisabeth Lindenmayer & Josie Lianna Kaye, *A Choice for Peace? The Story of 41 Days of Mediation in Kenya*, International Peace Institute (2009).

[33] Violence in 1991–1994, and after the 1997 elections in Kenya left more than 1,500 people dead and more than 300,000 people displaced, many of whom remained displaced at the time of the 2007 elections. For more detail, *see On the Brink of the Precipice: a Human Rights Account of the Post Election Violence in Kenya*, Kenya Human Rights Commission (2008); *Killing the Vote: State-Sponsored Violence and Flawed Elections in Kenya*, Kenya Human Rights Commission (1998).

[34] *See, e.g., How the Wagalla Massacre Occurred and its Extent*, Daily Nation, Feb. 5, 2010.

these events triggered the kind of international response seen in 2008.[35] The next section will explore in greater detail the response from regional and international actors.

III. REGIONAL AND INTERNATIONAL RESPONSE TO THE CRISIS

Within the structure of the mediation process, identifying means of halting the violence and addressing the humanitarian consequences were at the forefront of the agenda. The agenda for the KNDR, agreed at the first round of meetings with the two negotiating teams, included four items:

1. Immediate action to stop violence and restore fundamental rights and liberties
2. Immediate measures to address the humanitarian crisis, promote reconciliation, healing, and restoration
3. How to overcome the current political crisis
4. Long-term issues and solutions[36]

While RtoP was not referenced in the agenda, the first two items represent the focus of the process on responding to and preventing further violence. Tellingly, these two agenda items proved relatively easy to conclude agreements on, drawing consensus from the two parties, which led to the rapid signing of agreements on February 1 and 5, respectively. In contrast, the following several weeks of intense negotiations around Agenda Item Three, "How to Overcome the Current Political Crisis," was, as explained above, considerably more fraught and took the bulk of the international attention during the mediation process.

While the international community was engaged and supportive of the mediation from the outset—including public and private statements and behind-the-scenes pressure on the two parties, it was during the very political phase of the negotiations on the political settlement/power-sharing that interventions at a higher level in support of the Kofi Annan-led Panel were sought. These included the visits of U.S. Secretary of State Condoleezza Rice, and the interventions by Tanzanian President Jakaya Kikwete. Breaking the deadlock around the establishment of the Grand Coalition Government was strongly supported by the presence of Tanzanian President Jakaya Kikwete. His involvement had two important aspects. First, he applied pressure as a sitting East African head of state serving as Chairman of the African Union, underlining the importance of this agreement to the overall stability of the region as a whole. And second, he highlighted the successful model of Tanzania, with a strong president and a Prime Minister with broad powers. This model was an important aspect for consideration by the principals when finalizing the agreement around the responsibilities of the Prime Minister within the Grand Coalition.

International actions also exerted pressure on the parties to reach a political solution. Leaked information about plans by Western governments to impose travel bans

[35] Stephen Brown, *Donor Responses to the 2008 Crisis in Kenya: Finally Getting it Right?*, 27 J. Cont. Afr. Stud. 3 (Jul. 2009).

[36] *Kenya National Dialogue and Reconciliation Annotated Agenda*, Feb. 1, 2008, *available at* http://www.dialoguekenya.org.

and sanctions on individuals seen to be obstacles to a peaceful resolution of the crisis loomed large in the press during the two weeks of negotiation on Agenda Item Three.[37] The approach taken by the AU Panel throughout the process was also significant in terms of focusing on increasing public confidence in the process, demonstrating progress, and speaking directly to the Kenyan people to help to calm tensions and reduce the pace of the violence. Kofi Annan and the other members of the Panel held regular press conferences, and visited the affected areas of the country. While the role of some media in inflaming the violence during the crisis was a negative factor, the role of the mainstream press in covering the mediation process was very positive and important for getting public confidence that a solution could be sought through dialogue.[38]

On February 28, an agreement was reached on a Grand Coalition Government, under which Raila Odinga became Prime Minister while Mwai Kibaki retained the presidency. This deal had an important impact in stemming the violence. As Lord Mark Malloch Brown recalls, "the violence stopped because people saw light at the end of the tunnel: politicians were talking about a deal that would avoid real losers, e.g., where minorities in particular regions would be driven permanently out of their homes."[39]

The mediation then moved on to addressing long-term issues and solutions—essentially the issues that were viewed as being the root causes of the post-election violence. While the power-sharing deal helped stem the violence, the long-term issues and solutions were intended to develop a roadmap for reforms that would prevent such violence from occurring again.[40] Accordingly, Agenda Item Four, "Long-Term Issues and Solutions," offers an important framework for prevention of future atrocities in Kenya through broad-reaching structural and institutional reform. This is a key element of the Responsibility to Prevent, and is markedly different from past responses to violence in Kenya. As Stephen Brown argued in 2003:

> In its response [to the violence since 1991], ...there has been no strong, explicit attempt to prevent recurrence. The ad hoc efforts to forestall further conflict have been fatally handicapped by donors' reluctance to address the actual source of the violence. Instead, they implicitly (and erroneously) treat the root cause as "localized hatreds." As a result, the violence periodically arises anew and will continue to do so in the future unless there is a radical change in the international community's approach or in government strategies.[41]

However, assessing the interventions of the international community in this part of the mediation process—and hence also in the implementation of what is now commonly referred to as Agenda Four in Kenya—is more challenging as it is more diffuse. For instance, the mediation process around Agenda Four developed agreements which address both the direct responsibility for the post election violence as well as broader issues of truth and justice in Kenya. This is significant in that these pieces of the agree-

[37] *See, e.g.*, Matthew Weaver, *US Bans Kenyan Politicians Accused of Inciting Violence*, The Guardian, Feb. 7, 2008, *available at* http://www.guardian.co.uk/world/2008/feb/07/kenya.matthewweaver.

[38] Interview with Amb. Adam Wood (Nov. 5, 2010).

[39] Interview with Lord Mark Malloch Brown (Dec. 15, 2010).

[40] Notes, author's own, from the Kenya National Dialogue and Reconciliation, 2008.

[41] Stephen Brown, *Quiet Diplomacy and Recurring "Ethnic Clashes," in* Kenya, From Promise to Practice: Strengthening UN Capacities for the Prevention of Violent Conflict, 69–100 (2003).

ment deal not with ending the violence, as Agenda One and Two did, but with seeking redress. Further reforms through the constitutional review process, also an outcome of Agenda Four, led to a framework for judicial reform, which if implemented may also have an impact on preventing future violence through reducing impunity in Kenya.

The agreements reached in Agenda Item Four have resulted in a series of important reforms in Kenya. Significantly, on the August 4, 2010, through a referendum in Kenya, people voted in favor of a new constitution. The constitution brought about much-needed reforms in the areas of land, devolution, citizenship, and other key areas.[42] What became evident in the peaceful voting process was the identification with leaders from given ethnic communities. Support for the new constitution was high in those regions where political leaders from the area supported the constitution, and less so in areas where specific leaders opposed the draft. What this means in the longer term around ethnic identities and how these manifest themselves (peacefully or otherwise) in Kenya remains to be seen.[43]

Important judicial and electoral reforms have also moved ahead as a result of these agreements. The establishment of the National Cohesion and Integration Commission is another important step, particularly as its mandate includes addressing hate speech and broader reconciliation throughout the country.

A concerning failure has been a lack of an adequate domestic mechanism to prosecute victims of the post election violence. While the Commission of Inquiry on Post Election Violence (CIPEV or commonly known as the Waki Commission) was widely viewed as conducting an excellent inquiry, the primary recommendation for the establishment of a domestic mechanism to ensure accountability of those involved in the organization and conduct of the violence has not materialized.[44] However, the Commission has supported work by the International Criminal Court (ICC), which is now pursuing investigations of six senior figures in Kenya from the political, security, and media.[45] Of equal concern is the continued controversy that has undermined the Truth, Justice, and Reconciliation Commission. This is a real shortcoming, particularly in light of the importance of addressing longer-term grievances in Kenya as a cornerstone for prevention of future violence.[46] It is perhaps too early to tell whether these measures have put in motion a process of addressing impunity and violence related to political contests, which will have a long-term preventive impact in Kenya. However, many Kenyan civil society leaders credit the dialogue process with pushing forward reforms, which would not have otherwise been possible.[47]

[42] Tim Murithi, *Kenya's Constitutional Renewal: A Post-Referendum Analysis*, The Current Analyst, Jan. 23, 2011, *available at* http://www.currentanalyst.com/index.php/conflictsregional/136-kenyas-constitutional-renewal-a-post-referendum-analysis.

[43] Jeffrey Gettleman, *Kenyans Approve New Constitution*, New York Times, Aug. 5, 2010, *available at* http://www.nytimes.com/2010/08/06/world/africa/06kenya.html.

[44] Report of the Commission of Inquiry on Post Election Violence (CIPEV), Oct. 15, 2008.

[45] Lauren Gelfand, *ICC Indictments Put Kenya on Trial*, World Politics Review, Dec. 22, 2010, *available at* http://www.worldpoliticsreview.com/articles/7402/icc-indictments-put-kenya-on-trial.

[46] *See, e.g.*, *Kiplagat is Delaying TJRC's Work*, Daily Nation, Apr. 19, 2010, *available at* http://allafrica.com/stories/201004191690.html; Mike Plfanz, *US Professor Quits Truth Commission, Cites Confidence*, Christian Science Monitor, Oct. 22, 2010, *available at* http://www.csmonitor.com/World/Africa/2010/1022/US-professor-quits-Kenyan-truth-commission-citing-lack-of-confidence.

[47] Author discussions with Kenyan civil society leaders 2010–2011.

The mediation process officially concluded in June 2008, while the implementation of the agreements had already begun, and is continuing. At the conclusion of the crisis, an estimated 1,300 people had lost their lives and approximately 300,000 persons were displaced—disproportionately women and children—many of whom remain displaced today. The question of the level of organization of the violence and the premeditation surrounding the attacks was at the center of the deliberations of the CIPEV and remains a primary question for the ICC as it continues the investigations into high-level individuals involved in the organization and perpetration of the violence.[48]

In an interview reflecting on the situation in Kenya, Kofi Annan indicated that RtoP was the lens through which he viewed the crisis: "I saw the crisis in the RtoP prism with a Kenyan government unable to contain the situation or protect its people . . . I knew that if the international community did not intervene, things would go hopelessly wrong . . . Kenya is a successful example of RtoP at work."[49] UN actors, academics, policymakers, and civil society groups have similarly elected to treat the Kenya crisis as an exemplary case for RtoP. What is particularly interesting is the designation of this case as a model for RtoP, which suggests that it can be replicated in other situations. Gareth Evans has deemed it a "classic case of RtoP"[50] and Human Rights Watch has referred to the case as a model of diplomatic action under the "Responsibility to Protect."[51] Similarly, as Roger Cohen has argued: "RtoP . . . has had a rough start. But on a Kenyan model . . . it might have a brighter future."[52] The final section of this chapter will assess the role of RtoP in the resolution of the crisis.

IV. KENYA: A CLASSIC CASE OF RTOP?

On October 23, 2008, Chairman of the Commission of the African Union Jean Ping addressed a high-level meeting of experts on "The Responsibility to Protect in Africa." Within his remarks, Ping took note of the asserted connections between Kenya and the Responsibility to Protect, while questioning the extent to which the crisis may be considered an example of RtoP. According to Ping, there are "grey areas that remain to be clarified"[53] concerning the scope and application of RtoP in this case. The decision of the ICC pre-trial chamber to investigate "crimes against humanity" in Kenya—

[48] Kenya ratified the Rome Statute of the International Criminal Court on March 15, 2005. In November 2009, for the first time in the history of the Court, the Prosecutor invoked his *proprio motu* powers to commence an investigation. Subsequent to this, the Pre-Trial Chamber authorized the Prosecutor to conduct investigations into crimes against humanity that may have occurred in Kenya after June 1, 2005.

[49] Kofi Annan cited in Roger Cohen, *How Kofi Annan Rescued Kenya*, N.Y. Review of Books 55.2, Aug. 14, 2008.

[50] Lecture by Gareth Evans, President of the International Crisis Group to 10th Asia Pacific Programme for Senior Military Officers, S. Rajaratnam School of International Studies, Singapore, Aug. 5, 2008, *available at http://www.gevans.org/speeches/speech302.html*

[51] *Ballots to Bullets*, at 67.

[52] Cohen, *supra* note 49.

[53] Jean Ping, *Round-Table High-Level Meeting of Experts on "The Responsibility to Protect in Africa,"* Addis Ababa, Oct. 23, 2008.

one of the four crimes mentioned in the 2005 World Summit Outcome Document—has, however, served to corroborate the connections between RtoP and this case.[54]

For certain observers, the nature and scale of the violence, coupled with the state's failure to protect its citizens, was instantly reminiscent of the concerns that led to the development of RtoP. One of the first invocations of RtoP during the crisis was made by Ban Ki-moon on January 2, 2008: "The Secretary-General is increasingly troubled by the escalating tensions and violence in Kenya in the aftermath of last week's elections . . . The Secretary-General reminds the Government, as well as the political and religious leaders of Kenya, of their legal and moral responsibility to protect the lives of innocent people."[55] RtoP was also invoked by Francis Deng, the UN Special Adviser on the Prevention of Genocide[56] and in the report of the United Nations Office of the High Commissioner for Human Rights Fact-Finding Mission.[57] Similarly, French Foreign Minister Bernard Kouchner called for an international response on the basis of RtoP: "In the name of the responsibility to protect, it is urgent to help the people of Kenya. The United Nations Security Council must take up this question and act."[58] Further to this, Bishop Desmond Tutu referred to RtoP on February 19, 2008:

> [I]t should also be acknowledged that the international community has moved far faster in addressing this conflict than it has in similar situations elsewhere. The United Nations has engaged at the highest political levels, the Security Council has issued a statement deploring the violence, and the secretary general and the leadership of human rights offices have been mobilized. African leaders have provided invaluable mediation . . . I believe what we are seeing in Kenya is action on a fundamental principle—the Responsibility to Protect.[59]

Interestingly, when the UN Security Council took up the matter on February 6, 2008, the Presidential Statement took note of the violence and its impact on the region, but stopped short of referring to RtoP.[60]

To the extent that NGOs and civil society groups issued statements on the crisis, there was no explicit invocation of RtoP. International and regional media coverage of the crisis emphasized the scale of violence without direct references to RtoP.

[54] It should be noted that ICC Judge Kaul issued a dissenting opinion on the issue of whether attacks against civilians were organized at the State level. For a good discussion of the Pre-trial Chamber's judgment, *see*, Lionel Nichols, *ICC Pre-Trial Chamber Gives Ocampo the Green Light in Kenya*, EJIL Talk, Apr. 15, 2010.

[55] UN, *Secretary-General Troubled by Escalating Kenyan Tensions, Violence*, Jan. 2, 2008.

[56] *UN Genocide Adviser Urges End to Violence, Sends Staffers There*, UN News Centre, Jan. 28, 2008.

[57] Report from OHCHR Fact-Finding Mission to Kenya, Feb. 6–28, 2008, *available at* http://www.ohchr.org/Documents/Press/OHCHRKenyareport.pdf.

[58] Statement by Bernard Kouchner, *Violence in Kenya*, Jan. 31, 2008, *available at* http://www.diplomatie.gouv.fr/en/country-files_156/kenya_209/situation-in-kenya-2008_6019/situation-in-kenya-statement-by-bernard-kouchner-january-31–2008_10767.html.

[59] Desmond Tutu, *Responsibility to Protect*, Int'l Herald Tribune, Feb. 19, 2008.

[60] *Statement by the President of the Security Council*, S/PRST/2008/4, Feb. 6, 2008. According to Alex Bellamy, one can infer an implicit reference to RtoP within the statement. Failure to explicitly mention RtoP reflects how contentious RtoP-language continues to be within the Council.

Nevertheless, the global coverage of the crisis did recall previous instances of mass atrocity crimes that inspired the development of RtoP, most notably Rwanda. The analogies drawn between the unfolding crisis in Kenya and the 1994 genocide in Rwanda within the media were most apparent in the aftermath of the New Year's Day killings in Eldoret, in which a number of women and children were burned to death while seeking refuge in a church.[61] Similarly, the International Crisis Group referred to prospect of Kenya replicating "Rwanda-style killings,"[62] and Kofi Annan also drew a connection between the two cases, "when I got on the ground and saw the ethnic nature of the killings and the conflict that the responsibility to protect, and the Rwandan and the Yugoslavian stories came to my mind."[63]

Although the AU has been a trendsetter in the development of RtoP—particularly in light of Article 4(H) of the AU Charter[64] (the right of the Union to intervene in a Member State pursuant to a decision of the Assembly in respect of grave circumstances, namely: war crimes, genocide, and crimes against humanity), the AU did not make explicit references to RtoP around the Kenya crisis.[65]

As noted above, throughout the mediation process itself, RtoP was not mentioned in the agenda, press releases, or the agreements. Nevertheless, as Thomas Weiss has argued: "The best way to think about the contribution of RtoP to the mediation is as background music that contributed a sense of urgency, motivating Africans, the U.S. and the EU to enter the fray with seriousness and due speed."[66] Similarly, Michael Doyle has referred to the action as taking place in the shadow of RtoP.[67] Interestingly, Donald Steinberg has conceded: "given the backsliding and buyer's remorse in the international community regarding the RtoP norm, it is perhaps fortunate that no one labeled this as an RtoP situation."[68] Finally, as Mark Malloch Brown comments on Kenya and RtoP more broadly:

"On RtoP, its rhetorical use was very limited during the crisis. It remains an emotive and provocative term. My broader ministerial experience (e.g., Zimbabwe, Burma, and

[61] *Mob Torches Kenyan Church, 30 Die Inside*, Reuters, Jan.1, 2008, *available at* http://www.reuters.com/article/idUSL01651287; *A Massacre in a Kenyan Church*, Time, Jan. 1, 2008, at http://www.time.com/time/world/article/0,8599,1699181,00.html; *Mob Sets Kenya Church on Fire Killing Dozens*, New York Times, Jan. 2, 2008, *available at* http://www.nytimes.com/2008/01/02/world/africa/02kenya.html?_r=1&pagewanted=2; *Mob Kills up to 50 at Kenya Church*, MSNBC, Jan. 1, 2008, http://www.msnbc.msn.com/id/22460182/. Crisis Group also mentions the prospect of "Rwanda-style killings" in Kenya in Kenya in Crisis.

[62] *Kenya in Crisis, supra* note 21.

[63] *Prisoner of Peace: An Interview with Kofi Annan*, Kofi Annan Foundation and Centre for Humanitarian Dialogue, May 9, 2008.

[64] *Right of the Union to Intervene in a Member State Pursuant to a Decision of the Assembly in Respect of Grave Circumstances, Namely: War Crimes, Genocide and Crimes Against Humanity.*

[65] *Communiqué of the AU Peace and Security Council*, African Union, Mar. 14, 2008.

[66] Thomas Weiss, *Halting Atrocities in Kenya*, Great Decisions, 2010, *available at* www.fpa.org/info-url_nocat4705/info-url_nocat_show.htm?doc_id=1015755#KE.

[67] Michael Doyle, *Human Rights, Sovereignty and Military Intervention: A Dialogue with JS Mill*, Institute for Ethics Law and Armed Conflict Seminar Series, Feb. 9, 2010.

[68] Donald Steinberg, *Responsibility to Protect: Coming of Age?*, 1.4 Global Responsibility to Protect 432–441 (2009), *available at* http://responsibilitytoprotect.org/index.php/crises/-other-RtoP-concerns.

Sri Lanka) was reluctant to conclude that one should pursue its principles, but silently. For me, it was a stealth doctrine but one whose time will come. Also when politicians start to use it, they often indulge in dangerous imprecision about its scope."[69]

Although the key players involved in the mediation process did not explicitly invoke RtoP during the process, to what extent did external actors lend their support to this process in light of RtoP?

As Adam Wood, UK High Commissioner to Kenya at the time of the crisis commented:

> We would have done what we did—and worked to achieve what was in the end achieved—whether responsibility to protect had been debated in the UN and international circles or not. But the concept did help in gaining as quickly as we did the coherent international support and pressure for the crisis to be resolved. We learned a lot, and the coherence of that international response can be replicated.[70]

In further discussions with decision-makers involved in the crisis, concerns over regional instability appeared to be paramount: "I think Kenya was too important to too many actors to just stand by and watch."[71] This stands in marked contrast to the responses to political violence, which had plagued Kenya previously. While the incidents of violence around the 1992 and 1997 elections and the Wagalla massacre of 1984 all occurred prior to the articulation of RtoP, the lack of response on these events, particularly in comparison with the overwhelming international response in 2007–2008 is striking.[72]

The above statements tend to indicate that the international response would have been the same in the absence of RtoP. As the UN Secretary-General's Special Advisor on RtoP Edward C. Luck has acknowledged: "Operationally, did it change the way the UN went about its work in Kenya? I don't know. I'm not sure that it did in really observable ways. So whether one can show cause and effect, I'm not sure. But it was not after-the-fact labeling."[73] Similarly, Alex Bellamy has argued: "although Kenya is a notable success for RtoP, it is not clear that RtoP itself caused the intense international engagement."[74]

Although RtoP considerations did not prove to be a critical factor in the Kenya case, the resolution of this crisis has certainly made an impact on RtoP. As the remainder of this section will argue, the association drawn between the Kenya crisis and RtoP arguably owes much more to the conscious reprioritizing of prevention within RtoP debates.

[69] Interview with Lord Mark Malloch Brown, Dec. 15, 2010.

[70] Interview with Amb. Adam Wood, Nov. 5, 2010.

[71] Interview with Francis Deng, Jul. 13, 2010.

[72] Stephen Brown, *Quiet Diplomacy and Recurring "Ethnic Clashes" in Kenya, in* From Promise to Practice: Strengthening UN Capacities for the Prevention of Violent Conflict 69–100 (2003).

[73] Interview with Edward C. Luck, Jul. 14, 2010.

[74] Alex Bellamy, *The Responsibility to Protect–Five Years On*, 24.2 Ethics and International Affairs 165 (2010).

Prevention has occupied something of an ambiguous role in the intellectual and conceptual history of RtoP. Despite being deemed the "single most important dimension of the responsibility to protect,"[75] the responsibility to prevent has been habitually neglected.[76] Rather interestingly, this oversight goes back to the foundational documents of RtoP, the International Commission on Intervention and State Sovereignty (ICISS) report, where the responsibility to prevent is dealt with in considerably fewer pages than the other elements of the "continuum of responsibility."[77] The bulk of the report focused on the responsibility to react—a key component that included proposed criteria to guide prospective instances of intervention.

In recent years, the emphasis on reaction has begun to shift in favor of prevention. The renewed interest in prevention seems entirely appropriate in that it reintroduces a critical, yet often-neglected component of RtoP. However, this reorientation owes much more to pragmatism, cultivated in response to the political climate in which RtoP implementation has been forced to operate. Indeed, one of the principal challenges the UN has faced in its efforts to implement RtoP—particularly in light of the dubious humanitarian justifications offered for the U.S.-led invasion of Iraq in 2003 and Russia's 2008 military operation in Georgia—has been to downplay the reactionary component of RtoP. This comes across in the tone of the 2009 Secretary-General's report on implementing RtoP, which, among other things, goes to great lengths to distance the concept from the coercive measures, almost to the point of disavowing the use of force.[78] This has prompted leading scholars of RtoP such as Jennifer Welsh to identify a "lack of attention to 'hard power' within the report."[79] With the need to build consensus in mind, the report opts to elaborate on the preventive dimensions of the 2005 World Summit Outcome Document. Seen as a less divisive point of entry—the entire report is, in many respects, underpinned by a focus on prevention. This is evident in the report's regretful tone when recounting the failure to prevent atrocity crimes on previous occasions, and the specific proposals for implementation, which include plans for a shared office between the special advisors on RtoP and genocide prevention, and the proposed centralized UN early-warning system.

Arising precisely in between two critical benchmarks in the development of RtoP: the 2005 World Summit and the 2009 report on implementation, the crisis in Kenya overlapped with the efforts to translate RtoP from rhetoric to reality. Indeed, the crisis in Kenya coincided with the appointment of Edward C. Luck to his position as Special Advisor on RtoP. As the situation deteriorated, Luck took a decision, with the full

[75] The Responsibility to Protect, Report of the International Commission on Intervention and State Sovereignty, *International Development Research Centre* xi (2001).

[76] The ICISS Report conceptualizes a tripartite continuum of responsibilities: the responsibility to prevention, the responsibility to react, and the responsibility to rebuild.

[77] *Id.*

[78] The Report emphasizes that RtoP is "an ally of sovereignty, not an adversary." *Id.* at 7. It also reiterates that the principle is not "does not alter, indeed it reinforces the legal obligations of Members States to refrain from the use of force except in conformity with the Charter." *Id.* at 5. The responsibilities implied under RtoP not "confined to one part of the world. *Id.* at 6. For a good discussion of this *see*, Monica Serrano, *Implementing the Responsibility to Protect: The Power of RtoP Talk*, 2 Global Responsibility to Protect 167–77 (2010).

[79] Jennifer Welsh, *Turning Words Into Deeds: Implementing the Responsibility to Protect*, 2 Global Responsibility to Protect 152 (2010).

support of the Secretary-General and the other organs of the UN system, to treat the situation as the first "test-case" for RtoP:

> We were not set up in any way, shape, or manner. We hadn't even begun the bureaucratic debate. But the situation there looked like an RtoP contingency in terms of the risk of growing violence. It clearly was a case for prevention. Whether there was actually ethnic cleansing happening or not, it looked a lot like ethnic cleansing. And the numbers were getting pretty high and the possibility of escalation seemed very real. So it just seemed important to me to flag this one early, and to say it's an RtoP situation. Now we had no mechanism set up or anything. So it was a little premature, but other high-level UN officials agreed. So calling it an RtoP situation was not coincidental.[80]

Given that RtoP was devised in response to instances of international failure in the face of mass atrocities, the importance of locating a positive case study cannot be overemphasized—particularly with the ongoing efforts to institutionalize RtoP within the UN and broader international community. The manner in which the Kenya case was eventually resolved added weight to the emerging inclination within RtoP circles, as explored above, to downplay the use of force. What the Kenya case appeared to offer was a seamless illustration of RtoP's preventive dimension. It is, therefore, fitting that the Secretary-General refers to Kenya more than any other case in his 2009 report.[81] Most interesting is the reference to the Kenya crisis within the section on Pillar three (timely and decisive response), which might otherwise be understood to imply Chapter VII measures: "[P]illar three is generally understood too narrowly. As demonstrated by the successful bilateral regional and global efforts to avoid further bloodshed in early 2008 following the disputed election in Kenya, if the international community acts early enough, the choice need not be a stark one between doing nothing or using force."[82]

In short, while RtoP may not have been a critical factor in resolving the crisis in Kenya, the case has proven critical for proponents of RtoP.

To the extent that Kenya can be considered a successful illustration of the "responsibility to prevent," it should be noted that much depends on the implementation of Agenda Item Four of the Kenya National Dialogue and Reconciliation. Agenda Four deals with addressing the root causes of the 2007–2008 violence and therefore is ultimately concerned with preventing a recurrence of violence in the longer term. Accordingly, assessments of this case—particularly from a preventive standpoint—must go beyond the AU mediation and take into account the specific institutional measures put in place to prevent further violence, and indeed, their effectiveness.

V. CONCLUSION

The swift and sustained response to Kenya's post-election crisis in 2007–08 has been widely heralded as a success story for the Responsibility to Protect. This chapter has

[80] Interview with Edward C. Luck, Jul. 14, 2010.

[81] Report of the Secretary-General, *Implementing the Responsibility to Protect*, A/63/677), Jan. 12, 2009, at 9.

[82] *Id.*

endeavored to critically assess this claim. While official statements made throughout the unfolding crisis convey a genuine concern for the humanitarian consequences of the violence, underlying these concerns were a set of strategic considerations that stem from Kenya's regional importance. The prospect of the violence leading to instability beyond Kenya's borders ensured an unprecedented level of resolve among regional and international actors. Accordingly, the efforts to forestall the violence derive from a fortuitous convergence between humanitarian considerations and strategic interests, rather than a pure interest in saving lives.

Reflection on the Kenya case raises both some instructive lessons as well as some broader questions that will be important for proponents of RtoP as the discussion on the doctrine move forward.

The success of the mediation process points to some important lessons for RtoP interventions elsewhere. One of the primary lessons, as highlighted by Kofi Annan, is that "intervention" does not have to be considered as the use of force or more traditional peacekeeping elements. Mediation in itself can be a successful tool to prevent atrocities—and hence should be more widely considered.

On the one hand, the Kenya example indicates that some of the core standards for effective mediation are possible, and effective in preventing conflict and protecting civilians. Firstly, the rapidity of the response and ability of international and regional actors to pull together such a high-level mediation process so quickly was hugely important to counter the momentum of the violence with the momentum of dialogue. Related to this, the remarkable consensus of the international community and their discipline throughout the process of supporting the mediation and deferring to Kofi Annan's leadership was critical. The ability, with such a consensus, to use all different levers of influence to push forward for a resolution to the crisis was decisive for stemming the violence, and hence as an element of the success from an RtoP standpoint. Finally, the focus on both addressing the immediate triggers of the violence and the longer-term reforms required to prevent such future outbreaks in Kenya dealt both with immediate and broader prevention—an important lesson for RtoP. However, to what extent can this be replicated?

A further insight from the Kenya case—which points to its unique nature, particularly as the region is determining how to address the crisis in Côte d'Ivoire, is that Kenya was truly deadlocked—there was no clear winner and loser in this election. Despite the claims on both sides, there was no way to transparently and conclusively determine the winner of the December 2007 polls in Kenya. This meant, importantly from the perspective of intervention, that "taking sides" was not an issue for the international and regional players. This freed up intervention to be about responding more centrally to the political crisis and human consequences. What we have seen in other crises since is that with a recognized winner in the polls (both Zimbabwe and Côte d'Ivoire are examples), the international and regional community can be split, and it becomes more of a challenge for a mediation intervention to come in on impartial grounds. These therefore become very different mediation processes, and hence very different interventions from an RtoP standpoint.

While advocates of RtoP are keen to replicate the successes of the Kenya case, maintaining a position of impartiality may not only be difficult, but entirely inappropriate in other instances. This dilemma is indicative of the uneasy relationship between conflict prevention and the issue of atrocity prevention. As of yet, efforts to elaborate the preventive dimension of RtoP remain unclear on the precise relationship between these related, but distinct fields. This is certainly an issue that warrants further consideration in the ongoing efforts to implement RtoP.

An additional factor to consider in this case is the convergence between strategic considerations and humanitarian concerns. The fact that the response to this crisis was not wholly altruistic by no means undermines the credibility of this case from the perspective of RtoP. Indeed, the extent to which international actors responded to fears over regional instability should not be viewed as contradictory to the intentions of the Responsibility to Protect. Although the presence of mixed motives is not in and of itself a problem—the reality that strategic considerations provided an incentive to resolve the crisis brings to light an uncomfortable question: what of the cases in which strategic interests are not readily apparent, or in fact contradict an intervention on RtoP grounds?

While NATO's controversial intervention in Kosovo in 1999 may have been the catalyst to the ICISS process, at the other end of the spectrum is the problem of inaction—situations of little strategic interest that simply do not feature on the global agenda, such as Rwanda in 1994. It was with this case in mind that the ICISS commissioners delineated what is the crux of RtoP—the concept of "sovereignty as responsibility" and the attendant notion of a residual responsibility to act in cases where states fail to protect their populations. In spite of the conceptual shifts within RtoP debates over the past decade, encouraging the international community to assume this responsibility remains the foremost challenge in implementing RtoP. Given the level of strategic interest underlying the international response to this crisis, the Kenya case doesn't necessarily test the capacity of RtoP to galvanize international action in cases where intervention would otherwise be resisted. Indeed, according to high-level officials involved in the decision-making process throughout the crisis, the international response to this case would have likely been the same in the absence of any prior commitment to the principles of RtoP. The international community simply couldn't afford to fail in Kenya; however, it can afford to fail, and is failing, in places like Sudan, Democratic Republic of Congo, Sri Lanka and Syria. These remain the real test cases for RtoP.

Finally, apart from overstating the extent to which the Kenya crisis provides a sound test case for RtoP's preventive dimension—the responsibility to prevent—the tendency to designate this case a "success story" is premature. The agreements that were signed on February 28, 2008, were but one piece of the KNDR process. The substance of Agenda Item Four—long-term issues and solutions required for a durable peace—amount to a complete overhaul of the Kenyan state in order to prevent a recurrence of violence. Addressing the roots of the crisis will likely take years to resolve. In this respect, the full effects of the mediation process are far from conclusive. History should judge the Kenya process on the ability to put into motion reforms that, in the long term, prevent the events of 2007–2008 (and indeed the events of political violence throughout Kenya's history). This would be the ultimate test of prevention from an RtoP standpoint.

14 Sri Lanka

Damien Kingsbury

In the months between January and May 2009, the Sri Lanka Army (SLA) unleashed a full military offensive against the separatist Liberation Tigers of Tamil Eelam (LTTE, or Tamil Tigers) in Sri Lanka's northern districts. This was to be the final phase of a war for a separate Tamil state which killed more than 100,000 people, damaged the country's economy, and fundamentally changed and arguably diminished the Sri Lankan polity. According to a former UN spokesman, up to 40,000 people were killed in the final weeks of the war,[1] with a further 1,400 dying each week while in captivity following the end of fighting.[2]

Following the war, more than 250,000 Tamils were held in internment camps in which they did not have access to adequate food, clean water, or health care; with a death rate averaging 200 per day.[3] Also deeply disturbing, between 10,000 and 15,000 individuals "disappeared" from the internment camps,[4] consistent with previous practice and presumably murdered by soldiers or police without recourse to trial or any other form of justice. These actions continued as a profound reminder of the nature of the state that had evolved to assume authority of its sometimes reluctant peoples. Most internees were eventually released, if to an uncertain future, in many cases not being able to return to the homes or to the land they once owned. In some cases, their homes were destroyed but in many cases, they had also become the site of or in close proximity to army camps in what remained occupied areas. Continuing a long-standing

[1] Dateline (SBS television broadcast, Australia, 2009).

[2] Rhys Blakely, *Tamil Death Toll is 1400 a Week*, The Times, Jul. 10, 2009.

[3] Amnesty International, *Unlock the Camps in Sri Lanka* (2009).

[4] UN Office for the Coordination of Humanitarian Affairs, Sri Lanka: Vanni Emergency Situation report #19 (May 30, 2009).

policy of population displacement, poor Sinhalese were increasingly brought in to permanently displace them in what amounted to a state-sponsored program of "demogricide."[5]

In the period after the war, Tamils continued to flee Sri Lanka, in reasonable fear of persecution or for their lives. Despite the clear grounds they were able to present for seeking refugee status, receiving countries such as Australia and Canada treated them not with compassion but as, in effect, criminals or as potential criminals.[6] The Government of Sri Lanka, meanwhile called for Tamil asylum seekers to be returned to Sri Lanka, employing the logic that if they fled they would only be in fear if they were members or sympathizers of the LTTE.[7] Apart from the fact that many LTTE sympathizers simply sought equity, that many LTTE soldiers had been forced to join the organization, and that Tamils felt persecuted on the basis of their ethnicity rather than their political activity, the assumption was that they were all "terrorists."[8] Being returned to Sri Lanka, then, meant at least a brutal interrogation and a period of detention without trial,[9] and at worst, joining the legion of "disappeared." The grounds for international concern were overwhelming in practice, if consistently underwhelming in terms of responses.

Over the 12 months or more since the end of the fighting, increasing evidence has emerged of a military operation that systematically and deliberately ignored the lives of civilians in its pursuit of LTTE rebels or which targeted civilians as LTTE sympathizers. There is also growing evidence of war crimes having been committed by SLA troops[10] and some have argued that intentional disregard for or attack upon Tamil lives constituted an attempted genocide.[11] This all followed the formal and informal marginalization of, and, increasingly, attacks against, the Tamil people dating back to the period just after Sri Lanka's independence in 1948. The question, then, appears to be not whether there were grounds for invoking the principles of a Responsibility to Protect (RtoP) but, if they have meaning beyond words on paper, why such principles were not invoked.

Notably, assuming the Rome Statute constitutes the basis for determining and prosecuting war crimes, crimes against humanity and possibly genocide, as noted here it appeared there was evidence to support charges for such crimes. However, the Rome

[5] That is, the deliberate and systematic destruction of an ethnic group by permanent demographic displacement or expulsion.

[6] Paul Maley, *Boatpeople Facing Expulsion Over Security Concerns on Former Tamil Fighters*, The Australian, Oct. 6, 2009.

[7] Paul Maley, *200 Tamil Tigers "Sailing to Asylum,"* The Australian, Jun. 21, 2010.

[8] *Id.*

[9] Andra Jackson, *14 Lankan Tamil Refugees Caught While Trying to Flee*, Deccan Chronicle, Nov. 3, 2010; *Tamil Refugees "Questioned" by Sri Lankan Officials*, The Age, Jan. 9, 2010.

[10] Allegations of war crimes were being investigated by a UN investigative panel as this was being written, *see* UN News Center, "Ban appoints panel to advise on human rights issues during Sri Lanka conflict," Jun. 22, 2010.

[11] There was considerable debate about whether genocide was being committed, although the unremitting brutality and ethnic character of the war did tend to push it towards a conventional definition, *see* Bruce Fein, *Genocide in Sri Lanka*, The Boston Globe, Feb. 15, 2009; Suren Surendiram, *Genocide in Sri Lanka, The Great Debate*, Reuters, Jun. 4, 2009; M. Shaw, *Sri Lanka – camps, media . . . genocide?*, openDemocracy, Jun. 30, 2009, http://www.opendemocracy.net/article/sri-lanka-camps-media-genocide, last accessed Oct. 4, 2010; John Thompson, "Enough Already with the Genocide Talk" The Mackenzie Institute, Toronto, Oct. 4, 2010.

Statute applies only to those states that are signatories to it and Sri Lanka has never accepted its jurisdiction, not least because it has been involved in two wars in which its criteria for war crimes and crimes against humanity could, as noted below, be claimed to have been breached. However, while Sri Lanka is not a signatory to the Rome Statute, these key provisions are a part of international customary law and, as such, could be reasonably argued to constitute a basis for invoking RtoP.

I. A RESPONSIBILITY TO PROTECT IN SRI LANKA?

The idea of RtoP is relatively new in formal terms, bringing a sense of an international duty of care to the conduct world affairs. From inauspicious beginnings surrounding various mass killings, the principle of RtoP was endorsed by the General Assembly in 2005[12] under the explicit title of "Responsibility to protect populations from genocide, war crimes, ethnic cleansing and crimes against humanity" and unanimously reaffirmed by the Security Council in 2006.[13] Despite being adopted by the UN General Assembly, RtoP was, however, not universally endorsed in principle and is less committed to in practice. To illustrate this point, the still dominant "realist" interpretation of international relations posits, among other things, that the internal affairs of states are of no necessary interest or concern of other states; that international relations are conducted between states as free entities in an unregulated environment abstracted from their internal systems and conditions.[14] That is, what happens in one country is only relevant to the citizens of another country if they are directly affected. Thus there is a tension between notions of international law or international responsibility concerning globally acceptable behavior on one hand and the self-interest of states and disregard for others' internal affairs on the other.

There have been numerous other cases cited where RtoP has either applied in practice (if not identified as such), where it has been argued that it should be applied or where, after the fact, it appears that the international community has been remiss is not applying the RtoP principle. The UN's intervention in Kenya was the only formal employment of RtoP, although NATO's 1999 intervention in Kosovo stands, alongside Timor-Leste, as an example of the application in practice of RtoP, if prior to any formal adoption.[15] The situation in the Sudanese region of Darfur illustrates where RtoP has been argued should apply and the 1994 Rwandan genocide stands as a strong example of where after the fact it is widely agreed that RtoP should have applied.[16] The UN-mandated commander in Rwanda, Lieutenant General Romeo Dallaire, pleaded before and during the massacre for greater support and a more open mandate from the UN Security Council, which at that time included Rwanda as a non-permanent

[12] *2005 World Summit Outcome*, A/RES/60/1, Sept. 15, 2005, at ¶¶ 138–139.

[13] Resolution 1674.

[14] *See, e.g.*, Kenneth Waltz, Theory of International Politics (1979).

[15] Anne Orford, Reading Humanitarian Intervention 2 (2003). It is notable that RtoP could not have been applied prior to its adoption by the World Summit in 2005. However, the principles and practical application of RtoP can be said to have applied prior to this enunciation, notably in these two cases.

[16] Although RtoP could not have applied in Rwanda in 1994 because it had not yet been adopted, it was this situation in particular that highlighted the necessity of RtoP.

member and France, which has been argued to have supported the then Hutu-dominated government. The Security Council was, however, slow to respond and eventually offered too little too late. U.S. President Bill Clinton acknowledged that the international community had failed to act in Rwanda when it had a responsibility to do so. He vowed that it would "never again" happen.[17]

If the grounds for implementing RtoP in Sri Lanka were clear, the lack of such intervention illustrated much of the weakness with the idea of RtoP as it was constructed. Also clearly illustrated were the debilitating qualities of international division and sectional self-interest that precluded effective action and, in a time when much of the world and many of its leaders believe they had moved beyond barbarism, to allow it to continue. President Clinton might have said "never again" following the horrors of Rwanda, but all too often there have remained excuses to avoid a common responsibility, with little or nothing done to protect.

The limits to international law were nowhere more keenly felt than in 1999 when the UN Security Council failed to reach agreement on the Kosovo issue not because of debate about the severity of the situation but because of strategic infighting within the organization. Given the breach of promise by Serbia and its failure to comply with UN Security Council resolutions, it was, otherwise, a *prime facie* case of where external intervention was warranted and available under international law. In effect, the Kosovo intervention was less about pro-active but rather reactive international law; the challenge for the Security Council was not to endorse the intervention but rather, once it has taken place, to adopt a resolution terminating such action. In this, the "burden of veto" was reversed.[18] As a result, "[t]he central rule on the use of force, the prohibition of the threat or use of force contained in Article 2(4) of the UN Charter, is currently the subject of fundamental disagreement" (following Kosovo).[19]

The Security Council failure to act in its own right was self-diminishing, showing that the competing interests of the Security Council's permanent members was its greatest shortcoming and that which compromised its legitimacy in the eyes of the world, in particular among those people of states requiring intervention or, on the other hand, among those states feeling compelled to provide such intervention. It was out of this dilemma that Annan announced that it was the "core challenge to the Security Council and to the United Nations as a whole in the next century . . . to forge unity behind the principle that massive and systematic violations of human rights—wherever they take place—should not be allowed to stand."[20]

Reflecting the tensions that have arisen, however, between narrow self-interest and a moral responsibility to act, in light of the Security Council's failure and NATO's intervention in Kosovo, UN Secretary-General Kofi Annan noted that the global community increasingly accepted that it had "new responsibilities." He added that, implicitly, it had failed to act on those responsibilities, thus opening the way for a regional community to effectively supplant the UN in times of crisis. It was Annan's intention, as a consequence, that the UN rise to and address this challenge. In large

[17] *Newshour: Promoting Peace,* PBS, Mar. 25, 1998.

[18] ORFORD, *supra* note 15, at 2.

[19] CHRISTINE GRAY, INTERNATIONAL LAW AND THE USE OF FORCE 29 (2004).

[20] *Secretary-General's Annual Report to the General Assembly,* SG/SM/7136, Sept. 20, 1999.

part, Annan's recognition of this challenge highlighted both the limitations and the dynamism of law, and the debates that occur in relation to legal interpretation.[21]

There are, broadly, two schools of thought in regard to legal interpretation on such matters; that law is made by law-makers and should be applied in a literal and narrowly defined sense, and that law has a "natural" foundation, is open to interpretation, and should be applied according to context and changing values. The more formalistic argument in international law tends to arise among supporters of a "realist" position, in that they believe that law has little scope in largely unregulated international affairs, which is essentially a contest of self-interest, and should be limited in its application. An "idealist" perspective, on the other hand, suggests that not only should there be laws for the governing of the actions of the international community but that the extent of this law should be increased and more flexibly adapted to particular circumstances. The introduction, extension, and more open interpretation of such laws implies not global domination by a single entity (much less a conspiracy to this end), but an agreed system of mutual guarantees of protection. It is also possible to see the adoption of natural law by the state as providing grounds for RtoP within the state. However, a state that accepted this position would be unlikely to need to implement RtoP, given its prior disposition towards recognizing citizens' rights. Similarly, if RtoP was understood as deriving from positive law, it would necessarily be stronger. However, there remains little global acceptance of global law as such, but rather international agreements on less enforceable codes of behavior.

The Government of Sri Lanka has fallen very firmly into the literalist, realist camp of self-interest, and has been opposed to the idea and the practice of RtoP in all its nuanced forms since its inception. This meant that attempts at limiting Sri Lanka's internal behavior was and would likely have remained unsuccessful and would have made any last resort on-ground RtoP intervention very difficult, given that it would be likely to be militarily resisted. Illustrating the official Sri Lankan view, the "so-called responsibility to protect is nothing but a licence given by the white man to himself [to] intervene in the affairs of dark sovereign countries, whenever the white man thinks it fit to do so."[22]

This style of argument, in which both the logic is internally referential and externally exceptionalist, has been extensively used in arguments against the application of civil and political rights and even against environmental protection. The underlying assumption in this particular case is that there is a universal divide between "white" and "dark" peoples and that the states that represent them do so with the blessing of all of their citizens. In other applications, the division has been characterized as between developed and developing countries, between "Westerners" and "Asians" (notably around the "Asian values" debate).[23] The accusation that the argument is a "white" (or "Western") one is supported each time a person of European descent

[21] *See* Stephanie Carvin, *Threats, Challenges and Changes: International Law and the Evolution of "Threat" Since the End of the Cold War*, unpublished paper presented to *Bridging Multiple Divides*, International Studies Association, 49th Annual Convention (2008).

[22] Nalin Da Silva, *White Man's Burden in Black and White or RtoP the LTTE?*, The Island, Aug. 8, 2007; *CFA 5 Years*, Statement by the Sri Lanka Monitoring Mission, Feb. 22, 2007.

[23] *See, e.g.*, Leena Avonius & Damien Kingsbury, Asian Values and Human Rights Revisited (2009).

raises RtoP (or other ethical concerns), the logic being that "white" (or "Western") people are or should be disenfranchised from being able to legitimately comment on such matters.[24] Needless to say, one's skin color, ethnicity, or happenstance of place of birth should be the criterion by which humanitarian concern is legitimated. Moreover, such claims do not logically follow, confusing as they do the origins of an idea with their legitimacy. This is not to mention the widespread support for such ideas among more liberal and otherwise disenfranchised people from such countries. The argument, then, is not one of ethnicity or imperialism, but about the distinction between liberal humanitarian concern and authoritarian rejection of such concern.

II. THE TAMIL EELAM WAR

There is no precise date to mark the start of the Tamil (Eelam) separatist war, which led to the conditions that might otherwise have implied RtoP and in which "whites" have mostly shown limited interest. It was just a series of injustices which built up to the point where they were regarded by many Tamils as no longer tolerable. Militant unrest had begun to foment as early as 1970 with a young Tamil, Ponnuthurai Sivakumaran, attempting to assassinate a Sri Lankan government minister then visiting Jaffna. By 1975, radical young Tamils had conducted their first killing of a "turn-coat" government official, the Tamil mayor of Jaffna, Alfred Duraiappah. One of those involved in the assassination, allegedly the person who pulled the trigger[25] and who had been involved in other anti-government actions, was Velupillai Prabhakaran, later to become the leader of the LTTE and the Tamil resistance. After crushing or absorbing its rivals over the next several years, the LTTE eventually came to be the sole militant Tamil organization.

At the forefront of militant activities, the LTTE staged attacks against police officers, local politicians and robbed banks. In response, in 1979, the government passed the draconian Prevention of Terrorism Act and stationed a full Sri Lanka Army (SLA) brigade in Jaffna, the main Tamil city of the north. The LTTE was, at this time, proscribed as a terrorist organization. There is no doubt that the LTTE from the outset employed methods that fall under the conventional heading of "terrorism," including assassinations, generalized bombings, and attacking uninvolved civilians in a number of highly publicized cases. Similarly, however, the Sri Lankan state could similarly be accused of employing terrorism, notably in relation to mass killings of civilians, presiding over the "disappearances" of suspected activists and indiscriminate attacks against civilian populated areas. "When terrorists killed soldiers the SLA retaliated by going on a rampage and massacred civilians, burning and looting their properties,"[26] which simply drove more Tamils into the arms of the LTTE. Despite this, identifying the LTTE as a terrorist organization, especially forcefully at a time of "War on Terrorism," assisted the government of Sri Lanka is bringing international pressure to bear on the LTTE's increasingly sophisticated international operations. It also helped

[24] *See* Rajiva Wijesinha, *Letter to Brad Adams, Human Rights Watch*, Sri Lanka High Commission, Canberra, Aug. 14, 2008.

[25] Narayan Swamy, Tigers of Lanka 18 (6th ed. 2006).

[26] Nath Yogasundram, History of Sri Lanka: from Pre-History to Tsunami 313 (2006).

to delegitimize the goals of the LTTE and of Tamils more generally and was eventually used to internationally isolate the organization.

As LTTE attacks escalated, police and soldiers arbitrarily arrested and executed suspected LTTE members. On July 23, 1983, the LTTE hit back, ambushing an SLA jeep and truck near Jaffna, killing 13 soldiers, with two dying later. In response, soldiers killed 51 people in Jaffna and, following the funeral for the soldiers, anti-Tamil rioting broke out across the country, leading to many deaths—the toll was somewhere between a conservative 400[27] and a more probable 3,000. The rioting was the worst that had ever been seen in Sri Lanka, and it served to drive many Tamils living in the south of the country to the north or overseas, helping to establish what would become the LTTE's international network. Despite conflict having existed for years before, the LTTE's July 1983 attack is often regarded as marking the beginning of the Tamil separatist war.

These events in Sri Lanka caused considerable international concern, nowhere more so than in India with its own large and sympathetic Tamil population. Moreover, Tamil militants had for some years been receiving training and support in the Indian state of Tamil Nadu and increasingly from India's external intelligence agency, the Research and Analysis Wing (RAW). RAW's interest in the Tamil groups was in part based on their ethnic links to Tamils in India but also as a counter-measure to the government of Sri Lanka, which had allowed Pakistan to use Sri Lankan facilities for Pakistani ships to refuel in the Indo-Pakistani War of 1971, which had ultimately led to the creation of Bangladesh from East Pakistan. Pakistan, along with Israel, also provided military aid to the government of Sri Lanka, which India saw as a potentially threatening alliance. India therefore supported Tamil separatists in small part because of some Indian sympathy for their situation, but primarily as a counter to what was perceived to be an unfriendly regional government.

What is now referred to as Eelam War I is regarded as having run from 1983 until 1987, with a break in 1985 to allow for peace talks in Bhutan. By 1987, the SLA had cornered the LTTE in the Jaffna Peninsula and was preparing for a final assault. However, under pressure from its own ethnic Tamil population, the Indian government called for a halt to the offensive and, faced with rejection by the government of Sri Lanka, Indian Prime Minister Rajiv Ghandi attempted to send supply boats to relieve the LTTE. These supply boats were blocked by the Sri Lankan navy, so India supplied the LTTE with an air drop in what was known as Operation Poomalai (Garland). Following this intervention, Sri Lankan President Junius Jayewardene entered into talks with the government of India, which led, two months later, to the signing of the Indo-Sri Lankan Accord, the lifting of the siege of Jaffna and an agreement to send an Indian Peace Keeping Force (IPKF) to the island. This agreement brought to a conclusion the first stage of the conflict. The talks, relief efforts, and ultimately, the introduction of the IPKF could perhaps be understood as an early use of RtoP, even if its motives were less than pure and that it did ultimately go very wrong.

Despite the ostensible peacekeeping role of the IPKF, the LTTE refused to disarm, and fighting quickly broke out between the LTTE and the IPKF (with the LTTE in part

[27] *Id.* at 310.

being supported by the anti-Indian Sri Lankan government). Notably, at no stage did India support Tamil independence in Sri Lanka, but rather wished to see an arrangement that increased Tamil autonomy within the Sri Lankan state, in part because of concern for its own separatist issues.[28] Also in response to the Indian presence in Sri Lanka, there was also a leftist JVP uprising in the south. In suppressing the JVP uprising, by 1989 a conservatively estimated 40,000 people had been killed,[29] helping to inure the government of Sri Lanka to the idea that its first duty was to protect lives. Meanwhile, the IPKF, unprepared for a guerrilla war, only lightly armed and equipped and inadequately supplied, was unable to control its immediate strategic environment.[30] Having become a participant in the conflict rather than helping end it, the Indian government ordered the withdrawal of the IPKF in 1990. In discussion and RtoP, one of the criteria for intervention is that it will have "reasonable prospects of success,[31] the logic being that intervention would be counterproductive if it did not have such chances. The failure of the IPKF intervention, then, raised the RtoP spectre of "reasonable prospects" not able to be fulfilled in a future "peacekeeping" mission.

Following the withdrawal of the IPKF and the failure of peace talks between the government of Sri Lanka and the LTTE in 1990, almost 600 Tamil and Muslim police who had been ordered to surrender to the LTTE were massacred, initiating the second phase of the conflict, known as Eelam War II. The following year, in 1991, an LTTE suicide bomber assassinated the former Indian prime minister, Rajiv Gandhi, over India's handling of its intervention. The assassination of Ghandi effectively ended sympathy for the LTTE in India, including among many of India's 80 million ethnic Tamil community. In 1993, an LTTE suicide bomber assassinated Sri Lankan President Ranasinghe Premadasa at a political rally. These two events were hammered home by the government of Sri Lanka as evidence of the LTTE's "terrorist" status.

Following a three-month ceasefire, Eelam War III began in April 1995, quickly leading to a number of major clashes. After seven weeks of heavy fighting and the use of air attacks which led to high numbers of civilian casualties and around 2,500 SLA and LTTE troops being killed, following a decade of LTTE control the SLA retook the Jaffna Peninsula. However, despite this significant victory, the SLA also faced setbacks, with the LTTE using suicide bombers ("Black Tigers") to overrun the SLA base at Mullaitivu in July 1996, consolidating its position in the north of the country and establishing strong bases in the east.

The LTTE has been credited with inventing suicide bombings as a means of specific targeting, and often engaged in attacks well outside its principle geographic area of concern, notably in Colombo.[32] Its attacks were so successful that Colombo's business

[28] Anita Pratap, *Lessons from the Tiger Defeat*, The Week, May 31, 2009.

[29] *Information on the Janatha Vimukthi Peramuna - Sri Lanka*, Centre for Documentation on Refugees, UNHCR, Geneva, Jun. 1993.

[30] David Sandhu, Indian Peace keeping Force (IPKF) in Sri Lanka, *Order of Battles*, Sept. 8, 2002, *available at* http://orbat.com/site/cimh/india/ipkf.html/

[31] Nicole Deller & Sapna Chhatpar, *The Responsibility to Protect: Guidelines for the International Community to Prevent and React to Genocide and Mass Atrocities*, World Federalist Movement-Institute for Global Policy, 2006.

[32] By way of comparison, Aceh's Free Aceh Movement and Timor-Leste's Falintil both kept their attacks against state forces within their specific area of concern, thus assisting in avoiding

district was effectively shut down in 1996. The general justification for the attacks was that they were a legitimate response to government attacks within its claimed homeland and that it could not afford to limit its operational capacity by concerns about how it was externally viewed. In 2000, the LTTE pressed its growing advantage in the north, capturing the SLA's twin major bases of Iyakachchi and Elephant Pass, which remained in LTTE hands until 2008. While the LTTE used commandos to overrun Iyakichchi, in the case of Elephant Pass, rather than using suicide bombers or commandos, the LTTE employed heavy artillery, forcing the SLA's retreat. By 2000, it had been estimated that 64,000 people, mostly civilians, had been killed in the conflict.

III. AN EXTERNALLY BROKERED CEASEFIRE

As a consequence of what amounted to a strategic stalemate, on February 22, 2002, the LTTE and government signed a Norwegian-brokered ceasefire agreement (CFA), introducing the unarmed Norwegian-led Sri Lanka Monitoring Mission (SLMM). The SLMM was a muted version of RtoP,[33] of which type the Norwegians have been particularly engaged, both in Sri Lanka and elsewhere, if to date with little success. Part of the text of the agreement that allowed the SLMM read: "Responding to a proposal by the leadership of the LTTE, the parties agree to explore a political solution founded on the principle of internal self-determination in areas of historical habitation of the Tamil-speaking peoples, based on a federal structure within a united Sri Lanka. The parties acknowledge that the solution has to be acceptable to all communities."[34] In this there was a potential solution to the Sri Lanka problem. However, the SLMM did not have the capacity to ensure that such a solution was adequately pursued, much less achieved.

The CFA allowed the combatant forces to withdraw to their respective zones behind technical control lines, which quickly morphed into "borders," complete with immigration checks, visas and customs and tax.[35] The CFA also saw the opening of the A9 Highway through the LTTE controlled area to Jaffna in the north and the lifting of an embargo on goods to the LTTE-controlled Vanni. The opening of the A9 was widely considered to be symbolic of the renewed peace. Despite the LTTE pulling out of further peace talks the following year, the ceasefire continued to hold, with the LTTE establishing what amounted to a de facto state within a state in a northern area of Sri Lanka known as the Vanni.[36]

international proscription as terrorist organizations. This critical factor assisted successful international intervention in both cases.

33 This might be called "RtoP(2)L," or "Responsibility to Protect (Too) Lite."

34 Government of Sri Lanka/LTTE. *Oslo Declaration between the Government of Sri Lanka (GOSL) and the Liberation Tigers of Tamil Eelam (LTTE)*, Norway, Dec. 2–5, 2002.

35 *See* Christian Stokke, *Tamil Eelam - a De Facto State: Building the Tamil Eelam State: Emerging State Institutions and Forms of Governance in LTTE-controlled Areas in Sri Lanka*, Department of Sociology and Human Geography, University of Oslo; Raju Gopalakrishnan, *The Struggle for Tamil Eelam: Very little of Sri Lanka in Kilinochche*, Reuters, Feb. 2, 2006; This was also observed by the author at the northern and southern Vanni technical control lines in May 2006.

36 A northern, lightly forested area of about 7,500 square kilometers traditionally controlled by Tamil feudal chiefs, including the contemporary districts of Mannar, Mullaitivu, and Vavuniya.

After walking away from peace talks in April 2003, the LTTE followed up on the CFA by proposing to the government the establishment of an Interim Self-Governing Authority, which was immediately rejected. "Although the outright rejection by the government was predictable enough, the political backlash in Colombo was disproportionate."[37] Further, in what was to be a critical blow to the LTTE, in early 2004, the LTTE's eastern military commander, Colonel Vinayagamoorthy Muralitharan, better known as "Karuna," defected to the government after being called to account for alleged misallocated funds (Karuna claimed the defection was caused by northern Tamil high-handedness), which almost certainly meant going to his death. Although many of the 5,000 cadres under Karuna's command were said to have returned to the LTTE,[38] this defection fatally weakened the LTTE's hold on two eastern provinces, and confined the LTTE's military capacity to a relatively small area in the north.[39] Despite this strategic success, tensions between President Chandrika Kumaratunga and Prime Minister Wickremasignhe over what were claimed by the former and other nationalist groups to have been too many concessions to the LTTE meant that further progress on finding a political solution to the Tamil problem was effectively no longer available.

In reality, both the LTTE and the government had been using the period since the ceasefire agreement to build up stockpiles of weapons[40] and by the end of 2004 it appeared the two parties were ready to resume fighting. This perception was reinforced on August 12, 2005, when the LTTE was widely held responsible for the assassination of Sri Lankan foreign minister Lakshman Kadirgamar. Similarly, the government or front groups engaged in extra-judicial killings of public Tamil figures and political activists. The government in particular was using remaining Karuna group defectors and assistance from India's now anti-LTTE Research and Analysis Wing to conduct what amounted to an insurgency campaign against the LTTE.[41] As the government hardened its position in 2004, President Kumaratunga declared a state of emergency, suspended Parliament, took control of the mass media and Interior and Defense ministries, and called new elections for April 2004. The People's Freedom Alliance in coalition with the JVP won the elections, with Mahinda Rajapaksa becoming prime minister. Despite formally acknowledging the 2002 ceasefire agreement, from the outset Rajapaksa intended to seek a military victory over the LTTE.

At the end of 2004, Sri Lanka was hit by the Boxing Day Tsunami, killing some 30,000 and making homeless many more. Rather than bringing the two sides closer

[37] Chris Smith, *The LTTE: A National Liberation and Oppression Movement*, in Armed Militias of South Asia: Fundamentalists, Maoists and Separatists (Lauren Gayer and Christophe Jaffrelot, eds., 1990).

[38] Based on personal discussions with senior LTTE leaders, Kilinochchi, Jun. 2006.

[39] Neil Smith, *Understanding Sri Lanka's Defeat of the Tamil Tigers*, Joint Force Quarterly, No. 59, 43; *see also* C. Bryson Hull, *Sri Lanka Can Defeat Tigers, Top Ex-Rebel Says*, Reuters Nov. 13, 2008, *available at* http://in.reuters.com/article/southAsiaNews/idINIndia-36488720081113, accessed Nov. 3, 2010.

[40] Acknowledged by senior LTTE officers to the author, *see also* Rahul Bedi, *Sri Lanka Turns to China, Pakistan, for Military Needs*, Indo-Asian News Service, Feb. 6, 2007.

[41] The general belief this was the case was supported when RAW sent officers on a reconnaissance mission to Kilinochche after its recapture by the Sri Lankan army in late 2008, *see* Amarjeet Malik, *RAW Goes on Recce Mission*, Times of India, Jan. 7, 2009.

together around this natural disaster, as it did in Aceh, Indonesia, in Sri Lanka it only hardened divisions over the allocation and distribution of relief funds. In Aceh, there had been a much greater number of aid-workers in the disputed territory, relative to those in Sri Lanka, which helped cement a return to negotiations. Where Aceh and the Indonesian state both moved towards a democratic compromise, Sri Lanka was moving away from substantive democracy and towards electoral majoritarianism. How to address the problems caused by the tsunami was one more issue over which the government and the LTTE bitterly disagreed and which further fuelled animosity between them.

IV. THE RETURN TO WAR

In November 2005, Kumaratunga's presidency came to a conclusion, with presidential candidates Wickremasignhe standing on a pro-peace platform against Rajapaksa standing on a clear policy of militarily defeating the LTTE. The LTTE refused to allow Tamils under its control to vote in the election, which Rajapaksa won with the slim margin of just 1.8 per cent over Wickremasignhe. The LTTE's ban on Tamils under their control voting in the elections, their support otherwise going to Wickremasignhe, effectively handed power to Rajapakse. Following Rajapakse's election and the appointment of his brother, Gotabhaya Rajapaksa, as Defense Minister, the Sri Lankan government took a significantly more aggressive attitude towards the LTTE, escalating its attacks via proxy "militia," engaging in direct kidnappings, murders, and assaults, and eventually full-scale military confrontation. Notably, from this time, the Sri Lanka government stepped up its efforts to have the LTTE listed as a terrorist organization by a number of governments, including that of the USA, Canada, and the European Union. The purpose of this listing was principally to limit the raising of funds for the LTTE by expatriate Tamils, thereby denying it an important source of foreign income. The CFA more or less held until early 2006, when it began to fray, in particular following the abduction and murder of Tamil civilians, initiating escalating LTTE responses.[42] By July 2006, following full-scale government attacks in both the north and east, the CFA existed only on paper and what was commonly becoming referred to as Eelam War IV had begun. More than anything, the return to conflict from 2006 demonstrated that there was little taste for sustaining, much less pursuing, compromise in Sri Lanka, and little interest in coming to any sort of compromise other than through absolute material necessity.

While there were significant expressions of concern over a return to conflict by Tamil civil society groups,[43] there also remained profound impediments to returning to peace. From the perspective of the LTTE, there was a clear lack of trust in the intentions of the Sri Lanka government to genuinely pursue peace.[44] This lack of trust in a negotiated outcome was supported by the public announcement at the beginning of

[42] *War Victory Party in Sri Lanka*, BBC NEWS, Jul. 12, 2007.

[43] As directly communicated to the author in Jaffna and the Vanni in May 2006.

[44] This observation is based on discussions by the author with senior members of the LTTE international branch, in particular in 2006, a time in which there was also a marked breakdown in the 2002 Cease Fire Agreement. These views were supported in particular by interview with head of the LTTE Peace Secretariat, Pulidevan (single name attribution), May 10 and 12, 2006, the head of

January 2007, confirming what was already a reality on the ground, that the government intended to seek a military solution to the LTTE issue.[45] Moreover, Sri Lanka appeared to be moving away from open democratic processes and towards a type of bureaucratic authoritarianism.[46] Sri Lanka had shifted from a parliamentary to a presidential-led system in 1978. Since then, executive authority had been more and more located in the hands of the president, who appoints ministers as well as the Supreme Court judges who decide on constitutional issues. The role of the prime minister, in contrast, had become increasingly ceremonial. The president appoints, among others, the defense minister, who was from late 2005 an SLA brigadier-general and brother of the president. This has been accompanied by increasing failure of the judicial system,[47] which has granted effective impunity to extra-judicial killings and other grave human rights violations. Parliamentary politics continued, although the use of SLA-linked death squads,[48] torture, and denial of *habeas corpus*, contributed to an increasingly constrained political climate.[49] While an outcome that promoted democratization and political devolution could have theoretically worked, it appeared to have little real hope due to the organization of Sri Lanka's political parties and the voting patterns of its citizens, which ensured that ethnic Sinhalese parties dominated the parliament, if not always in mutual agreement, that the executive president has, to date and by default, been ethnic Sinhalese, and the increasingly extensive powers of that executive president.

The LTTE had offered a negotiated settlement, around a federated state model, but this was not engaged with by the Government of Sri Lanka. In 2006, this offer was effectively withdrawn as intended talks collapsed or failed to start. The capacity of the LTTE to negotiate was also severely limited by the serious illness (and, in December 2006, the death) of its chief negotiator and ideological strategist, Anton Balasingham. It was his illness and inability to attend negotiations in 2006 aimed at de-escalating violence that could in significant part be held responsible for their failure. It was around this time that the LTTE's earlier offer of a federal solution, based on unified northern and eastern provinces, was withdrawn, and it again called for a completely independent state.[50] The small, unarmed and, in terms of human rights violation monitoring, poorly trained SLMM, established to oversee the 2002 Cease Fire Agreement, was unable to prevent Sri Lanka's slide back into conflict. While all such

the LTTE International Secretariat, Castro (*nom de guerre*) on May 11, 2006, and with the political head of the LTTE, Suppiah Paramu Tamilchelvan, on May 13, 2006.

[45] B. Balachandran, *Lankan Army Hopes to Clear East by March,* HINDUSTAN TIMES, Jan. 3, 2007.

[46] In September 2010, a two-thirds majority of the parliament changed Sri Lanka's constitution to allow successive presidential terms beyond the prescribed two, handed control of the judiciary to the president, and effectively severed legal accountability.

[47] *Sri Lanka's Human Rights Crisis,* Asia Report No. 135, 6, International Crisis Group, Colombo/ Brussels (2007).

[48] Human Rights Watch, *Complicit in Crime: State Collusion in Abductions and Child recruitment by the Karuna Group,* Jan. 24, 2007.

[49] USAID, Mission in Sri Lanka, Democracy and Governance Program, *Democracy and Governance Program Initiative* (2006).

[50] Pirapaharan, Velupillai. Sinhala leaders "duplicity of war and peace has left Tamils with no choice but political independence Annual Heroes" Day Statement, Kilinochche, Sri Lanka, Nov. 27, 2006.

ceasefire agreements require the active support of all combatant parties,[51] the SLMM lacked the resources or political capacity to also impose its will on the combatant parties. In that the SLMM represented a type of RtoP, it was inadequately resourced relative to the situation on the ground, increasingly resented by the Sri Lanka government, and ultimately unable to prevent mass atrocities from occurring.

In the period from November 2005 until February 2007, it had been estimated that more than 4,000 people had been killed in the renewed fighting, with more than 250,000 made homeless.[52] Perhaps a further 1,000 or more were killed between February and August 2007 and a further 1,000 had disappeared and remained unaccounted for. Both sides thus resumed and escalated the conflict and both were seeking an effective military victory, or to be able to negotiate from a position of strength.

In large part, the LTTE's aspirations to the trappings of statehood were its undoing. The LTTE had evolved from a highly mobile if heavily armed and highly skilled guerrilla organization, the LTTE had become a conventional army fighting a largely conventional rather than asymmetric guerrilla war. In the final analysis, if the government put into the war as much determination as the LTTE had demonstrated, its overwhelming size and access to funds and military hardware meant that it would ultimately succeed. The LTTE had become a captive to its own dream and, along with its increasing international isolation, in particular from India, entered into the final phase of a conventional war that it could not possibly win.

The unfolding of a humanitarian disaster

The renewal of fighting in 2006 marked the beginning of the end of the Eelam wars. Despite initial LTTE signs of LTTE strength, the SLA conducted a series of successful campaigns. The first was to push the LTTE out of the eastern provinces including an LTTE artillery sight near Trincomalee, then the capture or destruction of LTTE-owned ships carrying weapons and supplies. The LTTE resumed its bombing campaign, with one suicide attack at Habaraba killing around 100 sailors in the single deadliest attack of the war. By 2007, the SLA felt ready to launch an assault on the LTTE's northern bases, initially targeting the LTTE's leadership with air strikes. In November 2007, the LTTE's political leader, Thamilchevan and five other senior leaders were killed in what was described by the LTTE as a precision air strike.[53] Despite these setbacks, LTTE forces on the ground put up a stiff defence against continuing SLA assaults. In a somewhat odd statement two years after the fact, the government formally withdrew from the 2002 ceasefire agreement in January 2008. After a number of setbacks, from August 2008 the SLA eventually advanced, taking Mannar in the west and then assaulting the

[51] This view was explicitly stated by Pieter Feith in discussions with GAM, at which the author was present, during negotiations that ultimately ended the Aceh conflict.

[52] SLMM 2007. *CFA 5 Years*, statement by the Sri Lanka Monitoring Mission, Feb. 22, 2007; *Sri Lanka's Human Rights Crisis*, Asia Report No. 135, 6, International Crisis Group, Colombo/Brussels (2007).

[53] This may have been an accurate account of events, although requiring close observation of this group in safe LTTE territory. An alternative account was growing divisions in the senior leadership of the LTTE over whether to fight or talk led the hard-line leadership to permanently remove soft-liners. Neither account was able to be substantiated.

LTTE's "capital" of Kilinochchie from three sides in November 2008, capturing it in January 2009. With the loss of their "capital," the LTTE, civilians under its protection and others retreated to Mullataivu where they underwent a sustained air attack, including against civilians sheltering with or being held by the LTTE. Again overwhelmed by the end of January 2009, the remaining LTTE forces and civilians retreated further.

Throughout this period, it was clear that a humanitarian disaster was unfolding. It is possible to mount a case that RtoP could have been applicable at several stages throughout the war in Sri Lanka, but towards the end of 2008 and into the first months of 2009, despite government efforts to restrict media coverage and to dissemble about the facts on the ground, it was becoming increasingly clear to the outside world that war crimes and crimes against humanity were being committed under the "complete operational freedom" granted to Sri Lanka army commanders to ensure the war's success.[54] It was this explicit "operational freedom" as a part of government policy that led to mass deaths that contravened the Rome Statute's Article 7 concerning "Crimes Against Humanity." Thus the grounds for RtoP were established, if not in terms so absolute that the UN Security Council could not help but take concrete steps (although recognizing China and Russia's role in limiting such steps). In that there had been arguments that genocide or ethnic cleansing was underway, this was more difficult to sustain. But genocide and ethnic cleansing were not required to be proven for war crimes and crimes against humanity to be committed.

Despite LTTE overtures that it was now willing to discuss a negotiated settlement, the government thus pressed the SLA's attack while foreign governments refused to intervene. The last months of the war were marked by unremitting brutality against civilians with consequently rapidly mounting civilian casualties. Human Rights Watch accused the SLA of "slaughtering" civilians through indiscriminate air and artillery attacks against positions where large numbers of civilians were known to be sheltering, making a mockery of President Rajapaksa's "zero civilian casualties" policy[55] and the SLA's claim that the area being shelled was a "no fire zone." The report also called on the government and the LTTE to release civilians being held by them, in particular some 200,000 who were pushed into a narrow, 14-kilometre strip of beach near Mullaitvu which had become the LTTE's last refuge. A UN confidential report estimated that 20,000 civilians were killed in the "no fire zone" in the last weeks of the war, at a rate of about 1,000 a day.[56] The Sri Lankan High Commissioner in London rejected that any civilians had been killed, and then qualified that by saying that: "If civilians had been killed, then that is because of the actions of the LTTE who were shooting and killing people when they tried to escape."[57] Government denials of the killings were common but increasingly unsustainable with mounting evidence showing the denials were at best a cover-up for the mass deaths. The government also routinely accused

[54] Neil Smith, *Understanding Sri Lanka's Defeat of the Tamil Tigers*, Joint Force Quarterly, No. 59, 40; *see also*, V.K. Shashikumar, *Lessons from the War in Sri Lanka*, Indian Defence Review, Oct. 3, 2009.

[55] Dean Nelson, *Tamil Tigers Prepare for Last Stand in Sri Lanka But Military Victory Is Not Political Peace*, The Daily Telegraph, Jan. 6, 2009.

[56] *Over 20,000 Tamils killed in Sri Lankan Onslaught*, Agence France Presse, May 29, 2009.

[57] *Id.*

anyone who raised such allegations of being either duped by LTTE propaganda or actively working for the LTTE.

In response to the unfolding humanitarian catastrophe, the United States said that it would block Sri Lanka's application for a $1.9 billion emergency loan from the International Monetary Fund because of its conduct in the war. The UK also said that it would not support the loan and also called for an investigation into allegations that Sri Lankan forces committed war crimes by shelling and bombing civilian targets, including hospitals.[58] Dissembling by the Sri Lanka government, however, created enough possible doubt about events at Mullaitivu within the UN Security Council to allow China to thwart any moves by the Security Council towards sanctions or intervention. RtoP was and remains based on a relatively small (if important) part of a larger international agreement that was subsequently dismissed by many of its signatories. As with most other international agreements, there was little capacity for the imposition of positive law to support it. RtoP had, therefore, always looked as though it would have weaknesses in application. That China thwarted Security Council resolutions regarding Sri Lanka meant that the requirements for implementing RtoP were not adequately established and its power of veto ensured that, even if such evidence was accepted as compelling, it would not allow the imposition of RtoP. Russia's support for the position only further weakened the case for RtoP in the Security Council. Undermining common agreement in the Security Council has been practiced since its establishment which, along with the power of veto, mean that the "realist" interests of member states will always trump agreement on a common humanitarian good.[59]

The Security Council did, however, express ". . . deep concern at the reports of continued use of heavy calibre weapons in areas with high concentrations of civilians, and expected the Government of Sri Lanka to fulfil its commitment in this regard." This "deep concern" and "expectation" may have been thought to have saved face for some UN Security Council members, but it did nothing to halt the mass killing in Sri Lanka. U.S. President Barack Obama ineffectually urged Sri Lanka to stop "indiscriminate shelling" of civilians and urged Tamil Tiger rebels to lay down their arms.[60] Despite this, "never again" continued to happen again.

V. THE FAILURE OF RTOP IN SRI LANKA

A major reason why the international community was not able to exercise more authority in relation to Sri Lanka, particularly in the final stages of the anti-LTTE war, was because it was both blocked in the UN Security Council by China and Russia and it was blocked on the ground by China and India both actively supporting the government of Sri Lanka. There was also considerable reluctance by Western states to do anything more than apply economic pressure to Sri Lanka, which might have been influential had it not been countered by China. It was particularly China's economic

[58] J. Page, *Sri Lanka Soldiers Fight Tamil Tigers, Trapping Civilians on Beach*, The Times, May 16, 2009.

[59] *See, e.g.*, Thomas Weiss, *The Illusion of UN Security Council Reform*, The Washington Quarterly Autumn 2003, 147–161.

[60] *Tamil War Zone Hospital Hit Again*, BBC News, May 13, 2009.

and military support for the government of Sri Lanka that effectively stopped international intervention and which limited the efficacy of economic sanctions. "The most remarkable aspect of Sri Lanka's recent victory over the Tamil Tigers is [that]. . . [w]ithout that Chinese backing, Rajapaksa's government would have had neither the wherewithal nor the will to ignore world opinion in its offensive against the Tigers."[61] China's involvement had compelled India to support the government of Sri Lanka, to ensure that its influence was not neutralized in favor of its regional competitor. "Sri Lanka was able to vanquish the Tigers also due to India's tacit support, which included providing training and logistical support such as naval surveillance to cut off Tigers' weapons supply." There were two motives: India wanted to be rid of the LTTE and, second, India could not sit back and see its regional influence overwhelmed by its main strategic competitor. "Against the combined military might of Sri Lanka, India and China, the LTTE was hopelessly outclassed."[62]

Setting aside India's mixed motives, Norway's efforts to achieve the 2002 Ceasefire Agreement (CFA) supported by the European Union, the United States, and Japan, was as close as Sri Lanka came to RtoP intervention. However, without a geo-political stake in its outcome, the international parties to the CFA were not able or willing to extend their involvement when the ceasefire began to break down from 2006.[63] Having initially backed peace efforts in Sri Lanka as a mechanism for resolving terrorism, the U.S. moved towards one of overall declining interest and increasing disenchantment with what it perceived to be the LTTE's problematic demands.[64] This corresponded with its War on Terror, a more global trend towards banning the LTTE as a terrorist organization, and U.S. positioning as a balance between India and China.[65]

Considering the above details and *prima facie* case for intervention and how it did not come about, it appears there were four key reasons why RtoP was not applied in Sri Lanka. The first reason was that the international community was (and remains) divided over whether or not RtoP is a legitimate form of international activity. In particular, a number of states with questionable human rights records, which include areas challenged by separatist movements or which have strategic alliances with such states have been reluctant to endorse or have been actively opposed to the implementation of RtoP principles. These included Sri Lanka and its main sponsor, China.

The second reason for the failure to invoke RtoP principles in the case of Sri Lanka was that, as a result of Sri Lankan appeals, the LTTE was widely classified as a proscribed terrorist organization, notably at a time when the U.S.-led "War on Terror" helped define much of the way in which otherwise more liberal states responded to "terrorist" threats. There was little international sympathy for the LTTE and considerable international support for the continued unity of the state of Sri Lanka. This should not have impacted upon international concern for the welfare of civilians, but the

[61] Wen Liao, *China Crosses the Rubicon*, AUSTRALIAN FINANCIAL REVIEW, Jun. 23, 2009.

[62] Anita Pratap, *Lessons from the Tiger Defeat*, THE WEEK, May 31, 2009.

[63] Jonathan Goodhand, *Aid, Conflict and Peace Building in Sri Lanka, Conflict Assessments*, Centre for Defence Studies King's College, University of London, 2001.

[64] Jeffrey Lundstead, *The United States' Role in Sri Lanka's Peace Process 2002–2006*, 33, 36–37 (2007).

[65] Robert Kaplan, *Center Stage for the Twenty-first Century*, FOREIGN AFFAIRS, March/April 2009, 16–32.

government of Sri Lanka was clever in the way it obscured the plight of and the circumstances under which Tamil civilians were with the LTTE.

The third reason for the failure to invoke RtoP principles in the case of Sri Lanka was that the economic sanctions that were applied were too little, too uncoordinated, too late, and ultimately countered by China's economic support. Beyond economic or other sanctions, should members of the international community have contemplated on-ground RtoP intervention, under its generally accepted (if not specifically endorsed) terms, it must have had a reasonable chance of success and must not have caused more harm than it resolved. Following India's unsuccessful intervention in 1987, neither of these criteria could be guaranteed. Indeed, given increasing Sri Lankan belligerence, there was a high likelihood of official military resistance, backed by China and possibly India.

Finally, the fourth reason for the failure to invoke RtoP principles in the case of Sri Lanka was that such an attempt would ordinarily require the endorsement if not active participation of the UN Security Council, which was blocked by China and actively opposed by Russia.

These four factors; international disagreement over RtoP, reservations about or being antithetical towards the LTTE, the likely human cost of intervention, and the lack of support from the UN Security Council, all contributed to making an RtoP intervention either ineffective as sanctions and all but impossible in an on-ground capacity.

In the end, no country cared enough about Sri Lanka's Tamils to want to go to the trouble of invoking RtoP. The UN Security Council was stymied by China and Russia, late and relatively minor sanctions by Western countries had little effect given that China had stepped into the military and economic breech, India vied with China to support the government, and the RtoP principle of benefits exceeding cost could not, reasonably, be established.

A resolution to the Sri Lankan conflict had not been likely, or possible, without significant international pressure to adopt measures which reflected a fundamental compromise on the part of both parties, and support for such measures once adopted. It may be that the earlier employment of RtoP could be produced this effect, especially if around the time of or as part of the SLMM (noting that this pre-dated the establishment of RtoP). Such an intervention would have implied, among other measures, a more substantial version of the SLMM, the promise of extra aid and the threat of serious sanctions on either party should they break the agreement. Having said that, the LTTE only came to a point of genuine preparedness to compromise in 2008–2009, well after the government of Sri Lanka had embarked on an opposite course.[66] From the election of Rajapaksa as president in 2005, the die was effectively cast, yet it was only at that time that the international community had formally adopted the idea of RtoP and had not yet moved to a position of enacting it. Had a sustainable solution been available at any time, Sri Lanka needed to return to being a more substantive democracy, working gradually back towards a notion of civic nationalism in which equity under rule of law rather than ethnicity was the effective basis for a sense of

[66] Based on discussions by the author with senior LTTE members in Sri Lanka in 2006 and outside Sri Lanka from that time until the defeat of the organization.

inclusion and participation, or at least the equitable management of different interest claims. This appeared an increasingly distant goal, following a change to the Sri Lanka constitution in September 2010 to end limits on presidential terms, the ending of the presidential advisory council and the direct political appointment of judges.[67] Assuming these changes did not imply "the last nail in the coffin of democracy"[68] or "absolute power,"[69] after perhaps generations, a sense of normalcy and unity might have returned to Sri Lanka, although not without deep and far reaching changes. Following the end of the war, such an outcome appeared to be further away than ever and such a potential path appeared littered with significant obstacles which the international community showed little interest in trying to surmount.

The world had a clear opportunity and, in terms of civilian deaths, a moral obligation to bring RtoP principles to bear in the Sri Lanka war. Instead, tens of thousands of people were killed in a relentless and barbaric act of warfare that only finds parallel with the mass killings of Bosnia and Kosovo, Rwanda, and Darfur. Indeed, it is probably inappropriate to try to compare acts of barbarity and inhumanity, as though there was some sliding scale by which some could be deemed more or less cruel and inhuman than others. All have the same intent and malignant lack of regard for human life; it has only been the efficacy of application that differentiated them. Sri Lanka was no different. Perhaps the timely application of RtoP could have averted the humanitarian disaster that was the Sri Lanka Eelam war, but by the time RtoP existed it was probably already too late, not least because of the structural impediments placed in its way by China, Russia, India, and the government of Sri Lanka and probably the LTTE itself.

It may be, had RtoP been properly implemented in a timely manner, Sri Lanka could now be rebuilding as a prospering, liberal democratic state with respect for civil and political rights and in which there was devolved authority for ethnically specific areas. At different times different relevant parties have aimed for such an outcome. The problem was that none of them aimed for such an outcome at corresponding times, the international community paid too little attention for too long and such opportunity, as it ever existed, was lost.

[67] The constitutional changes were approved by the Sri Lanka Supreme Court, which was also politically beholden.

[68] Jane Cowan, *Sri Lankan President Extends Grip on Power*, ABC News (Australia), Sept. 9, 2010.

[69] *Sri Lanka chief Mahinda Rajapakse Gets Total Power*, The Australian, Sept. 9, 2010.

15 Democratic Republic of Congo

Delphine Schrank

It has become commonplace to illustrate any article or report on the Democratic Republic of Congo (DRC) with vile assaults on civilian life. A random sampling since 2000 includes a doctor on the daily task of patching together another womb butchered from inside by something sharp and solid; a villager on neighbors locked in homes that were then burned to the ground; or a girl describing a gang rape that ended with sexual slavery for her and mutilation followed by slaughter for about a dozen companions. Or: a man is shot dead for refusing to violate his daughter; villagers are forced to eat chunks of their own flesh; and a woman hears her daughters screaming in an adjoining room as she watches her husband cut to pieces. Then, she later tells a reporter, she is forced to collect the body parts, lie on top and endure a gang rape herself.[1]

To tour through eastern Congo is to discover a land of incongruous natural beauty in which atrocities and abuses have become so commonplace, so numerous and frequent that some on initial meeting seem to be casually resigned to their

[1] For the particularities of each of these instances, and others across the years: Paul Salopek, *River of Blood Flows in War-Torn Congo*, Chicago Tribune, Dec. 11, 2000; Ishbel Matheson, *DR Congo's Women in the Frontline*, BBC News, Nov. 6, 2002; Emily Wax, *A Brutal Legacy of Congo War; Extent of Violence against Women Surfaces as Fighting Recedes*, Washington Post, Oct. 25, 2003; *Africa's Unmended Heart*, The Economist, Jun. 9, 2005; Jeffrey Gettleman, *Rape Epidemic Raises Trauma of Congo War*, New York Times, Oct. 7, 2007; *DR Congo Rebels Take Town In New Offensive*, Agence France Presse, Nov 6, 2008; Adam Hochschild, *Rape of the Congo*, 56(13) N.Y. Review of Books, Aug. 13, 2009, Human Rights Watch, *"You Will Be Punished;" Attacks On Civilians In Eastern Congo*, Dec. 2009; Nicholas D. Kristof, *The Grotesque Vocabulary in Congo*, New York Times, Feb. 11, 2010; Lisa Shannon, *No, Sexual Violence is Not "Cultural,"* Int'l Herald Tribune, Jun. 26, 2010; Jeffrey Gettleman, *Congo: "UN's Crowning Failure"; Peacekeepers Incapable of Protecting Civilians From Sexual Violence*, Int'l Herald Tribune, Oct. 5 2010.

occurrence. The horrific has become the ordinary. An urbane young woman I met one night in the eastern provincial capital of Goma told me with a shrug about the rape that day of a girlfriend whose husband then threw her out into the street because he couldn't stand the shame. Said another, a fisherman, on being thrown in jail for denouncing on local radio the national army's incompetence and complicity with militias camped near his village: "I'm not afraid. It's normal. That's Congo."[2]

Citizens from Congo's homegrown, cacophonous civil society—local journalists, pastors, community leaders, rights groups, and lone-dog activists—have long spoken out or tried however they might to pressure their government into staunching the suffering and violence.[3] In parallel, a substantial and ever-growing body of statements, documents, and reports from UN organs, aid groups, and other credible organizations allege that since 1993, and ongoing into early 2011 at the time of this writing, the scope, scale, and severity of sexual violence, killings, displacements, press-ganging, pillaging, torture, use of child soldiers, extortion, and other abuses against the inhabitants of Congo amount to serious crimes under international law that fall within the definition of crimes against humanity, war crimes and, at various points in the past decade, potentially acts of genocide.

Among the more devastating consequences: The number of internally displaced persons has since 2008 hovered around the 2 million mark which, depending on the period, makes DRC's displacement the third or fourth highest in the world. DRC has also been called, authoritatively, the world capital of rape, and six years after the nominal end of full-scale war, the rate (and brutality) of sexual violence has increased, reaching an all-time recorded high in 2009. A peer-reviewed mortality study has found that since 1998, 5.4 million people have died and 45,000 more die each month, largely from indirect consequences of conflict such as hunger and disease. This gives the Congolese crisis the claim to rank as most lethal since World War I.

[2] Interview with Adolphe Kakule Mambomingi, president of the Vishumbi fisherman's committee, Vishumbi, DRC, Oct. 14, 2008.

[3] *See* a joint letter dated Sept. 3, 2010, in which 220 Congolese human rights nonprofits pledged support for the just-released *UN mapping exercise on serious violations of human rights committed in DRC between 1993 and 2003* (*see* note 50, below). The groups "invite[d] the government to seize the occasion for a sincere reconciliation," and called for "new judicial policies based on the creation of judicial mechanisms," *available at* http://www.scribd.com/doc/36950742/Position-Des-Organ-is-at-Ions-de-La-Societe-Civile-Congolaise-Sur-Le-Rapport-Du-Projet-Mapping; *see also,* a 2010 letter of protest to the prime minister by South Kivu members of Congo's National Assembly, who wrote: "We find it sadistic and irresponsible that your government declares without embarrassment that there is peace throughout with only a few residual pockets of resistance in our province" quoted in Human Rights Watch, *Always on the Run: The Vicious Cycle of Displacement in Eastern Congo*, Sept., 2010, at 7; *available at* http://www.hrw.org/en/reports/2010/09/14/always-run-0; Or, in a typical example of civic disobedience and advocacy campaigns in which about 1,700 Congolese women marched against rape in Bukavu, South Kivu, in mid-Oct., 2010, *see DR Congo Women March Against Rape*, Al Jazeera, Oct. 17, 2010, *available at* http://english.aljazeera.net/news/africa/2010/10/20101017181314911798.html; Or, for examples of DRC's dynamic local media exposing government corruption and massive siphoning off of funds even amid the turmoil of the post-war transition government in 2005, *see* Ben-Clet, *Pillage Budgétaire*, Le Potentiel, Oct. 26, 2005; Faustin Kuediasala, *Selon le Rapport Conjoint Cour Des Comptes-Igf Dgi: Plus de 28 millions USD Des Crédits d'impôts Fictifs*, Le Potentiel, Nov. 8, 2005; *RDC. Le Budget 2005 et Ses Xontradictions*, Le Phare, Nov. 29, 2005.

History shows that the Congolese government has manifestly failed to prevent or stop the bleed, and other local mechanisms are at present unable to cope.[4] For all the apparent "slow burn" of the country's mortality crisis, the sheer number of affected civilians combined with the systemic and cumulative nature of decidedly non-slow-acting atrocities stagger the imagination. Both as a matter of clear and present danger to civilians in a country of unabated volatility, and as a humanitarian catastrophe occurring slowly over time, the question seems less whether the Responsibility to Protect (RtoP) applies than how, if at all, that assessment could translate into improving lives.

There is, after all, no easy diagnosis for the violence in DRC. It is messy. It is complex. It has in past years involved several interlocking crises rather then a single emergency: Fighting has taken place among Congolese, with the meddling of foreign governments, their proxies or their rebels, and within the broader context of a deeply impoverished country with a weak government mired by entrenched corruption, dysfunctional institutions and national security forces that have proven chronically predatory and incapable of controlling the territory or of adequately defending the population. Combatants from an alphabet soup of armed groups have regularly swapped uniforms and alliances, splintered and regrouped. On January 23, 2008, 22 warring parties sat around a table with the government to sign a truce for the restive eastern provinces of North and South Kivu. A more recent estimate whittled their number down to 20.[5] Their farrago of motives include localized land grievances and manipulated ethnic hatreds; shifting loyalties between clan, tribal groups, and the nation; self-defense in a chronic security vacuum; foreign patronage; control of natural resources; revenge; and personal power.[6] Also, too many young men with small prospects of employment in an area awash in small arms.[7] All this takes place on a stage the size of the United States east of the Mississippi composed largely of jungle or other inhospitable terrain, rendered the more inaccessible for want of basic infrastructure or functional transportation networks, and that consequently permits the

[4] This is the general view expressed in most credible reports. For instance, "In light of the gravity of the human rights situation, which has not improved over the course of the last year, the experts recommend that the Council once again consider the creation of a country-specific mandate, in particular if the level of access and response to thematic special procedures decreases," in *Technical Assistance and Capacity Building; Second joint report of seven United Nations Experts on the Situation in the Democratic Republic of Congo*, A/HRC/13/63, Mar. 8, 2010, at 3.

[5] List compiled by Jason Stearns, Jun. 9, 2010, *available at* http://congosiasa.blogspot.com/2010/06/list-of-armed-groups-in-kivus.html.

[6] *See* SEVERINE AUTESSERRE, THE TROUBLE WITH THE CONGO: LOCAL VIOLENCE AND THE FAILURE OF INTERNATIONAL PEACEBUILDING (2010); GERARD PRUNIER, AFRICA'S WORLD WAR; CONGO, THE RWANDAN GENOCIDE AND THE MAKING OF A CONTINENTAL CATASTROPHE (2008).

[7] Summed otherwise: "Impunity, the existence of non-state armed actors, the present state of the security and justice sectors, the illegal exploitation of natural resources, the political manipulation of ethnic cleavages and the lack of equality between men and women are identified as root causes of human rights concerns," in UN HRC, 10th Session, *Combined Report of Seven Thematic Special Procedures on Technical Assistance to the Government of the Democratic Republic of Congo and Urgent Examination of the Situation in the East of the Country*, A/HRC/10/59, Mar. 5, 2009.

entrenchment of thugs and criminal networks in remote borderlands or mineral-rich fiefdoms.[8]

Moreover, a cursory glance would suggest that the world has already exhibited a concerted commitment to bring Africa's third-largest nation toward peace and stability. The United Nations has since 1999 deployed a peacekeeping mission, which quickly evolved from a small observer mission into the largest UN operation in the world, with a Chapter VII mandate permitting lethal force to protect civilians under imminent threat. On the heels of several well-publicized failings to prevent fresh attacks on civilians, Security Council resolutions have since 2008 called on the mission—known by its French acronym as MONUC until it was renamed MONUSCO from July 1, 2010—to make civilian protection a priority. In 2006, the UN was also responsible for coordinating aid from the international community—at approximately $450 million about ten times the amount of funding from DRC itself—into the making of the world's most expensive multiparty elections.[9] These overcame massive logistical obstacles and succeeded in delivering to the Congolese their first democratically elected government in 40 years. Diplomats have since shuttled between regional capitals or rebel encampments or organized authoritative peace conferences; and international nonprofits or regional bodies such as the European Union have dispatched assistance to variously prevent hostilities, strengthen the architecture of state, or merely tether a lifeline to millions of civilians suffering from hunger, disease, grievous physical or psychic injury, or the more general collapse of their societal safety nets.

Yet if the crisis in DRC seems as hopeless as it is complex, the devil, as usual, is in the details. Strong arguments also indicate that deeper assumptions underlying Western-led international efforts, in DRC as throughout Africa, are badly flawed. This would explain floundering attempts to reform DRC's critically malfunctioning security sector. Or, as discussed below, the UN mandate has piled up complicated and often contradictory sets of tasks and roles within a broader effort to prevent hostilities or help reconstruct public institutions that never were.[10] Efforts to date to apply civilian protection as a priority, and what that means exactly and to whom, have been

[8] As the North Kivu provincial minister of mines put it when asked about the usurpation of the province's largest tin-ore mine by the renegade 85th Brigade of the Congolese armed forces: "The problem is that these zones are inaccessible. If we put roads, all those armed men wouldn't even be able to put up barriers;" Interview with Juma Balikwisha Mulhondi, provincial minister of mines for North Kivu, Goma, Nov., 2008. We were discussing the tin ore, or cassiterite, mine at Bisie, in the Walikale area of North Kivu, to which a South African-based multinational, Mining and Processing Congo, held the legal rights of exploration. But a renegade Congolese army unit's illegal exploitation of the mine, estimated to provide 80 percent of the tin ore exported from North Kivu, was an open national secret. To access Bisie would require chartering a plane (or sitting on bags of tin in a cargo hold) then walking a 26-mile, treacherous footpath through jungle. *See* Delphine Schrank, *Tin Fever*, 86(4) Virginia Q. Rev. (Fall 2010), *available at* http://www.vqronline.org/articles/2010/fall/scrank-tin-fever/.

[9] *Elections in the Democratic Republic of Congo in 2006*, Department For International Development, at 3; *available at* http://www.dfid.gov.uk/Documents/publications1/elections/elections-cd-2006.pdf.

[10] For the argument that the DRC government never possessed an effective bureaucracy, the rule of law, nor a coercive monopoly over its territory, *see* Thomas Callaghy, The State-Society Struggle: Zaire in Comparative Perspective (1984); Crawford Young & Thomas Turner, The Rise and Decline of the Zairian State (1984); *see also* Pierre Englebert & Denis M. Tull,

complicated by problems at all levels, from the political to the tactical. Nor has international will in reality been so forthcoming: MONUC has been chronically under-equipped and under-manned, political investment in resolving the crisis hampered by conflicting national interests, and analyses sometimes distorted by more appealing domestic narratives. Aid, for all the scholarly controversy surrounding its ability to deliver results in impoverished countries,[11] has been called "a drop in the ocean" in DRC, compared with the needs of the population.[12]

The people of DRC, in short, have often been given short shrift. Solutions may be neither palatable to domestic or international policy debates, but the urgency of the ongoing cost to Congo's 68 million people—compounded by the prioritization of RtoP as a legitimizing doctrine—make it incumbent on all stakeholders, primarily the Congolese government in concert with the international community, to consider their full range of options.

This chapter will first provide some necessary political background. Second, it applies the RtoP doctrine. Third, it analyzes international responses and their limitations. Finally, it surveys potential solutions. It concludes that if the Congolese must ultimately be empowered to help themselves, the international community must coordinate better; provide the means to match desired ends; and vastly improve the practical application of civilian protection, through the UN with potential help from controversial alternatives.

I. POLITICAL BACKGROUND

Congo's most recent, back-to-back conflicts are rooted in fallout from the 1994 slaughter of 800,000 Tutsis and moderate Hutus in tiny, neighboring Rwanda, combined with the collapse of the Congolese state after three decades of misrule by Mobutu Sese Seko. Two brutal wars, from 1996 to 1997 and then from 1998 to 2003, played out against a backdrop of longstanding economic and political decay. Smaller, more localized conflicts have since 2003 continued in eastern provinces, resulting in extreme violence and civilian suffering that has yet to show signs of abating.

As Paul Kagame's Tutsi-led Rwandan Patriotic Front swept through Rwanda to end the genocide, Hutus fled into Uganda, Tanzania, Burundi and about 2 million into in eastern DRC. Into that miles-long exodus melted Rwanda's genocidaires. From their new base in UN refugee camps in the Kivus, they periodically launched revenge attacks

Postconflict Reconstruction in Africa; Flawed Ideas about Failed States, 32(4) INT'L SEC. 106–139 (Spring 2008).

[11] *See* WILLIAM EASTERLY, THE WHITE MAN'S BURDEN: WHY THE WEST'S EFFORTS TO AID THE REST HAVE DONE SO MUCH ILL AND SO LITTLE GOOD (2006); PAUL COLLIER, THE BOTTOM BILLION: WHY THE POOREST COUNTRIES ARE FAILING AND WHAT CAN BE DONE ABOUT IT (2008).

[12] *Aid to DR Congo Province is "Drop in the Ocean": UNHCR*, AGENCE FRANCE PRESSE, Jul. 22, 2010. The head of the UN refugee agency was referring to aid to 210,000 people from restive Equateur province. This compounds the finding of the Humanitarian Response Index 2010 that donors are "disproportionately channeling to eastern conflict areas" and not adequately responding "to equally serious needs elsewhere," in *The Humanitarian Response Index 2010: The Problems of Politicization*, DARA, at 35 (2010), *available at* http://daraint.org/wp-content/uploads/2010/10/Complete-report_HRI-2010.pdf. The report found that 65% of the Humanitarian Action Plan funding was channeled to four provinces out of DRC's 11 provinces (10 plus the city of Kinshasa).

back over the border.[13] So began the first Congolese war: An incursion in 1996 from Kagame's Tutsi-led government to clear out Hutu extremists in Congo, resulting in the slaughter of an estimated 400,000 people, and a march on Kinshasa, the capital, under Congolese rebel leader Laurent-Desiree Kabila leading an alliance of rebel groups backed by Rwanda, Uganda, and Burundi. Mobutu's ramshackle and notoriously abusive army scattered. Newly installed as president, Kabila tried to oust his foreign patrons. His coalition fell apart, Rwanda and Uganda invaded, and DRC in 1998 descended anew into a bloody anarchy that eventually sucked in armies and mercenaries from nine countries fighting with, against, or among homegrown militias.[14]

In 1999, the Lusaka cease-fire agreement led to the creation of a small UN mission to oversee the terms of the truce. But fighting in "Africa's World War" raged until a nominal deal signed in December 2002, almost two years after Kabila's assassination. Foreign armies withdrew, and Joseph Kabila, Laurent's son, oversaw a power-sharing government until the 2006 elections, which returned Joseph to power as president buoyed by an overwhelming majority from the still-violent eastern provinces on the strength of his campaign promises to bring peace.

Much of the country has since been pacified, and investment has begun to return, particularly to mineral-rich southern Katanga province. But a dangerous volatility persisted through 2010. That same year, the Fund for Peace ranked DRC fifth in its Failed State Index, according to indicators that include group grievances, delegitimization of the state, factionalized elites and security-sector dsyfunction.[15] Hope has soured on Kabila's presidency. A new constitution, passed by referendum in 2005, promised to fulfill democratic aspirations lacking since independence from Belgium. Its implementation "clearly linked the return of lasting peace to the principle of a balance of power between central government and the provinces and the establishment of genuine checks and balances at both levels . . . Nearly four years on, however,

[13] On the uses of the camps as a political base for the ousted Hutu-led government, *see* John Pomfret, *Aid Dilemma: Keeping It from the Oppressors; UN, Charities Find Crises Make Them Tools of War*, WASHINGTON POST, Sept. 23, 1997. At this point there was no peacekeeping force in place, and the dilemma was posed as follows: "In Congo and several other post-Cold War regional crises, humanitarian action has become a substitute for Western military and diplomatic intervention. Yet the aid agencies lack the tools or the clout to handle the explosive situations they find themselves confronting. As such, the aid they bring often becomes a resource in a conflict, helping to fan its flames rather than damp then down." In this case, Pomfret writes, "Mobutu's army hijacked UN-chartered planes to transport guns," and "under the gaze of international aid workers, the planes flew into UN-run refugee camps where the arms were distributed to Rwandan Hutu refugees . . . who had become Mobutu's first line of defense. At the same time, the anti-Mobutu rebel army flew on stolen aid fuel, rolled in stolen aid trucks and grew strong on stolen aid food. As a Western ambassador put it: 'The failure of the West to deal with the Rwandan refugee crisis led directly to the fall of Mobutu.'" *Id.*

[14] PRUNIER, *supra* note 6; E. NEWMAN & O. RICHMOND, EDS., CHALLENGES TO PEACEBUILDING (2006).

[15] *Failed State Index 2010, available at* http://www.fundforpeace.org/web/index.php?option=com_content&task=view&id=99&Itemid=140. Likewise, for all its potential to rank among the wealthiest in Africa, DRC's 2010 human development index—based on education, health and income levels–ranked 168th out of 169 countries with comparable data; see *Human Development Indicators 2010: Congo (Democratic Republic of), Country Profiles, available at* http://hdrstats.undp.org/en/countries/profiles/COD.html.

the record is abysmal. [Kabila's] presidency is seeking to impose its power on all branches of the state and maintain parallel networks of decision-making."[16]

Since 2003, and in three agreements since 2007 in the Kivus, key protagonists have agreed to terms that would together enshrine a comprehensive peace. Foreign armies and proxies were meant to withdraw and Congolese combatants given the choice to demobilize or integrate into national forces through a process known as *brassage* that would involve training then breaking up former rebel groups by scattering members across army units. Many merely donned uniforms, retained their old structure, or never showed up for training, frittering into the jungle or other remote areas.[17] Among them were myriad local defense or Mai Mai militias.[18] All armed groups, including units of the army, continued to finance their efforts from minerals.[19] Two major rebel forces maintained fiefdoms in the east: the first, led by Rwandan Hutu extremists regrouped as the Democratic Forces for the Liberation of Rwanda (FDLR), and the second, an opposing force fighting in the name of Congolese Tutsis, the National Congress for the Defense of the People (CNDP) under a former Congolese army general, Laurent Nkunda, with clandestine military and financial backing from Rwanda.

This last situation violently and suddenly shape-shifted when Kagame's Rwandan government arrested its protégé, Nkunda, then joined the Congolese government and MONUC in a two-pronged military operation—a joint DRC-Rwanda "Umoja Wetu" campaign from January 20 to February 25, 2009, and then "Kimia II" with MONUC from February onward—aimed at ousting the FDLR from DRC. By most credible accounts, the operations failed miserably, at a devastating cost to civilians. Again rebel forces had been badly incorporated into DRC officialdom.[20] By fall 2010, the rank and file of the Congolese armed forces (FARDC), at about 120,000-strong, remained ill-disciplined, erratically paid and widely documented to prey on both population and land. Commands have often been given to men accused of serious crimes. Among the most flagrant is Bosco Ntaganda, CNDP ex-chief of staff, wanted by the International Criminal Court, rewarded instead with a generalship.[21]

[16] *Congo: A Stalled Democratic Agenda*, International Crisis Group, Africa Briefing No. 73 (Nairobi/Brussels, 2010), at 1, *available at* http://www.crisisgroup.org/en/regions/africa/central-africa/dr-congo/b073-congo-a-stalled-democratic-agenda.aspx.

[17] According to Government estimates, more than 100,000 fighters were by early July 2007 still waiting to be processed at training centers, noted in UN Human Rights Council 7th Session, *UN Special Rapporteur on Violence against Women, its Causes and Consequences, Yakin Ertuürk, Mission to the Democratic Republic of Congo*, A/HRC/7/6/Add.4, Feb. 28, 2008, at ¶ 89, *available at* http://www2.ohchr.org/english/bodies/hrcouncil/docs/7session/A.HRC.7.6.Add.4.doc.

[18] The Swahili term "Mai Mai" refers to the water amulets its fighters were said to wear to ward off bullets.

[19] UN reports by first a specially appointed Panel of Experts then a Group of Experts on the long-standing illegal exploitation of natural resources include S/2001/357, Apr. 12, 2001, and S/2010/596, Nov. 29, 2010.

[20] The integration of the CNDP into the Congolese armed forces was a requirement of a March 23, 2009 peace agreement.

[21] Others include: a Mai Mai Commander in Moba, where 45 women and girls were allegedly raped by Mai Mai fighters during 2002 to 2004, who has since been integrated into the FARDC with a command position at the Headquarters of the Naval Force; or Peter Karim Ugada (former FNI), Mathieu Ngudjolo of Mouvment revolutionnaire congolais, and Justin "Cobra" Matat (former FRPI), three former militia leaders in Ituri province each made FARDC colonels.

Meanwhile, a crisis erupted in northern Provence Orientale around the Lord's Resistance Army, a Ugandan militia renowned for chopping off lips and ears, that there found a conveniently un-policed foothold from which to massacre and attack civilians with impunity. Another erupted in late 2009 in the previously peaceful Equateur province when inter-ethnic armed clashes broke out over disputed farming and fishing rights, prompting an exodus of 192,000 people.[22]

II. MASS ATROCITIES THAT TRIGGER RTOP INTERVENTION

Though this discussion only looks at three key areas of mass distress, a more comprehensive analysis would include the recruitment and use of child soldiers within wider abuses of children, pillaging, arbitrary detentions, torture, and extortion. The devastating effects of the crisis on the young, however, can be glimpsed below, including findings that at least half Congo's conflict-related deaths are children, and that most sexual violence victims are adolescents.

The Democratic Republic of Congo is party to the main human rights treaties, including the Genocide Convention, the International Covenant on Civil and Political Rights (ICCPR), the Convention on the Elimination of All Forms of Discrimination Against Women (CEDAW), and the Convention on the Rights of the Child (CRC). It also ratified the Rome Statute for the International Criminal Court in 2002.

UN Special Advisor on RtoP, Ed Luck, has noted that where armed groups control territory, they should bear responsibility for protecting its population.[23] Major violators accordingly include the Congolese armed forces (FARDC), the Democratic Forces for the Liberation of Rwanda (FDLR) and its major factions, the National Congress for the Defense of the People (CNDP), and the Lord's Resistance Army (LRA).

A. Forced Displacement and Related Mortality

At the sound of gunfire—and fresh threats of atrocities—villagers flee. In flip-flops or barefoot, loaded down with jerry cans and a straw mat, perhaps a cooking pot or a bag of flour, they disappear into columns of escapees on the roads toward internally displaced persons (IDP) camps already overstocked with inhabitants, to distant relatives and acquaintances, or to makeshift refuges in open hangars, former schools, or churches.

For Congolese civilians, the flight from gunfire or the terror of fresh attacks has since 1993 acquired a haunting familiarity.[24] The number of IDPs has for several years

[22] *UN Takes New Security Steps After Deadly Attack in North-Western DR Congo*, UN NEWS, Apr. 7, 2010. *See also Democratic Republic Of Congo: Insecurity And Displacement*, UN Office for the Coordination Of Humanitarian Affairs, Apr. 2010, *available at* http://www.unhcr.org/refworld/category,COI,,MAP,,4bd691f92,0.html.

[23] Edward C. Luck, *The Responsibility to Protect: Growing Pains or Early Promise?* 24.4 Ethics and International Affairs, Vol. 24.4 (Winter 2010).

[24] Thus does Human Rights Watch call its report on the subject *Always on the Run*, *supra* note 3; *See also* an iconic photo of displacement that might as well date from 1994 as 2010: http://en.wikipedia.org/wiki/File:Kibativillagers.jpg

hovered around the 2 million mark, with more than 450,000 refugees in neighboring countries.[25] Of those, about 1.4 million are in the Kivu provinces alone.[26] In 2009, according to the Internal Displacement Monitoring Centre, DRC saw the highest number of new displacements both in Africa and, relative to itself, since 2004. At all stages of displacement IDPs in DRC endure vastly increased vulnerability to extreme violence. A 2008 UN report noted that victims in North Kivu have at times been "primarily" IDPs.[27] Displaced children face particular risks.[28]

They are also more likely to die. In a 2007 International Rescue Committee study that found a death toll of 5.4 million people in DRC since 1998 with 45,000 more dying a month,[29] the vast majority died of indirect public health effects of conflict, including higher rates of infectious diseases, such as malaria, diarrhea, pneumonia, increased prevalence of malnutrition and complications arising from neonatal- and pregnancy-related conditions—all "likely related to the social and economic disturbances caused by conflict, including disruption of health services, poor food security, deterioration of infrastructure and population displacement."[30] Nearly half the dead were children younger than five. The national crude mortality rate was 57 percent above the average for sub-Saharan Africa, with some zones seriously surpassing the accepted emergency threshold for determining humanitarian emergencies.[31] Ending in December 2006 before hostilities provoked at least another 400,000 to flee, the study noted its final tally represented a "conservative figure."

[25] See factsheet on the web site of Refugees International, *available at* http://www.refugeesinternational.org/where-we-work/africa/dr-congo.

[26] *Always on the Run, supra* note 3, at 5.

[27] *Twenty-Sixth Report of the Secretary-General on the United Nations Organization Mission in the Democratic Republic of the Congo*, Security Council, S/2008/433, Jul. 3, 2008, at ¶ 65, *available at* http://www.securitycouncilreport.org/atf/cf/%7B65BFCF9B-6D27–4E9C-8CD3-CF6E4FF96FF9%7D/DRC%20S2008433.pdf

[28] *Protection of Civilian Populations in the DRC Snapshot Report*, OCHA, Jan. 28, 2010, cited in *Always on the Run, supra* note 3, at 23, as follows: "Spontaneous settlements are crowded and chaotic environments without basic social services, leading to a breakdown in protective mechanisms for children. Children are more vulnerable to sexual violence, abuse and exploitation, recruitment into armed groups, abduction, social exclusion and emotional distress . . . In the majority of IDP sites, the extensive presence of armed elements inside and around the sites continues to put IDPs at risk. Not only does this presence of armed elements defy the civilian character of IDP sites, it exposes the IDPs to severe exactions including harassment, rape and looting."

[29] Benjamin Coghlan, Richard J. Brennan et al., *Mortality in the Democratic Republic of Congo: An Ongoing Crisis*, International Rescue Committee & Burnet Institute, 2007, at 1. Researchers visited 14,000 households in 35 districts of Congo's 11 provinces then combined the results with tallies in annual mortality surveys conducted since 2000. While the survey noted a tiny but significant decline in mortality rates in the unstable eastern provinces, a rare positive development attributed to the presence of UN peacekeepers, it also pointed to a rise in mortality in central regions otherwise free of combat, a change the authors said most likely reflected neglect by the government (and foreign aid programs) in an attempt to focus on the east. See also Benjamin Coghlan, Richard J. Brennan et al., *Mortality in the Democratic Republic of Congo: A Nationwide Survey*, 367 The Lancet 44–51, Jan. 7, 2006.

[30] *Id.* at iii.

[31] *Mortality In The Democratic Republic Of Congo: An Ongoing Crisis, supra* note 29, at 7.

A report released in January 2010 questioned the study's findings and methodology.[32] The IRC defended itself on grounds that its study had been subject to peer review, its methodological limitations widely examined and that the criticism was neither original nor itself free from "inconsistencies, conflicting evidence and poor scholarship."[33] Moreover, others have also shown conflict-related, slow-acting damage. A 2009 UNICEF report notes that DRC exceeds the established critical emergency threshold for the "wasting rate" in acute malnutrition among children,[34] a strong international determinant of urgent humanitarian need. Widespread malnutrition is particularly indicative of abnormality for occurring in a land with immense agricultural potential.[35]

IDPs typically abandon fields only to starve in the forest or depend on handouts in official IDP camps that have rarely been sufficient.[36] The majority seeks sanctuary with friends, relatives, or strangers, most of whom already barely scrape by, have little to no access to assistance,[37] and are as prone to attack as their guests.[38] As of May 2010, the UN estimated that 86 percent of IDPs had sought such refuge.[39] This figure came months after the near-overnight closing and emptying of five official camps housing 60,000 IDPs, when authorities toward the end of Kimia II deemed areas safe from FDLR. Diplomats and UN officials welcomed the initiative, but according to Human Rights Watch, the move "compromised the safety of at least some of the tens of thousands of people whose homes, fields and villages had been appropriated by locals or armed groups or whose return home otherwise remained perilous."[40]

[32] John Bohannon and John Travis, *How Many Have Died Due to Congo's Fighting? Scientists Battle Over How to Estimate War-Related Deaths*, Science Insider, Jan. 21, 2010, *available at* http://news.sciencemag.org/scienceinsider/2010/01/post-1.html. James Butty, *A New Study Finds Death Toll in Congo War Too High*, Voice Of America (English Service), Jan. 21, 2010.

[33] *Id.* The authors of the IRC study are explicit that they extrapolated a final death toll from an abstract rate based on conflicting estimates for the total Congolese population and difficulties establishing prewar mortality, which inevitably leads to imprecision. See *Mortality In The Democratic Republic Of Congo: An Ongoing Crisis*, *supra* note 29, at 4.

[34] *Machel Study 10-Year Strategic Review: Children and Conflict in a Changing World*, UNICEF, Apr. 2009, at 128.

[35] Though favored by extensive soil fertility and the climate, agricultural development has stalled subject to the general economic collapse, in which the conflicts have compounded corruption, vast numbers of overlapping taxes and pricing policies, and infrastructure problems. As a result, DRC now produces insufficient quantities of food for its population and imports about 1,25,000 tons a year. *See Trade Policy Review: Democratic Republic of Congo*, World Trade Organization, WT/TPR/S/240 (Nov. 24 and 26, 2010), *available at* http://www.wto.org/english/tratop_e/tpr_e/tp340_e.htm.

[36] *Id.*; *see also*, *Always on the Run*, *supra* note 3.

[37] Oxfam, *Out of Site, Building Better Responses to the Displacement in the DRC by Helping Host Families*, Oct. 1, 2008, *available at* http://www.oxfamamerica.org/publications/out-of-site.

[38] On the spread of humanitarian effects beyond IDP populations, a parish priest from Kaina told HRW: "In a culture in which visitors always eat first, many host family children end up with no food," in *Always on the Run*, *supra* note 3, at 38.

[39] *Monthly Report*, OCHA, May 2010 (cited in *id.* at 20).

[40] *Always on the Run*, *supra* note 3, at 5–6.

Assistance has long struggled to respond to DRC's unique displacement patterns.[41] Even within UN-administered camps, the safety of inhabitants has been a constant concern. Children have been press-ganged, and women regularly raped in trips outside to look for firewood or food.[42] With camps already filled to capacity, authorities have sometimes had to turn away waves of new arrivals.[43] In the 2008 CNDP offensive, a surge of 250,000 new IDPs coincided with the halving of rations to camp arrivals—from 2,000 calories a day per person to 1,000—compounded by the scrapping entirely of rations to those who had already been residing in the camps for more than few weeks, on account of inadequate funds from international donors who were prioritizing crises elsewhere.[44]

At present there is no international treaty governing the status of IDPs and the lack of an international legal framework has prevented their inclusion as a discrete area of protection in the RtoP principle. But the Guiding Principles on Internal Displacement set out responsibilities for states. As Roberta Cohen has argued, the concept of RtoP developed in the post-Cold War setting in which the plight of IDPs across an explosion of civil wars became apparent; that they continue to lack the rights accorded to refugees should have no effect on the promotion of the Guiding Principles on Internal Displacement within an RtoP strategy, which were themselves based on the concept of sovereignty as responsibility, albeit introduced into the UN a full seven years before the General Assembly's adoption of RtoP principles.[45] In the case of DRC, it seems moot to parse the atrocities committed against civilians from the context of displacements that have indubitably rendered them yet more vulnerable.

Moreover, the African Union adopted in October 2009 the binding Convention on the Protection and Assistance of Internally Displaced Persons in Africa, or the Kampala Convention. The convention aims to be a comprehensive instrument covering all phases of displacement, from prevention to protection, assistance, and durable solutions. Where the state is either unable or unwilling to effectively carry out its obligations, it is expected to seek, enable, and facilitate the assistance of the African Union. It represents significant *lex ferendi*, and by Article 18 of the Vienna Convention

[41] In most conflicts, IDPs seek refuge in one location then return home when fighting recedes. Many Congolese are IDPs twice or three times over. They choose to remain close to home—to cultivate their fields as their chief and sometimes only source of sustenance; move between displacement sites and vulnerable villages, in search of food or refuge; return home during lulls in violence only to flee again in fresh flare-ups; or occupy abandoned property or land, a situation that leads to inevitable disputes when previous owners return or perpetuates local frictions that have complicated resolution of the broader crisis. *Id.* at 20–21.

[42] *Annual Report of the UN Secretary General on Children and Armed Conflict*, Security Council, S/2007/757, Dec. 21, 2007; *see also Protection of Civilian Populations, supra* note 28.

[43] Delphine Schrank, *A Makeshift Existence; War in Eastern Congo has Driven 1 Million to a Life of Continual Wandering*, Washington Post, Nov. 9, 2008.

[44] Interview with Claude Kalinga, World Food Programme, Oct. 29, 2008; *see also Flash Info: Assistance Alimentaire du PAM en RDC*, World Food Programme, No. 2008/13, Aug. 8, 2008, which projected a food shortfall through July 2009.

[45] Roberta Cohen, *Reconciling RtoP with IDP Protection*, Brooking-Berns Project on Internal Displacement, May 25, 2010. Cohen notes, for example, that according to Principles 3 and 25, primary responsibility for displaced populations rests with their governments but if governments are unable to provide life-supporting protection and assistance, they are expected to request assistance from the international community, at 5.

on the Law of Treaties, DRC, as both signatory of the treaty and member of the AU,[46] is bound by its obligation not to defeat the convention's object and purpose prior to its entry into force.[47]

The condemnations of Congolese authorities in this regard are unanimous. A 2010 UN report found that the government "neglects its responsibilities to protect and assist internally displaced persons and returnees, who therefore have to rely entirely on the support provided by the international community."[48] A Human Rights Watch report on IDPs affected by hostilities from late 2008 to mid-2010 found that authorities were responsible for abuse: "during the attacks that uprooted them, following displacement, and after authorities decided it was time they return home." In the operations against the FDLR, "[g]overnment and rebel forces carried out widespread and vicious attacks on civilians . . . triggering renewed and massive displacement." On the basis of related high mortality rates, the DRC government has also proven incapable of protecting its people's right to life, enshrined in the ICCPR as Article 6 (1) and the most basic and fundamental of human rights without which all others are meaningless. Saving lives and ameliorating human suffering is at the core of RtoP. So too is the compulsion to respond to situations of compelling human need. The colossal scale of losses in DRC is likely the most significant metric for assessing the scale of its need. Consequences of such loss, moreover, not only include the wholesale destruction of potential and stunting of future generations of Congolese citizens—reason in itself for timely and decisive action to implement RtoP—but also future violence as a result of refugee outflows destabilizing neighboring countries or fractures and resource pressures deriving from a deeply aggrieved population. In that sense, the mortality crisis in DRC also invokes RtoP's preventive role (Pillar two), to assist populations under stress before crisis.

Finally, deliberate armed attack against camps could also amount to crimes against humanity or war crimes in violation of international humanitarian law as stipulated by the Geneva Conventions, including common Article 3, and implicate commanders as a matter of command responsibility.[49]

B. Killings

Since 1990, approximately 35,000 civilians have been massacred in one-sided violence. Reports have compiled evidence of atrocities that resulted in death in all phases of DRC's crises.[50] To note only examples recent to this writing: In 2009, in the Umoja

[46] DRC signed on 02/02/2010; *List of Countries Which Have Signed, Ratified/Accede to the African Union Convention for the Protection and Assistance of Internally Displaced Persons in Africa, available at* http://www.africa-union.org/root/au/Documents/Treaties/list/Convention%20on%20IDPs%20-%20displaced.pdf.

[47] The Kampala Convention has yet to come into force, with only a single ratification out of the minimum 15 AU countries as of August 2010.

[48] A/HRC/13/63, *supra* note 4, at 2.

[49] Deliberate attacks on IDPs have included: destruction of six IDP camps and public sites sheltering 27,000 by the CNDP near Kiwanja, in Nov. 2008.

[50] Among the most extensive for the formal war period, *see Report of the Mapping Exercise documenting the most serious violations of human rights and international humanitarian law committed within the territory of the Democratic Republic of Congo between March 1993 and June 2003,*

Wetu and Kimia II campaigns, Human Rights Watch researchers found that: "For every FDLR combatant that has been removed from combat through being repatriated, one civilian has been killed, seven women and girls have been raped, eight homes have been destroyed, and nearly 900 people have been forced to flee for their lives."[51]

All warring parties, including the UN mission, are accused of being implicated. In particular, HRW researchers found that Congolese forces and their allies violated their obligations under the laws of war to minimize harm to civilians on counts including failure to distinguish between civilians and combatants, with no advance warning to civilians when circumstances permitted and no opportunity to give them safe passage. Moreover, "they summarily executed hundreds of civilians under their effective control," amounting to at least 732 between January and September 2009, adding, "the figure is likely to be much higher."[52]

The FDLR left evidence as letters, public meetings, and oral threats of a strategy designed to "punish" civilians in the communities where they had lived. Killings by the FDLR have been recorded ever since their arrival in DRC. In November 2009, two leaders were arrested in Germany on suspicion of war crimes and crimes against humanity, but a number remained at-large and free of arrest warrants in Europe and elsewhere, despite credible allegations of serious human rights violations. But, notes Human Rights Watch of the 2009 operations, "this time the killings and abuses were more numerous and widespread and showed clear signs of being systematic." The final estimated tally: 701 civilians killed, many by machete or hoe, some burned to death in their home, some shot, and some dead from the after-effects of brutal rape. Community leaders and village chiefs were particular targets. One single incident saw the massacre of at least 76 civilians in the village of Busurungi. Villagers, some of whom knew their attackers by name, were tied up and then had their throats slit or locked in homes that were then burned to the ground.[53]

In a June 2010 report, Philip Alston, UN Special Rapporteur on Extrajudicial, Summary or Arbitrary Executions, noted that "many hundreds of civilians" were killed in 2009 in separate conflicts. Alston largely confirmed the HRW findings, noting that the numbers of FDLR killings in 2009 increased five-fold from an average of 10 civilian killings per month.[54] In the same operation, the FARDC had committed opportunistic killings and targeted massacres of civilians.[55] In those instances, the units involved were largely composed of ex-CNDP members under ex-CNDP commanders "with some extensive records of prior abuses."

UN OFFICE OF THE HIGH COMMISSIONER FOR HUMAN RIGHTS, Aug. 2010, Unofficial English Translation, *available at* http://www.ohchr.org/Documents/Countries/ZR/DRC_MAPPING_REPORT_FINAL_EN.pdf.

[51] "*You Will Be Punished,*" *supra* note 1, 45–46.

[52] *Id.* at 13–14.

[53] "*You Will Be Punished,*" *supra* note 1, at 14.

[54] *Report of the Special Rapporteur on Extrajudicial, Summary or Arbitrary Executions Philip Alston; Addendum–Mission to the Democratic Republic of Congo*, Human Rights Council, A/HRC/14/24/Add.3, Jun. 14, 2010, at ¶ 11–12.

[55] For instance, on April 27, 2009, at a makeshift refugee camp in Shalio, killings by the army immediately wiped out 50 Rwandan Hutu refugees, then a subsequent 50 people, a group of 40 women were raped and tortured and yet a further group remained unaccounted for. Other massacres took place near Shalio, and in August 2009 in Mashango and Ndoruma. *Id.* at 10.

The same report noted that since 2008 at least 1,300 Congolese civilians were killed in Province Orientale by the LRA, whose leader Joseph Kony and top commanders face arrest warrants from the ICC. Driven out of Uganda after waging a rebellion since the early 1980s, the LRA has a long and bloody record of massacres and mutilations coupled with a pattern of abducting children to turn them into killing machines. The LRA, Alston wrote, "has committed some of the most calculated and horrific killings I have encountered during my nearly six years as Special Rapporteur."[56] Others have similarly noted the group's capacity to "wreak absolute havoc" even when down.[57] Congolese armed forces and MONUC failed to push back the group in poorly planned operations in 2009; the result was a vicious litany of killings, rape, looting, and abductions, including of children.

Even without the larger context of interlocking crises, the resurgence of the LRA constitutes an immediate and imminent threat to civilians that, according to Alston and Human Rights Watch researchers, has spread regionally into Uganda, Sudan, and the Central African Republic. The risks of further massacres through early 2011 remained high. With a history of ties between the LRA and the regime in neighboring Khartoum, and in the absence of a strong and effective response on the part of the Congolese government, RtoP compels the international community to act as an urgent matter both for the stability of DRC and the region, and as protection to untold hundreds in DRC and beyond.

Alston's investigation also looked to deaths in prison, and vigilante and political killings, noting that hundreds of opposition supporters had been killed in 2007 and 2008. For the purposes of meeting any RtoP threshold, his findings were an ominous reminder of the fragility and volatility of the Congolese state: "Despite very real threat of further violence as the next election approaches," Alston noted, "little international attention is paid to the issue, and the Government has taken no steps to reform the security sector."[58] In sum, the possibility remains of massive violence across DRC, suggesting ongoing danger to the civilian population.

C. Sexual Violence

UN authorities have variously described DRC as the "rape capital of the world,"[59] and "the worst place in the world to be a woman or girl,"[60] with sexual violence so

[56] *Id.* at 13.

[57] John Holmes, UN Under Secretary-General for Humanitarian Affairs, quoted in *UN's Crowning Failure, supra* note 1. Notes Human Rights Watch of one massacre: "In Mabando village, the LRA sought to maximize the death toll by luring their victims to a central place, playing the radio and forcing their victims to sing songs and to call for others to join the party." Human Rights Watch, *The Christmas Massacres; LRA Attacks on Civilians in Congo*, Feb. 16, 2009, at 5.

[58] A/HRC/14/24/Add.3, *supra* note 54, at 2.

[59] Margot Wallstrom, UN Special Representative on Sexual Violence in Conflict, quoted in, among others, *Top UN Official Calls DR Congo "Rape Capital of the World,"* Agence France Presse, Apr. 27, 2010.

[60] Rebecca Feely & Colin Thomas-Jensen, *Getting Serious About Ending Conflict and Sexual Violence in Congo*, Enough Strategy Paper, Mar. 12, 2008, at 2. Other iterations, as "The sexual violence in Congo is the worst in the world," John Holmes, UN Under Secretary-General for Humanitarian Affairs, cited in Gettleman, *Rape Epidemic Raises Trauma of Congo War, supra* note 1.

widespread, violent, and systematic that it is "almost unimaginable."[61] Witnesses, including aid-workers, have often proven at a loss for language that adequately describes the horrors.[62] Alston, the UN Rapporteur on Executions notes in his June 2010 report on DRC that sexual violence also falls within his mandate "because it has reached such levels of brutality that women have literally been raped to death."[63]

Rape has always been a byproduct of war, but extensive and independent documentation from a wide array of sources, including medical reports, Congolese and international aid organizations, UN organs and credible media outlets, leads to the irrefutable conclusion that the sexual violence in DRC is epidemic and of a brutality unparalleled in globally recorded history.[64]

The collection of accurate data on numbers of victims, including those who died from their injuries, is nearly impossible. Information is gathered based on services provided to survivors;[65] survivors and family members often withhold reporting rape because of deep stigma, fear of reprisal, and sheer lack of access to support facilities; most violence takes place in remote areas to which NGOs do not have access—and in which victims lack life-saving medical support. Moreover, NGOs are not required to supply statistics to the United Nations Population Fund (UNFPA), which coordinates

[61] UN Under Secretary-General for Humanitarian Affairs and Emergency Relief Coordinator John Holmes quoted in Stephanie McCrummen, *Prevalence of Rape in E. Congo Described as Worst in World*, Washington Post, Sept. 9, 2007.

[62] "It's the scale and brutality of it," said UN Under Secretary-General for Humanitarian Affairs and Emergency Relief Coordinator John Holmes in September 2007. "It's the use of it as a weapon of terror. It's the way it's done publicly, for maximum humiliation. It's hard to understand." *Id.* "I have seen many many cases of rapes, and many cases of medical emergencies, but I have never seen anything so planned, so systematic, so animalistic," said Dr. Chris Baguma of the Los Angeles-based International Medical Corps, on treating victims of sexual violence from a July 2010 rebel rampage, in Michelle Faul, *Violence Spirals Out of Control in East Congo*, Associated Press, Sept. 17, 2010; "I have just returned from hell," began a 2007 magazine piece, by a playwright. "I am trying for the life of me to figure out how to communicate what I have seen and heard in the Democratic Republic of Congo . . . How do I tell you of girls as young as nine raped by gangs of soldiers, of women whose insides have been blown apart by rifle blasts and whose bodies now leak uncontrollable streams of urine and feces?" in Eve Ensler, *Women Left for Dead—And the Man Who's Saving Them*, Glamour, Apr. 1, 2007; "It is even worse than Rwanda during the genocide," noted an aid worker in *Rape Epidemic Raises Trauma*, *supra* note 1.

[63] A/HRC/14/24/Add.3, *supra* note 54, at ¶ 63.

[64] In 2003, in the earliest media usage in DRC of a new medical pathology that emerged as a result of the war and that has in many ways come to define a prevalent physical injury to sexual-violence victims in DRC, reporter Emily Wax noted that "gang rape has been so violent, so common in eastern Congo during the country's five years of war that thousands of women are suffering from vaginal fistula, leaving them unable to control their bodily functions and enduring ostracism and the threat of debilitating lifelong health problems." Fistulas result from ruptures in or between organs; Emily Wax, *A Brutal Legacy of Congo War; Extent of Violence Against Women Surfaces as Violence Recedes*, Washington Post, Oct. 25, 2003. Later reports include extensive accounts of uteruses displaced or ruptured from insertions of guns, wood, sand or glue, or fetuses ripped out.

[65] *Id.* at 34.

work on sexual violence in the country. As such, UNFPA and others acknowledges that their numbers likely represent a tiny fraction,[66] at the very least less than half.[67]

The UNFPA nonetheless registered 13,404 incidents in 2006; 13,247 in 2007; 14,245 or 15,996 in 2008, with 4,820 in North Kivu; and 17,507 cases in 2009.[68] For the first nine months of 2009 alone, UNFPA recorded more than double the figures for the same period the year before.[69] This correlated with military operations against the FDLR. Human Rights Watch further noted that, in 2008, 65 percent of victims of sexual violence were children, most of whom were adolescent girls, a figure that doubtless reflected a longstanding trend.[70]

Sexual violence has, according to all credible accounts, become a weapon of war, designed to shame, demoralize, and humiliate, sometimes intentionally provoking another group in population areas about which they felt possessive.[71] In an April 2010 study by the Harvard Humanitarian Initiative, researchers analyzed 4,311 records, or all post-rape interviews conducted between 2004 and 2008 at Panzi Hospital in Bukavu, South Kivu. They concluded that women in DRC were not safe anywhere—attacked while they farmed fields, collected firewood or, mostly, in their own homes at night.[72] Almost 60 percent of sexual violence survivors described gang rape. Captivity as sexual slaves often followed, particularly for young, single women. A pattern emerged of "extraordinary brutality, including genital mutilation, instrumentation with foreign objects, forced rape between victims and rape in the presence of family members." Children were slaughtered in front of parents and relatives killed and tortured. Rape was accompanied by a preponderance of pillaging: of cash, food, livestock, or other essentials on which depended rape survivors and their families—most of them illiterate subsistence farmers.[73]

[66] This is a disclaimer that is repeated in a number of reports analyzing sexual violence in DRC; including A/HRC/14/24/Add.3, *supra* note 54, at ¶¶ 63, 67, footnotes 21–3, or Human Rights Watch, *Soldiers Who Rape, Commanders Who Condone; Sexual Violence and Military Reform in the Democratic Republic of Congo*, Jul. 16, 2009; Harvard Humanitarian Initiative & Oxfam International, "*Now, the World Is Without Me:" An Investigation of Sexual Violence in the Eastern Democratic Republic of Congo*, Apr. 2010, at 1, *available at* http://hhi.harvard.edu/publications/hhi-program-publications.

[67] My calculation based on estimate of Nicola Dahrendorf, former Senior Advisor and Coordinator on Sexual Violence at MONUC, that less than 50 percent of raped women have such access, in *Soldiers Who Rape, supra* note 66, at 18, *available at* http://www.hrw.org/node/84369.

[68] A/HRC/14/24/Add.3, *supra* note 54, at 16. The higher estimate comes from a UNFPA report on file with Human Rights Watch, in *Soldiers Who Rape, supra* note 66, at 18.

[69] A/HRC/13/63, *supra* note 4, at ¶ 27. Varying estimates include 27,000 cases of sexual assault in 2006 in South Kivu alone, according to a separate UN body, in *Rape Epidemic Raises Trauma, supra* note 1, and, in 2009, more than 15,000 raped in the Kivus alone, according to Roger Meece, head of MONUSCO, citing the best data available, including more than 9,000 in the Kivus in Edith M. Lederer, *UN Envoy Says over 15,000 Raped in Eastern Congo*, Associated Press, Oct. 15, 2010.

[70] *Soldiers Who Rape, supra* note 66, at 18.

[71] This is particularly the case for groups of Mai Mai, local defense militias that have traditionally justified their existence in terms of self-protection against foreign invaders. *See also*, Jocelyn Kelly, *Rape in War: Motives of Militia in DRC*, U.S. Institute of Peace, Special Report 243, Jun. 2010, at 10.

[72] Harvard Humanitarian Initiative, *supra* note 66, at 18.

[73] *Id.*

Oxfam, Human Rights Watch, UN officials, and Congolese aid organizations have noted that, despite associated stigma preventing more than anecdotal reporting,[74] the number of male victims rose sharply in the joint Congolese-Rwandan operations against the FDLR, likely to inflict maximum humiliation and demoralization. (Reporters noted that four baby boys were among approximately 500 victims of gang rape in a rebel rampage in July 2010 on villages in North Kivu.)

Foreign and local researchers contend that there is nothing in Congolese history to suggest something culturally ingrained. There is evidence, instead, that the brutality and systemic nature of the violence emerged in the early 1990s, coinciding with the aftermath of the Rwandan genocide.[75] Sexual violence has since metastasized in the security forces—one estimate for six months of 2007 found 54 percent of all sexual violence cases committed by the FARDC and 43 percent by national police[76]—and, while predominantly militarized, has spread beyond conflict areas, on account of impunity, discrimination against women, and demobilization of fighters with minimal rehabilitation.[77]

Sexual violence is sufficiently widespread and systematic, with deliberate intent, to amount to war crimes and crimes against humanity as defined both under international humanitarian law (the Geneva Conventions, including an implicit ban in common Article 3, and an explicit prohibition on rape or other indecent assault in Article 4(2)(e) of Additional Protocol II, to which DRC is party) and international human rights law (including Article 7(g) of the Rome Statute of the International Criminal Court). It can be additionally argued that perpetrators have at times directly, or as a matter of command responsibility, wielded rape as a weapon of war with "intent to destroy, in whole or in part," entire communities designated according to their national, ethnic, racial, or religious identities, such as to fall within the definition of genocide in Article 2 of the 1948 Genocide Convention, which accordingly imposes obligations to act on DRC and the international community.

But efforts to address the problem by both remain woefully inadequate. In recognition of the need to take more pointed action, the Security Council in June 2008 redefined sexual violence in eastern DRC from a human-rights issue to a security issue. MONUC subsequently launched a comprehensive strategy in April 2009, but its implementation by late 2010 had been delayed by staffing issues. This coincided with a scandal surrounding the rebel rampage of July 2010 in which at least 500 people endured four days of rape and torture only 12 miles from a UN base. Local aid groups said MONUSCU had been duly warned of the impending attack, but it took days for

[74] A/HRC/14/24/Add.3, *supra* note 54, at note 22.

[75] As explained, for instance, by Wihelmine Ntakebuka, who coordinates a sexual violence program in Bukavu, South Kivu, to Gettleman in *Rape Epidemic Raises Trauma of Congo War*, *supra* note 1.

[76] Other major perpetrators have been found to include: the FDLR and its various factions, and CNDP or ex-CNDP commanders within State security forces, as told by the MONUC Human Rights Division to the UN Special Rapporteur on violence against women, in A/HRC/7/6/Add.4, *supra* note 17, at ¶ 13; *see also*, A/HRC/13/63, *supra* note 4, at ¶ 27. For further documentation on range of perpetrators wielding sexual violence as a weapon of war, *see also Soldiers Who Rape*, *supra* note 66; or Harvard Humanitarian Initiative, *supra* note 66, and most other reports cited herein.

[77] A/HRC/7/6/Add.4, *supra* note 17, at ¶ 15.

help to arrive.[78] A UN inquiry even found that peacekeepers had passively patrolled through one of the villages held by the fighters, but took no action because no one told them what was happening.[79] Thereafter, Resolution 1888 adopted September 20, 2009, explicitly mandated peacekeeping missions with the protection of women and girls from sexual violence in armed conflict.[80]

In 2006, the Congolese parliament passed a law on sexual violence that newly criminalized acts such as sexual mutilation and sexual slavery, thereby vastly improving the Congolese Penal Code and Code of Penal Procedure.[81] Four years later, Joseph Kabila called for a "moral revolution" to put an end to widespread rape.[82] But its ongoing prevalence corresponded with what one UN report appearing the same month as Kabila's statement called the "shocking lack of accountability in the country's domestic legal system." Between February and August 2009, less than 100 rape cases were prosecuted by the military justice system in the Kivus and most were of low-ranking officers.[83] Noted Yakin Ertürk, UN Special Rapporteur on Violence Against Women: "Due to political interference and corruption, perpetrators, especially those who belong to the state security forces, go unpunished. The limited support made available to the overburdened justice system raises questions as to whether there is political will to end impunity."[84]

Moreover, the Law on Sexual Violence coexists with laws and practices that continue to discriminate against women.[85] DRC ranked 137th out of 138 countries in UNDP's 2008 gender inequality index.[86] Reports also note a tendency among mid-level authorities and army commanders to dismiss the issue as largely fiction, or the fault of "unfaithful women."[87]

[78] Revised estimates doubling the number of victims of sexual violence at the time, from 250 to 500, emerged after a UN inquiry; *Violence Spirals Out of Control*, *supra* note 62; or *UN Peacekeepers "Failed" DR Congo Rape Victims*, BBC News, Sept. 7, 2010, *available at* http://www.bbc.co.uk/news/mobile/world-africa-11224656.

[79] *Violence Spirals out of control*, *supra* note 62.

[80] As stipulated in Article 7(g) of the Rome Statute of the International Criminal Court, rape and other forms of sexual violence including sexual slavery and enforced prostitution can be found to constitute crimes against humanity or war crimes as part of a widespread and systematic attack with deliberate intent. The Rome Statute codifies rape based on growing precedent that includes the 1998 decision in the case against Jean-Paul Akayesu before the International Criminal Tribunal for Rwanda.

[81] Law Number 06/018, Jul. 20, 2006.

[82] *Kabila calls for "Moral Revolution in DR Congo,"* Agence France Presse, Jun. 30, 2010.

[83] A/HRC/14/24/Add.3, *supra* note 54, at ¶ 68; *See also*, A/HRC/7/6/Add.4, *supra* note 17, at ¶ 66.

[84] *Id.* at 2.

[85] A/HRC/13/63, *supra* note 4, at ¶ 26.

[86] Gender Inequality Index, *available at* http://hdr.undp.org/en/media/HDR_2010_EN_Table4_reprint.pdf.

[87] *See* A/HRC/14/24/Add.3, *supra* note 54, at ¶ 66. In my interviews in October-November 2008, certain peacekeepers in the Indian battalions expressed similar sentiments, dismissing the rape problem as an exaggeration of aid-workers. His reflected deeper variations in practice among the donor militaries serving in MONUC, whereas soldiers in the Uruguan contingent, who formed the bulk of the force in Goma, said they individually volunteered to serve as peacekeepers, Indian soldiers, who filled up bases in the more remote areas, were called up with their regiments. There they were forbidden from interacting with locals other than in their vehicle patrols, and even then they were prevented from interacting with Congolese by language barriers.

Access to care, including life-saving surgery, remains seriously limited. The HHI study notes, for example, that Panzi hospital has only one specialty-trained gynecologist, despite the longstanding history and high volume of rape patients arriving for treatment in perhaps the most renowned of DRC's rare medical facilities focused on women or, since the mid-1990s, survivors of sexual violence.[88]

As Ertürk noted in February 2008 in a conclusion that holds through early 2011: "Given the multitude of actors . . . and the continuation of these crimes, the international community, in cooperation with Congolese authorities, has a responsibility to take all necessary measures to ensure that women in South Kivu are protected."

III. INTERNATIONAL RESPONSES AND THEIR LIMITATIONS

RtoP meets perhaps one of its greatest challenges in DRC.

The humanitarian and human-rights crises have persisted despite nearly two decades of international humanitarian, development and security sector assistance, including a $1.4 billion-a-year UN mission and extensive bilateral aid programs.[89] The World Bank and the International Monetary Fund approved a $12.3 billion debt relief package for DRC in July 2010,[90] and in November of that year, the Paris Club of international creditors forgave $7.35 billion in Congolese debt, a figure said to represent more than half of the country's overall foreign investment.[91] The Security Council has since 2004 imposed sanctions on DRC; in March 2008 it imposed an arms embargo and asset freezes against 22 individuals and companies, and in December 2008 expanded and extended these through November 2010.

A broad survey of the extant literature suggests, however, that there has been little comprehensive coordination in the international aid effort. While MONUC has been the chief vehicle for international assistance, a proliferation of other mechanisms has resulted in project overlap, disproportionate emphasis on some issues with neglect in others, and a lack of accountability. One analysis has catalogued nine simultaneous projects against sexual violence, illustrating confusion among stakeholders and difficulty bringing efforts into alignment.[92] Their overall impact, the analysis concludes,

[88] Harvard Humanitarian Initiative, *supra* note 66, at 14; Dr. Denis Mukwege estimates that he treats about 3,600 rape victims annually. Mukwege founded the hospital's special services for survivors of sexual violence upon noting their dramatic rise in the fighting of the 1990s. For more information, see web site, *available at* http://www.panzihospitalbukavu.org/drmukwege.php?weblang=1.

[89] Direct U.S. funding alone to DRC from 2007 to 2010, excluding funding through multilateral organizations such as the World Bank, has amounted to $2 billion, or 15 to 20 percent of the total contribution by the international community, in Spyros Demetriou and Salameh Magnuson, *Strengthening United States Foreign Policy in the Democratic Republic of Congo*, East Congo Initiative White Paper, Nov. 2010, at 28, *available at* http://www.easterncongo.org/whitepaper/.

[90] *IMF and World Bank Announed US$12.3 billion Debt Relief for the Democratic Republic of Congo*, International Monetary Fund, Press Release No. 10/274, Jul. 1, 2010, *available at* http://www.imf.org/external/np/sec/pr/2010/pr10274.htm.

[91] *Paris Club of Credits Forgives Congo Debt*, Associated Press, Nov. 18, 2010.

[92] These include: 1–2) Two unrelated efforts by OHCHR, one focused on grassroots justice in five provinces the other organizing a forum and mobile tribunals; 3) The STAREC program, which trains investigators; 4) A Goma-based UNDP program with a $1.5 million budget for three years;

has been fairly minimal, or at the very least problematic to assess. But elsewhere, the quandaries of prioritizing a "seemingly endless flow" of protection issues have hampered coordination efforts.[93]

In hindsight it is easy to criticize the poor coordination or overlap in a complex assistance operation that has inevitably played catch-up to the fits and starts of a shape-shifting crisis.

But at least one analysis sharply contends that flawed assumptions underpin international efforts. These include the implicit belief that Western state institutions can be successfully transferred to Africa, discounting the dynamics of local power structures and the importance of informal political institutions, including patronage networks within the security forces; a disconnect between the meanings of failure and reconstruction to international donors and the "spoilers" and warlords whom they instead empower as part of their "reconstruction" efforts; and donors' pie-in-the-sky faith that they can or will sustain the resources required for long-term reconstruction despite empirical evidence to the contrary.[94]

That damning thesis resonates in an analysis by Henri Boshoff *et al* of security sector reform (SSR) efforts in DRC.[95] The consensus holds that DRC's judicial, defense and police sectors are a shambles.[96] Boshoff points to fundamental differences in priorities between the international community and Kabila's government. The former seek broader organizational change. The latter opt for training and equipment, to cope with the short-term challenge of armed groups and the consolidation of their elite command. In parallel, SSR support in the DRC has been "essentially a collection of loosely connected donor-driven activists, implemented in isolation from essential political reforms, which are not resulting in the kinds of capacity and behavioral chances that could lead to significantly improved public security provision. It is key, for example, to complement training and other assistance with support that will tackle the culture of impunity."[97] Because of the ad hoc and bilateral nature of efforts,

5) A 15-month component program within the judicial-sector reformer REJUSCO; 6) UNFPA's separate data collecting initiative, along with attempts at workshops and "joint initiatives"; 7) Commissions at the provincial, territorial, and municipal level; 8) A variety of approaches by at least six separate INGOS "depending on the particular area of competence," with varying methods, and corresponding difficulties measuring impact, which "generally seems weak"; 9) Another batch of national NGOs with variable budgets and offerings of local legal assistance; in Henri Boshoff, Dylan Hendrickson, et al, *Supporting SSR in the DRC: between a Rock and a Hard Place*, Netherlands Institute of International Relations Clingendael, Apr. 2010, at 31–32.

93 *Always on the Run*, *supra* note 3, at 73.

94 Englebert and Tull, *supra* note 10. Another study, which evaluated the effectiveness of aid efforts and allocations, concluded: "In DRC, mass rapes by militias have raised concerns about the ability of the UN peacekeeping mission to provide effective protection to civilians and also . . . about donor willingness to invest in security sector reform to enable the DRC military and police to do so," *The Humanitarian Response Index 2010*, *supra* note 12, at 43.

95 Boshoff, Hendrickson, et al, *supra* note 92.

96 *See* International Crisis Group, *Congo: A Stalled Democratic Agenda*, AFRICA BRIEFING NO. 73 (2010), at 1, *available at* http://www.crisisgroup.org/en/regions/africa/central-africa/dr-congo/b073-congo-a-stalled-democratic-agenda.aspx.

97 "The fundamental challenge faced by international partners in the justice sector is that the interest of the Congolese authorities—both Government and judicial—in reform appears to a large degree rhetorical and opportunistic: a façade of support for the reform allows the system's actors to

international partners end up pandering to their interlocutors, without working toward the deep, managerial-level or grassroots behavioral changes that the authors deem critical to transforming the predatory and ill-trained army and police force, rooting out corruption (while recognizing the ongoing importance of patronage), and equipping the judicial system to viably begin dismantling the poisonous culture of impunity.

The international effort to reform the security sector has to a considerable extent been caught in a vicious circle. Until DRC is able to impose a monopoly of force as far as its borderlands and achieve a broad legitimacy, it will be incapable of protecting its citizens. This depends on a willing and committed central authority and strong, functional security institutions. But deep reform of the same security institutions—defense, police, and judicial—cannot happen in any meaningful way while violence persists, because the violence has created a self-sustaining dynamic.[98]

In the context of crucial programs to disarm, demobilize, and reintegrate combatants (DDR), the government has consequently been more concerned about mobilization than demobilization.[99] Under World Bank auspices, a $200 million-program aimed to disarm, demobilize, and reintegrate about 150,000 combatants; from September 2008 to June 2010, initial plans to process 70,000 army soldiers and 19,000 militia fighters were "severely disrupted" by hostilities and eventually reduced to about one-fifth.[100] Likewise, reintegration of militia forces into the army without appropriate vetting has perpetuated parallel structures and perceptions of impunity.

As such, SSR reform, and the critically linked process of DDR,[101] depends on a parallel political push at the national, regional, and international level. One, albeit limited, method has been the publication of authoritative investigations. At the height of the second Congolese war, a UN Panel of Experts exposed how all warring parties, including Rwanda and Uganda, were massively profiting from the illegal exploitation of DRC's natural resources. Another UN Group of Experts provided extensive damning evidence in 2008 and 2009.[102] Observers speculated that the revelations, chief among them Rwanda's evident support for Nkunda, led directly to Kagame's surprise turnaround in policy in 2009.

The UN reports, coming alongside a tide of others, undoubtedly amplified a central sticking point—the war economy—within domestic and international agendas. Pockmarked efforts to clean up the mining sector date back to 1997 at least, and in

attract financial resources and the Government to demonstrate its concern for good governance," Boshoff, Hendrickson, et al., *supra* note 92, at ii.

[98] *Id.* at 25.

[99] *DDR in the Democratic Republic of Congo; Program Update*, World Bank, Sept., 2009. About 132,000 men, women and children were demobilized in the programs first phase, between 2004–2006.

[100] *Id.*

[101] *See* Sean McFate, *The Link Between DDR and SSR in Conflict-Affected Countries*, U.S. Institute of Peace, Special Report 238 May, 2010.

[102] As Alan Doss, the UN Secretary-General's Special Representative to DRC, wrote in letter on December 3, 2009, in the *The Economist*: "By naming names and identifying the conduits for illegal exports of natural resources and supply lines for importing weapons, it presents the international community with abundant grounds for investigating further those with their fingers in the till as well as on the trigger—in the hope of stopping their activities."

February 2008 DRC joined the Extractive Industries Transparency Initiative (EITI), an international voluntary initiative designed to strengthen governance.[103] But the delays in implementing principles to reach the EITI's "validation" stage were mysteriously overcome by September 2010. Such attention also pushed U.S. legislators through the 2010 Financial Reforms Bill to require thousands of U.S. companies to disclose sourcing of minerals from DRC or its neighbors and to document due diligence ensuring no benefit to armed groups.[104]

Another report—a long-awaited, 544-page "mapping exercise" on crimes committed between 1993 and 2003, which investigated 617 incidents in all DRC provinces—definitively exposed the scale and nature of mass violence, including Rwandan troops' commission of violations that could amount to acts of genocide. This prompted calls in late 2010 to put DRC on the agenda of the Security Council—and forced the beginning of a re-examination of the deceptive politics behind regional peace deals, including the role of Rwanda, which had been given a free pass in Western political narratives after its genocide.[105] Rwanda, for its part, reacted to early leaks of the report by threatening to pull its forces from peacekeeping missions if the UN published a final version.

On other fronts, the government of the DRC referred crimes to the ICC on April 19, 2004. Investigations have thus far resulted in arrest warrants against five senior rebel leaders.[106] Though the reach of the ICC is small, its cases on DRC, among the first to be heard, are setting important precedents, including that use of children in armed

[103] After Joseph Kabila's administration took office, the government launched a major review of mining contracts from 1997 to 2002. As the U.S. State Department notes: "In theory, the purpose of this contract review was to determine which negotiations may have been colored by corruption and revisit/renegotiate their terms as need be. In practice, this process has itself been opaque, with little information provided by the government to foreign (including American) investors." *Background Note: Democratic Republic of Congo, U.S. Department of State*, Oct. 8, 2010, *available at* http://www.state.gov/r/pa/ei/bgn/2823.htm#econ.

[104] Mary Beth Sheriden, *Trying to Curb Trade of Conflict Minerals*, Washington Post, Jul. 21, 2010. That said, international rhetoric has sometimes outweighed substance. President Barack Obama signed into law the Lord's Resistance Army Disarmament and Northern Uganda Recovery Act on May 24, 2010, a breakthrough piece of legislation that obligated his administration to develop a strategy to protect civilians, work to apprehend the LRA leadership, and support the economic recovery of northern Uganda. Critics noted with some cynicism that the result lacked teeth, and, released four days before Thanksgiving, a major U.S. holiday conveniently evaded scrutiny.

[105] As one observer noted thereafter: "For the last decade, peace efforts have been based on the narrative that the two previous regional Congo wars and the war between the Congolese government and Rwandan-backed CNDP rebels were justified by the fight against the FDLR, the Rwandan Hutu armed group whose leadership was partly responsible for the 1994 genocide in Rwanda. . . [T]he collective guilt felt by the international community . . . led many powerful countries to turn a blind eye to the criminal and indiscriminant tactics used by Rwandan and Ugandan security forces during the two Congo wars as documented in the report. These same countries did not question the interests of Congo's neighbors in fighting not only the FDLR and other rebel groups, but maintaining a foothold in the wealthy mining regions of Congo," in Fabianne Hara of the International Crisis Group, *Congo Crimes Should be on the Agenda of the Security Council*, Huffington Post, Oct. 14, 2010, *available at* http://www.crisisgroup.org/en/regions/africa/central-africa/dr-congo/hara-congo-crimes-should-be-on-the-agenda-of-the-un-security-council.aspx.

[106] Four are in custody and undergoing hearings; the fifth, Bosco Ntganda, is a general in the Congolese army.

combat is a war crime that can and will be prosecuted at the international level.[107] But these advances coexist with other major failures beyond the ICC, to bring DRC's criminals to justice.

IV. ENHANCING CIVILIAN PROTECTION

The great vehicle for the international aid effort, and greatest target of reproach, has been the UN peacekeeping mission. Most agree that MONUSCO has generally stopped a bad situation from spiraling out of control. Where its forces show a presence, the thinking goes, atrocities and crime will fall. MONUSCO military and civilian personnel have built and repaired roads and airfields, shielded humanitarian workers, and maintained Radio Okapi, which arguably broadcasts the best, most reliable news available nationwide. Mandated tasks include mediating buffer zones and regional disputes; patrolling with and providing trainings to Congolese security services; preventing illegal traffic of arms and minerals; assisting the demobilization and disarmament of rebels and foreign insurgents; and monitoring peace deals.[108] When a fire broke out in a residential district in Goma in the fall of 2008, I watched it fall to peacekeepers to rush out their base to extinguish the flames in the absence of local firemen. It seemed an apt metaphor for their benign presence, and began to explain why civilians have repeatedly gathered by the thousands around UN bases in outbreaks of violence.[109]

On the other hand, huddled masses rallying to the blue flag have as often as not continued to be at the mercy of whichever armed group was nearby, and humanitarian actors have criticized MONUC not only for doing little or nothing to fulfill its civilian protection mandate but also for delaying the development of a protection strategy.[110]

Given the UN's very mixed record, military analyst Paul D. Williams suggests: first, manage expectations.[111] When MONUC was first mandated to protect civilians, in February 2000, it only met its projected troop ceiling of a meager 5,537 soldiers a full three years later. In 2004, the force was tasked with helping a transition process that was far from complete.[112] While permitted to use "all necessary means" to protect

[107] Param-Preet Singh, International Justice Program at Human Rights Watch, quoted in *DRC: ICC's First Trial Focuses on Child Soldiers*, Human Rights Watch, Jan. 23, 2009, *available at* http://www.hrw.org/en/news/2009/01/22/drc-icc-s-first-trial-focuses-child-soldiers.

[108] *See* Resolution 1856, Security Council, S/Res/1856, Dec. 22, 2008.

[109] *See Always on the Run, supra* note 3, at 40.

[110] *Id.* at 78.

[111] Paul D. Williams, *Lessons Learned: Despite Being the Largest UN Mission, MONUC Has Little Success to Show for It*, 4(4) J. Int'l Peace Operations 12–15 (Jan.-Feb. 2009).

[112] At the height of the massive Nkunda-led CNDP offensive in Oct. 2008, sufficient pressure led the Security Council in Nov. 2008 to authorize a "temporary increase" of up to 2,785 military and 300 police personnel to the 18,500 uniformed personnel. Noted Human Rights Watch: "The UN Security Council provided MONUC a strong mandate to protect civilians, but UN member states did not back up this commitment with adequate resources to ensure the full implementation of the mandate. The 3,000 additional peacekeepers . . . had still not arrived in eastern Congo by Oct. 2009, despite promises from council members that they would urge a rapid deployment. Alan Doss, the head of MONUC, repeatedly warned that, without such assets, MONUC's 'capacity to respond

civilians in 2008, blue helmets were meanwhile the neutral monitors in buffer zones established in a January 23, 2008 peace deal between a patchwork of rebel and army encampments, and, somewhat paradoxically, acting on behalf of the government to disarm, demobilize, and reintegrate militias. Such confusion pleased no one—rebels, authorities, or rock-throwing civilians—prompting UN troops to waste inordinate amounts of time on public relations.

This leads to a second lesson: craft achievable mandates. Key terms, such as "assist" or "illegal armed groups," have often been unclear. As for "protection," humanitarian agencies have traditionally understood it to mean legal protection, fulfillment of rights, and impartial delivery of assistance. But for militaries, the term is limited to physical defense. Compounded by operational-level vagueness, this has lead directly to problems of practical application, particularly among troops whose commitment to employing lethal force has already proved tepid.[113] Likewise, it has been self-defeating to task troops with assisting governments that have been unwilling to implement their commitments. The task of disarming and demobilizing members of the FDLR was particularly fraught given that it also required a commitment from Kagame's government, which never signed on to the UN mission in DRC in the first place.

And though a call to protect civilians was included in MONUC's mandate as early as 2000, it was not explicitly made top priority until 2008, then reinforced in Resolution 1925 of May 28, 2010. That same resolution renamed the mission: the UN Organization Stabilization Mission in the DRC, or MONUSCO by its French acronym, "in view of the new phase that has been reached" in the country.[114] But clarity remained elusive: "There are no details of how exactly MONUSCO is supposed to support the Congolese army—no mention, in particular, of vetting out abusive officers. No mention of pre-empting violence by taking offensive action against armed groups (not that it worked that well in the past); no new ideas of how to put pressure on the Congolese security forces to improve behavior—just a small reference to paragraphs about conditionality in the last resolution; and nothing on shifting some resources to deal with the LRA."[115]

Third: Size of the force. A rule of thumb for calculating troop numbers is 2 to 10 troops per 1,000 inhabitants. With the population of North Kivu estimated at 5 million, MONUC could therefore be expected to deploy about 10,000 to 50,000 military personnel to that region alone.[116] In 1999, a UN report estimated that MONUC

quickly to emerging threats and protect civilians would be curtailed,'" in Human Rights Watch, *'You Will Be Punished,' supra* note 1, at 143.

[113] Williams elsewhere writes that as late as July 2009 the authors of an important DPKO/OCHA study on civilian protection noted that no Security "Council document offers an operational definition of what protection of civilian means for peacekeeping missions." He adds that it has thus been a common complaint that "at a very practical level, it is not always clear to troops and police what is expected of them," in Paul D. Williams, *Enhancing Civilian Protection in Peace Operations: Insights from Africa*, Africa Center for Strategic Studies (Sept. 2010), at 15.

[114] Resolution 1925, Security Council, S/Res/1925 May 28, 2010.

[115] Stearns, May 26, 2010, *supra* note 5, at http://congosiasa.blogspot.com/2010_05_01_archive.html.

[116] For the entire population of the country, estimated at 68 million, the total might then roughly amount to 14 times that, between 136,000–680,000. Another method for calculating troop levels would suggest that the protection force must be equivalent to the largest indigenous armed force.

would require more than 100,000 troops. It was initially given under 6,000, and troop need has since always far outweighed actual levels.[117]

Add to that logistical challenges exceeding any previous UN operation:[118] Human Rights Watch researchers noted that it took months for news of the "Christmas" massacres of 2008 by the LRA to trickle out, so remote were some of the affected areas.[119] Massacres and atrocities took place within miles of both a UN base and an FARDC base. But: "With only some 200 troops in the area who were designated primarily to provide logistical support to the Congolese army—not to protect civilians—MONUC peacekeepers were too few and too ill-equipped to assist civilians who came under attack." In another twist, the new mandate instructed MONUC to provide highest priority to operations in North Kivu, which obstructed officials from moving troops to areas under LRA attack.[120]

Successes have often proved exceptions. In 2003, fighting broke out in Ituri province. With a skeleton force at its disposal, MONUC had little means to protect the affected population. The UN Secretary-General asked France for a military intervention, and the result was Operation Artemis, a UN-sanctioned European Union operation of 1,500 soldiers for a three-month deployment to restore order in the city of Bunia. But analysts noted that it "was narrowly conceived and for that reason more likely to achieve its goals. First, it intervened within a well-known, tightly constrained time period and geographic scope and armed elements had only to withdraw to beyond the force's reach and wait out the mission. While the situation in Bunia was stabilized, the rest of Ituri continued to grapple with insecurity and during the period of its deployment massacres did occur not too far from where the force was on the ground."[121] Artemis was also equipped with surveillance devices, air support, an intelligence apparatus, including soldiers who could communicate with the Congolese (in French), a field doctor, a liaison with the civilian aid effort, all organized by a professional Western army. These ingredients have been noted as critical to operational success but MONUC, and MONUSCO, have always lacked them.[122]

Other successes have been smaller, but reveal the possibilities if and when blue helmets have the will or creative initiative. In 2005, the Pakistani brigade in South

By that estimate, when the rebel forces in North Kivu were at 6000 for the CNDP and 6000–7000 for the FDLR, MONUC's numbers fared better; but it must be noted that the 120,000-strong Congolese army, together with dozens of Mai Mai rebels, were likewise major sources of abuse.

[117] In a Security Council presentation on August 6, 2010, Lieutenant General Babacar Gaye, Force Commander of MONUSCU pointed out: "In the eastern provinces of the Kivus alone, the entire Force could be spread out to just one peacekeepers per 20 square kilometers."

[118] For example, see former complex operations in relatively tiny Bosnia, Kosovo or Timor-Leste.

[119] Only thereafter were two researchers able to find the sites, with motorcycles and help from local rights activists. Two lone journalists following in their footsteps said they first had to charter planes and transport to reach the area for $17,000; Ida Sawyer of Human Rights Watch and journalists Marcus Bleasdale and Joe Bavier speaking at a panel on the Lord's Resistance Army, George Washington University, Jan. 13, 2011; *See also The Christmas Massacres, supra* note 58.

[120] *Id.* at 6.

[121] *Operation Artemis: Lessons of the Interim Emergency Multinational Force*, Peacekeeping Best Practices Unit Military Division, Oct. 2004, at 16.

[122] Nor was there even a temporary transfer of expertise or equipment to the UN forces tasked with holding down Ituri after the French-led force withdrew.

Kivu organized local communities to alert peacekeepers of imminent attacks by banging pots and blowing whistles. Recent initiatives have included the creation of Joint Protection Teams (mobile teams of civilians that assess situations in brief field missions) and regular meetings between military and civilian staff, a development that led quickly to the creation of mobile bases in newly identified "must protect" areas.

Military thinkers have also begun to overcome the doctrinal gap that existed on protection operations. A collaborative effort between the U.S. Army Peacekeeping and Stability Operations Initiative and Harvard University's Carr Center for Human Rights Policy resulted in a military planning handbook whose primary objective is to stop the killing of civilians. Though directed at the United States, analysts contend that it contains transferable insights, aiming to distill the particularly complex dynamics of mass atrocities and to shift the debate from "whether" to "how."[123]

Such initiatives, however, remain limited and unlikely to yield results in the near future. In that environment, it seems fair to ask whether there is a role for other non-state actors to engage in the kind of work that the UN or regional bodies cannot or will not.

In the period that saw RtoP evolve out of recognition that civilians have become the greatest victims of war, private military companies have demonstrated and expanded their peacekeeping capabilities in challenging environments from Sierra Leone to Iraq. In 2005, at the height of the turmoil in DRC, a voluntary association of such firms approached the UN and the United States offering its services to complement the floundering UN mission and ensure its success as a "force multiplier." Hundreds of thousands of deaths later, a renewed offer gives pause.[124]

A non-traditional approach to DRC might look something like this: Engage under the auspices of the United Nations one or several private security firms with NATO-level professionalism and years of experience in challenging environments, set clear boundaries and ethical standards for their rules of engagement, and allow them to deploy with high-tech equipment, including aerial surveillance, and armed rapid deployment police. They could be assigned specifically to protect vulnerable populations, backed by a helicopter firm that could quickly transport police to hot spots as well as assist with emergency evacuations and humanitarian supply. Other firms would be responsible for training gendarmes and police. An independent foundation, outside Congo, could make sure police and soldiers were paid in a timely manner.[125]

A related idea that has the advantage of empowering and strengthening Congolese security forces suggests: First, embed a small team of international military advisors in each battalion or appropriate unit to provide external "eyes on" the internal

[123] Sarah Sewell, Dwight Raymond and Sally Chin, Mass Atrocity Response Operations: A Military Planning Book (Cambridge 2010), *available at* http://www.hks.harvard.edu/cchrp/maro/.

[124] Doug Brooks, *Monuc, Inc., Plan A Has Not Worked So Well. How About a Privatized Plan B?*, 4(4) J. Int'l Peace Ops. 20–21 (Jan. 2009).

[125] Writes Doug Brooks in a 2009 followup to his original 2003 plan: "The private consortium would be a 'force multiplier,' making the UN operation substantially more effective for a fraction of the cost of its current budget. This private sector model option could even be a model for improved peace operations in the future." *Id.*

operations of the unit. History is rich with examples of army units refraining from the commission of atrocities if and when they operate with the embedded presence of international, highly professional military staff. Second, ensure that Congolese troops are uniformed, garrisoned, and accounted for at barracks, rather than living mixed within the population. To support this, conduct biometric identification of every soldier or police, which allows positive identification in case of investigation of abuses and also reduces fraud when it comes to payment of salary or benefits. The technology for this exists already in DRC, where portable retinal scanners have been used in UNDP-funded programs to record and identify child soldiers. Third, in instances of an imminent or recent attack with risks of massive violence, deploy a rapid reaction force of Congolese soldiers and/or police mixed with embedded international advisors. Fourth, use private sector firms to advise and help set up professional, accountable administrative structures (such as pay, vetting, record-keeping, or promotions). Although governmental or UN groups can do this, private sector advisors are more likely to be non-political, specialized and qualified in the specific topics, can employ "lessons learned" from similar work elsewhere, and can maintain continuity longer than bilateral or multilateral advisors who often have short-term assignments.[126]

Benefits of employing private military contractors, otherwise known as mercenaries, include a clear chain of command, more readily compatible military equipment and training, a handpicked pool of combat-hardened elite veterans, and the financial efficiency of a for-profit corporation with none of the political baggage and bureaucratic foot-dragging of a multinational force.[127] Training and intelligence, two areas in DRC where international efforts have thus far proved deficient, sluggish, or nonexistent, would be particular strong points. Clear instances where private firms have had successes stopping bloodletting include South African-based Executive Outcomes conclusively halting insurgencies in Angola and Sierra Leone where the UN mission had failed;[128] and the U.S. government contracted out the overhaul of the Liberian army after a brutal civil war to U.S.-based DynCorp, a process which involved scrapping the entire force and rebuilding it after thorough and painstaking vetting.

Disadvantages have, however, often proved more weighty. The use and abuses of mercenaries are long, from employment by strongmen in Africa to the case of Blackwater, a U.S.-based private security firm whose employees were accused of killing civilians while under contract with the U.S. government in Iraq. Ongoing serious concerns include difficulty of controlling the quality of a firm's personnel, its daily interactions with locals, or its readiness to sub-contract to unaccountable firms.[129]

[126] These suggestions were drawn from an interview Dec. 18, 2010, with Laura Englebrecht, U.S. diplomat in DRC during 2001–2003 and current President of New Century U.S., a private company which is contracted by the U.S. government to conduct capacity building of foreign security forces.

[127] *See* Herbert M. Howe, *Private Security Forces and African Stability: The Case of Executive Outcomes*, 36(2) J. Mod. Afr. Stud. 307–331 (Jun. 1998).

[128] *Id.* There were controversies involving the allocation of minerals and other mines to EO, but the firm is generally credited with stopping the brutalities, in an ad hoc and innovative scenario, in uniforms, under Sierra Leonean auspices.

[129] T.X. Hammes, *Private Contractors in Conflict Zones: The Good, the Bad and the Strategic Impact*, Institute for National Strategic Studies Strategic Forum, Nov. 2010, at 37; *available at* http://www.ndu.edu/inss/docUploaded/SF%20260_Hammes.pdf, *see also*, Howe, *supra* note 125.

In the eyes of the population, personnel may critically lack the legitimacy of uniformed forces. Most worrying, they may have few qualms resisting hire by a wealthy "spoiler."

Some of these concerns have begun to be addressed by regulation that would constrain firms to abide by international legal standards.[130] On September 17, 2008, 17 countries adopted the Montreux Document on private military and security companies, a non-binding agreement that is nonetheless the first international framework to set out the duties, obligations, and best practices for employing private military or security firms.[131] In November 2010, 50 global firms signed an International Code of Conduct for Private Security Contractors, with an additional 20 signing thereafter.[132]

That the effort to conform to international norms is evolving into law in parallel to RtoP bears special consideration for purposes of RtoP application, which has thus far been largely discussed or considered conceptually only in terms of the traditional state-centric system. But history continues to show that such a system, premised as it is on the domestic whims and political compromises of individual states, has its limits.[133]

Moreover, the reality is that U.S. and Western governments engaged in peace and stability operations routinely—and increasingly—contract out an array of jobs including personnel protection, training, logistics, surveillance, and other support services,[134] and proponents have circulated proposals for their employment in a wider variety of roles, from medical support under fire to taking the lead in security sector reform.[135] Not only are former soldiers on the lookout for jobs, particularly as engagement in

[130] *See* the International Stability Operations Association, formerly the International Peace Operations Association, a not-for-profit, trade association whose mission includes the promotion of "high operational and ethical standards of firms active in the peace and stability operations industry." The organization and its Code of Conduct were the brainchild of Doug Brooks, an academic fellow in 2000 and 2001 in Sierra Leone where he noticed the professionalism and ethical practice of the private sector in support of UNAMSIL, *available at* http://ipoaworld.org/eng/codeofconducthistory.html.

[131] Montreux Document, *Permanent Representative of Switzerland to the United Nations addressed to the Secretary-General*, General Assembly, A/63/467-S/2008/636, Oct. 6, 2008.

[132] *International Code of Conduct for Private Security Contractors*, *available at* http://www.news.admin.ch/NSBSubscriber/message/attachments/21143.pdf.

[133] As of January 31, 2008, just 0.3% of MONUC's 18,385 personnel were Western, echoing a general and longstanding trend in which the best-equipped, most professional militaries have largely abandoned peace operations that do not directly support national interests; J.J. Messner, *Still Waiting for the West: Since This Time Last Year, Very Little Has Changed*, 3(5) J. Int'l Peace Ops. (March–April 2008).

[134] As of March 31, 2010, the United States deployed 175,000 troops and 207,000 contractors in Iraq and Afghanistan; Hammes, *supra* note 129; or Peter W. Singer, *Outsourcing the Fight*, FORBES, Jun. 5, 2008, *available at* http://www.forbes.com/2008/06/05/outsourcing-army-halliburton-tech-cx_ps_logistics08_0605outsource.html.

[135] Some have used the media to broadcast their intentions, including Erik Prince, founder of the notorious Blackwater. Prince told a reporter he sees a future using the mobility and flexibility of Blackwater's ex-SEALs, former Coast Guard officersm and FBI agents to seek out and quickly fill other gaps that others present. When he noticed a shortage of U.S. combat medics, he developed a school and program to train his own and was now looking for customers who want to hire medics as contractors; Mike Baker, *Blackwater Mixes Business Glitz with Military Glitz*, Associated Press, Jul. 28, 2008.

Afghanistan and Iraq wanes,[136] but private donors and individual nonprofits have in discrete instances reached out to them to take action in a vacuum of effective international action. The case of Mia Farrow is instructive. According to news reports in the summer of 2008, the Hollywood actress-turned-activist reached out to Erik Prince, founder of Blackwater, to discuss the possibility of military intervention on behalf of civilians in Darfur.[137]

Though the plan never came to fruition, it seems fair to wonder whether the right set of conditions, or the impetus of the RtoP spirit, could in a future situation lead a corporation or wealthy individual donor to bypass altogether the UN system—unless the UN buys in from the start. Regarding DRC and other crisis areas, the Genocide Intervention Network, a U.S.-based nonprofit, has talked with private firms about the possibility of deploying unmanned aerial vehicles—expensive surveillance still out of reach of UN budget considerations—or discussed other creative or high-tech methods to inform peacekeepers, humanitarian actors and members of the diplomatic corps in real time about imminent attacks on civilians in remote areas.[138]

Consider the 1998 lament of Kofi Annan, UN Secretary-General, recalling the Rwandan genocide and its aftermath in DRC: "When we had need of skilled soldiers to separate fighters from refugees in the Rwandan refugee camps in Goma, I even considered the possibility of engaging a private firm. But the world may not be ready to privatize peace."[139] In all likelihood, that firm was Executive Outcomes.[140] In an unpublished letter after the genocide, Chris Grove, EO's former chief of staff wrote that in 14 days, the company could have had armed troops on the ground, and within six weeks deployed 1,527 personnel, complete with air and communications sup-

[136] *See Mercenaries in Africa: The Fog and Dogs of War,* The Economist, Mar 18, 2004.

[137] "The people in the camps would say 'we don't care whether it's Blackwater, any-water, as long as they help us,'" Farrow told a reporter, in Harvey Morris, *Activists turn to Blackwater over Darfur,* Financial Times, Jun. 19, 2008, *available at* http://www.ft.com/cms/s/0/4699eda6–3d65–11dd-bbb5–0000779fd2ac.html#ixzz18mnNkZWa; Anna Schecter, *Breakfast With Blackwater; Mia Farrow and Blackwater CEO Prince Met to Discuss a Possible Collaboration,* ABC NEWS, Aug. 20, 2008, *available at* http://abcnews.go.com/Blotter/story?id=5617186&page=2

[138] Interview with Mark Hanis, President, Genocide Intervention Network/Save Darfur Coalition, Jan. 10, 2011. The talks have stopped short of action largely on the basis of prohibitive cost for non-state actors, potential moral hazard, and the necessity of engaging with local governments about the use of their airspace.

[139] Secretary-General Kofi Annan, Ditchley Foundation Lecture XXXV, Jun. 26, 1998, *available at* http://www.ditchley.co.uk/page/173/lecture-xxxv.html. Annan was, he said, "haunted by the experience of Rwanda in 1994 . . . Surely things would have been different if the Security Council had had at its disposal a small rapid reaction force, ready to move at a few days' notice. I believe that if we are to avert further such disasters in the future we need such a capacity; that Member States must have appropriately trained stand-by forces immediately available, and must be willing to send them quickly when the Security Council requests it." *Id.*

[140] "During the Rwanda genocide we believe Executive Outcomes could have stopped the massacres if given the opportunity to intervene on behalf of the UN . . . The then CEO of EO made comments to journalists during that time of how we viewed the situation and how EO could possibly go about to resolving the conflict if approached by the UN." Chris Grove, *A Possible Role of Executive Outcomes (A Private Military Company, Now Disbanded) During the Rwandan Genocide of 1993/1994,* Letter with Detailed Budget and Plan, undated, *available at* http://www.hoosier84.com/00–06eor-wanda.pdf.

port—sufficient to "have stopped the massacres if given the opportunity to intervene on behalf of the UN." A budget for the six-month operation amounted to $150 million.[141] In comparison, a "dysfunctional" peacekeeping operation in Sierra Leone at that time cost almost $100 million a month.

Counterfactuals can often be empty academic exercises. Still: What if RtoP had already established itself as a doctrine? Would Kofi Annan, then-head of the Department of Peacekeeping Operations, have felt compelled to take another route? And—now that the RtoP principle both exists and provides an impetus for action—what if the crisis of Lord's Resistance Army in the DRC were a contender for a viable "force multiplier" option, where MONUSCU working with the Congolese forces alone has thus far conclusively failed?

V. CONCLUSION

In conclusion, though there are no easy answers, there are ways forward. Private contractors are an option, but chiefly to bolster a more efficient UN peacekeeping force that is both capable and willing to live up to an achievable mandate, with a clear plan for the practical application of civilian protection. This includes managing expectations and delivering on troop needs, such as manpower, intelligence systems, and equipment. Simultaneously, political pressure must continue, albeit harmonized; and the UN or other another group must find ways to coordinate ad hoc assistance and assess their projects, particularly in the vital area of security sector reform. Therein, an examination of flawed assumptions, or the mismatch between the ends of donors and aid groups and their Congolese recipients, might cause significant adjustments. With its mass of funds and experience, the international community must first strive to do no harm while carefully strengthening a legitimate Congolese government and the considerable forces within Congolese civil society so that they can at last protect their own.

[141] *Id.*

16 Democratic People's Republic of Korea

Kjell Magne Bondevik and
Kristen Abrams

I. INTRODUCTION

Despite the Democratic People's Republic of Korea's (DPRK), or North Korea's, formal commitment to human rights through the ratification of several international treaties, the human rights situation in this reclusive, isolated country is characterized by widespread, systematic, and severe violations of its citizen's fundamental freedoms and human rights. The Government of North Korea routinely disregards its obligation to protect its citizens from starvation, persecution, imprisonment, torture, enslavement, and even murder. Former United Nations Special Rapporteur on the Situation of Human Rights in the Democratic People's Republic of Korea, Vitit Muntarbhorn, characterized the human rights situation in North Korea as "harrowing and horrific"[1] and recently said that "freedoms from want, from fear, from discrimination, from persecution and from exploitation are regrettably transgressed with impunity by [the] authorities, in an astonishing setting of abuse after abuse, multiplied incessantly."[2]

This chapter first provides a brief historical background of North Korea and discusses the political and economic indicators that have allowed massive human rights violations to take place. Next, this chapter explains the severe food crisis and the

[1] The Special Rapporteur on the Situation of Human Rights in the Democratic People's Republic of Korea–Vitit Muntarbhorn, *Report of the Special Rapporteur on the Situation of Human Rights in the Democratic People's Republic of Korea,* A/HRC/13/47, Feb. 17, 2010, at ¶ 86 [hereinafter Special Rapporteur Feb. 2010 Report].

[2] The Special Rapporteur on the Situation of Human Rights in the Democratic People's Republic of Korea–Vitit Muntarbhorn, *Situation of Human Rights in the Democratic People's Republic of Korea,* A/64/224, Aug. 4, 2009, at ¶ 72 [hereinafter Special Rapporteur Aug. 2009 Report.]

kwan-li-so political prison system. Following an introduction to crimes against humanity and the Responsibility to Protect doctrine, this chapter analyzes the facts presented against the elements that constitute crimes against humanity and concludes that North Korea is committing crimes against humanity by starving millions of its people and maintaining a political gulag system. After demonstrating that North Korea is committing crimes against humanity, an overview of the actions recently taken by the international community—including the United Nations, regional bodies, states and non-governmental actors—which acknowledge the severity and state responsibility for these atrocities is explored. This evidence supports the conclusion reached in the prior section that North Korea is indeed committing crimes against humanity and that the international community is taking note. Finally, this chapter ends with several recommendations that should be taken to alleviate the suffering of the North Korean people.

II. BACKGROUND ON NORTH KOREA

A. Politics and Economics

North Korea has been appropriately labeled the world's most isolated and reclusive nation. Its estimated 23 million people live in absolute global isolation; freedom of movement does not exist and emigration is illegal, akin to treason. North Korean leaders maintain power through militaristic dictatorial rule and the government operates in total secrecy. The government is the "ultimate source of power, virtue, spiritual wisdom, and truth for the North Korean people."[3]

Since Kim Il-sung, the "Great Leader," took leadership of the country following the Korean War, North Korea has been governed by a Marxist-Leninist political model of autonomy and self-reliance, called *juche*.[4] The government relies on a Soviet-style, centrally planned economy. Until the Soviet Union's collapse, poor domestic production was routinely offset by aid and subsidies from Soviet bloc countries. After the disintegration of the Soviet Union, aid halted and the economy all but collapsed.[5] By the early 1990s, economic mismanagement, political and economic isolation, and over-militarization had left the country in economic shambles.[6]

Following Kim Il-sung's unexpected death in 1994, his oldest recognized son, Kim Jong-il, the "Dear Leader," assumed leadership of the country. Under Kim Jong-il's rule, North Korea maintains a centralized, socialist government under the rigid control of the communist Korean Workers' Party (KWP), to which all government

[3] Michael Cromartie, *Preface* to DAVID HAWK, THANK YOU FATHER KIM IL-SUNG, EYEWITNESS ACCOUNTS OF SEVERE VIOLATIONS OF FREEDOM OF THOUGHT, CONSCIENCE, AND RELIGION IN NORTH KOREA iv (United States Commission on International Freedom, 2005), *available at* http://hirc.house.gov/archives/109/NKwitnesses.pdf.

[4] *See* U.S. Library of Congress, Federal Research Division, *Country Profile: North Korea* (Jul. 2007), 4–5, *available at* http://lcweb2.loc.gov/frd/cs/profiles/North_Korea.pdf.

[5] *See id.* at 8.

[6] *See* DLA Piper US LLP & US Committee for Human Rights in North Korea, *Failure to Protect: A Call for the UN Security Council to Act in North Korea* 6 (2006) [hereinafter *Failure to Protect*].

officials belong.[7] Former UN Special Rapporteur Vitit Muntarbhorn describes the government as "a form of ruler-based nationalism . . . bent on personal survival, under which the ordinary people . . . undergo intolerable and interminable suffering."[8] Combined with decades of economic mismanagement, the country's largely self-imposed global isolation severely hinders economic progress.[9] Large-scale military expenditures consume much-needed resources for investment, while ineffective collective, state-run farming, government mismanagement, and weather-related problems, have left millions of North Koreans malnourished or starved.[10]

In recent years, rumors of Kim Jong-il's declining health have led to intense speculation as to who will succeed him. By September 2010, it became widely regarded that Kim Jong-il's youngest son, Kim Jong-un, is the heir apparent.[11] Most observers believe that Kim Jong-un will continue the totalitarian regime, global isolation, and *juche* philosophy of his father and grandfather.

B. Food Policy and Famine

To control the population, Kim Il-sung instituted a public food rationing system that favored certain classes of citizens, particularly the ruling party and high-ranking military, intelligence, and police officers.[12] This public distribution system, when combined with other disastrous government policies, such as the state's monopoly on food and the degradation of the country's agricultural sector, as well as natural weather challenges, subjected the people of North Korea in the 1990s to a catastrophic famine that killed at least one million people, and stunted the development of surviving children for life.[13] Following the famine, the regime was forced to accept foreign food aid to prevent additional widespread starvation. But, the government ignored commonly accepted aid distribution norms and instead pursued policies that hindered effective monitoring and created opportunities for regime control and diversion.[14]

[7] *See* U.S. Department of State, *Background Note: North Korea* (Sept. 2010), http://www.state.gov/r/pa/ei/bgn/2792.htm.

[8] The Special Rapporteur on the Situation of Human Rights in the Democratic People's Republic of Korea–Vitit Muntarbhorn, *Report of the Special Rapporteur on the Situation of Human Rights in the Democratic People's Republic of Korea*, A/HRC/10/18, Feb. 24, 2009, at *¶ 4* [hereinafter Special Rapporteur Feb. 2009 Report].

[9] Marcus Noland, *A New International Engagement Framework for North Korea? Political Economy of North Korea: Historic Background and Present Situation* (2005), International Institute for Economics, at 36 [hereinafter Noland: A New Int'l Engagement].

[10] *See* Special Rapporteur Feb. 2009 Report, *supra* note 8; Noland: A New Int'l Engagement, *supra* note 9, at 36.

[11] *See generally* Mark McDonald, *Kim Jong-il's Heir Attends Parade*, New York Times, Oct. 9, 2010.

[12] *See* Human Rights Watch, *A Matter of Survival: The North Korean Government's Control of Food and the Risk of Hunger* (May 2006) [hereinafter *A Matter of Survival*].

[13] *See generally Failure to Protect*, *supra* note 6; Stephan Haggard & Marcus Noland, Hunger and Human Rights: The Politics of Famine in North Korea (U.S. Committee for Human Rights in North Korea, 2005), at 21 [Hereinafter Haggard & Noland, Hunger and Human Rights]; *A Matter of Survival*, *supra* note 12.

[14] *See Failure to Protect*, *supra* note 6, at 24; Stephan Haggard & Marcus Noland, Famine in North Korea: Markets, Aid and Reform (Columbia University Press, 2007) [hereinafter Haggard & Nolan, Famine], at 25–26.

In an effort to increase food output, in 2002 the government permitted some private farming and private "farmers' markets." But by the end of 2005, the government had reversed course by forbidding private sales of grains, reinstituting the food rationing system, and terminating most international humanitarian assistance operations to curb what it believed was outside influence. Described as "unconscionable"[15] by Special Rapporteur Muntarbhorn, other observers warned that these measures were a "recipe for disaster."[16] When faced with devastating floods in 2006 and 2007, again, the people of North Korea experienced aggravated chronic food shortages and widespread hunger.

Even in a year of good harvests, the government cannot produce enough food to properly feed its 23 million citizens.[17] Still, since mid-2008, North Korea has wavered between accepting and rejecting U.S. and other foreign shipments of food. For example, Pyongyang began receiving U.S. shipments of food aid in mid-2008, but in March 2009 rejected all additional U.S. aid shipments and asked American non-governmental organizations to leave the country.[18] These uneven policies were compounded by the disastrous November 2009 currency devaluation. This so-called monetary "reform" effectively wiped out the cash savings of many citizens, stripping them of all power to purchase food.

Today, the public food distribution system is all but defunct, only distributing food to high-level government and military officials and security forces. The United Nations World Food Programme (WFP) reported in 2010 that more than one in four North Koreas need food aid, but only about one in 17 will receive it.[19] Crippling food shortages have caused widespread illness as thousands are forced to subsist on "wild foods" such as grass, tree bark, and roots, according to Amnesty International.[20] Hoarding and barter trade are prevalent, but the government remains insistent on punishing those engaging in these private-market, but life-saving, activities.[21] A North Korean woman who spoke to a *New York Times* reporter in mid-2010 summarized the predicament she and her family face, "If you don't trade, you die."[22]

Chronic food shortages leading to perpetual hunger have had a dramatic impact on the health and well-being of the people of North Korea. Malnutrition is widespread, affecting much of the North Korean population. Children, the elderly, as well

[15] Special Rapporteur Feb. 2009 Report, *supra* note 8, at ¶ 13.

[16] Human Rights Watch, *North Korea: Policy Changes May Foster New Hunger*, May 2006.

[17] *See* Mark McDonald and Kevin Drew, UN *Urges Food Aid for North Korea*, New York Times, Nov. 17, 2010.

[18] *See* Choe Sang-Hun, *Convoy Carries South Korean Rice Donations to the North*, New York Times, Sept. 19, 2010; Special Rapporteur Feb. 2010 Report, *supra* note 1, at ¶ 15.

[19] *See* Sharon LaFraniere, *Views Show How North Korea Policy Spread Misery*, New York Times, Jun. 9, 2010.

[20] Amnesty International, *Starving North Koreans Forced to Survive on Diet of Grass and Tree Bark*, Jul. 15, 2010, *available at* http://www.amnesty.org/en/news-and-updates/starving-north-koreans-forced-survive-diet-grass-and-tree-bark-2010–07-14.

[21] *See* Kay Seok, *Handling the Next North Korean Famine: When Pyongyang Needs Food Aid, Donors Can—and Must—Insist on Meaningful Monitoring*, Wall Street Journal, Apr. 13, 2010.

[22] *See* LaFraniere, *supra* note 19.

as pregnant and breast-feeding women are most severely impacted.[23] According to the WFP, 25 percent of pregnant and breast-feeding women and 33 percent of children are chronically undernourished.[24] UNICEF has warned that this malnourishment has resulted in as high as 45 percent of North Korean children experiencing permanent stunted growth.[25] Perhaps the two most striking examples of the impacts of the food crisis is that the average seven-year-old boy in North Korea weighs 20 pounds less and is 8 inches shorter than his South Korean counterpart; and, in 2003, the military reduced its height requirement from four feet, nine inches (150cm) to four feet, one inch (125cm).[26]

Nevertheless, the government continues to ignore this serious problem and refuses to take action to remedy the fundamental circumstances that led to these conditions. Instead, the government continues to spend excessively on military armaments. In fact, an estimated 15 to 30 percent of North Korea's GDP is used to support the army, even during times of famine and food insecurity.[27] Pyongyang has repeatedly demonstrated that keeping its population properly fed is a low priority. Rather than focusing on the suffering of its people, the North Korean government prioritizes exerting control over its people, maintaining global isolation, building a nuclear weapons program, and maintaining an oversized military.[28]

C. *Kwan-li-so* Political Prison Camps

The array of human rights violations perpetrated by the North Korean government extends far beyond the government's reckless food policy. These violations, which are fueled by the brutal suppression of all forms of political dissent, most flagrantly include the government's operation of a massive political prison system, or gulag, known as *kwan-li-so*.[29]

[23] *See generally* Report of the Working Group on the Universal Period Review, *Democratic People's Republic of Korea*, A/HRC/13/13, Jan. 4, 2010, at 3; *Failure to Protect*, *supra* note 6, at 12.

[24] World Food Programme, Country Report–Democratic People's Republic of Korea, *available at* http://www.wfp.org/countries/korea-democratic-peoples-republic-dprk.

[25] *See Poor Nutrition Stunting Growth of 200 Million Children*, Telegraph (UK), Nov. 12, 2009.

[26] *See* Marcus Noland, *Famine and Reform in North Korea*, International Institute for Economics (2003), at 10, n.16; Craig Simmons, *North Korea's Famine Believed to be Escalating*, Austin American-Statesman, May 18, 2007.

[27] *See* Lee Young-sun & Yoon Deok-Ryong, *The Structure of North Korea's Economy: Changes and Effects, A New International Framework for North Korea?* American Enterprise Institute (2005), at 52; Yoel Sano, *Military Holds the Key*, Asia Times, Feb. 18, 2005; Marcus Noland, Sherman Robinson & Tao Wang, *Famine in North Korea: Causes and Cure*, Institute for International Economics (2002), at 1–2.

[28] It is estimated that the armed forces total over 1 million armed personnel, with another 7.7 million reserve component. U.S. Library of Congress, *supra* note 4, at 9.

[29] *See* Choi Sung-Choi, *The International Community and Human Rights in North Korea*, Center for Advancement of North Korean Human Rights (1996), at 11; David Hawk, *The Hidden Gulag–Exposing North Korea's Prison Camps*, U.S. Committee for Human Rights in North Korea, at 24, *available at* http://www.hrnk.org/download/The_Hidden_Gulag.pdf [hereinafter Hidden Gulag]; *see generally* Korea Institute for National Unification, *White Paper on Human Rights in North Korea* (2008) (providing a highly detailed overview of the human rights situation in North Korea).

In North Korea, one may be accused of a political crime for taking the following actions, among others: expressing anti-socialist sentiment, having "unsound ideology," criticizing the regime in any manner (including, for example, expressing "negative influences [on] the process of amassing slush funds for Kim Jong-il"), reading a foreign newspaper, or even expressing exasperation with the difficulty of life in North Korea.[30] Religious belief—apart from state authorized *juche* ideology—is also grounds for being accused of a political crime. Several escapees reported that after being repatriated from China, after failed escape attempts, they were sent to a prison camp after confessing that they were "followers of Jesus."[31]

Once accused of a political crime, rather than being formally charged or arrested, an accused is placed in an interrogation facility and sometimes tortured until he or she confesses to the alleged crime.[32] Deemed guilty of a political crime, the criminal is punished in one of two ways—execution or incarceration in a *kwan-li-so* political prison.[33]

In existence since 1947, political prisons were first created to hold landowners, religious persons, and those who supported the Japanese during its occupation of Korea.[34] Religious groups, in particular, were viewed as political competition to Kim Il-sung's Korean Workers Party.[35] During the 1950s and 1960s, to purge political foes, thereby containing the proliferation of their influence, the regime either executed or confined those who expressed anti-regime sentiments, together with their families, in prison camps in remote areas.[36] By 1982, the government had sentenced over 100,000 undesirables to permanent hard labor in North Korea's expanding network of prison camps.[37] Generally, the number of operational prison camps has risen and fallen together with the anxieties and insecurities of Kim Il-sung and Kim Jong-il. Today, it is believed that approximately 200,000 people are held in *kwan-li-so* camps.[38]

While the existence of labor camps is common knowledge both within North Korea and outside, detailed information about life in a North Korean gulag has only relatively recently begun to filter out of North Korea via the growing number of defectors and former inmate escapees. While much of this information is anecdotal and, naturally, unverifiable, escapee and defector reports present a horrifying depiction of life in a North Korean gulag. Escapees and defectors report that once inside a camp, prisoners face numerous impediments to their survival, including starvation, forced labor, sickness, and torture.

Inmates in political prison camps are always subjected to forced hard labor. Typical types of labor include mountain logging, stone quarrying, farming, and factory work,

[30] *See* Choi Sung-Choi, *supra* note 29 at 110–12; Anne Applebaum, *Preface* to David Hawk, *supra* note 29.

[31] See David Hawk, *supra* note 3.

[32] *See* Hidden Gulag, *supra* note 29, at 24–25.

[33] *See id.* at 24; Choi Sung-Choi, The International Community and Human Rights in North Korea, Center for Advancement of North Korean Human Rights (1996), at 11.

[34] *See* Choi Sung-Choi, *supra* note 29 at 107–108.

[35] *Id.* at 107, 232.

[36] *See* Korea Institute for National Unification, *supra* note 29.

[37] *See id.* at 109.

[38] *See Hidden Gulag, supra* note 32, at 24, fn. 16; Amnesty International, *North Korea: Torture, Death Penalty and Abductions*, Aug. 2009, *available at* http://www.amnesty.org/en/library/asset/ASA24/003/2009/zh/544fbfdc-941c-4bb4-89b8-92dd08c62d92/asa240032009en.pdf.

often for 10 hours or more per day, seven days a week. Prisoners are given strict and unrealistic daily production quotas.[39] A former guard reported that at one prison camp, there were so many deaths from beatings of prisoners who failed to meet their production quotas, guards were instructed to be less violent.[40]

Though they are forced to engage in long hours of demanding physical labor, inmates are provided only starvation-level food rations. One defector described the daily ration as 20 grains of corn per inmate.[41] This defector further reported that to stave off death, prisoners dug through cow dung in search of undigested grain.[42] A former prison guard reported that at a very large prison camp, 1,500 to 2,000 prisoners died annually from malnutrition.[43]

Inmates are prohibited from having any contact with the outside world.[44] Living conditions are primitive and access to health care is non-existent, with many prisoners suffering from pneumonia, tuberculosis, pellagra, and other diseases. With little more than rags for clothing, frostbite—resulting in amputation—is commonplace.[45] When a prisoner falls so ill that he or she can no longer work, the prisoner is sent to a sanatorium and essentially abandoned.[46] Failure to meet one's work quota, being accused of lying, not working fast enough, or forgetting seemingly innocuous prison rules result in reduced food rations or other forms of physical punishment.[47] Forms of punishment include beatings, forced exercise, sitting still for prolonged periods of time, and humiliating public criticism.

The combination of hard labor, inadequate food, physical abuse, lack of medical care, and poor living conditions have turned North Korean political prison camps into death camps. Some reports indicate that more than 400,000 prisoners have died in these camps in the past 30 years.[48]

III. APPLYING THE RTOP DOCTRINE TO THE FACTS

A. Defining Responsibility to Protect and Crimes Against Humanity

The Responsibility to Protect doctrine directs states to take responsibility to protect its population from genocide, war crimes, ethic cleansing, and crimes against humanity. In the event a state fails in its responsibility to protect its population, the United Nations has directed that it holds the responsibility to take collective action in a timely

[39] *See* Korea Institute for National Unification, *supra* note 29 at 110–112; Applebaum, *supra* note *30* at 8.

[40] *See* Hidden Gulag, *supra* note 32, at 40.

[41] *See* John Gittelsohn, *Defections and Doubts*, Orange County Register, Jun. 23, 2003.

[42] *See id.*

[43] Kang Chol-Hwan & Pierre Rigoulot, Aquariums of Pyongyang (Basic Books 2001), at 86.

[44] *See* Korea Institute for National Unification, *supra* note 29 at 126.

[45] *Hidden Gulag, supra* note 32, at 25.

[46] *See* Korea Institute for National Unification, *supra* note 29 at 127.

[47] *See Failure to Protect, supra* note 6, at 91.

[48] Choi Sung-Choi, *supra* note 29 at 11.

and decisive manner up to and including action by the UN Security Council.[49] As thoroughly discussed in prior chapters, the Responsibility to Protect doctrine includes four key elements:

1. The primary responsibility for protecting a state's population from these most egregious of human rights abuses resides with that country's government;
2. The international community has a duty to help states in meeting this responsibility;
3. When a state manifestly fails in its obligation to protect its own citizens, it is the international community's responsibility to help protect that population; and
4. If multilateral action through the UN and regional entities fail to address the problem, it is the Security Council's responsibility to intervene.[50]

The legal definition of "crimes against humanity" was also thoroughly explored in prior chapters and will not be repeated here. For purposes of this analysis, "crimes against humanity" will be defined according to the Rome Statute. Specifically, crimes against humanity are crimes including, among others, murder, enslavement, torture, rape, persecution, and all other inhumane acts of a similar character (willfully causing great suffering, or serious injury to body or to mental or physical health), committed "as part of a widespread or systematic attack directed against any civilian population, with knowledge of the attack."[51] The following section will apply international law to North Korean government conduct with respect to its food policy and treatment of

[49] *See 2005 World Summit Outcome*, A/RES/60/1, Sept. 15, 2005, at ¶¶ 138–139 [hereinafter 2005 WSOD]; S.C. Res. 1674, S/RES/1674, Apr. 28, 2006.

[50] *See, e.g.*, William R. Pace & Nicole Deller, *Preventing Future Genocides: An International Responsibility to Protect*, World Order, Vol. 36, No. 4 (2005), citing Secretary-General's High-Level Panel on Threats, Challenges and Change, *A More Secure World: Our Shared Responsibility*, A/59/565, Dec. 2, 2004, at ¶¶ 29, 201.

[51] Specifically, the following elements must be satisfied under customary law:

1. There must be an attack;
2. The acts of the accused must be part of the attack;
3. The attack must be directed against any civilian population;
4. The attack must be widespread or systematic; and
5. The accused must know that the acts constitute part of a pattern of widespread or systematic crimes directed against a civilian population, know that the accused's acts fit into such a pattern, and intend to commit the underlying prohibited act.

The Rome Statute proscribes eleven acts which constitute crimes against humanity under customary international law. Those eleven acts include:

- Murder;
- Extermination;
- Enslavement;
- Deportation or forcible transfer of population;
- Imprisonment or other severe deprivation of physical liberty in violation of fundamental rules of international law;
- Torture;
- Rape, sexual slavery, enforced prostitution, forced pregnancy, enforced sterilization, or any other form of sexual violence of comparable gravity;

political prisoners. This analysis will conclude that North Korea has committed and continues to commit crimes against humanity and is failing in its Responsibility to Protect its own citizens from such atrocities.

B. North Korean Food Policy: Crimes Against Humanity

As demonstrated above, North Korea's protracted food crisis has led to widespread malnutrition, disease and death. International agencies warn that North Korea is on the brink of a major humanitarian crisis due to the severe shortage of food. Nonetheless, ensuring that its population is adequately fed appears not to concern the North Korean government. Instead, it maintains an intentional, disastrous food policy that starves and malnourishes millions of North Korean citizens.

By starving and malnourishing large segments of its population, the North Korea government is committing extermination and other inhumane acts, as defined by the Rome Statute. "Extermination" includes inflicting life conditions, such as depriving access to food and medicine, calculated to bring about the destruction of part of a population.[52] "Other inhumane acts" include the "causing of great suffering, or serious injury to body or to mental or physical health."[53]

1. Public Distribution System and *Songum* Policy

Examples abound of intentional government conduct that has deprived millions of North Koreans of adequate nourishment and caused great human suffering.[54] Since the earliest days of the regime, the public food rationing system has been used as a means of controlling the population. Food is provided by the state along political lines; the government rewards those persons favored by the regime with food and denies food to the less privileged. And, even those who manage to obtain food through the public distribution system (which is largely nonoperational today), the portion is inadequate as the government remains wholly unable to produce or import enough food to sufficiently feed its people. Moreover, the long-standing principle of *songum*, a policy which prioritizes the military over the rest of North Korean society is reflected in the government's food distribution system. This policy, in addition to the

- Persecution based on political, racial, national, ethnic, cultural, religious, gender or other grounds that are universally recognized as impermissible under international law;
- Enforced disappearance;
- The crime of apartheid;
- Other inhumane acts of a similar character intentionally causing great suffering, or serious injury to body or to mental or physical health.

North Korea is not a signatory to the Rome Statute. The Rome Statute of the International Criminal Court, *opened for signature*, Jul. 17, 1998, A/CONF.183/9 (1998), 2187 U.N.T.S. 90, at art. 7 §1(k) [hereinafter Rome Statute].

[52] *See* Machteld Boot, *Nullum Crimen Sine Lege and the Subject Matter Jurisdiction of the International Criminal Court*, School of Human Rights Research (2002), at 498; Draft Finalized Text of the Elements of Crimes, PCNICC/2000/INF/3/Add.2 (2000), at 10; Rome Statute, *supra* note 51, at art. 7(2)(b).

[53] Rome Statute, *supra* note 51, at art. 7(2).

[54] *See* Special Rapporteur Aug. 2009 Report, *supra* note 2, at ¶ 11.

government's policy of distributing food through the political caste system, depletes the resources of the country while leaving large segments of the population without any of the food provided by international relief agencies or donor countries.

2. Juche Ideology and International Food Aid

Further compounding the deprivation and great suffering that unfavored North Koreans experience is the government's adherence to *juche* ideology. *Juche* was implemented at the founding of the nation and advocates self-reliance, among other tenants. In North Korea, only 19 to 22 percent of the country's land is arable[55] and even in a year of good harvest, the government cannot come close to producing enough food to feed its population. Accordingly, outside food aid is essential to even attempt to adequately nourish North Korean citizens. Ignoring these simple facts, Pyongyang maintains an incoherent policy on international food aid and regularly forbids international food aid monitors from entering the country. When organizations like the World Food Programme are prohibited from monitoring their deliveries, they halt food aid. The government's decision to ban international aid monitors results in valuable, available food aid that never reaches the thousands of starving North Koreans for which it was intended. International aid organizations worry that the catastrophic government decisions during the famine of the 1990s, which included ignoring commonly accepted norms for aid distribution and pursuing policies that diverted aid for government and military purposes, are being repeated today.

3. Criminalization of Private Coping Mechanisms

Furthermore, the North Korean government has criminalized many of the coping strategies adopted by its people. By reversing earlier policies that permitted some small scale private farming, the government's decision to forbid private sales of grains results in thousands of politically unfavored citizens without food. According to a 2007 Central Committee communication, Kim Jong-il believed the underground markets had become a "birthplace of all sorts of non-socialist practices."[56] In his 2008 report, former UN Special Rapporteur Muntarbhorn described this situation as a "painful paradox" for non-elites. He said, "[O]n the one hand, the social safety nets [such as the food ration system] which the State offered in the past are now no longer reliable and [the non-elite people of North Korea] must seek other ways to fend for themselves; on the other hand, when they undertake various livelihood initiatives to supplement their income, the authorities clamp down on them for fear of losing their grip on the population."[57] Moreover, because the government heavily regulates free movement, North Koreans are prevented form searching for food themselves or relocating to areas with less acute food shortages.

[55] *Failure to Protect*, *supra* note 6, at 89, *citing* World Fact Book, U.S. Central Intelligence Agency.

[56] Sharon LaFraniere, *supra* note 19.

[57] The Special Rapporteur on the Situation of Human Rights in the Democratic People's Republic of Korea–Vitit Muntarbhorn, *Report of the Special Rapporteur on the Situation of Human Rights in the Democratic People's Republic of Korea*, A/HRC/7/20, Feb. 15, 2008, at ¶ 13 [hereinafter Special Rapporteur Feb. 2008 Report].

4. Global Aggression

Pyongyang's decisions to conduct nuclear and missile tests, expand its nuclear weapons program, and its presumed role in the sinking of the South Korean ship the Cheonan, has had serious consequences for the well-being of its people. By reaffirming the government's prioritization of its weapons program over feeding its people, potential food donors have been driven away while others have canceled food shipments in protest. Josette Sheeran, Executive Director of the UN's WFP, said in November 2010 that her agency has only about 20 percent of the money it needs to fund its project to combat malnutrition in North Korea.[58] WFP operations are funded by donations from world governments, corporations, and private donors.

Furthermore, in an attempt to stockpile food in the event of a protracted standoff with South Korea and/or the United States, Pyongyang at times has suspended all food deliveries. Commenting on the report of government stockpiling, the WFP cautioned, "it's a bit of a perfect storm."[59]

5. 2009 Currency Devaluation

Finally, the government's devastating November 2009 currency devaluation wiped out many families' life savings—the very money that allowed them to purchase food on the black market to fend off starvation. Rather than prop up the economy, experts believe that the currency devaluation fueled the food crisis.

While acute famine conditions reminiscent of the 1990s does not exist today, millions of North Koreans remain food insecure, and the circumstances and decisions that led to the famine have not changed. North Korea cannot produce enough food to provide sufficient nutrition to its people, yet it continues to take actions that prevent its people from receiving the nourishment they deserve.

Unquestionably, the government of North Korea's actions are starving millions of its citizens and are carried out in a highly organized manner. There is no doubt that limiting access to the country, limiting or banning private marks, favoring the military and politically elite as part of its food distribution system, suspending or curtailing the food ration system, and preventing the transparent distribution of food aid are systematic as well as widespread actions.

Ensuring that all North Korean people are adequately fed is a fundamental responsibility of the government of North Korea. Since the founding of the country more than 60 years ago, North Korea has failed its responsibility as a sovereign to meet this universal humanitarian imperative and instead pursues policies which have resulted in the death of hundreds of thousands of North Koreans and subjected those who survive to serious bodily harm and ill-health. By committing extermination and other inhumane acts, the government of North Korea's food policy and its refusal to feed substantial segments of its own population constitute crimes against humanity.

[58] *North Korean Defections Continue Amid Food Shortage*, Voice of America, Nov. 15, 2010.

[59] Tania Branigan, *UN Fears Tragedy over North Korean Food Shortages*, The Guardian (UK), Apr. 17, 2008.

C. Operation of *Kwan-li-so* Camps: Crimes Against Humanity

Earlier sections of this chapter explored in detail the existence and operation of the North Korean political prison camp system, known as *kwan-li-so*. This complex system aids in the commission of several international crimes, including enforced disappearance, imprisonment, persecution based on political and religious grounds, extermination, enslavement, and torture. Pyongyang's intentional operation of this system and the commission of the aforementioned acts, explained and analyzed below, constitutes crimes against humanity.

1. Enforced Disappearance

The Rome Statute defines enforced disappearance as "the arrest, detention or abduction of persons by, or with the authorization, support or acquiescence of, a State or a political organization, followed by a refusal to acknowledge that deprivation of freedom or to give information on the fate or whereabouts of those persons, with the intention of removing them from the protection of the law for a prolonged period of time."[60] In the DPRK, those opposed to or perceived to be opposed to the regime, and possibly their family members, are subjected to "enforced disappearances."

Persons accused of subversive thoughts or actions are routinely apprehended by government officials and forcibly transferred to a remote prison labor camp. Government authorities do not possess arrest warrants, do not legally charge under domestic criminal code and often fail to even notify the accused of his or her alleged "crime."

The intent of the DPRK's abduction or "enforced disappearance" policy is to remove the accused from society and the protection of the law for an indefinite period of time.[61] Disappeared persons are generally told that they are "traitors to the nation" in a political declaration read to the accused shortly following his or her abduction. Disappeared persons are not told for how long, or where, they will be detained. Family members, if not also detained, are provided little to no information about their arrested relative and many never learn of their relative's fate or whereabouts.

North Korea's practice of detaining and abducting perceived political wrong-doers and transferring them to political labor camps for indefinite detention, all without notifying the family of the abducted person as to his or her whereabouts, constitutes an "enforced disappearance" under international law.

[60] Rome Statute, *supra* note 51, at art. 7(2)(i).

[61] David Hawk, *Concentrations of Inhumanity: An Analysis of the Phenomena of Repression Associated With North Korea's Kwan-li-so Political Penal Labor Camps According to the Terms and Provisions of Article 7 of the Rome Statute of the International Criminal Court and the Parallel Provisions of Customary International Law on Crimes Against Humanity*, Freedom House (2007), at 38–39 [hereinafter *Concentrations of Inhumanity*].

2. Imprisonment or Other Severe Deprivation of Physical Liberty

Under international law, a person is considered "imprisoned" if he or she is (1) deprived of his or her liberty, and (2) the deprivation is imposed arbitrarily, or without due process of the law.[62] According to the International Covenant on Civil and Political Rights (ICCPR), "due process of law" means the right to a fair and public hearing by independent and impartial tribunal, the right to be informed of the charges against him or her, the right to counsel, the right to presumption of innocence, and the right to appeal.[63]

Persons "disappeared" in North Korea are deported to penal labor camps where they are imprisoned and deprived of all physical liberties. Estimates suggest that 200,000 people are now imprisoned in North Korean prison gulags. Without question, those detained in *kwan-li-so* camps consider themselves prisoners and understand that any attempt to try to leave or escape would result in likely execution. As *Concentrations of Inhumanity* reports, "there are few situations in today's world with a more 'severe deprivation of physical liberty' than DPRK's political penal colonies."[64]

Those imprisoned in *kwan-li-so* camps are being held without due process of the law. As outlined above, prisoners are not informed of the charges against him or her, have never been given the opportunity to appear before an independent tribunal, and certainly have no right to counsel or the ability to appeal. Accordingly, under international law, these political prisoners are considered "imprisoned" and "severely deprived of physical liberties."

3. Persecution Based on Political or Religious Grounds

As discussed thoroughly above, political opposition or perceived political opposition may result in an indefinite detention in one of North Korea's *kwan-li-so* prison camps. North Korean defectors have reported similar punishment for those practicing any form of non-state sanctioned religion, or any practice, thought, or belief other than the monolithic *juche* ideology, known previously as "Kimilsungism."

In 1974, Kim Il-sung said that "factionalists or enemies of class, whoever they are, their seed must be eliminated through three generations."[65] Holding true to the Great Leader's proclamation, Pyongyang maintains a practice of detaining in its massive prison camp system not only the person accused of subversive acts or thoughts, but up to three generations of the accused's family.

Persecution is defined as "the intentional and severe deprivation of fundamental rights contrary to international law by reason of the identity of the group or collectivity."[66] The Rome Statue prohibits persecution based on political or religious grounds, in addition to other bases.[67] Further refining the definition, the ICTR said

[62] *Prosecutor v. Simic, Tadic, and Zaric* (Case No. IT-95–9-T), Oct. 17, 2003, at ¶ 64.

[63] North Korea acceded to the ICCPR on September 14, 1981. *See* International Covenant on Civil and Political Rights, G.A. Res. 2200A (XXI), 21 UN GAOR Supp. (No. 16), at 52, A/6316 (1966), 999 U.N.T.S. 171, *entered into force* Mar. 23, 1976.

[64] *Concentrations of Inhumanity*, *supra* note 61, at 41.

[65] *Hidden Gulag*, *supra* note 32, at 25.

[66] Rome Statute, *supra* note 51, at art. 7(2)(g).

[67] *Id.* at art. 7(1)(h).

that political grounds include "party political beliefs and political ideology."[68] In this context, an identifiable group or collectivity is all those who are perceived to be opposed to the regime as well as the family members of known or suspected political or religious opponents.[69] North Korea's policy of abducting and detaining large segments of the population based on political opposition, alleged political opposition, or unauthorized religious belief constitutes persecution.

4. Enslavement

The treatment of prisoners in *kwan-li-so* camps is tantamount to enslavement. Enslavement is defined as "the exercise of any or all of the powers attaching to the rights of ownership over a person. . . ."[70] The ad hoc international criminal tribunals help clarify whether enslavement can been established in this context. The International Criminal Tribunal for the former Yugoslavia (ICTY) held that indicia of enslavement include: control of someone's movement, control of physical environment, psychological control, measure taken to prevent or deter escape, force, threat of force or coercion, duration, assertion of exclusivity, subjection to cruel treatment and abuse, control of sexuality, and forced labor.[71]

As described in previous sections, prisoners in *kwan-li-so* camps are forced to engage in hard labor every day. Prisoners are assigned to physically dangerous and demanding jobs in factories, agricultural fields, logging, and mining. The brutality of the labor conditions that prisoners are subject to, including the imposition of strict production quotas, together with starvation level food rations, the threat of execution if escape is attempted, physical abuse, and indefinite physical confinement constitutes enslavement.

5. Extermination

Severe malnutrition combined with demanding, and often dangerous, forced labor conditions has resulted in staggeringly high death rates in detention camps. The provision of insufficient food rations is designed to maintain absolute control over the prison population. First-hand accounts from escaped prisoners and defected guards have established that thousands of people die from malnutrition in camps each year. In his 2010 report, Special Rapporteur Muntarbhorn said that "the lives of inmates are lost only too easily to hunger and slave labour, brutality and atrocity."[72]

Extermination is the "intentional infliction of conditions of life, *inter alia*, the deprivation of access to food . . . calculated to bring about the destruction of part of a population."[73] Because there is a presumption in international law that "persons who

[68] *Prosecutor v. Kayishema and Ruzindana* (Case No. ICTR-95–1-T), Judgment, May 21, 1999, at ¶ 130.

[69] *See Concentrations of Inhumanity*, *supra* note 61, at 53–54.

[70] Rome Statute, *supra* note 51, at art. 7(2)(c).

[71] *Prosecutor v. Kunarac, Kovac and Vokovic* (Case No. IT-96–23-A & IT-96–23/1-A), Judgment, Jun. 12, 2002, at ¶ 112.

[72] Special Rapporteur Feb. 2010 Report, *supra* note 1, at 10.

[73] Rome Statute, *supra* note 51, at art. 7(2)(b).

commit acts or omissions do so intentionally, absent indications to the contrary,"[74] it is reasonable to conclude that the practice of providing prisoners with starvation-level food rations, combined with demanding forced labor conditions, resulting in many prisoner deaths, constitutes extermination.

6. Murder, Torture, and Other Inhumane Acts

To maintain control, gain information, and punish misbehaving prisoners, guards in *kwan-li-so* camps routinely torture and sometimes murder prisoners. Murder, torture, and other forms of inhumane acts are crimes against humanity.

a) Torture and Other Forms of Inhumane Treatment Torture is "the intentional infliction of severe pain or suffering, whether physical or mental, upon a person in the custody or under the control of the accused; except that torture shall not include pain or suffering arising only from, inherent in or incident to, lawful sanctions."[75] The ICTY and ICTR (International Criminal Tribunal for Rwanda) added that torture is the infliction of pain or suffering for a particular purpose, such as obtaining information or a confession, punishing, intimidating or coercing the victim.[76]

Defectors and escapees have reported that prisoners are subjected to frequent beatings and that interrogation routinely involves physical abuse, sometimes leading to injury or death. Reports of cruel treatment include suspending prisoners from the ceiling by their wrists and using clubs, guns, poles, and other objects to physically strike prisoners. Prisoners are sometimes confirmed in spaces that are so small that a person cannot fully stand or lie down. Psychological and verbal abuse is also reported. There are also reports that prisoners are used in experiments to train new medical doctors.[77]

Taking place clearly outside acceptable standards for the treatment of prisoners in international law, conduct of this nature constitutes torture because it is intentional, for a particular purpose, and inflicts pain and suffering upon prisoners under control of the North Korean government.

b) Murder First-hand reports describe public executions by firing squad or hanging. Prisoners may be executed for stealing or foraging for food, fighting, assaulting guards, engaging in sexual relations, refusing to abandon religious beliefs, criticizing the North Korean regime, or attempting to escape.[78] Similar to the disbursement of food, executions are carried out as a means of controlling and installing fear in the prison population.

[74] William A. Schabas, The UN International Criminal Tribunals (Cambridge University Press 2006), at 295.

[75] Rome Statute, *supra* note 51, at art. 7(2)(e)

[76] *See Kunarac, Kovac and Vokovic, supra* note 71, at ¶ 142; *Prosecutor v. Akayesu* (Case No. ICTR-96–4-T), Judgment, Sept. 2, 1998, at ¶¶ 593–95.

[77] *See* Christian Solidarity Worldwide, *North Korea: A Case to Answer, A Call to Act* (2007), at 50.

[78] *See id.* at 36.

Guards are trained and authorized to beat and kill prisoners and are told not to think of prisoners as human beings. There are numerous reports of death occurring both during torture and subsequently as a result of injuries inflicted from torture.

Moreover, though sexual activity is prohibited in the camps, pregnancy does happen. Those found to be pregnant are punished and are generally subjected to a forced abortion.[79] Women who somehow progress to a late stage of pregnancy have disappeared or are killed. There are also reports that babies born in detention are killed upon birth.[80]

As defined by international jurisprudence, murder is a death resulting from the act of another which was motivated by the intention to kill the victim or cause grievous bodily harm which will likely result in death.[81] The many first-hand reports of executions and death resulting from torture at the hands of prison guards demonstrates a pattern of activity consistent with murder.

7. Systematic and Widespread

Organizing and maintaining labor camps, and carrying out the acts described above, requires tens of thousands of prison officials. These actions are carried out "systematically." The organized nature of the acts and the improbability of their random occurrence are beyond doubt. Furthermore, the massive nature of the prison camp system, and the hundreds of thousands of North Koreans who are subjected to this brutal network, can be characterized as "widespread." Though it is not required that prohibited acts satisfy both the widespread and systematic element, the *kwan-li-so* political camp prison system certainly does.

IV. RECOGNIZING THE CRIMES: THE INTERNATIONAL COMMUNITY RESPONDS

Though North Korea remains shrouded in secrecy and has intentionally isolated itself from the international community, in the last twenty years international attention to human rights in North Korea has greatly expanded. Increased numbers of North Koreans have escaped the country and have shared information about life inside North Korea, including information about the food crisis and the existence of the gulag system. As the number of defectors has grown—reports indicate that more than 20,000 are currently living in South Korea[82]—the international community has begun paying careful attention to the grave human rights and humanitarian situation in North Korea. Recent pronouncements from governments, nongovernmental organizations, and many United Nations bodies have reported grave, systematic, and widespread violations of human rights and humanitarian law in North Korea. The carefully

[79] *See id.* at 39.

[80] The killing of infants constitutes murder. Forced abortion, while it may not constitute murder, certainly constitutes inhumane treatment.

[81] *Prosecutor v. Blaskic* (Case No. IT-95–14-T), Judgment, Mar. 3, 2000, at ¶ 217.

[82] Hyung-jin Kim, *Number of N. Korean Defectors to South Tops 20,000*, Washington Times, Nov. 15, 2010. Additionally, other estimates indicate that between 100,000 and 400,000 North Korean refugees are in China. *See How to Help North Korea's Refugees*, Wall Street Journal, Jun. 16, 2009.

selected language in these pronouncements reaffirms our conclusion that North Korea has and continues to commit crimes against humanity and is failing in its Responsibility to Protect its citizens.

A. United Nations

Since 2003, many United Nations bodies, including the General Assembly, the (former) Commission on Human Rights, the Special Rapporteur for Human Rights in the Democratic People's Republic of Korea, and the Human Rights Council, have condemned—at least annually, if not more often—the human rights situation in North Korea, including the grave food situation and the existence of the prison labor camps.

1. Commission on Human Rights

The United Nations Commission on Human Rights[83] adopted its first resolution on North Korea in April 2003, expressing the Commission's deep concern about the patterns of human rights abuses including the country's prison camp system, the prevalence of malnutrition and the violation of fundamental freedoms.[84] In addition to reiterating the concerns it listed in its 2003 resolution, the Commission's 2004 and 2005 resolutions called on North Korea to "put an immediate end to maltreatment and infanticide in prison and labour camps."[85] The Commission's 2004 resolution called for the appointment of a Special Rapporteur on the situation of human rights in North Korea.[86] Since then, the Special Rapporteur has submitted at least annual reports expressing deep concern about continuing human rights abuses in North Korea.

2. Special Rapporteur

Professor Vitit Muntarbhorn was appointed Special Rapporteur in July 2004 and submitted his first report on January 10, 2005.[87] Listing numerous human rights concerns, the Special Rapporteur articulated concerns about: the right to food and the right to life; the right to security of the person, humane treatment, non-discrimination and access to justice . . . and the right to self-determination/political participation.[88] Special Rapporteur Muntarbhorn paid specific attention to the catastrophic food shortages and expressed concern that food aid was being diverted away from people in need to

[83] The UN Commission on Human Rights was replaced by the Human Rights Council in March 2006. *See* G.A. Res. 60/251, A/RES/60/251, Mar. 15, 2006.

[84] UN Comm'n on Human Rights Res. 2003/10, E/CN.4/RES/2003/10, Apr. 16, 2003.

[85] UN Comm'n on Human Rights Res. 2004/13, E/CN.4/RES/2004/13, Apr. 15, 2004, at ¶ 2(e) [hereinafter Comm'n on Human Rights 2004 Resolution]; *see also* UN Comm'n on Human Rights Resolution, 2005/11, E/CN.4/RES/2005/11, Apr. 15, 2005.

[86] Comm'n on Human Rights 2004 Resolution, *supra* note 85, at ¶ 5.

[87] *See* Special Rapporteur for the Comm'n on Human Rights, *Question of Violation of Human Rights and Fundamental Freedom In Any Part of the World: Situation of Human Rights in the Democratic People's Republic of Korea*, E/CN.4/2005/34, Jan. 10, 2005.

[88] *See id.* at 2.

clandestine uses as well as the "disconcerting practice" of collective punishment based on guilt by association whereby families of political criminals are also punished.[89]

Since his first report, the Special Rapporteur has submitted eight additional reports, each growing more critical. In each report, the Special Rapporteur calls attention to the seriousness of the food crisis and the prison labor camps. The Special Rapporteur's 2007 reports emphasized the validity of claims of torture and inhuman and degrading treatment committed by state authorities inside *kwan-li-so* camps.[90] In 2008, after discussing what he described as a great disparity between access by government allies to food and the rest of the population, the Special Rapporteur called on North Korea to "overcome the disparities in access to food and other basic necessities, and build food security through sustainable agricultural development with broad-based people's participation."[91]

In one of the Special Rapporteur's 2009 reports, he highlighted the use of collective punishment and public executions and described the "intolerable suffering" the people of North Korea are subjected to by means of starvation, torture, and almost universal spying. More specifically, he noted that torture was used extensively, and in the country's prisons, the lack of food and forced labor helped ensure that "many prisons are a death trap for the inmates."[92] The report also clearly attributed the egregious human rights violations to the government, saying that "those at the top . . . are behind the environment leading to these transgressions, with entrenched impunity."[93] Calling for immediate attention, the report described "[w]idespread, systematic and reprehensive human rights violations of a long-standing and insidious nature, which demand attention and commitments nationally and internationally to improve the situation."[94]

In 2009, the Special Rapporteur also affirmed the need to address impunity for these violations through state responsibility. The Special Rapporteur's pronouncement signals the United Nations' commitment to holding nations accountable for their actions and advances the doctrine of Responsibility to Protect. Citing to reports by non-governmental organizations calling for UN involvement at the highest levels to hold North Korea to its Responsibility to Protect,[95] Special Rapporteur Muntarbhorn said that the "totality of the United Nations system, especially the Security Council," must be enabled "to take measures to prevent egregious violations [and] protect people from victimization."[96]

The Special Rapporteur's February 2010 report is the strongest and most critical of any UN pronouncement to date. In this report, the Special Rapporteur questions why

[89] *See id.* at ¶ 34.

[90] The Special Rapporteur on the Situation of Human Rights in the Democratic People's Republic of Korea–Vitit Muntarbhorn, *Report of the Special Rapporteur on the Situation of Human Rights in the Democratic People's Republic of Korea*, A/HRC/4/15, Feb. 7, 2007, at ¶ 13 [hereinafter Special Rapporteur Feb. 2007 Report].

[91] The Special Rapporteur on the Situation of Human Rights in the Democratic People's Republic of Korea–Vitit Muntarbhorn, *Report of the Special Rapporteur on the Situation of Human Rights in the Democratic People's Republic of Korea*, A/HRC/7/20, Feb. 15, 2008, at ¶¶ 15, 82 [hereinafter Special Rapporteur Feb. 2008 Report].

[92] Special Rapporteur Feb. 2009 Report, *supra* note 8, at ¶ 24.

[93] *Id.* at summary.

[94] *Id.* at ¶ 50.

[95] *See* Special Rapporteur Feb. 2009 Report, *supra* note 8, at 15 fn. 20.

[96] *Id.* at ¶ 81(e).

those who are responsible for these horrific crimes have enjoyed impunity for so long. Discussing the various options for holding the perpetrators responsible for their actions and tying those actions to specific international crimes, the Special Rapporteur concludes that "the international crime . . . most closely related to the happenings in the country in question is 'crimes against humanity.' . . . ."[97] Having concluded that North Korea is committing crimes against humanity, the Special Rapporteur recommends, among other things, that the international community advocate strongly for the responsibility of the [government of North Korea] to protect the people of the country, taking on that responsibility should the national authorities fail to do so. . . ."[98]

3. The United Nations General Assembly

For its part, the United Nations General Assembly has adopted five resolutions expressing its serious concern with persistent reports of "systemic [or systematic], widespread and grave violations of human rights" in North Korea.[99] Since its first report in 2005, UN General Assembly resolutions have increasingly expressed more robust criticism of North Korea and have attracted additional votes and sponsors.

Echoing the sentiments of the Special Rapporteur, UN General Assembly resolutions have expressed serious concern with the continued reports of "torture and other cruel, inhuman or degrading treatment or punishment, public execution, extrajudicial and arbitrary detention, the absence of due process and the rule of law, the imposition of the death penalty for political reasons, and the existence of a large number of prison camps and the extensive use of forced labor."[100] In addition to calling attention to the consequences for real or perceived political opposition, the General Assembly has been very clear in its condemnation of the regime's failure to properly feed its population. Since December 2006, the General Assembly has resolved annually that "violations of economic, social and cultural rights" . . . "have led to severe malnutrition and hardship for the population in [North Korea]."[101] The General Assembly's 2007, 2008, and 2009 resolutions addressed specifically the prevalence of maternal and infant malnutrition and attributed this humanitarian failure, in part, to the "misallocation of resources away from the satisfaction of basic needs."[102] The 2009 resolution added the State's "restriction on the cultivation and trade in foodstuffs"[103] to the list of factors contributing to the precarious humanitarian situation in North Korea.

Underscoring the General Assembly's serious concern for the state of human rights in North Korea, contained in its annual resolution, the General Assembly reaffirms its commitment to examine the issue and requests that the Secretary-General submit a

[97] Special Rapporteur Feb. 2010 Report, *supra* note 1, at ¶ 60.

[98] *Id.* at ¶ 89(b).

[99] G.A. Res. 60/173, A/60/1Dec 73, 16, 2005, at ¶ 1(b); *see also* G.A. Res. 61/174, A/RES/61/174, Dec. 19, 2006, at ¶ 1(b); G.A. Res. 62/167, A/RES/62/167, Dec. 18, 2007, at ¶ 1(b); G.A. Res. 63/190, A/RES/63/190, Dec. 18, 2008, at ¶ 1(a); G.A. Res. 64/175, A/RES/64/175, Dec. 18, 2009, at ¶ 1(a)

[100] G.A. Res. 61/174, A/RES/61/174, Dec. 19, 2006, at ¶ 1(b)(i).

[101] *Id.* at ¶ 2.; G.A. Res. 62/167, A/RES/62/167, Dec. 18, 2007, at ¶ 3.

[102] *Id.*; G.A. Res. 63/190, A/RES/63/190, Dec. 18, 2008, at ¶ 3; G.A. Res. 64/175, A/RES/64/175, Dec. 18, 2009, at ¶ 3.

[103] *Id.*

comprehensive report on the situation. In September 2010, Secretary-General Ban Ki-moon submitted a scathing report on the deteriorating humanitarian and human rights situation in North Korea. The Secretary-General confirmed reports of chronic food insecurity, high malnutrition rates, and spiraling economic problems.[104] He also called to the General Assembly's attention the use of torture, forced labor, and harsh treatment in prison camps.[105] Most recently, in November 2010, the Secretary-General said that he was "deeply concerned about chronic hunger and poverty in North Korea, 'especially among very young children.'"[106]

Beyond the General Assembly's direction to Pyongyang to take immediate preventive and remedial action to end all human rights violations, in its five resolutions, the General Assembly has called on the North Korean government to cooperate with the Special Rapporteur and engage in discussion with UN bodies regarding human rights issues. To date, North Korea has refused both requests and instead has leveled accusations that UN criticism of North Korea is merely a thinly veiled plot to overthrow the country's government.

Finally, beyond simply supporting the annual DPRK resolution with an affirmative vote, there is a group of UN member states that have elevated the dialogue by specifically evoking the Responsibility to Protect doctrine. For example, the statement made by Portugal, then President of the Council of the European Union (the sponsor of the annual DPRK resolution), at the introduction of the 2008 resolution, "express[ed] . . . grave concern at the persistence of continuing reports of widespread, systematic and grave violations of human rights in the country, reflecting the Government of the DPRK's absence of willingness to uphold its responsibility to protect its populations."[107] This statement was repeated the following year by France, then serving as EU President. Leaving little room for doubt that the DPRK is committing crimes against humanity, the statement expressed concern over the following state-sanctioned violations:

> instances of torture and other cruel, inhuman or degrading treatment or punishment, namely inhuman conditions of detention; the absence of due process and the rule of law, *inter alia*, fair trial guarantees and an independent judiciary; the imposition of the death penalty for political and religious reasons; the situation of refugees and asylum seekers expelled or returned to the DPRK and the punishment of those who leave or try to leave the country without permission and of individuals exercising their freedom of opinion and expression, and of their families.[108]

[104] Situation of Human Rights in the Democratic People's Republic of Korea, *Report of the Secretary-General*, A/65/391, Sep. 24, 2010, at ¶ 1.

[105] *Id.* at ¶¶ 17–18.

[106] *Keeping Development on the G-20 Agenda*, New York Times, Nov. 10, 2010.

[107] EU Presidency Statement, Statement by Jorge Lobo de Mesquita, Deputy Permanent Representative, Permanent Mission of Portugal to the United Nations on behalf of the European Union and Japan, United Nations 62nd Session of the General Assembly, 3rd Committee, *The Situation of Human Rights in the Democratic People's Republic of Korea*, Nov. 8, 2007, *available at* http://www.europa-eu-un.org/articles/en/article_7505_en.htm.

[108] EU Presidency Statement, *supra* note 107.

4. Human Rights Council

The Human Rights Council (HRC), which in 2006 replaced the former Commission on Human Rights, was created to address human rights violations and make recommendations thereon. As part of its work, the HRC adopts resolutions calling international attention to gross and systematic human rights violations. The HRC also engages in periodic reviews of human rights practices in all 192 UN Member States.

The HRC's most recent resolution on North Korea recognized the "use of torture and labor camps against political prisoners" as part of the regime's system of "grave, widespread and systematic human rights abuses."[109] Importantly, after deploring the prevalence of "widespread and systematic" human rights abuses—a clear nod to the definition of "crimes against humanity"—the 2010 HRC resolution reaffirmed that "it is the responsibility of the Government of Democratic People's Republic of Korea to ensure the full enjoyment of all human rights and fundamental freedoms of its entire population."[110] Pyongyang has categorically rejected all resolutions as the extreme manifestation of "politicization, selectivity and double standards in the area of human rights."[111]

As part of the Human Right's Council's quadrennial universal periodic review, states have the opportunity to submit a national report with their own comments on human rights in their country. States also have the opportunity to comment on and respond to the issues raised by other States during the review process.[112]

During the Human Rights Council's 2009 review of the country, North Korea denied the existence of all human rights violations, despite a great majority of participating States expressing deep concern with the human rights situation in North Korea. Of the 52 States that participated in the periodic review's interactive dialogue, at least 16 raised specific concerns about the food situation and 13 addressed the operation of North Korea's prison system and/or the treatment of political dissenters. Selecting language that follows the definition of crimes against humanity, many states raised specific concern about "public executions," "extrajudicial execution," "torture," "deprivation of due process," "forced labor," and "enforced disappearances."

Nonetheless, demonstrating the difficulty in achieving consensus within the UN system, several delegations spoke in support of the North Korean government. For example, China, Iran, Belarus, Yemen, Zimbabwe, and Palestine commended government successes on human rights. And, China and Palestine said that "North Korea's constitution clearly outlines necessary instruments for the promotion and protection of human rights and freedoms. . . [And] hopes this will allow [other parties] to adopt an unbiased view of the country."[113]

North Korea's national report and its response to questions from member states demonstrated that Pyongyang is in absolute denial of alleged human rights abuses and

[109] Human Rights Council Res. 13/14, A/HRC/RES/13/14, Mar. 24, 2010, at ¶ 2.

[110] *Id.*

[111] Report of the Working Group on the Universal Period Review, *Democratic People's Republic of Korea*, 3, *submitted to the Human Rights Council*, A/HRC/13/13, Jan. 4, 2010.

[112] *See id.*

[113] *See* Working Group on the Universal Period Review, *supra* note 111, at ¶¶ 17–79.

lacks the political commitment to adhere to international standards of human rights and humanitarian law. In direct response to questions from Member States about political prison camps, the North Korean delegation said that because the term "political prisoner" is not part of North Korean vocabulary, so-called political prison camps do not exist.[114] Responding to allegations of government classification of its people, North Korea said that because the constitution provides that citizens have equal rights, such practices are inconceivable.[115] Equally as offensive given the numerous, credible reports of a food crisis in North Korea, the government said that it gives top priority to the solution of food problems and that "in the near future, [the government will] meet the domestic demands for food on its own."[116]

5. The Security Council

Like most of the international community, the UN Security Council has been largely preoccupied with North Korea's nuclear weapons and missiles tests. Discussion about the human rights and humanitarian challenge within the Security Council—the sole UN body that can authorize intervention in North Korea for its failure to protect its citizens from crimes against humanity—has been neglected. Several international NGOs have recommended that the Security Council take up human rights and humanitarian issues because they have clear implications for the stability of the region. Nonetheless, it is unlikely that the Security Council would consider introducing a resolution on the situation given divisions among permanent members of the Security Council. Rather, a more realistic option would be for a Security Council member to raise the issue informally and work toward more formal consideration of the issue in the future.

B. European Union

In June 2006, the European Parliament adopted its first Urgency Resolution condemning human rights in North Korea.[117] Again in 2010, it adopted a resolution deploring the horrific human rights situation, noting that "large parts of the population are suffering from starvation."[118] The resolution further denounced reports of "state authorities systematically carrying out extrajudicial killings, arbitrary detentions and disappearances," and state practices which subject political prisoners to "gross human rights violations, torture, starvation, slave labor" and death.[119] Importantly, this resolution considers that the "ongoing grave, *widespread and systematic* human rights

[114] *Id.* at ¶ 45.

[115] *Id.* at ¶ 44.

[116] *Id.* at ¶ 47.

[117] European Parliament Resolution on North Korea, Eur. Parl. Doc. RC/619804EN, Art. L7 (2006).

[118] European Parliament Resolution on North Korea, Eur. Parl. Doc. P7_TA-PROV(2010)0290 (2010).

[119] *Id.*

violations perpetrated [by the government] against its own people, *may amount to crimes against humanity and thus be subject to international criminal jurisdiction.*"[120]

Although there is no practical effect to these resolutions, they demonstrate the engagement of this body in recognizing the severity of the violations, attribute the violations directly to the government of North Korea and suggest that these violations amount to crimes against humanity.

C. United States

National legislatures have also censured North Korea for their human rights transgressions. In October 2004, the U.S. Congress adopted the North Korean Human Rights Act, which sets forth a long list of known human rights violations.[121]

Establishing context, the Act states that "the Government of North Korea is 'a dictatorship under the absolute rule of Kim Jong-il' that continues to commit numerous, serious human rights abuses."[122] The Act further reports that millions of North Korean citizens are estimated to have starved to death since the 1990s, and an estimated 200,000 political prisoners are held in camps where they are subjected to forced labor, beatings, human testing of chemical and biological poisons, forced abortions, infanticide, torture, and executions.[123]

Sending an important message that human rights should play a central role in U.S. relations with North Korea, the Act expressed the "sense of Congress" that human rights is a key element in negotiations with North Korea and established the position of Special Envoy on Human Rights in North Korea.[124] Though the North Korean Human Rights Act was reauthorized in 2008 with overwhelming congressional support, the Unites States government, like most, remains focused on North Korea's nuclear threat and has devoted little public attention to the human rights issue.

D. South Korea

The Sunshine Policy, an effort by South Korea to pursue reconciliation, interaction, and economic cooperation with North Korea, dominated North-South Korean relations for the better part of the last 20 years. As articulated, the Sunshine Policy separated politics from economics and led to the South providing vast amounts of no-strings-attached economic aid in the hopes of gradually convincing North Korea to more productively engage the outside world. During the years the Sunshine Policy directed relations between the neighbors, South Korea focused on finding cooperation, seeking reconciliation, and avoided criticizing the North, particularly with respect to human rights. However, the response from the North—and resulting policy decisions and political engagement—was not as hoped for in the South.

With the inauguration of President Lee Myung-bak in early 2008, South Korea's approach to North-South relations began to change, including its interest in

[120] *Id.* (emphasis added).

[121] North Korean Human Rights Act of 2004, 22 U.S.C. §7801.

[122] *Id.* at § 3(1).

[123] *See* North Korean Human Rights Act, *supra* note 121.

[124] This position was filled for the first time in 2009 by Ambassador Robert King.

addressing human rights atrocities in North Korea. Many observers were hoping for immediate, specific public condemnation of the human rights tragedies taking place in the North, but instead, throughout 2009, North Korea's missile tests and nuclear weapons program dominated South Korean—and international—dialogue and energy. Still, President Lee recently reaffirmed his commitment to pushing the North Korean government on human rights. In October 2010, the president said that before his government would rush aid to North Korea, the country will have to demonstrate goodwill toward its own people and the rest of the world, adding "[w]hat my government is most interested in is whether North Korean leaders are serious about the nuclear issue, inter-Korean peace and its people's human rights and happiness."[125]

While tensions remain high after the sinking of a South Korean warship, which Seoul and many capitals have blamed on North Korea, very recently there have been some slight positive signs of improving relations between the two Koreas. Both nations agreed to resume reunions for families divided by the Korean War, and South Korea is considering a proposal by North Korea to restart talks about a joint tourism project.

E. NGO Community

Within the NGO community, there is growing momentum to invoke the Responsibility to Protect doctrine in the case of North Korea. In October 2006, former Czech Republic President Václav Havel, former Norwegian Prime Minister Kjell Magne Bondevik, and Nobel Peace Prize Laureate Elie Wiesel commissioned the Committee for Human Rights in North Korea and the global law firm DLA Piper to prepare an account of the humanitarian and human rights situation in North Korea. The resulting report concluded that North Korea had failed in its Responsibility to Protect its citizens from the most severe violations of international law—crimes against humanity—and urged an international response through the UN Security Council.

Bringing additional international attention to North Korea's human rights record, Christian Solidarity Worldwide's (CSW) illuminating 2007 report, *North Korea: A Case to Answer—A Call to Act*, concluded that there is *prima facie* evidence of crimes again humanity occurring in North Korea, namely murder, extermination, enslavement/forced labor, forcible transfer of a population, arbitrary imprisonment, torture, persecution, enforced disappearance of persons, other inhumane acts and, perhaps, rape and sexual violence.[126] CSW further detailed the obligations of states, and the United Nations, to prevent and punish international crimes. CSW invokes the Responsibility to Protect doctrine in the case of North Korea, arguing that "a growing body of evidence points to the ongoing commission of a range of crimes as 'state crimes.' It is manifest evident that the national authorities are failing to protect their population from international crimes, because they are the very authorities and persons responsible for such crimes."[127]

[125] Donald Kirk, *South Korea's Lee Expects Kim Jong-un to Rule North Korea*, Christian Science Monitor, Oct. 11, 2010.

[126] Christian Solidarity Worldwide, *supra* note 77, at 8.

[127] *Id.* at 9.

Likewise, Freedom House's report *Concentrations of Inhumanity* added yet another highly respected voice to international calls for North Korea's actions to be appropriately termed crimes against humanity. In the report, author David Hawk applied international legal standards of crimes against humanity to the evidence obtained from survivors of *kwan-li-so* camps and concluded that the repression associated with the political prison camp system in North Korea are clear and massive crimes against humanity as defined by law.

The chorus of condemnation by multilateral, regional, and state actors is unmistakably clear and growing in volume. The serious nature of these pronouncements supports the conclusion outlined above that by committing crimes against humanity, North Korea is failing in its Responsibility to Protect its citizens. Simply put, in the words of Special Rapporteur Muntarbhorn in his February 2010 report, "The voice of the international community . . . indicates that the powerbase in the Democratic People's Republic of Korea has failed in its responsibility [to protect the rights and daily needs of ordinary people of North Korea.]"[128]

V. CONCLUSION

The international community—including the Untied Nations, regional bodies, states, and NGO actors—has demonstrated in very clear terms that North Korea's systematic starvation of its population and the operation of a massive political prison system is unacceptable and is in violation of international law. Undoubtedly, over the past five years, awareness of the human rights situation and an understanding that the government is committing crimes against humanity has generated significant international attention. That said, though North Korea is party to four major international human rights treaties,[129] Pyongyang has repeatedly refused to address concerns raised by the international community. It has refused access to the Special Rapporteur, has denied all allegations of wrongdoing to the Human Rights Council and continues to ignore calls from the UN General Assembly, regional bodies, and other states, all while "the sufferings of the ordinary people of the country continue every day, waiting for light at the end of a long and dark tunnel."[130]

A myriad of recommendations have been made as to how to address this situation, including increasing UN attention (through the UNGA, Security Council, and Human Rights Council), increasing foreign diplomatic presence in the country, increasing economic cooperation and mutual exchanges, initiating regional bodies of inquiry, and adopting national legislation condemning the situation. Some of these recommendations have been accepted, but sadly, the situation for the people of North Korea remains largely unchanged.

[128] Special Rapporteur Feb. 2010 Report, *supra* note 1, at 1.

[129] The Democratic People's Republic of Korea is party to the International Covenant on Civil and Political Rights (ICCPR) (acceded on Sept. 14, 1981), the International Covenant on Economic, Social and Cultural Rights (ICESCR) (acceded on Sept. 14, 1981), the Convention on the Elimination of All Forms of Discrimination Against Women (CEDAW) (acceded on Feb. 27, 2001), and the Convention on the Rights of the Child (CRC) (acceded on Sept. 21, 1990).

[130] Special Rapporteur Feb. 2010 Report, *supra* note 1, at 1.

A significant hurdle in achieving more serious international pressure on North Korea to address human rights stems from the almost-exclusive international focus on the nuclear issue. States and regional actors have been reluctant to take up human rights in negotiations with North Korea for fear that their criticism might derail any progress made on security topics. Still, the political will largely does not exist in most capitals, and at the United Nations, to raise North Korea's flagrant human rights record with Pyongyang and demand that it take action to end all state-sanctioned human rights abuses.

With specific respect to the Security Council, though the technical elements have been satisfied to conclude that by committing crimes against humanity, North Korea is failing in its Responsibility to Protect its citizens, it is unlikely that the Security Council will make any movement to classify North Korean action as such or authorize international intervention in the near term.

Instead, bilateral and multilateral activities including the following would be productive first steps to ending the suffering of the millions of North Korean people.

- Because North Korea has shown little willingness to fairly negotiate with international actors on any issue—from food aid through nuclear questions—there is no reason to demonstrate additional restraint in raising human rights concerns. The international community must demand that multilateral engagement with North Korea include human rights and humanitarian issues;
- The international community should take all necessary steps, including increasing bilateral food aid and funding at committed levels international organizations such as the World Food Programme, to alleviate the severe food shortage in North Korea;
- The international community should insist on immediate, safe, and unhindered access to all of North Korea to ensure food distribution channels are secured;
- North Korea should be urged to allow the International Committee of the Red Cross access to all detention facilities in North Korea, including the *kwan-li-so* labor camps;
- Should the dormant Six-Party talks resume, human rights must be added to the agenda and should be addressed in selected working groups and subsidiary negotiations;
- The UN General Assembly should strengthen its annual resolution by endorsing the applicability of the Responsibility to Protect doctrine to the situation in North Korea; and,
- The UN General Assembly should ask the Secretary-General to establish a commission of inquiry empowered to investigate the nature and scale of serious violations of international human rights in North Korea and propose steps to halt ongoing violations.

PART IV
THE FUTURE OF THE RESPONSIBILITY TO PROTECT

Lessons and Challenges

Gareth Evans

Acceptance by the global community of the new principle of the responsibility to protect—unanimously by heads of state and government in 2005, and overwhelmingly in hard-fought UN General Assembly debates since then—has involved a profound normative shift. For centuries, right up to the beginning of our own, mass atrocity crimes perpetrated behind state borders were seen essentially as nobody else's business. Now, at least in principle, they are regarded as everyone's business. And that really does hold out the prospect that genocide, ethnic cleansing, and other major crimes against humanity and war crimes can be stopped, once and for all, in our time.

The significance of that shift must not be underplayed: it is huge. But it is also only half the story. As every contributor to this book has acknowledged—with varying degrees of passion, resignation, or skepticism—what ultimately matters is translating principle into practice. It is not just a matter of acknowledging the intellectual and moral force of the new norm, but implementing it. One doesn't have to be an acolyte of Karl Marx to appreciate, in this context, his observation that the point is not just to observe the world, but to change it.[1] And right now that process is, at most, a work in progress.

From the journey so far we have learned a lot—perhaps most of all about the power of ideas both for good and ill, the omnipresent reality of politics as both positive and negative force in international as in domestic affairs, and the necessity for more patience than most reformers possess if there is to be lasting change for good.

[1] "The philosophers have only interpreted the world, in various ways. The point, however, is to change it." Karl Marx, Theses on Feuerbach 11 (1845).

Those lessons will need to be absorbed by policymakers, and those who seek to influence them, as they face the challenges still ahead—conceptual, institutional, and political—that must be met if RtoP is to be established not only as benchmark ideal but rock-solid reality.

I. THREE LESSONS

A. Ideas Matter

John Maynard Keynes put it best: "ideas . . . both when they are right and when they are wrong, are more powerful than is commonly understood. Indeed the world is ruled by little else. Practical men, who believe themselves to be quite exempt from any intellectual influence, are usually the slaves of some defunct economist."[2]

The problem, before RtoP was articulated, was that for all the force of the human rights, humanitarian, and human security principles articulated in the Universal Declaration, Geneva Conventions, Genocide Convention and elsewhere, when it came to mass atrocity crimes committed behind the walls of a sovereign state, there was simply no idea in international political currency powerful enough to match the force of the very traditional concept of sovereignty thought to be embodied in Article 2(7) of the UN Charter, which states "nothing shall authorize the United Nations to intervene in matters which are essentially within the jurisdiction of any State." The only competing idea was Bernard Kouchner's *droit d'ingerence*: "the right to intervene" or "the right to humanitarian intervention." But that—while it had real resonance in the Global North, particularly in the context of genocidal catastrophes in Rwanda and Bosnia—commanded only negative traction in the Global South, and simply could not generate the necessary consensus for action.

The great achievement of the International Commission on Intervention and State Sovereignty (ICISS) was to identify a new idea that *could* compete, in a way that "humanitarian intervention" had proved unable to, with the old, narrow idea of sovereignty as immunity. "The Responsibility to Protect," a phrase almost banal in its simplicity, captured two critical themes: at issue here was not anyone's "right" to act, but everyone's "responsibility," and the action in question was framed not as "intervention" but "protection." As fully explained in the language of the 2005 World Summit Outcome Document, it was even clearer that RtoP was not an assault upon state sovereignty so much as an embrace and refinement of it: the primary responsibility to protect against mass atrocity crimes remained with the state itself; others had a responsibility to assist it to do so; and it was only in the case of that state "manifestly failing" to exercise its own responsibility that any more general obligation to engage, including if necessary through more coercive measures, would cut in.

There is a lingering tendency in some quarters (partially reflected in this volume in the chapter on Sudan by Andrew Natsios and Zachary Scott) to argue that RtoP is not a new idea at all, just old doctrine—and in some respects even old practice—in a new bottle. Certainly, as a number of contributions note, the idea of "sovereignty as

[2] John Maynard Keynes, The General Theory of Employment Interest and Money (1935), at Ch. 24.

responsibility" had been articulated and actively promoted earlier by Francis Deng (and his Brookings Institution colleague Roberta Cohen) in the context of Internally Displaced Persons (IDPs). It is also manifest that the idea of limitations on absolute state sovereignty is inherent in the UN Charter and the major human rights instruments. And it is certainly arguable that RtoP involves a political call to for all states to abide by legal obligations already in treaty instruments and international humanitarian law.

All true, but perhaps missing the point. Substantive obligations were simply not being observed; Article 2(7) of the Charter was being given more weight than the rest of the corpus of treaty instruments put together; no one was actually using "sovereignty as responsibility" or "responsibility to protect" language in any generally prescriptive way; the only conceptual framework for the intervention debate was "humanitarian intervention," about which there was not only zero consensus, but a bitter international contest. What was needed was a *political* game-changer. And what exercised the original ICISS Commission was the need to find a way—as simple as possible, and if it had some resonances in pre-existing literature and international law so much the better—to rearticulate the issues, which would build a bridge between the absolute-sovereignty and limited-sovereignty brigades, getting them to find some common ground which previously simply did not exist. The model that the Commission expressly had in mind was Gro Harlem Brundtland's World Commission on Environment and Development, which a few years earlier had come up with the bridge-building leitmotif, in that context, of "sustainable development."[3]

A rather less subtle variation on the theme that RtoP is not really a new idea at all is the suggestion, not much in evidence in this volume but certainly in a good deal of post-colonial and self-consciously anti-imperialist writing, that the concept is simply old militarism in a new bottle, a "facile rebranding of interventionist doctrine."[4] But when properly understood, RtoP and "humanitarian intervention" could hardly be more different. The very core of the traditional meaning of humanitarian intervention is coercive military intervention for humanitarian purposes—nothing more or less. But RtoP is about much more than that. It is about taking effective preventive action, and at the earliest possible stage. It implies encouragement and support being given to those states struggling with situations that have not yet deteriorated to the point where genocide or other atrocity crimes are a reality, but where it is foreseeable that if effective preventive action is not taken, with or without outside support, they could so deteriorate. It recognizes the need to bring to bear every appropriate preventive response: be it political, diplomatic, legal, economic, or in the security sector, while falling short of coercive action (e.g., a "preventive deployment" of troops, as in Macedonia in 1995).

Of course there will be situations when prevention fails, crises and conflicts do break out, and some interventionary reaction becomes necessary. But that does not have to

[3] *Our Common Future*, Report of the World Commission on Environment and Development (Oxford University Press 1987). This and some later passages in this chapter draw directly on a previously published article by the author. *See* Gareth Evans, *Ethnopolitical Conflict: When is it Right to Intervene*, 10:1 Ethnopolitics 117–125 (Mar. 2011).

[4] The quote is from Tom Hazeldine, writing about the International Crisis Group in *New Left Review* 63 (May–Jun. 2010).

mean military intervention: it can involve political, diplomatic, economic, and legal pressure, measures which can themselves each cross the spectrum from persuasive to intrusive, and from less coercive (e.g., economic incentives, offers of political mediation, or legal arbitration) to more coercive (e.g., economic sanctions, political and diplomatic isolation, or threats or decisions to refer to the International Criminal Court). Coercive military action cannot be excluded when it is the only possible way to stop large-scale killing and other atrocity crimes, as few doubt was the case, for example, in Rwanda or Srebrenica. But it is a travesty of the responsibility to protect principle to say that it is about military force and nothing else. That's what "humanitarian intervention" is about, but it's not RtoP.

B. Politics Matters

The reason that ideas matter, and that it is so important that efforts be made to articulate new ways of thinking about old problems, is that they do have—or at least *can* have, if they are taken up—real political force. As William Burke-White puts it in Chapter 2, the power of norms is their "ability to alter the cost-benefit calculations, preference sets, or value choices of actors in the international system." They provide a frame of reference, making it easier for policymakers to take one course rather than another, because they can articulate clear reasons to the various constituencies they have to satisfy. Getting a big, new idea more or less universally recognized as *the* appropriate frame within a particular problem should be addressed is getting at least half way toward ensuring that the outcome will be consistent with that idea. If one looks at a Rwanda situation through the lens of *prima facie* sovereign immunity from intervention on "internal matters," excuses for non-intervention are easy to find; look at it through the lens of RtoP and this becomes very much harder.

In the minds of those who initiated it, RtoP was designed from the outset primarily to have political effect. The ICISS commissioners were concerned to build new doctrine on sound philosophical and legal foundations, but our overwhelming preoccupation was with stopping mass killing, raping, forced population shifts, and property destruction. The whole point of trying to craft a new conceptual framework for addressing mass atrocity crimes was to generate among international policymakers and those who influenced them a reflex consensus reaction when any such new case came along—that such man-made catastrophes were everybody's business, not nobody's—and to energize effective collective action accordingly.

Given that action-oriented political focus, the Commission tried to design and express the RtoP concept in a way that would guarantee it the maximum possible take-up and real-world impact. But we had something more to learn in this respect. There were some conceptual and presentational refinements that needed to be made if it was to have maximum possible political force and effect. That is exactly what took place between the release of the ICISS report in 2001 and the unanimous embrace of the responsibility to protect by the UN General Assembly sitting at head-of-state and government level in 2005, and the process has continued to some extent with the further articulation of the issues in the Secretary-General's reports prepared by his Adviser Edward Luck and debated, with practically no dissent evident on the key issues, by the General Assembly in July 2009 and again in August 2010.

One important step was to define the threshold for the application of the doctrine more narrowly—in terms of the occurrence or anticipation of "four crimes" ("genocide, war crimes, ethnic cleansing, and crimes against humanity"); the ICISS report, while essentially focusing on that same group of mass atrocity crimes, had used a broader and more ambiguous formulation—"a population suffering serious harm, as a result of internal war, insurgency, repression or state failure"—which made some states nervous about potential overreach. A second change, more presentational than substantive, was to characterize the relevant responsibilities in terms of "three pillars"—with what was implicit in Paragraphs 138 and 139 of the 2005 Outcome Document in this respect being made explicit in the 2009 Secretary-General's report. As has been described in earlier chapters, Pillar One is the responsibility of each state to protect its own population from the atrocity crimes in question; Pillar Two is the responsibility of others to assist it to do so; and Pillar Three is the responsibility of the wider international community to respond in a "timely and decisive" fashion and by all appropriate means (not excluding coercive military action, in accordance with the UN Charter) if this becomes necessary because the state in question is "manifestly failing" to protect its people.

Characterizing the different responsibilities in this way has proved extremely helpful in practice in getting the great majority of states to understand and accept what is involved. As Edward Luck himself rightly says in Chapter 5 of this volume—describing as "narrow but deep" the formulation to emerge in 2005—"the product of the [World Summit] bargaining process was a stronger, not weaker RtoP." Certainly the ICISS commissioners have not been at all unhappy about the way in which the concept, as originally articulated, has evolved in response to the need to gain the widest political acceptance. Some commentators, including perhaps Noel Morada in Chapter 7, have made rather too much of the distinction between the "three pillars" approach and that in the original ICISS report (and, for what it's worth, my own book on the subject[5]), which primarily describes the responsibilities in question as being "to prevent, react, and rebuild." The point is simply that these are simply alternative ways of organizing and presenting exactly the same material. Think of a cake with three layers—labeled respectively, from the bottom up, "prevention," "reaction," and "rebuilding"—which is then sliced vertically into three big wedges, labeled respectively Pillars One, Two, and Three. The State itself has the responsibility under Pillar One to perform all three roles of prevention, reaction, and rebuilding, as circumstances require; as does any State assisting it under Pillar Two; and as does the wider international community when playing an even more activist role under Pillar Three.

Because RtoP was designed essentially as a political rather than legal concept, with its intended impact on policymakers rather than prosecutors and judges, there is a risk—as Tarun Chhabra and Jeremy Zucker acknowledge in Chapter 3 (after conducting their own meticulous analysis of the legal meaning of genocide, war crimes, ethnic cleansing, and crimes against humanity!) that "too narrow a focus on the legal content of RtoP crimes may muddle more than it sharpens the debate over the application of the concept." Exactly so. RtoP was unashamedly designed to break a North-South

[5] Gareth Evans, The Responsibility to Protect: Ending Mass Atrocity Crimes Once and For All (Brookings Institution Press 2008). This passage, and some later ones in this chapter, draw directly on another previously published article by the author: Gareth Evans, Response to Reviews by Michael Barnett, Chris Brown, and Robert Jackson, 2 Global Responsibility to Protect 320–327 (2010).

political impasse, and the whole point of the exercise, to repeat, was not to create new legal liability, but to create the conditions for a reflexively *consensual* rather than conflictual response to new internal conflict and atrocity crime situations as they arose in the future. Nicole Deller in Chapter 4, after noting that "ethnic cleansing" is not an established legal term of art in the same way as the other three crimes (though it can be seen as actionable under each of them), makes the interesting point, quoting Ekkehard Strauss, that "Hopefully, the identification of ethnic cleansing as a separate case for the application of the responsibility to protect will enable the international community to address some situations based on their factual appearance rather than their legal qualifications."

All that said, it would certainly be desirable if, over time, the various layers of responsibility built into RtoP were to evolve into rules of customary international law, as distinct from simply being, as they are now, normative principles of political and moral, but not legal, weight. But that will depend on how comprehensively the new norm is implemented and applied in practice, as well as recognized in principle, in the years ahead.

C. Patience Matters

In this respect, as with more immediate issues about impact and practical effectiveness, it is important that RtoP advocates fully internalize and act in accordance with a lesson we should all by now have learned: that this is all going to be a long haul, with progress slow and often disappointing. William Burke-White argues very cogently in Chapter 2, that to try to force the pace now in codifying RtoP as binding law would be to risk a significant dilution of its content: "as is often the case in international law and politics, when states are asked to transform norm to law, political considerations get in the way. Moving too fast risks undermining that [present strong and growing] consensus, as some states step back from forward-leaning rhetorical positions to avoid legal codification."

Patience is harder to summon, but is equally necessary, on the question of how effective RtoP is proving to be in its primary intended role as political energizer. It will just take more time for the new norm to become as effective a mobilizer of appropriate international action as its advocates would like it to be. Obvious successes are so far thin on the ground. Kenya in early 2008, for all the qualifications that Meredith Preston-McGhie and Serena Sharma quite properly spell out in their Chapter 13 case study, does probably constitute the best example we have so far of the Responsibility to Protect appearing to play an important energizing role in stimulating an effective response—here diplomatic rather than military—to a rapidly emerging large-scale atrocity crime situation. Kofi Annan, who made clear that RtoP was the "lens" through which he viewed the whole crisis, and Ban Ki-moon, who very early on articulated the necessary international response in RtoP terms, would certainly be inclined to resist the authors' perhaps slightly overly cynical suggestion that Kenya may have been more important for RtoP than RtoP was for Kenya.

Failures or weaknesses are easier to identify. Darfur is a case where the international community's response has been from the outset, and remains, much less focused and effective than it could and should have been, although Andrew Natsios and Zachary Scott in their excellent Chapter 11 analysis of that shortfall (and of some of the evident weaknesses in civil society advocacy strategy as well) could perhaps have acknowledged a little more clearly that it was only in 2005 that RtoP emerged as an accepted international principle, whereas most of the damage in Darfur was done earlier, in 2003 and 2004. Sri Lanka in 2009 was another case where the international community largely dropped the ball, as well documented by Damien Kingsbury in Chapter 14. The Democratic Republic of Congo can perhaps be regarded as another, although the UN, EU, and African Union have made large-scale efforts to halt the slide into further violent chaos, and—as Delphine Schrank very lucidly points out in Chapter 14—the problems in that continent-sized country are nightmarishly intractable. But the lesson from these and other disappointments so far is not that the RtoP norm is inherently ineffective, or irrelevant. Rather it is that we just have to do much better in applying it in future.

II. THREE CHALLENGES

A. Conceptual

It has been clear from the outset that there are three interrelated but distinct hurdles that RtoP will have to overcome if it is to be really effective in practice: securing close to unanimous understanding of just what kinds of real-world cases the norm is meant to embrace, and what kind of policy responses it actually requires case by case; having in place the institutional capacity to deliver that response; and having the political will to do so. Of these, the first—conceptual—challenge, still stirs by far the most academic controversy, but is probably now in practice the least problematic.

It was not ever thus. But the six years of experience that have elapsed since 2005 have seen much debate about how to characterize particular situations in the UN General Assembly, other international forums and in the literature—much of it reflected in the excellent case studies in this volume. And as a result it is now clear that there is something much closer to international consensus about what are, and are not, cases of RtoP concern, and—although this is always harder—what are the most appropriate policy options for dealing with them at each stage.

Of course there is a risk that even the best designed and developed doctrine will from time to time be subject to misuse or abuse, as happened to some extent with the coalition invasion of Iraq in 2003 (although before the norm's formal adoption by the UN two years later), and Russia's justification in these terms of its invasion of Georgia in 2008 (a try-on which persuaded practically no one else). More work does need to be done to bed down general understanding and acceptance of these definitional issues and what follows from them—and the regular publication of an authoritative Watch List of countries of RtoP concern, of the kind that is now being developed by the Global Centre for the Responsibility to Protect in New York, would be very helpful in this respect.

But as time goes on, consensus is growing about what *are* clear RtoP cases, with Darfur, Eastern Congo, Kenya, and Sri Lanka pre-eminent examples in recent years (and with Sri Lanka serving the useful purpose of showing that the responsibility to protect populations can be regarded as extending beyond governments to non-state actors, here the LTTE). And in a crucial breakthrough, just as this chapter was going to press, the Security Council passed two resolutions in quick succession in February and March 2011 explicitly invoking "the Libyan authorities' responsibility to protect its population" in response to the violence being waged against its own citizens by the

Gaddafi regime, desperate to avoid a repetition of the peaceful revolutions that had just occurred in Tunisia and Libya. Resolution 1970 condemned the violence, demanded that it stop, and sought to concentrate Gaddafi's mind by applying targeted sanctions, an arms embargo and the threat of International Criminal Court prosecution for crimes against humanity. Then, three weeks later, as it became apparent that Gaddafi was not only ignoring that resolution but planning a major assault on Benghazi in which no mercy would be shown to perceived opponents, armed or otherwise, Resolution 1973 was passed, another historic first, explicitly authorizing military intervention to ensure the protection of civilians, by means of an enforced no-fly-zone and all other "necessary measures" short of a foreign occupation force.

These two resolutions amounted to a textbook example of RtoP working sequentially, exactly as intended in the 2005 UN resolution, with the Security Council taking "collective action, in a timely and decisive manner" under Chapter VII following evidence of State authorities "manifestly fail[ing]" to protect their own people from mass atrocity crimes. It is to be hoped that the military force being applied by NATO in Libya at the time of writing will not only successfully achieve its civilian protection objective, but also respect the carefully defined limits of the Security Council mandate. If it overreaches that mandate, there is a risk that Libya, far from setting a new benchmark for future commitment in extreme cases, will prove to be a high water mark from which the tide will rapidly recede.

Consensus is also growing on what are *not* such cases—in particular Iraq and Georgia. And there is an increasing willingness to recognize that there have been some more *ambiguous* cases, the preeminent example being Burma (Myanmar) in the immediate aftermath of the 2008 cyclone when it appeared for a time that the military government was being recklessly indifferent to large-scale loss of life to the extent of committing a major crime against humanity.

Other cases might be thought to be ambiguous for different reasons, for example Israel-Palestine, discussed by Mohamed Helal in Chapter 10. He is right that there is no real doubt, conceptually, that some instances of Israel's treatment of Palestinians in the territories under its control properly qualify as situations of RtoP concern. The present author would only add the caveat that in his experience of discussing this issue with Palestinians in the past there has been an evident preference to characterize the situation as not so much an "internal" one, of the kind on which RtoP has always been sharply focused, but rather as one of conflict between two essentially sovereign states, with the issue being as a result better characterized in the more traditional international humanitarian law terms. If that is in fact the view of those most wanting to energize an international response, it deserves to be respected, but majority sentiment on this may well be different now, and nothing of wider analytical significance turns on the choice.

The greatest continuing conceptual precondition for RtoP's practical effectiveness is not just defining and refining, but *confining* its scope to manageable dimensions, to avoid what Nicole Deller in her chapter calls the "dilemma of comprehensiveness." It is easy, linguistically, to extend the idea of "the responsibility to protect" to a whole variety of human security situations that extend well beyond the core group of mass atrocity crimes around which the 2005 consensus is founded. But that temptation should be resisted. RtoP should be seen not as about conflict generally, or human rights generally, let alone human security generally, but rather about that small subset of cases where atrocity crimes are occurring, imminent, or likely to occur in the readily foreseeable future if preventive strategies are not adopted. In contrast to the one hundred or so countries at any given time that are the subject of reasonable human rights concern (as identified by organisations like Human Rights Watch), and the seventy or so countries at any given time that justify attention on conflict prevention or resolution grounds (as identified, e.g., by the International Crisis Group), there will usually only be a dozen or so countries that can properly be regarded at any given time as being of RtoP concern.

There will always be borderline cases like North Korea (the continuing ugly human rights situation in which is well documented in Chapter 11 by Kjell Magne Bondevik and Kristen Adams). But if the scope of any Watch List is expanded beyond a relatively small number of situations of unequivocal mass atrocity concern, RtoP will run a serious risk of losing its basic value-adding role as a vehicle for energizing responses to those "never again" cases, small in number but immense in their tragic significance, that have been so grievously neglected in the past.

There is a related "comprehensiveness" problem concerning the *preventive* reach—and possible overreach—of RtoP, which needs to be recognized and addressed. The kind of advice, assistance, and support strategies involved in a good many Pillar One and Two contexts, notably those of a long-term structural prevention character, are likely to involve exactly the same kinds of strategies—for example, governance and rule of law capacity building and economic development designed to redress inequalities between ethnic and other groups—as those one would deploy in addressing conflict-prevention and human rights protection objectives more generally. The problem is that actively describing them as RtoP strategies may cause conceptual confusion, creating the impression that RtoP is all about everything, rather than being specifically designed to improve the international community's lamentable record of inaction in the face of mass atrocity crimes actually or imminently occurring.

This is a legitimate concern, which can be addressed in this way. By all means, let us continue to recognize that there is a long-term preventive dimension to the Responsibility to Protect concept, and that there is every reason to work away at strategies designed to reduce the kind of ethnopolitical and other tensions and grievances that may have the potential, if not addressed, to build to explosion point in the distant future. But let us also recognize that there is no particular utility, and some downside risk, in *labeling* these strategies as RtoP ones. Better rather to just describe them as related to conflict prevention or the advancement of human rights, and confine the RtoP label to that small subset of cases where atrocity crimes are occurring, imminent, or likely to occur in the readily foreseeable future if effective preventive or reactive strategies are not immediately embraced, which, as already stated, are likely at any given time to amount only to a small subset of the universe of situations of human rights and conflict concern. That way the RtoP norm stays manageable in its reach, and most likely to be politically effective.

Beyond these matters of characterization, there are not many other conceptual issues that are presently creating any serious difficulty for RtoP's acceptance or effectiveness. One that was initially very important, but is much less so now, was the disposition in many quarters, particularly in the Global South, to regard RtoP as just a more polite synonym for "humanitarian intervention." It is now broadly accepted that RtoP is multi-layered and multi-textured, embracing a responsibility to prevent and rebuild as well as just to react to catastrophic situations, and that the responsibility to react—if it does come to that—involves the use of coercive military force only as an absolute last resort. In retrospect it is clear that most of the trouble stemmed from the preoccupation of the original ICISS report with the military intervention issue, because that was just about the only context in which the protection issue had been framed during the 1990s: the choice had been to "send in the Marines" or "do nothing." Subsequent reports, of the High-Level Panel in 2004, and successive Secretaries-General in 2005, 2009, and 2010,[6] were careful to give the other themes inherent in RtoP—prevention, rebuilding, and non-military forms of reaction—much more relative prominence, and the cruder debate is now effectively over.

That said, there is still a need—so long as there remain strong in collective memory cases like the coalition invasion of Iraq in 2003, and Russian invocation of RtoP to try to justify its invasion of Georgia in 2008—to have greater clarity, and if possible international agreement, on what the actual criteria for the use of coercive military force should be.

On the question of legal criteria, there is in fact not much room for anyone to maneuver, and not much practical disposition now to do so. It is generally acknowledged that, self-defense apart (covered by Article 51 of the UN Charter), the threat or use of coercive military force against another state can only be legal under international law if it is expressly authorized by the UN Security Council under Chapter VII of the Charter, although there is growing acceptance that Chapter VIII allows some additional room for such action when it is taken by a recognized regional or sub-regional organization acting within its own agreed rules, at least when that action is ultimately later endorsed by the Security Council (an option well discussed by Ademola Abass in Chapter 6 on Africa). It is not seriously contested that "coalition of the willing" action taken without any form of UN authorization must be seen as unlawful: the only qualification being that if that action is taken (according to overwhelming international sentiment) in a manifestly principled way, and in the face of a manifestly unreasonable veto in the Security Council, then the illegality will be regarded by the wider international community as somewhat mitigated by the circumstances.

On the question of prudential criteria—or what would count as acting or not in a "manifestly principled" way—much effort was expended by ICISS, and the High-Level Panel and Secretary-General Annan in their own subsequent reports, in identifying a set of guidelines that might eventually command international consensus. The five "criteria of legitimacy" which emerge from these reports, and about which there now seems to be a significant measure of intellectual if not political consensus, involve the seriousness of the harm being threatened; the primary intent or purpose of the proposed military action (whether it is to halt or avert that harm or for something else); the issue of last resort (whether there are reasonably available peaceful alternatives); the proportionality of the response; and the balance of consequences—whether more good than harm would be done.

The argument for having a set of agreed such guidelines, with moral but not legal force, is not that they would be self-executing, producing agreed outcomes with

[6] *A More Secure World: Our Shared Responsibility*, Report of the Secretary General's High-Level Panel on Threats, Challenges and Change (2004); *In Larger Freedom: Towards Development, Security and Human Rights for All*, Report of the Secretary General (2005); *Implementing the responsibility to protect*, Report of the Secretary-General, A/63/677, Jan. 12, 2009); *Early Warning, Assessment and the Responsibility to Protect*, Report of the Secretary-General, A/64/864, Jul. 14, 2010.

push-button consistency: rather simply that the prospects of finding real consensus on what are, and are not, suitable cases for military treatment would be much enhanced. For the foreseeable future, however, it seems that intergovernmental agreement on these conceptual underpinnings—however informal that agreement might be identified as being—will stay out of reach. Some Security Council members will argue for absolute freedom of ad hoc action; others, usually outside it, will argue, however implausibly, that any guidelines at all for military action will only serve to encourage it. But there remains every reason for independent analysts and experts to continue to argue for the salience of the kind of criteria that have emerged, and to evaluate Security Council decision-making by reference to them: by that route, over time, new norms can be established and observed.

There is one remaining conceptual challenge to the embrace of RtoP for which there is no easy answer, except to say that it arises in every area of human rights and security policy as well, making RtoP not at all unique. That is the problem of selectivity, or double standards: major powers, including Security Council veto wielders, will always be able to resist pressure, and ultimately intervention, in a way that smaller and weaker powers cannot. That basic reality about the balance of international power is not going to be changed by RtoP.

True, there are some qualifications and consolations. It can be argued, for example, that no state, however big and powerful, is wholly immune from peer group pressure, as shown in an RtoP context by Indonesia's reluctant acceptance, after heavy lobbying by the United States and others, of an Australian-led stabilizing military mission in East Timor which it would never otherwise have agreed to, and nobody could have forced it to. Again, it can be plausibly stated that application of the "balance of consequences" criterion would preclude military action against any of the five permanent members of the Security Council, or other major powers, even if all the other prudential criteria for the use of force, discussed above, were manifestly applicable: a bigger conflagration would almost certainly be triggered, and the original RtoP objective remain unmet. But at the end of the day the only answer to the problem of double standards is this: the reality that military intervention or other effective enforcement action may not be able to be mounted in every case where there is justification for doing so is no reason for them not to be mounted in *any* case.

B. Institutional

If RtoP is not to remain more theoretical than real, conceptual understanding has to be matched both by institutional preparedness, and—always the biggest challenge of all—the political will to deploy that capability when and where it is required. As Andrew Natsios and Zachary Scott put it, with feeling, in their chapter on Darfur, "RtoP . . . can only be implemented through institutions, and the strengths and weaknesses of those institutions will determine whether the doctrine actually results in the protection." The institutional challenges here are essentially threefold: to ensure that there are early warning and response focal points established within all the key governments and intergovernmental organizations; to have in place civilian capability able to be utilized, as occasion arises, for diplomatic mediation, civilian policing and other critical administrative support; and to have in place capable military resources, available both for rapid "fire-brigade" deployment in the most extreme cases which cannot be otherwise addressed (like Rwanda in 1994), and for longer-haul stabilization operations (like those in Sudan and the Congo).

The most immediate institutional need is for dedicated early warning and response mechanisms. Gathering the information is less the problem these days—there is a mass of it about, in real time, for anyone who cares to look—than capturing policymakers' attention and energizing an appropriate response. Those who have never been involved in decision-making at the highest levels can scarcely begin to imagine how many problems and issues are simultaneously clamoring for attention at any given time, how hard it is to get anyone to focus on anything but the most immediate and urgent, and how tempting it is to deny, diminish, or defer a problem in the hope that it will disappear entirely or be seen as someone else's. Governments and large intergovernmental organizations need—in addition to whatever else might usefully be done to "mainstream" consideration of RtoP issues—dedicated focal points within their systems staffed by officials whose full-time day job it is to keep track of this information, evaluate it, ensure that it gets on to the relevant desks, identify response options, and follow them through, and whose status in the systems in question is high enough to ensure that their voice will be heard.

While there is a long way to go in universalizing this practice, the required capacity is beginning to be developed in a number of key governments—notably in the U.S. where the Obama administration has established a special White House office under Samantha Power's direction to perform just this role, and it would appear, to major useful preventive effect already in at least one context, that of the South Sudan referendum in early 2011, where major violence had been widely feared. Within the UN system this function now seems likely to be effectively performed by the newly formed joint office, bringing together the Office of the Special Adviser on the Prevention of Genocide and the Special Adviser on RtoP, with newly agreed processes (as described by Edward Luck in Chapter 5) which will have now at least a fighting chance of mobilizing the many notoriously fissiparous and occasionally lethargic sections of the UN bureaucracy which have an RtoP role to play. It would be useful if that office could be supported by a revitalized standing Secretary-General's Advisory Committee on the prevention of genocide and mass atrocity crimes, constituted by independent experts outside the UN system, able to make reinforcing waves as occasion demands and ensure that serious early warnings never again fall into the black hole of indifference that confronted General Romeo Dallaire in Rwanda in 1994.

An important role for the focal-point incumbents is to work systematically on refining and developing, in advance of their application in any actual situation, the "toolboxes" of available strategies which might need be applied, according to the circumstances of individual cases—and every one is different—across the whole spectrum of prevention, reaction, and rebuilding responses. A particular need is to develop a repertoire of carefully thought-through targeted sanctions measures, with an effective, professionally resourced mechanism ready to be put in place immediately to monitor the application and effectiveness of those sanctions once applied. But sanctions are just one subset of a large range of potential economic and social, political and diplomatic, legal and constitutional, and security-sector measures, both long-term and short-term, that could possibly be relevant and useful, and likely to be much more effective if carefully prepared rather than designed and delivered on the run.[7]

A second institutional need is to have the necessary civilian response capability, with personnel trained and available to play the many roles that the effective exercise of RtoP requires, again at all three of the prevention, reaction, and post-crisis rebuilding stages. This means diplomatic capacity, for a start, ready and available to negotiate and mediate those situations which are capable of being stopped by effective early intervention of this kind, and to lead the peacekeeping and peace-building missions which are so critical in holding troubled situations together through often extended transition periods, and ensuring that the underlying causes of whatever went wrong are addressed. The UN system, through UNITAR in particular, has been paying much more attention in recent years to training negotiators, mediators, and mission-leading Special Representatives, who need to be paragons of many more virtues than those to which most mortals can aspire. The regional organizations—EU, OSCE, AU, OAS, ASEAN, and all those others whose multiple potential roles are stressed in all the chapters in Part II of this volume—could all do significantly more in this respect.

A full range of civilian capabilities needs to be available to assist states under Pillar Two, when they are trying to put in place preventive measures to avoid catastrophe. This is a need which can usually be met in the context of contemporary development assistance programs, which for good reason tend now to focus as strongly on capacity-building and governance generally as on direct poverty reduction. As the Secretary-General's 2009 report put it, "Experience and common sense suggest that many of the elements of what is commonly accepted as good governance—the rule of law, a competent and independent judiciary, human rights, security sector reform, a robust civil society, an independent press and a political culture that favors tolerance, dialogue, and mobility over the rigidities and injustices of identity politics—tend to serve objectives relating to the responsibility to protect as well."

What much attention needs to be focused on is providing that same range of capabilities when any international peace operation is mounted requiring the deployment of forces in the context of post-conflict peace-building. The civilian components here—covering everything from policing and human rights protection, to rehabilitation and repatriation, to election administration and specialist civil administration—are at least as important, if not more so, than the military, but in practice very hard to find. A great deal of self-congratulatory effort has gone into building standby capability, particularly of police officers, but hard experience has shown over and again that formal commitments by government are one thing, and the timely honoring of those commitments is something else. Months of delay remain the norm, and many missions never get the total numbers that their planning demands.

Probably the most difficult of all the institutional challenges is to have the right kind of military capability available when and where it is needed, bearing in mind that this is relevant not just in the extreme context of coercive interventions, against the will of

[7] The "toolboxes" are tabulated in Gareth Evans, The Responsibility to Protect, *supra* note 5, at app. B, and described in detail, along with all the other institutional and political needs addressed here, in Part II, "Operationalizing the Responsibility to Protect," Chapters 4–10.

the government concerned, but also for fully consensual preventive deployments (as in Macedonia) and stabilization operations (again with the consent, if perhaps reluctant, of the government involved) in both reaction and rebuilding situations. In all these cases, skill sets of a kind rather unfamiliar for the military are required: RtoP civilian-protection operations involve neither traditional war-fighting (where the object is not to stop violence as such, but to defeat an enemy, usually overturning its governing regime in the process) and peacekeeping operations (which although these days usually involving much more than the traditional passive monitoring, have still not come to grips with the kind of responses needed to cope with the threat or reality of atrocity crimes). The experience of the current mission in Darfur, fully described in Chapter 10, is a classic demonstration of the problem of military capacity in a consensual intervention situation—too few troops, too poorly equipped, and too immobile to perform effectively even the limited civilian protection task required by their present mandate.

It is not just a matter of having troops available in the necessary number, with the right equipment and logistic support, and with the required levels of basic competence. It is a matter of even the most sophisticated and best-resourced militaries in the world struggling with inappropriate force configurations, and needing to develop new doctrine, new concepts of operations, new kinds of rules of engagement, and new kinds of training. The better news is that some excellent work is now being done on all these issues, not least in the context of a joint exercise by Harvard University's John F. Kennedy School of Government's Carr Center for Human Rights Policy and the U.S. Military, which has developed a new descriptive title for this new military role—Mass Atrocity Response Operations (MARO)—and a published handbook and other work in progress to go with it, all of which offers excellent guidance for national militaries and intergovernmental organizations elsewhere.[8] But there is a long way to go in these respects, just as there is in having in place in practice—not just on paper—the rapidly deployable standby military capability that the EU, AU, and NATO, among others, have for years now been announcing, but never quite delivering.

There are a number of other institutional issues which any more comprehensive and systematic checklist than this would need to address, including systematic strengthening of the capability of the regional and sub-regional organizations on which so much of the RtoP operationalization agenda is going to depend, more government support around the world for the International Criminal Court—not least in supporting its writ so that those indicted can be apprehended and tried, and those convicted effectively punished, and more comprehensive reform of the United Nations and its multiple agencies. As to the UN, it is important to keep in perspective what is and is not achievable, given the realities of international politics, and Edward Luck's chapter is a useful corrective to over-optimism in this respect.

A case in point is the veto power, which is likely to continue to make extremely unlikely Security Council support for coercive military action in RtoP cases in all but the most exceptional cases. No permanent member is going to vote in the foreseeable

[8] *See MARO: Mass Atrocity Response Operations – A Military Planning Handbook* (2010), accessible, along with a full description of the project, *available at* http://www.hks.harvard.edu/cchrp/maro/index.php.

future for a Charter amendment that removes or dilutes its veto power. A more modest proposal advanced by ICISS (after some indication of support from France), for permanent members to agree voluntarily not to utilize their veto to block action for which there was otherwise a Council majority and where their own vital national interests were not engaged, received little support. Proposals continue to be advanced by civil society organizations for a voluntary agreement that the veto not be exercised in cases of evident mass atrocity crimes. But the trouble with all such proposals is that they tend to run into the stumbling block immortally characterized by an Australian Prime Minister of the 1940s, Ben Chifley: "The trouble with gentleman's agreements is that there are not enough bloody gentlemen."

C. Political

What emerges most clearly from the preceding discussion is that, in meeting the challenge of operationalizing RtoP, overwhelmingly the most important players, for good or ill, are individual states and their governments. Other actors do play important roles, but not the central one. Intergovernmental organizations can only decide if their member states agree and can only act if their member states deliver, and nongovernmental organizations can only be influential in their advice or effective in their program delivery if individual states listen and allow them to act. It is the inability or unwillingness of national governments to exercise their sovereign responsibility to protect all their own people from catastrophic human rights violations that creates the problem in the first place. And it is the ability and willingness of national governments to act as good friends and neighbors, as generous donors, as persuasive diplomats, and—if the circumstances demand it—as appliers of coercive pressure and, in really extreme cases, military intervention, that is crucial to any solution. States remain, for better or worse, and will be for the foreseeable future, the primary actors in international affairs.

So how is it possible to get them to do the right thing when it comes to RtoP? Generating the necessary political will to do anything hard, or expensive, or politically sensitive, or seen as not directly relevant to national interests, is just a given in public affairs. The point is that its absence should not be a matter for lamentation, but mobilization. Political will is not hiding in a cupboard or under a stone somewhere waiting to be discovered: it has to be painstakingly built, and the only way to do that is through the time-honored trio of good information, good arguments, and good organization.

When it comes to information, there are few excuses these days for any decision-making system, national or intergovernmental, not to know about RtoP situations occurring or emerging. Officials on the ground report back up through their communication lines, there are sometimes graphic descriptions in the print and electronic media, and above all, there are now nongovernmental organizations—including recently established ones with worldwide field resources, like the International Crisis Group—pumping out the necessary information through all the real-time forms of electronic communication that earlier generations of advocates and activists could only dream about. Advocates can always do more in shaping and presenting material to cut through the competing cacophony—and it is important, as Andrew Natsios and Zachary Scott point out in their not unreasonable criticisms of a good deal of the "Save Darfur" campaigning, that in doing so they stay right on top of the data and adjust the story as the situation on the ground changes—but inability to get and communicate the necessary information is not the problem it may once have been.

What matters most in persuading policymakers is the presentation of good arguments, intelligently and energetically advanced. It is critical, for a start, that the RtoP concept itself be able to be articulated and explained with precision and clarity: thus the importance of meeting the conceptual challenges already discussed above. When it comes to energizing responses to particular cases, moral arguments—which are at the heart of RtoPs intellectual and emotional appeal—will always be persuasive, because however base politicians' real motives may be, they always like to be seen as acting from higher ones. But they won't necessarily be decisive. They need to be supplemented by a variety of hardheaded arguments, beginning if at all possible with an appeal to traditional national interests. These are rather easier to make now in relation to "quarrels in far away countries between people of whom we know nothing," in Chamberlain's terms, because of what we do know now about the capacity of failed states, in this globalized world, to be a source of havoc for others: states that can't or wont stop internal atrocity crimes are the kind of rogue states, or failed or failing states, that can't or won't stop terrorism, weapons proliferation, drug and people trafficking, the spread of health pandemics and other global risks.

Financial arguments can also be importantly reinforcing, in terms of a million dollars worth of preventive action now saving a billion dollars worth of military intervention later. And finally, there are more directly political arguments. Political risk and reward calculations are bound to come into play for any government when the expenditure of blood or treasure is on the line, and it is important to be able to meet them head on if at all possible. Mounting arguments that will address domestic political concerns is, however, a subtler business than just calculating what majority reactions will be. What can on occasion matter even more to governments is having arguments that will appeal to, or at least not alienate, their own political support base, and which they can use to deflate, or at least defend against, the attacks of their political opponents: considerations of this kind, involving the support of the Christian right, were an important factor in George W. Bush's strong commitment in Sudan.

Without effective organization, even the most compelling information and argument may not have the impact it should. Noel Morada properly emphasizes in Chapter 7 the critical importance of effective "bottom up" civil society activity, regionally as well as nationally and globally, with enthusiasm being matched by professionalism in the quality of analysis and advocacy presented. Strenuous efforts have been made in recent times to build that capacity and they need to be maintained and enhanced.

The three most important organizational structures in this respect, all based in New York but with outreach around the world, are the Global Centre for the Responsibility to Protect (www.globalr2p.org), designed as an information clearing house and research and advocacy resource for both governments and the global NGO community, focusing both on consolidating understanding and acceptance of the norm, and ensuring its effective practical implementation; the International Coalition for the Responsibility to Protect (www.responsibilitytoprotect.org), designed as an umbrella organization bringing together NGOs all over the world committed to advancing those same RtoP objectives; and the UN "Friends of RtoP," currently co-chaired by the Netherlands and Rwanda, which has worked generally to promote the norm among governments through their missions in New York and to coordinate like-minded input into General Assembly and related debates.

To some extent, those of us passionate about making the responsibility to protect a reality will always be pushing at a partly open door. There *is* goodwill out there, in the wider community, and among government policymakers and decision-makers around the world. There is a basic willingness to accept and embrace the RtoP norm, and to ensure that we don't ever again have to confront failures of will and action on the scale of Rwanda or Srebrenica—not just as a matter of national self-interest but as a function of our common humanity. But we know from long, hard, depressing experience that mobilizing that goodwill, and actually producing the necessary action, are not things that just happen. They have to be *made* to happen. And that is the responsibility of us all.

Index